Gulfport
New Orleans Cem.
P.S. 3 classroom
Fred Nude
New Orleans Canal
World Trade Center
Auto Show
G.M. Building
Gas Mask [illegible]

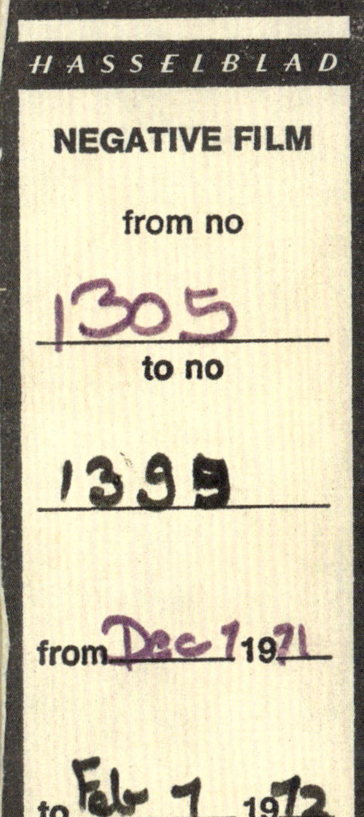

Jim Shields writing
Baton Rouge
East Hampton
Lonely Road
Country clubs
Doors with Jim
S.I. commune
R.S.D. park with head
Unemployment agency
City college
Ladies strike
Elizabeth Burge
in auto junky ard

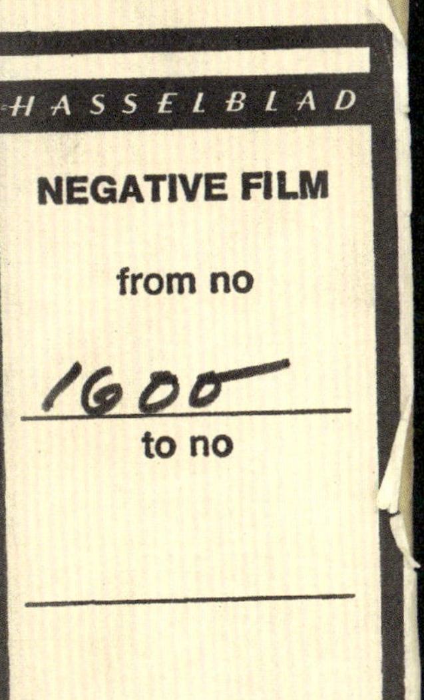

City College
South Seaport
man with plastic in C.P.
Philadelphia Flood
Wilkes Barre flood
Adam + Rut
Prospect Park + Bronx Park

BALI
San Francisco
JAPAN
N.J. State Fair
Virginia State Fair
Adam + Fr[illegible]
Dentist

SMOKE
World Trade
2 Rakes on chaise Lounges

HASSELBLAD
NEGATIVE FILM
from no
1800
to no
1899
from Oct 1972
to Nov. 1972

Nantucket
Provincetown
DANBURY
Virginia Beach
Norfolk
Lester Marks
DREAM CITY
CONEY ISLAND
BLANKETS
moon rock
Harlem River
San Francisco
Barber. Violin

STAR-TREK
Bicycle C.I.
MIAMI BEACH
FONTAINBLEAU HOTEL POOL
Weehawken

HASSELBLAD
NEGATIVE FILM
from no
1900
to no
1999
from Dec 1972
to Jan 1973

Statue of Liberty
Washington D.C.
MARCH
Coney Island
Boy in Squash
Santa Claus
Ice. Snug Harbor. Nature
History museum
R. REYNOLDS
BETTY BERSH
RED GROOMS
C. Park ZOO

ASTLE. DAS
ANKS. S.I.
Aim. ST. PAT
BOBO. CLOWN
CARACAS.
DUPONT ESTATE
CAMDEN.
REGTON. PREP SCHOOL
CHESTER.
WASHINGTON CAT.

HASSELBLAD

NEGATIVE FILM

from no 2000

to no 2100

from Feb 1973

to March 1973

INVENTORS CON
DRAG BALL
BETTY BERSH
NEWARK
BRONX STAINS
BEAUTY SCHOOL
DAY CARE PROT
EDISON LAB
LONG BEACH
ICE FACTORY
CIRCUS parade
BALTIMORE
BURNS
ENSWICK, N.J.
Leisure CONV.
Dog. SHOW

costumes
metal union
car show
taxidermist
5 corners
American Indian Express
Poly Technic Inst

HASSELBLAD

NEGATIVE FILM

from no 2100

to no 2198

from April 1973

to June 1973

Scientist Berk

CORNELL SPAC
N.Y. DENTIST
PAPA-BABY
WASHINGTON D.C.
STATEN ISLE
BIKE RACE
CROOKED FACTORIES
QUEENS TOWER
POLICE DAY
N.Y.U. Police
1 to I Day
C.I. Golem
I.B.M.
CLOCKTOWER
RADIATOR REPAIR
WORLD Fair Science
Starring Forest
A.M.A. PENN Hotel

Bronx - Tires
Ice Boxes
Hunts Pt. Junk

Sound Speaker
Chemical Conv.
Thanksgiving Day Parade
Bronx - Dead Chicken
A.S.P.C.A.
CO-OP city
Long Island City
Ithaca. KOTEX
Prospect Park
man + child.
S.F. Information
Headless shadow
Grant's Tomb
Bird Cage - Tokyo
S.F. gate

HASSELBLAD

MAPPAR

Bruce
Van Etten Snow

fr. o. m. nr 2400 —

t.o.m. nr 2499

under tiden

från Nov 1 1973

till Dec 31 1973

Dragon

NEW LONDON, CONN
Rose garden Queens
Boys FootBALL
C.I. Dragon
Municipal Trash Can
Rockaway Chess Board man
C.I. girls in Window
St Anthonys Boys
Floyd Bennett Beach
Ocean ave graveyard
HACKENSACK

Puerto Rico Shadows
Coney Island Shadows
central park shadows
marble hill
down town

HASSELBLAD

MAPPAR

fr. o. m. nr 2500

t.o.m. nr 2599

under tiden

från Jan 7 1974

till Jan 30 1974

magic show
blind children
Thayer's Parade
Bob Axelrod Studio
Schools garbage

Florida East Coast
Key West with Bruce
teenage photo in pond
Yankee Stadium old couple
Martin + Heart Health Care Center
Maine sardine
French chateau
Lady Cop
couple in Sativus

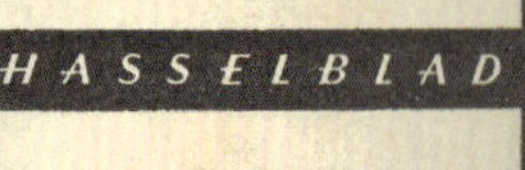

HASSELBLAD

NEGATIVE FILM

from no 3300

to no 3399

from Dec 1974

to Jan 1975

CO

ARTHUR TRESS

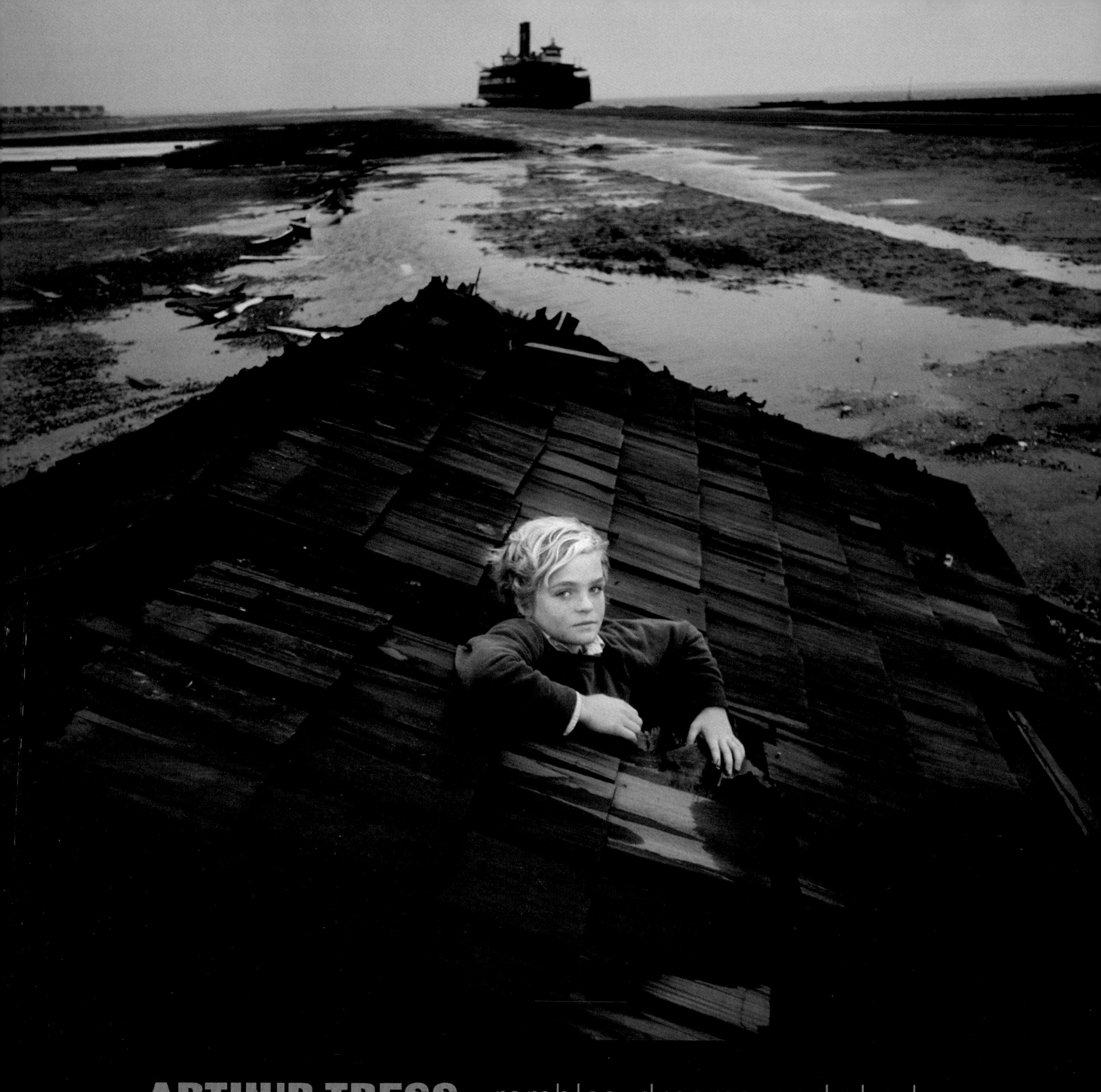

ARTHUR TRESS rambles dreams and shadows

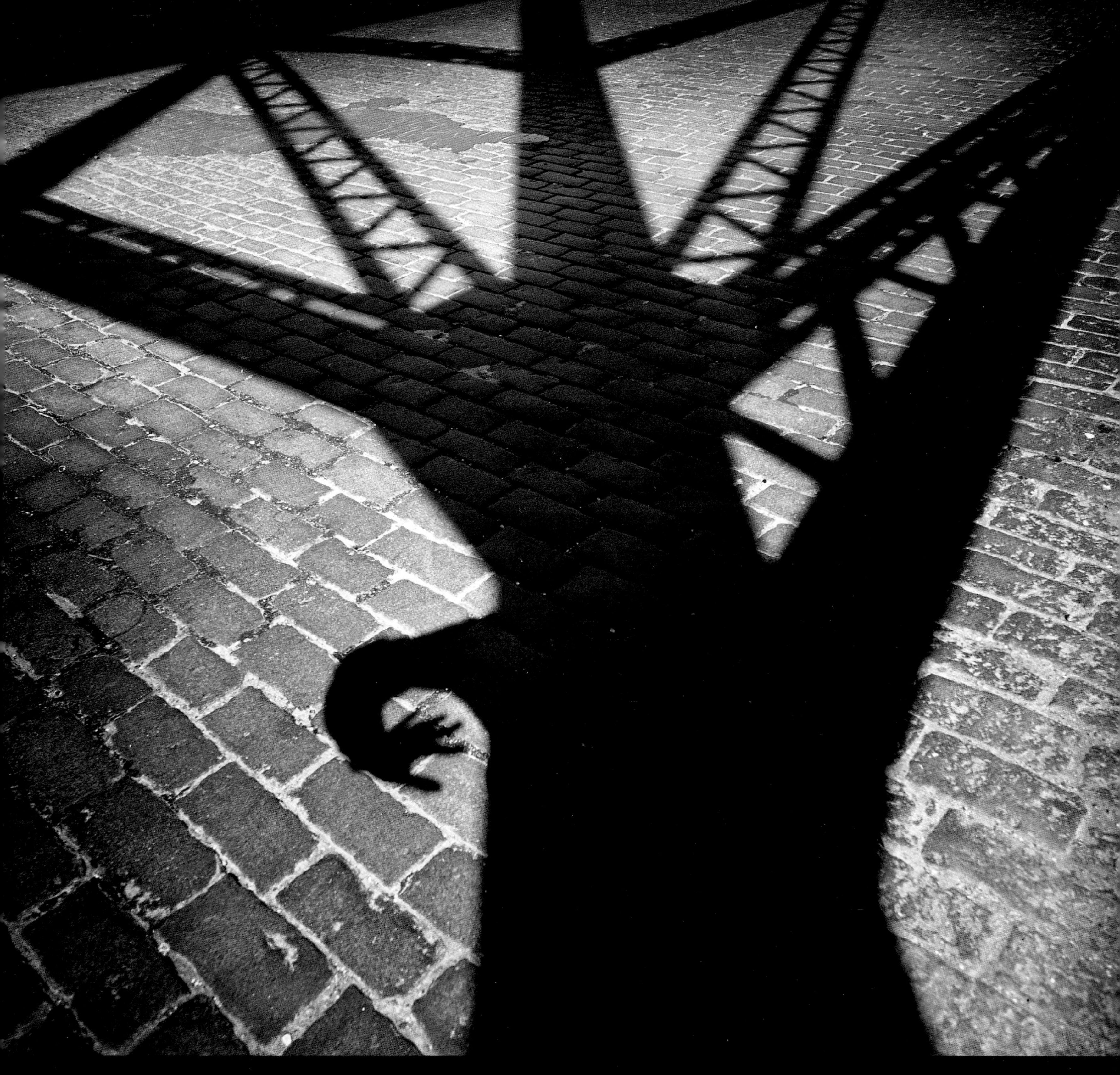

Edited by James A. Ganz

With essays by
James A. Ganz
Mazie M. Harris
Paul Martineau

J. Paul Getty Museum
Los Angeles

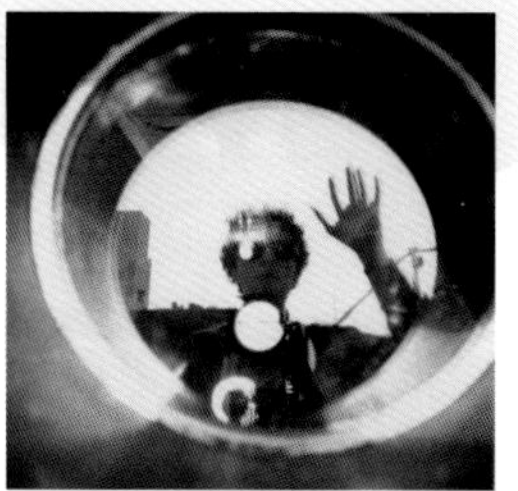
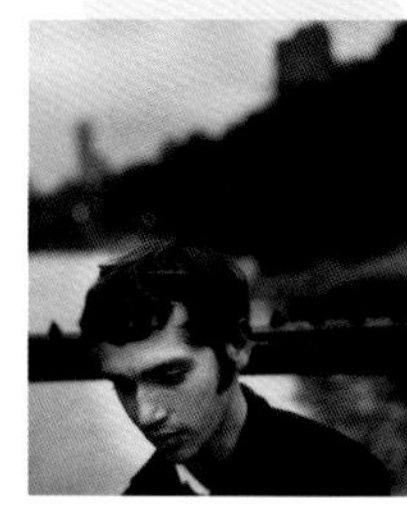
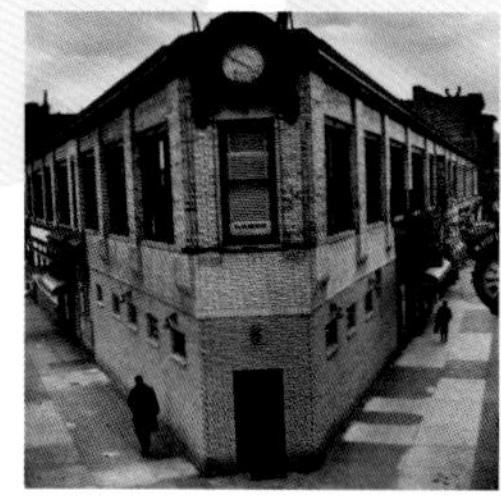
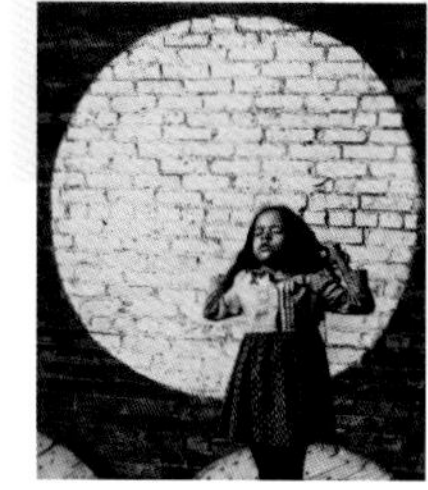

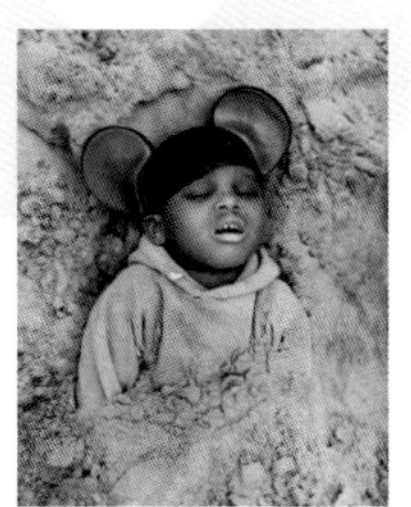

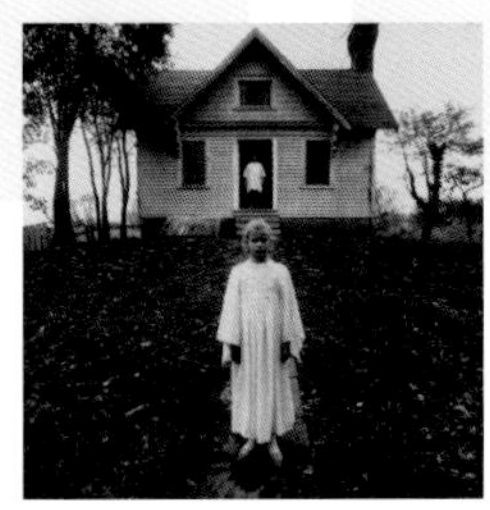

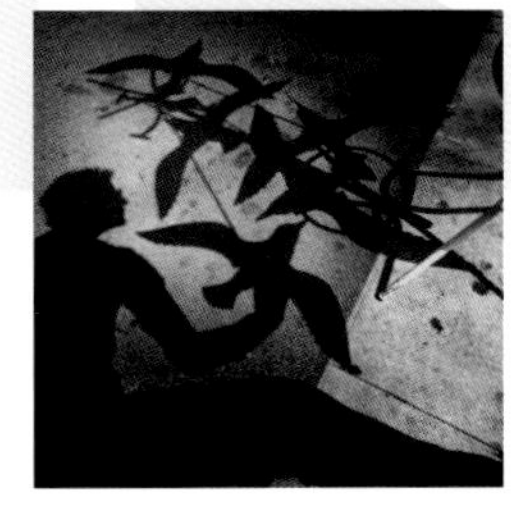

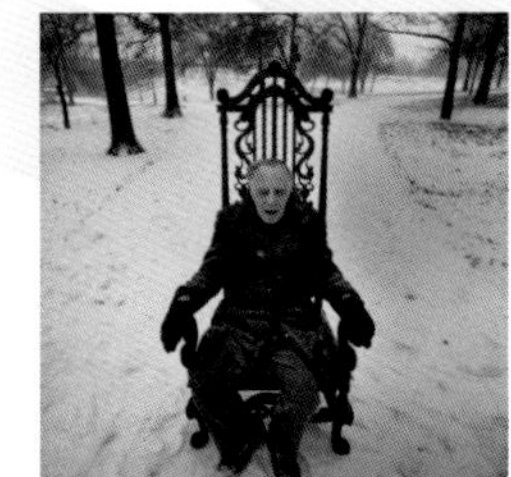

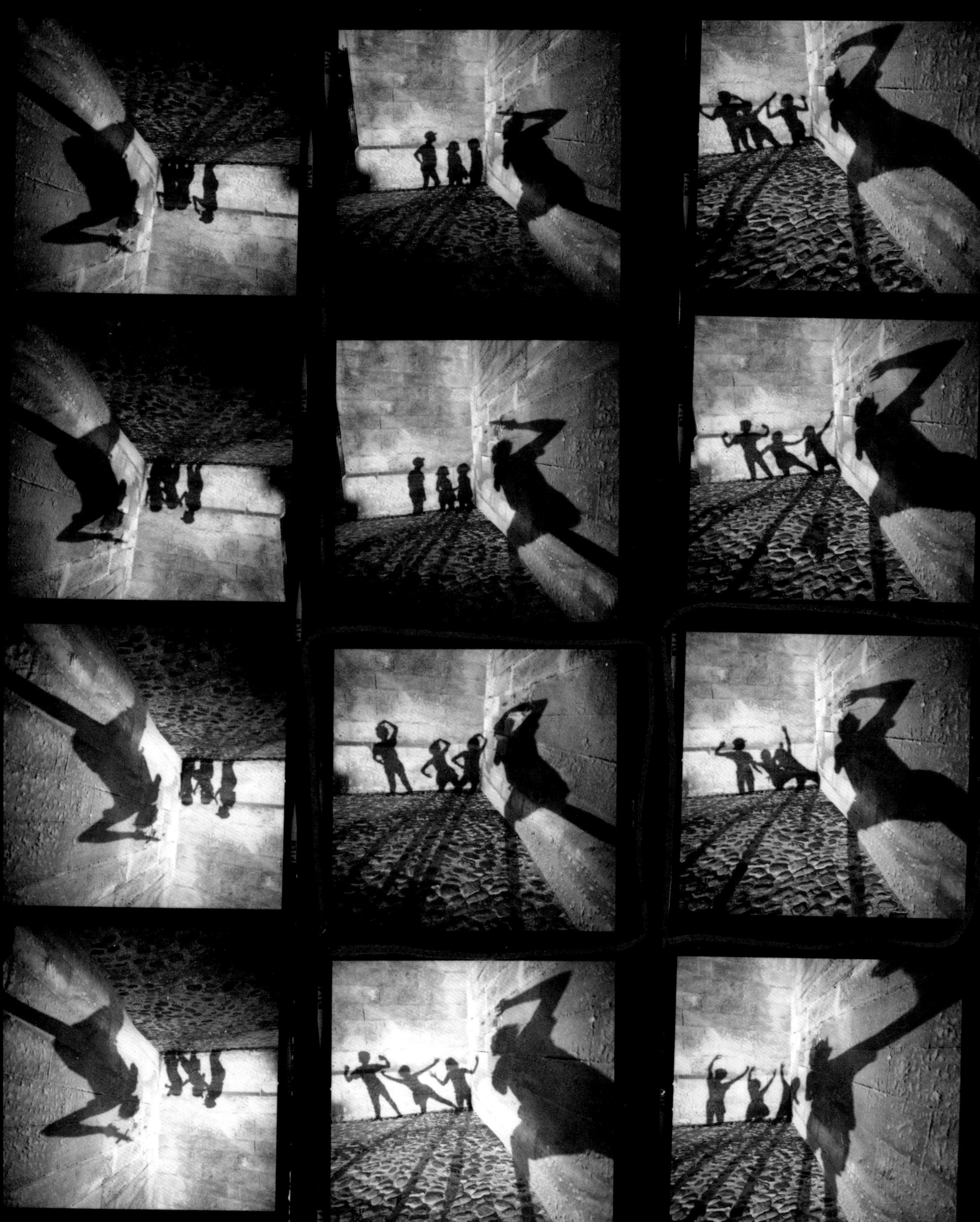

Foreword

Arthur Tress: Rambles, Dreams, and Shadows is the first exhibition to chronicle the early career of a singular figure in the landscape of postwar American photography. Born in 1940 in Brooklyn and educated at Bard College, Arthur Tress traveled internationally as a social documentary photographer in the mid-1960s. He journeyed through Europe to Egypt, Mexico, India, Japan, Thailand, and Cambodia, ending with an extended residence in Sweden and publishing his growing portfolio of commercial work in a variety of magazines and stock agencies. After returning to the United States, Tress embarked on series devoted to the people of Appalachia and New York City before pursuing more personal exhibition and book projects that delved deeper into the worlds of surrealism, fantasy, and his own queer identity. Along with a handful of his contemporaries, including Duane Michals and Les Krims, Tress was a true maverick in the field of staged photography at a time when the prevailing aesthetic emphasized prosaic realism rather than performative invention.

While Tress has been the subject of several museum exhibitions, most notably the retrospective *Arthur Tress: Fantastic Voyage, Photographs 1956–2000* at the Corcoran Gallery of Art in 2001, the depth of his artistic achievement has yet to be fully recognized. In his previous role as curator of the Achenbach Foundation for Graphic Arts, the Getty's senior curator of photographs, James Ganz, organized *Arthur Tress: San Francisco 1964* at the de Young Museum in 2012, which did much to increase recognition of the artist's early work. That exhibition and its accompanying publication served, in effect, as the prequel to the Getty's current offering, which showcases the fascinating first chapter of Tress's long career. An introductory essay by Ganz provides a biographical overview of Tress's early years, followed by a series of focused essays by Ganz, Mazie M. Harris, and Paul Martineau that elucidate the major projects Tress undertook from 1968 to 1978: *Appalachia: People and Places, Open Space in the Inner City: Ecology and the Urban Environment, The Dream Collector, Shadow*, and *Theater of the Mind*.

We are fortunate at the Getty Museum to have a strong representation of Tress's photographs, which we have been actively collecting since 2013. We are especially grateful to David Knaus, a founding member of the Getty's Photographs Council, who shepherded Tress's archive for many years and personally donated many works to the Museum, as well as facilitating other gifts. Thanks to David's generosity, we are able to organize this exhibition primarily from our own holdings. We are also delighted to have received support for this exhibition from Photographs Council members Michael Hawley, Daniel Greenberg and Susan Steinhauser through The Greenberg Trust, Alison and Richard Crowell, Al Uzielli, Willard Huyck and Teleia Montgomery, and Paula Ely and Cesar Rueda.

Finally, we are greatly indebted to the artist himself. Tress has generously shared his rich archive of primary source material, enabling the authors of this publication to painstakingly reconstruct his personal and artistic evolution within the blossoming New York photography world of the 1970s. Appropriately, these new essays on Tress's early work are bracketed by the artist's 1970 text "The Photograph as Magical Image" and a newly composed postscript, "Looking Back." Tress's distinctive images occupy a special place in the modern canon of photography and have inspired generations of artists. We trust that this book and the exhibition it accompanies will provide further insights into his innovative and, at times, provocative oeuvre.

TIMOTHY POTTS
Maria Hummer-Tuttle and Robert Tuttle Director
J. Paul Getty Museum

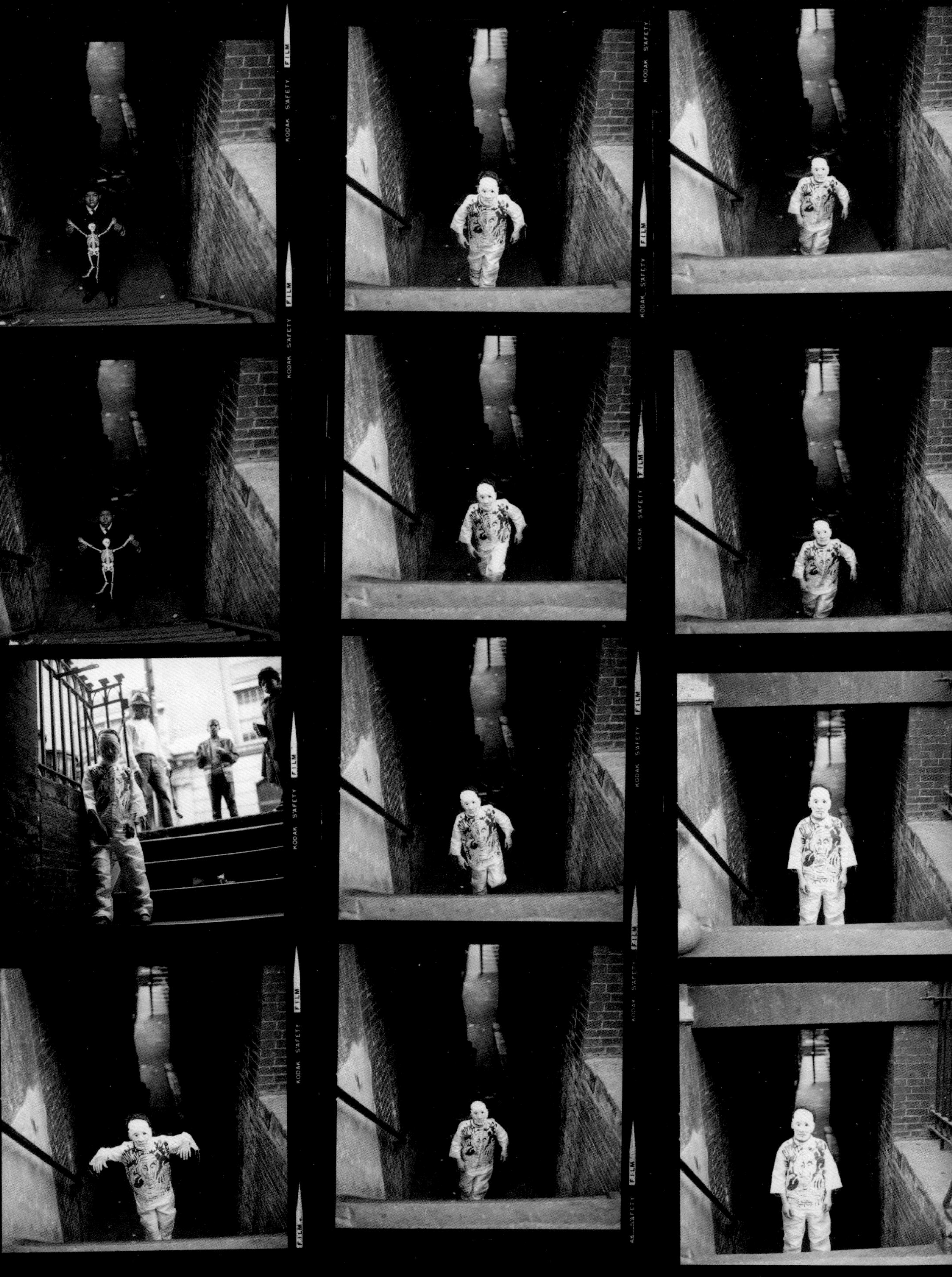

Preface

The Photograph as Magical Image (1970)

ARTHUR TRESS

A photographer could be considered a kind of magician—a being possessed of very special powers that enable him to control mysterious forces and energies outside himself. The photographer's intensely heightened sense perception, product of the brutal discipline of constantly seeing at 1/250 of a second, unevenly evolves his visual faculties to an almost superhuman degree. With these highly developed instincts he seems to be able to almost anticipate the activities of his subjects and sometimes actually appears to cause their occurrence by some mental willpower of his own that projects outward, making reality conform to his mentally conceived image of it that he records on film. Often his best photographs are taken in a trancelike state where there is an almost unspoken mystical communication between his subject and himself and action is directed through nonverbal gesture and psychic transference. As a trained observer he can foretell the potential movements of his subjects and perhaps even by mental intimidation and expansion actually cause them to happen. The photographer participates in an almost ritual dance with the world whereupon his own intense response to its rhythms corresponds to his being able to predict its following certain predetermined patterns.

The photographic image itself has great magical possibilities. Like the ceremonial mask, the ritual incantation, the protective amulet, or magical mandala, the photograph has the potency of releasing in the viewer preconditioned reactions that cause him to physically change or be mentally transformed. In fact, because of our intense belief in the factual literalness of the photograph, it can provoke even stronger reactions than other graphic media. A photograph can more often "grab our guts" or arouse our sexual desires than other art forms because of its purported realness, but it can also more subtly stimulate unconscious responses that we are hardly aware of. The grotesque or frightening image may stir forgotten animal instincts of primordial helplessness and fear, reaching back to the basic insecurity of early man and our own personal childhoods. Images of great peace and harmony have the curative possibility of restoring tranquility and balance to a disturbed soul or agitated body. The photographic image which hints to the essential mystery of growing things and the unknown qualities of life itself can make the viewer aware of higher states of nature to which we are faintly sensitive. The magical photograph is simply one that attempts by its mere assertive presence to go beyond the immediate context of the recorded experience into realms of the undefinable. The photographer as magician is just someone who is more acutely aware of the subliminal "vibrations" of the everyday world which can call forth hidden emotions or states of feeling that are usually tightly wrapped up in our unconscious selves. He is himself totally "opened" to the multiplicities of associations that are submerged behind the appearances of the objective world. He uses the repressed mythology of dreams and the archetypical designs of geometry to magically conjure up deep and irrational reactions from the viewer.

Perhaps why so much of today's photography doesn't "grab us" or mean anything to our personal lives is that it fails to touch upon the hidden life of the imagination and fantasy, which is hungry for stimulation. The documentary photographer supplies us with facts or drowns in humanity, while the pictorialist, avant-garde or conservative, pleases us with mere aesthetically correct compositions, but where are the photographs *we can pray to, that will make us well again, or scare the hell out of us?* Most of mankind's art for the past 5,000 years was created for just those purposes. It seems absurd to stop now.

Originally published as "The Photograph as Magical Image," *Album*, no. 2 (March 1970), 1.

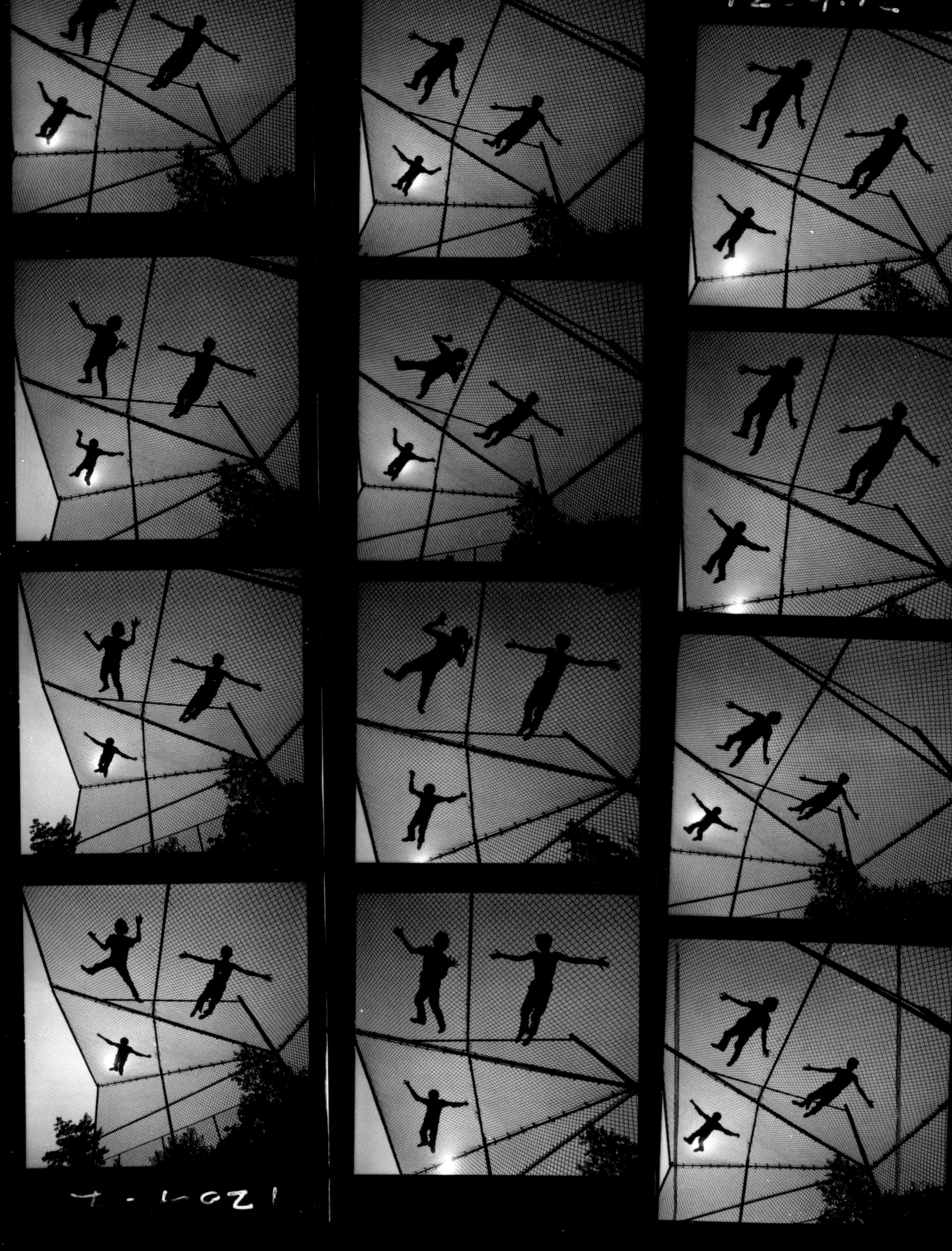

JAMES A. GANZ

Arthur Tress, Dreams and Variations

During his first decade in the New York photography world, Arthur Tress (fig. 1) transformed his artistic approach, which was initially rooted in the social documentary tradition, and shifted to drawing primary inspiration from his dreams and fantasies. Between 1968 and 1978 he forged a daring path for himself that defied art historical conventions, broke taboos, and laid bare his soul. For Tress, the camera became more than a mechanical tool; it was an object of enchantment that transformed the mild-mannered and shy young man into a confident stage director taking complete control of his craft and his vision. Despite its originality and potency, much of this work is little known today, and the remarkable story behind Tress's early career has remained untold.

> Have decided to leave Paris, really don't know why. It's mostly a feeling of restlessness. I had here everything I could have possibly wanted—a little room, a good working space, heat, a record player, light, friends, the cinema musée, plenty of free time to work . . . but I just couldn't get settled down and also sit quietly enough for doing anything that requires thought. So in usual Tress manner . . . "je partir pour voir le monde." Will go down the Mediterranean coast until I hit Gibraltar, perhaps hop over to Tangiers and see Egypt. If you know any people there or interesting things to see send me their address at American Express Paris, + they can send on to me.[1]

This brief note from twenty-two-year-old Arthur to his sister, Madeleine, an insurance executive in San Francisco, records his decision in December 1962 to leave Paris, where he had briefly attended the Institut des Hautes Études Cinématographiques, and begin a multiyear travel odyssey. A cache of the artist's unpublished letters—from which this note is

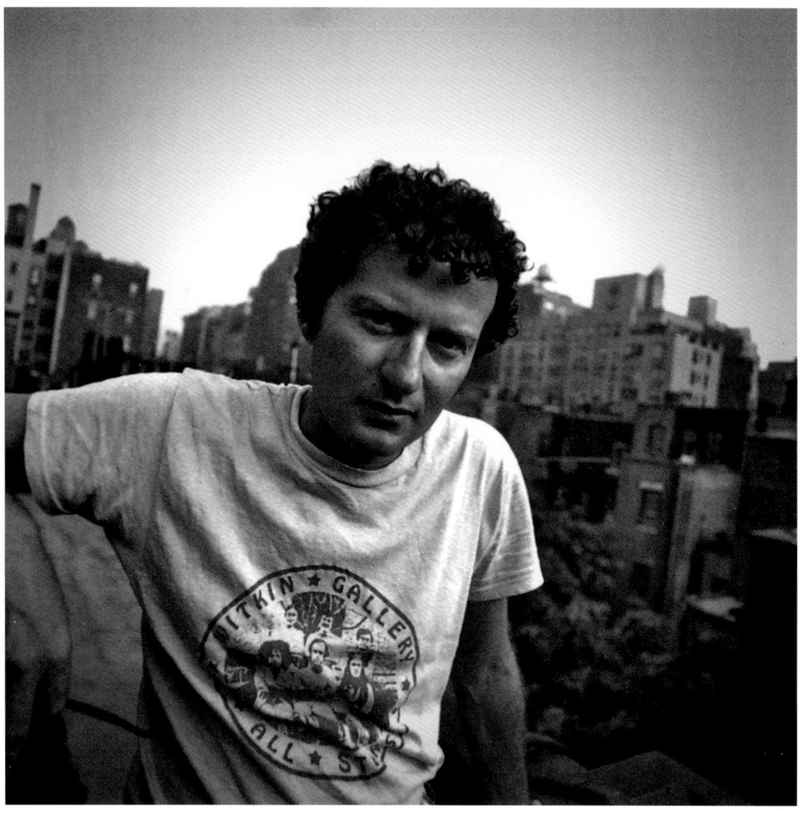

Figure 1
Anonymous
Arthur Tress in New York, New York, ca. 1971
Gelatin silver print,
5.7 × 5.7 cm (2 ¼ × 2 ¼ in.)
Collection of Arthur Tress

Figure 2
"Blodig Lek i Färg"
From November 1966 issue of *Foto och Filmteknik* with portrait of Tress by Douglas Kneedler
Collection of Arthur Tress

drawn—sheds light on his activities and aspirations during the formative period of his career.[2] Besides Madeleine, his principal correspondents were his brother, David, an aspiring actor in New York; his father, Martin, a New York businessman; and, starting in 1967, his Swedish boyfriend, Torbjörn (Tobi) Astner, an acting student in Skara with whom he shared his first serious and openly gay relationship.

The youngest of three children, Tress spent his formative years shuttling between his divorced parents in different neighborhoods around New York City. Both of his siblings encouraged his interests in filmmaking and photography and gave him his first cameras. Tress attended Abraham Lincoln High School in Brighton Beach, which had a strong program in applied arts, and Bard College in Annandale-on-Hudson, New York, where he studied art history and painting and developed a special interest in ethnography. Tress came of age during the time of Edward Steichen's monumental *Family of Man* exhibition (1955) at the Museum of Modern Art, a period that also saw the publication of seminal photobooks like William Klein's *New York 1954.55* (1956) and Robert Frank's *The Americans* (1959). Essentially self-taught as a photographer, Tress idolized Henri Cartier-Bresson, whose books from that time, *People of Moscow* (1955) and *China in Transition* (1956), made a strong impression.

After graduating with his BFA from Bard, Tress traveled abroad between 1962 and 1967, motivated by a wish to avoid the draft and the risk of being sent to Vietnam. He spent time in Spain, Italy, Egypt, Mexico, Japan, Thailand, Cambodia, and India, with a memorable summer in San Francisco (1964)[3] and finally an extended stay in Sweden (1966–67), during which he made additional excursions to parts of West Africa as well as Lapland, Leningrad, Paris, and London. During this odyssey Tress continued to send documents to the draft board claiming to be a graduate student while making films, painting, and photographing. He was undoubtedly among the best-traveled American photographers of his generation, a circumstance made possible by the financial support of his family. On his twenty-fourth birthday Tress wrote to his father from Mexico: "I feel a little guilty that I haven't achieved more success than I have, but I don't want to push myself until I have found what I really want to say. Most people don't have the time + must sell themselves to the world before they are ready. Thank you for the opportunity."[4]

When Tress arrived in Stockholm in the spring of 1966, he was exhausted from four years of travel. While wandering around Norra Djurgården, the Stockholm Royal Seaport to the northeast of the city, he noticed a historic house called Södra Villervallan that offered inexpensive lodging. It was a peaceful place on the water, surrounded by

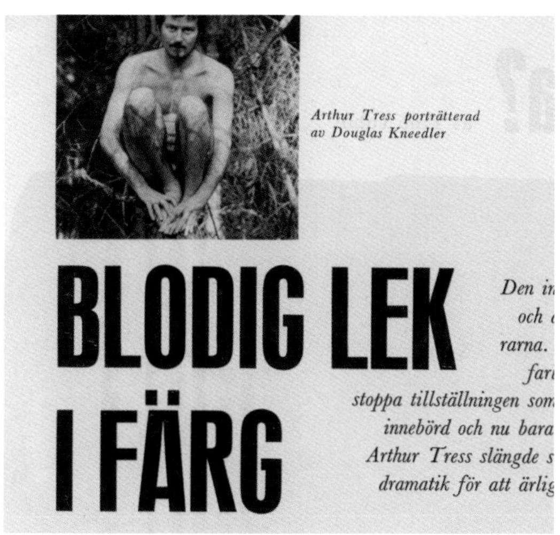
Arthur Tress porträtterad
av Douglas Kneedler

BLODIG LEK
I FÄRG

Den i
och
rarna.
far
stoppa tillställningen som
innebörd och nu bara
Arthur Tress slängde s
dramatik för att ärlig

birch trees. “My apartment is going to be beautiful,” Tress wrote to his brother on May 3. “I finished painting the bedroom white with bright blue windows. The living room I’m going to make into a studio. I am going to join a Foto School attached to the University so perhaps I can avoid the army for another year.”[5] He was struck by the city’s spotlessness. “There really isn’t anything very dramatic to photograph, no poor people, junkyards, anything. People sit around very neatly dressed in clean little houses or parks with their quiet pretty children.”[6] A few months later he wrote to Madeleine, “This morning I walked along the shore collecting bits of rubbish to put into my collages. It’s very difficult. Swedish people are so damn neat there’s hardly any junk around.”[7]

Despite his initial concerns about Stockholm’s austerity, Tress plunged into his new life, taking Swedish-language classes and focusing his creative time on painting and making collages, with a brief excursion to Lapland to photograph the annual reindeer slaughter. After going around to galleries with slides of his birchbark collages, he finally secured a venue to present his work, but at the last minute the gallerist canceled the show. The experience led Tress to an important realization, which he recounted to his brother: “You really should concentrate on something for a longer period of time if you want to accomplish anything. I can’t really keep switching back between painting, photography + filmmaking. I really have to organize myself in one + push ahead in that even if it gets boring or difficult.”[8] While he did not entirely abandon his other artistic activities, Tress increasingly directed his efforts to the medium of photography, which he saw as the best opportunity to earn a living.

The first published profile of Tress appeared in the November 1966 issue of the Swedish magazine *Foto och Filmteknik* under the title “Blodig Lek i Färg” (Bloody Game in Color) (fig. 2), illustrating his images of the bull-taming festival in the southern Indian village of Avaniapuram that he had shot before he arrived in Stockholm. Pointing out the blurring of his action shots, which Tress made with a Rolleiflex on Ektachrome film purchased on the black market, the writer concludes: “Tress is not really a photographer. He is a folklorist and portrayer of folk life. His camera is just an instrument that records what he experiences.”[9] Accompanying the article is a portrait by Douglas Kneedler, another American expatriate, of the bare-chested artist crouching in a tree. Although he clearly welcomed the publicity, Tress was bemused by the piece. “You may think that the photograph of myself is a little strange,” he wrote to his brother, “but it goes very well with the article, which represents me as a kind of eccentric ‘folklorist,’ a semi-nut who goes around collecting bizarre folk material.”[10]

For Tress, Stockholm’s Etnografiska museet served as an important resource, though contrary to assertions in published biographies, he was never employed by this venerable ethnological institution. As a freelance photographer he received several commissions from the Swedish

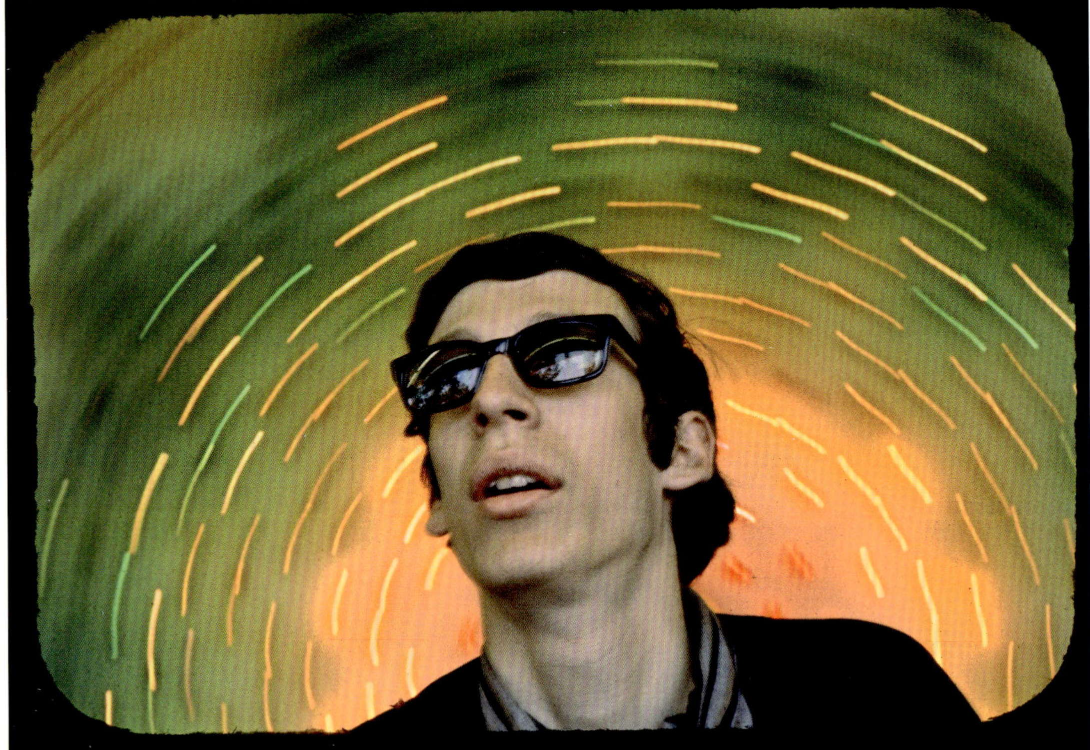

Figure 3
Arthur Tress
LSD Trip from *Narcotics in Sweden*, 1967
Kodachrome slide,
2.5 × 3.8 cm (1 × 1 ½ in.)
Collection of the artist

educational publisher Natur & Kultur, which produced textbooks, filmstrips, and other pedagogical materials for schoolchildren on a variety of topics. Tress was particularly drawn to the medium of the 35 mm color filmstrip, a ubiquitous teaching tool in 1960s classrooms that served as a cheaper alternative to 16 mm films. He enjoyed the research process, which reminded him of assignments at Bard, then going out in the field and photographing his subject, and finally writing the narration. He made a point of retaining his image copyrights so he could recycle them for pictorial features in magazines and eventually in self-published artist books. More than half a century later, some of these images continue to appear in online stock-agency picture libraries, available for licensing.[11]

One of Tress's more prophetic assignments from Natur & Kultur, in that it prefigured the imagery of disaffected youth that would permeate his *Open Space in the Inner City* series, was to produce a filmstrip on teenage drug addiction.[12] Although he was not a user himself, his Swedish girlfriend had abused amphetamines, which had led to their breakup. At the time he wrote to his brother that "drugs have replaced alcohol as the Swedish way 'out' of the social situation and half the local youth is on them."[13] Tress began on *Narcotics in Sweden*, a carousel of 140 color slides and a ten-page typescript of captions, in the spring of 1967, working simultaneously on a 16 mm short on the drug scene called *Morphine Fix*.[14] The imagery of *Narcotics in Sweden* ranges from candid views of alienated teens hanging out in the subway to addicts shooting up in public and domestic spaces, a drug user participating in a therapy session, and the visualization of an LSD trip that Tress devised by posing a friend in front of swirling lights at a carnival (fig. 3).

While much of his work for Natur & Kultur was circumscribed by conventions of documentary photography, Tress's social and cultural circles expanded to members of the vanguard, including individuals affiliated with the Pistolteatern (Pistol Theatre), a cutting-edge venue in Stockholm's Old Town founded by Pi Lind and Staffan Olzon, whose abbreviated names formed the

Dear David + Dawn, Oct 1, 1966
Please write about how your doing + living.
I am sending some blurred no good Lapp pictures that you can throw away just to give you an idea of what the atmosphere + colors rocks like.. I wish I could show you the good ones.
Two nites ago an eccentric american body musician came to town + I knew her from the avant-garde concerts at Judson Hall so I helped her with her concert - She did a John Cage piece + then her own composition - which was playing "Swan Lake" in a transparent cellophane formal on her cello - stopping in the middle + getting into a tank of water coming out dripping wet + then finishing the piece. She created a quite a scandal in all the newspapers + lots of people came. I had to help her get on to the ladder so she

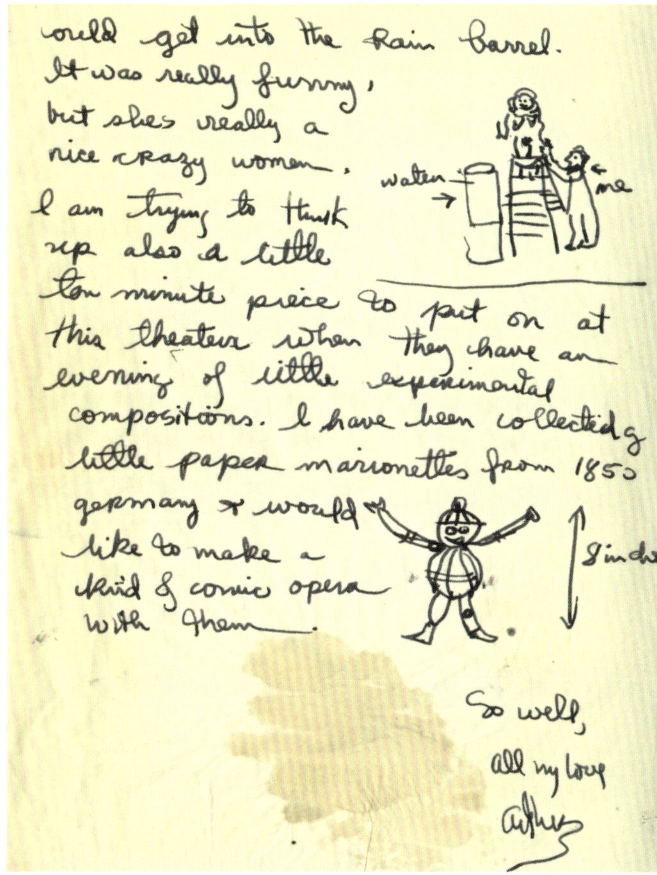

would get into the Rain barrel.
It was really funny,
but shes really a nice crazy women.
I am trying to think up also a little ten minute piece to put on at this theater when they have an evening of little experimental compositions. I have been collecting little paper marionettes from 1850 germany + would like to make a kind of comic opera with them.

So well,
All my love
Arthur

Figure 4
Arthur Tress
Letter to David Tress, October 1, 1966
Collection of the artist

word *pistol*.[15] The Pistolteatern was the site of numerous Fluxus "happenings" and experimental performances, and Tress was a regular attendee. On September 28, 1966, the cellist Charlotte Moorman gave a concert that included Nam June Paik's "Variations on a Theme by Saint-Saëns" (1965). To perform the piece Moorman would wear a formal gown of transparent cellophane, and halfway through she would immerse herself in a barrel of water. An assistant, usually Paik, would help her in and out of the barrel, but in her appearance at the Pistolteatern, Tress volunteered for that role. "Two nites ago an eccentric American body musician came to town," he wrote to his brother, "and I knew her from the avant-garde concerts at [New York City's] Judson Hall, so I helped her with her concert."[16] He included a small sketch showing himself guiding Moorman on a stepladder (fig. 4). Tress went on to say he hoped to present a ten-minute comic opera at the theater using the nineteenth-century German marionettes that he had been collecting (these would be featured in his *Teapot Opera* series twelve years later).

Although Tress failed to follow through on his puppet show, he did exhibit one of his most original photographic projects in the Pistolteatern's lobby: a series depicting the members of a rifle club at a shooting range (*skjutbana*) near his apartment in Norra Djurgården. Tress conceived the *Skjutbana* series—an independent project rather than a commission—as a photo essay on a form of contemporary ritual, something deeply embedded in Swedish culture. "I was very interested at the time in finding modern versions of ancient rituals and ceremonies as psychosocial vestiges in contemporary life," he recently recalled.[17] He loaded his Hasselblad with black-and-white film to capture the vaguely malevolent figures going about their exercises in the misty autumnal landscape. What sets the work apart from his previous documentary oeuvre is the degree to which he interacted with his subjects, choreographing their poses with the hand-painted targets to create dreamlike tableaux (fig. 5). A cross between social documentary, satire, and surrealism, the *Skjutbana* series represented a real breakthrough that would prefigure his more directorial work of the next decade.[18]

Tress was still considering a career in photojournalism and set his sights on Magnum Photos, the world's most celebrated press photo agency. Founded in 1947 in Paris by Robert Capa, Henri Cartier-Bresson, David Seymour, and George Rodger, the cooperative organization had an exclusive, invitation-only membership, a humanistic interest in world cultures and events, and a house style that favored 35 mm and emphasized candid realism. Despite its prestige, Tress recognized early on that the Magnum approach to photojournalism did not exactly align with his own sensibility. By chance he had found himself staying in the Ryokan Inn next to Cartier-Bresson's room during a visit to Kyoto in November 1965 and had taken advantage of the opportunity to show his recent prints from Mexico. The French photographer had commented that his square-format photographs, made with a Rolleiflex, were "over rationalized," "academic," and lacking in "spontaneity," but Tress still wrote

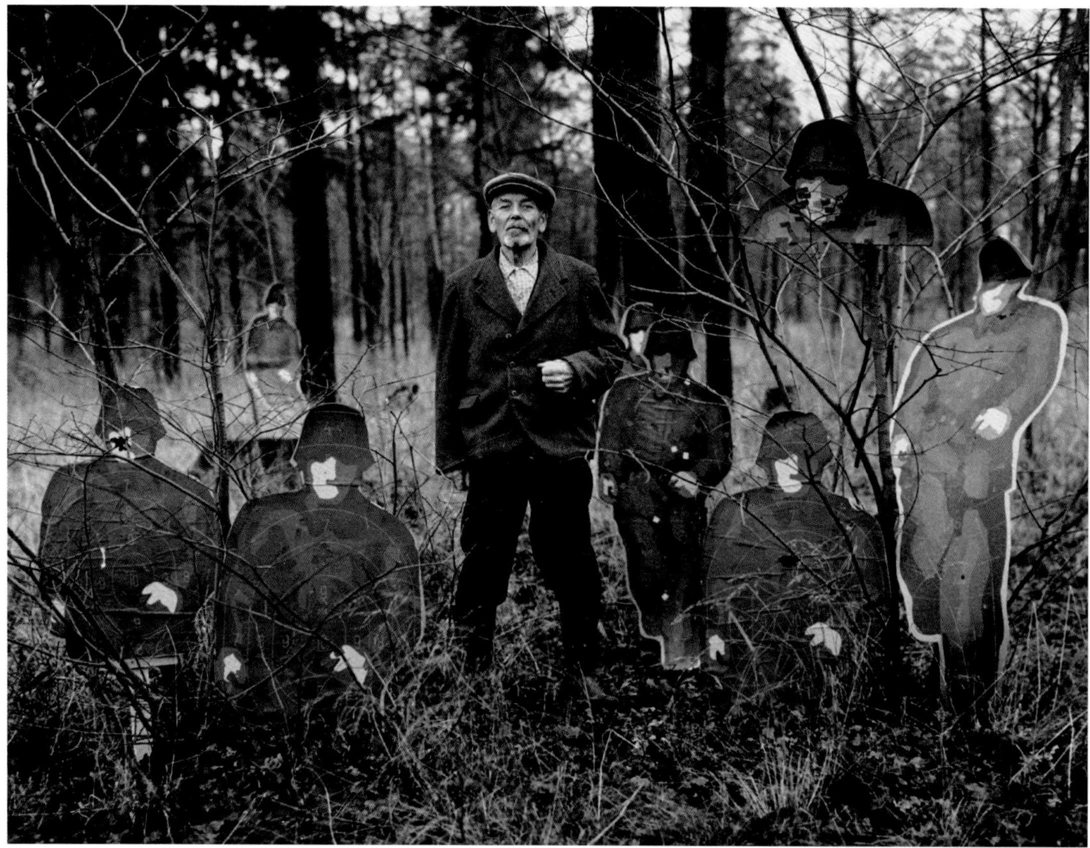

Figure 5
Arthur Tress
Target Keeper, Stockholm, Sweden, 1966
Gelatin silver print, 26.1 × 33.6 cm (10 ¼ × 13 ¼ in.)
Los Angeles, J. Paul Getty Museum, Gift of Jon and Ellen Vein Family, 2019.171.10

enthusiastically to his sister about getting to know "perhaps the greatest photographer working in that [Magnum] style."[19]

During his final year in Stockholm, focusing on his photographic output and attempting to vary his approach, Tress acquired a Leica for 35 mm color work. In January 1967 he struck a deal with a travel agency to document Swedish tourists and their excursions around the island city of Bathurst (now Banjul) in the Gambia—a popular destination for Scandinavians escaping the dark winter months—in exchange for his flights and hotel expenses. At the same time he entered into an agreement with Natur & Kultur to produce filmstrips on African life in the kingdoms along the Niger. He spent two weeks with an expedition sponsored by Radio Gambia gathering folk music from various villages, and in a stroke of luck he was able to photograph the Sigui mask festival in Mali's Dogon country, which takes place only every sixty years. Tress traveled as far as the mountains of North Dahomey, where he rented a motorbike to reach outlying villages. The trip was eye-opening and productive but physically challenging; he was afflicted with malaria, dysentery, meningitis, and finally a serious case of hepatitis, and in Mali the police confiscated his film on two occasions.[20] During his return flight he had an epiphany somewhere over the Pyrenees. The Swedish tourists on the plane "remind me of how terribly dull + conventional Sweden is + spoiled," he wrote to his sister, "so unless something happens with the book publisher I shall probably be coming back to New York which at least has the illusion of something happening."[21]

Back in Stockholm, he photographed the first public session of the International War Crimes Tribunal, co-organized by Bertrand Russell and Jean-Paul Sartre, and a kite-flying contest at the Swedish Academy of Art and Design, as well as his series on teenage drug use. "Now I am working with a Leica in 35 mm and in color and my style is changing," he wrote to his brother, "to put much more spontaneous action in my pictures." He added that it might be "an unfortunate change, because the pictures become too casual and sloppy and also 'human story' quality which is boring to me, but which magazines like."[22] At the Russell Tribunal, Tress made the crucial acquaintance of the Magnum photographer (and at the time Magnum's European vice-president) Marc Riboud, who agreed to meet later in Paris to review his work.

Tress visited Magnum's Paris office on Bastille Day 1967, and excitedly wrote to his family that Riboud liked his kite and narcotics photographs, which were done in the style of Cartier-Bresson. Riboud's enthusiasm "made me very happy as you have to be a better photographer to work with such ordinary material."[23] Riboud agreed to take the work to Magnum's New York bureau, but Tress continued to doubt his own suitability for the firm. "With this agency you must work in their style which is very spontaneous, natural photo-journalism which is not exactly the way I think or work," he wrote, adding, "I hate this snap! snap!—I still want to do my artistic flower photos etc. I am not such a man of the world—to go running about to wars and elections and riots."[24]

Tress's final summer in Sweden was spent finishing his filmstrips for Natur & Kultur (including *The Lapps*, *Empires of the Sudan—Timbuktu*, *Why Study African Religion?*, *African Religion and World View*, and *Young People of West Africa*) while slowly recovering from hepatitis. Without his usual nervous energy, he stayed close to home, photographing flowers in Djurgården.[25] Anticipating his twenty-seventh birthday in late November, which would mean he was no longer of draft age and could end the ruse of being a PhD student and return home, he quipped to his brother, "After all these years—8—of student deferments they must be getting suspicious. I should be the head of a university by now."[26] Although he was desperate to leave before another Swedish winter, he delayed his departure when he stumbled on the opportunity to buy a cheap ferryboat ticket to Leningrad (now Saint Petersburg) and attend the fiftieth-anniversary celebrations of the Bolshevik Revolution in early November. "It's going to be fabulous," he wrote to his sister, "flowers + vodka + Leningrad + drunk Russians waving red flags," adding, "I must do a lot of reading before the 3rd because I know nothing about it at all."[27] After a summer spent photographing still lifes with his Hasselblad, he worried that he might no longer have the reflexes for action photography, so he used his Leica, with no film in the camera, to practice shooting.[28]

Tress made the most of his seventy-two hours in Leningrad (fig. 6). In a long letter to David he described marching in the "People's Parade" with a group of female textile workers, "one enormous MASS moving by its own unstoppable momentum," but added, "This is all very bad for my liver as I am getting slightly squashed."[29] After the parade, he noted, the mood changed abruptly as people had difficulty navigating the blockades:

> This is where I made a mistake + took a photograph of some people angry + being pushed back by the police at a barricade. The police got angry + put me on a motorcycle: took me to a police station. They all began shouting at me like I was a little child, scolding me + shaking their heads, of course in Russian. I kept on saying I'm sorry + tried to look very apologetic, confessing immediately to everything they accused me of. I pointed to the camera + went through the motions of opening it up . . . they all examined the film, holding up to the light, very pleased as though they had caught a C.I.A. agent . . . I could see they were actually in a good mood + a little drunk so I wasn't afraid or nervous even (as) they waggled their fingers at me as a last warning + escorted me back to the hotel.[30]

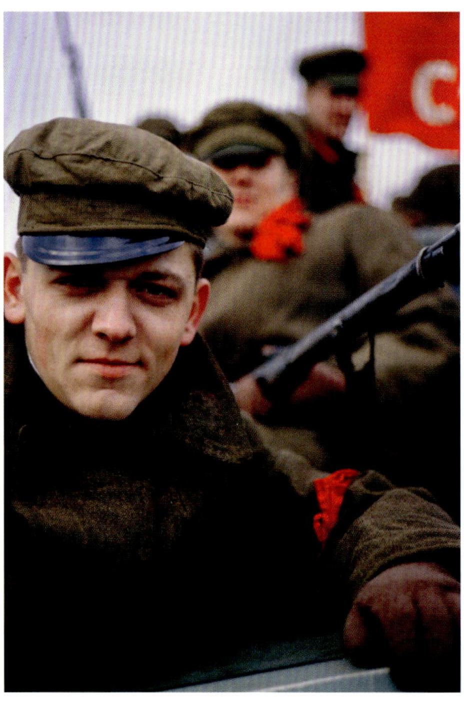

Figure 6
Arthur Tress
Untitled (Leningrad), 1967
Kodachrome slide, 3.8 × 2.5 cm (1½ × 1 in.)
Collection of the artist

Tress was dismayed to learn, upon returning to Stockholm, that his slow ferry cruise meant that his photographs were no longer newsworthy and would be passed over by the Swedish press, who had already contracted images from big agencies or magazines like *Paris Match*.[31]

In his final letters from Stockholm, Tress summarized his professional achievements during his years of travel. He had completed eighteen photo essays on a range of topics, among them "Japanese Fishing Village," "India Bull Fight," "Nepalese Buddhism," "Timbuktu," and "Teenage Drug Addiction." He had thrived in the field of

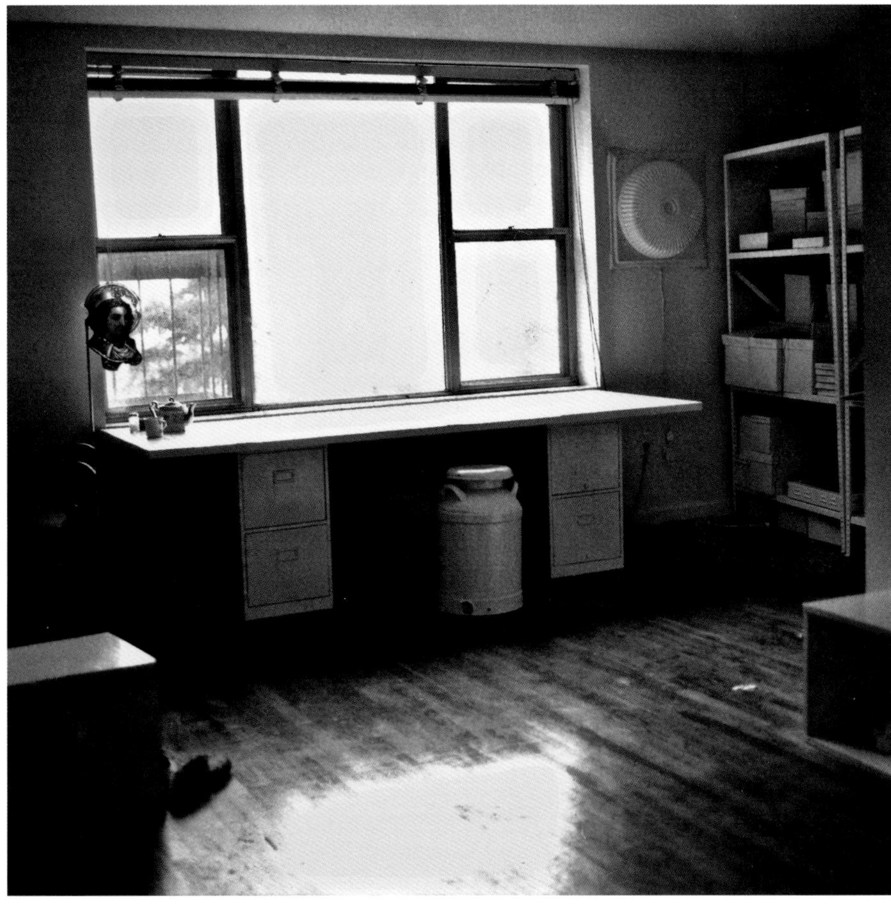

Figure 7
Arthur Tress
Apartment Interior, 2 Riverside Drive, New York, New York, 1970
Gelatin silver print, 5.7 × 5.7 cm (2 ¼ × 2 ¼ in.)
Collection of the artist

educational filmstrips, and his photographs had appeared in several Swedish magazines, including *Foto och Filmteknik*, *Fotografisk årsbok*, and *Popular Fotografi*. But just as he was on the cusp of acceptance in the tiny Swedish photography world, he felt the magnetic pull of New York. "I'm afraid I can't just go on like this the rest of my life," he wrote to his boyfriend Tobi, "moving from one city to another." He confided, however, that "the idea of N.Y. frightens me . . . so brutal + impersonal + you feel so small. I felt people were beginning to know me in Stockholm . . . I belonged a little bit . . . you could never feel that way in New York."[32]

Soon after Tress's return to Manhattan in December 1967, he rented a loft in the camera district near Herald Square, and his fears about the big city were quickly realized. Early in the new year he complained to Tobi about his "very bad neighborhood, full of factories + trucks + bad air and dust," and reported that he was robbed on his first night and his Leica stolen, "so I feel very depressed + vulnerable."[33] But as if to convince himself, he added, "I don't have any plans, but I am going to become very successful in New York, in spite of myself, + be making lots of money. Inside I am all 'mixed up'—New York is so violent + noisy + so many people. I am really frightened, but it has so much interesting culture + people."[34]

After a year, Tress moved to a 450-square-foot studio apartment at 2 Riverside Drive, a quiet neighborhood on the Upper West Side, five blocks south of his father's address (fig. 7). Its large window overlooked Riverside Drive Park at 72nd Street and the Hudson River, the site of a number of photographs in his *Dream Collector* series. He painted the walls white to match those of his Stockholm apartment and kept the small space

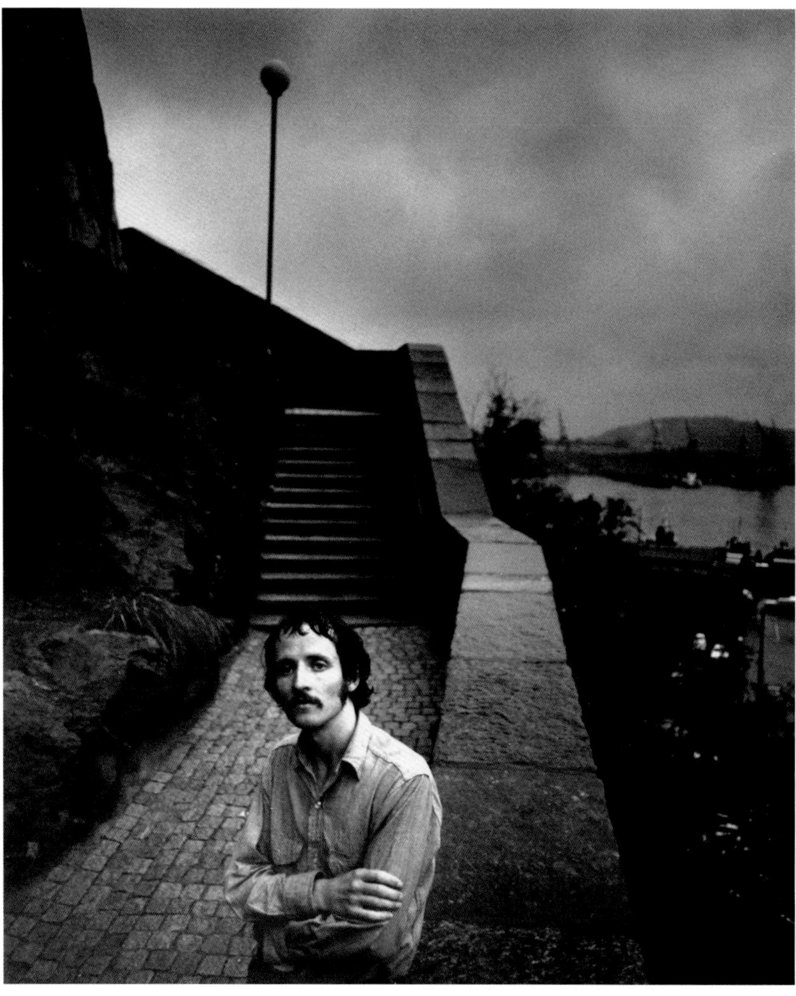

Figure 8
Arthur Tress
Tobi Astner in Gothenburg, Sweden, 1969
Gelatin silver print, 25.4 × 20.3 cm (10 × 8 in.)
Collection of the artist

minimally furnished, with a door resting on two file cabinets to serve as a desk and austere steel shelving holding boxes of prints and negatives. He slept on a futon and converted a closet into a small darkroom with film tanks, an enlarger, trays, and a dry mount press. He would wash his prints in the bathtub, squeegee them on the tile bathroom wall, and dry them on a wire hanging from the shower.

Contributing to Tress's anxiety after his move from Stockholm to New York was the hostility he felt from others toward his sexual orientation. In high school, when he had begun experimenting with men, his father had sent him to a psychiatrist to undergo a form of conversion therapy. Naturally it did not work; Tress continued hooking up with people of both sexes during and after his college years. In Sweden his much more serious relationship with Tobi brought him to the realization of his authentic identity as a gay man (fig. 8). After he moved back to New York, letters he received from Tobi and another male friend, Jan Gunnar, were intercepted by Tress's father, who read aloud his correspondence over the phone when he was traveling. That practice led to some awkward conversations. "I didn't read your last letter," Tress wrote to Tobi from North Carolina in the spring of 1968, "but my father did, + he said in it how much you loved me, which I appreciate, but you must be a little more discreet in the future. Don't worry he seems to think you're a girl."[35]

Between March and October 1969, Tress created an extraordinary series of photographs of men in the Ramble, a section of Central Park known as a gay cruising ground (plates 13–20). His *Ramble* series was a personal body of work that he did not exhibit or publish, because doing so could have exposed the photographer and his subjects to embarrassment or harassment.[36] In some ways it might be seen as a sequel to the *Skjutbana* series and his earlier documentary projects, in which he approached his subjects as forms of contemporary ritual. The critical difference with the *Ramble* photographs was that he was now a member of the tribe he was documenting and therefore emotionally invested in its customs. In a letter to Tobi, he described a lonely experience wandering into Central Park after watching a film at the Museum of Modern Art: "At the fountain I spoke to a boy with lovely red hair and a camera but was too embarrassed to try and make it with him—so I wandered off to look for some pond pollution which I didn't find; then into the Ramble—where I felt that at least they would all be queer—but no one seemed interested + I began getting a headache."[37] Looking back on this time, he recently wrote:

> I had myself spent many, many hours steadfastly "cruising" usually without much success. I just didn't seem to have the knack or the correct sexual pheromones so I seemed, to my frustration and anger, to be a perpetual outsider, even within my own peer group. In taking on the *Ramble* series I already knew first-hand the furtive glances, the poses, the false flirtations, the quick rejections, the masquerades of hyper "machismo" or fey passivity as indicated by tokens of strategically placed articles of clothing, the endless turns around the same paths again and again, often with feelings of great guilt and self-loathing and the avoiding of any conversation or eye contact in surreptitious, anonymous comings together.[38]

What had attracted Tress to New York City was its status as the center of the photography world. Soon after his arrival he made the rounds of the photo venues and composed a remarkable gallery guide that would later be published in the British magazine *Creative Camera*.[39] In it he described Louis Bernstein's retrospective at Dorothy Koppelman's Terrain Gallery in Greenwich Village; Lawrence Weissman's solo show at the Hicks Street Gallery in Brooklyn Heights; displays of Eliot Porter and Ansel Adams prints at the Sierra Club Gallery on East 53rd Street; *The People Protest*, a group exhibition organized by Larry Fink at Columbia University's Crypt Gallery; a show of Magnum photographers at the Riverside Museum; a Julia Margaret Cameron exhibition at Robert Schoelkopf's gallery on Madison Avenue; and displays at the Metropolitan Museum of Art and the Museum of Modern Art. He lavished particular attention on Norbert Kleber's Underground Gallery, a long, narrow space connected to Kleber's basement apartment in Greenwich Village. Despite being one of the most prominent photography venues in the city, the Underground Gallery operated on a shoestring budget. "Because of the gallery's high expenses the photographer must pay a hanging fee of $25," Tress explained, "plus $25 electricity per monthly show. He must also pay for his own publicity and mailing costs. At each exhibition prints are for sale for about $25—one-third going to the gallery and two-thirds to the photographer." Kleber's 1967 holiday exhibition included photographs by Minor White, Bruce Davidson, and Duane Michals.

Tress had arrived just as the nascent photo scene was starting to heat up, with the critic A. D. Coleman commencing his "Latent Image" column in the *Village Voice* in June 1968; Lee Witkin inaugurating his gallery on East 60th Street in March 1969; Maggie Sherwood establishing the Floating Foundation of Photography at the 79th Street Boat Basin in 1970; Tennyson Schad opening LIGHT Gallery at Madison Avenue and 78th Street in November 1971; Soho Photo, an artists' co-op founded by a group of *New York Times* photographers, opening on Prince Street in December 1971 (the site of Tress's exhibitions *Vision Seekers* in 1973 and *Phallic Phantasies* in 1977); Larry Siegel establishing the Midtown Y Photography Gallery, the first nonprofit exhibition space for photography in Manhattan, in 1972; Alex Harley founding the non-profit 4th Street Photo Gallery in 1973, a year that was also marked by the publication of the first volumn of *The Black Photographers Annual*; and Cornell Capa founding the city's first museum of photography, the International Center of Photography, in a Fifth Avenue townhouse in November 1974. Small exhibitions were also mounted in various camera shops and processing labs around the city, including Discovery Gallery/Modernage in several locations[40] and Raffi Photo Lab's gallery at 21 West 46th Street, where Tress exhibited *Daymares*, as his *Dream Collector* series was originally called, in the summer of 1972.

Tress's career thrived in the new environment. During his first two years in New York he concentrated on establishing his commercial practice and took on commissions in social documentary photography. Early in 1968 he visited the George Eastman House in Rochester, the site of a dynamic contemporary exhibition program under the curator Nathan Lyons. He also met Lyons's wife, Joan, who was freelancing as a designer on an ambitious exhibition project co-organized by the Genesee Valley School Development Association and the Memorial Art Gallery.[41] It was a fortuitous encounter, resulting in Tress's commission to spend the month of May in Appalachia photographing indigenous craftspeople and folk musicians and gathering examples of their handiwork for an exhibit to be circulated in Rochester's public schools. During a subsequent summer trip, he spent two weeks in residence at the Penland School of Craft in North Carolina, where he turned his attention from crafts to the subject of rural poverty.

The Sierra Club Gallery in New York exhibited Tress's Appalachia photographs—*The "Disturbed" Land*—in October,[42] and A. D. Coleman, who would become an important champion of Tress's work, published an enthusiastic review in the *Village Voice* of this first solo show: "By turns lyrical, dramatic, and shocking, the photographs are telling revelations of a lifestyle rapidly being shattered." Coleman compared Tress to the classic Farm Security Administration photographers Walker Evans and Dorothea Lange, while affirming that despite their influence, "he is entirely his own man."[43] In his article "American Documentary Photography," published with a selection of his Appalachia images in *Fotografisk årsbok 1970*, Tress wrote: "For these photographs I very consciously used the earlier style of 1930s Depression documentary photography. One reason for this is that too many people believe the situation to have changed, that there are no more poor white people starving to death in the southern mountains. I wanted to show that the poor whites are still there and look exactly the same as they did twenty years ago."[44]

In 1968 Tress began receiving commissions from the government organization Volunteers in Service to America (VISTA). Assignments included photographing Black sharecroppers in South Carolina, the effects of strip mining in Kentucky, and the impoverished lives of newly arrived immigrants in San Francisco's Chinatown and the Hassidic community in the Williamsburg section of Brooklyn.[45] His social documentary work appeared in *VISTA Volunteer* magazine, the Methodist Church publication *World Outlook*, *Harper's Magazine*, and several Swedish periodicals. The fundamental tension that underscored Tress's photographic practice during this period was expressed by the photographer in his text "Shooting for VISTA" (1969), in which he described his decision to earn a living in photography: "I was too much interested in the world and people for fashion or advertising, and photo-journalism seemed the best way. By luck I got these assignments from VISTA and was able to experience what photo-reporting is all about." But he expressed ambivalence about this kind of work. "I'm still not convinced it's really me, all this life and reality and action," he wrote, adding, "I'm a bit too removed and a dreamer—but it has expanded my thinking technically (shooting in difficult light); personally (meeting people, travelling, arranging interviews); and visually (working rapidly by intuition)."[46]

In letters to Tobi he often complained about the financial necessity of taking on editorial assignments documenting pollution and poverty while putting aside the creation of more personal artistic work projecting his own emotions. During a particularly miserable trip to Point Hope, Alaska, to photograph Inuit people for the educational publisher Holt, Rinehart & Winston in September 1969, he wrote to Tobi: "Well here I sit as the rain drizzles down. I am looking at a sled dog who is looking worriedly at me. The damn sun is out until about nine at night. I am not in the mood for this at all + feel like going home as soon as can be."[47] A few months later he wrote, "It's hard to do 'projects' on one's own. I want to be completely free but it scares me . . . I keep thinking up reasons to take pictures, but I just want to wander . . . I'll probably starve to death. I guess I just want to be an artist again."[48] In his contemporaneous text "The Photograph as Magical Image," published in *Album* (1970),[49] Tress suggested that "perhaps why so much of today's photography doesn't 'grab us' or mean anything to our personal lives is that it fails to touch upon the hidden life of the imagination and fantasy, which is hungry for stimulation. The documentary photographer supplies us with facts or drowns in humanity, while the pictorialist, avant-garde or conservative, pleases us with mere aesthetically correct compositions." In conclusion he asked the reader, "Where are the photographs *we can pray to, that will make us well again, or scare the hell out of us?*"[50]

Despite his increasing angst over his many professional assignments, as expressed not only in his letters but also in a New Year's 1969 message to himself in his notebook ("avoid becoming an academic producer of stock photos"), commissions from newspaper and magazine editors and stock photo licensing would be Tress's bread and butter throughout the 1970s. Even the images he created for his artistic photobooks found their way into other kinds of commercial publications. The same notebook lists an eclectic international array of publishers, editors, and periodicals he was in contact with, including Afro-American Heritage House, *After Dark*, Almqvist & Wiksell (Stockholm), American Craftsmen's Council, American Education Publishers, *American Heritage* magazine, *Atlas* (Paris), *Audubon* magazine, *Avant Garde*, *Black Star*, Da Capo Press, *Dance* magazine, *Du* (Zurich), *Esquire*, *Eye*, Eye Gate House, Filmstrip House, Grolier, Guidance Associates (filmstrip producer), Harcourt, Brace & World, *Harper's*, Holt, Rinehart & Winston, Alfred A. Knopf, Laidlaw Brothers (textbook producer), *Life*, *Look*, Macmillan, *National Geographic*, *National Wilderness* magazine, *Natural History*, Natur & Kultur (Stockholm), *New York Post*, *New York Times*, *Newsweek*, Norstedts förlag (Stockholm), *Pageant* magazine, *Planète* (Paris), *Psychology Today*, Random House, Religious News Service, *Scholastic* magazine, Simon & Schuster, *Smithsonian* magazine, True, *Venture*, VISTA, Franklin Watts, and *World Outlook*.[51]

Also listed in Tress's late 1960s notebook are several photo-licensing agencies that carried his images, including Magnum, Photo Researchers, Pictorial Parade, and Photo Trends. "Photographers of my generation kind of cobbled together a living," Tress later recalled. "I had a portfolio that I'd bring around weekly to Condé Nast and various educational publications, *New York* magazine, *Time*, *Newsweek*, *Business Week*, to get editorial jobs: small, fairly insignificant images on pages."[52] Tress's own typescript stock list from around 1970 (fig. 9), bearing his Riverside Drive address, includes a range of social documentary images drawn from his international and domestic travels. Under "New York City," Tress listed subjects from his *Open Space* and *Dream Collector* series, including vest pocket parks, traffic congestion, dream studies, fantasies, and nightmares.

In his quest to make a name for himself in the New York art world, Tress focused more on work than on socializing, spending his days photographing and hawking his images to publishers and many of his evenings in the darkroom. His

Figure 9
Arthur Tress
Stock list, ca. 1970
Collection of the artist

STOCK

ARTHUR TRESS/ 2 RIVERSIDE DRIVE,NEW YORK,NEW YORK,10023

TEL:(212) 877-1305

A: AFRICA: TRIBAL RITES AND CEREMONIES:DOGON:GAMBIA:NIGER
B: BUDDHISM:JAPAN:THAILAND:NEPAL
C: COUPLES:COURTING:MARRIAGE:DIVORCE
CANADA:MONTREAL:VANCOUVER:HALIFAX
D: DEATH:WIDOWS:FUNERALS
E: ETHNIC GROUPS:CHINESE,ITALIAN,PUERTO RICAN,JEWISH
F: FISHING:NEW ENGLAND,LOUISIANA,CALIFORNIA
G: GAY LIFE:LIBERATION,MALE & FEMALE
H: HEALTH:HOSPITALS,NURSING, CLINICS
I: INDIANS:CHEROKEE,NAVAJO
M: MATH CONCEPTS:ADDITION,SUBTRACTION,NUMBERS
N: NATIONAL PARKS:ANIMALS AND PLANTS,DEATH VALLEY, BIG BEND
NATURE:FOUR SEASONS IN CLOSE UP ,DESTUCTION OF ENVIRONMENT
O: OLD AGE: LONLINESS, HOMES, JOBS
P: POVERTY: APPALACHIA,COAL MINING, SCHOOLS, NUTRITION, HOUSING
BLACKS:HOUSING, SCHOOLS, GHETTO
POLLUTION:AIR,CAR,WATER,VISUAL,RIVER,OCEAN,OIL,NOISE,SMOKE,STRIPMINE
R: RECYCLING:GARBAGE,PAPER,BOTTLES, SEWERAGE:ECOLOGY
S: SOLAR ENERGY: HOUSES,OFFICES, POOLS, SOUTHWEST
T: TRIBES:ESKIMOES,LAPPS,MAYANS, SHAMANS,DANCES, LIFESTYLE
TEENAGERS: SCHOOLS,PROBLEMS,LUST
W: WOMEN:LIBERATION,OLDER WOMEN,MOTHERS
U: UNEMPLOYMENT:WHITE,BLACK,INDUSTRIAL &RURAL
URBAN ENVIRONMENT:ALIENATION,RENEWAL,GARDENS:HOUSING,ECONOMY

SOCIOLOGY PHOTOGRAPHS

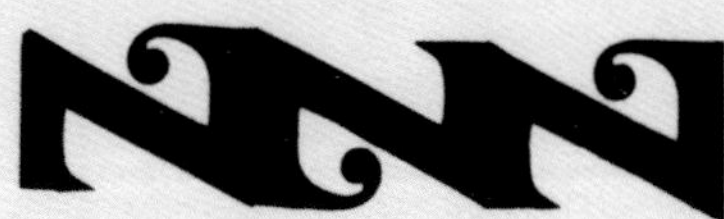

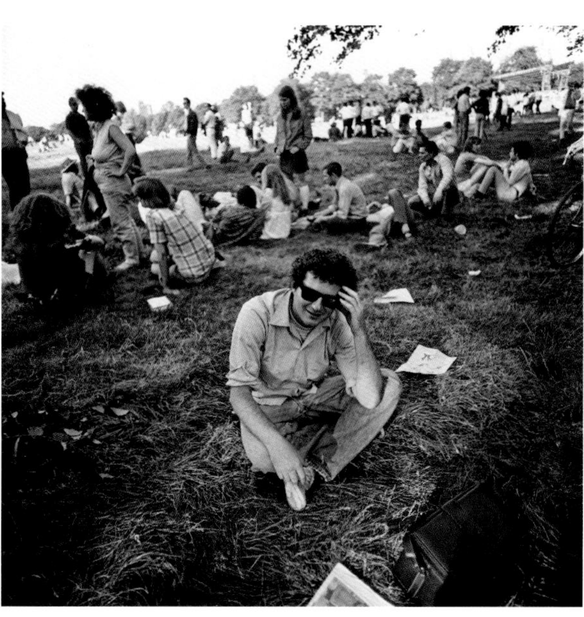

Figure 10
Anonymous
Arthur Tress in Central Park after Gay Pride Rally, 1970
Gelatin silver print, 5.7 × 5.7 cm (2 ¼ × 2 ¼ in.)
Collection of Arthur Tress

notebook mentions several of the photographers with whom he crossed paths, such as Bruce Davidson, Joel Meyerowitz, George Tice, Diane Arbus, and Leonard Freed, but his own circle of friends was quite small, including the photographers Duane Michals (to whom he introduced himself after Michals's *Sequences* exhibition at the Underground Gallery in 1968, a major source of inspiration[53]), Laurence Salzmann, Marcia Keegan, and Charles Henri Ford. He continued his correspondence with Tobi Astner, and the two reconnected in New York (in the summer of 1970) and Sweden (in the summer of 1971), but in time they naturally drifted apart. Aside from Tobi and an aspiring writer named Bruce, the dedicatee of his photobook *Shadow*, whom he began seeing in 1972, Tress had few protracted romantic relationships and instead sought hookups in gay bars and bathhouses, the Ramble, and the West Side piers.

While Tress kept his Ramble portfolio under wraps, New York's first gay pride parade (officially called the Christopher Street Liberation Day March), held in June 1970 on the first anniversary of the Stonewall uprising, gave him the courage to turn his camera on the LGBTQIA+ community. He photographed a gay couple on their Christopher Street stoop before the parade (plate 21), and later recalled, "I was so impressed that they were actually holding hands in public, it changed me a lot."[54] An acquaintance used Tress's camera to capture him sitting on the lawn in Central Park near the parade's terminus (fig. 10). That summer Tress also photographed the morning after a rooftop sleepover on the Lower East Side (plate 22). "The boy under the flag lived on the top floor of the walk up," Tress recollected recently.

> He stayed mostly in his tiny apartment and made paper flowers that his friends would sell in the streets, and during the summer had frequent all-night slumber parties on the roof for his neighborhood gay buddies. I had a bit of a crush on him which was not really reciprocated. I think he sensed I was a bit too Uptown for his scene. We would bring some food, candles, pot, and chat and play music. The mattresses were already in situ and there was occasionally friendly fraternization during the night. I took the photo at dawn when everyone was just waking up to a rather cool gray morning. I remember walking, a bit sadly, down the deserted gray Second Avenue at that early hour to the subway entrance to go back Uptown, leaving a sort of fantasy bohemian scene which did not quite accept me nor I its freedom from growing up.[55]

This photograph, and the slightly melancholic memories that it conjures up for the artist today, was unusual in Tress's oeuvre at the time, which was generally directed to the outside world rather than to his personal experiences and relationships.

One of Tress's most important professional associates was Peter Schults, the head of the stock agency Photo Researchers, whom he met through his sister, Madeleine, when he was in high school. Schults carried Tress's stock photographs and copublished *The Dream Collector* (1972). It

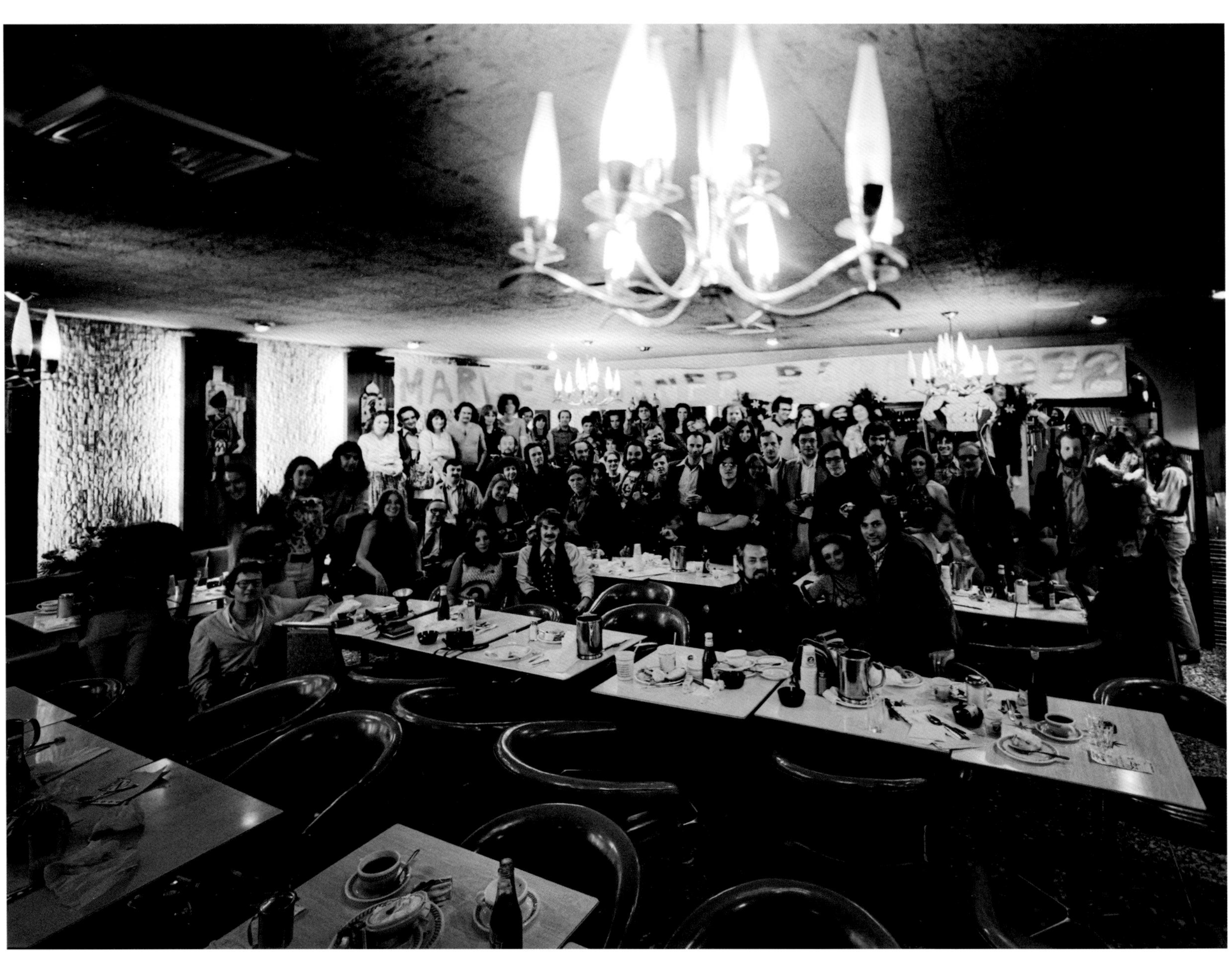

Figure 11
Neal Slavin
(American, born 1941)
Market Diner Bash, 1972
Courtesy of Neal Slavin

was through Schults that Tress met Robert David Lion Gardiner, the fabulously wealthy and eccentric owner of Gardiner's Island in East Hampton, where Schults lived while working on a biography of the self-proclaimed "16th Lord of the Manor." (Gardiner and Schults eventually severed ties, and the biography was never completed.) Gardiner's private grounds provided an important setting for Tress's *Theater of the Mind* photographs (plate 125). Schults also introduced Tress to James Shields Jr., a professor in the School of Education at the City College of New York, who became a lifelong friend. Tress gave Shields lessons in photography, which he put to use in his own publications, and in return Shields helped Tress expand his network. Through Shields he met John Melser, the innovative principal at the newly opened P.S. 3 in the West Village, where he made a series of photographs for *The Dream Collector*.

Both Tress and Shields participated in the legendary Market Diner Bash of May 14, 1972, a "happening" attended by a hundred or so members of the New York photography world (and a few out-of-towners) at a restaurant on 11th Avenue, organized by A. D. Coleman and the photographer Neal Slavin. "Boiled down to its essence," Coleman explained in his *Village Voice* column, "the idea was to ask a roomful of photographers to bring their own cameras to a celebration at the Market Diner, said celebration to serve as both the opening for the invitational group exhibit and its subject."[56] The attendees—including Les Krims, Judy Dater, Eva Rubinstein, Bea Nettles, Robert D'Alessandro, Harry Wilks, Wolf von dem Bussche, Betty Hahn, Norman Rothschild, James Enyeart, the dealers Lee Witkin and Norbert Kleber, and the up-and-coming curators Harold Jones, Anne Tucker, and Weston Naef—were invited to create their own photographs of the event that would be shown, a month later, in a group exhibition at the Underground Gallery. (Tress brought a Batman torso standee as a prop; it appears in the rear of Slavin's group portrait behind the distant chandelier at right [fig. 11]. Tress sits in the left foreground, in front of Mary Ellen Mark.)[57] Also in attendance was Maggie Sherwood, the entrepreneurial founder and director of the Floating Foundation of Photography (FFP), a houseboat serving as an exhibition and education space. The boat was moored at the 79th Street Boat Basin, not far from Tress's apartment, and occasionally traveled on the Hudson River. Notably absent from the gathering were John Szarkowski, head of MoMA's photography department, and the artists he championed, including Garry Winogrand and Lee Friedlander, and the artists associated with the Kamoinge Workshop, the collective of Black photographers founded in 1963.

Tress participated in one of the FFP's most innovative programs—conducting photography workshops in New York–area prisons. In 1974 he and several other photographers traveled on a yellow school bus to the Sing Sing Correctional Facility in Ossining to share their work with inmates. Tress created a series of staged photographs in the prison yard that he considered an extension of his *Theater of the Mind* series, though his book had already gone to press. Participating in a similar FFP program at the Bedford Hills Correctional Facility for Women, Tress made his *Portrait of Number 74G96* (fig. 12), which was selected as one of the "ten 'toughest' photographs of 1975" by Douglas Davis for *Esquire* magazine, along with works by Judy Dater, George Tice, Neal Slavin, Emmet Gowin, and Stephen Shore, among others.[58]

The tension between documentary realism and social surrealism colors much of Tress's work of the 1970s, including *Open Space in the Inner City*. That series, which occupied his attention from 1969 to 1971, ultimately intersected with his first major photo book, *The Dream Collector* (1972). His work on the *Dream Collector* series continued after the

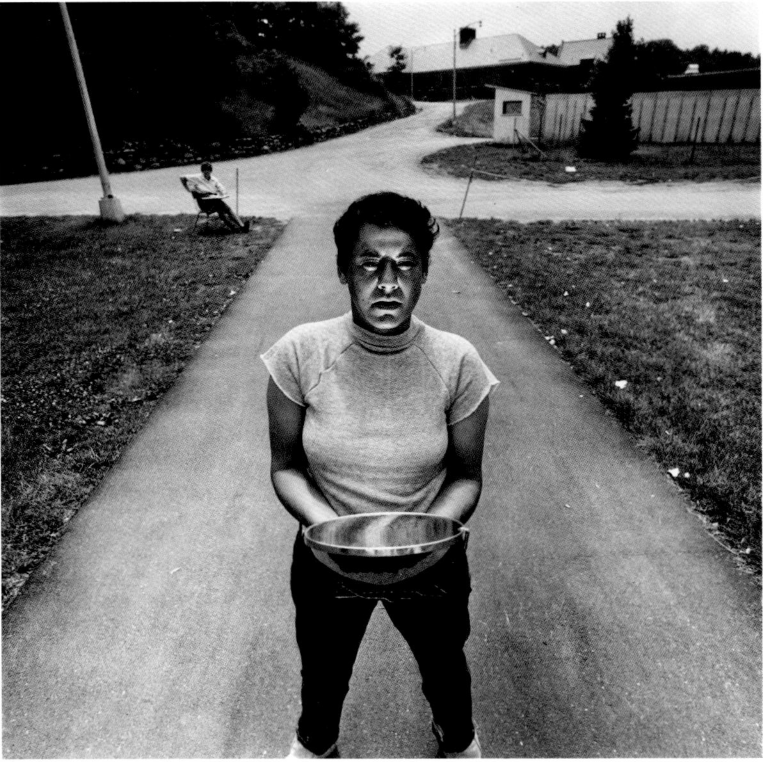

Figure 12
Arthur Tress
Portrait of Number 74G96, Bedford Hills, New York, 1975
Gelatin silver print, 25.4 × 25.4 cm (10 × 10 in.)
Collection of the artist

book's publication, with new images appearing in the "Child's Play" section of *Theater of the Mind* (1976).[59] The publication of *Theater of the Mind*, which included an introduction by A. D. Coleman, coincided with the appearance of Coleman's seminal article "The Directorial Mode: Notes toward a Definition" in the September 1976 issue of *Artforum*, which used one of Tress's *Theater* plates as an illustration.[60] In both of his essays Coleman discussed the historical antecedents of directorial, or staged, photography as practiced by Tress and a handful of his contemporaries, including Les Krims, William Wegman, Lucas Samaras, and Duane Michals. Michals, too, contributed a brief text, "Tress's Vaudeville," to *Theater of the Mind*. "Tress will upset you," he warned the reader. "When he photographs you with a friend or lover, you will become an actor. You will perform in his theater and that drama one soon realizes is one's own. Don't be surprised if Arthur suddenly asks you to put your mother in a wheelbarrow, and don't be amazed to find yourself doing it."[61]

The subcurrent of kink and sexual symbolism that cropped up in Tress's *Theater of the Mind* series surfaced more explicitly in his exhibition *Phallic Phantasies* at the Alfred Stieglitz Gallery of Soho Photo in October 1977, which he has described as "my first coming out as a specifically gay artist."[62] Eight months after selections from Robert Mapplethorpe's *X Portfolio* were first exhibited at The Kitchen, Tress's show did not receive the same level of attention, but Marcia Wooding published an interview with Tress in *SoHo Weekly News* in which he revealed that this body of work derived from his next planned photobook, *Priapus, Study of Phallic Phantasies*. "In my book *Theater of the Mind*, I began to use a certain amount of phallic symbolism," he explained. "People were holding out gas pumps towards one another and women were stroking snakes' heads and there were lighthouses in the background. I thought it would be interesting to do a whole book on that motif."[63] It was a remarkably bold series for the time, featuring graphic sadomasochistic imagery and male genitalia, and some of the images would reappear in gay men's magazines, including *Christopher*

Street, Mandate, Drummer—which also showcased Mapplethorpe's work—and *Honcho*.[64] In an artist statement for the *Phallic Phantasies* exhibition Tress openly proclaimed his queer orientation. "Photography is one of the most directly sensual of the arts," he wrote, "and it is important for every photographer to express and confront his own sexuality in an open and direct way through his work. This project is important to me in that it expresses many of my own erotic desires and interests that in the past I have been timid to deal with."[65] In the spring of 1978 the Robert Samuel Gallery opened under the direction of Sam Hardison on Broadway in Greenwich Village with a program devoted to "the masculine image in art," hosting a series of exhibitions of work by Paul Cadmus, George Platt Lynes, David Hockney, Duane Michals, Robert Mapplethorpe, and Lucas Samaras.[66] In April 1979 the gallery featured Tress's exhibition *Men between Themselves: Images of Male Self Sexuality*, and the following year this body of work appeared under the imprint of the Geneva publisher Bernard Letu as the photobook *Facing Up*.

One can find no clearer example of the essential conservatism of the 1970s art world concerning explicit male nudity than the *New York Times* photography critic Gene Thornton's review of *The Male Nude: A Survey in Photography* at the Marcuse Pfeifer Gallery in June 1978. "There is something to be said for old-fashioned prudery when the unclothed human body is a man's body," Thornton wrote. "No one denies that men's bodies are sexually attractive to most women and also to some men. Nor does anyone deny that the place of the male nude in art is an old and honorable one. Nevertheless, there is something disconcerting about the sight of a man's naked body being presented primarily as a sex object."[67] In his review in the *Village Voice*, Ben Lifson expressed similar concerns: "The nude is a matter of convention. In photography it's difficult, because everyday experience doesn't readily proffer naked people, to say nothing of men with phallic symbols between their legs. A nude in a photograph is presumed to be naked in order to be photographed. The male nude is harder still. A man's body doesn't lend itself to abstraction like a woman's."

One of the settings for Tress's *Phallic Phantasies* was the former YMCA at 72nd Street and the Hudson River, built in the 1940s to house employees of the New York Central Railroad. Tress began using rooms in the boarded-up building as a makeshift studio during the late 1970s (fig. 13). Marcia Wooding described being led by Tress into the Railroad Y in her article "Further Adventures in the Theater of the Mind," published in the summer 1978 issue of *35 mm Photography*: "Arthur jiggles the screwdriver in the hole of a knobless door. It springs open with a loud creak. Tress leads the way . . . [T]he interior of the place is a wreck. Plaster and paint are falling off the wall in multi-sized chunks. Some kind of breakfast cereal is spilled out on the floor. In this environment even a bunch of little red o's take on an ominous glow."[68] Tress had long been attracted to such ruined and marginalized places. As a teenager in the late 1950s he loved to photograph decaying Coney Island on gray winter days, when he could find himself alone amid the closed attractions. While an undergraduate at Bard, he briefly squatted in an abandoned greenhouse on the grounds of Blithewood, an early twentieth-century estate adjacent to the campus, turning it into a secret art studio that he decorated with antique scientific charts the school had discarded.[69] And as a queer New Yorker he became a regular visitor to the abandoned Hudson River piers, both as settings for his art and as safe spaces for sexual encounters with other gay men. Later, in the mid-1980s, he would spend three years creating and photographing dozens of elaborate

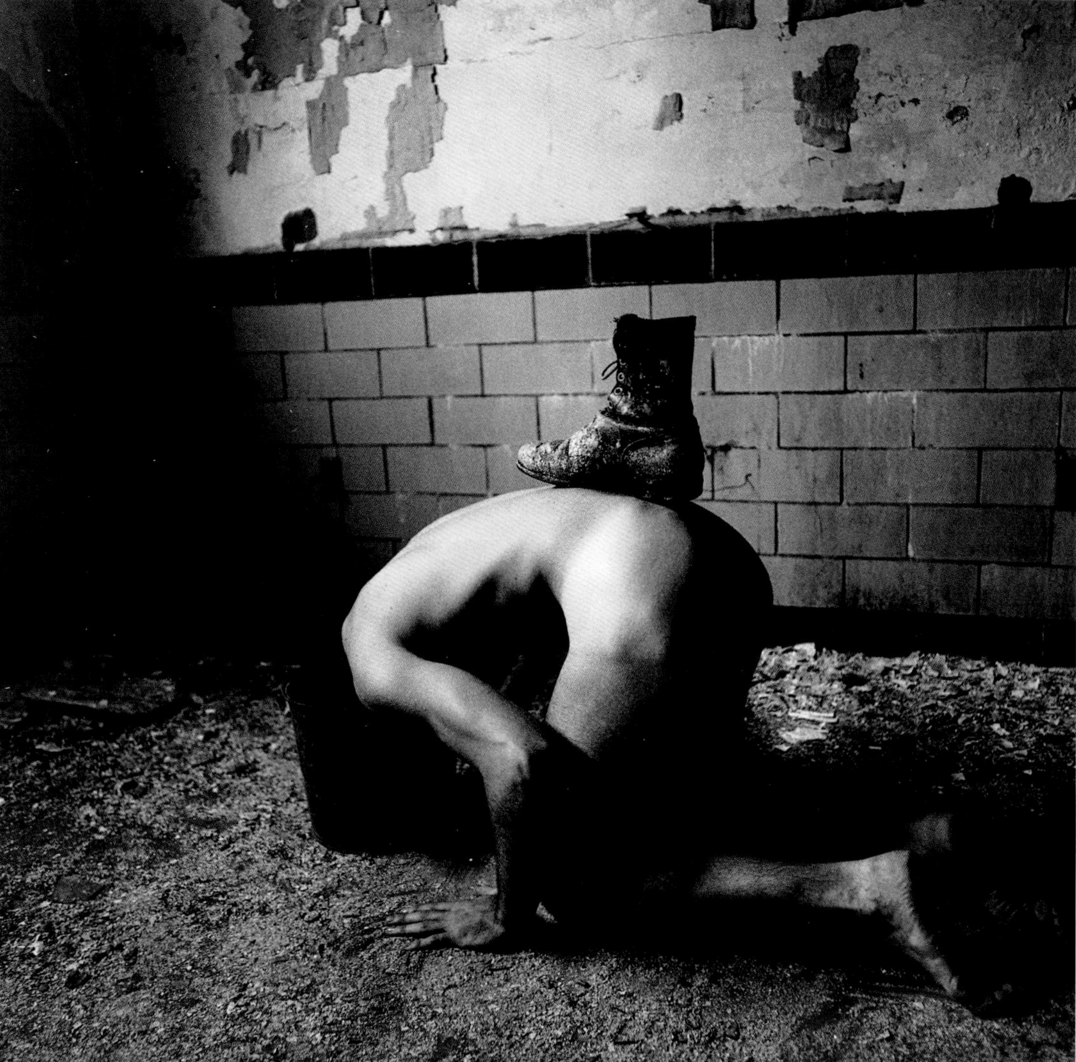

Figure 13
Arthur Tress
Boot Fantasy, New York, New York, 1977
Gelatin silver print,
26 × 26 cm (10 ¼ × 10 ¼ in.)
Los Angeles, J. Paul Getty Museum, Gift of David Knaus, 2015.116.12

mixed-media installations made from abandoned medical equipment in a boarded-up training hospital on New York's Roosevelt Island. He described this extraordinary *Hospital Constructions* series in one interview as "Disneyland meets Franz Kafka."[70]

Among art historians there has been new interest in examining the piers as a locus of artistic production for queer artists of the 1970s and 1980s, including Tress's contemporaries Vito Acconci, Alvin Baltrop, Leonard Fink, Peter Hujar, Stanley Stellar, and David Wojnarowicz. In his book *Pier Groups: Art and Sex along New York's Waterfront* (2019), Jonathan Weinberg sees Tress's influence on Wojnarowicz's work as stemming from an intense sexual encounter in the spring of 1978 between the two men on the piers, described in extensive detail in the latter artist's memoirs. "Although Tress's effect on Wojnarowicz's art and life never rivaled that of Peter Hujar," Weinberg writes, "their relationship was nevertheless transformative at a time when the young artist was searching for new inspiration and aesthetic directions."[71]

Aside from the relatively small group of like-minded photographers who trafficked in fantastic imagery drawn from the inner worlds of dreams and the imagination, Tress was an outlier with his performative approach, generally out of sync with the modernist traditions of pure or "straight" photography and, later, with the photo world's emphasis in the 1970s on stylistic anonymity and

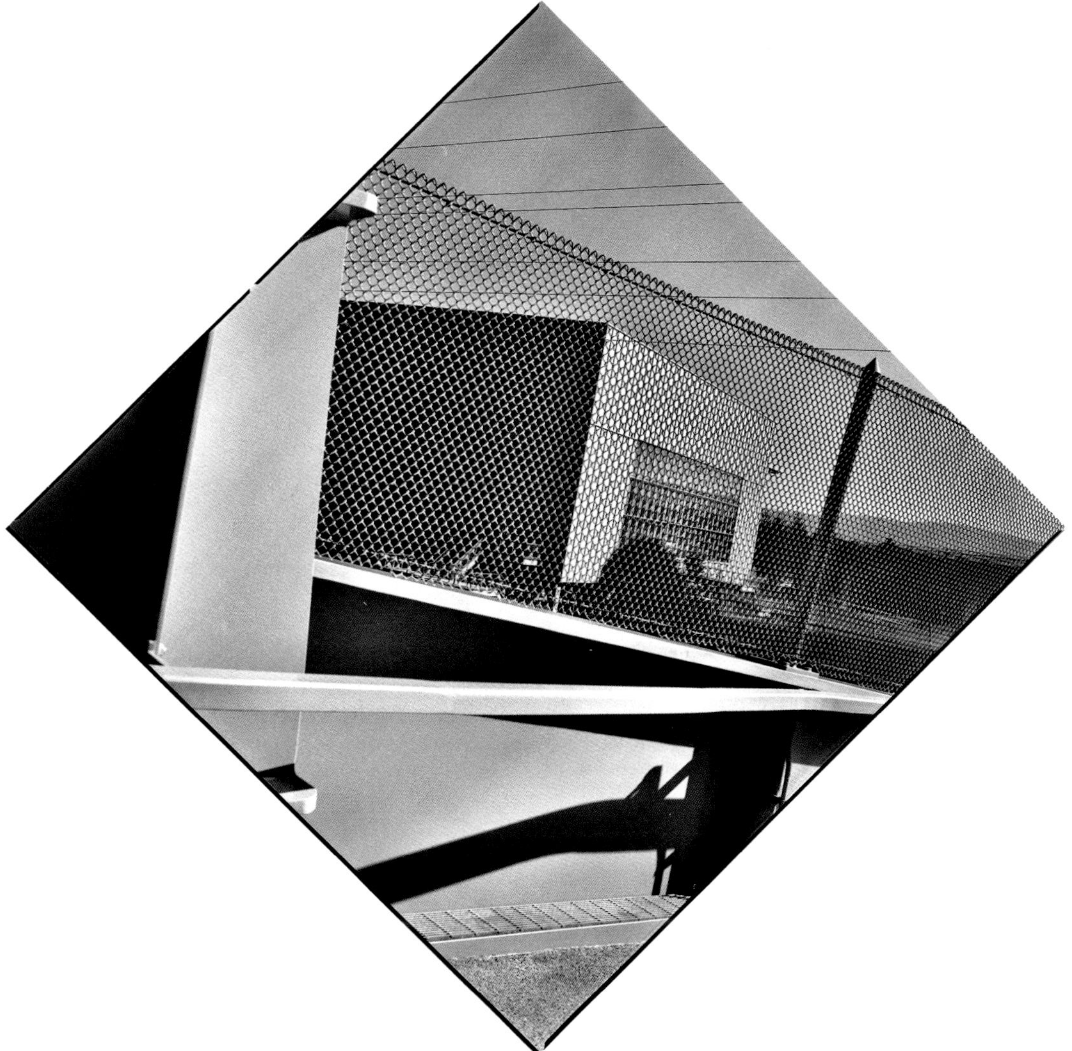

Figure 14
Arthur Tress
Facebook Meta Building, Menlo Park, California, 2022
Gelatin silver print, 12.7 × 12.7 cm (5 × 5 in.)
Collection of the artist

mundane subject matter. But Tress and his contemporaries Michals, Krims, and Samaras paved the way for the broader emergence of staged photography in the 1980s as practiced by artists like Joel-Peter Witkin, Jeff Wall, Cindy Sherman, and Gregory Crewdson.[72] Meanwhile, the irrepressible creative energy that fueled Tress's commercial and artistic productivity during his early career in New York has sustained an unbroken succession of new photographic series and book projects into the present decade, covering such diverse subjects as fish tanks installed with elaborate tableaux (*Fish Tank Sonata*, 2000), skate parks (*Skate Park*, 2010), traffic cones (*The Life Circle of the Orange Rubber Traffic Cone*, 2019), and, most recently, deserted schoolyards and empty Silicon Valley office campuses during the Covid-19 pandemic (*In Recess: Closed Schools of Northern California*, 2022). Tress sees a link between his most recent work (fig. 14) and his earlier concerns with urban planning, reflected in his *Open Space* photographs. "My recent revisiting of that distant body of imagery," he now says, "seeing its significance with unprejudiced eyes, has inspired me anew to continue exploring, always with the simplest means and equipment, the visual potential of the basic photo image, born out of a committed aspiration to improve the world around us."[73]

Notes

1 Letter to Madeleine Tress, December 1962, from Paris, collection of the artist.

2 Tress retrieved the letters he sent to various recipients as he was organizing his archives in the early 2010s.

3 Documented in James Ganz, *Arthur Tress: San Francisco 1964*, exh. cat. (San Francisco: Fine Arts Museums of San Francisco, 2012).

4 Letter to Martin Tress, November 24, 1964, from Mexico, collection of the artist.

5 Letter to David and Dawn Tress, May 3, 1966, from Stockholm, collection of the artist.

6 Ibid.

7 Letter to Madeleine Tress, August 2, 1966, from Stockholm, collection of the artist.

8 Letter to David and Dawn Tress, October 10, 1966, from Stockholm, collection of the artist.

9 Åke Emmer, "Blodig Lek i Färg," *Foto och Filmteknik* 28, no. 11 (November 1966): 26.

10 Letter to David and Dawn Tress, November 3, 1966, from Stockholm, collection of the artist.

11 For instance, his photograph *Heroin Addict Shoots Up* (1967) is available for licensing from Science Source Images; https://www.sciencesource.com/archive/Image/Heroin-addict-shoots-up-SS2184903.html, accessed August 29, 2022. Science Source was originally a division of Photo Researchers, Inc.

12 Tress describes the assignment in a letter to David and Dawn Tress, June 10, 1967, from Stockholm, collection of the artist.

13 Letter to David and Dawn Tress, November 22, 1966, from Stockholm, collection of the artist.

14 Typescript in the collection of the artist. Tress mentions the five-minute film *Morphine Fix* in a letter to Tobi Astner from late 1967, collection of the artist.

15 See Per Ringby, translated by Jesper Olsson, "Pistol-teatern—Avant-Garde Performance and Political Theatre," in *A Cultural History of the Avant-Garde in the Nordic Countries, 1950–1975*, ed. Tania Ørum and Jesper Olsson (Leiden and Boston: Koninklijke Brill, 2016), 528–33.

16 Letter to David and Dawn Tress, October 1, 1966, from Stockholm, collection of the artist.

17 Email to the author, October 13, 2022.

18 Tress exhibited one of the shooting-range photographs (*The Frontiersman*) in the 11th European Photo Exhibition for Students at the Uplandmuseet, September 29–October 29, 1967, and won a bronze medal. He published several of the photographs in *Popular Fotografi*, February 1968, and submitted one to Nathan Lyons's *Vision and Expression* exhibition at the George Eastman House, 1969. The work is also reproduced as the ninth plate in *The Dream Collector*. Tress self-published a compendium entitled *Shooting Range: Stockholm 1966* (Blurb Books, 2011), https://www.blurb.com/b/2200449-shooting-range-stockholm-1966, accessed January 2023.

19 Letter to Madeline Tress, November 27, 1965, from Hiroshima, collection of the artist.

20 Tress's 1967 notebook includes a partial draft of a letter dated March 20, 1967, to his editor, Mr. Hüsen, at Natur & Kultur, in which he describes his illnesses and his desire to cut short his travels in Africa; collection of the artist.

21 Letter to Madeline Tress, undated (April 1967), from Stockholm, collection of the artist.

22 Letter to David and Dawn Tress, May 16, 1967, from Stockholm, collection of the artist.

23 Letter to Martin Tress and David Tress, July 14, 1967, from Paris, collection of the artist.

24 Ibid.

25 The flower photographs appeared in the December 1967 issue of *Foto och Filmteknik* (vol. 27, no. 12) as "Flower Power på Djurgården."

26 Letter to David and Dawn Tress, September 29/October 1, 1967, from Stockholm, collection of the artist.

27 Letter to Madeline Tress, undated (late October 1967), from Stockholm, collection of the artist.

28 Letter to Tobi Astner, undated (late October 1967), from Stockholm, collection of the artist.

29 Letter to David and Dawn Tress, November 8, 1967, from Stockholm, collection of the artist.

30 Ibid.

31 A slideshow of Tress's Russia photographs appeared in the online Lens blog of the *New York Times*. See Evelyn Nieves, "Back in the U.S.S.R.," February 26, 2015. https://archive.nytimes.com/lens.blogs.nytimes.com/2015/02/26/back-in-the-ussr/, accessed August 2022.

32 Letter to Tobi Astner, undated (November–December 1967), from England, collection of the artist.

33 Letter to Tobi Astner, January 20, 1968, from New York, collection of the artist.

34 Ibid.

35 Letter to Tobi Astner, undated (July 1968), from Penland, North Carolina, collection of the artist.

36 The body of work appears in Tress's print-on-demand Blurb book *The Ramble 1968* (2009); https://www.blurb.com/b/670671-the-ramble-1968/, accessed August 2022. The photographs in the Blurb book are misdated 1968; Tress has more recently confirmed that they were all created between March and October 1969. Email to the author, October 21, 2022.

37 Letter to Tobi Astner, undated with later inscription 1969, from New York, collection of the artist.

38 Email to the author, October 13, 2022.
39 Arthur Tress, "Gallery Guide: Photographs for Show and Sale," *Creative Camera*, no. 57 (March 1969): 148–49.
40 A. D. Coleman, "Toward Some Future History of Photography, 1965–2000: Part I" (1999), http://www.nearbycafe.com/photocriticism/members/archivetexts/photocriticism/coleman/colemanfuture1.html, accessed January 2023.
41 Julie K. Brown, who worked on the project with Mary Lipscom, Peggy Fleming, and Joan Lyons, shared her recollections with the author in an email, September 8, 2022.
42 See the essay by Mazie M. Harris in this volume.
43 A. D. Coleman, "Arthur Tress," Latent Image column, *Village Voice*, October 10, 1968.
44 Arthur Tress, "Amerikansk dokumentärfotografi," *Fotografisk årsbok* 25 (1970): 67. The article appeared in a Swedish translation; quoted here from the original English-language typescript in the collection of the artist.
45 Tress's photographs are used to illustrate the following articles in *VISTA Volunteer*: Eileen Wilansky, "To Live and Die in Dixie," vol. 4, no. 9 (October 1968): 3–13; Phyllis Franck, "On Being Hasidic in New York City," vol. 5, no. 2 (February 1969): 24–30; Eileen Wilansky, "On Being Chinese in San Francisco," vol. 5, no. 2 (February 1969): 18–22.
46 Marco Livingstone, ed., *Arthur Tress: Talisman* (London: Thames & Hudson, 1986), 148.
47 Letter to Tobi Astner, September 1969, from Point Hope, Alaska, collection of the photographer.
48 Letter to Tobi Astner, December 1969, from New York, collection of the photographer.
49 *Album*, no. 2 (March 1970): 1. The article from the British journal appears in its entirety as the preface to this volume.
50 Ibid.
51 The notebook is in the collection of the artist.
52 James A. Ganz, "Arthur Tress: Dreaming in Color," *ESOPUS*, no. 24 (2017): 215.
53 Tress recalls meeting Michals in Zelda Cheatle, ed., *The Photograph That Changed My Life* (London: Art Cinema, 2022), 14–15.
54 Email to the author, September 17, 2022.
55 Email to the author, July 7, 2021.
56 A. D. Coleman, "Confirming her fatalism (q.v.)," *Village Voice* 17, no. 25 (June 22, 1972): 30.
57 Coleman and Neal Slavin reproduced a key to Slavin's photograph on a limited poster for the exhibition; email from Neil Slavin to the author, October 12, 2022.
58 Douglas Davis, "The Ten 'Toughest' Photographs of 1975," *Esquire* 85, no. 2 (February 1976): 108–15.
59 See Paul Martineau's "All the World's a Stage" essay in this volume.
60 A. D. Coleman, "The Directorial Mode: Notes toward a Definition," *Artforum* 15, no. 1 (September 1976): 55–61.
61 Duane Michals, "Tress' Vaudeville," in *Theater of the Mind* (Dobbs Ferry, NY: Morgan & Morgan, 1976), pages unnumbered.
62 From an artist statement for the exhibition *Stonewall: 50 Years* at the Harvey Milk Photo Center, San Francisco, June 22–July 21, 2019.
63 Marcia Wooding, "Phallic Fantasies," *SoHo Weekly News*, October 1977, pp. 14, 33.
64 According to Jack Fritscher, the publisher of *Drummer*, Robert Mapplethorpe saw Tress as a competitor; Fritscher, *Mapplethorpe: Assault with a Deadly Camera* (New York: Hastings House, 1994), 268.
65 Excerpt from "Phallic Phantasy," unpublished text, 1978, in Marco Livingstone, ed., *Arthur Tress: Talisman* (London: Thames & Hudson, 1986), 152.
66 Shelley Rice, "Image-Making," *SoHo Weekly News*, April 1979, p. 42. See also "The Art and Politics of the Male Image: A Conversation between Sam Hardison and George Stambolian," *Christopher Street* 4, no. 7 (March 1980): 14–22.
67 "From the Ideal to the Erotic," *New York Times*, June 18, 1978, p. D27. See also https://www.artspace.com/magazine/interviews_features/body-of-art/body-of-art-philip-gefter-mapplethorpe-wagstaff-53224, accessed January 2023.
68 Marcia Wooding, "Further Adventures in the Theater of the Mind," *35 mm Photography* (Summer 1978): 75.
69 Interview with the author on Zoom, September 19, 2022.
70 PhotoProfiles presents Arthur Tress, https://www.youtube.com/watch?v=Y4xswBBvJDA&t=695s at 10:40, accessed January 2023.
71 Jonathan Weinberg, *Pier Groups: Art and Sex along New York's Waterfront* (University Park: Pennsylvania State University Press, 2019), 100–101.
72 Moa Goysdotter, *Impure Vision: American Staged Art Photography of the 1970s* (Lund: Nordic Academic Press, 2013). In Jonathan Weinberg's interview of the artist on December 26, 2002, Tress told him, "When Joel Peter Witkin came along, I got out of the grotesquery and said I cannot compete with this guy" (p. 3 of unpublished transcript in the collection of the artist).
73 Email to the author, October 19, 2022.

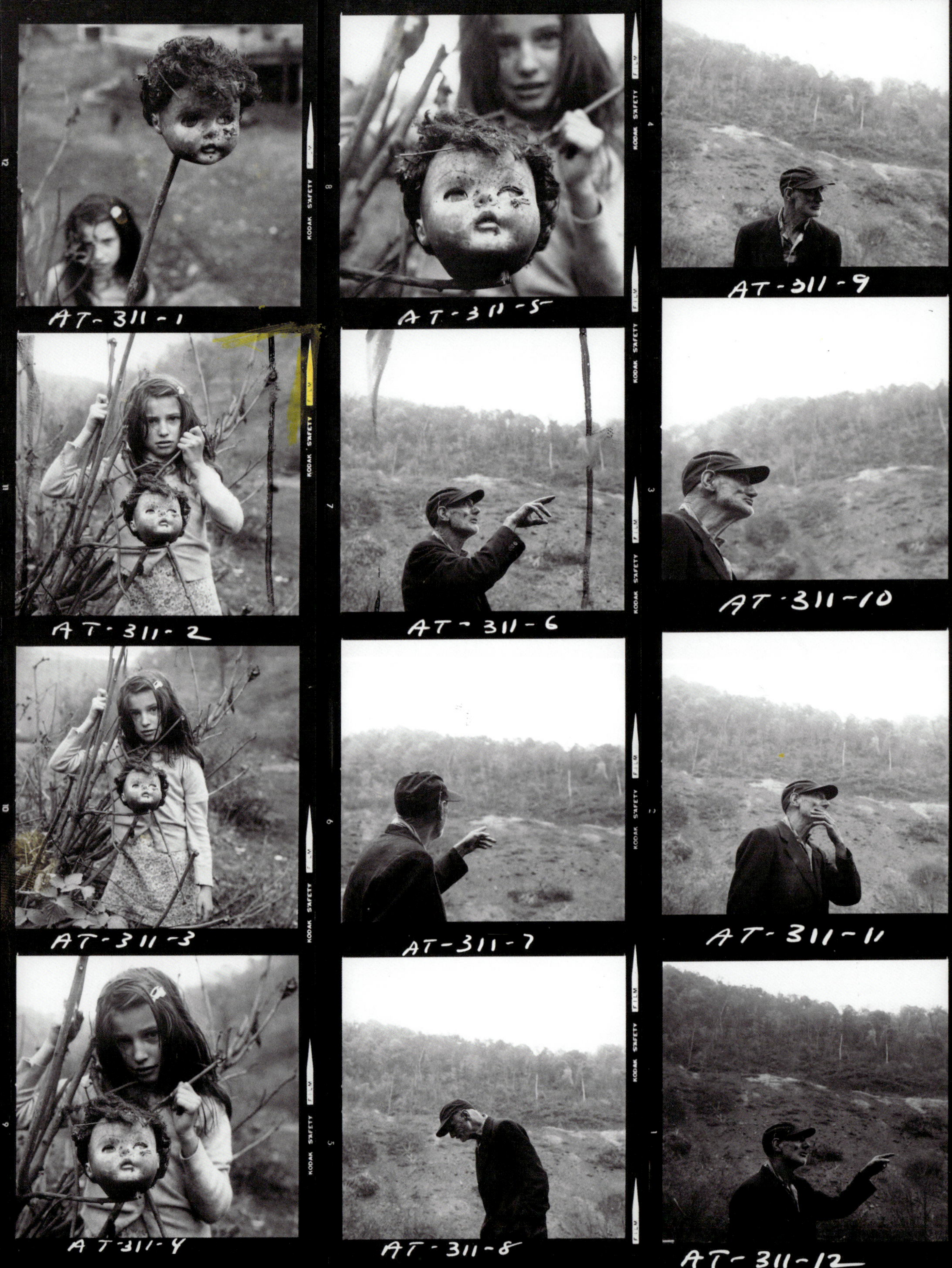
AT-311-1
AT-311-2
AT-311-3
AT-311-4
AT-311-5
AT-311-6
AT-311-7
AT-311-8
AT-311-9
AT-311-10
AT-311-11
AT-311-12
KODAK SAFETY FILM

MAZIE M. HARRIS

Crossroads: Arthur Tress in Appalachia

Arthur Tress first visited Appalachia in May 1968 and returned to the region several times that year, wrestling with his past and present as well as with the popular imagination of the place. With each visit his interests and encounters varied. Working in a manner he thought of as ethnographic, he combined portraits and landscapes with "poetic details of textures."[1] His film background led him to seek out establishing shots to give a sense of place, intermixing them with more intimate images of people and the particulars of their lives.

Looking for photographic opportunities upon his return to the United States from Sweden, he had traveled to Rochester, New York, in the spring of 1968 to meet with Nathan Lyons, an influential curator and editor at the George Eastman House. Lyons introduced Tress to his wife, Joan Lyons, and would later include Tress's work in the February 1969 Eastman exhibition *Vision and Expression*. At the time Tress met her, Joan Lyons was working with the Rochester University Memorial Art Gallery to pull together small exhibits of images and objects for local school district classrooms to connect Rochester students with the wider world.[2] Together, Tress and Lyons created an exhibition of some of his materials from Mali and Niger. She next suggested a showcase on Appalachian folk crafts. Funded by the Memorial Art Gallery, Tress traveled to North Carolina to gather examples of local crafts and to make images of the people who created them. While inclusion in the prominent roster of exhibitions at the George Eastman House probably felt more significant to the young photographer at the time, the Appalachia assignment would prove deeply formative for his development as an artist.

On his first trip to Appalachia, in May 1968, Tress traveled to Asheville, North Carolina, where he was put in touch with the Southern Highland Handicraft Guild, the same group that the photographer Doris Ulmann had worked with in the 1930s

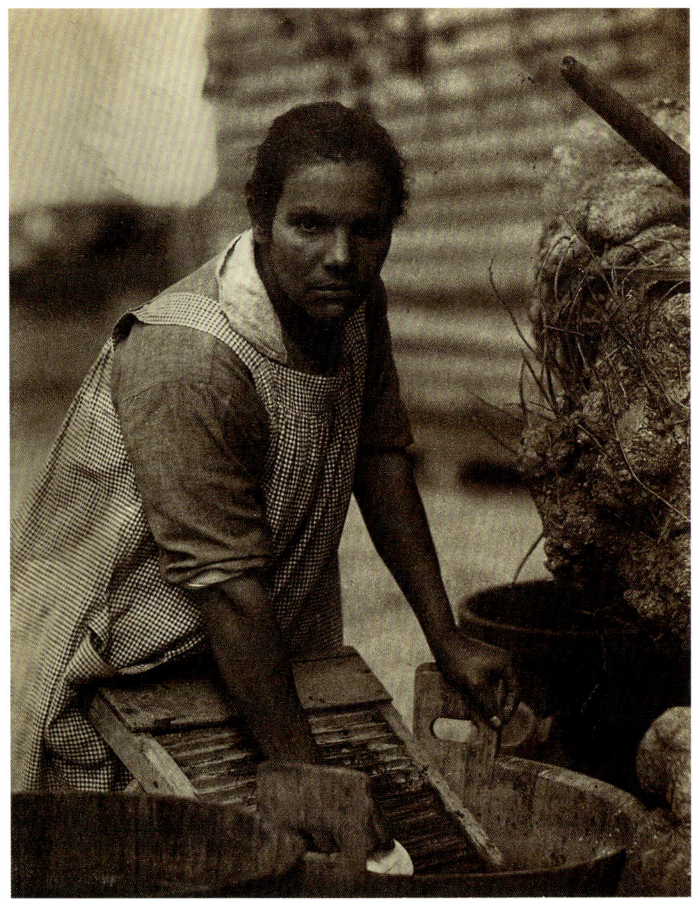

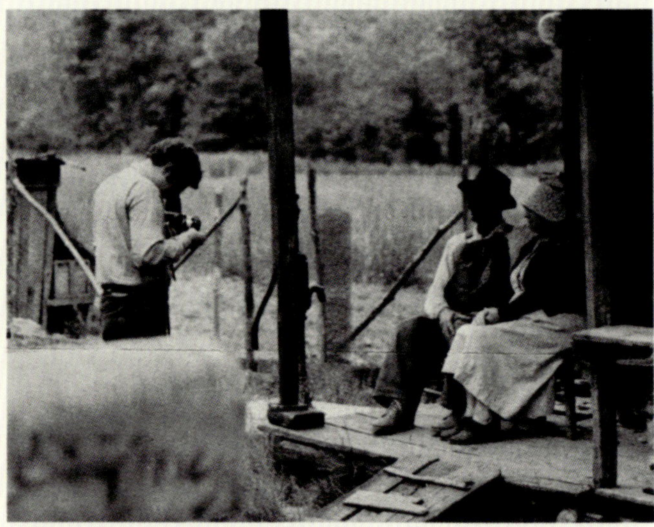
PHOTO ACTIVITIES

Above—Arthur Tress, widely traveled photographer from New York City, takes a portrait of a mountain couple living near Mars Hill, N. C. Arthur spent several weeks in the Guild area, working on a slide presentation to accompany a traveling craft exhibit in upper New York state schools. The exhibit and the photo presentation are being prepared by the Memorial Art Gallery, the University of Rochester, Rochester, New York.

Figure 15
Doris Ulmann (American, 1882–1934)
Laundry Day, North Carolina, ca. 1929
Platinum print, 20.2 × 15.5 cm (7 15⁄16 × 6 1⁄8 in.)
Los Angeles, J. Paul Getty Museum, 87.XM.89.73

Figure 16
Clipping from *Highland Handicraft Guild Bulletin*, May 1968
Collection of Arthur Tress

for her own photographic study of the area (fig. 15). Tress's visit was featured in the guild's May newsletter with an image that showed him making a portrait with his Hasselblad camera of a local couple on their porch (fig. 16). In using the Hasselblad Tress was limited to only twelve photos on each roll of film, forcing him to work selectively and methodically (fig. 17). Rather than shooting spontaneously as a photojournalist might, accumulating roll upon roll of film, Tress searchingly composed each frame, his subjects aware of his presence and participating in their own depiction.

As he had for earlier ethnographic projects, Tress wrote texts to accompany the photographs intended for Rochester school use (fig. 18). With his edit characterizing early settlers to the region as not just the sort who "go beyond" hardships but "endure" them, he suggested both stubborn stasis and a resolute spirit of survival. The tone was in keeping with the details he chose to include in his visual framing of craftsmen (plate 6) and musicians in photographs he made on that first trip south to Asheville, Boone, Cherokee, and nearby small towns in North Carolina, with stops in Gatlinburg, Tennessee, and Pikeville, Kentucky, on his way back north.

Tress and the members of the Rochester committee who appointed him were not alone in their interest in Appalachia or in a commitment to portraying southern life as representative of resilient American character. As in the 1930s, growing industrialization in the 1960s and an accompanying concern that mechanization was cleaving the country from its handwrought customs prompted renewed interest in American folk culture. In the years after Alan Lomax labored to capture field recordings of folk songs, Joan Baez, Bob Dylan, and the Folkways Records Anthology of American

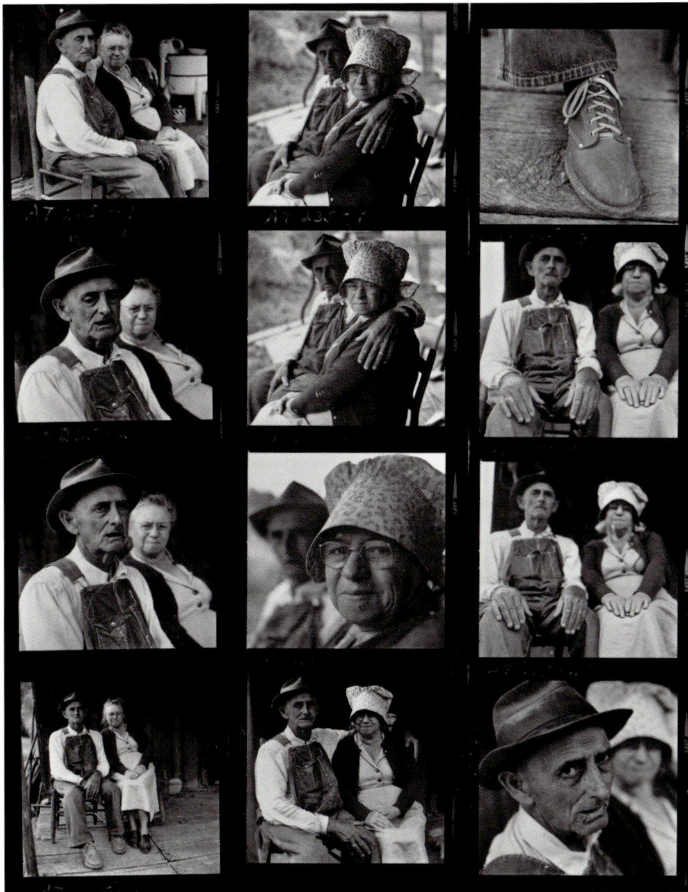

Handicrafts of the Southern Appalachians 1
photographs and text by Arthur Tress.

1. In the early mornings a foggy mist hangs over the hills and thus the mountains get their nickname "smoky" or "blue ridge". The mountain area known as Appalachia includes parts of Maryland, Virgina, nearly all of West Virginia, eastern Kentucky and eastern Tennessee, western North Carolina, and the mountainous counties of South Carolina and Georgia.

2. The area is vast and often still difficult of access. The early pioneers followed Indian trials into the mountains looking for new land. The routes were dangerous thickly covered with woods and impassable vines, but beyond lay losh untouched valleys of fertile earth that encouraged the first settlers to ~~go beyond~~ endure the hardships of frontier life.

6. In these mountains natural beauty could be found pure and lovely hardly equaled elsewhere in America. From the coming of the wild flowers in the Spring to the autumn foliage of the many varieties of hardwoods. This is a rare Jack-in-the Pulpit wildflower that blooms in early May.

Figure 17
Arthur Tress
Contact sheet, Mars Hill, North Carolina, 1968
Gelatin silver print, 25.4 × 20.3 cm (10 × 8 in.)
Collection of the artist

Figure 18
Arthur Tress
Handwritten text, "Handicrafts of the Southern Appalachians," ca. 1968
Collection of the artist

Folk Music intensified popular interest in music that was seen as authentically American. Oral historians sought out tales of ways of life thought to be endangered, and a resurgence of attention to American handicraft was under way.

In a letter he wrote to his brother and sister-in-law while in Appalachia, Tress marveled at the determined spirit of the people he encountered, who drew strength from "the morality of 'old time religion' and the individuality of the frontiersman."[3] Echoing the refrain of a 1964 Bob Dylan song, Tress closed the letter by noting, "But the times are a changing . . tourists coming in . . poverty . . factories . . construction . . ."[4]

In the context of the uncanny tenor of much of Tress's later work, it is tempting to see images such as *Pearl Norwood, Maker of Raggedy Ann Dolls, Banner Elk, North Carolina* (plate 7) in a surrealistic light. But as part of his project to document craftspeople and their wares, the image is movingly effective. The woman is shown absorbed in her task and surrounded by her handiwork. It is an efficient composition, foregrounding the dolls as much as their maker, their smiling faces and open embraces a product of her focused attention. But Tress's framing—the hard light casting a deep shadow at the left side of the image, the image tightly cropped to exclude any sense of space—hints at the ways in which the modern world was closing in on tradition, shrinking the window of possibility for artisans.

Compared with that image of devoted labor, a photograph made on a subsequent trip to Appalachia, *Girl with Doll's Head, Capels, West Virginia* (plate 12), gives a sense of the ways in which Tress's attitude toward the region shifted over the course of his visits. In place of a lovingly handcrafted doll, the later work shows the type of manufactured plastic product that supplanted it. No longer heirlooms passed from generation to generation, toys were increasingly discarded just as quickly as they rolled off a factory conveyor belt. Dirtied and impaled, the doll's head eerily doubles the girl's own stare, foreshadowing the artist's interest in the psychology of child's play in later photographic series. The empty and broken branches that ensnare both the girl and the discarded doll suggest the barren future of the region. While the artist's initial visit to Appalachia had been focused on the endurance of nativist American traditions, in subsequent trips he began more and more to foreground threats to the fragile human and environmental ecosystems of local communities.

Tress's work in Appalachia coincided not only with a resurgence of interest in American folk crafts but also with a growing awareness of environmental and regional inequities. A 1962 exposé by Harry Caudill, *Night Comes to the Cumberlands: A Biography of a Depressed Area*, brought attention to the exploitation of Appalachia by outside business interests. The book prompted a federal investigation and an infusion of government aid, catalyzing President Johnson's 1964 declaration of the War on Poverty and the 1965 Appalachian Regional Development Act. VISTA (Volunteers in Service to America) was created at that time to help provide staffing for programs intended to alleviate poverty.

Just back from his first trip south, Tress received an assignment from the Office of Economic Opportunity to return under the auspices of VISTA. Tress's images from Appalachia—and later from assignments elsewhere in the United States—would be sent to various newspapers and magazines to promote antipoverty programs. In July 1968 he wrote to his family that he was happy to have the VISTA job, his "first professional assignment—like one you would get from *Life* or *Look*—I hope I can get involved in it and do it well."[5]

During that second trip, in the summer of 1968, Tress was given access to a darkroom at the Penland School of Craft in the Blue Ridge Mountains, where he came across a copy of *Handicrafts of the Southern Highlands: A Book on Rural Arts* (1937), illustrated with photographs by Doris Ulmann. Inspired by her work, he sought out the same people she had photographed, on occasion finding their children instead, many of whom were carrying on the craft traditions of their parents (fig. 19).

Although he was stirred by the sensitivity of Ulmann's images, her intimate style of portraiture did not come easily to the shy photographer. On that trip back to the Carolinas Tress's work was eased by the presence of Sandra Hutchings, a Penland student who accompanied him in his travels. Tress did not drive at the time, so Hutchings steered them through North Carolina back roads. She was personable and at ease in starting conversations, making both Tress and the people they met comfortable.

For his third trip to Appalachia, in the fall of 1968, Tress took a bus to southern Kentucky and was introduced to community members by social service agencies. Working with local welfare advocates deeply committed to the region and its people, he was able to make inroads with families facing environmental and financial devastation (fig. 20). Their hardships, their waterways polluted by strip mining, and their desolate landscapes brought Tress's attention to environmental concerns.

In late 1968, on his fourth trip, Tress traveled to small towns in West Virginia, making photographs of an Appalachia that seemed nearly unimaginable to Americans hyped up on postwar affluence.
So recently exposed to the strong social welfare systems of Sweden, he was shocked by the sight of children scrambling over coal heaps scrounging for fuel for their home fires. It was on that trip that

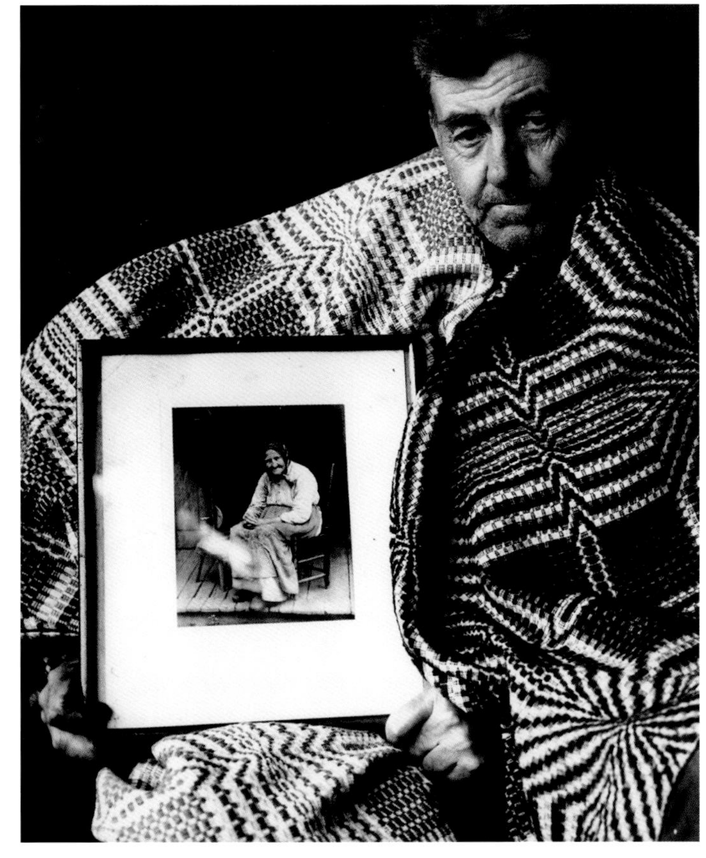

Figure 19
Arthur Tress
Taft Greer, Trade, Tennessee, 1968
Gelatin silver print, 25.4 × 20.3 cm (10 × 8 in.)
Taft Greer is pictured holding a portrait of his mother made by Doris Ulmann.
Georgia Museum of Art, University of Georgia, Gift of J. Patrick and Patricia A. Kennedy, GMOA 2020.2055

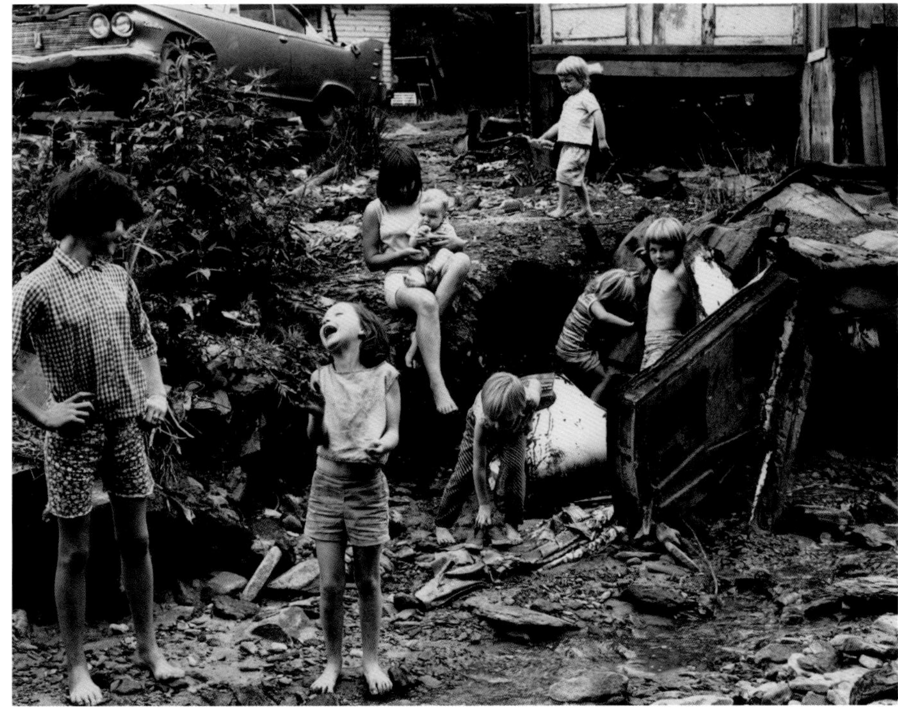

Figure 20
Arthur Tress
Children Play in Coal-Mined Area, Whitesburg, Kentucky, 1968
Gelatin silver print, 19.5 × 24.4 cm (7 11⁄16 × 9 5⁄8 in.)
Los Angeles, J. Paul Getty Museum, Gift of the Ottersons, 2018.114.7

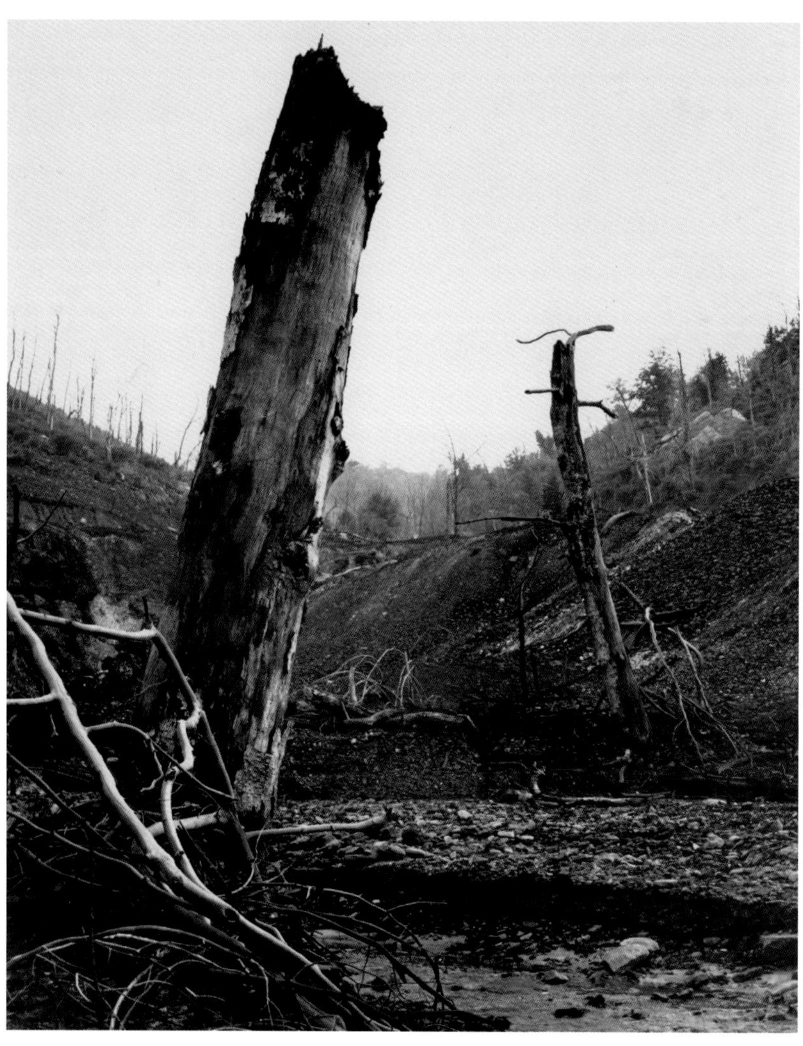

Figure 21
Arthur Tress
Strip-Mined Land, Pikeville, Kentucky, 1968
Gelatin silver print,
24.6 × 19.3 cm (9 11⁄16 × 7 5⁄8 in.)
Los Angeles, J. Paul Getty Museum, Gift of the Ottersons, 2018.114.28

he made the bleak image of the girl with the doll's head (plate 12), his early interest in endurance supplanted by a deep concern that the region's resources were being irrevocably depleted. Tress wrote to Tobi Astner: "I'm back in the hills again—this time amongst the coal miners of West Virginia . . . gaunt starving faces, freezing children, and all slightly out of their minds. It's a little too easy to get effective dramatic photographs under such extreme conditions and the problem is to transcend the condition."[6]

As he became more deeply distressed by what he saw in Appalachia, he made abject images of environmental destruction (fig. 21) and people burdened by the weight of their situation (plate 8). At the same time, he found himself increasingly able to draw attention to the conditions he encountered. He began submitting images not only to VISTA but also to stock agencies, including Magnum, with typewritten captions describing in detail what he had witnessed (fig. 22). The evocative tone of his classroom scripts was supplanted by the staccato intensity of captions aimed at garnering the attention of news agencies.

In November 1967 the Sierra Club opened a New York gallery to bring greater awareness to environmental issues, and Tress showed photographs from Appalachia in an October 1968 exhibition, *The "Disturbed" Land*, with the goal of highlighting "the effects of coal mining on the human and natural ecology of Southern Appalachia."[7] Noting in his review of the exhibition the resemblance of Tress's work to that of Depression-era photographers, A. D. Coleman wrote that he found it "almost hallucinatory" that contemporary images so strongly resembled images made in the depths of the economic devastation of what many Americans assumed to be a bygone era.[8]

In contrast, the article "On Aging" by Simone de Beauvoir in the leftist magazine *Ramparts*

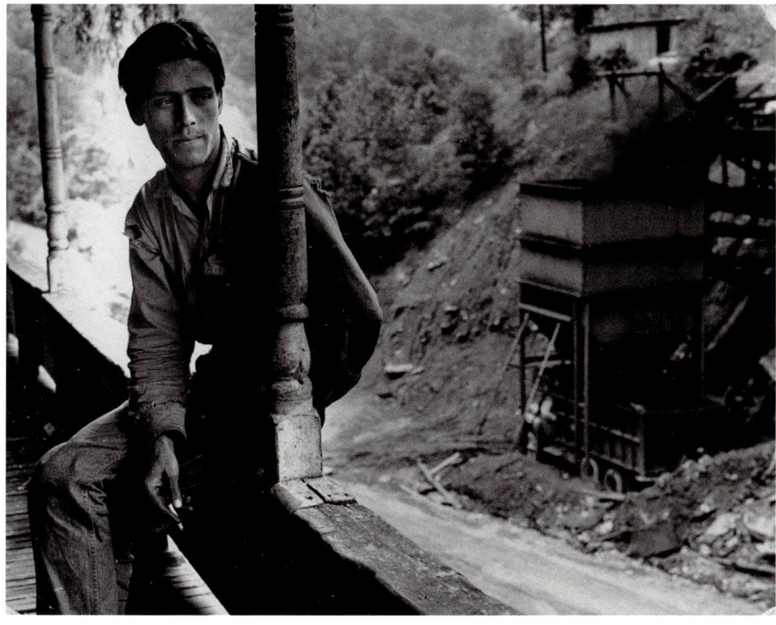

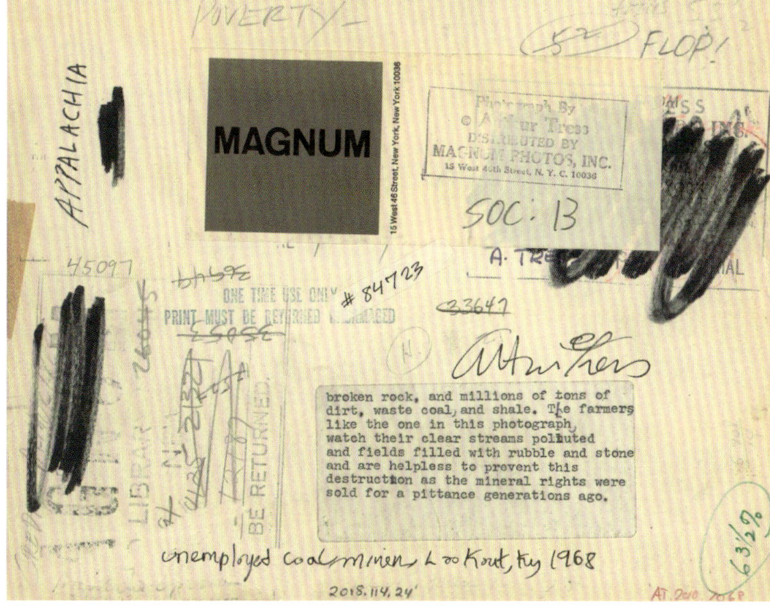

Figure 22
Arthur Tress
Unemployed Coal Miner, Lookout, Kentucky, 1968
Gelatin silver print, 19.9 x 25 cm (7 13⁄16 × 9 13⁄16 in.), recto and verso
Los Angeles, J. Paul Getty Museum, Gift of the Ottersons, 2018.114.24

exemplifies how the sorts of images Tress was making could be read differently when circulated by stock agencies.[9] De Beauvoir framed Tress's images of hardscrabble Appalachian lives as meditations on aging rather than on regional collapse. Within the pages of *Folk Songs of the Blue Ridge Mountains*, a 1968 publication by Herbert Shellans that paired Tress's images of Appalachia with regional music and lyrics, the photographs helped readers to visualize the isolated communities whose ballads were compiled during Shellans's research visits in the late 1950s.

The summer after Tress's visits to Appalachia, several photographs from his time there were shown for two months in the rotunda outside the Smithsonian National Museum of History and Technology gift shop. Opening at the same time as the third annual American Folklife Festival—held July 1–6, 1969, in Washington, DC—Tress's Smithsonian installation, titled *Appalachia: People & Places*, focused primarily on portraits of Appalachian artisans, with a few graveyard images included to hint that folk ways were endangered.[10] The artist sold several large-scale photographs of craftspeople, marking interest in the southern crafts that were geographically close at hand yet seemingly a world away.

Along with making photographs that were commercially marketable, Tress began to focus in some of his work on details that might previously have crept in at the margins of his images, now allowing them to fill the frame. Tress's work for stock agencies, for exhibitions, and for use as illustrations had to be relatively straightforward—lending themselves to accompany various texts that spoke to a range of audiences—but hints of his later, more surrealistic style were becoming apparent in images such as *Twisted Tree Roots, Lookout, Kentucky* (plate 9). In other images from Appalachia, Tress implied the erosion of generational promise more overtly. In a West Virginia composition (plate 10), for example, he focused

Figure 23
Arthur Tress
Railroad Sign, Welch, West Virginia, 1968
Gelatin silver print, 17.4 × 17.5 cm (6 7/8 × 6 7/8 in.)
Los Angeles, J. Paul Getty Museum, Gift of the Ottersons, 2018.114.21

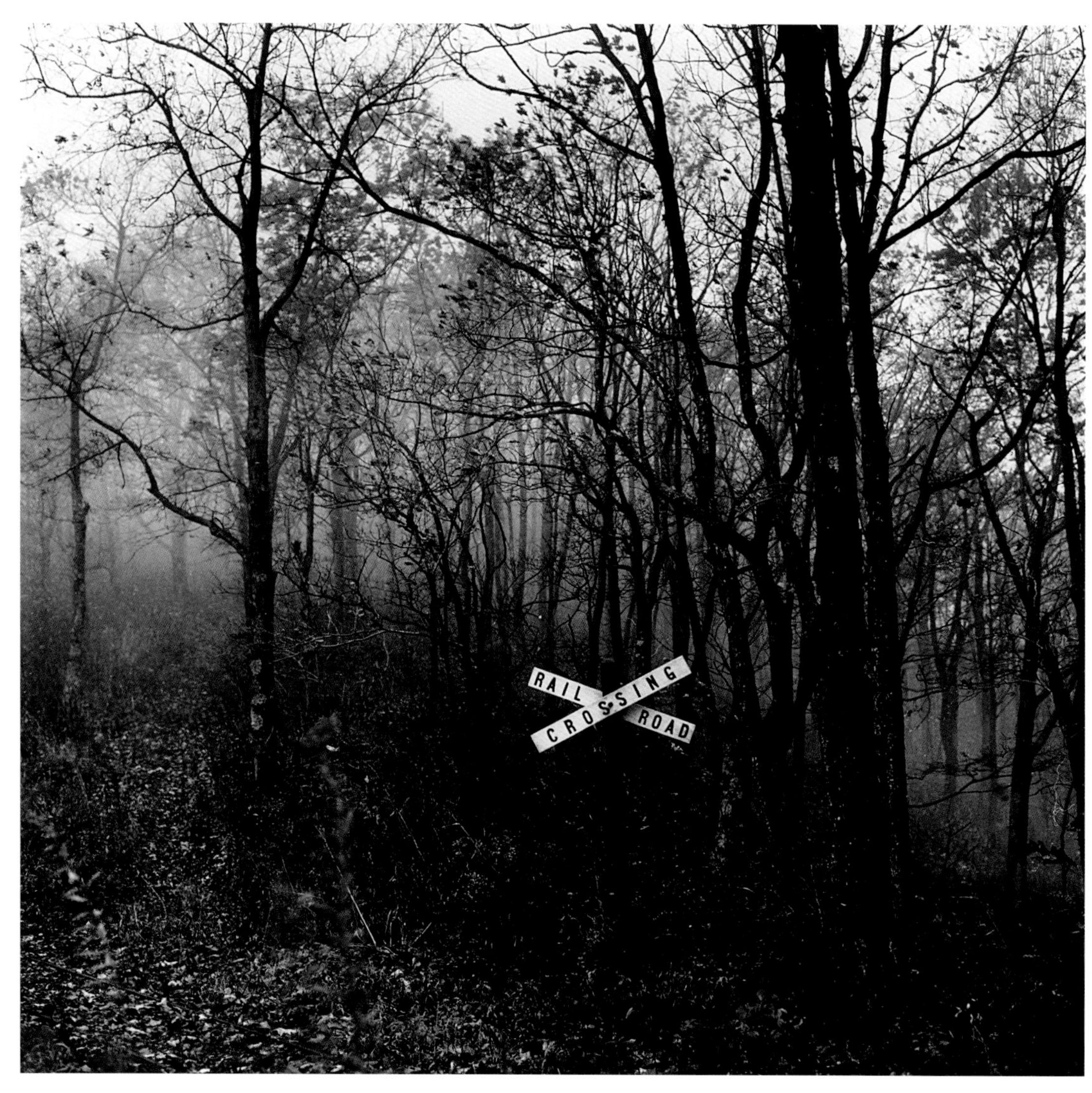

in on a faded family photograph—partially buried amid coal rubble—of a mother clutching a child, with a large glove beside the photograph. No caption necessary: the glove connotes labor in the coal mines, and the portrait evokes the human potential stripped away along with the region's natural resources.

Looking back at his time in Appalachia now, decades later, Tress links his experiences there to his earlier work photographing communities in other parts of the globe. He began to focus more and more on themes that he felt surfaced in communities anywhere. Seeking out collective archetypes increasingly interested Tress and continues to captivate him today.

The original goal of his Appalachia work was for educational purposes—to expose schoolchildren to varied modes of living and creating. But Tress himself was educated by his experience as well, moving from mere observation of the communities he visited to a commitment to social justice.

Tress's Appalachia pictures capture changes to the people and places of the region but also register the transformation of the artist himself as he forged a career path. Tress was at a crossroads, trying to determine how best to support himself while carrying on his search for signs and symbols through which to make meaning from the fog of everyday experience (fig. 23). During his trips to Appalachia he found a way forward: making images suited to a wide range of applications while also seeking out more evocative images—photographs that insinuate and unsettle, hinting at direction even when the path is not yet clear.

Notes

1. Interview with the author, October 13, 2021.
2. With thanks to the scholar Julie Brown for her recollections about this program. Brown worked with the Memorial Art Gallery to introduce students to creative expression and visual culture through firsthand access to artists and objects.
3. Letter to David and Dawn Tress, May 1968, from North Carolina, collection of the artist.
4. Aside from the final ellipsis, the punctuation follows that of the original letter.
5. Letter to Madeleine Tress and her partner, July 16, 1968, from Charleston, South Carolina, collection of the artist.
6. Letter to Tobi Astner, October 1968, from West Virginia, collection of the artist.
7. Sierra Club Gallery exhibition announcement.
8. A. D. Coleman, "Latent Image" column, *Village Voice*, October 19, 1968.
9. The article is undated in archive files, but presumably it was published in advance of the author's 1970, *La Vieillesse*. Simone de Beauvoir, "On Aging," *Ramparts*, year unknown, 19–20.
10. Carl Fox, later director of the Smithsonian Museum Shops, sought to innovate museum stores by selling original work by artists and artisans rather than replicas. He initiated this strategy at the Brooklyn Museum, where Tress first met him.

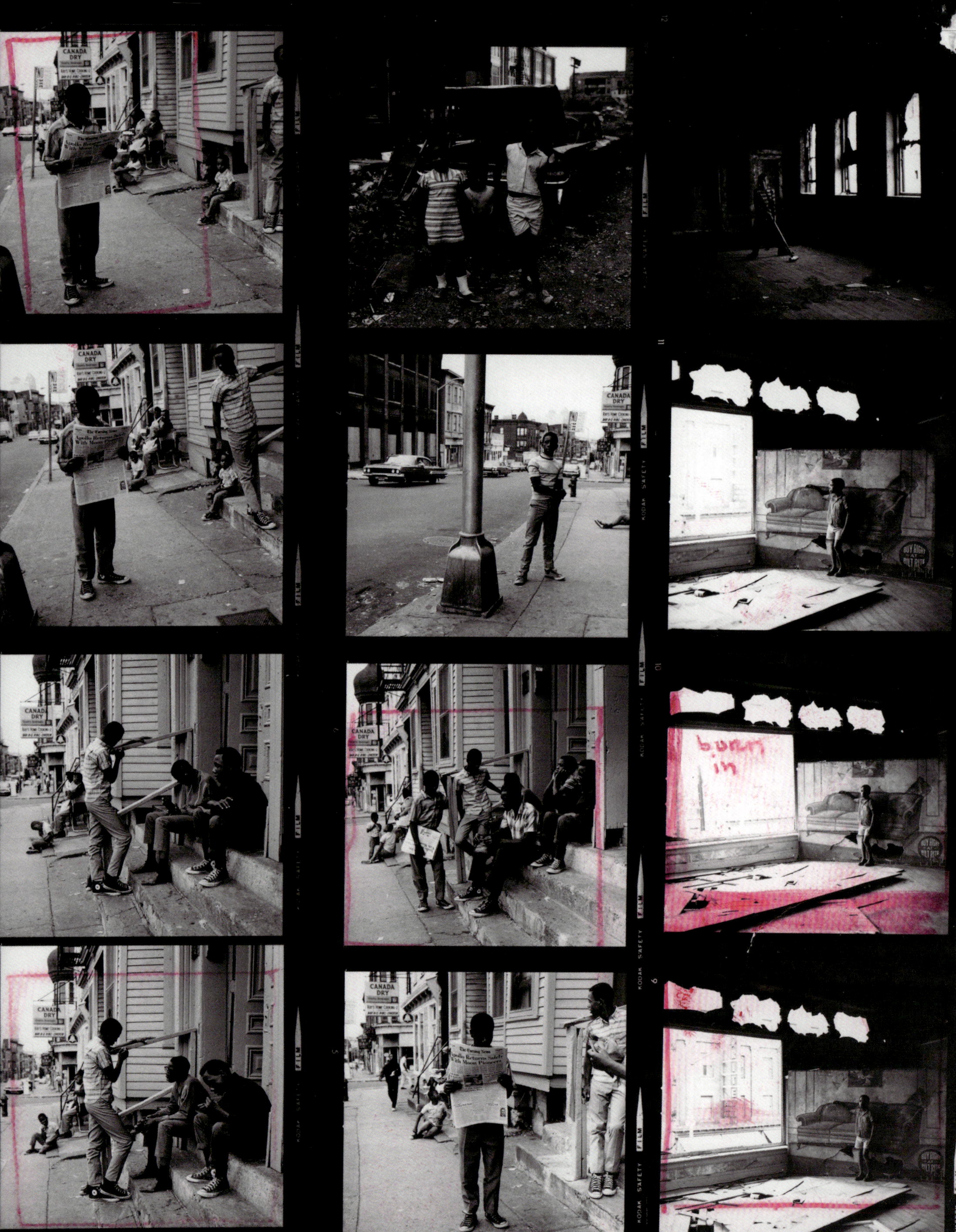
CANADA DRY
The Evening News
Apollo Returns Safely With Moon Pioneers
burn in
KODAK SAFETY FILM

JAMES A. GANZ

Seeking Open Space

Open Space in the Inner City, Tress's most ambitious photographic project to date, occupied much of his attention from 1969 to 1971.[1] It represented a continuation of his environmentalism, which characterized his work for VISTA, as well as his interest in documenting contemporary problems facing young people, as in his photo essay on teenage drug addiction in Stockholm. Set primarily in New York City and its environs, the *Open Space* series emphasized urban blight and crowding—focusing on polluted streetscapes and waterways, housing projects, urban parks, junkyards, factories, and parking lots—and included candid and posed images of children, teenagers, families, and commuters. The photographs appeared in gallery exhibitions, newspapers, magazines, and printed portfolios, and many resurfaced in Tress's later photobooks, most notably *The Dream Collector*, and formed a large percentage of his growing library of stock photos.

When he took up residence in the United States after living in Sweden, Tress experienced the contrast between the laid-back environment of Stockholm and the chaotic and congested Manhattan as a culture shock. New York City was suffering through a marked period of decline, with a depressed economy and rising levels of crime and pollution. Tress spent much of his first year back in the United States traveling outside of New York, photographing struggling rural communities, and it was this body of work that paved the way for his series devoted to the challenges of city life.

The topic of Tress's new project, of central concern to urban planners and environmentalists at the time, was articulated in publications like *Open Space Action*, the journal of the nonprofit Open Space Institute. Based in New York City, the institute sought to encourage developers and municipalities to set aside recreational areas for urban dwellers. Tress knew the environmentalist

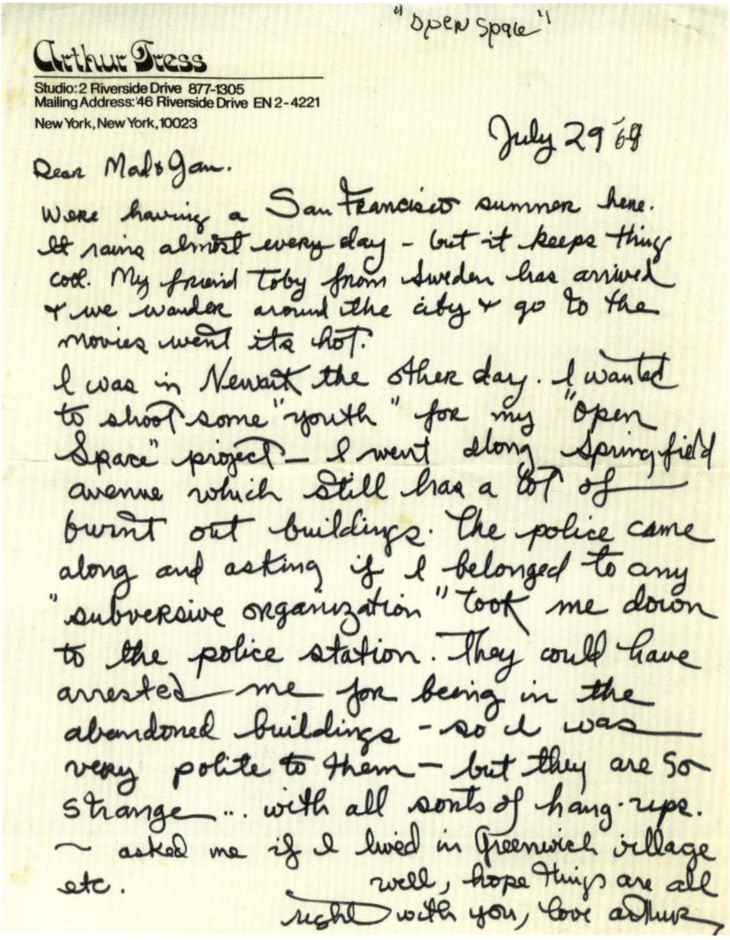

"Open Space"

Arthur Tress
Studio: 2 Riverside Drive 877-1305
Mailing Address: 46 Riverside Drive EN 2-4221
New York, New York, 10023

July 29 '69

Dear Mad & Jan.

Were having a San Francisco summer here. It rains almost every day - but it keeps things cool. My friend Toby from Sweden has arrived & we wander around the city & go to the movies when its hot.

I was in Newark the other day. I wanted to shoot some "youth" for my "Open Space" project - I went along Springfield avenue which still has a lot of burnt out buildings. The police came along and asking if I belonged to any "subversive organization" took me down to the police station. They could have arrested me for being in the abandoned buildings - so I was very polite to them - but they are so strange... with all sorts of hang-ups. - asked me if I lived in Greenwich village etc.

well, hope things are all right with you, love arthur

Figure 24
Arthur Tress
Letter to Madeleine Tress, July 29, 1969
Collection of the artist

John G. Mitchell, the institute's director of publications and editor of its magazine, who was also the editor-in-chief of Sierra Club Books. The genesis of Tress's *Open Space* project may be traced directly to the inaugural issue of *Open Space Action* (October–November 1968), which included an article entitled "Open Space and the Inner City," in which the staff writer Lynn Young argued that a lack of recreational facilities contributed to the race riots in cities across the United States during the "long, hot summer of 1967."[2]

The first mention of the project in Tress's correspondence came in a letter to his sister dated July 29, 1969, describing a visit to the site of the Newark riots two years earlier (fig. 24): "I wanted to shoot some 'youth' for my 'Open Space' project—I went along Springfield Avenue which still has a lot of burnt out buildings. The police came along and asking if I belonged to any 'subversive organization' [they] took me down to the police station. They could have arrested me for being in the abandoned buildings—so I was very polite to them—but they are so strange . . . with all sorts of hang-ups—asked me if I lived in Greenwich Village, etc." On that day Tress photographed a child posing against a painted wall in the former Biltrite furniture store (plate 80). It would become one of his most frequently reproduced images from the *Open Space* series and would also be included in *The Dream Collector*.

Tress's *Open Space* photographs began to reach the public eye in August 1969, when two of his New York waterfront views appeared in *Open Space Action*.[3] The following month he published a five-page article, "Open Space in the Inner City," consisting of an introductory text and eight captioned photographs, in *World Outlook* magazine.[4] "The enjoyable quality of urban life has not kept up with the advances of our modern life," he wrote. "We have put a man on the moon before we have solved the problem of collecting our cities' garbage." Several passages of his text are clearly derived from Lynn Young's *Open Space Action* article. Tress's assertion that "the American city is a cage and the smoke and ashes of civil disorder are the explosive efforts of the young to escape from its claustrophobic walls" is essentially lifted from the opening of Young's piece: "From Washington, Cincinnati and New York, the voices differ but the message is the same: Without open space for recreation, the American city is a cage. This special two-part section on open space and the inner city explores that cage from its claustrophobic walls to its only exit. The walls, of course, also carry the message. It was etched there last summer in the smoke and ashes of civil disorder."[5]

Tress first exhibited photographs from the series in November 1969 at the Focus Coffee

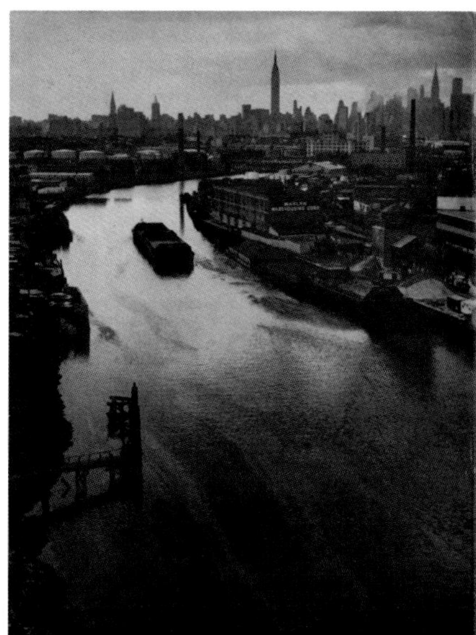

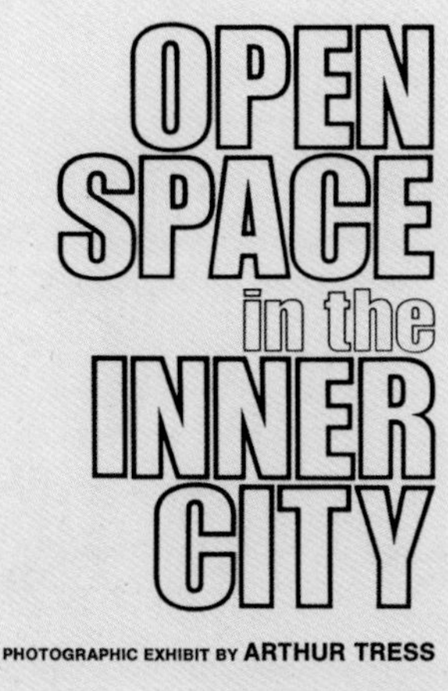

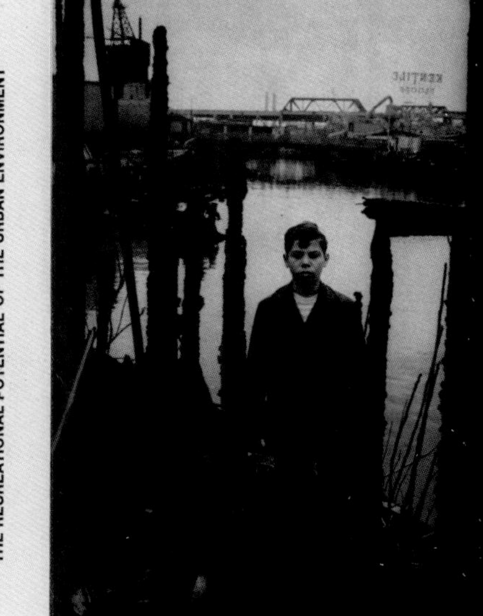

Figure 25
Open Space in the Inner City, 1970
Exhibition leaflet,
17.8 × 38.1 cm (7 × 15 in.)
Collection of Arthur Tress

House/Photographic Gallery. Focus was a cozy new venue on the ground floor of a townhouse on West 74th Street and Amsterdam Avenue run by Larry Brezner and George Gruber, former public school teachers.[6] According to the press release (presumably written by Tress), the photographer "has gone beyond the documentary approach, and uses dream, fantasy, and myth to express and extend these urban social problems. It is, in effect, social surrealism" (a term that appears in Tress's notebooks of that era). Tress is quoted in the press release as saying that photography is "a kind of autobiography, a continual cataloguing of perceptions. I'm like an eccentric collector creating my own archives, filling insights on photographic index cards."[7]

A. D. Coleman described the show as "a set of montages by mounting groups of small prints side by side on panels—perhaps 20 pictures per panel—in order to convey the almost-claustrophobic congestion of urban life which is one of the exhibit's themes."[8] Sean Callahan, photo editor of *Life* magazine, also saw the work. Particularly admiring Tress's photograph of Calvary Cemetery in Queens (plate 23), he subsequently published it in a two-page spread in *Life*, a major milestone of public exposure for the photographer.[9] "Tress believes that the living have greater need for the space than the dead," Callahan wrote, "and he shot the picture as part of an essay encouraging the more rational use of city land."

The Focus show was a warmup for a larger *Open Space in the Inner City* exhibition, which ran from February 16 through March 31, 1970, at the Sierra Club's new gallery on West 57th Street (fig. 25). The press release articulates the three sections of the installation:

> The first part of the exhibit deals with some of our cities' space problems:
> **Overpopulation, air and water pollution, traffic congestion, and ghetto violence**
> The second section demonstrates where to find open space in such areas as:
> **Waterfront**: abandoned piers, under bridges, river freight yards.
> **Vacant lots**: between buildings, backyards, and parking lots.
> **Roofs**: apartment house gardens, office and school buildings, garages.
> **Rights of way**: unused streets, railroad tracks, canals and aqueducts.
> **Coastal areas**: swamps, bays, landfill.
> The third section combines architects' and landscape designers' plans for various projects throughout the Metropolitan area that incorporate these kinds of space possibilities.

Coleman described the multimedia installation in his *New York Times* review, entitled "Finding a Place to Breathe, to Live": "For this new version, the prints have been hung separately. Many of them have been enlarged to 16 x 20, and the exhibit has been expanded by the addition of newspaper headlines, magazine articles and architect's drawings which relate to the exhibit's multiple themes . . . Tress's combination of pictures with relevant non-photographic material is an ingenious and successful experiment, for it helps to bind together many disparate images, and, further, directs the viewer beyond the appalling conditions depicted to the potential solutions thereof."[11] Coleman applauded Tress's visual wit and his efforts to stage certain images to dramatize the problems. He called attention to the photograph of "a businessman emerging from the miasmic mist of a sewer (which has been made into a fine poster)" and noted the appropriate caption (fig. 26).

By a lucky coincidence, the offices of the New York State Council on the Arts (NYSCA) were located in the same building as the Sierra Club Gallery, and Allon Schoener, the council's visual arts director, saw Tress's exhibition and entered into an agreement with the photographer. Tress wrote excitedly to Tobi Astner, his Swedish boyfriend: "The New York State Council on the Arts bought the whole show to send around New York State museums + have commissioned me to do 2 other exhibits for them. That means $ thousands. I want ever so much to go to Japan for a few weeks to soothe my soul in Zen gardens after so many months of New York ugliness + materialism."[12]

Tress had hoped his exhibition would travel—in his notebook he indicated that the Sierra Club and the Open Space Institute were preparing to make that happen—but instead the work circulated in a novel manner conceived by Allon Schoener. "Traditionally the travelling exhibition has been conceived of as a unique one-of-a-kind installation," Schoener explained. "Recognizing that there is a need throughout the State for the same thing at the same time, the council is now working to supplement unique exhibitions by multiple editions of the originals—so that four, six, or possibly dozens of exhibitions with the same content can be viewed simultaneously in as many different places."[13] At the end of his review Coleman noted that copies of the exhibit, "consisting of a set of 8 x 10 glossy prints of the photographs," were "available on loan, at no cost, to any school, church, business or other organization interested in preparing its own presentation," and he provided contact information at the NYSCA office. In fact, the first edition of an "exhibit portfolio" called *Open Space and the Inner City*, consisting of fifty 11 x 14-inch halftone reproductions, was rushed into production for distribution around the first Earth Day, which took place with great fanfare on April 22, 1970.[14] A statement accompanying the photographs explains their intended use and audience:

> These photographs have been selected to provide you with the opportunity to arrange your own exhibition demonstrating good and bad environmental conditions in New York City. You should feel free to use as many or as few of these photographs as you desire. They have been divided into four categories: Pollution, Congestion, Alienation, and Pleasure. However, you may feel free to follow these divisions or disregard them. A fifth category—Solution to our Environmental Problems—is suggested. Use your imagination to describe or illustrate new solutions. In arranging your own exhibition, you may use press clippings, your own photographs, your own drawings, your own statements, or anything else which you feel is appropriate. When you are through with it, you

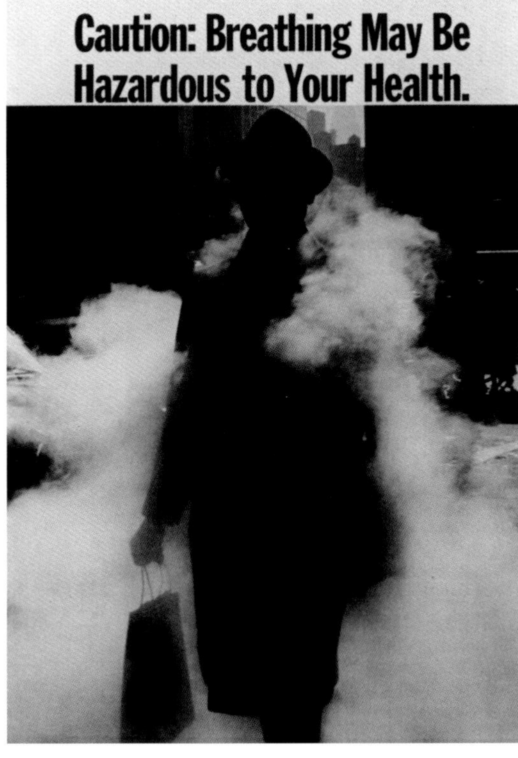

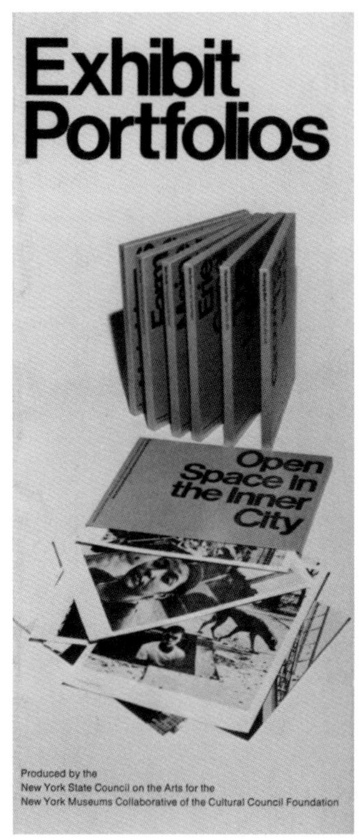

Figure 26
"Caution: Breathing May Be Hazardous to Your Health," 1970
Poster, 71.2 × 45.7 cm (28 × 18 in.)
Collection of Arthur Tress

Figure 27
New York State Council on the Arts Exhibit Portfolios, 1971
Printed advertisement, 22.9 × 12.7 cm (9 x 5 in.)
Collection of Arthur Tress

> may do with it whatever you want. There is no reason to return it.

NYSCA's first disposable exhibit portfolio having been deemed a success, it was followed by a second edition in 1971 with a new title, *Open Space in the Inner City: Ecology and the Urban Environment*. It would be one of seven portfolios in the same format produced by NYSCA's Visual Arts Program (fig. 27).[15] For the second edition Schoener slightly revised the selection and replaced the thematic captions with locations; the prints were packaged in a cardboard slipcase with an introductory statement by the artist that recycled and expanded his text from *World Outlook*. Unlike Tress's artist statement for the Focus exhibition, which had emphasized his artistic vision and interest in social surrealism, this text concentrated on the subject matter of the photographs and on how they illustrated the various problems and solutions relating to recreational space in the urban environment.

Tress's *Open Space* series represented his first extended engagement with the genre of street photography. During the roughly two and a half years that he worked on this project, he produced thousands of photographs, only a small percentage of which appeared in his exhibitions, exhibit portfolios, or publications. Some made their way into his own stock lists and other photo-agency files, and from there into books and periodicals in contexts unimagined by the artist; others reappeared in his *Dream Collector* photobook. On some shoots he used both Kodak Plus-X Pan black-and-white and Ektachrome transparency films, producing color variants that he filed with stock agencies (fig. 28). His approach to the project was both intuitive and methodical. He kept a map of the city on which he highlighted areas to photograph, and taking public transit, he gravitated, Atget-like, to marginalized areas rather than to central tourist sites. He described how he went about it:

> I will almost arbitrarily select an area of New York out of an enormous street atlas that I have of all the boroughs. I open my atlas and look at the configurations of routes and intersections and try to sense what area might be visually productive. Perhaps a housing development

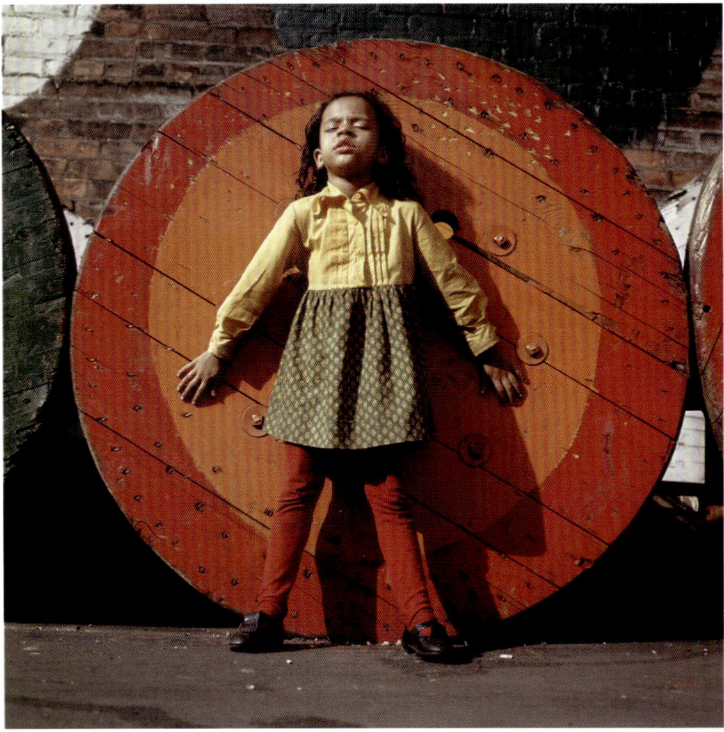

built around the circular course of an abandoned racetrack on Staten Island or indications of streets that end in enormous stairways in the hilly Bronx. Perhaps for a few days I will follow the edge of a river or bay and pick up upon paths of the Elevated subways that run like streams through canyons of housing.[16]

The *Open Space* project incorporates a range of photographic approaches, from straightforward documentary-style vistas of the urban environment to candid images of life in the parks and on the streets, portrait-style photographs in which Tress engaged the sitters to pose, and more deliberately staged scenes revealing his surrealist sensibility and love of visual non sequiturs. Like Cartier-Bresson he sought out large gatherings, such as parades, political rallies, or protests, where he aimed his lens toward spectators rather than participants (plates 52–53). The cast of New Yorkers featured in *Open Space* represents diverse communities, with an emphasis on disaffected young people whose facial expressions range from anxious to threatened. "My newest project is doing high school students," Tress wrote to Tobi in April 1970, "just going around to different neighborhoods + outside the schools—contrasting their alive energies against the prison-like schools."[17] In another letter from a few months earlier, he described the challenge of photographing industrial sites with his new Distagon lens:

> Doing gas + coal works in New Jersey—with my new wide angle lens which is sometimes a pain as it sort of shrinks everything together + they lose dramatic impact. I planned today with such hopes . . . putting myself in a "creative mood"—not getting nervous . . . resting my mind + trying to clarify what I wanted to do . . . calmly going into the subway + then to the bus station + then walking over to the gas works in my big green boots. Then being chased off the railroad bridge + then followed by police cars + then being given hostile looks by the coal company employees (everyone is getting very uptight about pollution).[18]

Although the original *Open Space* photographs were taken in New York City and its immediate environs, NYSCA awarded Tress a commission after his Sierra Club exhibition to photograph around Albany and Buffalo for a potential new exhibit portfolio devoted to poverty and pollution in upstate New York. Tress was inspired by the work he produced there in the fall and early winter of 1970 (plates 38, 48, 62), writing to Tobi from Albany: "I am more involved with the world—the streets, faces, trees, people—than ever before. I am doing this

Figure 28
Arthur Tress
Girl in Vest Pocket Park, Upper West Side, New York, 1968
Ektachrome transparency, 5.7 × 5.7 cm (2 ¼ × 2 ¼ in.)
Collection of the artist

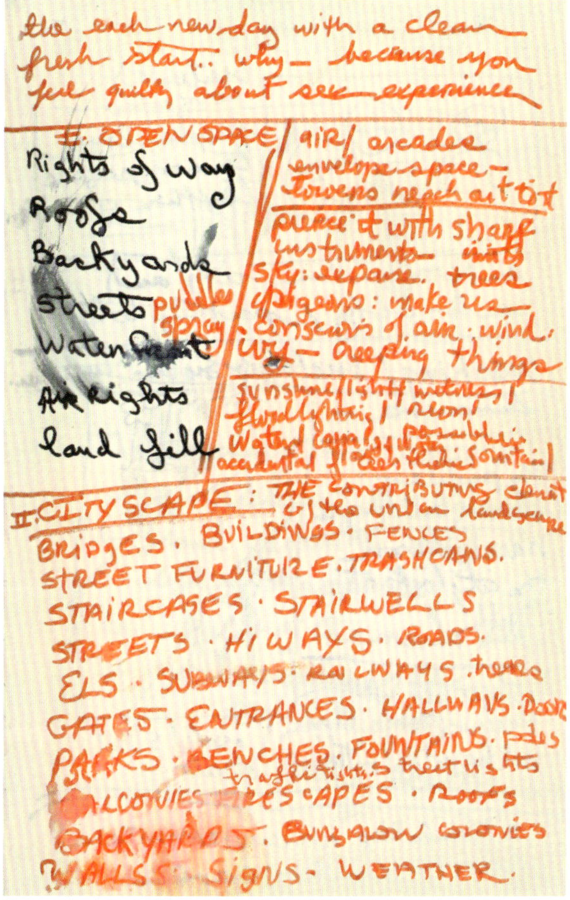

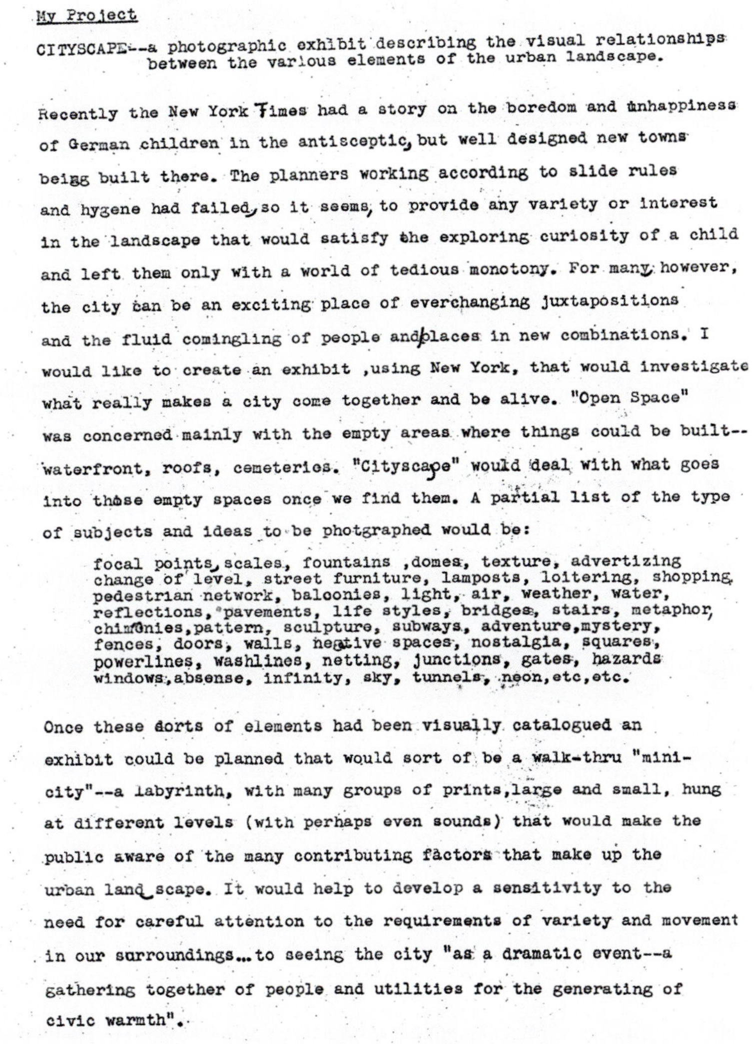

My Project

CITYSCAPE--a photographic exhibit describing the visual relationships between the various elements of the urban landscape.

Recently the New York Times had a story on the boredom and unhappiness of German children in the antisceptic, but well designed new towns beigg built there. The planners working according to slide rules and hygene had failed, so it seems, to provide any variety or interest in the landscape that would satisfy the exploring curiosity of a child and left them only with a world of tedious monotony. For many, however, the city can be an exciting place of everchanging juxtapositions and the fluid comingling of people and places in new combinations. I would like to create an exhibit ,using New York, that would investigate what really makes a city come together and be alive. "Open Space" was concerned mainly with the empty areas where things could be built--waterfront, roofs, cemeteries. "Cityscape" would deal with what goes into these empty spaces once we find them. A partial list of the type of subjects and ideas to be photgraphed would be:

focal points, scales, fountains ,domes, texture, advertizing change of level, street furniture, lamposts, loitering, shopping pedestrian network, balconies, light, air, weather, water, reflections, pavements, life styles, bridges, stairs, metaphor, chimnies, pattern, sculpture, subways, adventure, mystery, fences, doors, walls, negative spaces, nostalgia, squares, powerlines, washlines, netting, junctions, gates, hazards windows, absense, infinity, sky, tunnels, neon, etc, etc.

Once these sorts of elements had been visually catalogued an exhibit could be planned that would sort of be a walk-thru "mini-city"--a labyrinth, with many groups of prints, large and small, hung at different levels (with perhaps even sounds) that would make the public aware of the many contributing factors that make up the urban landscape. It would help to develop a sensitivity to the need for careful attention to the requirements of variety and movement in our surroundings...to seeing the city "as a dramatic event--a gathering together of people and utilities for the generating of civic warmth".

extraordinary project which no other photographer has ever had so much freedom or responsibility to do before."[19] But Schoener was dissatisfied with the results, as Tress now recalls, because he was looking for rural scenes more along the lines of Appalachia. With Schoener's departure shortly thereafter from NYSCA, the exhibit portfolio series was abandoned.[20] Tress considers the upstate photographs an extension of his *Open Space* project.

On an undated notebook page Tress jotted down ideas for a planned sequel to *Open Space*, which he called *Cityscape* (fig. 29). His archive also includes a single-page typescript proposal for *Cityscape*, "a photographic exhibit describing the visual relationships between the various elements of the urban landscape" (fig. 30).[21] In it, Tress explains that "'Open Space' was concerned mainly with the empty areas where things could be built—waterfront, roofs, cemeteries. 'Cityscape' would deal with what goes into those empty spaces once we find them." He provides a partial list of subjects to be photographed, including fountains, advertising, street furniture, lampposts, balconies, pavements, bridges, stairs, chimneys, sculpture, subways, fences, doors, walls, power lines, wash lines, gates, windows, and neon; this list is intermingled with abstract ideas, including lifestyles, metaphor, adventure, mystery, nostalgia, absence,

Figure 29
Arthur Tress
Notebook page, ca. 1971
Collection of the artist

Figure 30
Arthur Tress
Cityscape exhibition proposal, 1971
Collection of the artist

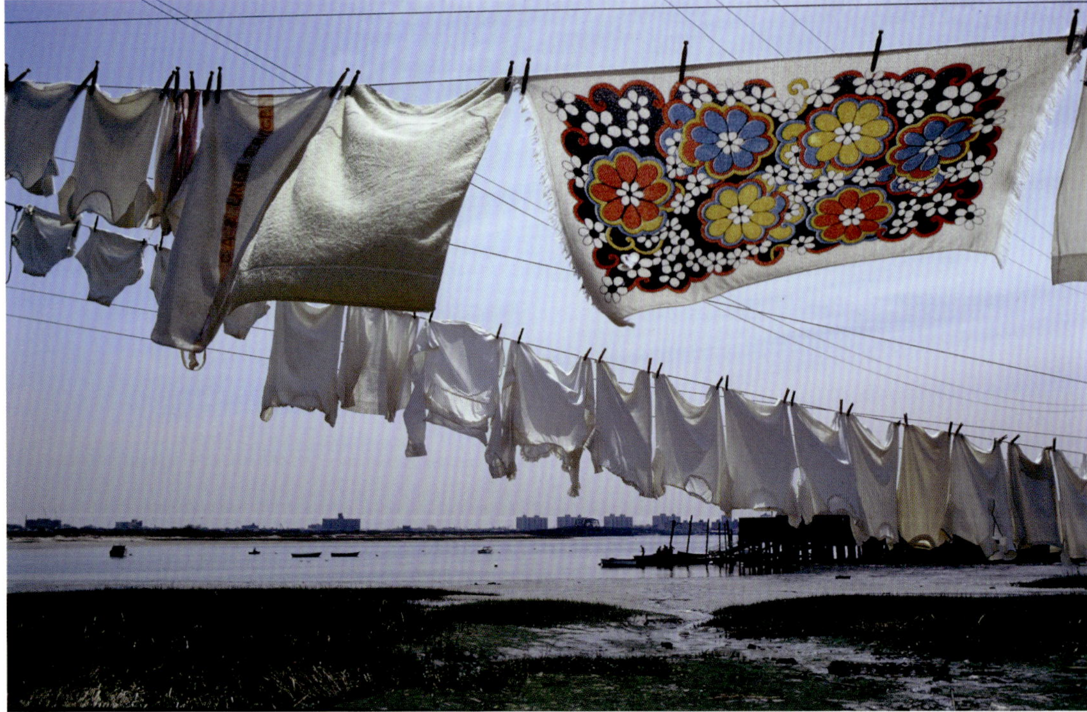

Figure 31
Arthur Tress
Laundry Day, Broad Channel, Queens, New York, 1973
Kodachrome slide, 2.5 × 3.8 cm (1 × 1½ in.)
Collection of the artist

and infinity. Tress imagines the installation as "a walk-thru 'mini-city'—a labyrinth, with many groups of prints, large and small, hung at different levels (with perhaps even sounds) that would make the public aware of the many contributing factors that make up the urban landscape." Tress's ambitious proposal was clearly inspired by experiential photo-based exhibitions like Edward Steichen's *Family of Man* (Museum of Modern Art, 1955), Schoener's *Portal to America: The Lower East Side, 1870–1925* (Jewish Museum, 1967), and Schoener's controversial *Harlem on My Mind: Cultural Capital of Black America, 1900–1968* (Metropolitan Museum of Art, 1969), which led to protests because it did not include any works by Black artists. Tress's plans for a *Cityscape* exhibition would remain unrealized, but he created a significant number of images for this project even as he increasingly redirected his creative energy to his photographs of children's dreams that would coalesce into his *Daymares* exhibition and *Dream Collector* photobook.

What might be seen as a postscript to Tress's *Open Space* work was his participation in the ambitious Documerica photography project (fig. 31). Created by Gifford Hampshire of the Environmental Protection Agency, Documerica took inspiration from the Farm Security Administration photography project of the 1930s.[22] Along with dozens of other freelance photographers in various regions of the country, including Ken Heyman, Danny Lyon, and Chester Higgins, Tress was selected to document the societal effects of pollution using 35 mm Kodachrome slides. Tress's Documerica work was relatively limited in scope. In May 1973 he received a commission to shoot over the course of a week to ten days at the standard rate of $150 a day plus expenses and the cost of film. He used the opportunity to revisit areas that he explored for his *Open Space* project, particularly around Staten Island, Sheepshead Bay, Jamaica Bay, Sandy Hook, and Coney Island. After the agency made its selection, he placed the rejects in stock-agency files. The photographs Tress contributed to the project generally lack the element of social surrealism that characterized his *Open Space* work, but they make striking use of color, and in a few instances they transcend the stock-photography aesthetic of the overall project.

Notes

1 Despite the importance of this project and its prominence around the time of the first Earth Day, it has received little attention outside of the literature on Tress. Katherine Bussard gave an overview of the work in Katherine A. Bussard, Alison Fisher, and Greg Foster-Rice, *The City Lost and Found: Capturing New York, Chicago, and Los Angeles, 1960–1980* (Princeton, NJ: Princeton University Art Museum, 2015), 88–89, and lectured on the topic at Rutgers University on March 24, 2017, in the symposium "Reinventing Documentary Photography in the 1970s." Her talk was entitled "'Beyond the Documentary Approach': Arthur Tress' Open Space in the Inner City."

2 Lynn Young, "Open Space and the Inner City," *Open Space Action* 1, no. 1 (October–November 1968): 11–17. Tress has confirmed (email to the author, October 6, 2022) that this article was one of several sources that led him to focus on "open space" as a major theme in the fall of 1968, and the texts he wrote to accompany publications of his work draw directly from Young's article.

3 Tress's photographs illustrate the article "On the Waterfront" in *Open Space Action* 1, no. 5 (August 1969): 4–5, 9.

4 Arthur Tress, "Open Space in the Inner City," *World Outlook* 10, no. 10 (September 1969): 20–27.

5 Young, "Open Space and the Inner City," 12.

6 It would later evolve into a performance space featuring vocalists and improvisational comedy. Brezner went on to become an important agent for major comic personalities as well as a prominent film producer.

7 A copy of the press release is in the collection of the artist.

8 This description of the Focus Gallery show appears in Coleman's published review of the later exhibition at the Sierra Club Gallery, "Finding a Place to Breathe, to Live," *New York Times*, March 15, 1970, p. D31.

9 Email to the author, October 6, 2022. The photograph was featured on the Gallery page of *Life* 70, no. 23 (June 18, 1971): 6–7.

10 Original document in the collection of the artist.

11 Coleman, "Finding a Place to Breathe, to Live," p. D31.

12 Letter to Tobi Astner, February–March 1970, from New York, collection of the artist.

13 Quoted in "Arthur Tress, Open Space in the Inner City, photographs for the New York State Council on the Arts," *Creative Camera* 10, no. 10 (December 1970): 362–63.

14 Allon Schoener in *NYSCA Annual Report*, 1970–71: "For the first Earth Day celebration in New York City, the Council served as coordinator of the State's displays in Union Square and produced the first edition of Arthur Tress's *Open Space in the Inner City*" (p. 89). Around the time of Tress's Sierra Club exhibition, the Washington, DC urban planning firm Marcou, O'Leary, & Associates published a selection of his *Open Space* photographs in its report *Open Space for Human Needs*, prepared for the National Urban Coalition in 1970.

15 The others were *Farm Life Today* (photographs by Joseph Consentino), *Main Street* (Milo Stewart), *Neighbors on the Block* (Upper West Side residential hotel residents photographed by Laurence Salzmann), *Growing Up Black* (Leroy Lucas), *The Erie Canal* (reproductions of nineteenth-century prints and photographs), and *The Lower East Side* (turn-of-the-century images from the Jewish Museum). *NYSCA Annual Report*, 1970–71, p. 108.

16 Previously unpublished text, "Open Space" (1970), in Marco Livingstone, ed., *Arthur Tress: Talisman* (London: Thames & Hudson, 1986), 148.

17 Letter to Tobi Astner, April 16, 1970, from New York, collection of the artist.

18 Letter to Tobi Astner, January 1970, from New York, collection of the artist.

19 Letter to Tobi Astner, September 1970, from Albany, collection of the artist.

20 Email to the author, October 6, 2022.

21 This text is also undated but refers to a "recent" *New York Times* article—"Psychologists' Report Finds New Towns in West Germany Boring to Children," by Lawrence Fellows—that was published on May 9, 1971, providing a terminus post quem for the document.

22 See Bruce I. Bustard, *Searching for the Seventies: The DOCUMERICA Photography Project* (Washington, DC: Foundation for the National Archives, in association with D. Giles Ltd., London, 2013). Tress's Documerica work is discussed in Barbara Lynn Shubinski, "From FSA to EPA: Project DOCUMERICA, the Dustbowl Legacy, and the Quest to Photograph 1970s America," PhD diss., Graduate College of the University of Iowa, December 2009. Tress's 164 Documerica photographs in the National Archives are viewable at https://catalog.archives.gov/search?q=record.contributors.naId%3A10582020&ancestorNaId=542493, accessed January 2023.

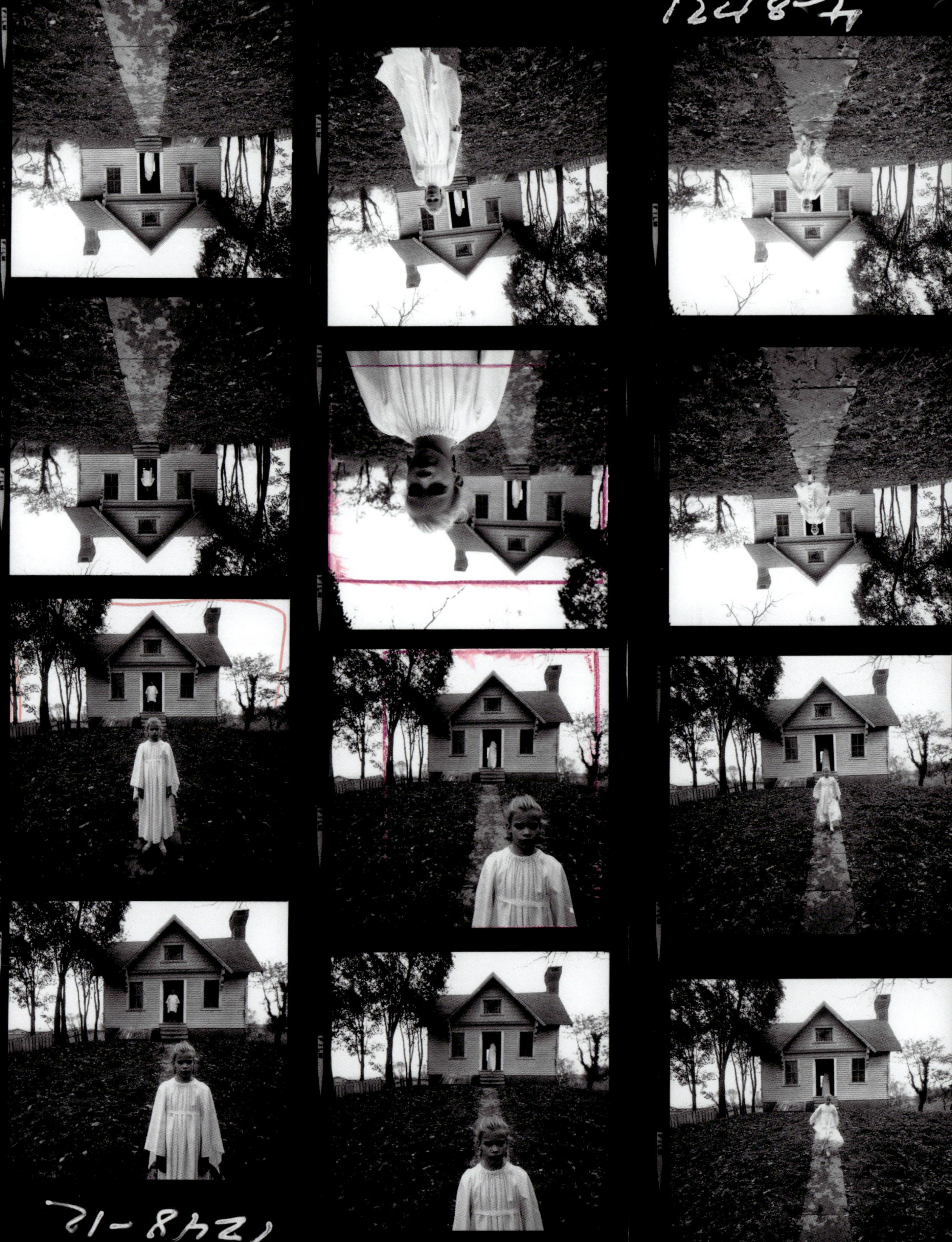
1248-7

JAMES A. GANZ

Collecting Dreams

Informed by his readings of classic texts by Sigmund Freud and Carl Jung, Tress's 16 mm film *Daymares* (1965) represented the first manifestation in his oeuvre of visualizing daydreams and nightmares, which would become a lifelong source of artistic inspiration. The film also reflected his love of European avant-garde cinema of the 1920s and 1930s as practiced by figures like Fernand Léger, Luis Buñuel, and Jean Cocteau, and incorporated a number of radical techniques, including the use of multiple exposures and found footage. With a soundtrack of distorted recordings of electronic and Asian music, *Daymares* offered a succession of dream montages attributed to people representing different stages of life from infancy through old age. In a typescript description dating from one of its few screenings, Tress wrote that "dreams are circular trips to the underworld of our unfulfilled desires. The dream-hero travels into the dark labyrinth and returns with the mythical gift that will save mankind."[1] He described the dream sequences as "variations on the terrors, confusions and triumphs of such nocturnal journeys." Along with the rest of Tress's early cinematic efforts, *Daymares* was quickly forgotten, but its title and themes would resurface a few years later in his seminal photographic series devoted to children's dreams.

Among the reservoir of proto–*Dream Collector* photographs that predated the project and essentially pointed the way forward, one of the most striking is the image he made in West Virginia capturing the fear and vulnerability of a young girl posing with a creepy doll's head (plate 12).[2] It would be published in *The Dream Collector* accompanied by a short text: "The little girl was dressed in rags, didn't go to school, didn't have shoes, didn't have enough to eat. Her family had stuck this doll's head on a bush in front of the house. She told Tress it frightened her and she sometimes dreamed about

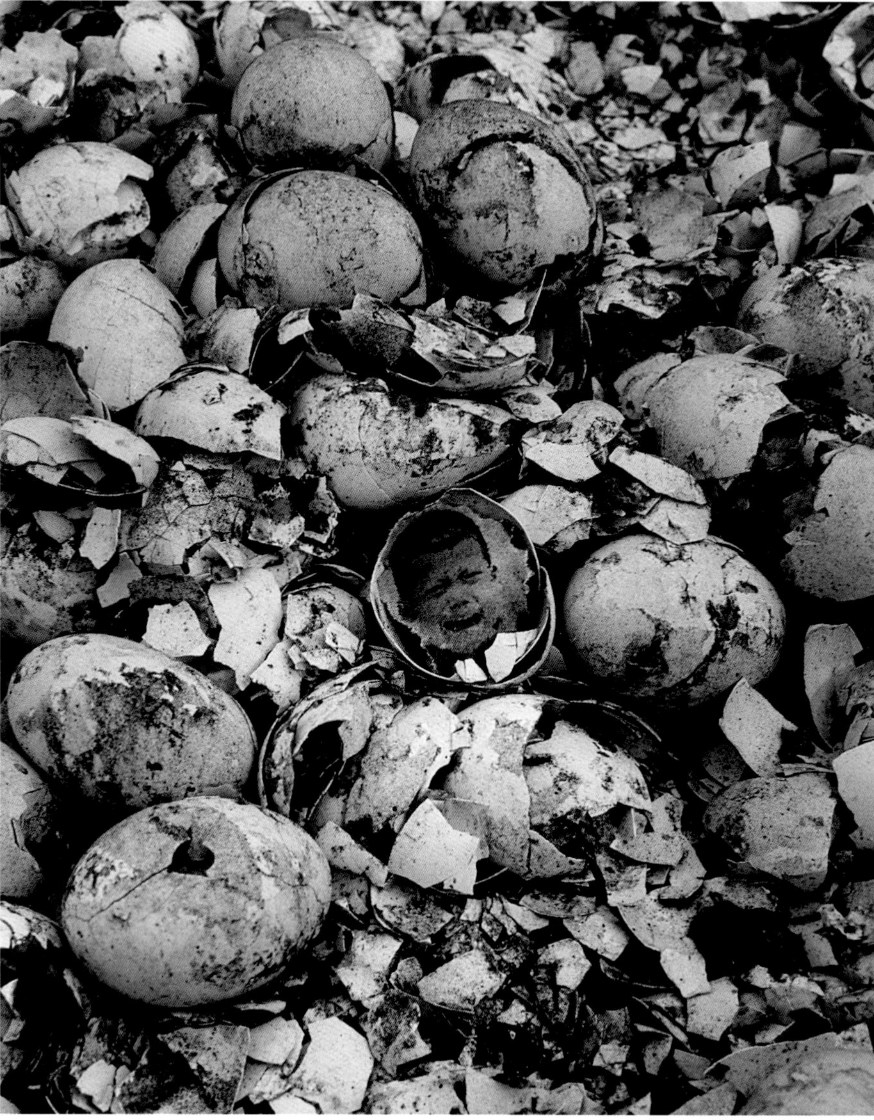

Figure 32
Arthur Tress
Face in Broken Egg Shells, New York, New York, 1969
Gelatin silver print, 34 × 26.5 cm (13 3/8 × 10 7/16 in.)
Los Angeles, J. Paul Getty Museum, Gift of Trixy Castro, 2019.167.10

it."[3] While making a good living photographing poverty and pollution in Appalachia and around New York, Tress confided in a January 1970 letter that he wanted to transcend the mundane subject matter and achieve something more profound in his work. "I want to use the external world to express my inner feelings," he told his boyfriend Tobi Astner. He had the audacity to voice this ambition a few months later to an international photography world that was preoccupied with journalistic verisimilitude. In his essay-manifesto "The Photograph as Magical Image," published in the March 1970 issue of *Album* magazine along with the image of the girl and the doll's head, he wrote: "A photographer could be considered a kind of magician—a being possessed of very special powers that enable him to control mysterious forces and energies outside himself. . . . The grotesque or frightening image may stir forgotten animal instincts of primordial helplessness and fear, reaching back to the basic insecurity of early man and our own personal childhoods."[4]

The immediate origins of Tress's *Dream Collector* series are the more surreal photographs of children he produced during his work on his *Open Space* project. A primary theme of the *Open Space* photographs was the lack of proper recreational facilities for urban youths, a scarcity that led them to play in peculiar—and occasionally hazardous—sites. As Tress has noted, "The desolate piers, warehouses, and trash dumps were often used by kids as impromptu recreation areas and had already in themselves a feeling of surreal dislocation and melancholy peculiar to a dream-like atmosphere."[5] Indeed, the two projects were intertwined geographically, chronologically, and thematically, with a significant number of *Open Space* images resurfacing in the *Dream Collector* book. Among these are *Wild Man of the Forest, Central Park, New York* (plate 65), *Boy in Water under Bridge, Queens, New York* (plate 67), and *Boy with Chalk Face, Coney Island, New York* (plate 99). Other *Dream Collector* images created by Tress during his work on *Open Space* include *Child Buried in the Sand, Coney Island, New York* (plate 66), *Face in Broken Egg Shells, New York, New York* (fig. 32), and *Boy with Duck Decoy, Passaic, New Jersey* (plate 87).

A major turning point for Tress, marking his transition from merely injecting his *Open Space* images with elements of social surrealism to redirecting his creative energy into a new series of photographs exploring children's dreams, occurred in the early months of 1971 when he was contacted by the poet Richard Lewis, a fellow Bard graduate. Tress has described his subsequent work with Lewis as "a mind-expanding moment for me . . . a kind of mental can-opener that had me questioning the 'fabric of knowing' and the 'multiplicity of realities' that are usually not accorded full rights under the norms of narrowly accepted photographic procedures."[6] Lewis had recently founded a nonprofit educational organization called the Touchstone Center for Children "in the belief that all persons have natural creative and artistic capacities, which, when encouraged and allowed to develop, find unique expression in each individual."[7] One of the first grants awarded by the New York State Council on the Arts went to the Touchstone Center to organize a series of "Creative Imagination Workshops" in three elementary schools during the 1970–71 academic year: the Children's Community Workshop School on the Upper West Side, the Manhattan Country School on the Upper East Side, and P.S. 198 at Third Avenue and East 96th Street, which served a diverse student body from the luxury apartment buildings in the immediate neighborhood as well as housing projects in East Harlem.[8]

During regular hour-long sessions, Lewis encouraged small groups of children to explore various artistic outlets to express their daydreams. Looking back on the workshops, Lewis wrote that they revealed to him how accessible dreams were to preteens. The participants not only recounted their nightmares but focused on the experience of daydreaming "as a crucial step in approaching the mythic and poetic sensibility within as well as the flow of intimations, images, and feelings that make up the inward state."[9] He reported that "as the months passed, we experimented with evolving dream 'dramas' that could be taken outside and performed in the schoolyard or in the park. We asked the photographer Arthur Tress to film what took place, and to make still-picture dramas, which were developed and made into a series of 'dream books'—which could be read as a sequence of unfolding images and interpreted in endless ways."[10] A May 1971 *New York Times* article on the project at P.S. 198, illustrated with a photograph by Tress from a few months earlier, described how Tress "arrived with a duffle full of costumes—capes, crowns, horns, swords and monster masks. The children dressed themselves and took parts." One of the children, "functioning as a director, . . . arranged the other children in a series of tableaux that Mr. Tress photographed. In the school's playground, in less than an hour, the children created an elaborate

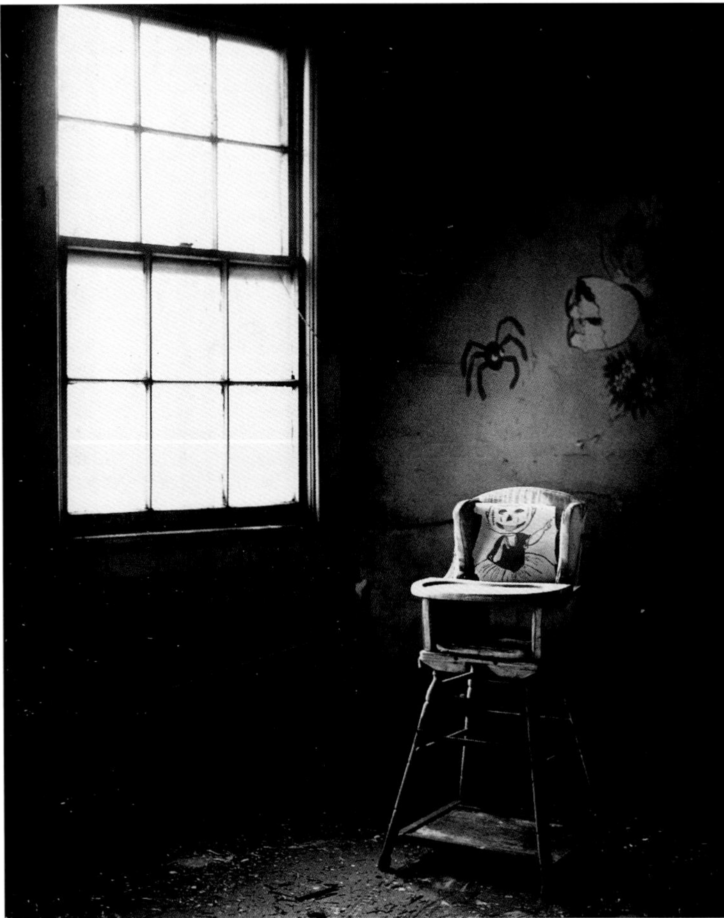

THE TOUCHSTONE CENTER FOR CHILDREN
In Association With
THE MANHATTAN THEATRE CLUB

Present

A DREAM EVENT

Directed
by
Richard Lewis

DANCE AND MOVEMENT:	Laura Simms
FILMS: 'YOU, THE DREAMER':	Photographs by Arthur Tress Text by Richard Lewis Film Realization and Direction:Robert Carroll
'DREAM CREATURES':	Drawings by children from the Dream Workshop: P.S. 198, Children's Community Workshop, Manhattan Country School. Music by Richard Lewis and Robert Carroll Film Realization and Direction: Robert Carroll
SLIDES:	Arthur Tress
LIGHTING:	Keith Michael
CREATURES:	Created by Children on CREATURE MAKING DAY, May 6th, at the Manhattan Theatre Club

TEXTS: I Once Has This Feeling - Julie Gluck - Age 9
The Window Turns... - Elizabeth John - Age 10
Where Are My Dreams Taking Me? - Jackie Foy - Age 10
Falling, Falling.... - Caroline Kane - Age 9
The Eye in the Scenery - Mazaki Kiyonori - Age 10
It's Raining and Snowing - David Usdan - Age 9
There was once a Laughing Monster - Louis Jones - Age 10
The Bird Crashed.... Nicola - Age 8
My Cave - Ishikawa Sekiko - Age 10
Sometimes I Think - Jessica Roth - Age 9
The Dream of Chuang Tzu

ADMINISTRATIVE ASSISTANTS: FOR TOUCHSTONE CENTER: Laura Simms
FOR MTC: Margaret Brown and Anne Roby

WE WOULD LIKE TO THANK APRIL HAMILTON FOR HER WORK ON CREATURE-MAKING DAY, THE STAFF OF MERC FOR THEIR ASSISTANCE AND USE OF FACILITIES FOR OUR FILMS, AND TO ALL THE CHILDREN WHO CONTRIBUTED MATERIAL FOR THE DREAM EVENT. PRODUCTION MADE POSSIBLE BY A GRANT FROM THE NEW YORK STATE COUNCIL ON THE ARTS.

Figure 33
Arthur Tress
Children's Ward, Welfare Island, New York, ca. 1971
Gelatin silver print, 24.2 × 19.4 cm (9 1/2 × 7 5/8 in.)
Los Angeles, J. Paul Getty Museum, 2013.68.66

Figure 34
Touchstone Center for Children
A Dream Event program, New York, 1972
Collection of Arthur Tress

narrative in pictures."[11] Tress also brought the costumes, borrowed from a friend who worked at a children's theater, for the students from the Children's Community Workshop School to use in Riverside Drive Park, subsequently the site of a number of his *Dream Collector* photographs, including *Boy with Root Hands, New York, New York* (plate 81).

Beyond his participation in Touchstone's Creative Imagination Workshops, Tress collaborated with Lewis on several related projects. Lewis made a four-minute film called *You, the Dreamer* (1972), which consisted of a montage of around fifty of Tress's photographs accompanied by Lewis's voice-over narration of his poem of the same title (fig. 33). The film was shown at *A Dream Event*, directed by Lewis and staged for children and their parents at the Manhattan Theatre Club on May 13 and May 20, 1972 (fig. 34).[12] The presentation also included a slide show of Tress's *Daymare* images. Tress and Lewis intended to produce a book version of *You, the Dreamer* and prepared a maquette now in the archives of the Touchstone Center, but they did not in the end pursue it. On his own, Tress lectured and organized workshops relating to children, dreams, and photography at the Floating Foundation of Photography, the American Society of Picture Professionals, and other venues, and started planning a children's book called *The Child's First Book of Dreams*, for which he hoped to engage a professional nonfiction children's book writer. This publication failed to materialize, as did

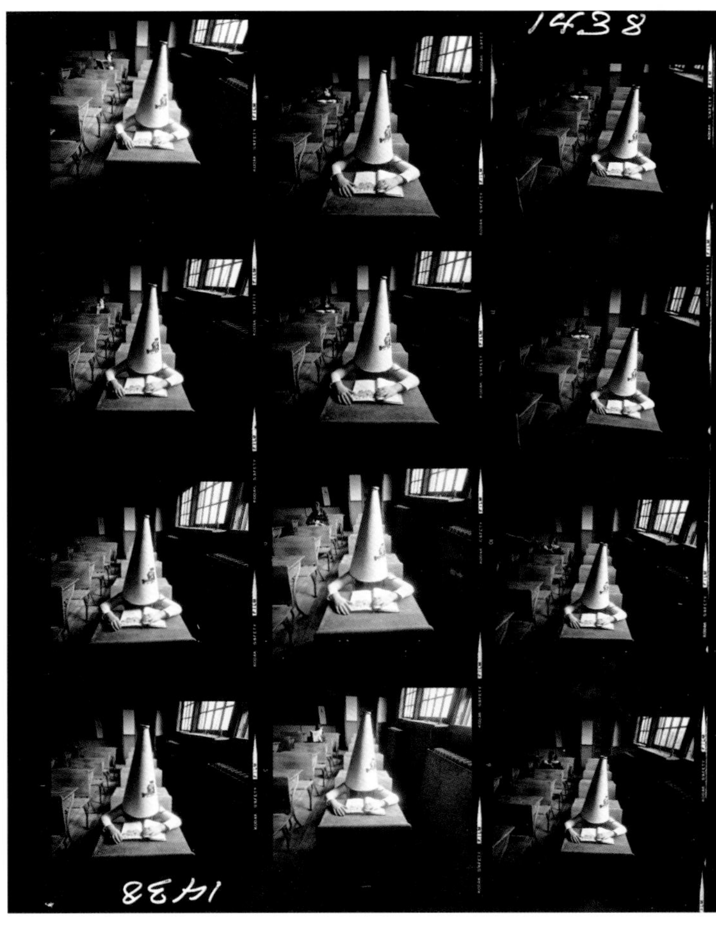

Figure 35
Arthur Tress
Contact sheet, P.S. 3, New York, New York, 1972
Gelatin silver print, 25.4 × 20.3 cm (10 × 8 in.)
Collection of the artist

a later book project called *A World of Children's Dreams* (ca. 1974–75) with a proposed text by the clinical social worker Lilo Plaschkes.

Inspired by his collaborations with Lewis and independent research of his own on dream psychology, which he had begun studying in scholarly journals, Tress began to focus his efforts on a new photographic series relating to children's dreams. As he delved deeper into the project, he sought advice from the celebrated author Maurice Sendak, whose work tapped into the world of children's dreams and nightmares. Tress was introduced to Sendak through Justin G. Schiller, a rare book dealer based in New York City who specialized in juvenile literature and had a particularly close relationship with Sendak.[13] Tress visited Sendak's Greenwich Village rowhouse with a box of 11 x 14-inch *Daymare* photographs in late 1971 or early 1972 to solicit his response to the work and ask for advice on how to proceed. "He was a bit taken aback by them actually," Tress recalled recently. "He thought they were a bit too direct and I think too dark in tone. From his point of view, where the illustrated dreams in his own work are more lyrical and not frightening, perhaps my more gothic and sinister interpretations were a bit over the top." Sendak recommended that Tress research Winsor McCay's *Little Nemo in Slumberland* comic strip from the early twentieth century for an alternative method of illustrating a child's dream world. The visit ended with an artistic exchange: Sendak gave Tress a small signed copy of a German edition of one of his books, and Tress let him choose one of the *Daymare* photographs for his collection. To his surprise, Sendak selected *Wild Man of the Forest, Central Park, New York* (plate 65), perhaps one of the most visually disturbing images Tress had produced to date, in which he embedded his photograph of a grizzled ragpicker in a muddy pile of leaves, intending to evoke the archetypal figure of the medieval wild man of the woods.[14]

Around this time Tress also made the acquaintance of John Melser, the founding principal of P.S. 3 in the West Village. P.S. 3 was launched in 1971 as a progressive school with open, multi-age classrooms and a special emphasis on the creative arts. In an unpublished passage from the original *Dream Collector* manuscript, it was described as "an old granite and brick building, dating from 1905—similar to the grade school [Tress] suffered through in his childhood. But, ironically, P.S. 3 today is one of the most exciting 'experimental' schools in the country, with virtually all the old teaching methods abandoned."[15] From late 1971 through the early spring of 1972, Tress was able to work with third- to fifth-grade students at P.S. 3 on his own informal "dream workshops," producing a series of improvised photographs—destined for his spring

Figure 36
Arthur Tress
Notebook page, 1972
Collection of the artist

exhibition—with the children in classrooms, corridors, and stairways (plates 70–72; fig. 35). *Boy with Tangled Strips, New York, New York* (also known as *School Boy's Dream*) is one of the few images for which Tress has noted a direct connection between a child's described dream and the staging of a specific photograph. In his notebook he recorded the dream of ten-year-old Blaise, a new student at P.S. 3 who had lived on a farm upstate and described being chased by a piece of harvesting equipment (fig. 36). As Tress recently explained, "Blaise and I, after he told me the dream, went to a staircase corridor and I found some plastic slats that I wrapped the boy in where he is looking anxiously out as he struggles to become free."[16]

Tress's *Daymares: Photographs of Children's Dreams* was shown in a small gallery space connected to the Raffi Photo Lab on West 46th Street from May 3 to June 21, 1972. "You entered from an elevator in an industrial building," Tress has recalled. "At the far end of the room was a large desk where a lab worker would take in your film order and deliver it back to you. One wall was windows overlooking the street. The photos were along one wall above a seating area and some were behind the reception desk. At the time there was no embarrassment for photographers to show in places like that. It was one step above showing in a folk café."[17] According to the artist's press release, the exhibition presented "a series of photographs that attempts to interpret the dreams and fantasies of young children through the medium of documentary photography":

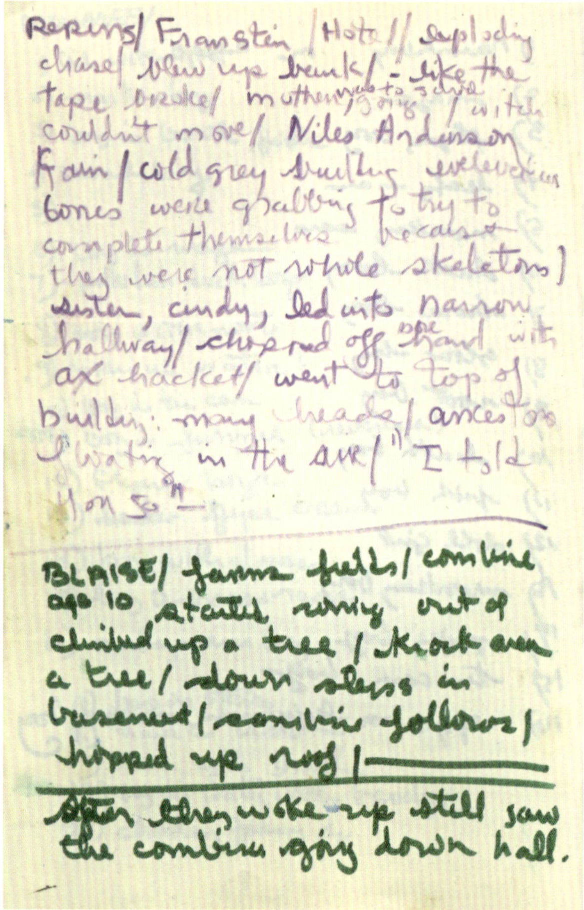

> Dreams or nightmares were collected by conversations with children in schools, streets, or neighborhood playgrounds . . . Often the location itself, such as an automobile graveyard or abandoned merry-go-round, would provide the possibility of dreamlike themes and spontaneous improvisation to the photographer and his subjects. In recreating these fantasies there is often a combination of actual dream, mythical archetypes, fairy tale, horror movie, comic book, and imaginative play. These inventions often reflect the child's inner life, his hopes and fears, as well as his symbolic transmutation of the external environment, his home or school, into manageable forms.[18]

Tress took special care in making richly toned gelatin silver prints and mounting them on black matboard suggestive of the nocturnal subject

Figure 37
Cover of *Arthur Tress: The Dream Collector*, 1972
28.6 × 21. 9 cm (11 1/4 × 8 5/8 in.)

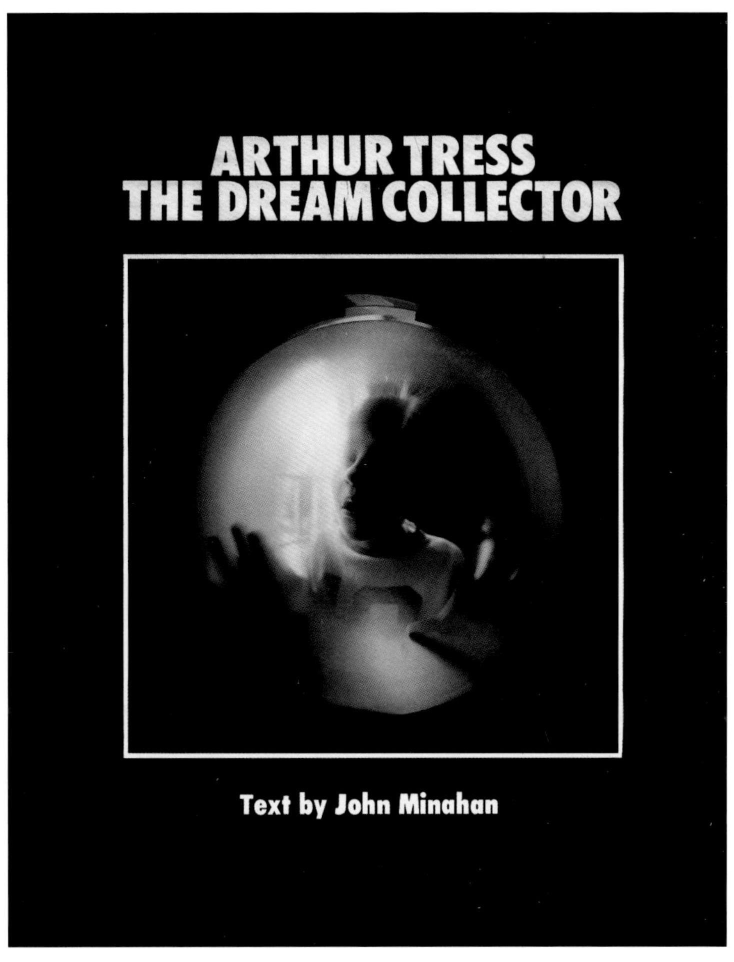

matter, a visual scheme that would carry over into the design of the *Dream Collector* book with its black pages and cover. He showed approximately twenty photographs from the series, which were priced at $25 each, although none sold. A. D. Coleman, who had previously taken note of Tress's exhibitions *The "Disturbed" Land* and *Open Space in the Inner City*, published a positive review: "A childlike openness which I've noted before as part of his vision has here stood him in good stead, as has his attraction to fantasy, his enjoyment in staging events, and his tendency toward controlled melodrama."[19] Coleman added that plans were already under way for a book to come out in the fall.

The key figure in the relatively quick evolution of *Daymares* from gallery exhibition to monograph was Peter Schults, the charismatic founder and head of the stock agency Photo Researchers, which represented Tress's work. Schults attended the small opening of the Raffi Lab show, just a few blocks away from his office on Fifth Avenue and 42nd Street, and immediately saw the potential for a photobook. Schults brought the idea to his old friend Earl Cooley, the chief editor and manager of a new press called Westover Publishing Company in Richmond, Virginia. Given Westover's relatively conventional nonfiction list, which focused on nature topics, parenting, wine, and cookbooks, it is perhaps surprising that Cooley agreed to copublish with Photo Researchers the macabre *Arthur Tress: The Dream Collector* in its first hardcover edition (fig. 37). But Schults was persuasive and threw himself into the project, his own initial foray into book publishing.

Because Schults was assuming the financial risk for *The Dream Collector*, he took certain decisions out of Tress's hands. In particular, believing that the images could not stand on their own, he hired John Minahan, a novelist who had worked as a staff writer for *Time* magazine and in television advertising, to produce an introductory essay as well as extended captions for the sixty plates. This didactic approach stood in marked contrast to a recently published photobook by Ralph Gibson, *The Somnambulist* (1970), which was also concerned with dreamlike imagery (fig. 38) but which functioned as a (photo)graphic novel composed exclusively of pictures. Like Tress, Gibson had started his career working in the photojournalistic mold of Robert Frank but chose a new path into the subconscious world. Despite his efforts to secure a publisher, Gibson was unsuccessful, so he opted

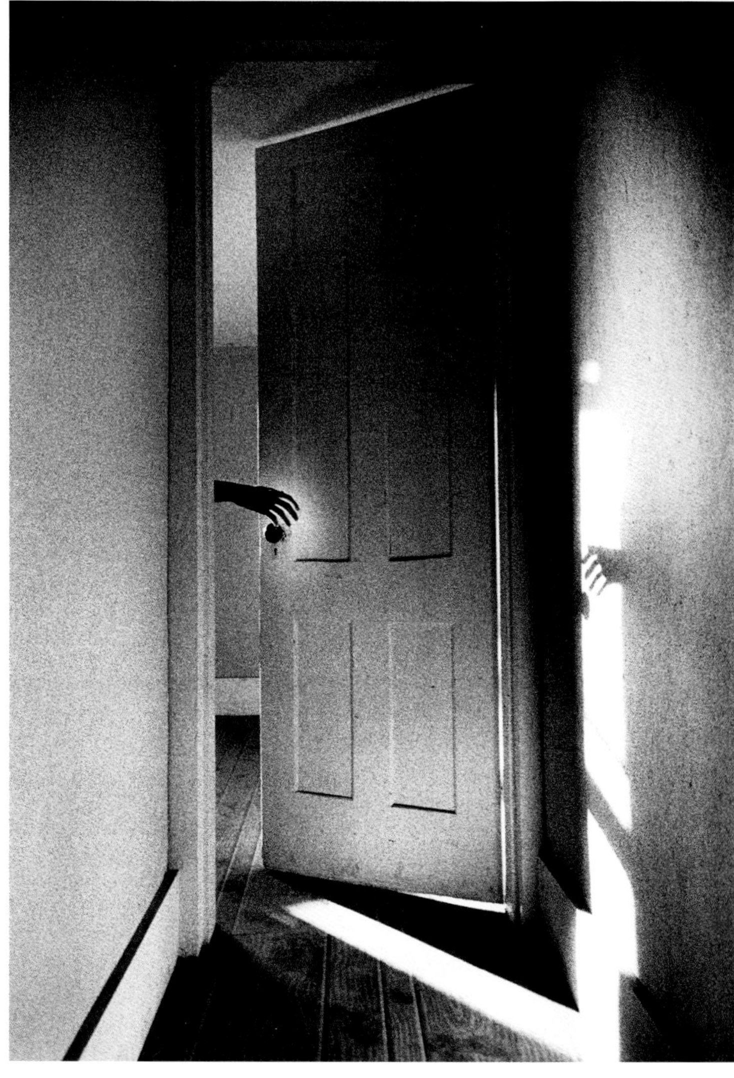

Figure 38
Ralph Gibson
(American, born 1939)
Hand through Doorway, 1969, plate from *The Somnambulist* (New York: Lustrum Press, 1970)
20.5 × 13.5 cm (8 1⁄16 × 5 5⁄16 in.)
Private collection

to self-finance and self-publish *The Somnambulist* and two sequels, *Déjà-Vu* (1973) and *Days at Sea* (1974), under his own imprint, Lustrum Press. At least one contemporary critic made the insightful connection between Tress's and Gibson's work; George Cruger, publications editor at the Virginia Museum of Fine Arts, drew parallels between *The Somnambulist* and *The Dream Collector*, noting the difference that "Gibson related disparate fragments from his own dreams." The two books were "imaginative companion studies of dream imagery," Cruger wrote. "Neither is all-inclusive, but they could be used as valuable adjuncts to the standard and modern texts on the subject (with which, incidentally, Tress is very familiar)."[20] Gibson conceived of his book as a sequence of fragmentary images that form a cohesive narrative, while Tress's *Dream Collector* photographs are self-contained variations on a theme. With *Shadow*, Tress would more closely follow Gibson's approach to creating a wordless photographic novel.

Minahan's introduction includes a biographical sketch of Tress, emphasizing his "unusually difficult and often unhappy childhood," and mentions a visit to his apartment studio, which Minahan describes as "a total environment of stark, antiseptic white, not unlike a hospital"[21] (see fig. 7). His thumbnail sketch of Tress is in many ways a fictionalized persona engineered at least in part by Schults, with the collusion of the photographer himself. Minahan characterizes Tress as a kind of dream detective, scouring obscure corners of the city with a tape recorder and camera to document children's recollections of their dreams. One story Minahan tells is of a Saturday he spent with the photographer in June 1972, when Tress interviewed and photographed a young boy at the South Street Seaport in Lower Manhattan. Looking back, Tress has confessed that he never owned a tape recorder and relied on his own sharp memory and notebook jottings to document his own dreams and those of friends, strangers, and children. But Minahan portrayed the "dream detective" character so evocatively that, about a year after the book came out, Dick Clark Productions approached Schults with the unlikely proposal of turning the concept of a photographer who goes around collecting young people's dreams into a television special, with several of the dreams staged as musical numbers. A *New York Times* article at the time focused on Clark's attempts to find creative approaches to staging pop music performances on television.[22] "Unfortunately, the rights negotiations bogged down over minor details," Tress recently

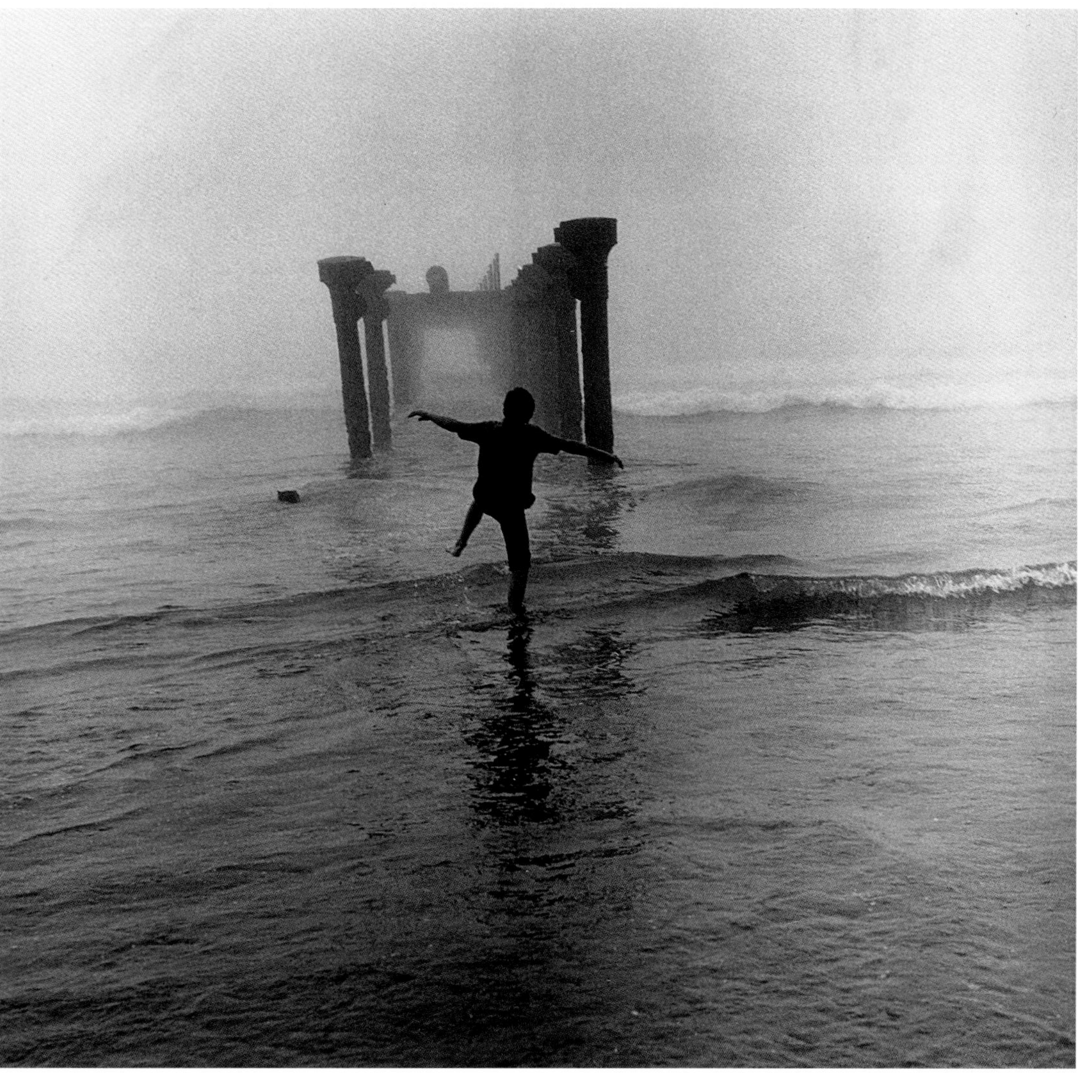

Figure 39
Arthur Tress
Boy in Front of Sea Gate, San Francisco, California, 1965
Gelatin silver print, 26.7 × 26.5 cm (10 ½ × 10 7⁄16 in.)
Los Angeles, J. Paul Getty Museum, Gift of Wes and Julie Nichols, 2019.170.8

recalled, "as Peter perhaps was overly protective of future use internationally, and so the matter was dropped. I was quite excited by the idea at the time, both monetarily and fame-wise, as I would have been hired as a consultant to the program and perhaps would even have been in it."[23]

In addition to writing the introduction, Minahan sat down with Tress to discuss the individual images. His extended captions for the sixty plates documented their locations and provided information about some of the sitters. In the end, Schults and Cooley chose to substantially edit these texts for publication, generally reducing them to one or two suggestive sentences.[24] Another change from the preliminary manuscript to the finished book was the elimination of the six one-word section headers—Emergence, Possession, Identity, Disaster, Death, and Return—that Tress had originally suggested to explicitly demarcate the thematic arc of the plates, from birth to death to rebirth.

Although Minahan's introduction to *The Dream Collector* would have the reader believe that Tress followed a uniform artistic program, a number of the images derived from earlier, unrelated projects and assignments. For instance, the final plate, of a boy strutting in the icy waters of San Francisco's Ocean Beach in front of the ruins of the Lurline Pier (fig. 39), is actually the earliest photograph in the book, most likely dating from the fall of 1965 when Tress stopped in San Francisco to visit his sister on his way to Japan. Minahan wrote in his caption that Tress asked the boy to reenact his dream of a dead man walking out to sea toward a distant gate, but clearly he fabricated this narrative and retroactively assigned it to the earlier image.[25] Another photograph derived from Tress's years of travel is the plate depicting a target keeper from his 1966 photo essay devoted to the Stockholm shooting range (see fig. 5). While the image appears somewhat out of place in the book, Minahan justifies its presence by explaining, "In children's dreams, the authority symbol sometimes emerges as a force so powerful that it cannot be understood or challenged, at times causing such acute anxiety that it becomes the target in later aggression dreams."[26] In his extended description, which was edited out of the final copy for publication, he offers a psychoanalytical interpretation of the image's significance to the photographer: "I think this is certainly one of Tress's most openly aggressive compositions. To him, the old man represents precisely the kind of arrogant and tenacious authority figure that damaged him as a child, dominated his dreams and continues to inculcate feelings of frustration and hostility."[27]

Despite Minahan's claim that Tress carried out tape-recorded interviews, his actual methodology was entirely intuitive and improvisational. "Throughout the project I never preplanned any image," Tress has confirmed. "It was my instinct as a documentary photographer to let things appear as they would and I just wandered around certain areas of the city like Coney Island, zoos, or the Jersey Shore and the images would present themselves for me as though my own mind were projecting my needs outward for providence to make them happen."[28] Emphasizing the autobiographical nature of this body of work as a projection of his own complexes and fears, he explains:

> I began working out of not only my research into dream structures but also to bring in my own darkest feelings about my own childhood traumas. I began to look more inside my own mind and its hidden anxious recesses as the central source for producing my artwork. . . . For most of the photos I had several dream theme ideas already in my mind and just by wandering around the city I would serendipitously find children playing in odd locations that would suggest a possible reenactment like being born, or being bitten, or dying.[29]

Boy in Flood Dream, Ocean City, Maryland (plate 85), one of Tress's most frequently reproduced photographs, provides an illuminating case study of his working method. The image came out of a photographic field trip down the New Jersey and Maryland coasts during the early winter of 1971. At the time Tress was consciously looking to produce *Daymare* photographs, and he thought off-season seaside resorts would provide suitably surreal locations. In Ocean City, Maryland, the southernmost point in his journey, he encountered a striking scene: "I noticed on the Bay side of the long thin peninsula a large asphalt pier reaching far into the water and at the end of it what appeared to be an abandoned ferry boat called the 'Knickerbocker' whose name could still be seen painted on its weathered foredeck tilted over to one side."[30] Tress was in luck: two young boys were playing in the area and agreed to pose for a series of photographs around the boat, as well as on the ruin of a shingle roof lying inexplicably nearby with no house underneath. "I asked [one] boy if he would put his head through a gaping hole and rest his arms on the wet shingles. He assumed different expressions as I shot two rolls of film of him, some closer and some further away [fig. 40]. The variations in the expressions provide

Figure 40
Arthur Tress
Contact sheet, Ocean City, Maryland, 1971
Gelatin silver print, 25.4 × 20.4 cm (10 × 8 1/16 in.)
Collection of the artist

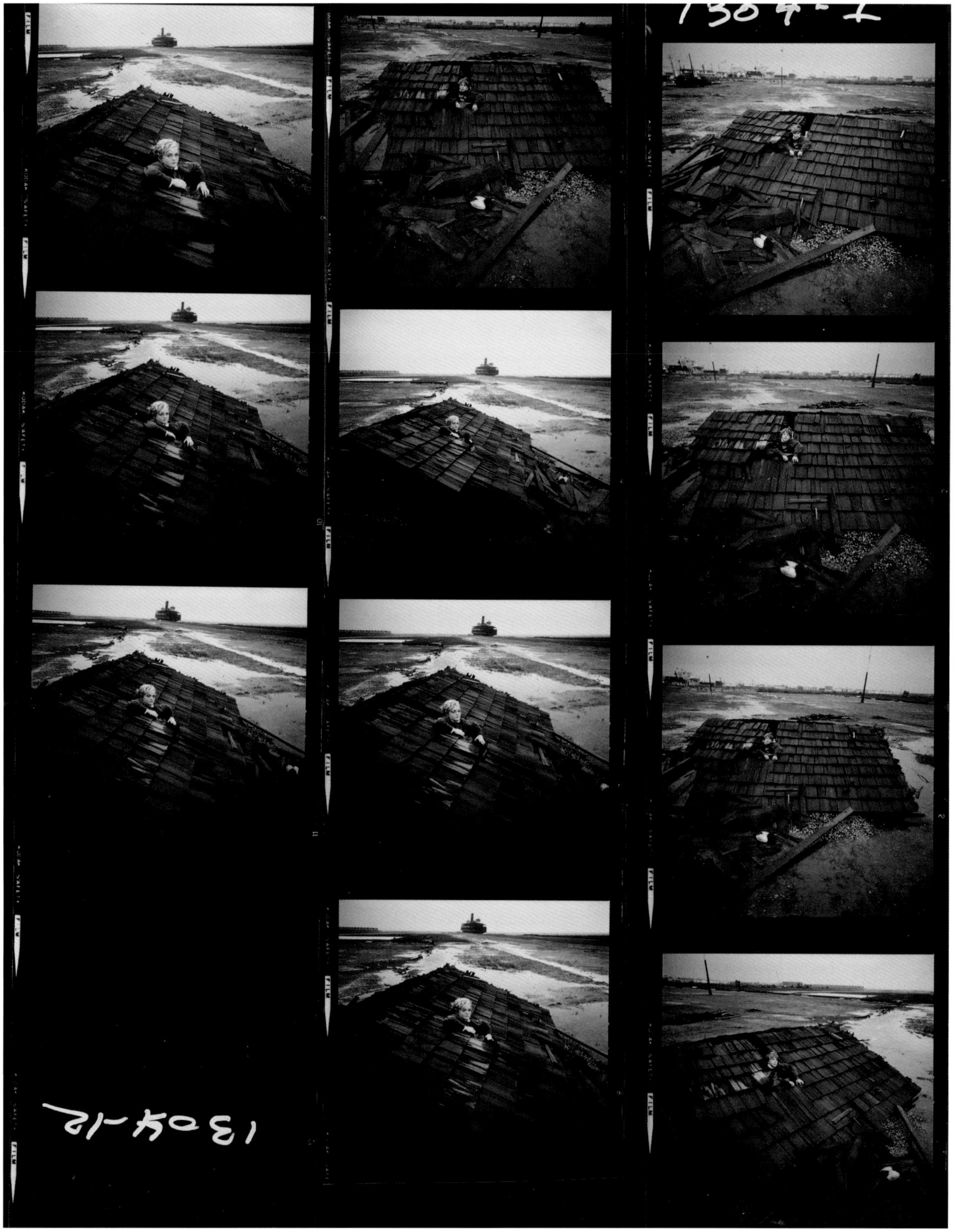

interesting expectations of interpretation. In the well-known version, the boy appears tranquil in the midst of disaster."[31]

Tress's iconic *Boy in Flood Dream* is in many ways a miraculous product of creative improvisation. As is often the case in this series, his method followed a pattern of (1) random serendipitous amalgamation of setting, prop(s), and child "actor," (2) spontaneous playacting for the camera, with Tress directing the action, and (3) retroactive interpretation of the finished work. In Minahan's extended caption, he attempts to describe the scene, though he misidentifies its location as Ocean City, New Jersey, and then relates the photograph to a specific dream that the photographer tape-recorded, "in which a child explained that his house was washed into the sea by a flood and he watched it all from the roof," but the final caption in the book simply reads, "Resignation and peace in the midst of disaster."[32] Tress's notebooks of this period contain several records of his recurrent drowning dreams, which he has connected to a specific incident within his personal storehouse of repressed childhood traumas, when at age five he fell out of a rowboat into the cold, muddy waters of Brooklyn's Prospect Park Lake during a Sunday family excursion. "Although I was quickly rescued, the memory has stuck with me to this day—the feeling of sinking and struggling towards the surface and perhaps that nasty nautical experience could have permeated several of the *Dream Collector* series."[33]

Of the book, which appeared in hardcover in October 1972, A. D. Coleman wrote:

> Tress's dream photographs come at you on three levels: First, they are a sequence of Tress's personal statements, and as such this book can be taken as a sort of "Self Portrait," with children instead of shadows as the central symbol (especially in light of Tress's saintly self-portrait on the back flap [plate 107]). Secondly, they are photographic interpretations of actual children's dreams recounted to Tress, and thus metaphors for deep-rooted fears within all of us—psychic Rorschachs. Finally, as records, they indicate the specific threats felt by a specific generation, which gives them considerable moral (and dare I say it, even political) significance as well as great informational value.

Coleman concludes:

> On all three of these levels, the book works well, but the interplay among them is particularly rich. It has a peculiarity and a forcefulness which is quite distinctive; it poses provocative challenges; and it is also one of the few photographic books I've seen over the past five years which could easily become a bestseller, as I'm quite sure it will.[34]

Following the appearance of *The Dream Collector* in October 1972, Tress sought additional avenues for disseminating the work. He shared a group of the prints with the influential educator-photographer Minor White, who was then still teaching at the Massachusetts Institute of Technology. White had a special interest in the spiritual nature of photography and noted that "dreams and photographs have something in common; those photographs that yield to contemplation at least have a quality about them that tempt one to set associations going."[35] After incorporating Tress's work into his idiosyncratic "Creative Audience" class in the spring term of 1973, White wrote to Tress: "We had an interesting reaction with the class in audience training that we showed your pictures to. Let me give you a bit of background.

We had been working up to using photographs as dream symbols by making sketches of responses to a slide and then each person acting out his own sketch according to gestalt therapy analytical practice. When we tried your photographs in the same manner they were found to be very effective."[36]

Westover arranged for a group of about ten of the *Dream Collector* photographs to be included in a four-venue trade show of camera equipment circulated by the International Photo Optical Show Association in Minnesota (October 1972), San Francisco (November 1972), Atlanta (January 1973), and Washington, DC (March 1973). Tress showed a selection of *Dream Collector* photographs, along with newer work that would eventually form the basis for *Theater of the Mind*, in the exhibition *The Vision Seekers* at the Soho Photo Gallery in September 1973. That same month, his *Dream Collector* and *Theater of the Mind* photographs were featured in the exhibition *Surrealism in Photography*, which combined three one-man shows devoted to Tress, Adál Maldonado, and Vilem Kriz at Helen Johnson's Focus Gallery in San Francisco (fig. 41). Thomas Albright, writing for the *San Francisco Chronicle*, called Tress "the most venturesome of these photographers; at least he risks being unsubtle, and the theatricality of his images is undisguised."[37] The Soho Photo and Focus Gallery exhibitions coincided with the publication of *The Dream Collector* as a mass-market paperback by Avon Books, where it was championed by the legendary editor-in-chief Peter Mayer. In 1975 Tress published the *Dream Collector Portfolio*, a selection of twelve 11 x 14-inch prints mounted on 16 x 20-inch museum board in an edition of fifty, though only twelve were made. He included the text Duane Michals wrote for *Theater of the Mind* (1976), the first section of which, "Child's Play," consisted of fourteen new *Dream Collector* images.[38]

Looking back recently on this rich body of work that helped establish his reputation, including the *Dream Collector* photographs as well as the related jottings throughout his early 1970s notebooks and hundreds of index cards on which he recorded his own dreams, Tress emphasizes their autobiographical foundation. "In these long compendiums of literally hundreds of these dream scenarios culled from dozens of sources," he says, "there is this kind of academic 'bucket list' of visual items to be acquired and checked off that could have been mere *Psychology Today*–type magazine illustrations, but perhaps saved from that fate in being supplemented, at that time, by my own rather disquieting anxiety-driven emotional turmoil and struggles for a new more assertive personality." He describes "a very potent mix of an objective research study in a subconscious frothy stew of angry encounters with family members and the private passions of frustrated intimacies with rejecting lovers and friends, that lends the *Dream Collector* photographs, almost unintentionally, the kind of latent communicative power of myth, that is both particular and universal." He concludes, "Perhaps doing these kinds of revelatory photos and the making of the *Dream Collector* book were also a kind of artistic and therapeutic 'rite of passage' where I came out the other side, after my trip to the gloomy underworld, with the light-filled illuminations of *Shadow*."[39]

Figure 41
Anonymous
Arthur Tress in exhibition *Surrealism in Photography*, Focus Gallery, San Francisco, 1973
Gelatin silver print, 6.4 × 6.4 cm (2 ½ × 2 ½ in.)
Collection of Arthur Tress

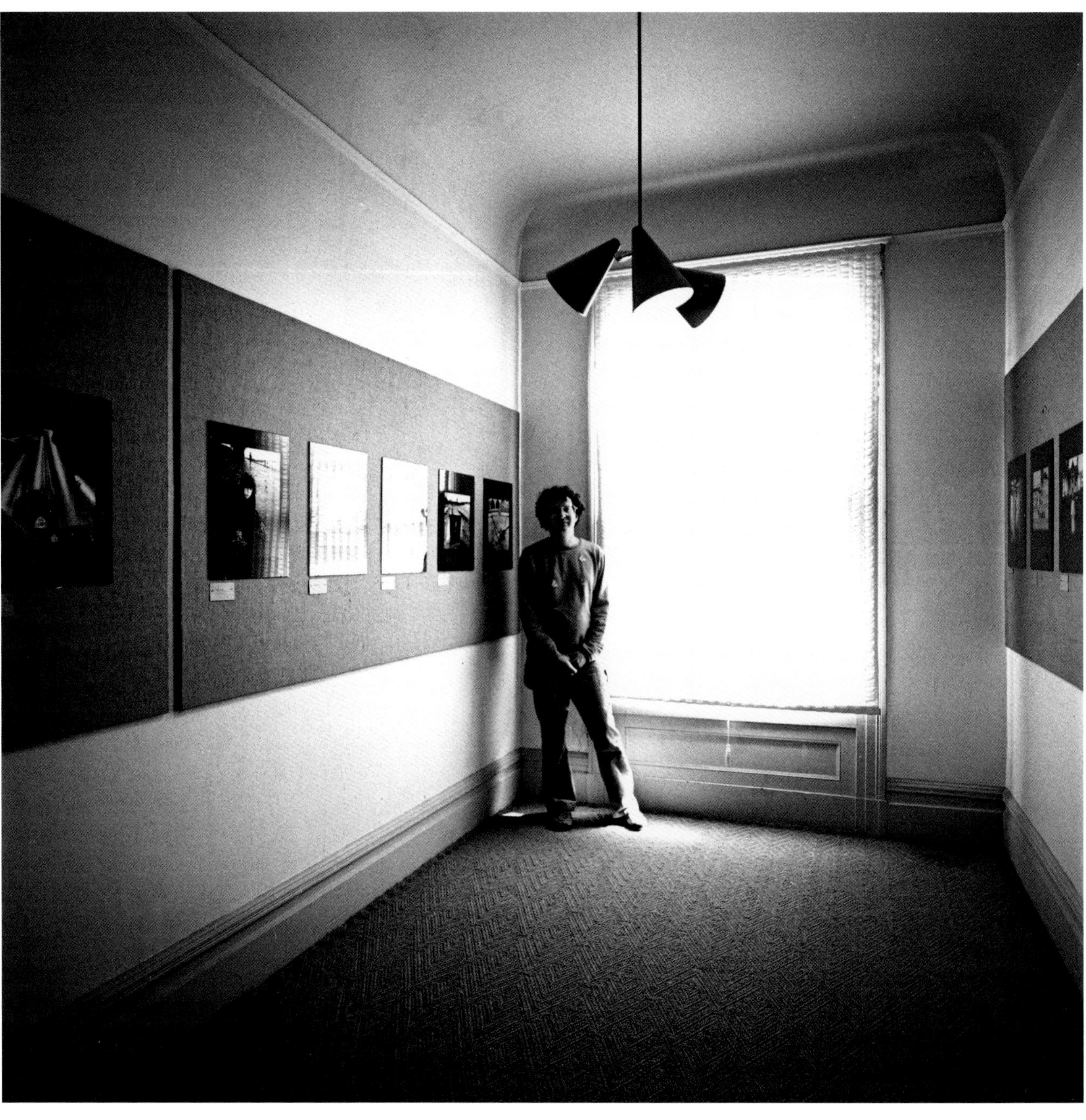

Notes

1 Undated typescript in the collection of the artist. The indication that the film cost approximately 35 pounds sterling to produce suggests that it derives from a screening held in London in 1966.
2 See Mazie M. Harris's essay in this volume.
3 The image appears as the twenty-fourth unnumbered plate in *The Dream Collector.*
4 The complete essay serves as the preface to this volume.
5 This quote derives from a text by Tress dating from September 2010 for an unpublished exhibition catalogue by A. D. Coleman. Tress emailed his text to the author on January 15, 2020.
6 From Tress's unpublished essay (2010) for A. D. Coleman; see note 5.
7 https://touchstonecenter.net/archival-project/, accessed January 2023.
8 From *New York State Council on the Arts Annual Report*, 1971–72, p. 31: "The Touchstone Center for Children, New York City. $1,000 for twenty-six weekly writing workshops for twenty children at The Children's Community Workshop, an experimental open-corridor elementary school, and for videotaping participating students' stories and drawings on the origins of the world." In a subsequent grant application made by the Touchstone Center to NYSCA dated June 7, 1971, the program is described in more detail, revealing that the dream workshops are taking place at P.S. 198, the Children's Community Workshop, and the Manhattan Country School; copy of the grant application in the collection of the artist.
9 Richard Lewis, *Living by Wonder: The Imaginative Life of Childhood* (New York: Touchstone Center Publications, 1998), 57.
10 Ibid., 60.
11 Joseph Lelyveld, "Class 4-4: Childish Fantasy Is More Than Make Believe," *New York Times*, May 1, 1971, second section, pp. 1, 54.
12 Program from the collection of the artist. The film *You, the Dreamer* is in the archives of the Touchstone Center.
13 Steven Heller, "Maurice Sendak, Mao Zedong, and the Man Who Collects Them," *The Atlantic* (July 25, 2013); https://www.theatlantic.com/entertainment/archive/2013/07/maurice-sendak-mao-zedong-and-the-man-who-collects-them/278101/, accessed January 2023.
14 Email to the author, November 1, 2022.
15 John Minahan, original unedited manuscript for *The Dream Collector*, 1972, p. 37; from the collection of the artist.
16 Email to the author, May 14, 2020.
17 Email to the author, October 29, 2022.
18 A copy of the press release is in the collection of the artist.
19 The published source of this review is unidentified; from a clipping in the collection of the artist.
20 George Cruger, "Photograpy: Collecting Childhood Dreams," *Richmond Mercury* 1, no. 22 (February 7, 1973).
21 John Minahan, from the introduction to *The Dream Collector*, unpaginated.
22 John J. O'Connor, "TV: Dick Clark's Originality Enhances Pop Music," *New York Times*, July 17, 1973, p. 79. Tress kept a clipping of this article.
23 Email to the author, May 25, 2022.
24 A copy of the original *Dream Collector* manuscript (1972) is in the collection of the artist.
25 Minahan, *The Dream Collector* manuscript, p. 86.
26 Minahan, *The Dream Collector*, unpaginated.
27 Minahan, *The Dream Collector* manuscript, p. 34.
28 From Tress's unpublished essay (2010) for A. D. Coleman; see note 5.
29 Ibid.
30 Email to the author, January 29, 2020.
31 Ibid.
32 Minahan, *The Dream Collector* manuscript, p. 58.
33 Email to the author, May 24, 2020.
34 A. D. Coleman, Latent Image column, *Village Voice* 17, no. 41 (October 12, 1972): 29.
35 Paul Martineau, *Minor White: Manifestations of the Spirit* (Los Angeles: J. Paul Getty Museum, 2014), 1.
36 Minor White, letter to Arthur Tress, May 18, 1973, collection of the artist.
37 Thomas Albright, "The Pitfalls of Theatricality: Three Surrealist Photographers," *San Francisco Chronicle*, September 7, 1973.
38 See Paul Martineau's "All the World's a Stage" essay in this volume.
39 Email to the author, May 16, 2020.

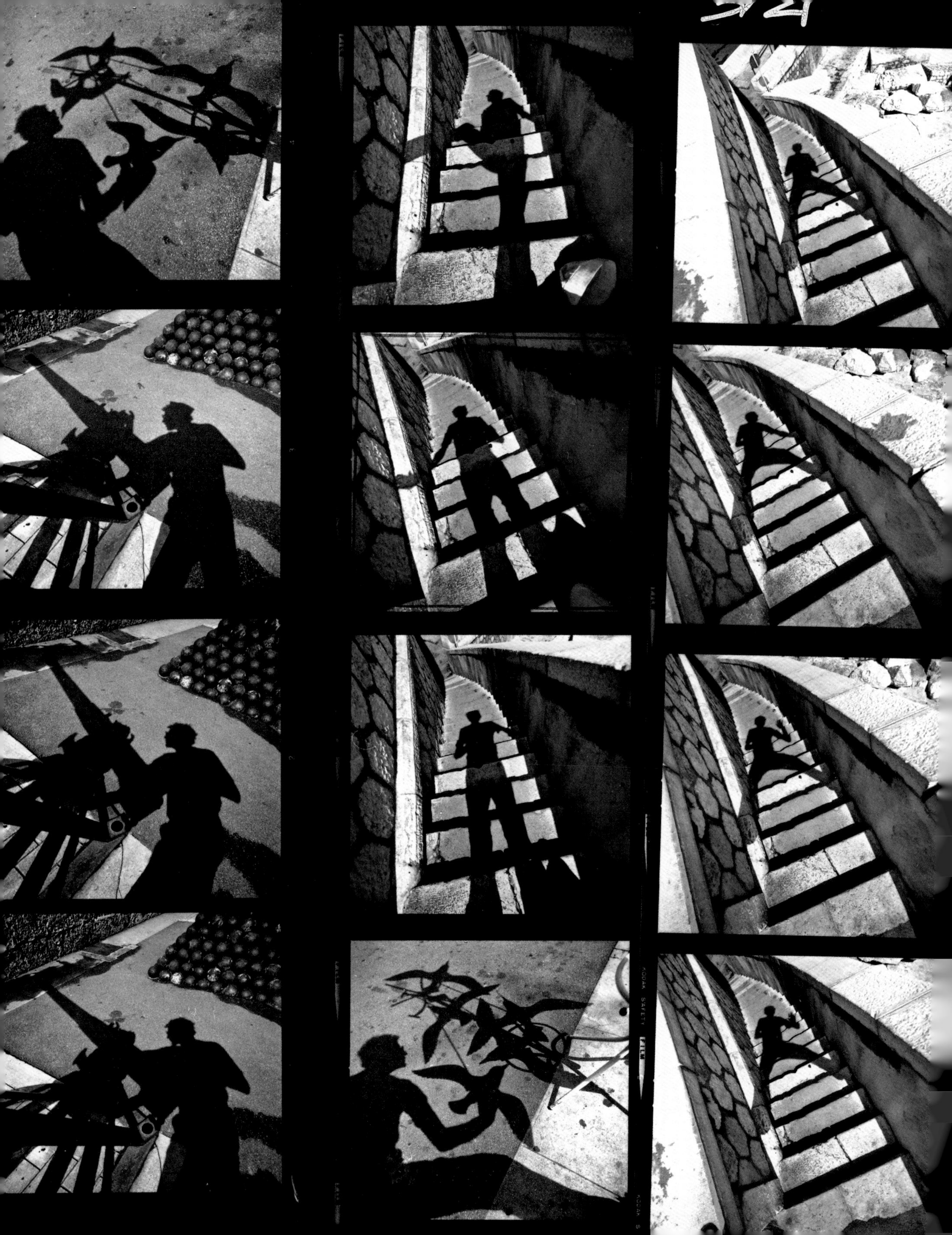
KODAK SAFETY FILM

PAUL MARTINEAU

The Enigma of the Shadow

Everyone who has picked up a camera and stood with their back to the sun or another strong source of light has had to decide whether their cast shadow is a welcome addition to the picture. The self-shadow is always a sign of the photographer's double presence—before and behind the camera—but in some cases it serves also to reinforce pictorial goals.[1] In Lewis Hine's 1914 *Newsboy, Mobile, Alabama* (fig. 42), for example, the inclusion of the photographer's shadow gives the composition a somewhat menacing aspect, helping to emphasize the small size and vulnerability of the subject. Although it is unlikely that Hine had his shadow in mind as he approached the newsboy, he recognized immediately how it could aid him in communicating the evils of child labor.

Between 1972 and 1975 Arthur Tress created a new body of work centered on his own shadow, ninety photographs in all. He organized them into thirteen chapters and then assembled them into a graphic novel (fig. 43). *Shadow* traces a mystical dream journey of an individual soul from the past to the present and into the future, through birth, death, and enlightenment. Although individual images are strong enough to stand on their own, it is only within the context of the book that the project's deeper meanings can be fully appreciated. Other than the short chapter titles—"The Prisoner" and "The Journey," to cite two—and two quotes, one to open the book and another to close it, there is no expository text; the reader must piece together the narrative. Tress was impressed by *The Journey of the Spirit after Death*, a sequence of photographs published in 1970 by his friend Duane Michals, and saw *Shadow* as an opportunity to create his own "shaman vision quest dream journey."[2]

Tress, who was thirty-two in 1972, had successfully transitioned from photojournalist to artistic photographer, but he was still trying to find his

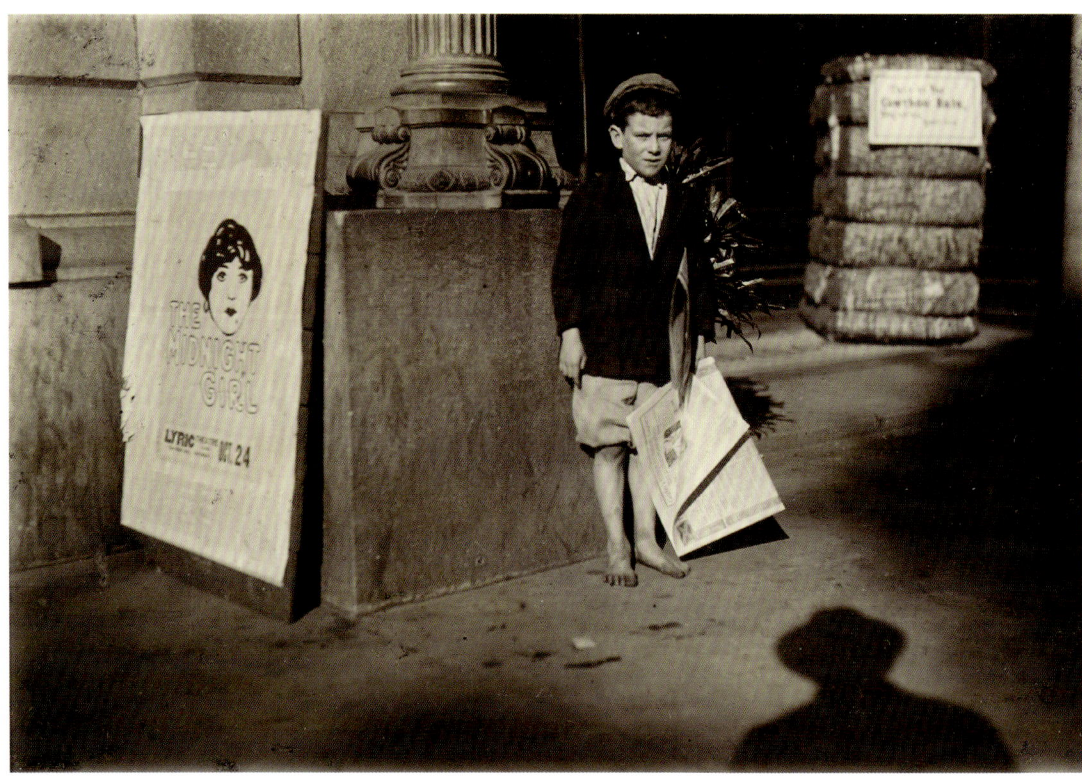

Figure 42
Lewis W. Hine
(American, 1874–1940)
Newsboy, Mobile, Alabama, 1914
Gelatin silver print, 11.8 × 16.8 cm (4 5/8 × 6 5/8 in.)
Los Angeles, J. Paul Getty Museum, 84.XM.132.33

footing in a world that he saw as hostile and anxiety provoking. He took temporary refuge in the life of the mind, reading a wide variety of books on psychiatry, philosophy, religion, ethnography, and art. His new knowledge sparked his curiosity and provided him with the intellectual energy he needed to engage with the chaotic world outside his door.

Shadow was produced during a period of intense intellectual and creative activity, after publication of *The Dream Collector* (1972) and before the release of *Theater of the Mind* (1976). The ghostly figure in *Shadow* represents Tress himself only obliquely, he has said, but he has described it as addressing his adolescence in the way that *The Dream Collector* expresses his childhood fears and *Theater of the Mind* his adult anxieties and sexual eccentricities.[3] Tress, part voyeur and part creator, recalls Monsieur G., the "passionate spectator" of nineteenth-century Paris as described by the French poet Charles Baudelaire:

> For the perfect flâneur, the passionate spectator, it is an immense joy to set up house in the heart of the multitude, amid the ebb and flow of movement, in the midst of the fugitive and infinite . . . Thus the lover of universal life enters into the crowd as though it were an immense reservoir of electrical energy . . . Few men are gifted with the capacity of seeing; there are fewer still who possess the power of expression. So, at a time when others are asleep, Monsieur G. is bending over his table, darting onto a sheet of paper the same glance

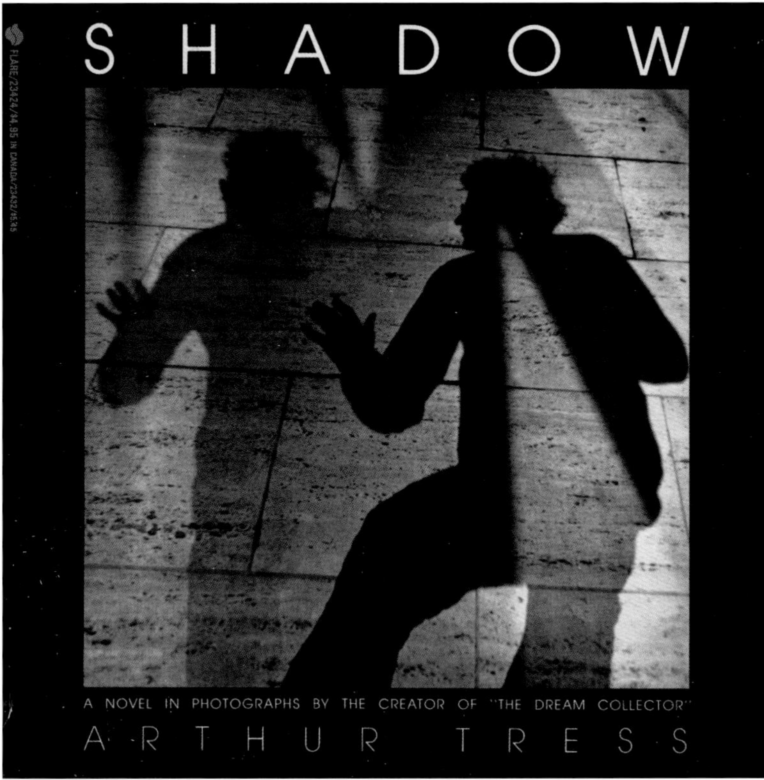

Figure 43
Cover of *Shadow*, 1975
20 × 20.3 cm (7 ⅞ × 8 in.)

> that a moment ago he was directing towards external things, skirmishing with his pencil, his pen, his brush, splashing his glass of water up to the ceiling, wiping his pen on his shirt, in a ferment of violent activity, as though afraid that the image might escape him, cantankerous though alone, elbowing himself on. And the external world is reborn upon his paper, natural and more natural, beautiful, and more than beautiful, strange and endowed with an impulsive life like the soul of his creator.[4]

Tress organized his thoughts and documented his dreams on notecards that he kept close at hand. He must have sensed that he was at a crossroads in his life and career when he wrote: "At certain points in our lives we are between old and new, childhood and adolescence, solitude and marriage, and life and death. Even our society today is thrown very much into this problem of past and future—initiations, fragments, rites of passage are our mind's imagination trying to help us through and over these transitions."[5]

Particularly important to the *Shadow* series was Tress's keen interest in beliefs held by tribal peoples in remote parts of the world. As he saw it, in addition to their personal dreams they had visionary dreams, which they believed included instructions from the gods. Trying to represent the universal nature of these dreams in pictures, Tress searched for "equivalents," modern activities that derive their power from vestiges of a forgotten past. "These recurrent mystical strivings perhaps demonstrate that our psyches are composed of primordial residue of religious symbolism thousands of years old which keeps reappearing in the unconscious and will continue to do so as long as our basic human experiences and structures remain the same," Tress has explained.[6] These ideas were part of his *Vision Seekers* series of photographs, but after it was exhibited at the Soho Photo Gallery in September 1973, Tress concluded that the pictures were lacking the vitality of the *Dream Collector* series and decided to incorporate these concepts into *Shadow*.[7]

As Tress's thoughts about the *Shadow* project began to coalesce, he devised lists of visual motifs that might be of use. On a card bearing the title "Ideas from Greek vases," for example, he scribbled, "Holding branches, chasing butterflies, giving a wreath, shooting a bow and victim of arrow, pouring wine to someone seated, pursuing a woman and she is looking back."[8] To anyone with even a cursory knowledge of ancient Greek art, these words evoke elegant red and black figures posing, gesturing, and dancing across the glazed surface of a slender lekythos or a broad bell

Figure 44
Frans Masereel
(Belgian, 1889–1972)
Untitled plate from *Die Sonne*, 1926
Page size 15.2 × 11.6 cm (6 × 4 9⁄16 in.)
Collection of Arthur Tress

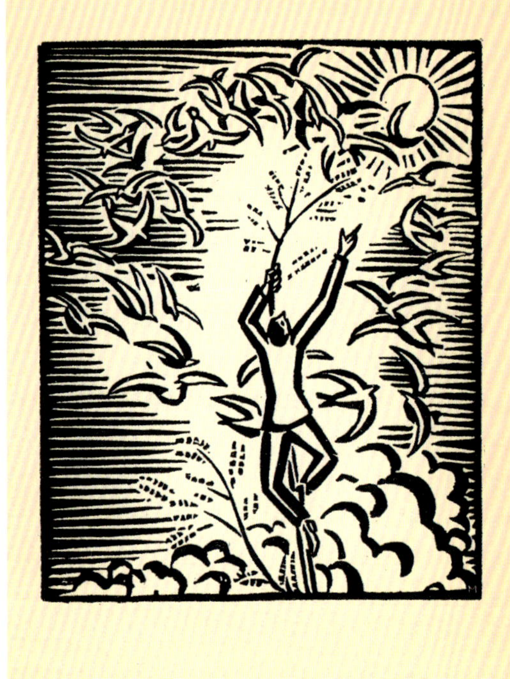

krater. Whether we can find an exact match in the photographer's subsequent images is unimportant. What matters is knowing that he was actively mining the past to excite his mental faculties, expanding his ability to recognize pictorial opportunities as he moved through the urban landscape with his camera.

Tress was a collector of many things, from antique books to ceremonial masks, obtained at home in New York City and while traveling in Asia and Africa. His interest in works on paper led him to acquire woodcut engravings by the Belgian artist Frans Masereel and the American printmaker Lynd Ward. Tress's use of tight framing and bold forms owes a certain debt to these artists (fig. 44), as does his idea of creating a graphic novel.[9] He adjusted his compositional technique to fill the frame. "My composition tends to be extremely simple," Tress later recalled, "but to photograph my own shadow, I was forced to use new areas of the square, mostly the corners. The shadow had to be in odd places, so the pictures are freer visually than my earlier things."[10] During a trip to Bali in 1973, Tress attended a cremation ceremony and convinced the locals to allow him to have a large, hand-carved wooden figurehead that had escaped the flames. Back in New York, he quickly found a use for it as a prop (fig. 45).

In *Shadow, New York, New York [Signs]*, a dark figure rises from the lower right, counterbalancing the shadow of a building on the lower left (plate 109). The figure appears to be wearing a cloak and cap, recalling the Magician, the first trump card in a tarot deck. As an archetype, this powerful man is associated with positive transformation through determination and skill. Here, the shadow points to a sign with an extended index finger, a gesture that recalls the director F. W. Murnau's use of the shadow to frighten viewers of his 1922 silent horror film *Nosferatu*. By selecting one sign from among others, that pointing finger may also be suggesting that when we have a variety of options there is only one correct choice. *Shadow [Signs]* appears in an early section of the book, the chapter called "The Search," alongside other photographs that represent the pursuit of knowledge.

In *Shadow, Cannes, France [Birds]*, the dark figure emerges from the lower left grasping a bird, perhaps a gull, from the flock rising into the sky (plate 113). The outsize shadow of the artist's right leg grounds the picture; the shadow cast by the sculpture of birds moves from the lower right to the upper left. Tress has adroitly counterbalanced that trajectory by selecting a position for himself at a right angle to the line of pavement that runs diagonally from the lower center to the upper right corner. The photograph appears in the book's tenth section, entitled "Magic Flight." Within the context of images featuring

Figure 45
Arthur Tress
Transformations 2, New York, New York, 1974
Gelatin silver print,
19.4 × 19.4 cm
(7 5/8 × 7 5/8 in.)
San Francisco, SFMOMA,
Gift of Dr. Pat Kennedy,
2019.114.89

Figure 46
Arthur Tress
The Prisoner 5, Paris, France, 1974
Gelatin silver print,
19.1 × 19.1 cm
(7 1/2 × 7 1/2 in.)
San Francisco, SFMOMA,
Gift of Dr. Pat Kennedy,
2019.114.64

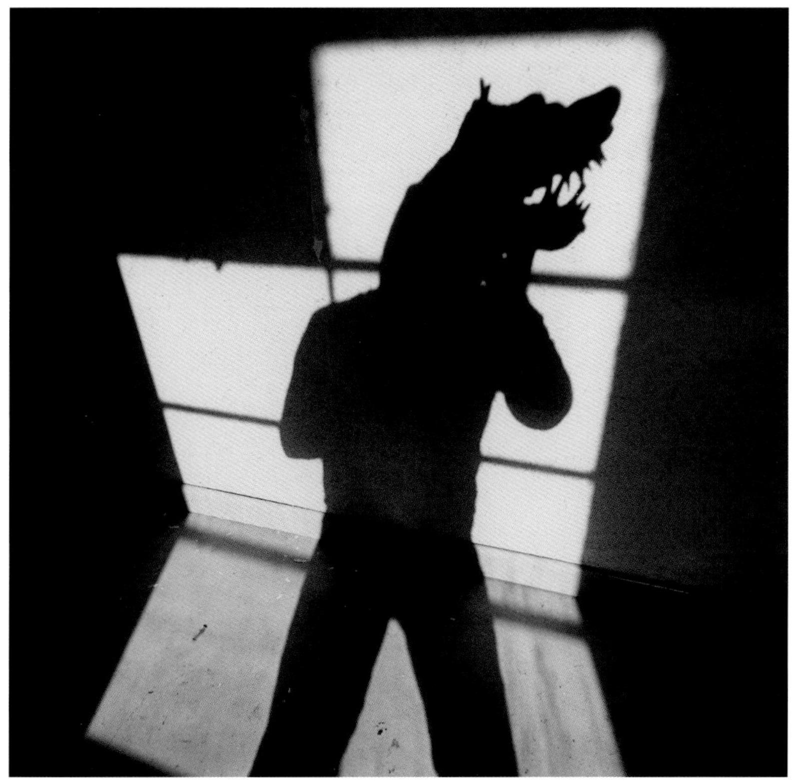

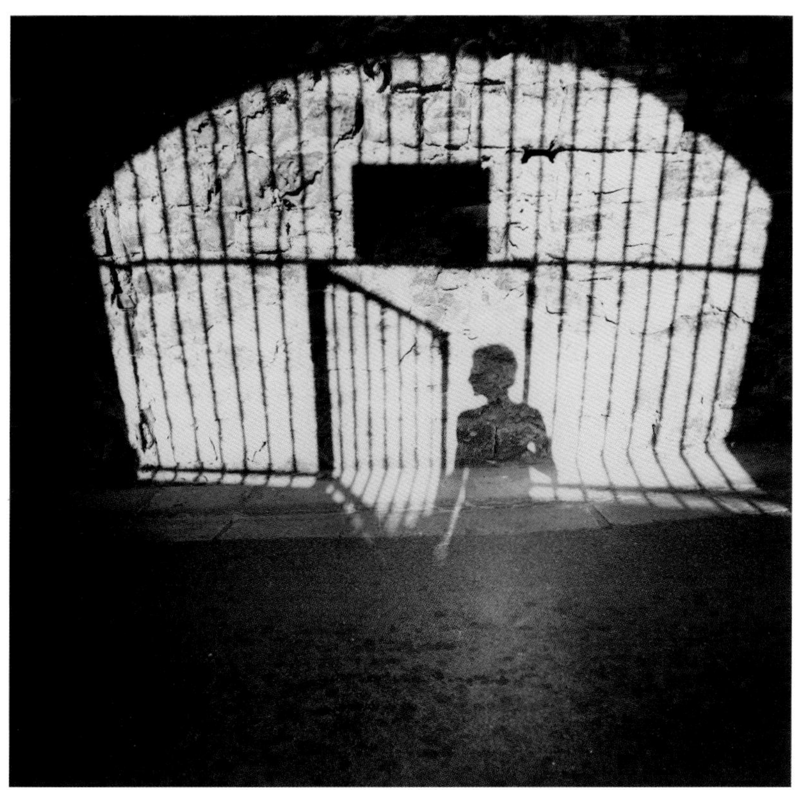

the shadow ascending staircases and ladders, *Shadow, Cannes, France* represents freedom. It is the perfect foil for the first section's images of the shadow imprisoned (fig. 46).

The figure in *Shadow, New York, New York [Bridge]* has been subsumed into the shadow of the truss of a bridge (plate 114). In this way it appears to have been transformed into the hydra, the many-headed sea monster of ancient Greek mythology. An arm and a hand, the only human attributes visible, appear as a sort of a curled vestigial tail, which contains the power to anthropomorphize the rest—the truss—as it bends to the left to take a better look at the viewer outside the frame. *Shadow [Bridge]* comes in the penultimate section of the book, entitled "Transformations." Here, the scope of imagery suggests the results of the gradual but wondrous shift between immature and mature stages of development, the larva emerging from the chrysalis as a butterfly.

Why are Tress's shadow pictures so compelling? Certainly a contributing factor is that they were created with intention. Over the course of three years Tress pursued the motif with an obsessive intensity, exposing some six thousand frames and making approximately five hundred contact sheets before editing these down to the hundred or so images that best represented his vision. Another factor is that the compositions are simple but ambiguous, allowing for a multiplicity of interpretations. Tress was well versed in the meaning and centrality of the shadow in the history of art and culture. "The shadow is the basic primal image," Tress explained in a piece he wrote in 1974. "Man's first art as an outline of his hand against a cave wall, formed with black paint. A stark silhouette warning that we were entering the hunter's sacred space—a sign of trespass, it is man's first attempt to define form and place; it is the essential creative act, black ciphers or letters structuring life, humanizing, and colonizing the unknown."[11]

Tress did not allow himself to get bogged down in technical concerns. He kept his equipment straightforward, using a Hasselblad 500C camera fitted with a 40 mm Distagon lens. The choice of a wide-angle lens with dynamic perspectival effects gave a dreamlike quality to the images. The source of light was the sun, which made the early morning or late afternoon the ideal time to shoot. The raking light lengthened his shadow, making the lower parts of his body look large and the upper parts of his body small. With practice, Tress became adept at holding the camera close to his chest in the crook of his arm, so that it would be hidden in the image, and releasing the shutter with one hand while gesturing or steadying himself with the other. In *Shadow, New York, New York [Bicycle]* (plate 112), however, one can glimpse the lens protruding from the shadow of his torso. Here and in other examples, the shadow has a dimensionality that disrupts our perspective, introducing a sense of instability and movement into what was, for a moment, a static mise en scène. In the darkroom Tress made adjustments, dodging and burning his prints to darken the penumbra and brighten areas around his shadow's edges to make them glow a bit.[12]

Location was of great importance to him. Tress created many of the photographs in New York City and added others while traveling in France, Monaco, and Puerto Rico. Interested in psychogeography as espoused by the Situationist movement of the late 1950s as well as the novels and short stories of the Bohemian writer Franz Kafka, Tress saw the city as a labyrinth of the imagination and would navigate urban spaces in a dreamlike state, taking in its sites and moods at different times of day. Tress's knowledge of locations in and around New York City played a role; he often returned to sites he had visited before, such as

Chase Manhattan Plaza or Grant's Tomb.[13] When he traveled, his lack of familiarity with a new city became a point of departure that matched his attempts at discovering the right composition.

In 1975 Tress's *Shadow* photographs were exhibited in solo shows at Neikrug Gallery, New York, New York; La Photogalerie, Paris, France; the Gallery of Photography, Washington, DC; and the Shadow Gallery in Oregon City, Oregon. When the French novelist Michel Tournier saw the photographs in Paris, he wrote:

> The photographs immediately blew me away, dazzled me, amazed me. . . . All of them precede one and the same vision, but this common key is so deep, so secret, so encrypted that none of its images really resembles the others, although they all translate the same thing. . . . It is exactly the opposite of a photo novel, whose images illustrate an imposed text. Here, the photographs go off on their own and find a poetry and even a metaphysics that only they can express.[14]

While countless photographers have included their shadows in their pictures, a much smaller number have made their shadows a regular part of their practice. Lee Friedlander comes to mind in the smaller group, but he appears to have used his shadow as a form of self-portraiture rather than as a representation of a character or to tell a story. Tress understood intuitively that what he was doing was different: he was exploring the limits of the motif, extending it into new areas.[15] When asked what he hoped people would take away from the series, he said, "I hope they'll say, 'This is an interesting use of someone's imagination.' That's what I really want—to celebrate the imagination."[16]

Notes

1 William Chapman Sharpe, *Grasping Shadows: The Dark Side of Literature, Painting, Photography, and Film* (New York: Oxford University Press, 2017), 265–66.
2 Arthur Tress, interview by the author, August 18, 2022.
3 Interview by the author, August 18, 2022.
4 Charles Baudelaire, "The Painter of Modern Life," in *The Painter of Modern Life and Other Essays*, trans. and ed. Thom Mayne (London: Phaidon, 1995), 9–11.
5 Notecard, May 4 [no year]. The artist provided the Department of Photographs at the J. Paul Getty Museum with two bound books of photocopies of the notecards that he donated to the International Center of Photography in New York City.
6 "The Vision Seekers" (press release for the exhibition at the Soho Photo Gallery, September 4–29, 1973), as published in Marco Livingstone, ed., *Arthur Tress: Talisman* (New York: Thames & Hudson, 1986), 150.
7 Ibid.
8 Notecard, n.d.
9 Arthur Tress, interview by the author, August 18, 2022.
10 Sheila Turner-Seed, "Arthur Tress," *Popular Photography* (August 1976): 224.
11 Arthur Tress, "Apropos 'the shadows'" (unpublished manuscript, 1974), as published in Livingstone, *Arthur Tress: Talisman*, 151.
12 Arthur Tress, interview by the author, August 18, 2022.
13 Turner-Seed, "Arthur Tress," 224.
14 Michel Tournier, "Arthur Tress au royaume des ombres," *Le Nouvel Observateur*, July 12, 1975, p. 58. Translated from the original French by the author.
15 Arthur Tress, email to the author, September 7, 2022.
16 Turner-Seed, "Arthur Tress," 224.

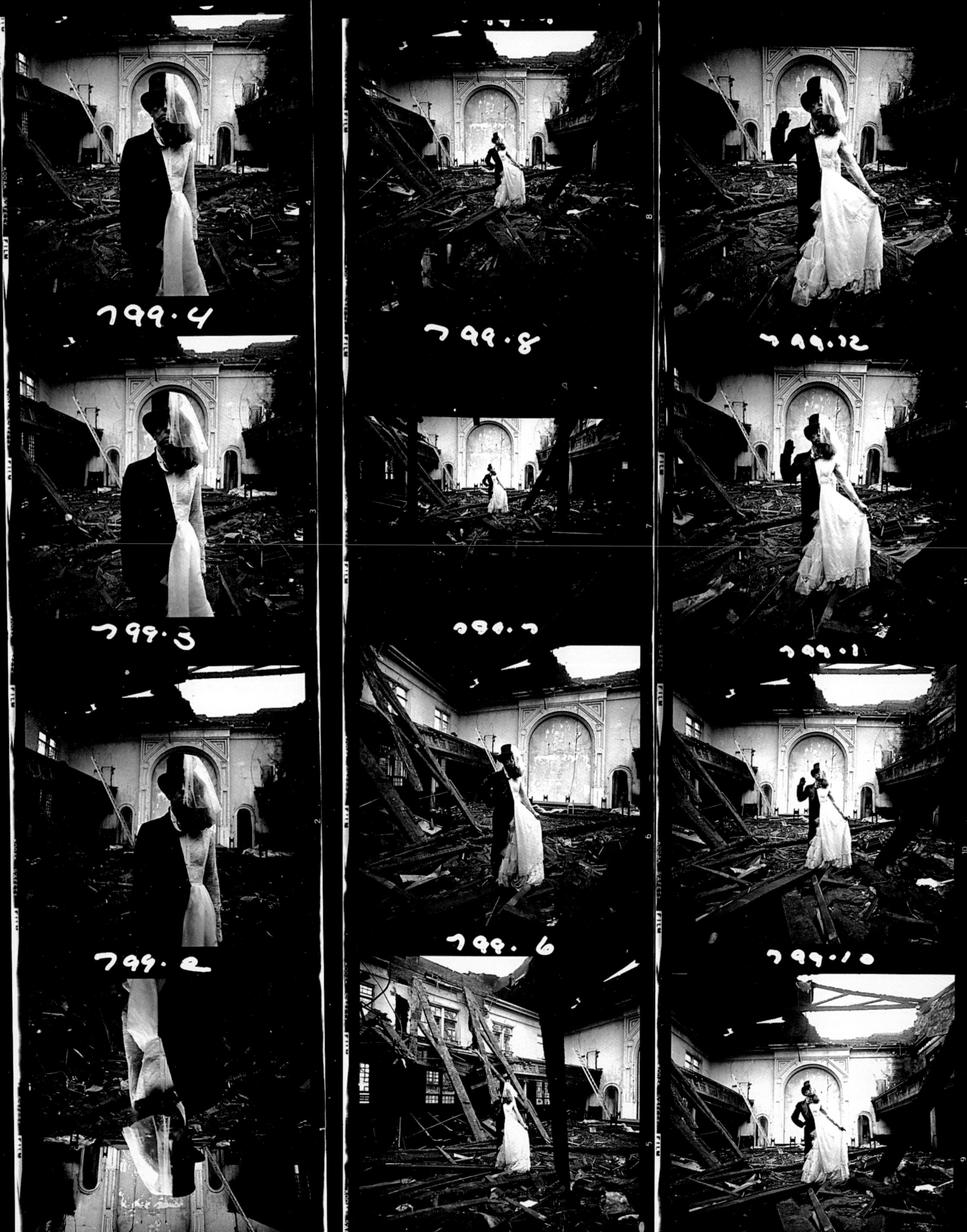

799·4
799·8
799·12
799·3
799·7
799·11
799·2
799·6
799·10
KODAK SAFETY FILM

PAUL MARTINEAU

All the World's a Stage

In 1976, close on the heels of his *Shadow* photographs, Arthur Tress published *Theater of the Mind* (fig. 47). The *Shadow* series had provided Tress with a much-needed break from working with others. Emerging from that experience energized and determined to move away from his focus on children, Tress took the methods he had devised for *The Dream Collector* and applied them to exploring the complexities of family relationships, specifically the ones lying beneath the surface, for *Theater of the Mind*. Rather than interview his subjects at length, he convinced them to play out scenes on the fly, taking advantage of the peculiarities of the built environment and props at hand. Having given much thought to the dynamics of his own family situation, he was keen to portray the dysfunctional aspects of these connections through psychological dissonance, the perception of contradictory information. The photographer relied on what he has described as "almost psychic intuitions" or "impressions" that came to him soon after meeting his subjects.[1] Afterward, when he shared the photographs with them, they often remarked on his having illuminated an important but hitherto hidden aspect of the relationship.[2]

Helpful to understanding *Theater of the Mind* are the titles of the six sections into which Tress organized the photographs in the book: "Child's Play," "Private Acts," "Domestic Scenes," "Stage Properties," "Directors of Darkness," and "Final Curtain." The chapters are arranged in loose chronological fashion, from the younger subjects to the older ones, with the themes becoming progressively darker.[3]

"Child's Play" includes pictures that would have been featured in *The Dream Collector* if they had been created before the book went into production. They focus on the way children use play to express their fears. For *Boy and Cut-Out Face, New York, New York* (plate 119), an image of

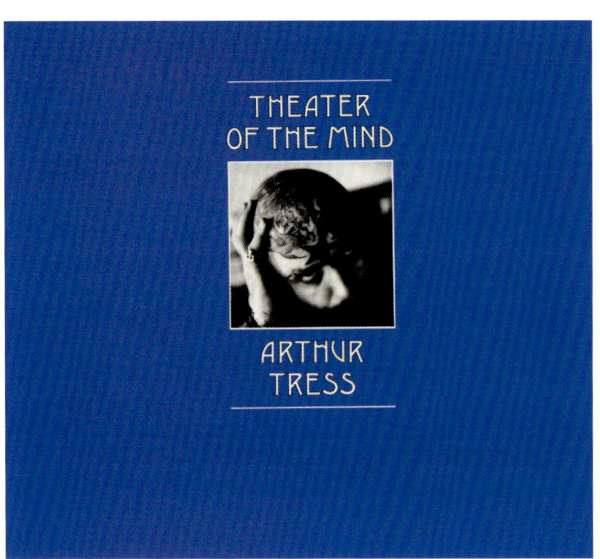

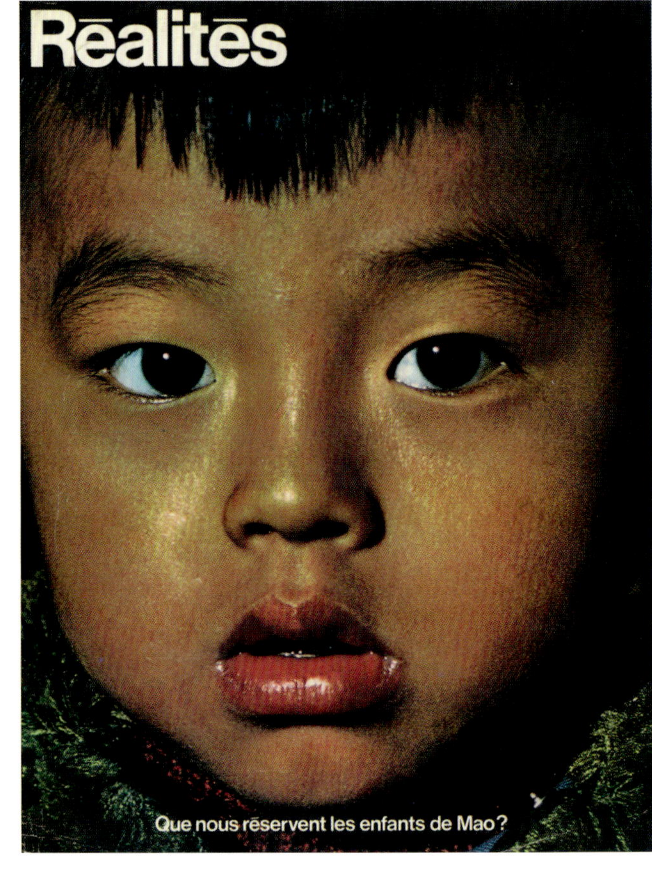

Figure 47
Cover of *Theater of the Mind*, 1976
22.9 × 22.7 cm (9 × 8 15⁄16 in.)

Figure 48
Emil Schulthess
(Swiss, 1913–1996)
Chinese-American Boy, as reproduced on cover of *Réalités*, no. 280, May 1969
27.9 × 21.5 cm (11 × 8 1⁄2 in.)
Private collection

a boy in a park in Chinatown, Tress came across a discarded magazine with a close-up of a boy's face on the cover. The boy in the magazine image appeared to be around the same age as the boy Tress wanted to photograph, and there was a resemblance between the two (fig. 48). Tress removed the magazine from the trash, tore off its cover, and placed the cover under the subject's jacket, which looks in Tress's photograph as if it has just been unzipped to reveal a second face. The child seems relaxed while his printed counterpart appears insecure, worried. Does the second face represent a portal into the hidden depths of the psyche? Do these feelings of unease belong to the past or to the future? In *Girl with Eagle, Cape Cod, Massachusetts* (fig. 49), a large dark bird towers over a girl sprawled out on the sand. Tress has cleverly aligned the bird's sharp beak with the girl's facial features, contorted into an expression of pain. Does the subject represent Prometheus, the bringer of fire, who was condemned by Zeus to have his immortal liver eaten by an eagle for all eternity? The photographs' open, ambiguous nature allows viewers to bring their own visual vocabulary to bear when analyzing the images.

"Private Acts" features environmental portraits of adults (alone or in pairs) and a self-portrait. They deal with hidden desires and relationships that are marked by silence and tension. *Androgynous Figure between Venus and Mercury, East Hampton, New York* (plate 125) was created in the formal gardens on the estate of Robert David Lion Gardiner. It features the gymnast Robert Axman, who represents Hermaphroditos, the androgynous offspring of the Greek gods Hermes and Aphrodite (or their Roman equivalents, Mercury and

Figure 49
Arthur Tress
Girl with Eagle, Cape Cod, Massachusetts, 1974
Gelatin silver print,
17.7 × 17.7 cm (7 × 7 in.)
Collection of the artist

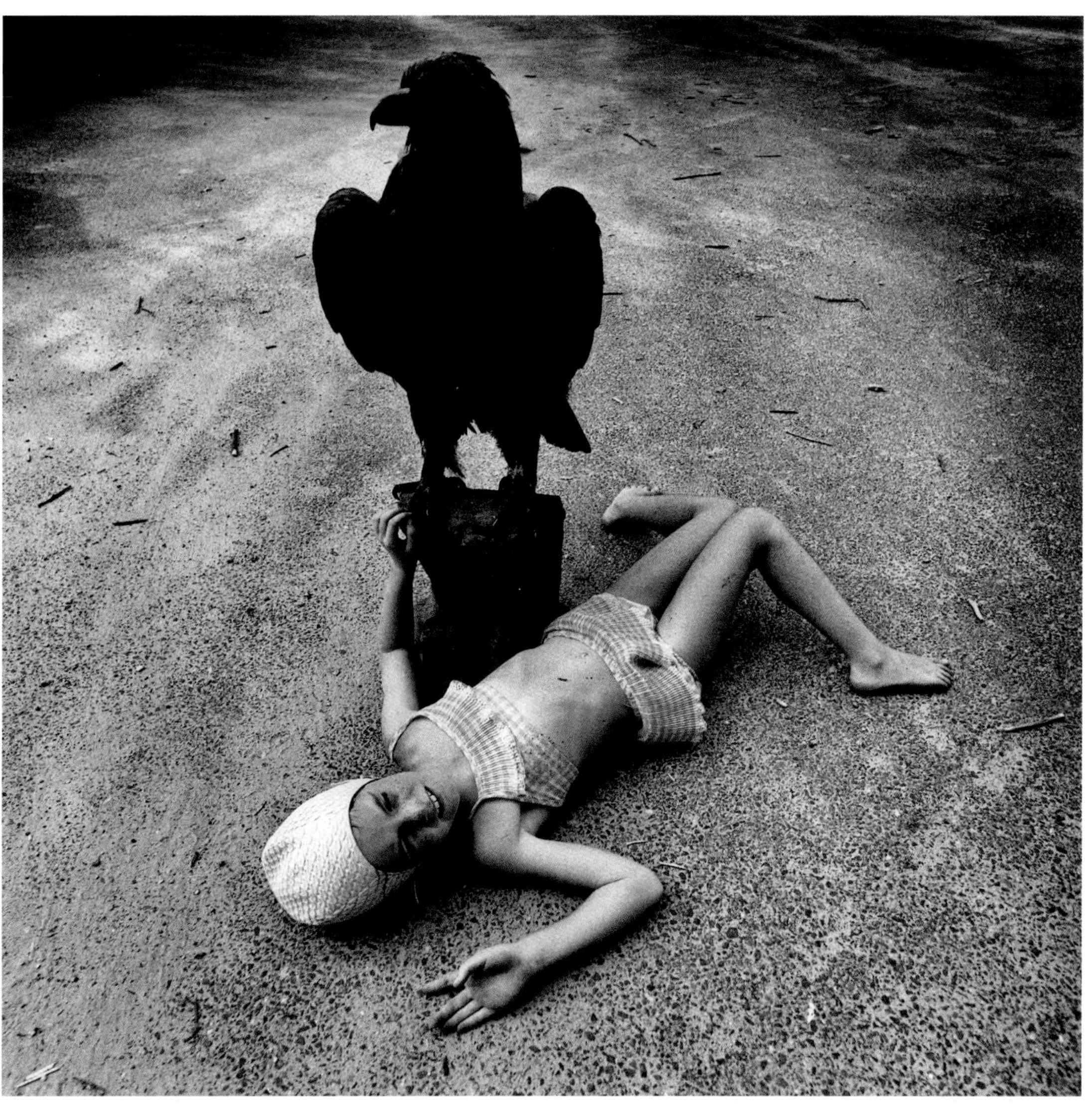

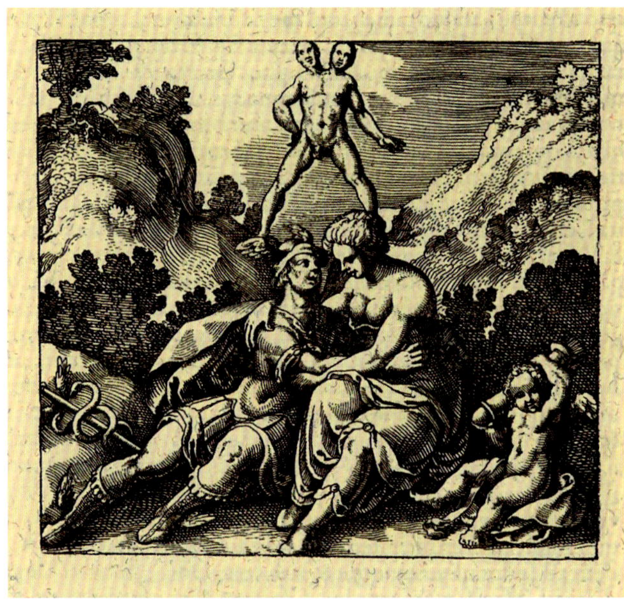

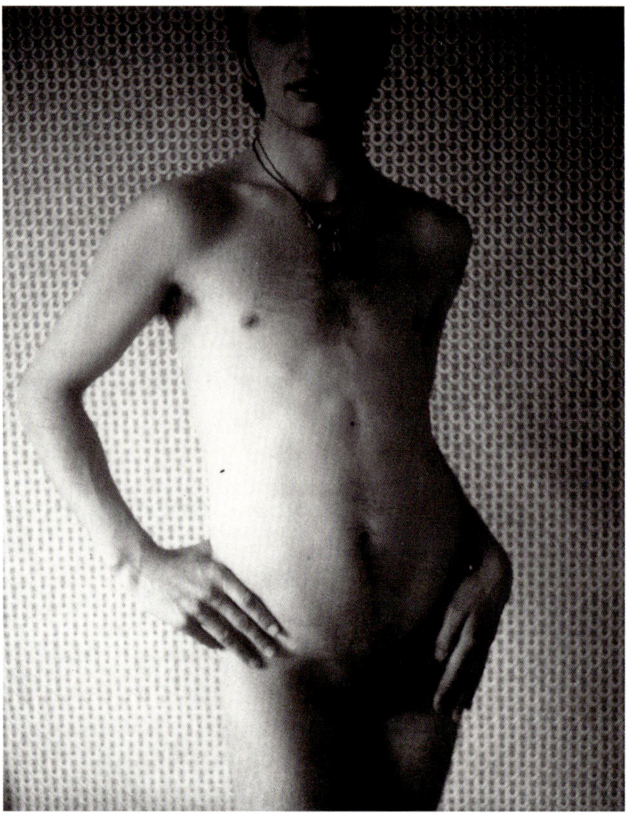

Figure 50
Matthäus Merian the Elder
(Swiss, 1593–1650)
Mercury and Venus in Unison, Giving Birth to the Alchemical Hermaphrodite (Emblem 38), ca. 1618
Woodcut, as published in H. M. E. De Jong, *Michael Maier's Atalanta Fugiens: Sources of an Alchemical Book of Emblems* (Leiden: E. J. Brill, 1969), 414

Figure 51
Robert Mapplethorpe
(American, 1946–1989)
Untitled (Nicholas, London), ca. 1972
Dye diffusion print (Polaroid), 9.5 × 7.3 cm (3 3/4 × 2 7/8 in.)
Los Angeles, jointly acquired by the J. Paul Getty Trust and the Los Angeles County Museum of Art; partial gift of The Robert Mapplethorpe Foundation; partial purchase with funds provided by the J. Paul Getty Trust and the David Geffen Foundation, 2011.9.64.3

Venus). The inspiration for this composition came to Tress from a seventeenth-century engraving found in a book of emblems (fig. 50). "This fusion of male and female energies seemed to mirror my own inner feelings of artist balance," Tress later recalled. "I thought to make a photograph that would have this same kind of hieroglyphic symbolic atmosphere and archetypal resonance."[4] The New York photographer Robert Mapplethorpe created a composition that featured a male nude with his genitals tucked between his legs (fig. 51). Just as the gender-bending aspects of these photographs were in the air, so were the classicizing aspects of the male nude, something that Mapplethorpe would master and which Tress would continue to explore with *Phallic Phantasy*, a series of homoerotic nudes in which Tress used the body to express what he saw as the base and divine parts of homosexual desire.

Self-Portrait with Lobster, Bar Harbor, Maine (fig. 52) is an image of the photographer in the bath with a lobster balanced on his lap. The lobster, of interest to artists since antiquity, was prominently featured in *Incostanza: An Allegory of Fickleness* by the Flemish artist Abraham Janssens (fig. 53). Janssens's painting was a response to an engraving in Cesare Ripa's *Iconologia* (1603), which shows a woman holding a crescent moon in her right hand while she steps on a crab with her left foot. Ripa explained why the crab was considered a symbol of faithlessness: "The crab is an animal, walking forward and backward, with equal disposition, as do those who, being irresolute, now praise contemplation, now action, now war, now peace, now science, now ignorance, now conversation, and now loneliness."[5] During the late 1930s, the Spanish painter Salvador Dalí, who viewed the lobster as a symbol of libidinous dreams, helped to popularize it as a Surrealist motif (fig. 54). In his self-portrait Tress used the crustacean to cover his genitals, a fact that points to issues that he was having with his own sexuality, particularly his difficulties dealing with an unpredictable bisexual partner whose emotions ran hot and cold.[6]

Figure 52
Arthur Tress
Self-Portrait with Lobster, Bar Harbor, Maine, 1974
Gelatin silver print
17.7 × 17.7 cm (7 × 7 in.)
Collection of the artist

Figure 53
Attributed to Abraham Janssens
(Flemish, 1567–1632)
Incostanza: An Allegory of Fickleness, 1615–18
Oil on canvas, 106.5 × 82 cm (42 × 32 3⁄8 in.)
Copenhagen, Statens Museum for Kunst, KMSst387

Figure 54
George Platt Lynes
(American, 1907–1955)
Salvador Dalí, 1939
Gelatin silver print with applied pigment, 16.7 × 14.5 cm (6 9⁄16 × 5 11⁄16 in.)
New York, Metropolitan Museum of Art, David Hunter McAlpin Fund, 1941, 41.65.28

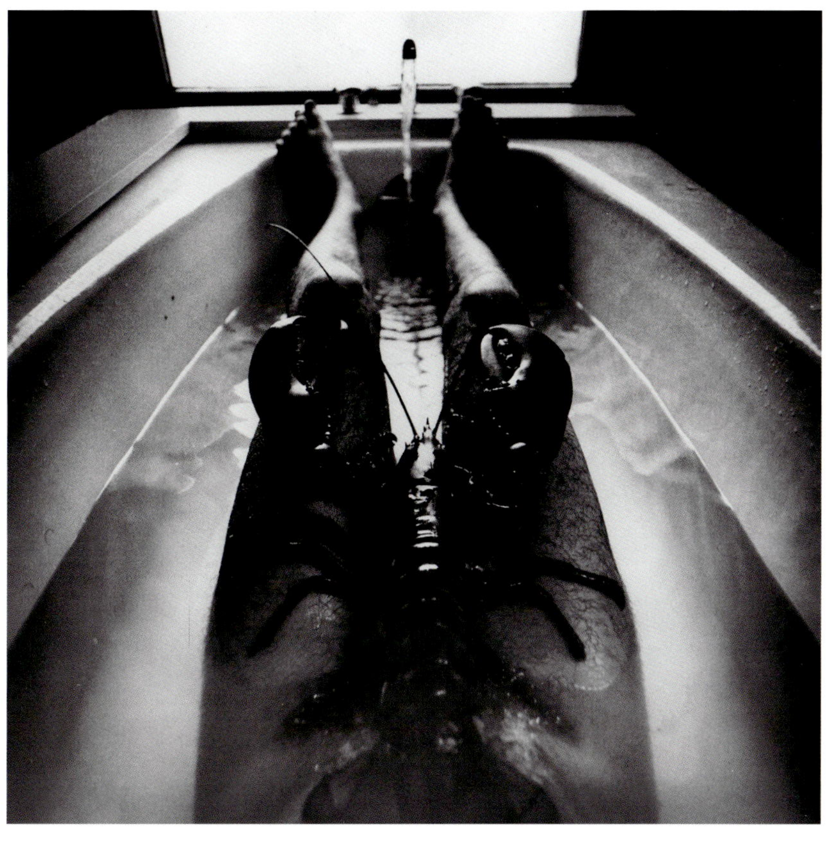

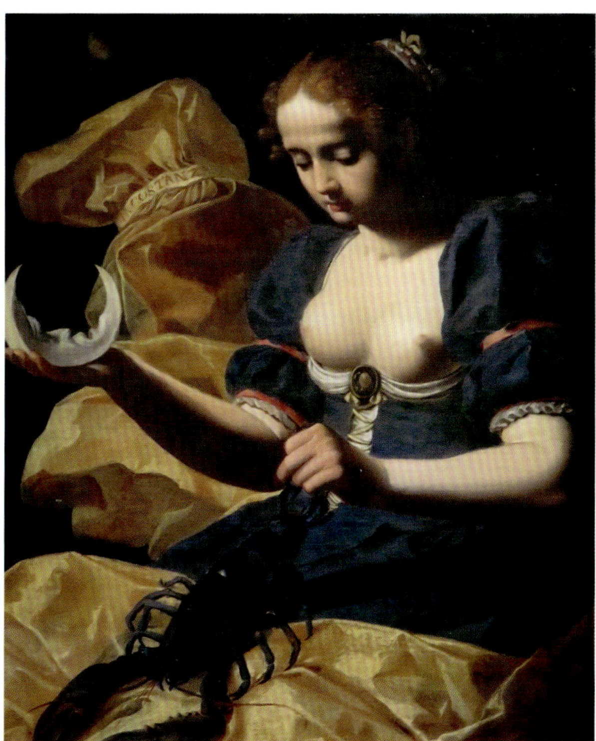

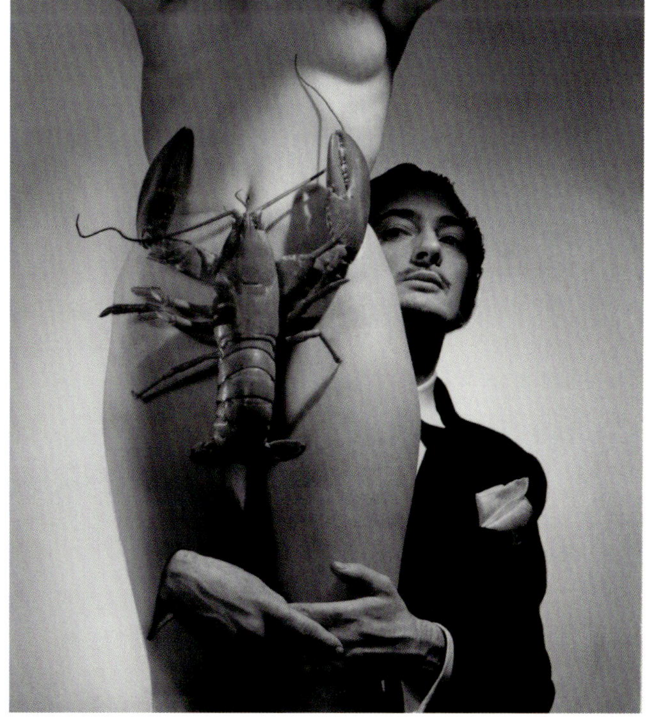

"Domestic Scenes" focuses on how our ideas about familial relationships (mother and son, brother and sister, father and daughter, and so on) do not always match our real experiences of them. The creation of *Ed Berman and His Mother, Brooklyn, New York* (plate 123) provides a good example of the complex ways in which many of the artist's photographic sittings came to be. Tress and Berman were friends during their freshman year of high school (1954–55) but drifted apart when Tress became more interested in art and began hanging out with a different crowd. Twenty years later, Berman phoned Tress to let him know that he had come to Brooklyn from his home in Portland, Oregon, to help care for his sick mother. Tress asked Berman if he could photograph him and his mother for his latest project, and Berman agreed. "We met in her apartment in the rather dismal Coney Island housing projects," Tress explained recently. "I did a few typical images but then I noticed the stained ironing board and just on an impulse I asked Ed if he would put the cold iron over his mother's hand. Later when I sent him a copy of the print Ed told me it was right on as he could do whatever he wanted to do to his mother, and she never minded."[7] Tress's relationship with his own mother was a source of discomfort. For fear of rejection, Tress never came out to his mother as a gay man. Keeping that from her, he said recently, "created a kind of separation between us and perhaps anger on my part, and we were never openly affectionate, which is sad as we both probably needed someone to honestly confide in. And when she had a series of strokes in the late 80s, I was reluctant and perhaps incapable of giving her the kind of attention she needed at the end of her life."[8]

"Stage Properties" consists of photographs—all taken in interior spaces—of people and their collections. Although the photographs in "Stage Properties" lack the dynamism found in other sections, the questions they raise are interesting. Is collecting an attempt to order and gain control over a chaotic world? Can collecting take the place of important social or familial relationships, and if so, does the desire to acquire spring from loneliness or from some other deeply rooted psychological need? Tress, who was an avid collector, understood instinctively that there was a line between being a collector of things and being controlled by one's need to collect. For *Mr. X, Clock Collector, New York City*, Tress asked Kelly Edde to stand on the staircase of his Victorian brownstone and hold an ornate mantel clock in front of his face, effectively dehumanizing him. One thinks of the unfeeling automaton, a frightening specter of a progressively mechanized world. "All photographs are *memento mori*," Susan Sontag wrote, pointing out the unsettling nature of photography and its relation to the passage of time. "To take a photograph is to participate in another person's mortality, vulnerability, mutability. Precisely by slicing out this moment and freezing it, all photographs testify to time's relentless melt."[9]

"Directors of Darkness" contains portraits of creative people (among them a magician, a chanteuse, a clairvoyant, an actor, and a dream therapist) who live outside the mainstream and whose esoteric beliefs and unusual personalities seem to give them a special place in the world. One of these people was the singer and drag performer Minette, who was a friend of Tress's father when he was living at 46 Riverside Drive on Manhattan's Upper West Side. The elder Tress enjoyed the company of theater people, often inviting them to join his family for holiday meals. Although Minette liked to go out in women's clothes during the daytime and used feminine pronouns, she was accepted in Vaseline Flats, a close-knit neighborhood of Italian immigrant families in Brooklyn, one of the places

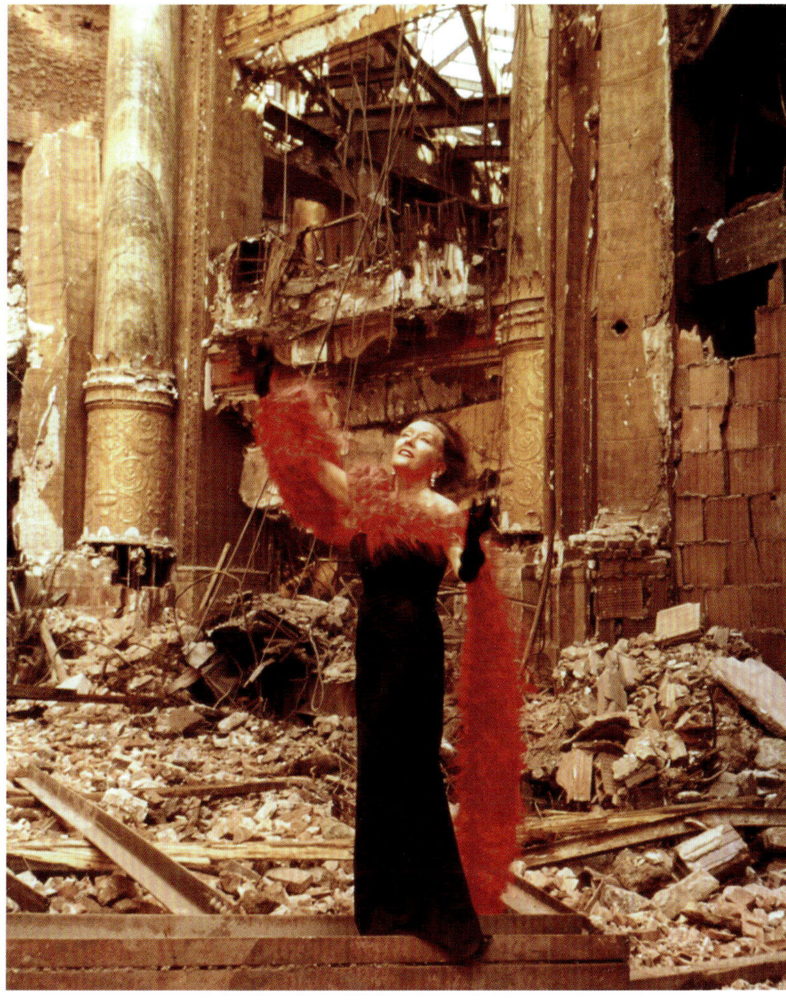

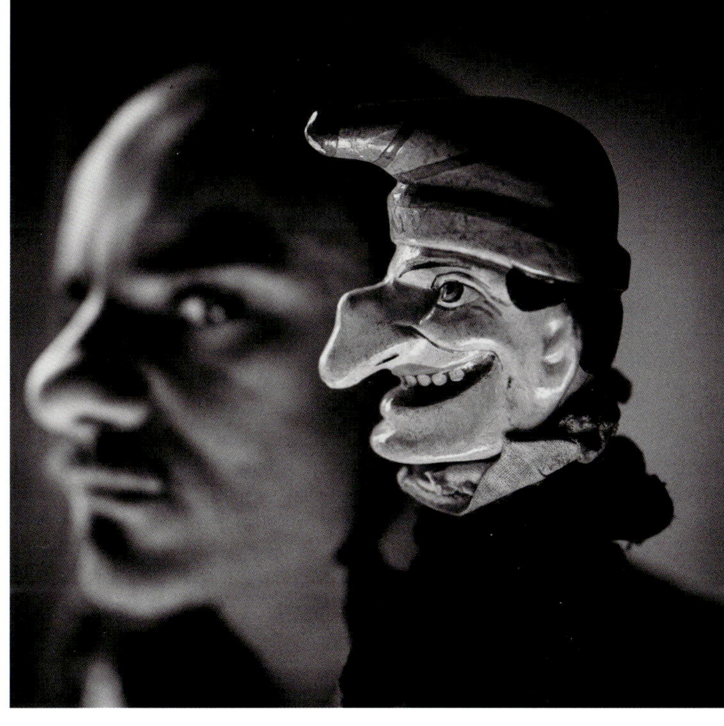

Figure 55
Eliot Elisofon (American, 1911–1973)
Gloria Swanson at Roxy, 1960, as published in *Life* magazine, November 7, 1960, p. 46
Private collection

Figure 56
Arthur Tress
Charles Ludlam, Punchman, New York, New York, 1976
Gelatin silver print
17.7 × 17.7 cm (7 × 7 in.)
Collection of the artist

where Tress photographed her.[10] For *Minette as Gloria Swanson in Ruins of Fox Theater, Brooklyn, New York* (plate 131), Tress cast Minette in the role of the film star Gloria Swanson as she appeared in 1960, posing amid the rubble of the Roxy Theatre in Manhattan (fig. 55).[11] Minette idolized Swanson, whose glamorous starring roles in dozens of silent films during the 1920s brought her international acclaim. Although Swanson's movie career foundered in the 1930s, she had a spectacular comeback in 1950 playing the role of Norma Desmond in Billy Wilder's classic film *Sunset Boulevard*. Wearing a feather boa and gloves, Minette strikes a defiant pose in the partially demolished movie house at 20 Flatbush Avenue.[12] In a scene pulsing with drama and pathos, one can almost hear the voice of Norma Desmond bellowing through the ruined hall: "There once was a time in this business when I had the eyes of the whole world! But that wasn't good enough for them, oh no! They had to have the ears of the whole world too. So they opened their big mouths and out came talk . . . Oh, those idiot producers. Those imbeciles. Haven't they got any eyes? Have they forgotten what a star looks like? I'll show them! I'll be up there again, so help me!"[13]

Minette introduced Tress to the actor, director, and playwright Charles Ludlam, who formed the Ridiculous Theatrical Company in 1967, which brought together comedy, queer themes, and experimental theater to shock audiences by its outrageousness. In *Charles Ludlam, Punchman,*

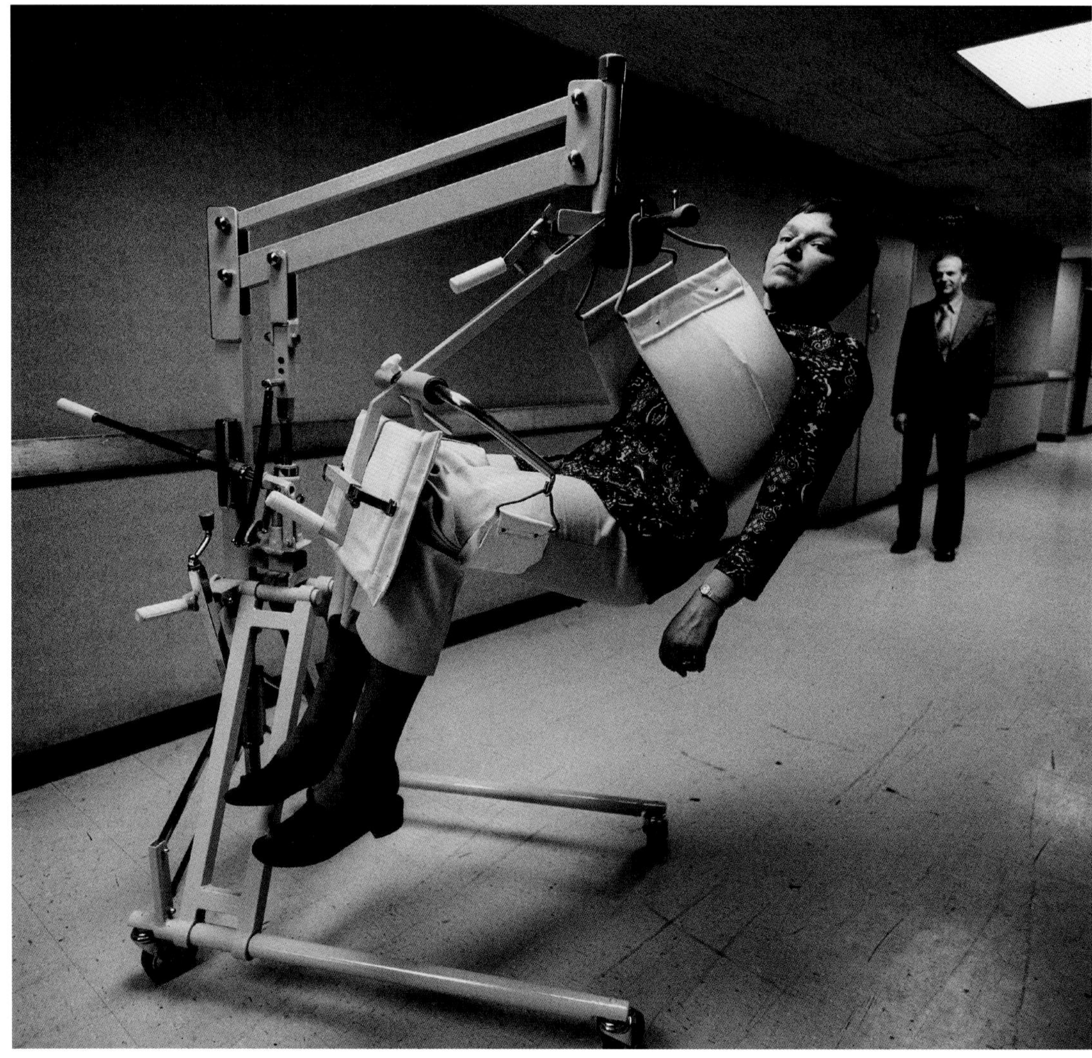

New York, New York (fig. 56), Tress encourages the viewer to compare the sitter's profile with that of Mr. Punch, making use of natural light from a nearby window and selective focus to draw attention to the wooden puppet's grotesque features. Ludlam collected Mr. Punch puppets, which have their origins in Pulcinella, a stock character in the Italian commedia dell'arte—an apt prop, considering the improvisational nature of this form of theater and Ludlam's productions. Here, Mr. Punch, who is generally considered a clever and fearless opportunist, becomes Ludlam's alter ego.[14]

The actor Stefan Brecht, son of the playwright Bertolt Brecht, was also a member of Ludlam's Ridiculous Theatrical Company. Tress photographed him wearing a costume made by Brecht's wife, Mary, for the play *The Grand Tarot*, which represents marriage as an androgynous figure with male and female attributes (plate 132). Wandering around Greenwich Village, Tress and Brecht found the perfect location for the shoot—a vandalized church, a place where many marriages had been solemnized. As a portrait of gender ambiguity, the image relates to *Minette as Gloria Swanson in Ruins of Fox Theater* and to *Androgynous Figure between Venus and Mercury*.

The "Final Curtain" section of the book features photographs that revolve around themes such as science, medicine, and death. Tress was intrigued by how the first two seek to understand

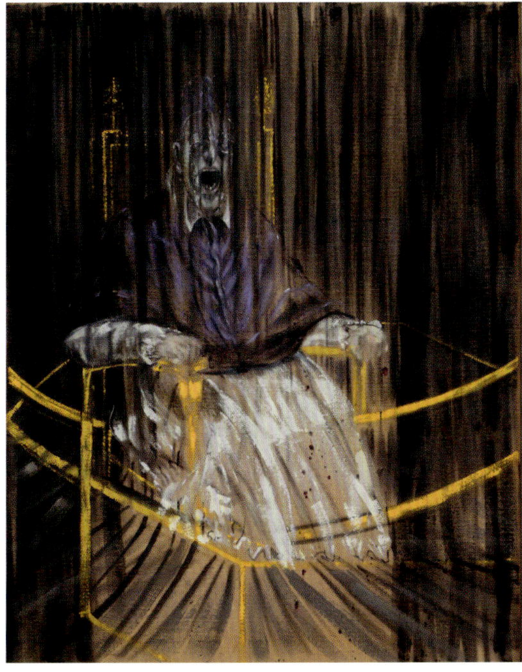

Figure 57
Arthur Tress
Doctor and Patient, Bellevue, New York, New York, 1973
Gelatin silver print, 25.7 × 26.2 cm (10 1⁄8 × 10 5⁄16 in.)
Los Angeles, J. Paul Getty Museum, Gift of Wes and Julie Nichols, 2019.170.7

Figure 58
Francis Bacon
(British, 1909–1992)
Study after Velázquez's Portrait of Pope Innocent X, 1953
Oil on canvas, 152.1 × 117.8 cm (59 7⁄8 × 46 3⁄8 in.)
Des Moines, Des Moines Art Center, Purchased with funds from the Coffin Fine Arts Trust; Nathan Emory Coffin Collection of the Des Moines Art Center, 1980.1

and manipulate human existence in ways that sometimes threaten to destroy it. *Doctor and Patient, Bellevue, New York, New York* (fig. 57) depicts a woman in a hoist used to move patients in and out of bed. Contrary to the title, the photograph was made at a medical convention at the New York Coliseum in Columbus Circle.[15] Tress chose the inventor of this machine and his wife to be the players in this narrative, and through a gradual series of simple requests he got his subjects to comply. First he asked the inventor to push the device into an empty hallway so he could photograph it. Then Tress asked him if he would demonstrate how the machine worked, using his wife as the "patient."[16] Removed from its context of the display in the main exhibition hall, the hoist takes on ominous connotations, raising fears about the loss of mobility and independence.

Last Portrait of My Father, New York, New York (plate 126) deals with some of the same themes as *Doctor and Patient* but is personal in nature. Tress recalled its making:

> I took the rather large ornate chair that I normally sit in myself at my writing desk and placed it in a nearby park at the beginning of a snowstorm. My father lived a few streets away and I telephoned him to meet me. Although ill, he was excited that I was interested in photographing him. The cold white flakes falling on his black coat in the vast landscape seem to symbolize the sense of the unescapable finality of his approaching death and possible release from his painful condition. . . . [t]his photograph of my father in a snowstorm is, in fact, a kind of surrogate self-portrait that mirrors my own hollow fearfulness about my own body's decline and disappearance into a cold emptiness.[17]

The rich associations that the image evokes are an integral part of its power. And while many of Tress's photographs rely on the way the subjects look at each other or at the camera, here it is the open mouth that is the most striking detail. Tress's father appears to be bracing himself for transfiguration like the screaming figure in Francis Bacon's painting *Study after Velázquez's Portrait of Pope Innocent X* (fig. 58). Interestingly, the elder Tress could pass for the horror movie actor Boris Karloff, and the highbacked seat recalls a throne or perhaps even an electric chair.

Tress worked his list of contacts, sharing his idea for the book with Duane Michals, Michel Tournier, and A. D. Coleman. They agreed to be part of the project. Michals issues a warning to the reader in his preface: "If Arthur Tress comes to photograph you beware. Do not be taken in by that innocent smile and shy demeanor. They are his disguises . . . he intuits all those unseen ties of a relationship and brings them to our attention. Now we understand and nothing more needs to be said . . . I don't think that I want Arthur to photograph me. I might not be prepared to deal with what he sees. And I know he will be right."[18] Michals astutely points out the split in Tress's character, his gentle, easygoing demeanor in contrast to the steely determination that underpins what he does. Michals also suggests, even if subtly, that in Tress's hands the camera is an instrument with magical properties, one that allows him to unearth our deepest secrets and put them on display.

In his introduction Coleman places Tress's work within the history of the constructed photograph, explaining that "certain uses of the directorial mode have been accepted as legitimate, while others have been rejected out of hand." These value judgments have nothing to do with logic, Coleman says, but are the result of the conservatism of a few influential historians, and Tress and other photographers of his generation (think Clarence John Laughlin, Ralph Eugene Meatyard, and Duane Michals) are pushing against these limits. Coleman goes on to characterize *Theater of the Mind* as an expression of the artist's "ongoing concerns and obsessions"—in other words, they say more about Tress than they do about his subjects. In Coleman's view, the photographer's best images are the ones that elicit the most provocative questions. "We might eventually be led to ask: Who are these people?" he writes. "And because these photographs make it apparent that there is someone interested in their ritualistic revelations, adept at evoking them from his subject and capable of embodying them in direct, effective, exorcistic images, the question follows: Who is this photographer?"[19]

Tress developed an intricate network of personal and professional relationships that benefited his career. He was introduced to the publisher Douglas Morgan, son of the photographer Barbara Morgan and *Life* magazine editor Willard Morgan, by the photographer Eva Rubinstein, daughter of the pianist Arthur Rubinstein.[20] Photographs from *Theater of the Mind* were shown at several galleries following the book's publication, including in the exhibition *Arthur Tress: A Twelve-Year Survey* at the Robert Samuel Gallery in New York City in 1980. Critical response was mixed. Van Deren Coke characterized the photographs as "thin" and lacking the ability to "transcend the staging of the episode recorded by the camera."[21] Roxanne Enyeart pointed out the artist's ability to evoke "laughter, dismay, or outright disgust" and praised the series as "a marvelous visual opportunity to share in another's assessment of existence."[22] In her article "Further Adventures in the Theater of the Mind," Marcia Wooding claimed that "critics expressed shock and moralized about the kind of people who would expose 'their darker side to the camera,'" but she did not cite her sources. She went on to marvel at the artist's uncanny ability to coax the actors in his little play to do as he liked.[23]

"People who have watched or filmed me doing a portrait session see how quickly and spontaneously the camera activity takes place," Tress said recently. "I create sort of a scenario that I believe might be true to the players' lives involved in this immediate improvisation or perhaps echoing some deeply felt injury dwelling inside my own psyche."[24] The results, which are often influenced by a variety of visual sources, from the covers of trashy novels to old Hollywood films, resonate with viewers of these pictures as well as those being pictured. Tress uses the camera as a tool for finding order amid chaos; it is his way of exploring and gaining control of half-formed ideas that need expression. His desire to photograph is part of his obsessive search for meaning, even if that search generates more questions than answers.[25]

Notes

1 Arthur Tress, "Family Portraits: The Techniques of Theatre of the Mind" (unpublished manuscript, 1976), as published in Marco Livingstone, ed., *Arthur Tress: Talisman* (New York: Thames & Hudson, 1986), 151.
2 Livingstone, *Arthur Tress: Talisman*, 13.
3 Arthur Tress, interview with the author, September 25, 2022.
4 Arthur Tress, letter to Francesca Richer, March 10, 2005, from Cambria, collection of the artist.
5 Cesare Ripa, *Iconologia* (Torino: Fògola, 1986), 210–11.
6 Arthur Tress, interview with the author, September 25, 2022.
7 Email to Jim Ganz, January 17, 2020.
8 Ibid.
9 Susan Sontag, *On Photography* (New York: Farrar, Straus & Giroux, 1977), 15.
10 Arthur Tress, interview with the author, September 25, 2022. A review of the contact sheets shows children whom Minette had befriended in some of the frames.
11 The Roxy Theatre, a 5,920-seat movie palace located at 153 West 50th Street in Manhattan, opened on March 11, 1927, with the premiere of *The Love of Sunya*, starring Swanson. The theater was demolished in 1960. For the shoot, Swanson was wearing a gown by the Hollywood designer Jean Louis and $170,000 worth of jewelry. She had to be carried and placed on top of the rubble of the crumbling building so as not to injure herself or ruin her dress or shoes.
12 The Fox Theater was a 4,305-seat movie palace built in 1928 and demolished in 1971.
13 From *Sunset Boulevard* (1950), directed by Billy Wilder.
14 Arthur Tress, interview with the author, September 25, 2022.
15 The New York Coliseum was a convention center that consisted of windowless exhibition spaces in a low-rise building and an office tower. It was completed in 1956 and demolished in 2000.
16 Arthur Tress, interview with the author, September 25, 2022.
17 Arthur Tress, "Portrait of My Father" (unpublished manuscript, 1991), emailed to the author, September 26, 2022.
18 Duane Michals, "Tress' Vaudeville," in *Arthur Tress: Theater of the Mind* (Dobbs Ferry, NY: Morgan & Morgan, 1976), unpaginated.
19 A. D. Coleman, "Introduction," in *Arthur Tress: Theater of the Mind*, unpaginated.
20 Arthur Tress, interview with the author, September 25, 2022.
21 Van Deren Coke, "Arthur Tress, Theater of the Mind," *Society for Photographic Education Newsletter*, n.d., photocopy from the artist's archive.
22 Roxanne Enyeart, "Arthur Tress, Theater of the Mind," *Society for Photographic Education Newsletter*, n.d., photocopy from the artist's archive.
23 Marcia Wooding, "Further Adventures in the Theater of the Mind," *35 mm Photography* (Summer 1978): 74.
24 Email to the author, October 6, 2022.
25 Arthur Tress, "Statement about Myself and Photography" (unpublished manuscript, 1968), as published in Livingstone, *Arthur Tress: Talisman*, 147.

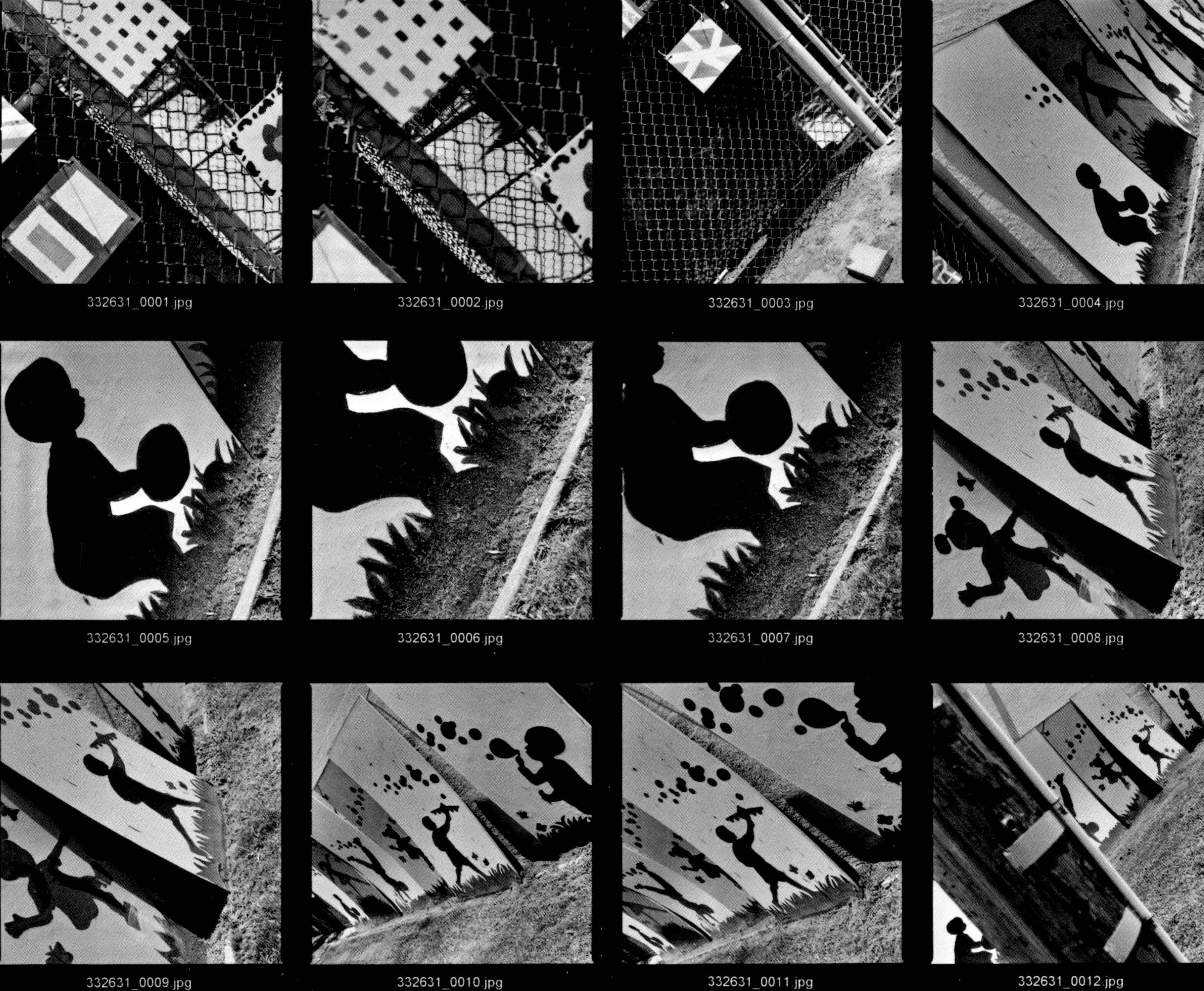
332631_0001.jpg
332631_0002.jpg
332631_0003.jpg
332631_0004.jpg
332631_0005.jpg
332631_0006.jpg
332631_0007.jpg
332631_0008.jpg
332631_0009.jpg
332631_0010.jpg
332631_0011.jpg
332631_0012.jpg

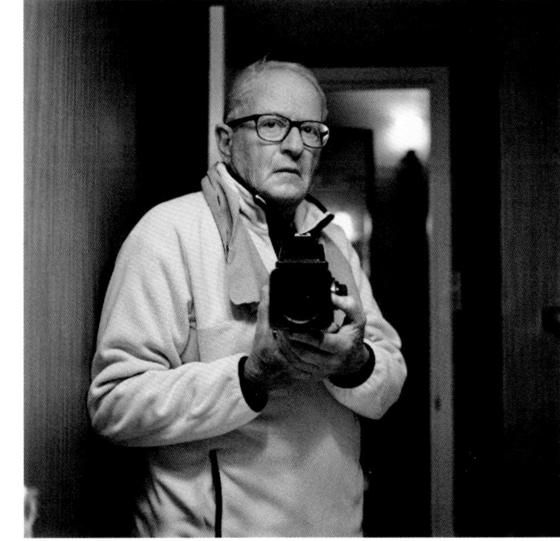

Figure 59
Arthur Tress
Self-Portrait with Hasselblad, Lake Tahoe, California, 2018
Gelatin silver print,
20.4 × 20.4 cm (8 × 8 in.)
Collection of the artist

Postscript
Looking Back (2022)

Over the past few years I have been revisiting a unique decade of my early career, looking through old contacts, worn prints, tattered magazine tear sheets, barely legible notebook pages, and folded and faded personal letters from myself and sweetly saved by family, friends, and lovers. They brought back to me so much forgotten information about the stressful struggles and quiet joys of those youthful days. It was a re-immersion into a time, almost half a century ago, when I was just beginning to assert myself as a full-time professional in the hotly competitive world of New York photojournalism and the burgeoning cosmos of galleries and museums with their new interest in the photographic medium.

Intensely searching these materials again brought back hundreds of memories—of anxious disappointments over editorial rejections, confidence-building elation when work was appreciated and published or bought as fine art, economic insecurities when I could barely manage the rent . . . and also of my personal challenges and evolution through nightly dream journals, men's therapy groups, and gay rights activism, where I found more confidence in the validity of my own unconventional sexual identity.

What an era that was—of experimental theater, film, dance, happenings, and avant-garde music, all done on the cheap, and how lucky I was to be part of it and to absorb its daring. And now as an older person, age eighty-two, I can almost envy the youthful enthusiasm and energy that pushed through almost any disparaging barriers, optimistic in its belief that the photo image could bring about social change or insights into the human predicament. It was an incentive for working hard and being extravagantly productive. Also, I am amazed, a bit, at how imaginative and perhaps even innovative my way of working was, as it evolved during that era from a documentary adhesion to the factual to a more brazen approach to the psychological manipulation of subject matter. I can see now that it was also a time when certain persistent themes or potential avenues of expression became nascent, which were to sustain my curiosity and explorations over the following many years of stylistic probing.

Amazingly, even my most recent art project of the past five years—photographing the vast and now mostly empty office "campuses" in a changing Silicon Valley—harkens back to some of my earlier concerns with irresponsible urban planning, environmental degradation, and unrestrained, dehumanizing corporate power. These were perhaps the subtext for my very first widely distributed portfolio, *Open Space in the Inner City* (1970–71), with its images of polluted waterways, cramped tenements, and an alienated work force. The freshly made images are different in that they contain no people, just the faceless, monolithic aluminum-clad structures, plazas, or parking lots devoid of all humanity—filled with a strange and disconcerting quality, but again somehow still touching upon the very disturbing resonant "surrealness" of the 1970s accomplishments. My recent revisiting of that distant body of imagery, seeing its significance with unprejudiced eyes, has inspired me anew to continue exploring, always with the simplest means and equipment, the visual potential of the basic photo image, born out of a committed aspiration to expand the possibilities of what photography is capable of exploring and make the world a better place.

Plates

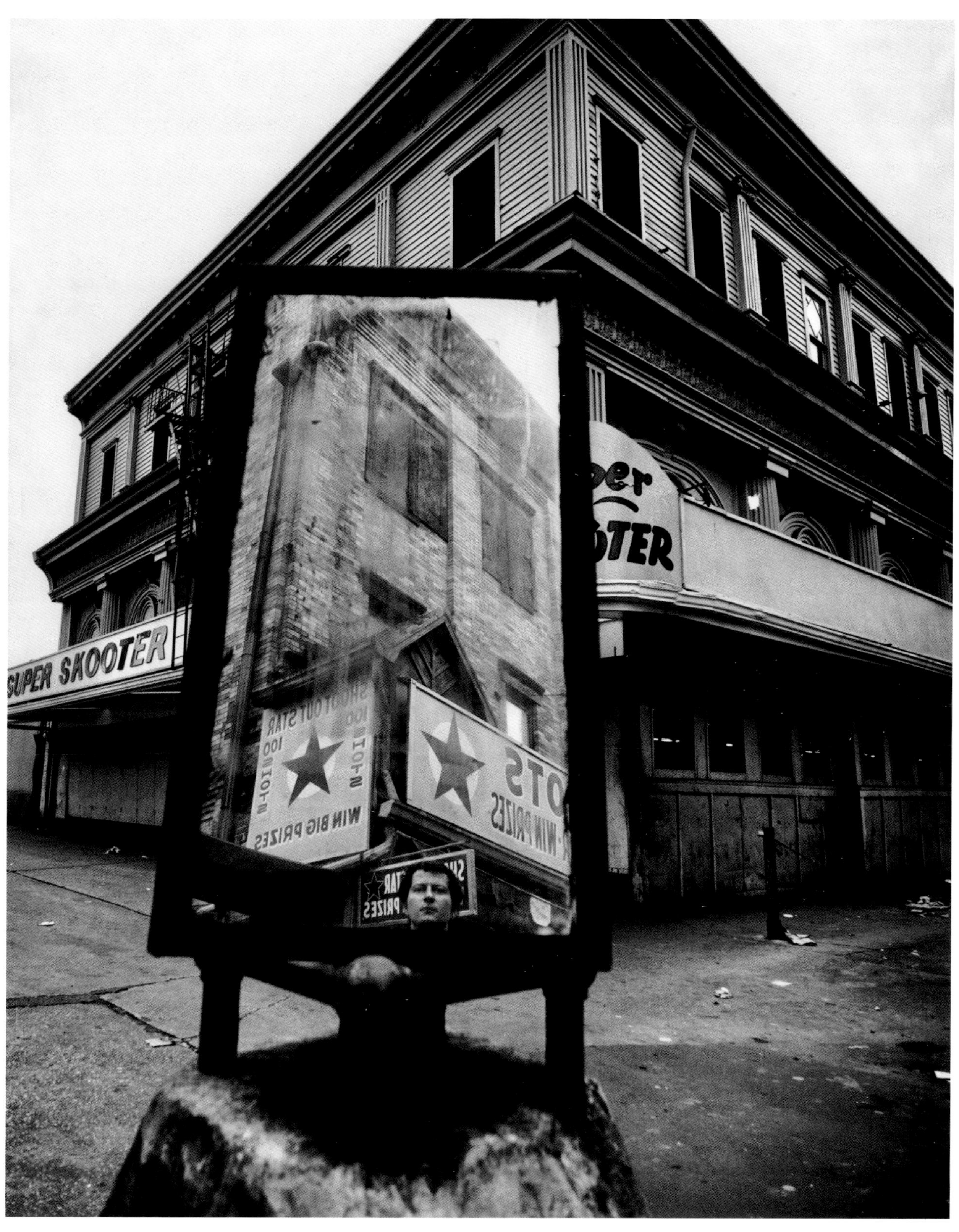

PLATE 1
Self-Portrait in Mirror, Coney Island, New York, 1969

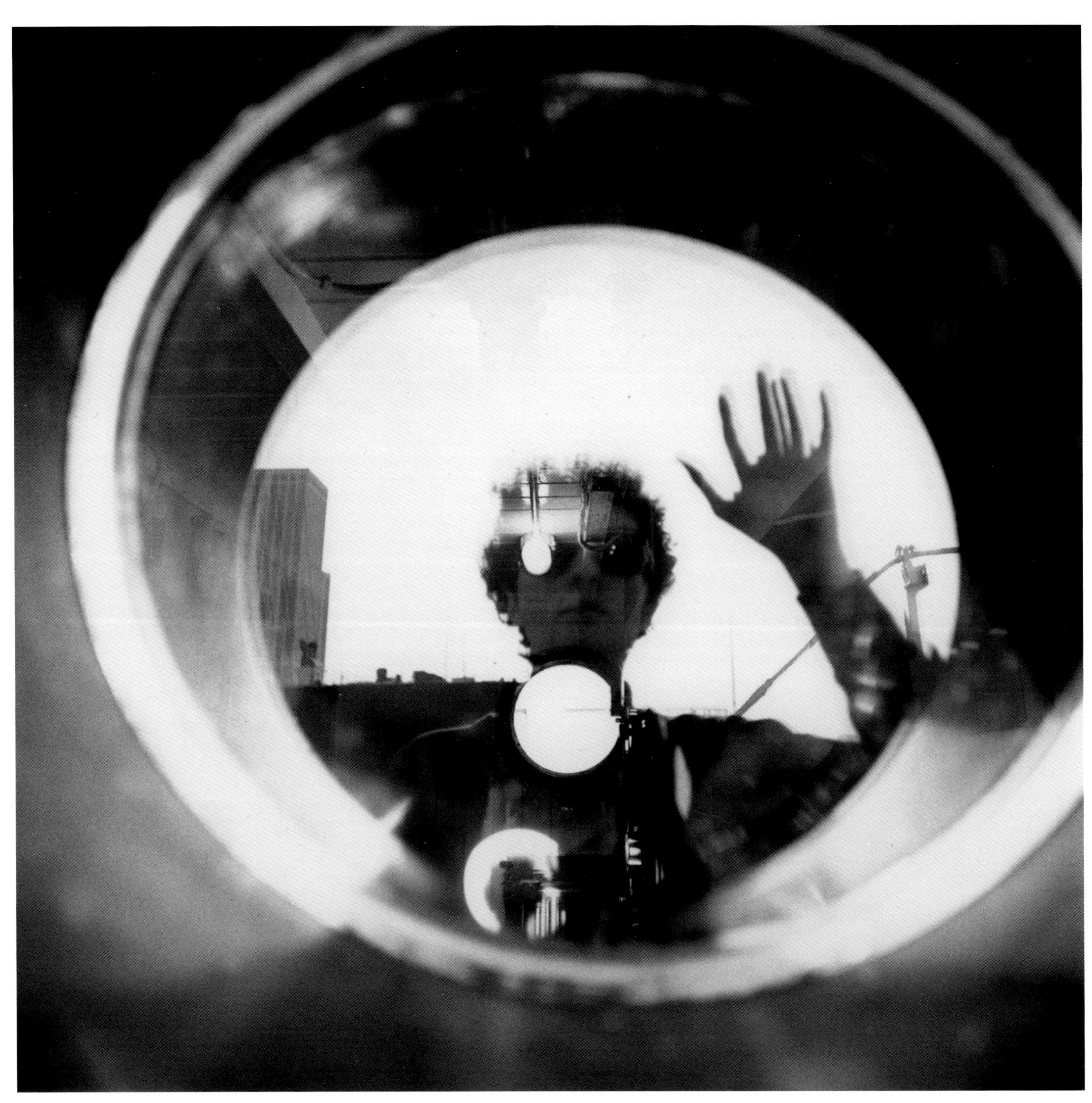

PLATE 2
My Face in Store Window, New York, New York, 1969

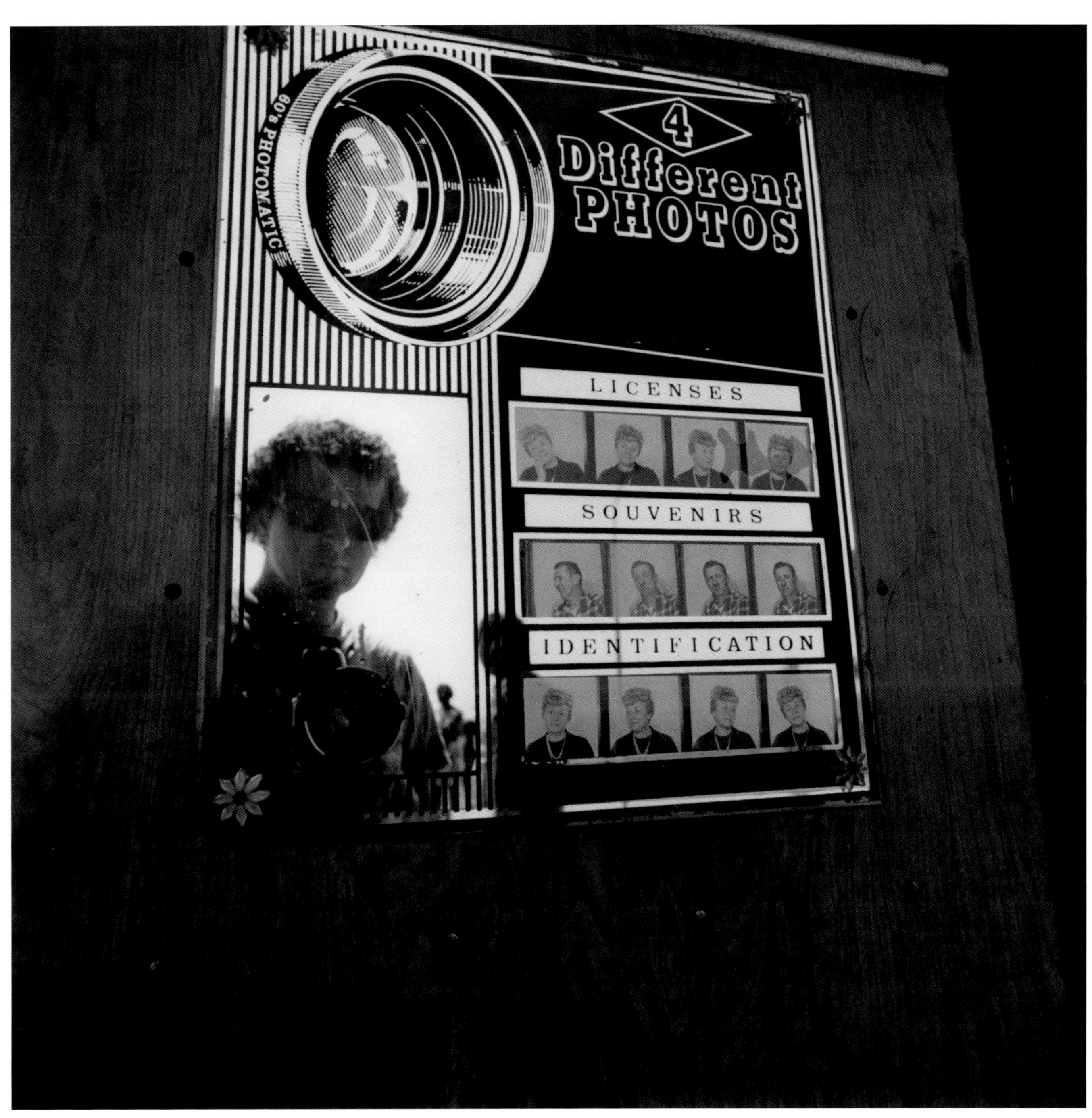

PLATE 3
Self-Portrait in Photomat Mirror, Coney Island, New York, negative 1970; print 2021

Appalachia: People and Places

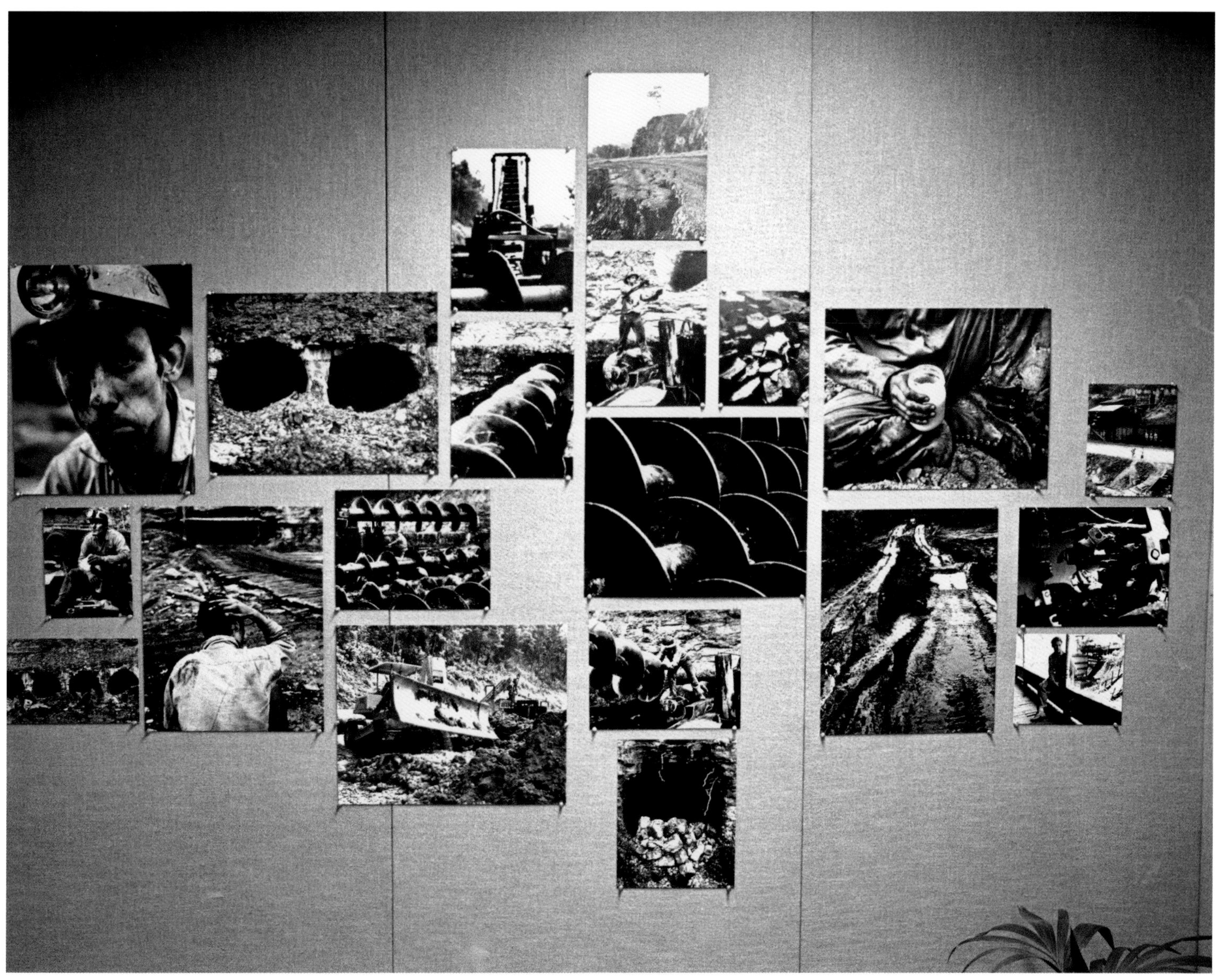

Installation view of *The "Disturbed" Land* at the Sierra Club Gallery, New York, New York, 1968
Gelatin silver print, 20.3 x 25.4 cm (8 x 10 in.)
Collection of Arthur Tress

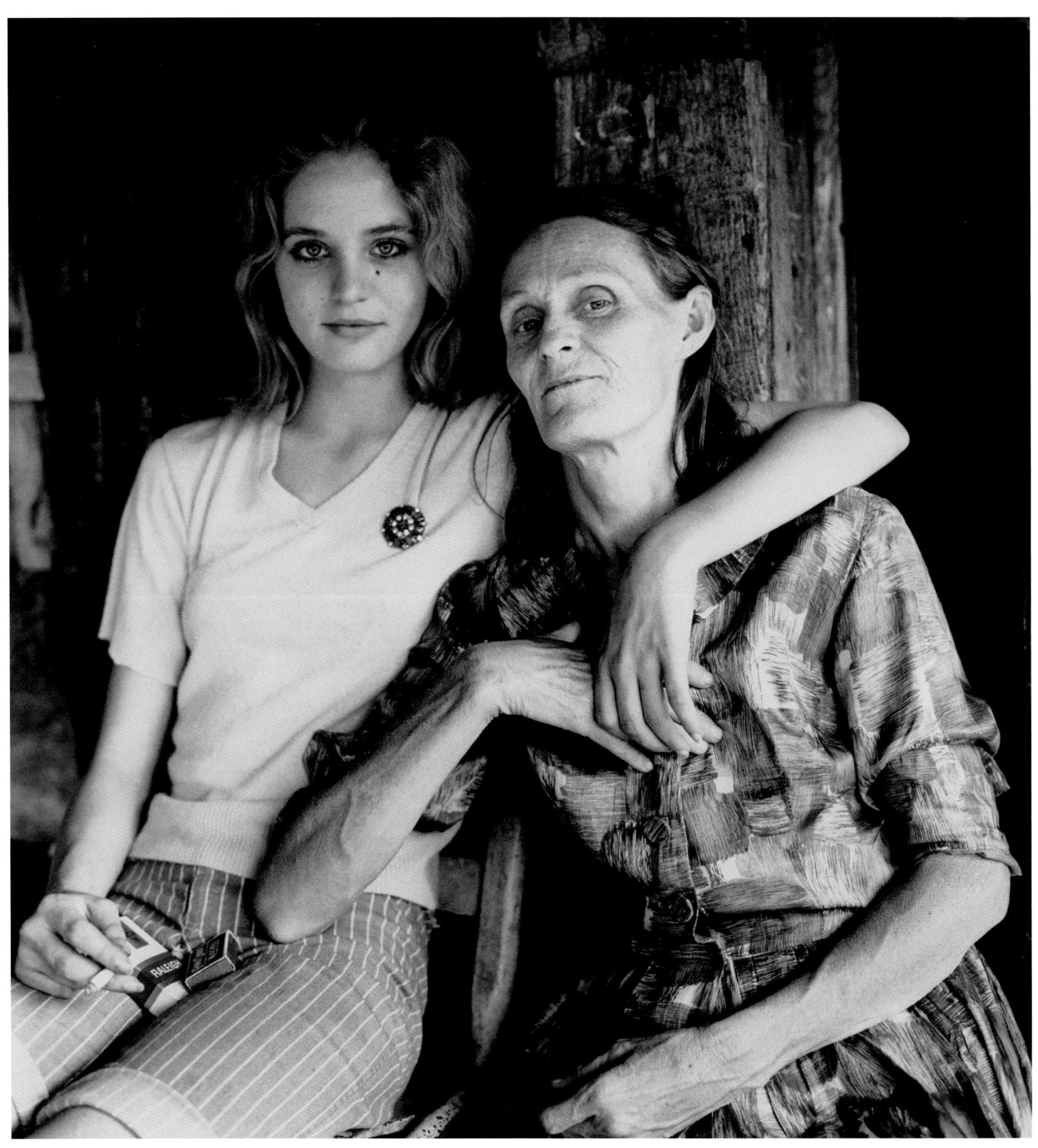

PLATE 4
Mrs. C. W. Boone and Her Daughter, Barnardsville, North Carolina, 1968

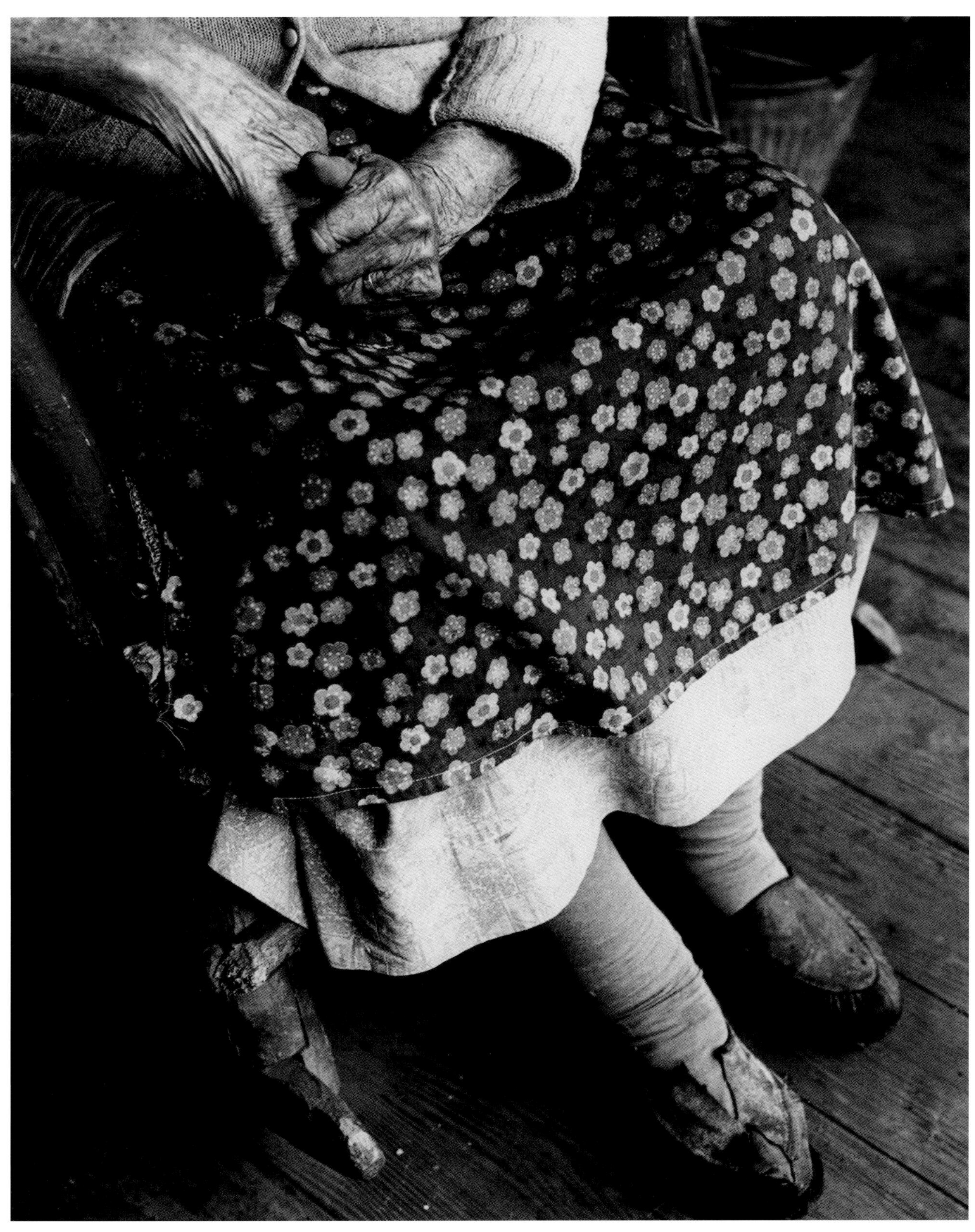

PLATE 5
Mrs. B. Riddle, Pensacola, North Carolina, 1968

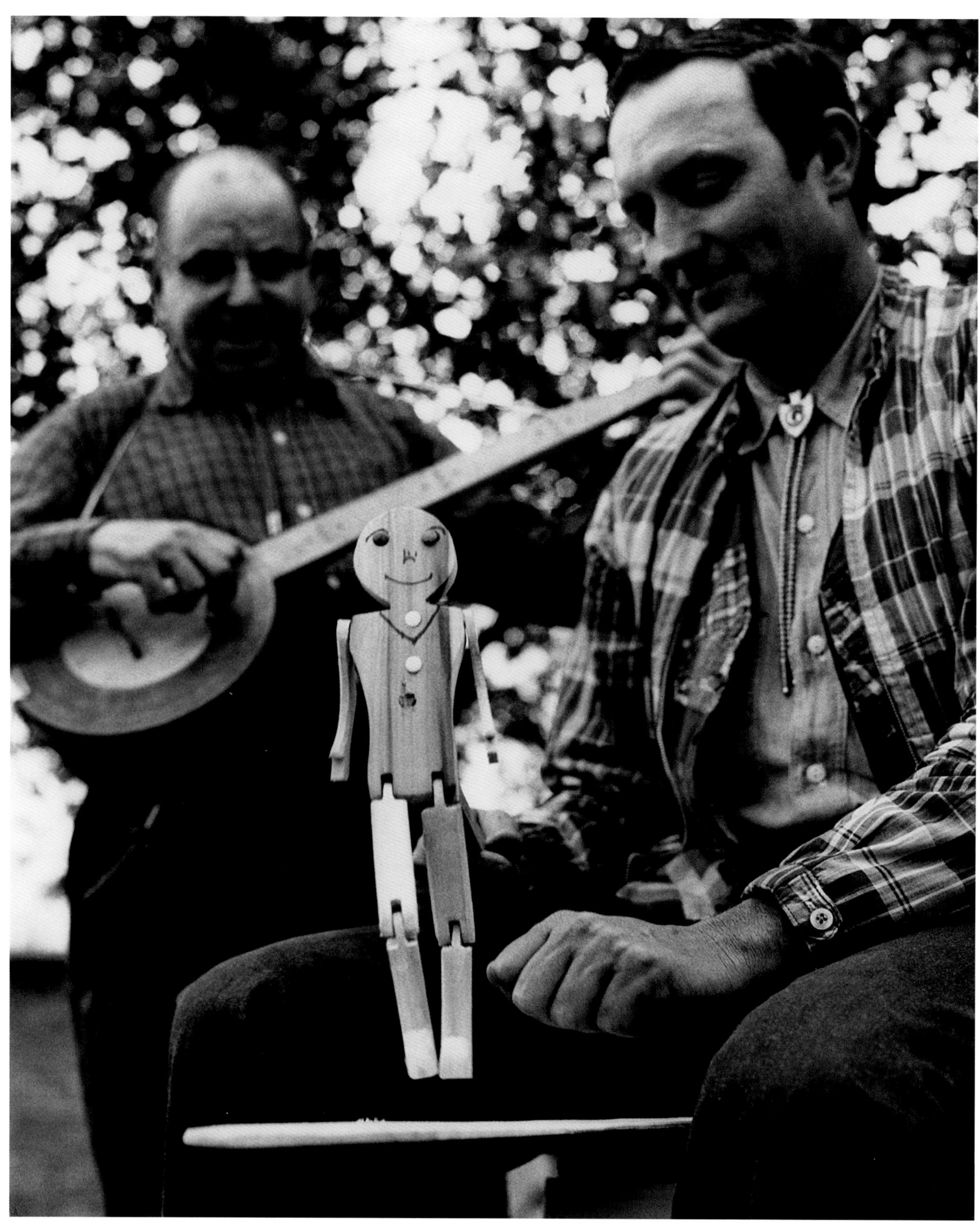

PLATE 6
Jumping Jack Man and Dancing Board, Beech Creek, North Carolina, 1968

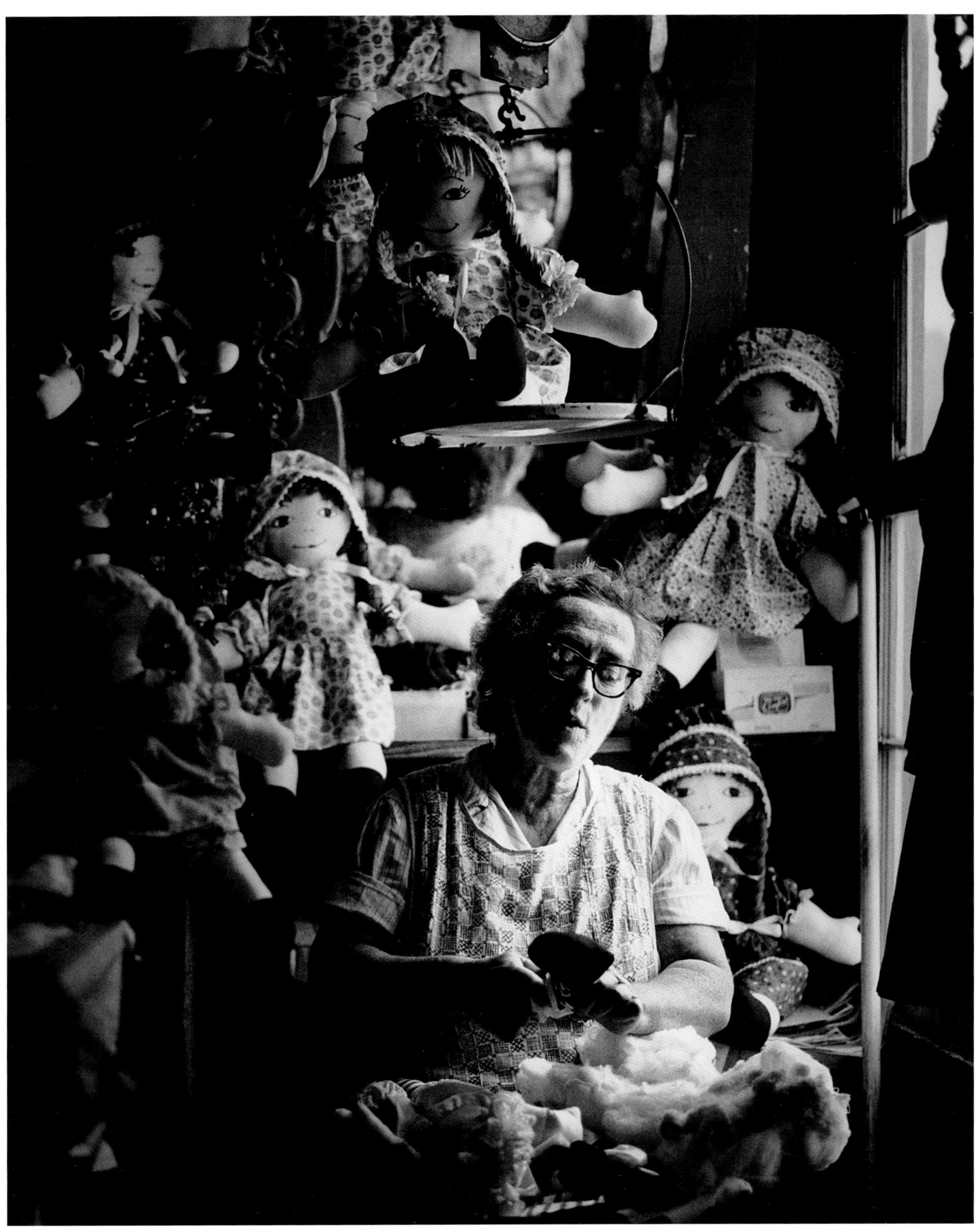

PLATE 7

Pearl Norwood, Maker of Raggedy Ann Dolls, Banner Elk, North Carolina, 1968

Contact sheet, Vicco, Kentucky, 1968
Gelatin silver print, 25.4 × 20.3 cm (10 × 8 in.)
Collection of the artist

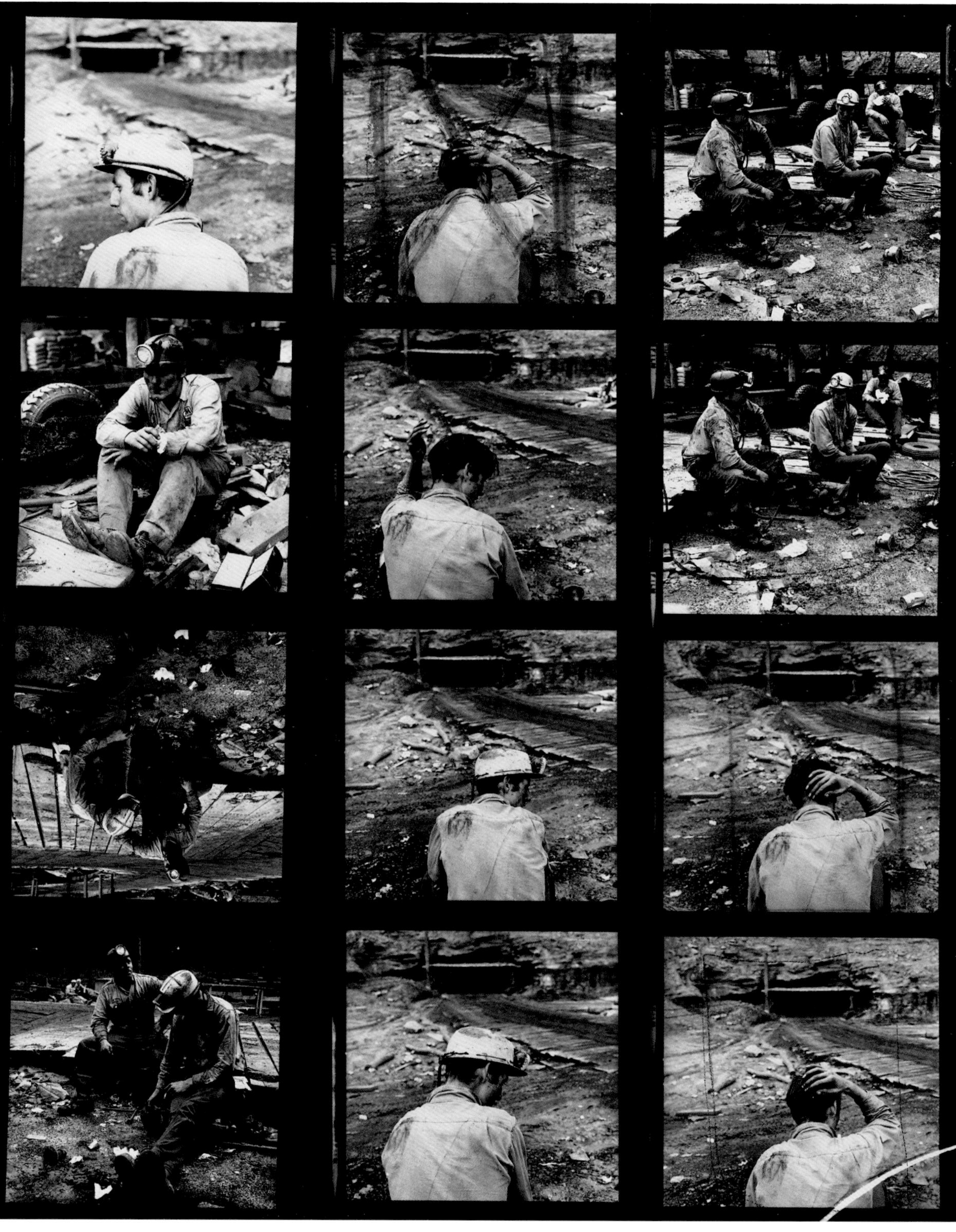

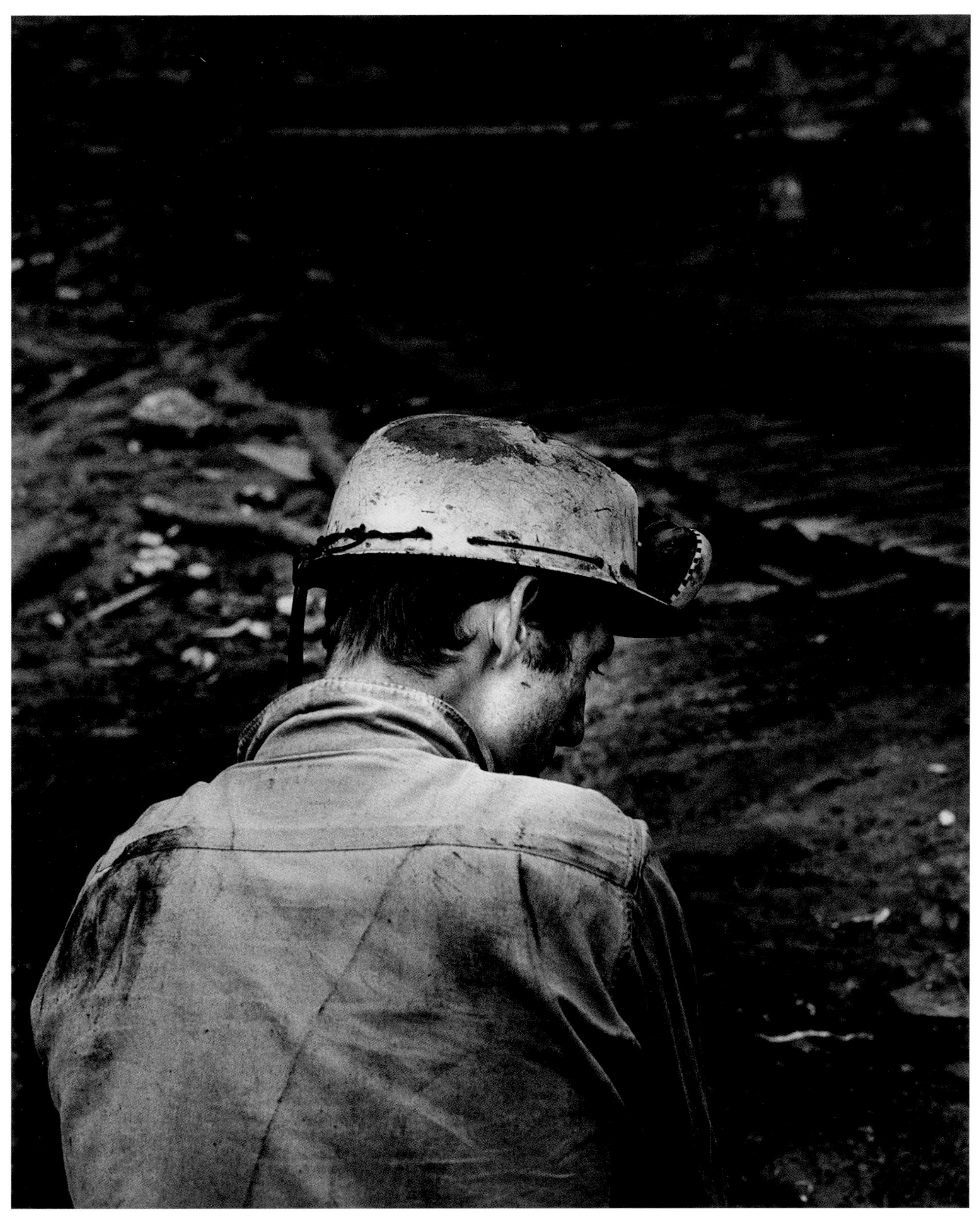

PLATE 8
Miner's Back, Vicco, Kentucky, 1968

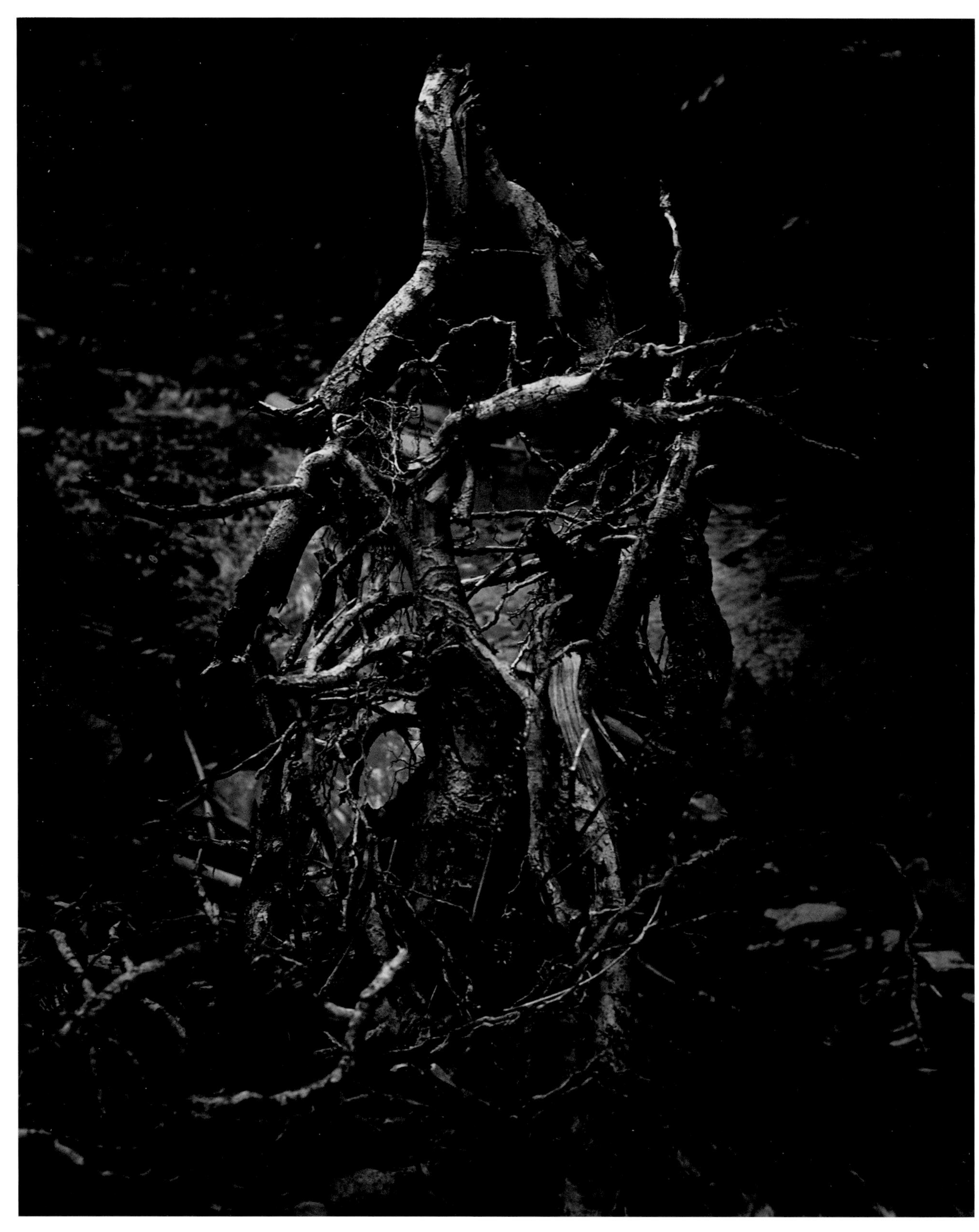

PLATE 9
Twisted Tree Roots, Lookout, Kentucky, 1968

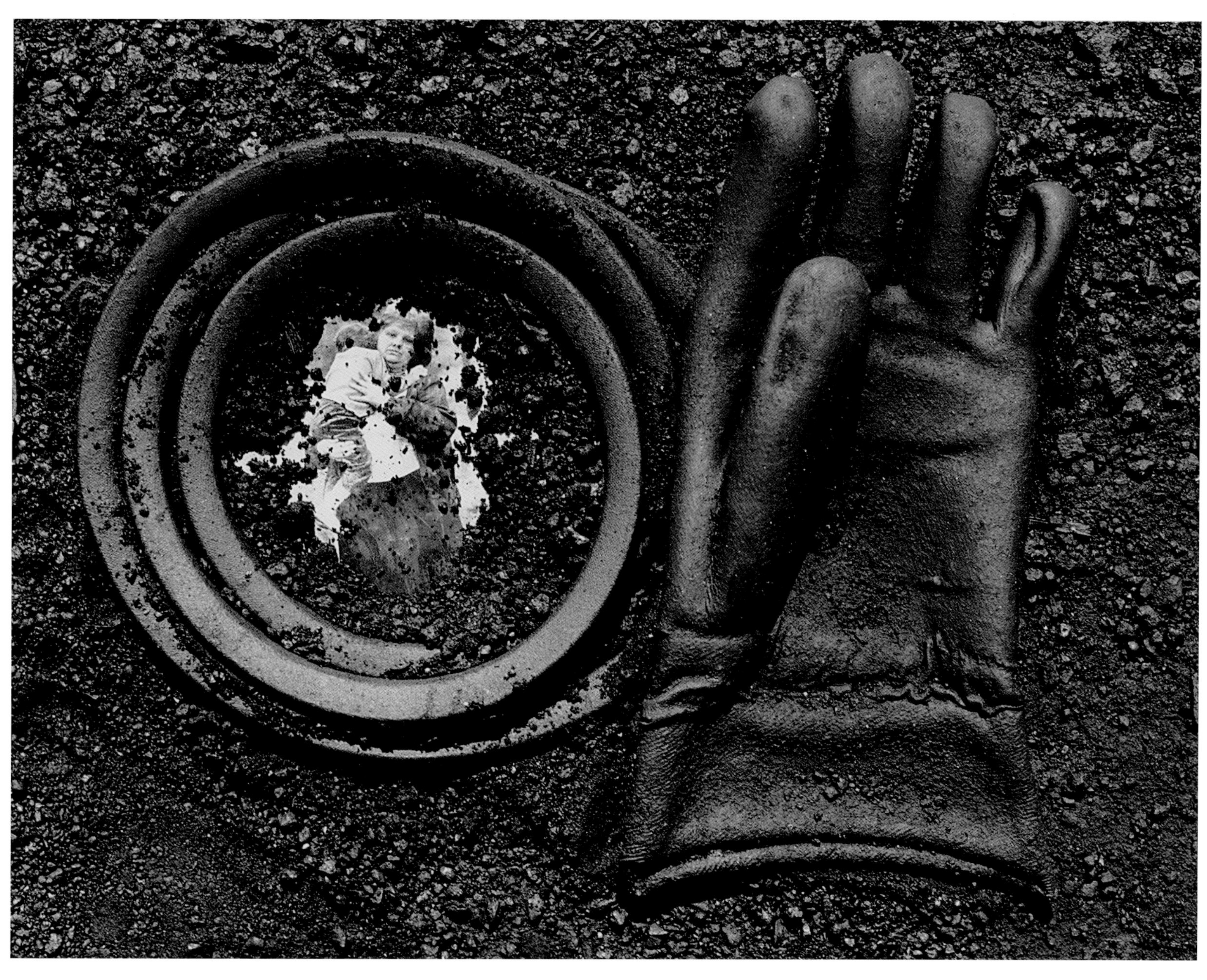

PLATE 10
Glove and Portrait, Welch, West Virginia, 1968

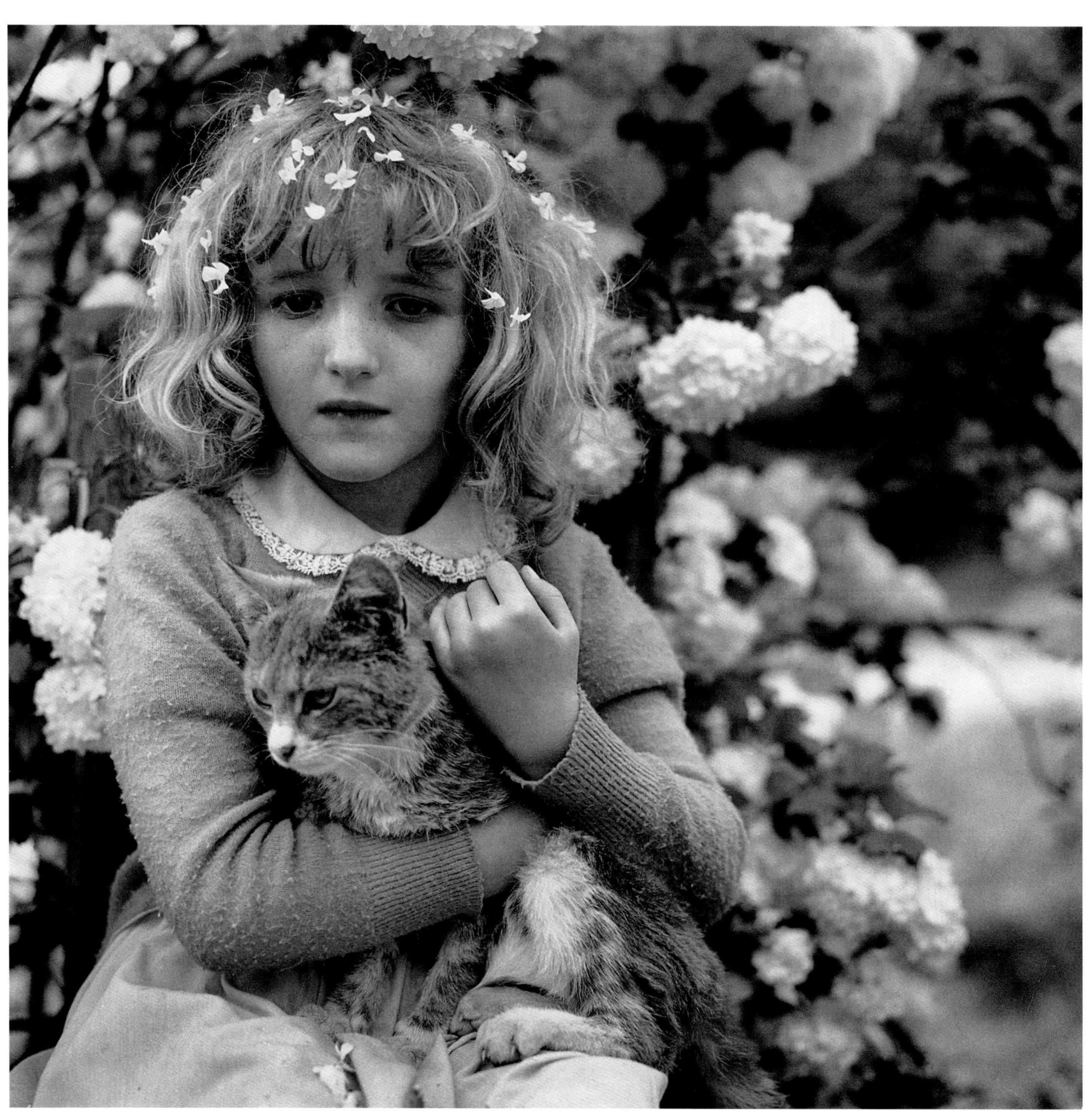

PLATE 11
Appalachian Girl Who Is Sick with Anemia, Lookout, Kentucky, 1968

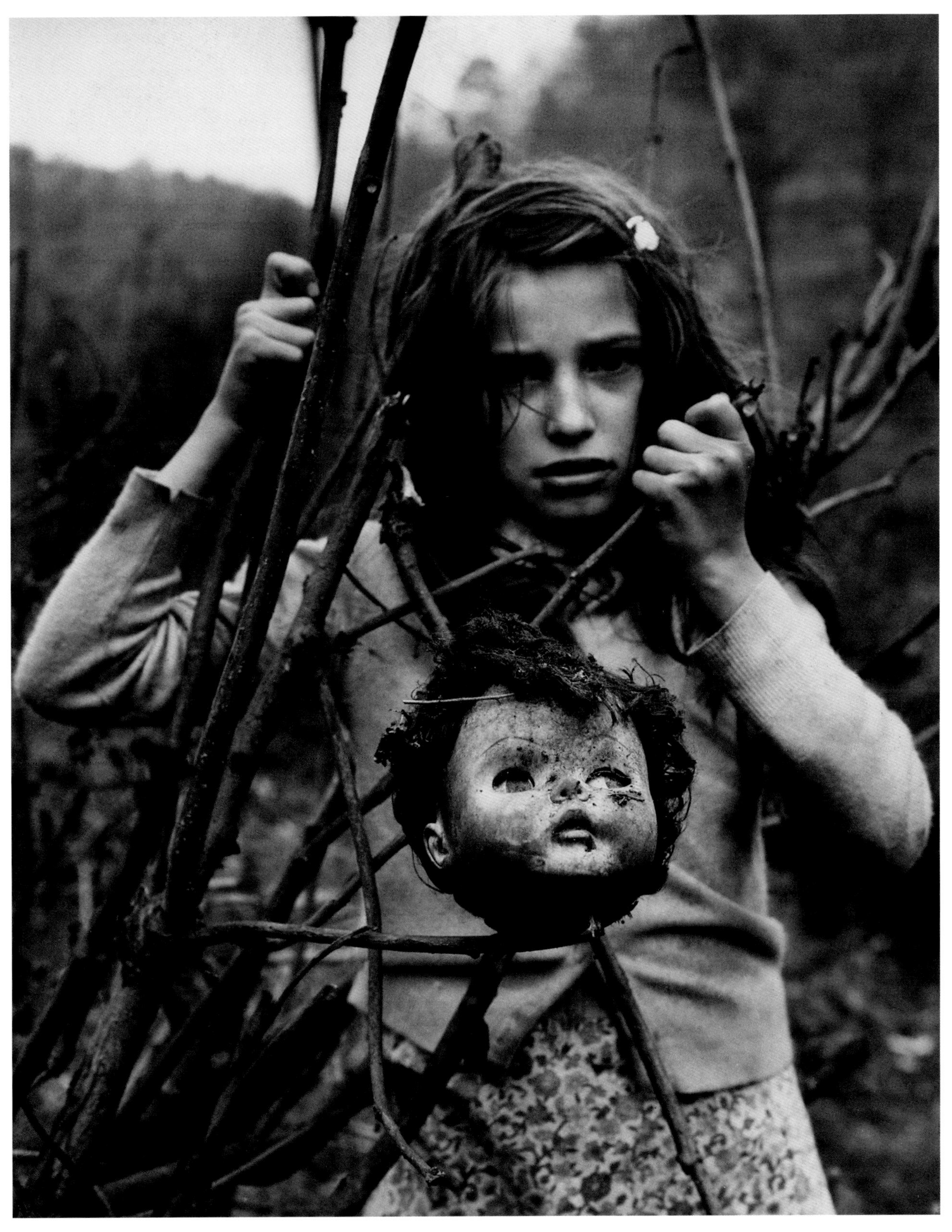

PLATE 12
Girl with Doll's Head, Capels, West Virginia, 1968

The Ramble

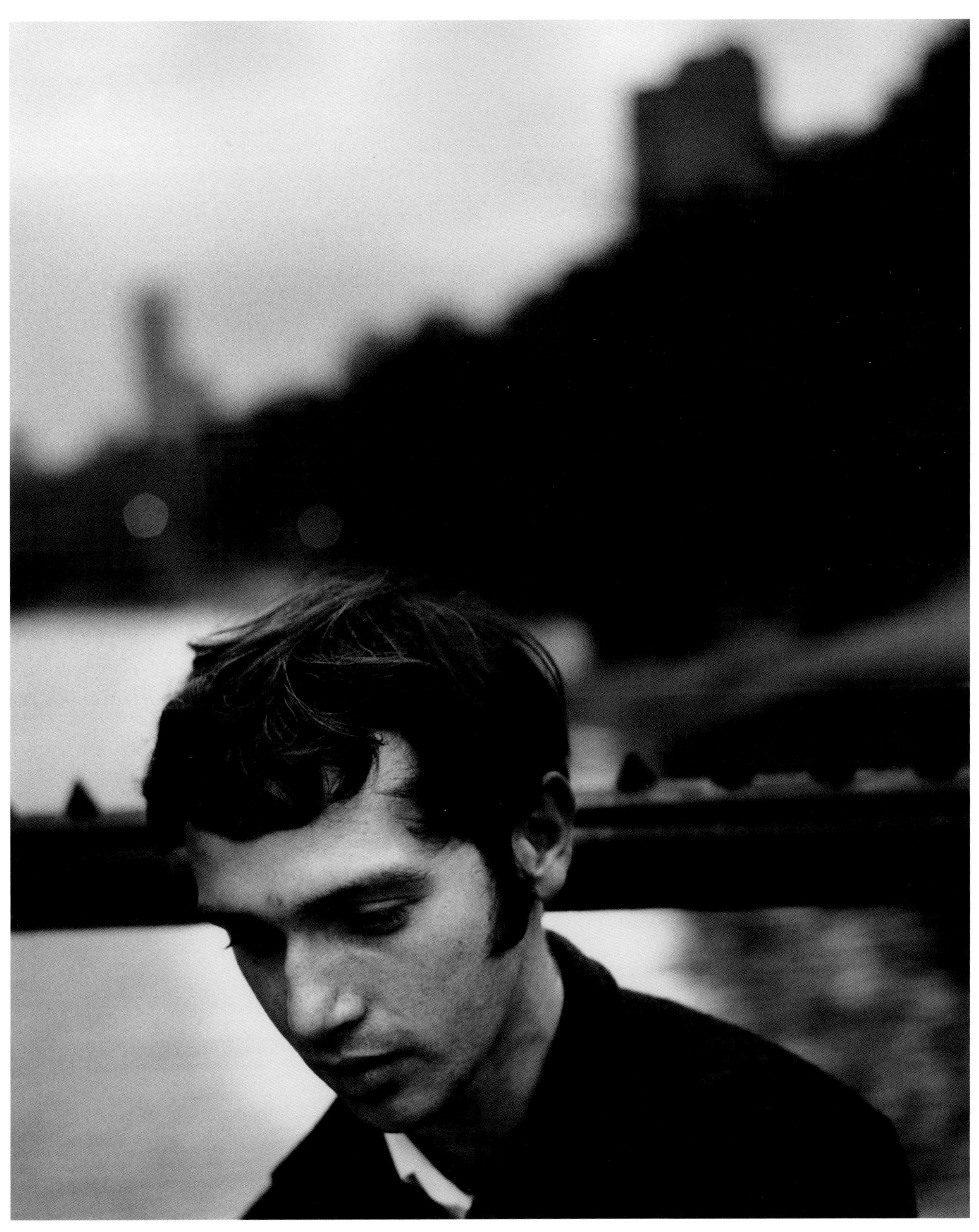

PLATE 13
Young Man on Bridge, Central Park, New York, 1969

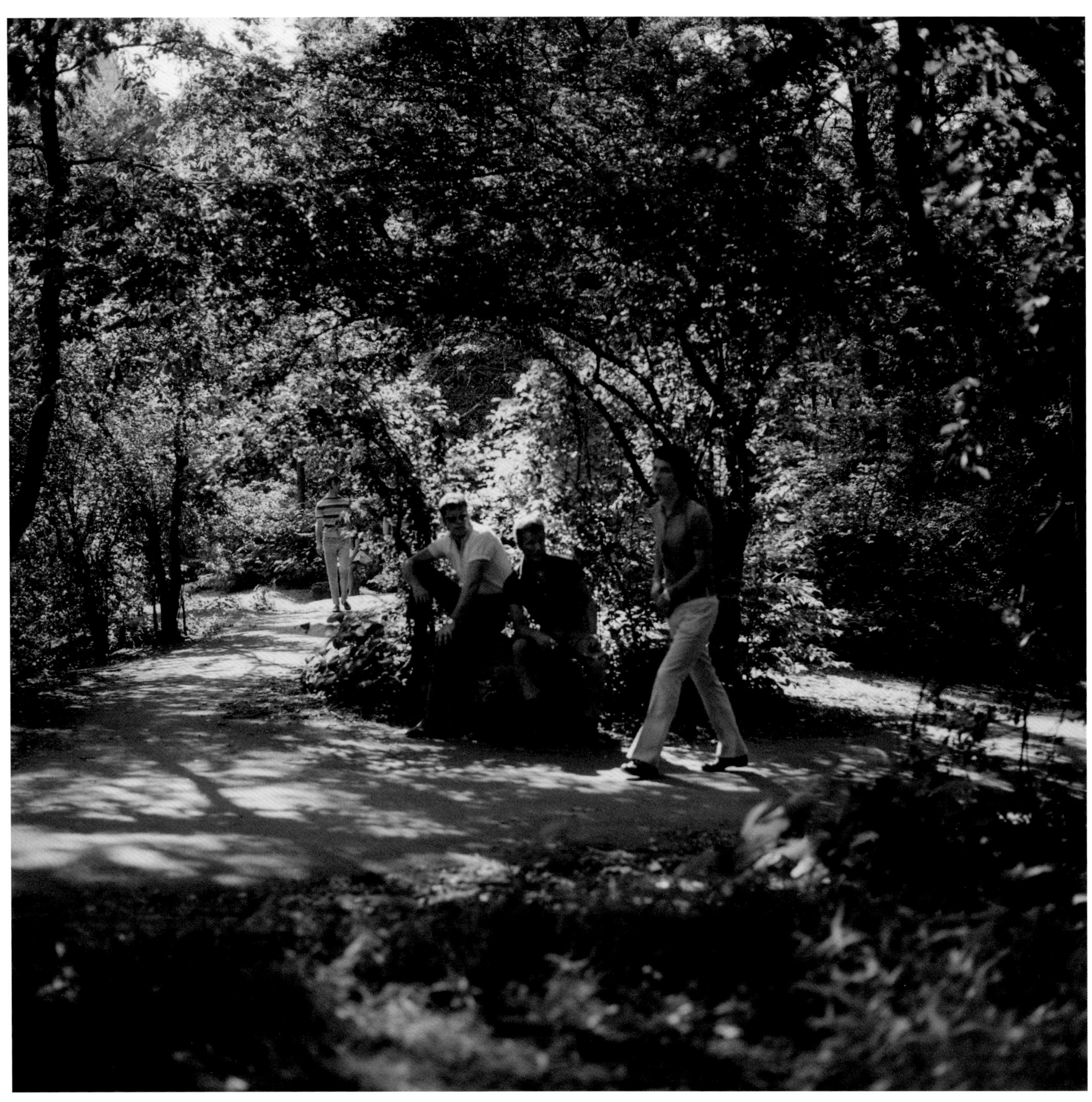

PLATE 14
Watching, Central Park, New York, negative, 1969; print 2007

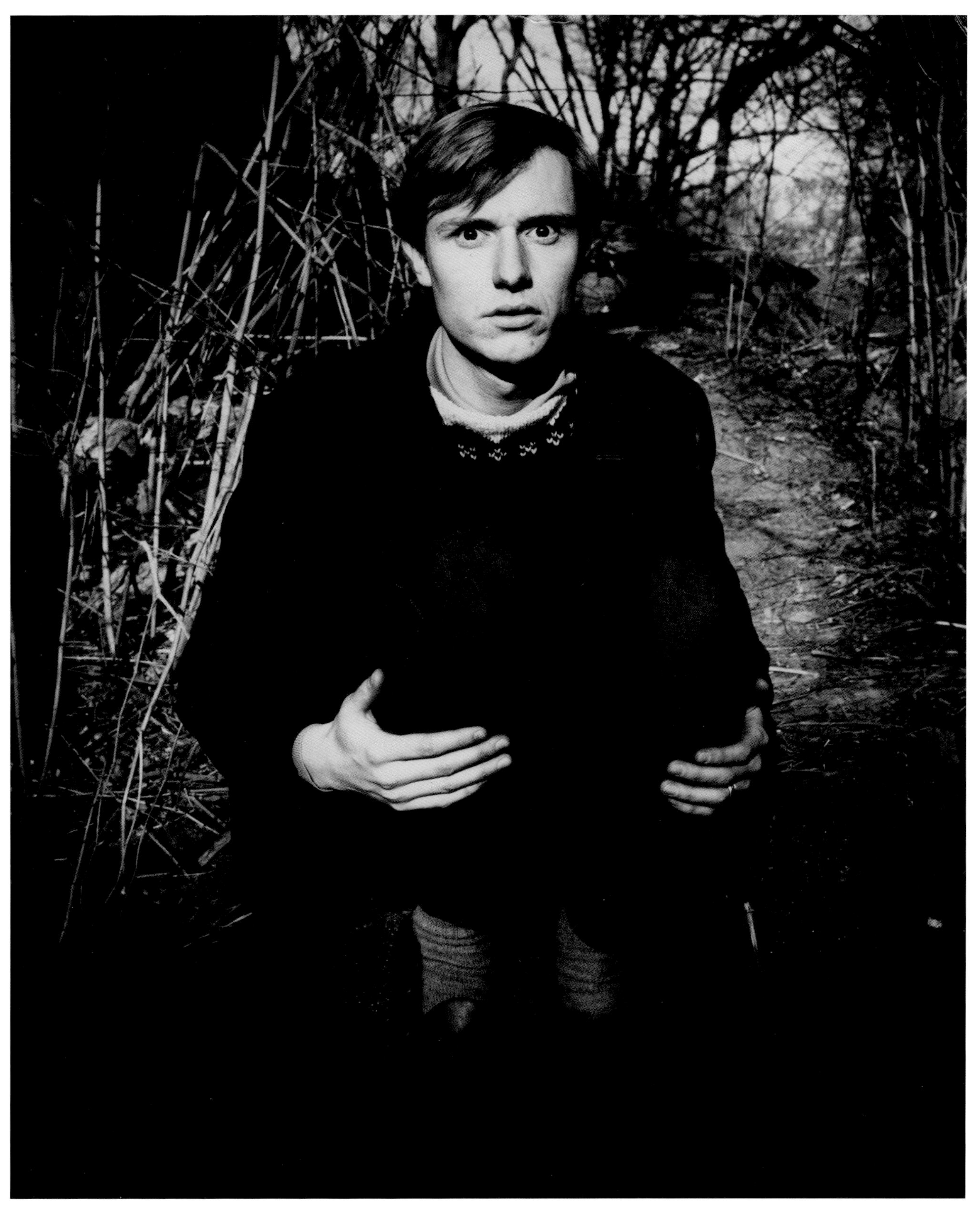

PLATE 15
Young Man in Woods, Central Park, New York, 1969

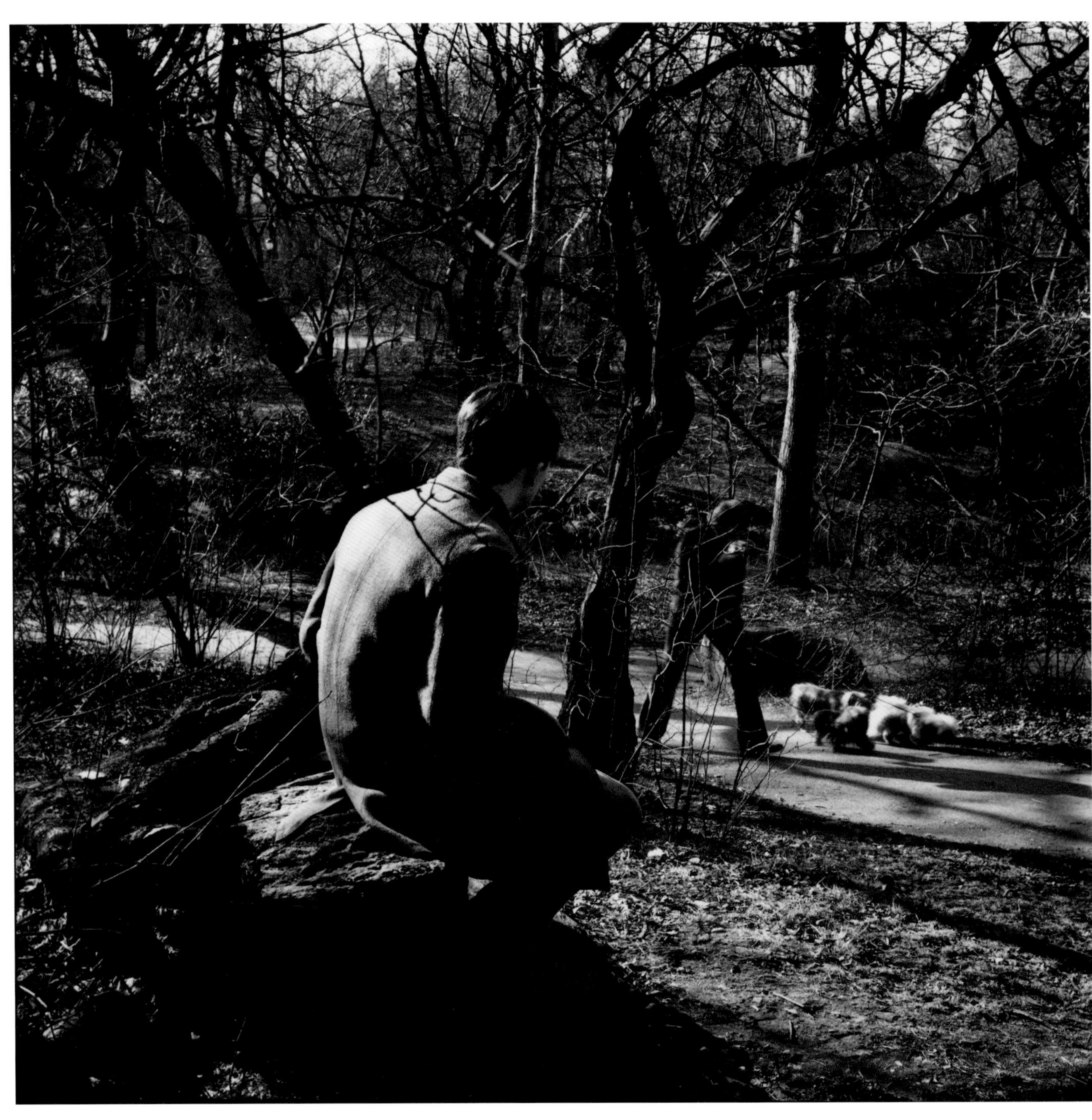

PLATE 16
Dog Walker, Central Park, New York, negative 1969; print 2007

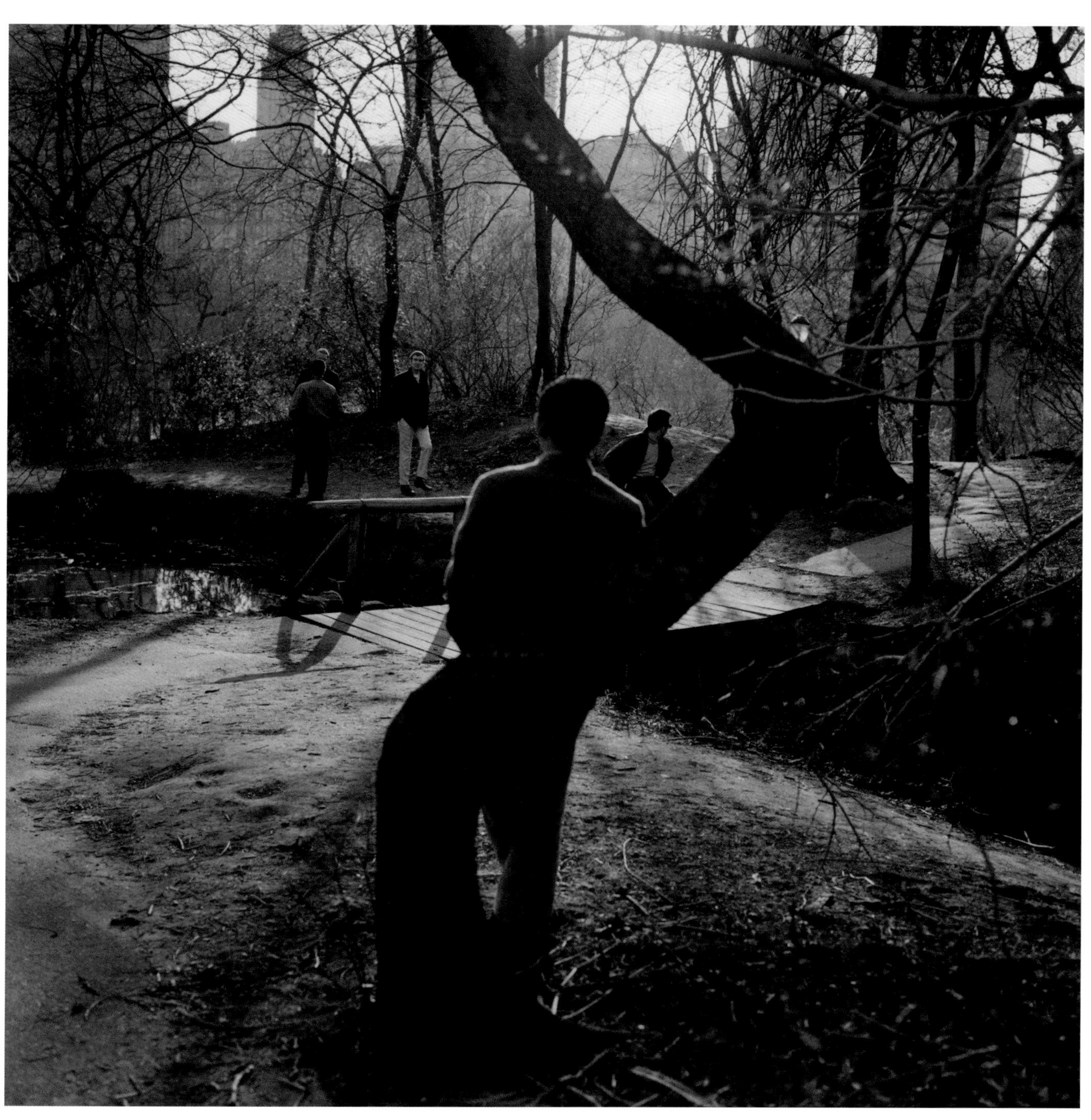

PLATE 17
In the Woods, Central Park, New York, negative 1969; print 2007

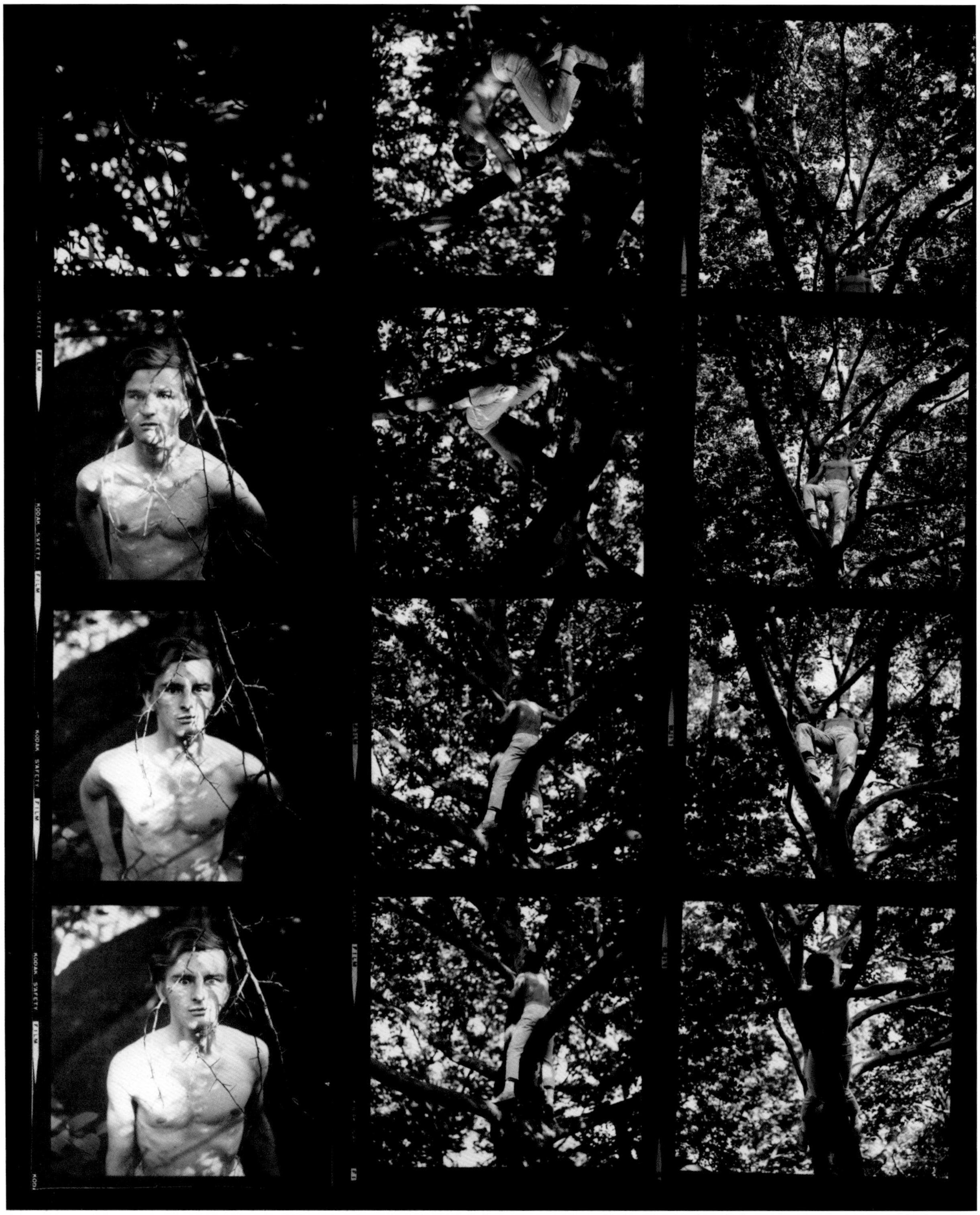

Contact sheet, Central Park,
New York, 1969
Gelatin silver print,
25.4 × 20.3 cm
(10 × 8 in.)
Collection of the artist

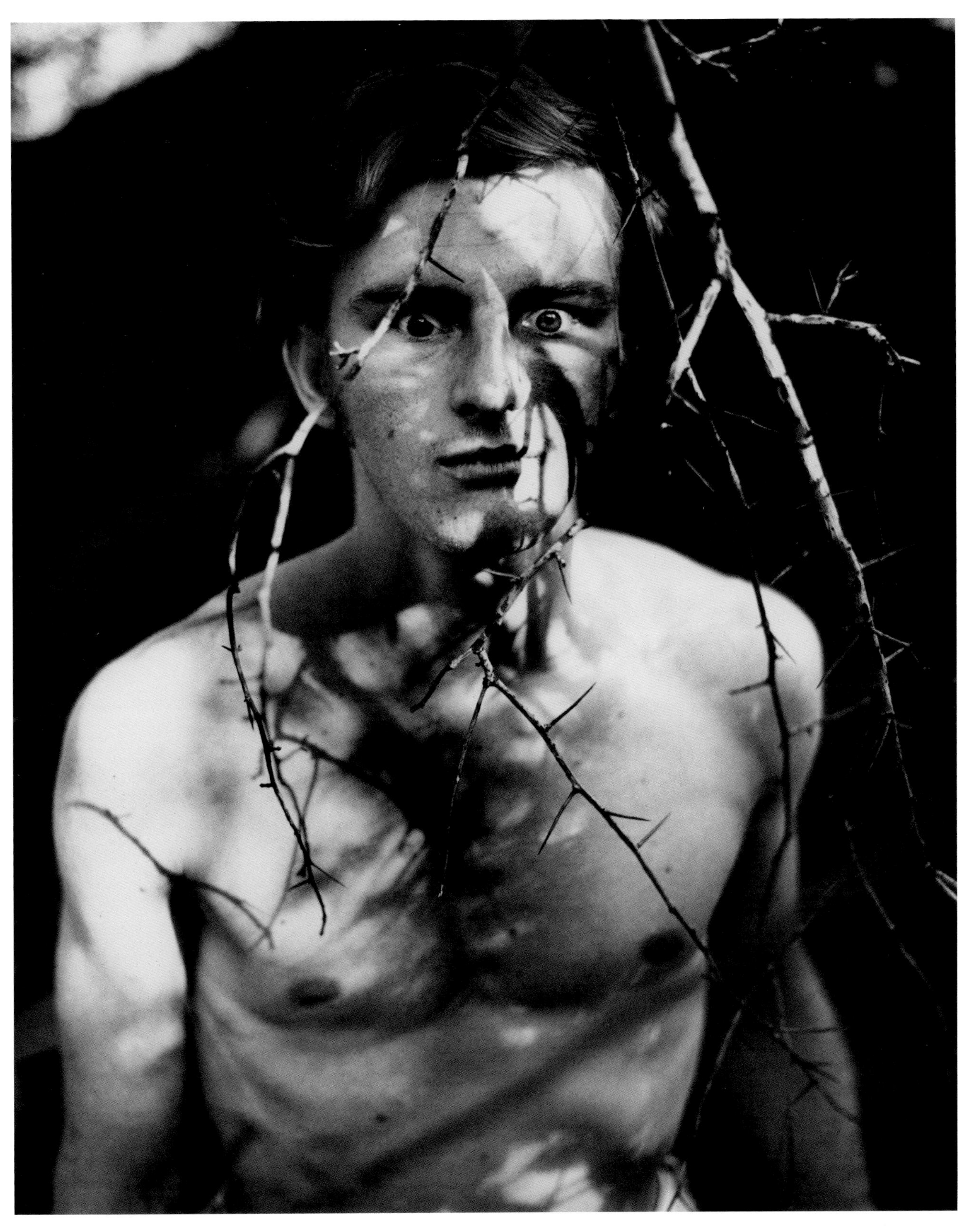

PLATE 18
Boy in Central Park, New York, 1969

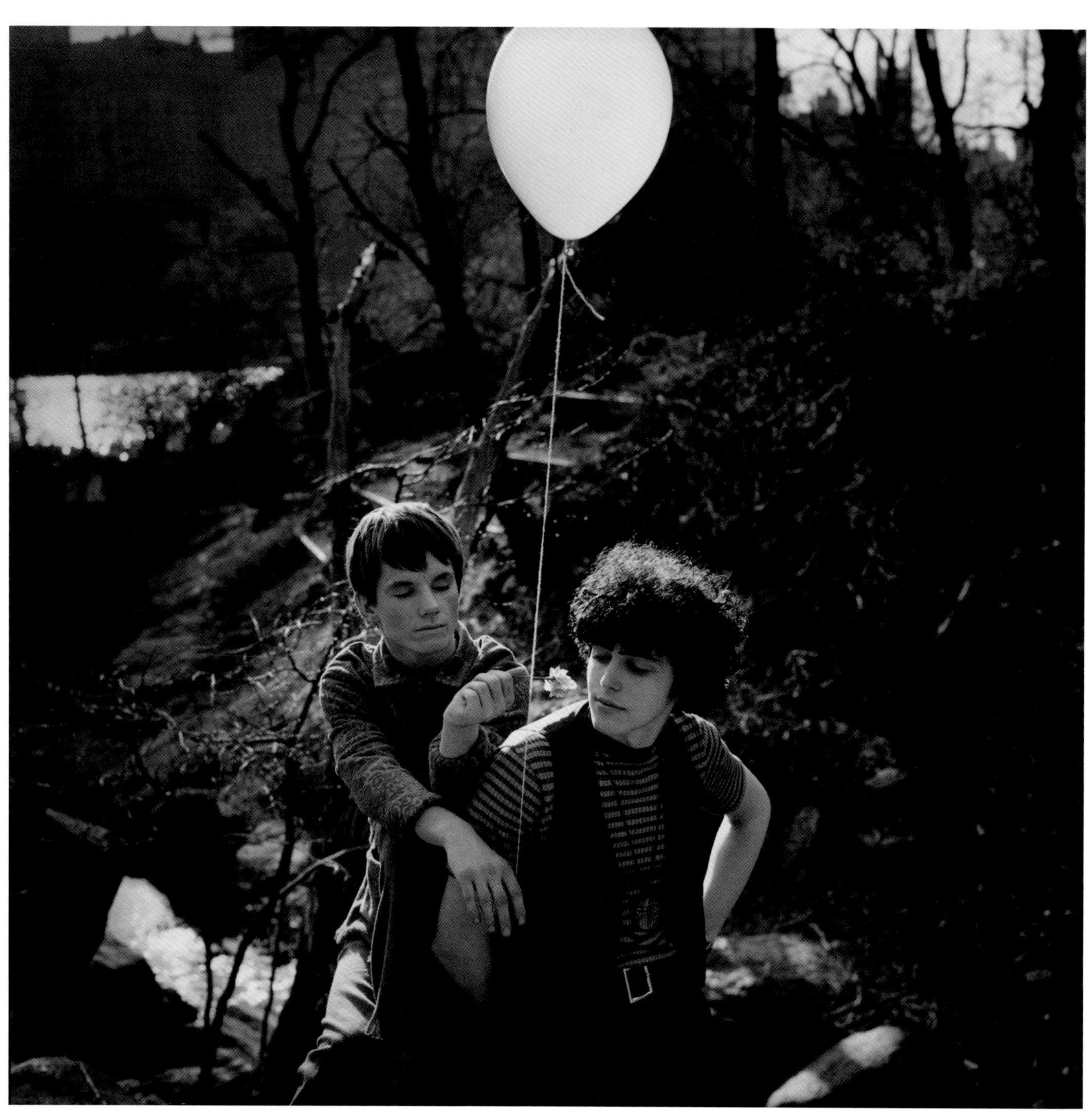

PLATE 19
Two Boys in Central Park, New York, negative 1969; print 2007

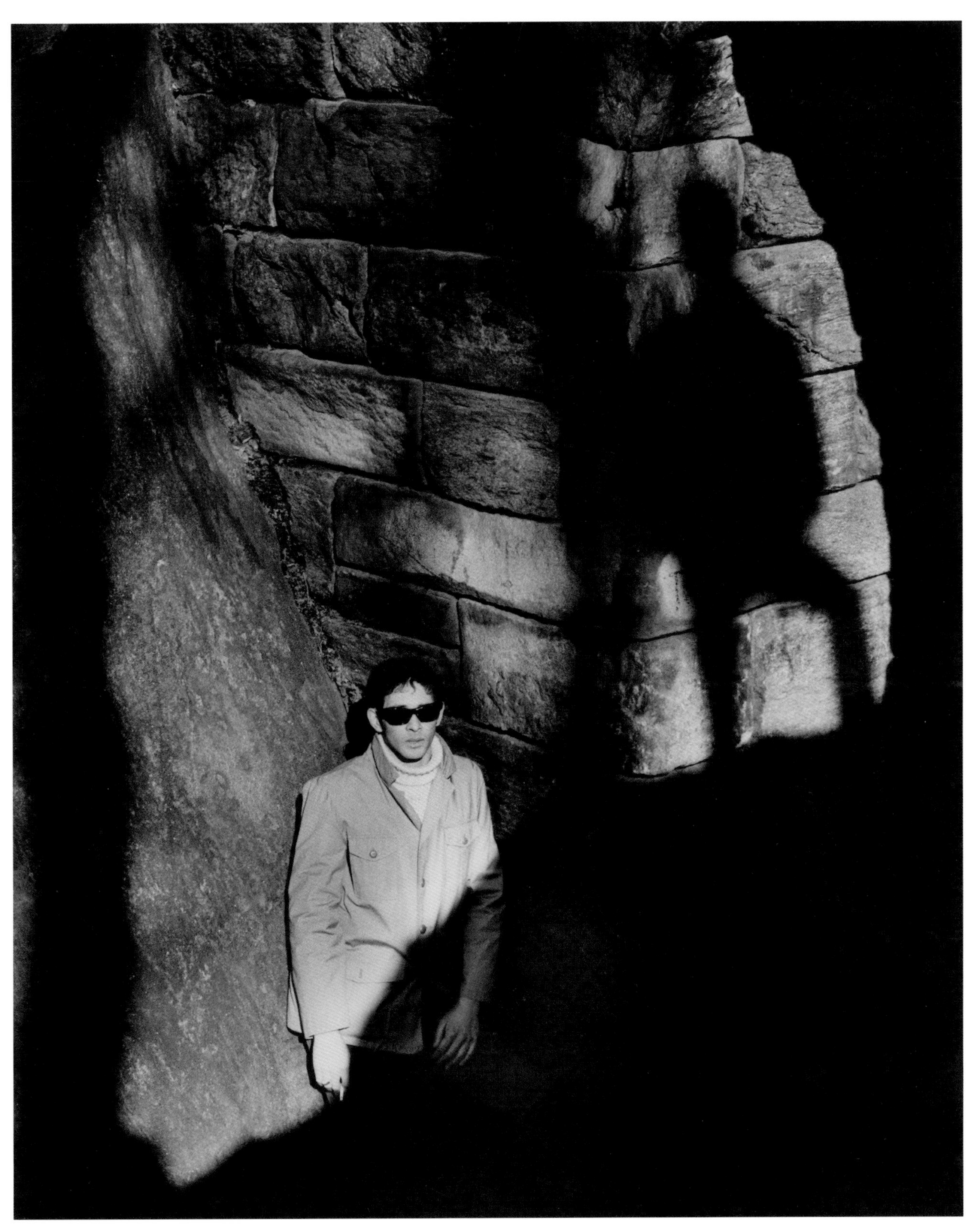

PLATE 20
Two Men Cruising, Central Park, New York, 1969

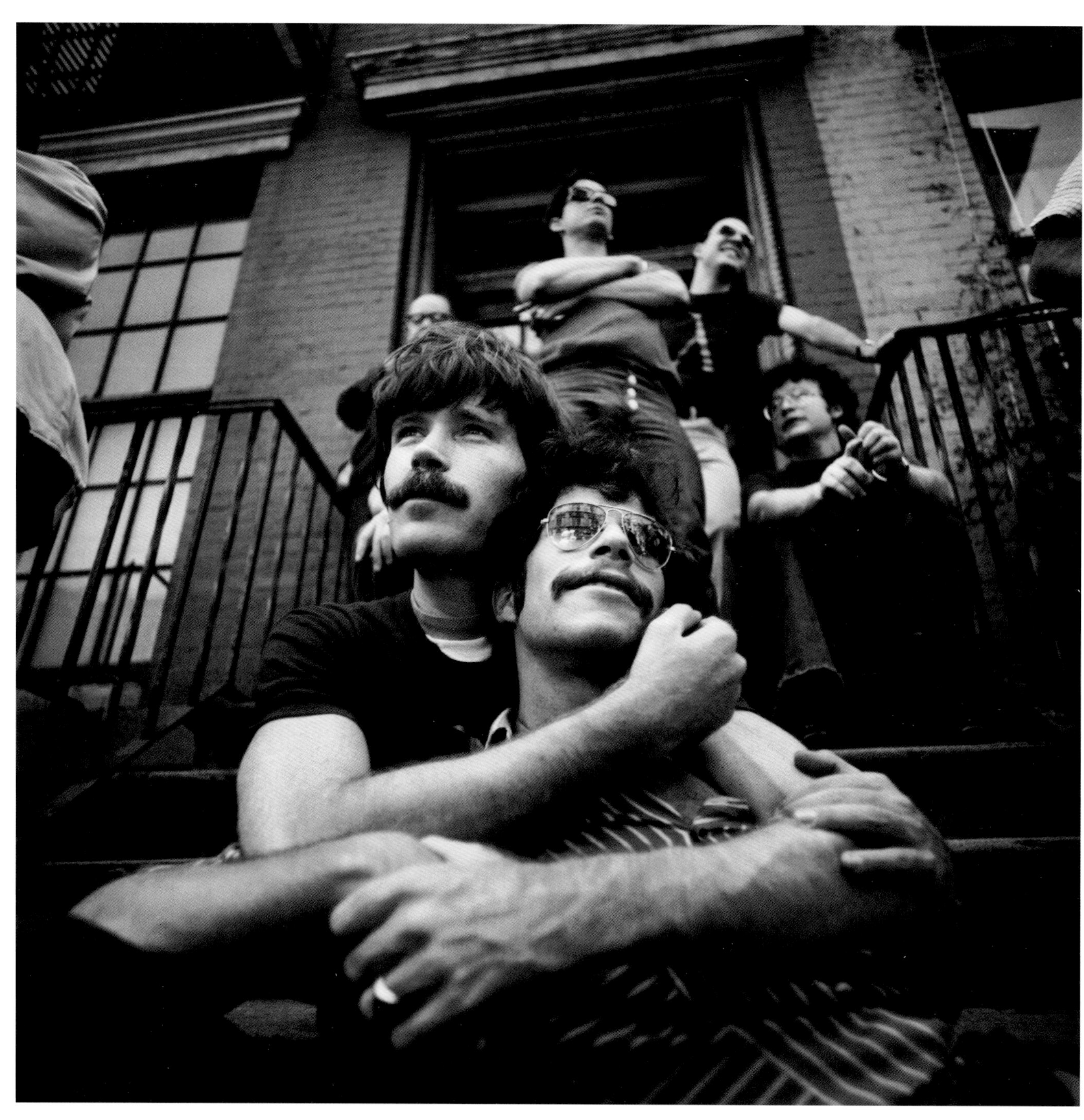

PLATE 21
Gay Activists at First Gay Pride Parade, Christopher Street, New York, negative 1970; print 2021

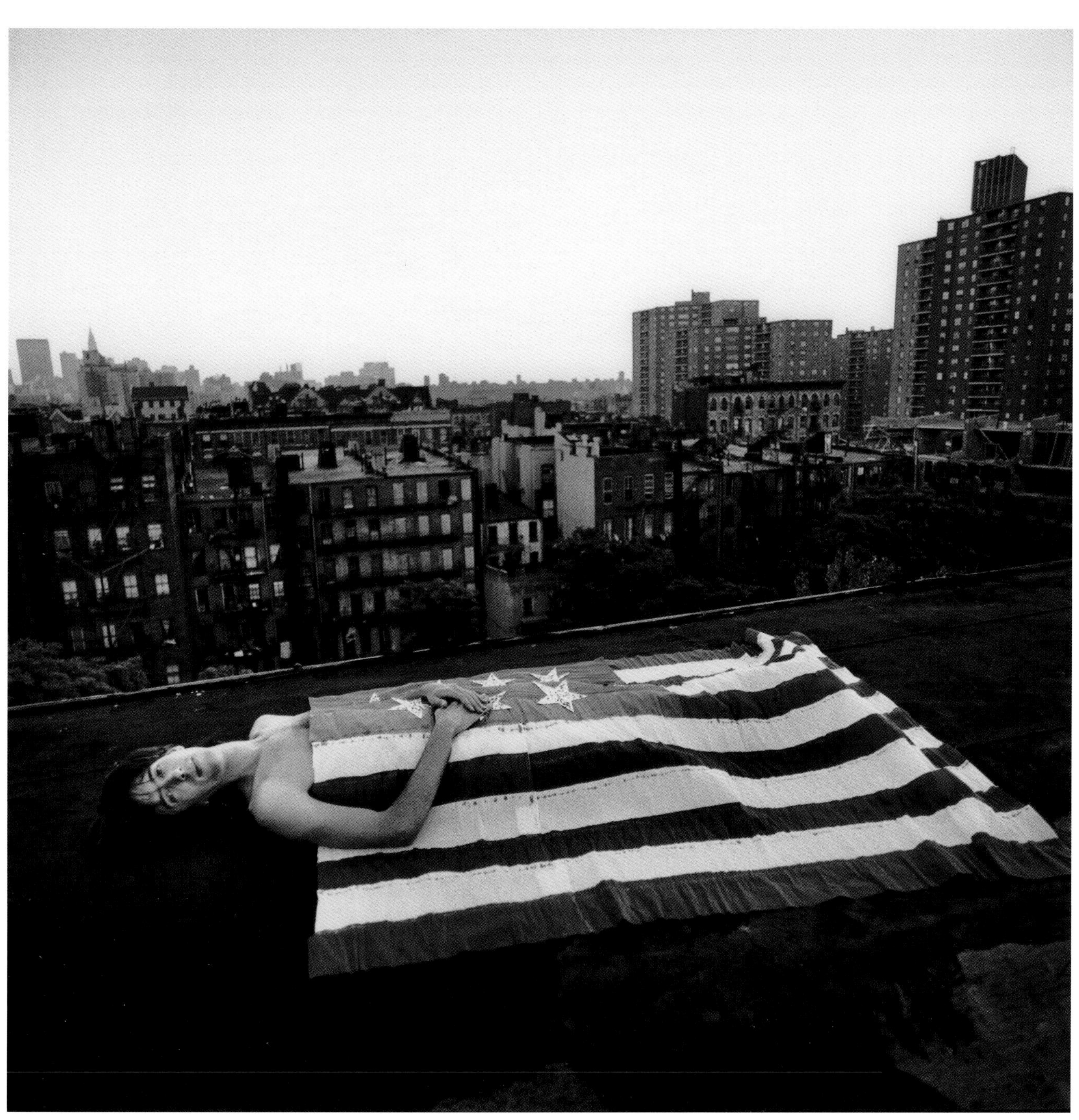

PLATE 22
Bruce at Dawn, Paper Flower Maker, East Village, New York, negative 1970; print 2021

Open Space in the Inner City

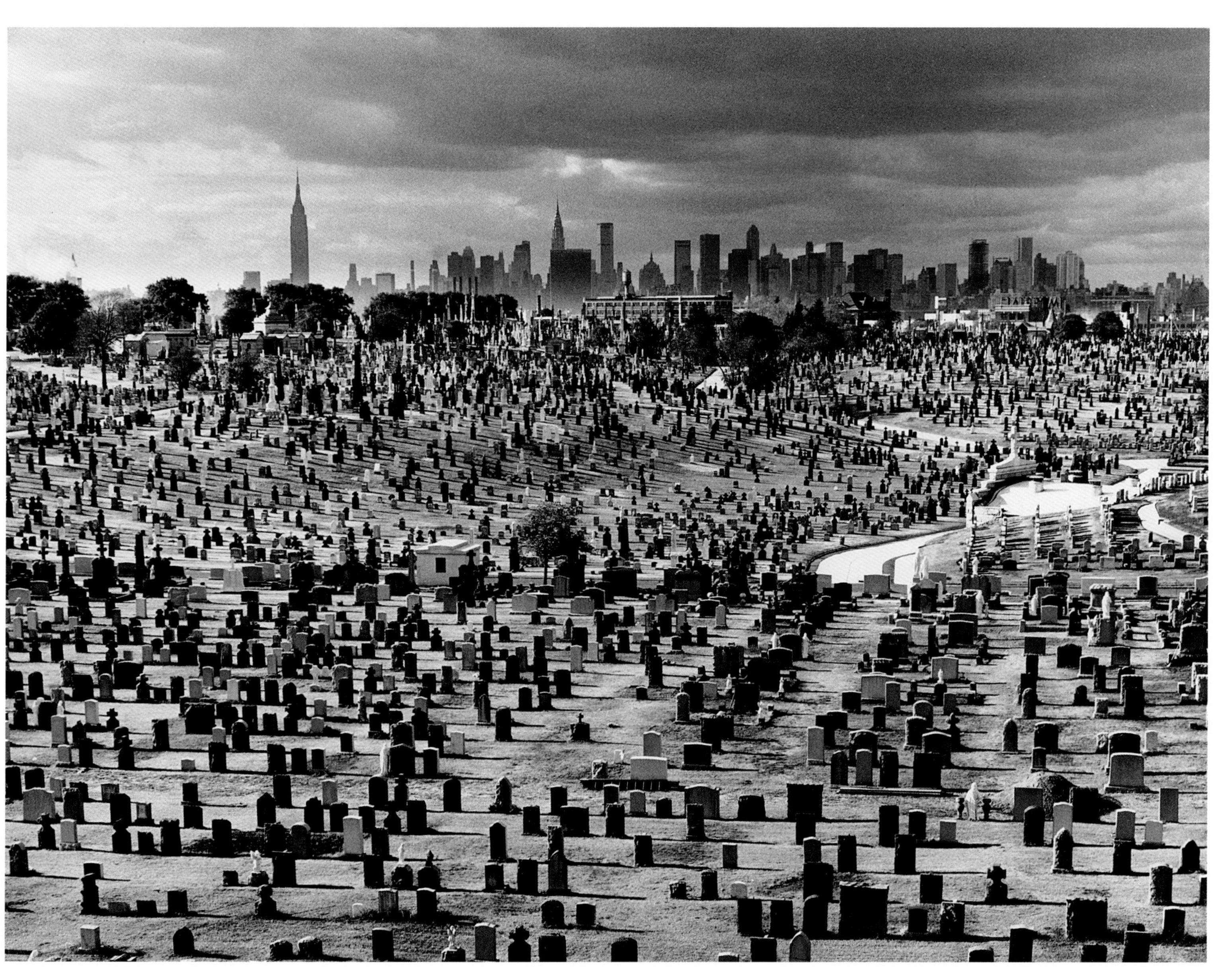

PLATE 23
Cemetery, Queens, New York, 1969

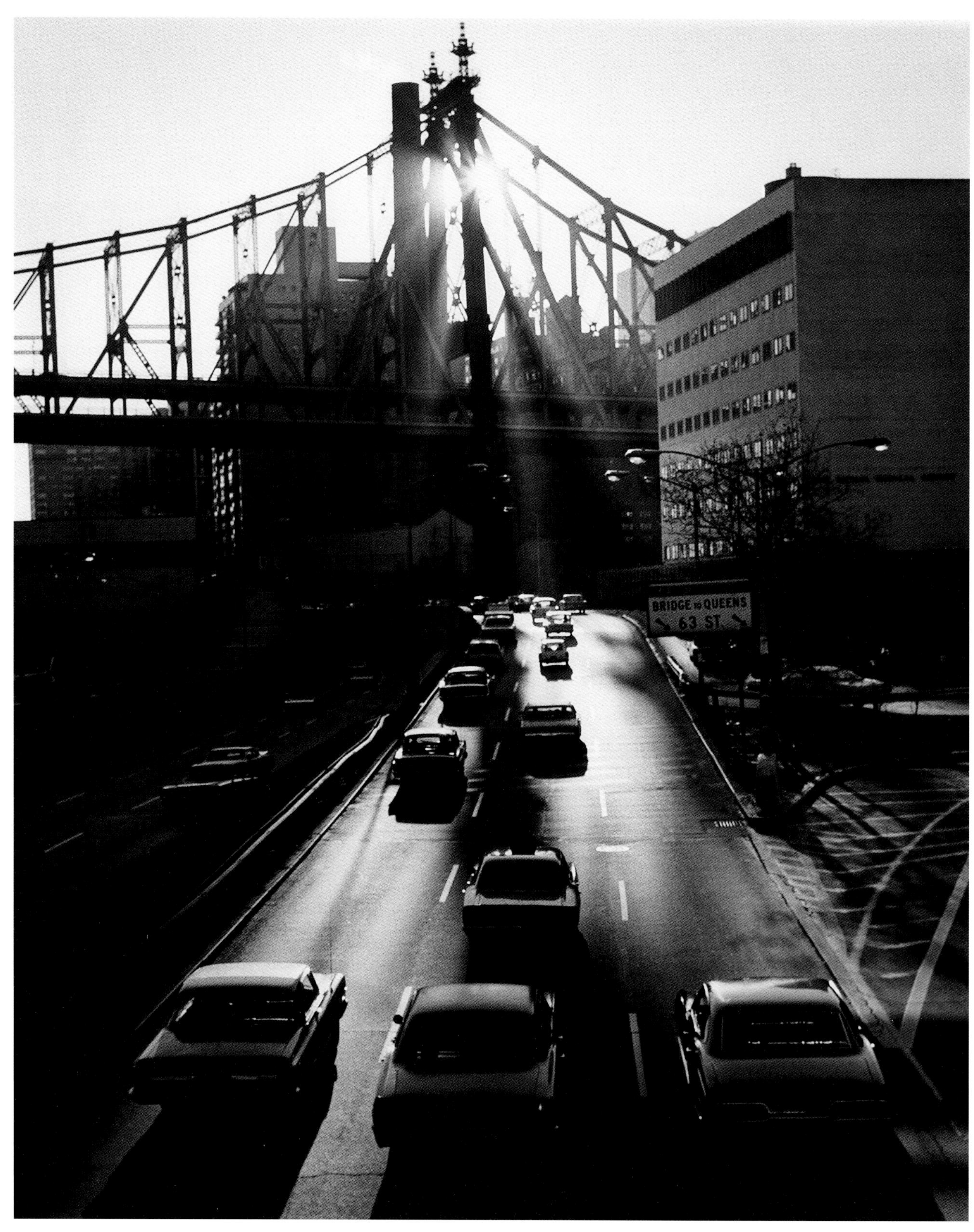

PLATE 24
Expressway, New York, New York, 1969

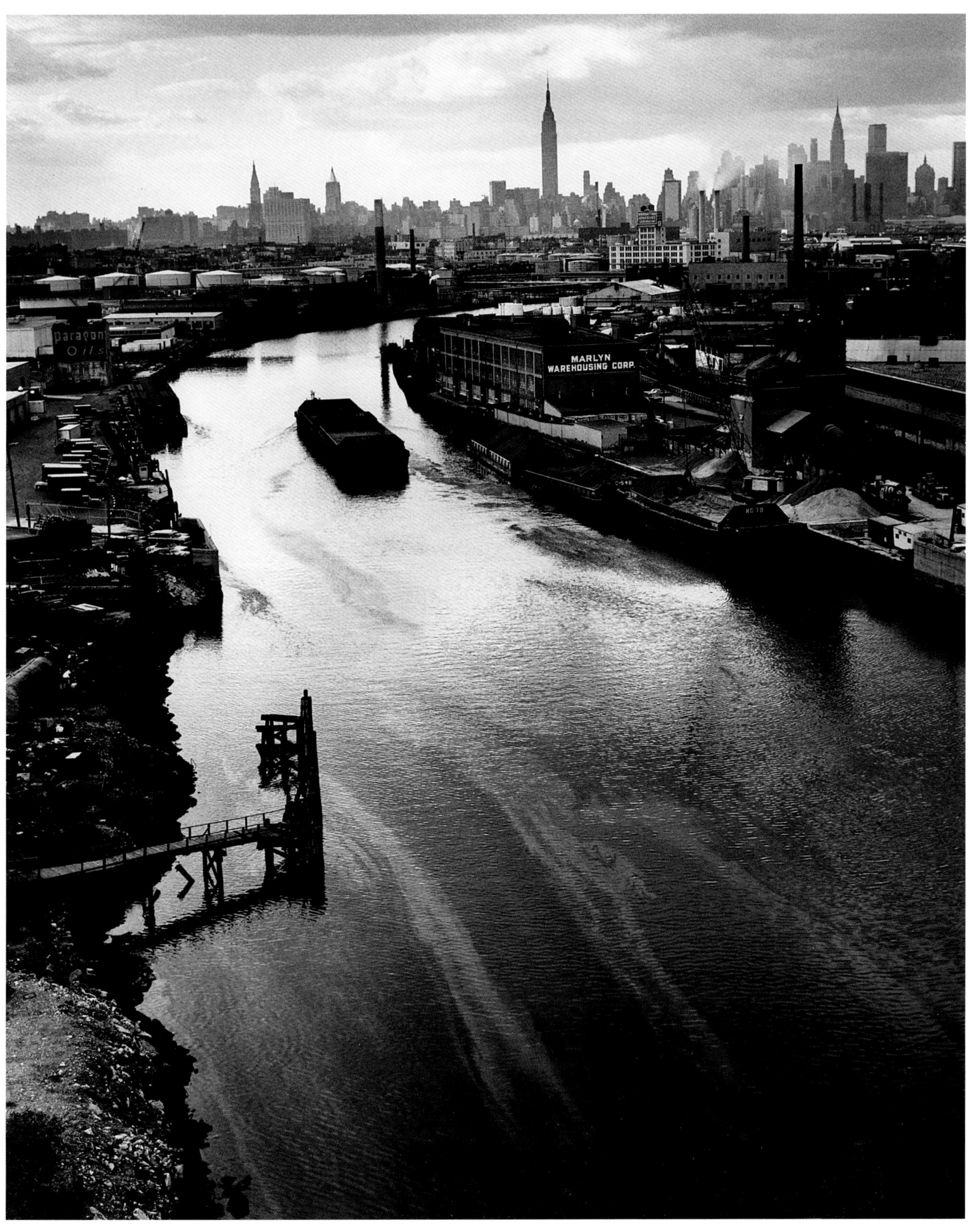

PLATE 25
Newton Creek, New York, New York, 1969

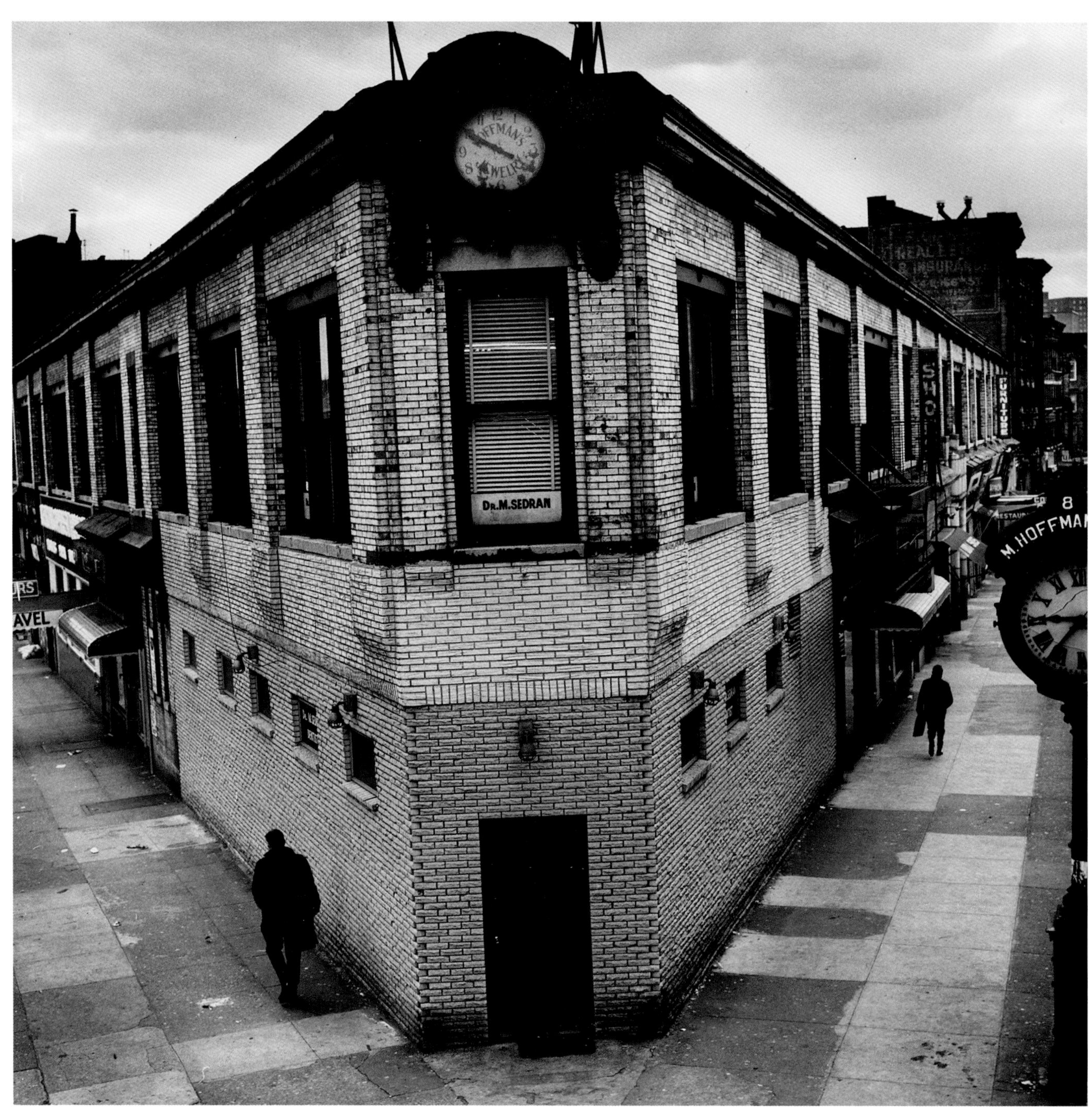

PLATE 26
Two Streets, Two Clocks, Bronx, New York, 1969

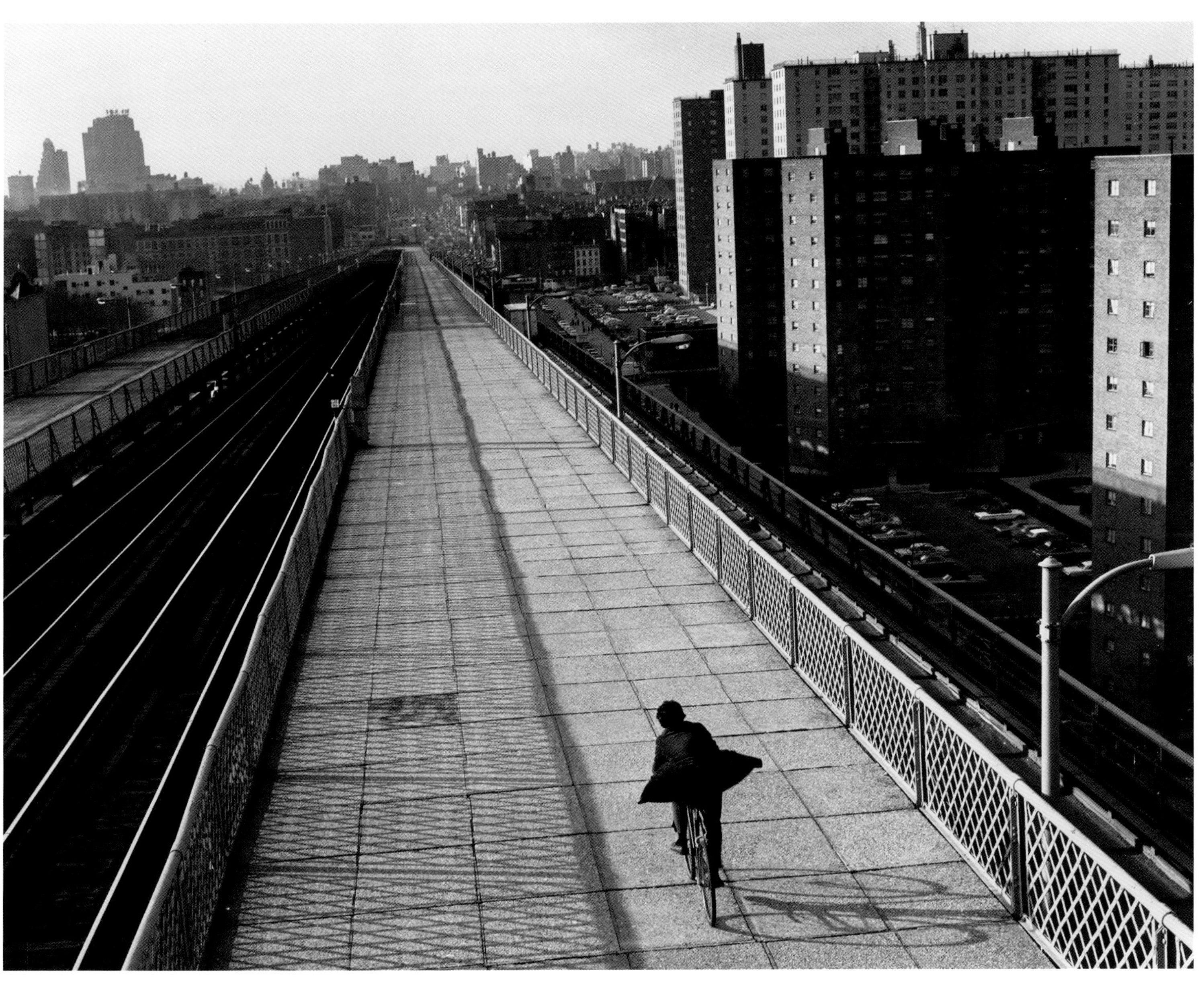

PLATE 27
Boy on Bike Crossing Williamsburg Bridge, New York, 1969

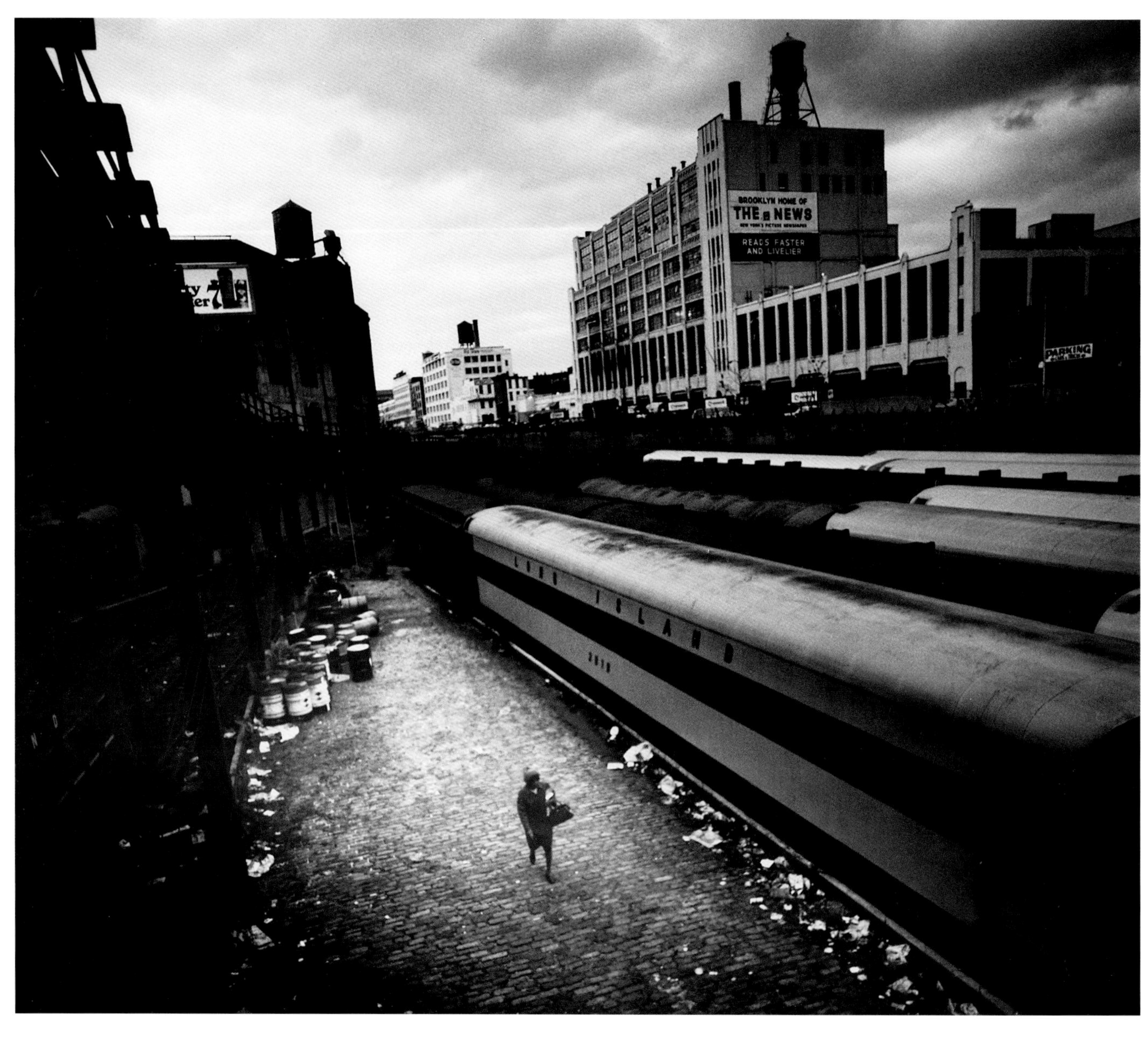

PLATE 28
Woman in Railroad Yard, Brooklyn, New York, 1969

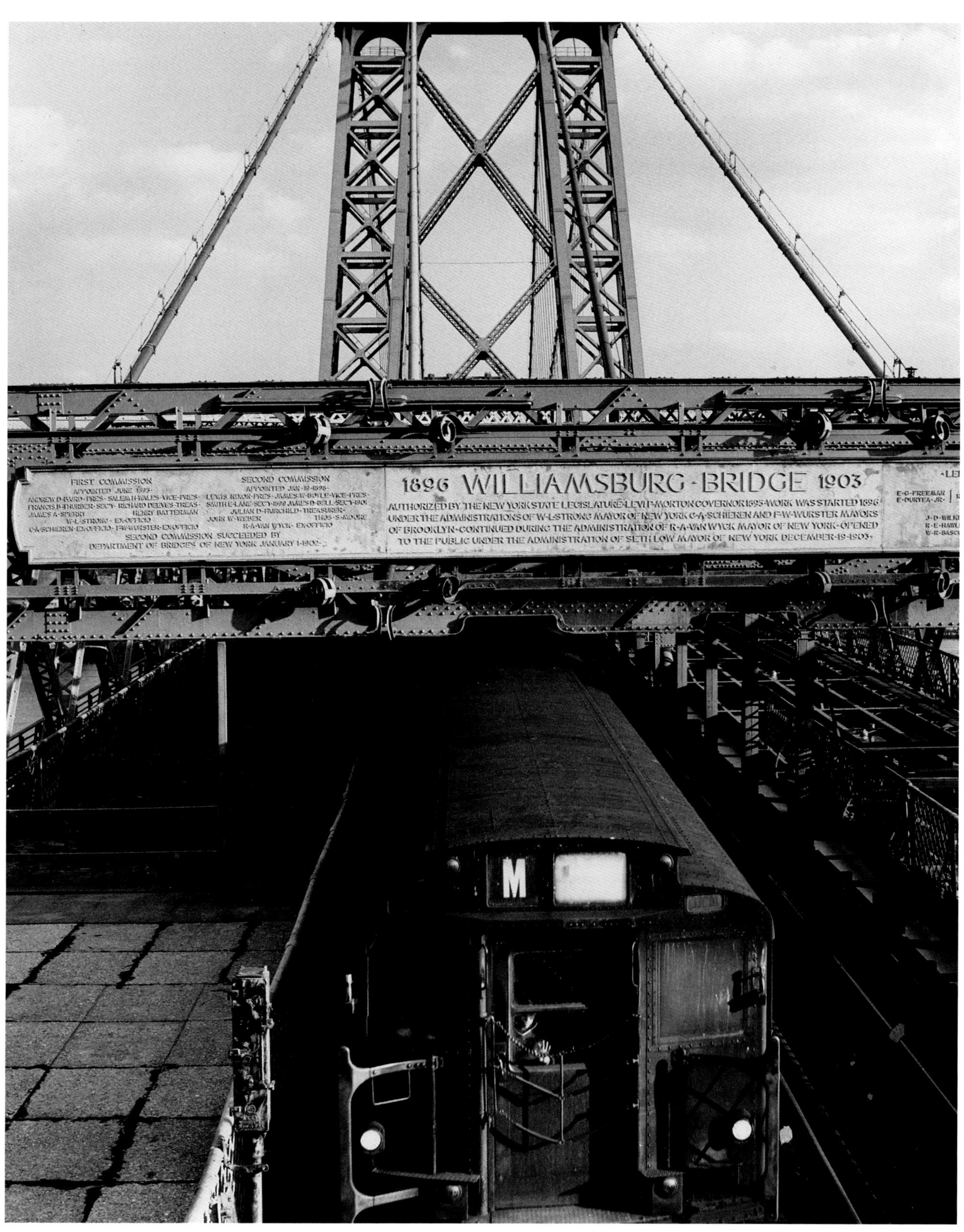

PLATE 29
Boy on Subway Car, Williamsburg Bridge, New York, 1969

Contact sheet, New York,
New York, 1969
Gelatin silver print,
25.4 × 20.3 cm
(10 × 8 in.)
Collection of the artist

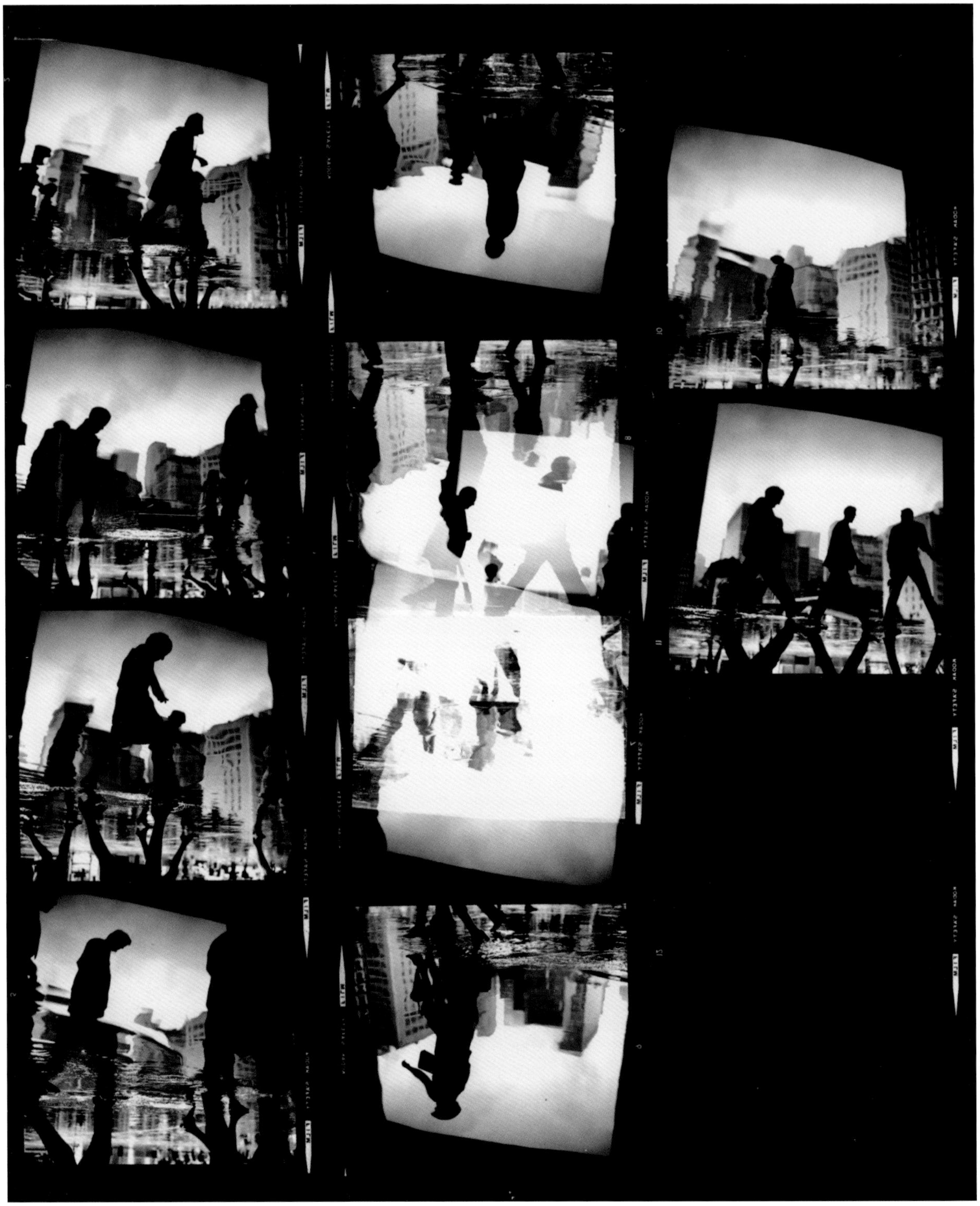

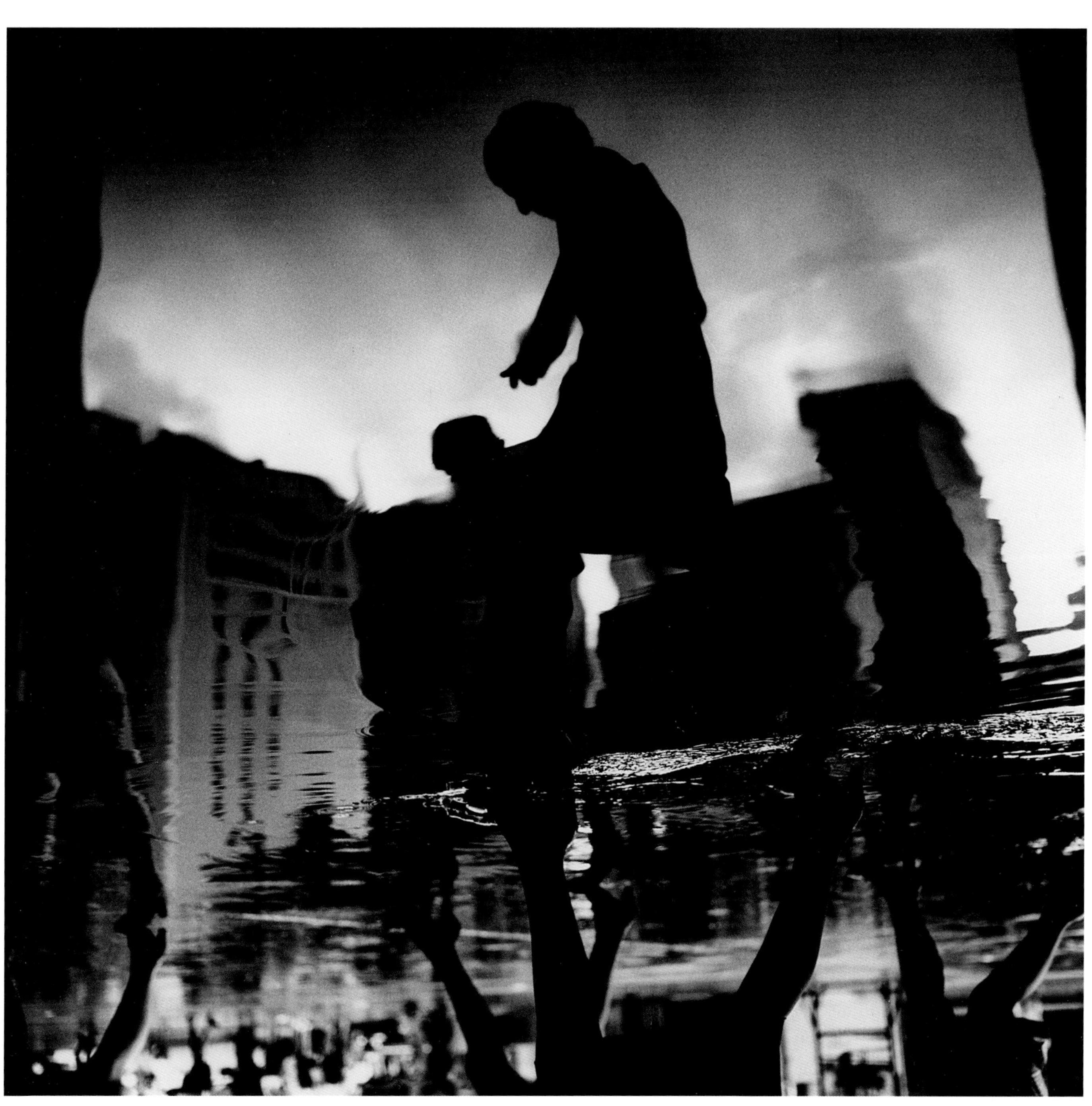

PLATE 30
Office Workers Returning Home, New York, New York, negative 1969; print later

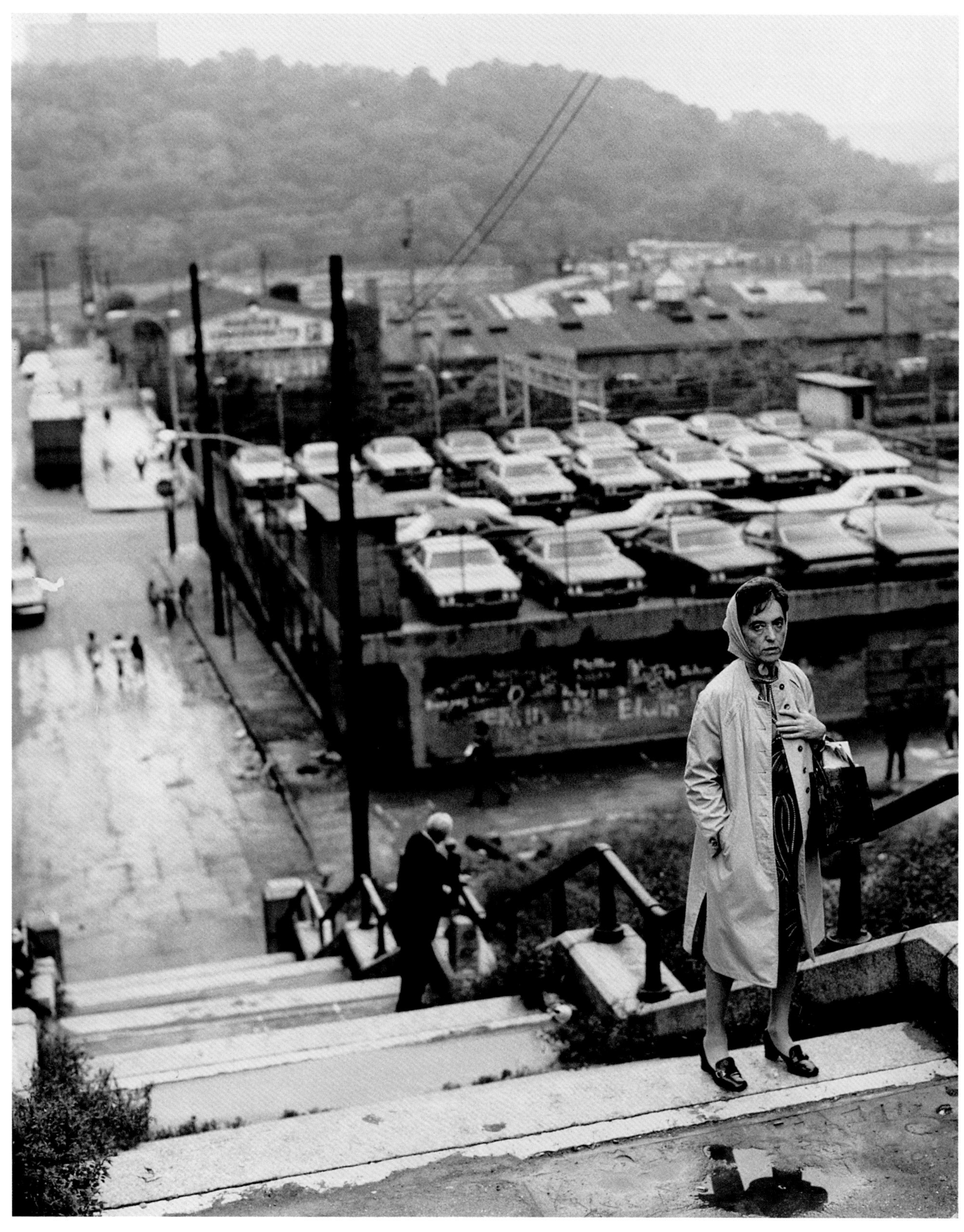

PLATE 31
Woman Climbing Steps, Bronx, New York, 1969

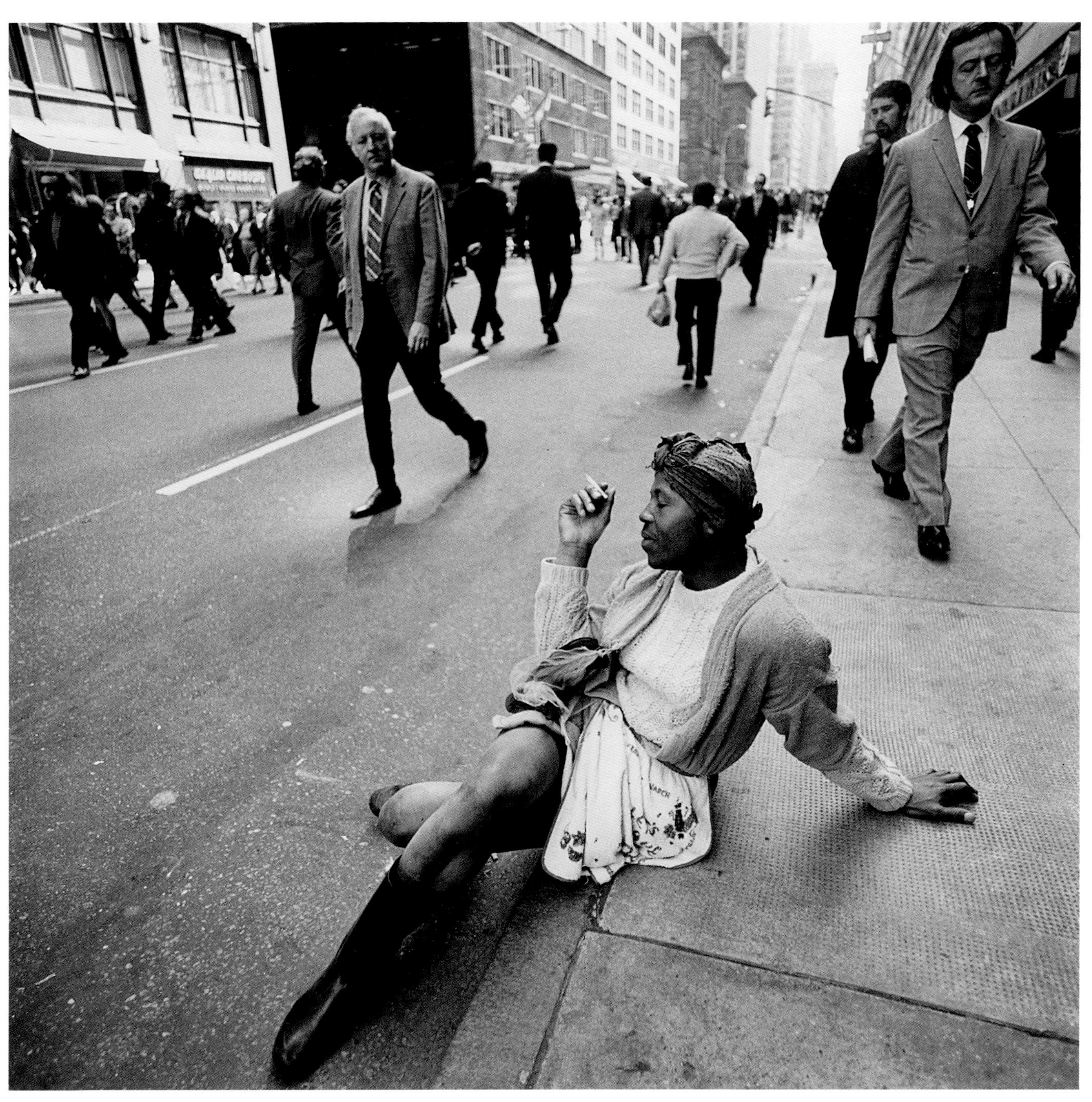

PLATE 32
Resting on Fifth Avenue, New York, New York, 1971

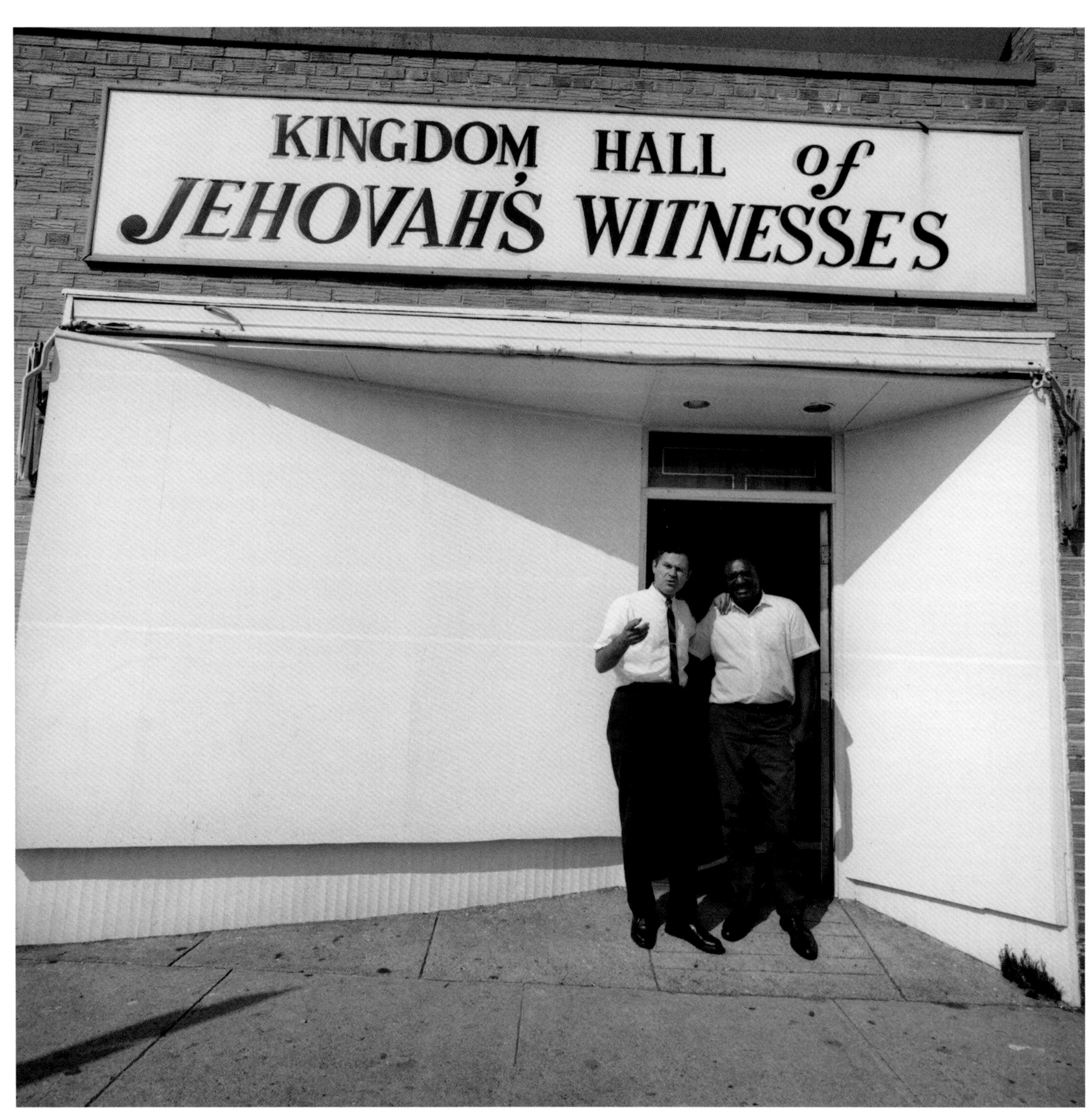

PLATE 33
Jehovah's Witnesses, New York, New York, negative 1970; print 2021

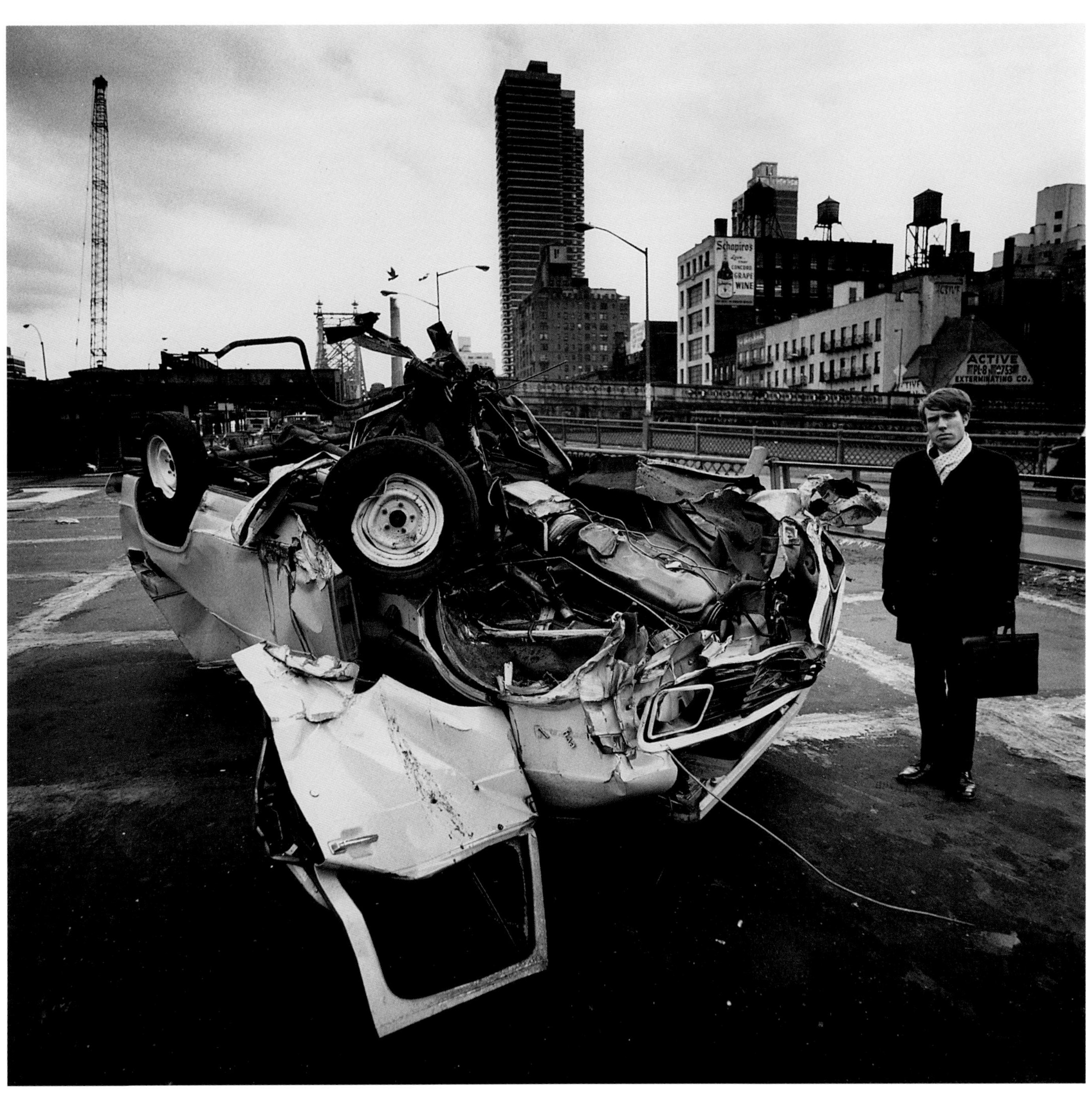

PLATE 34
Man on Way to Work Next to Wrecked Auto, New York, New York, 1976

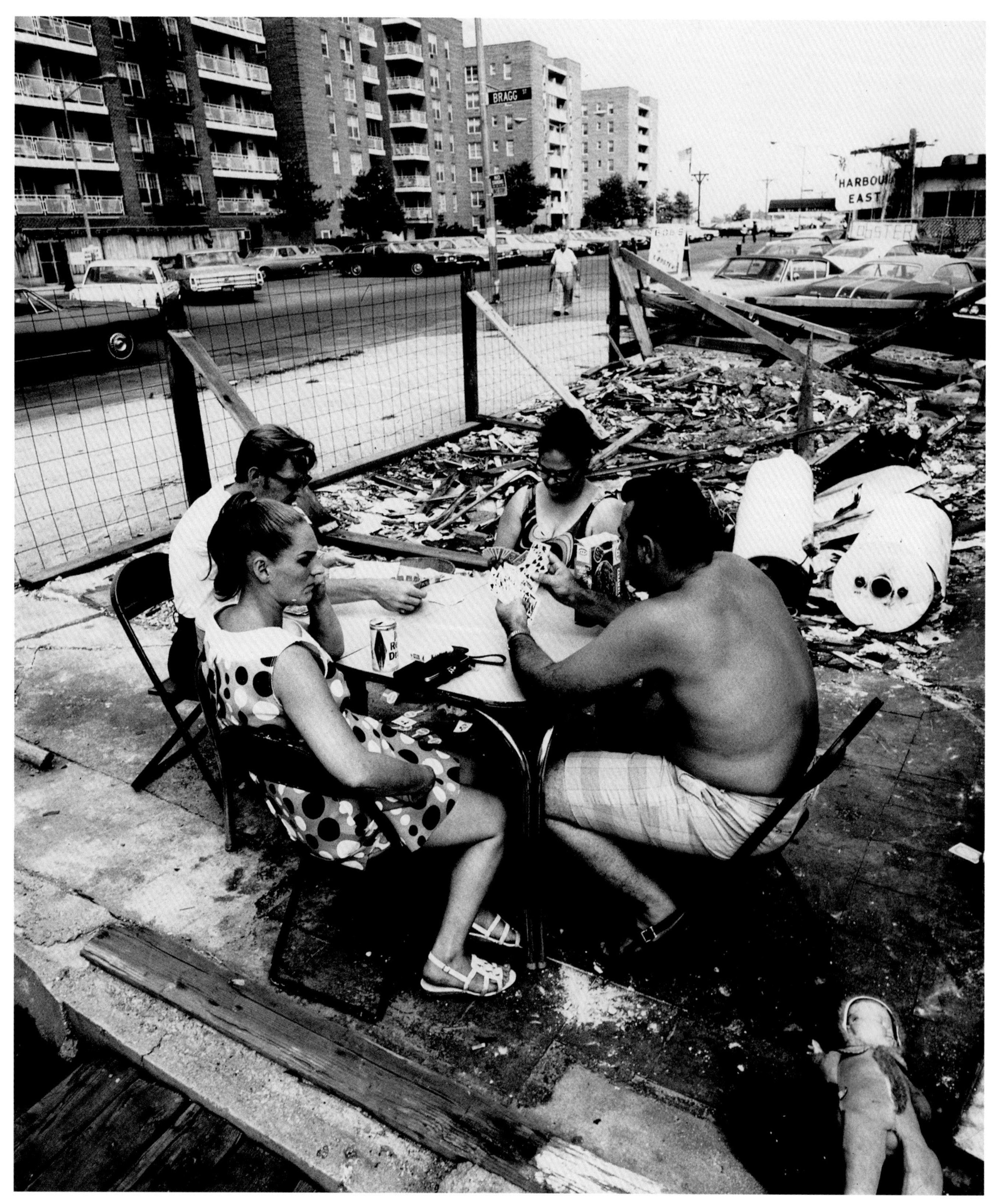

PLATE 35

Friends Playing Cards, Sheepshead Bay, Brooklyn, New York, 1970

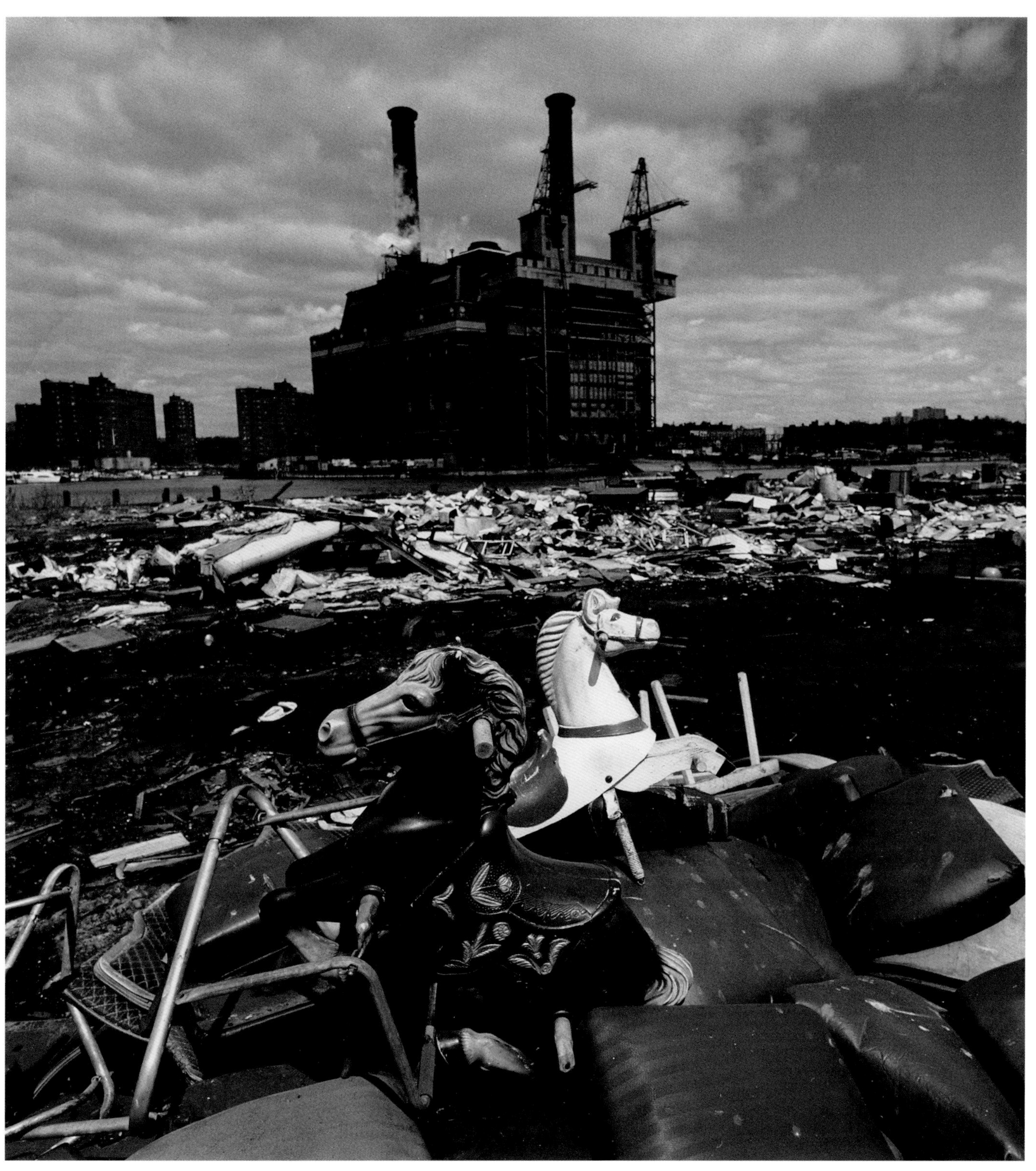

PLATE 36
Hobby Horses, Harlem River, Bronx, New York, 1970

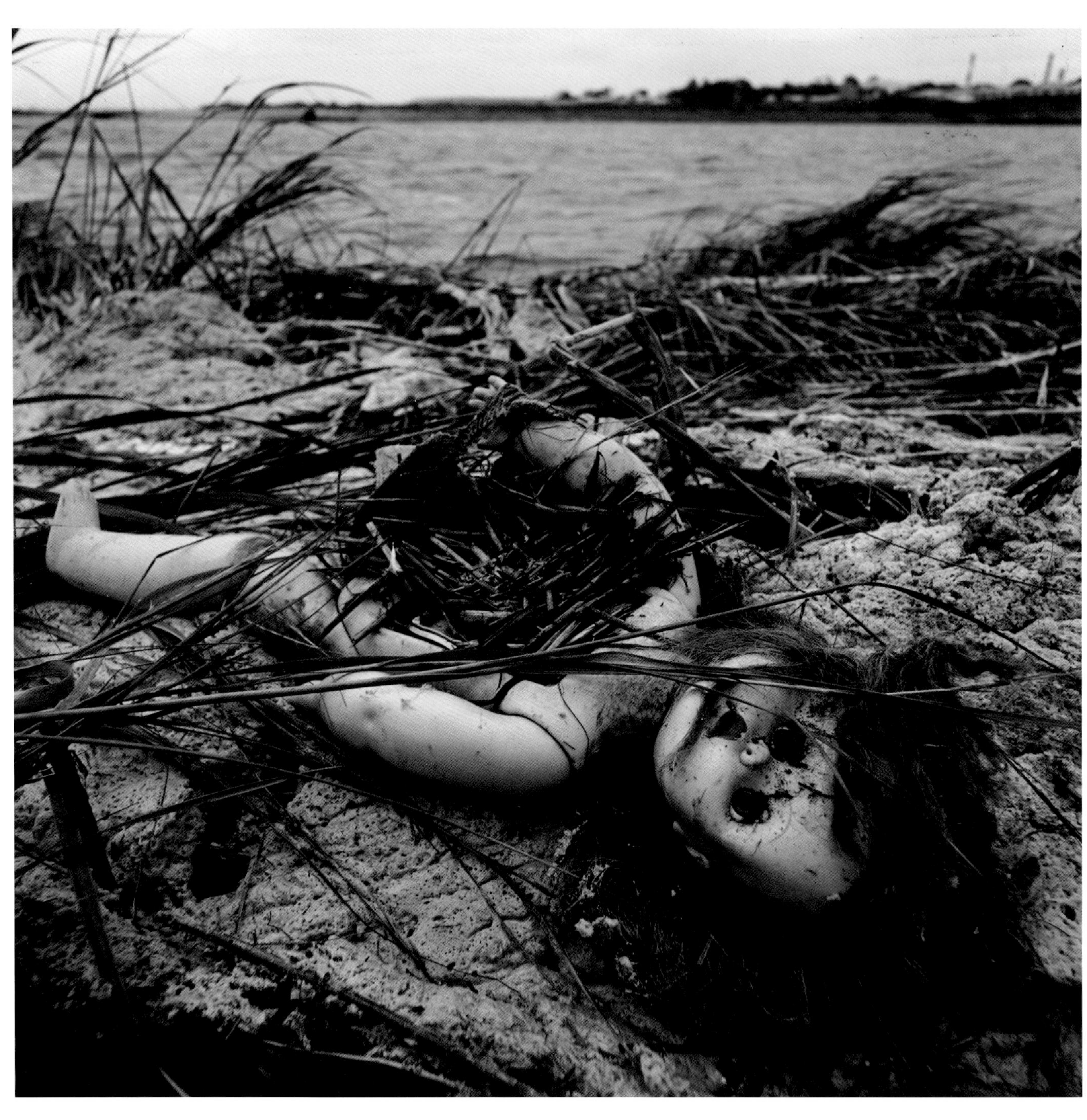

PLATE 37

Abandoned Doll, Jamaica Bay, Queens, New York, 1971

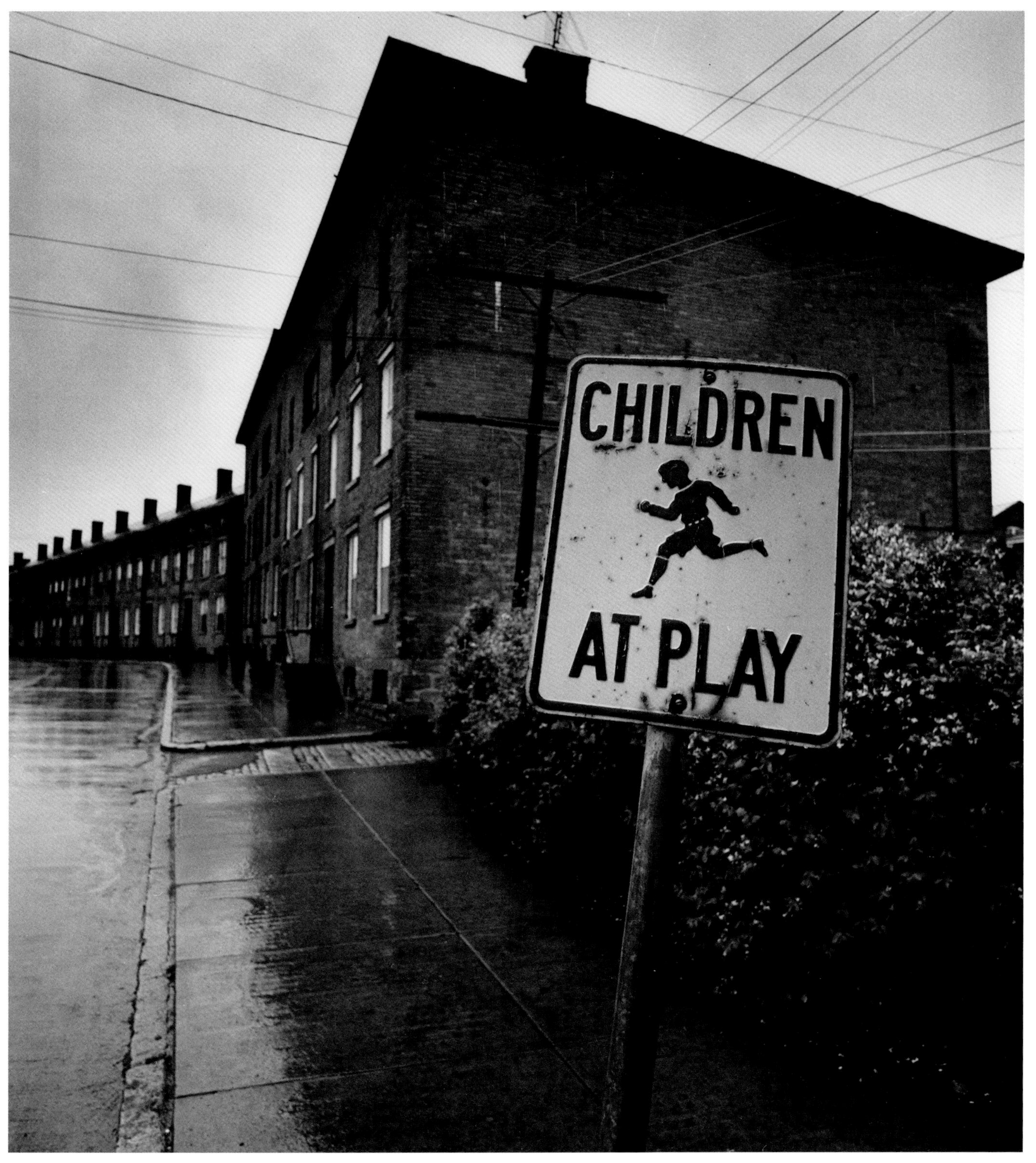

PLATE 38

Workers' Housing, Cohoes, New York, 1970

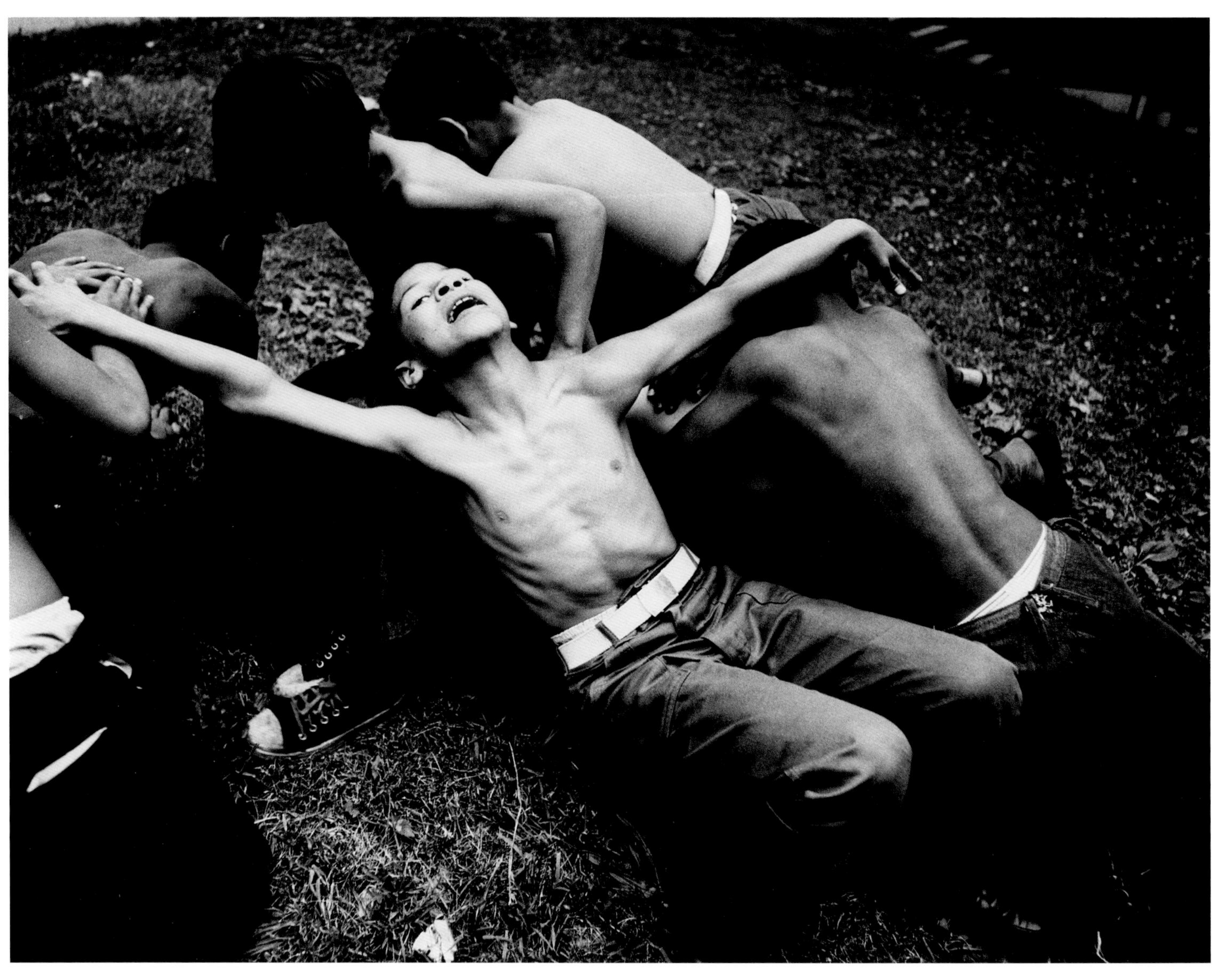

PLATE 39
Boys Playing in Van Cortlandt Park, Bronx, New York, 1970

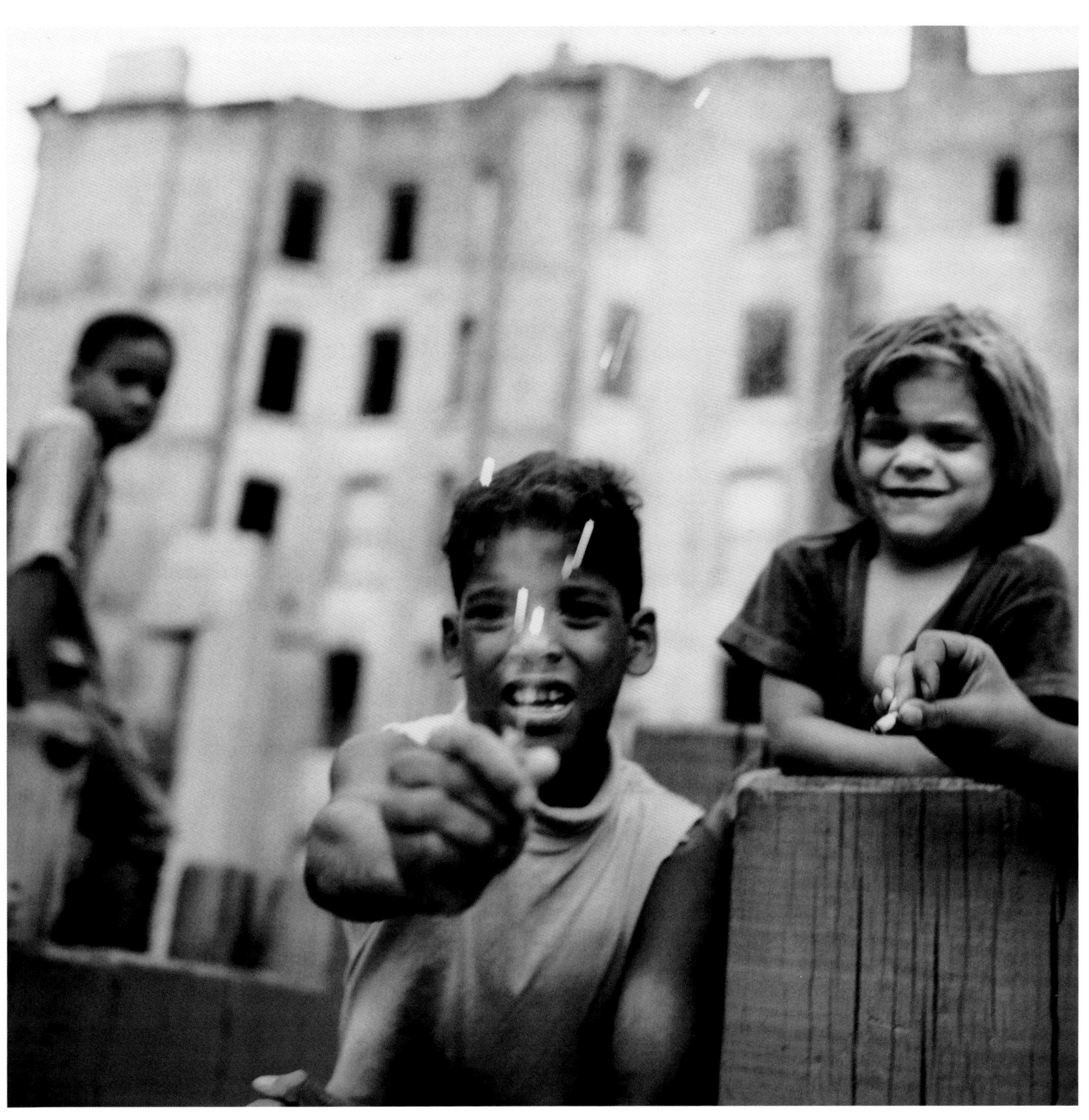

PLATE 40
Kids with Sparklers, Lower East Side, New York, negative 1969; print 2021

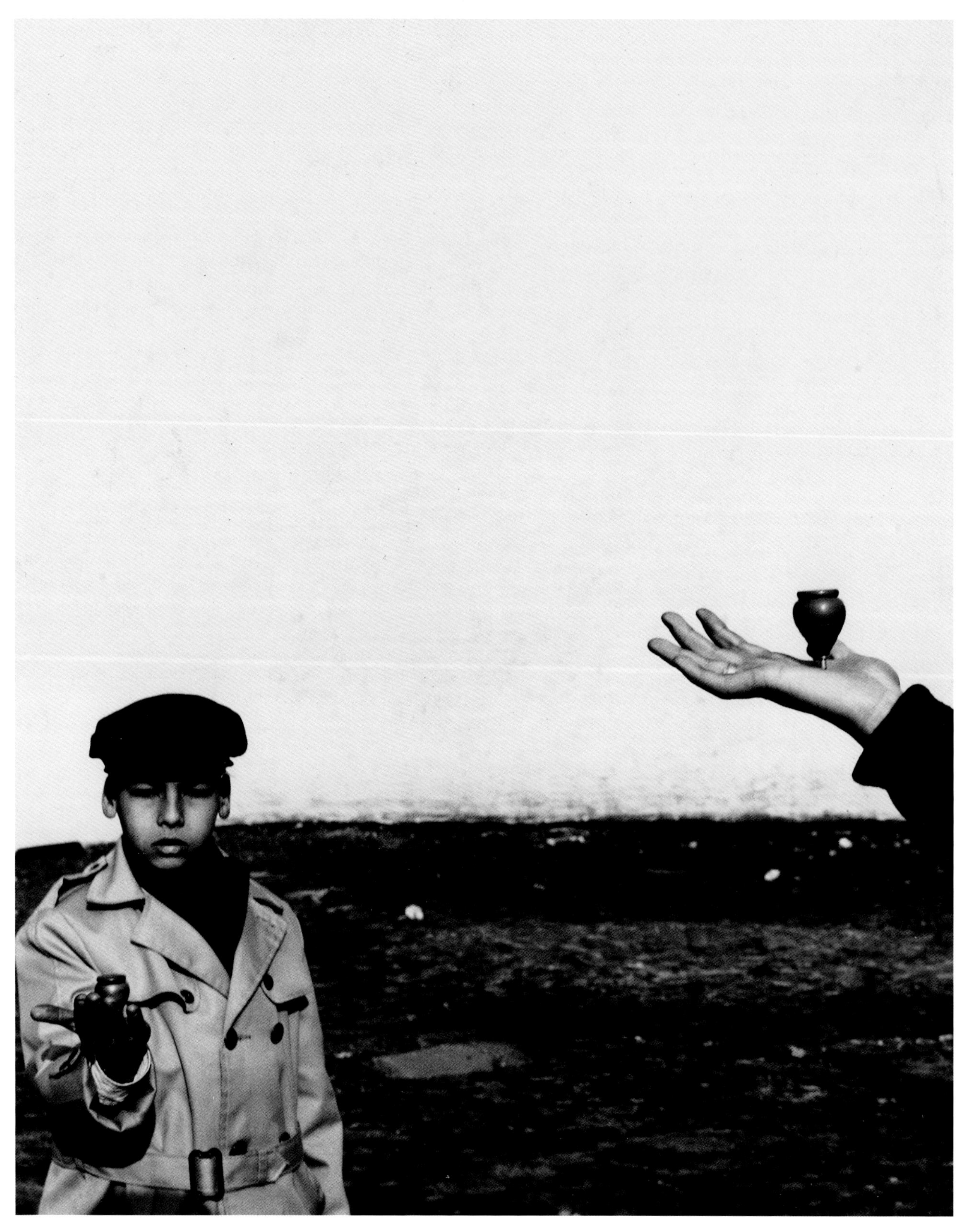

PLATE 41
Boys with Tops, Weehawken, New Jersey, 1969

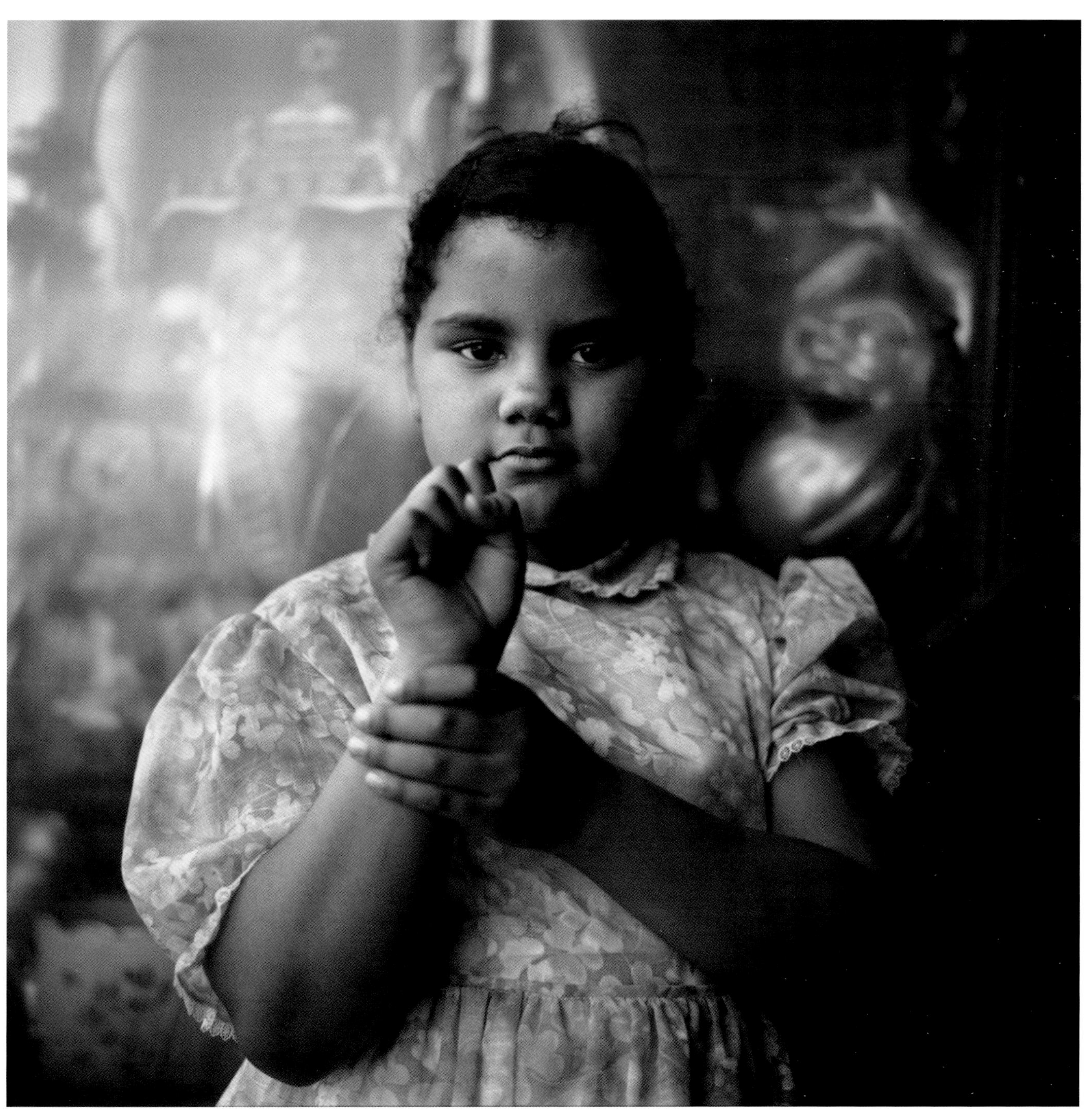

PLATE 42
Girl and Botanica Store, Spanish Harlem, New York, negative 1969; print 2021

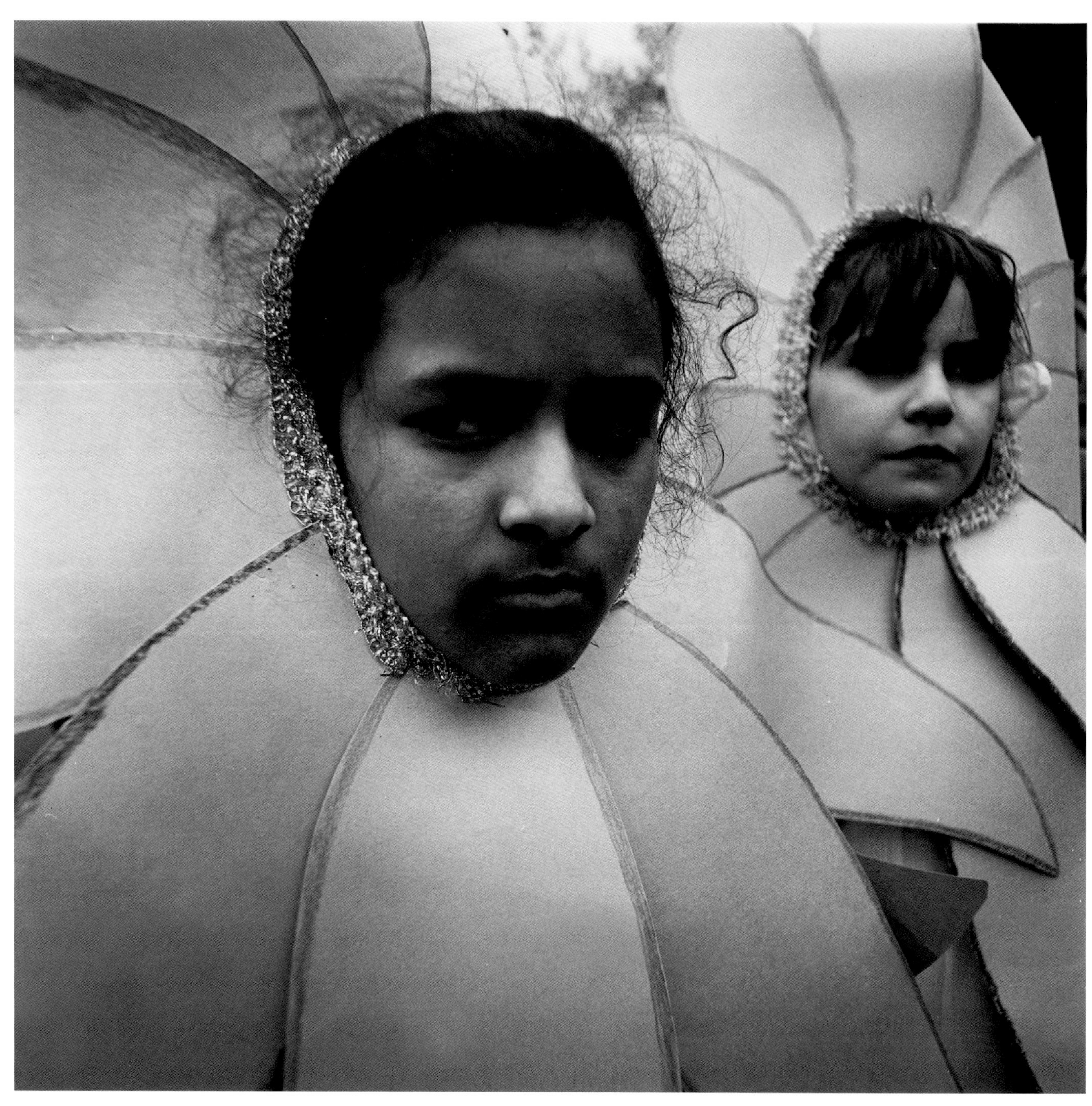

PLATE 43
Two Girls in Puerto Rican Parade, New York, New York, 1970

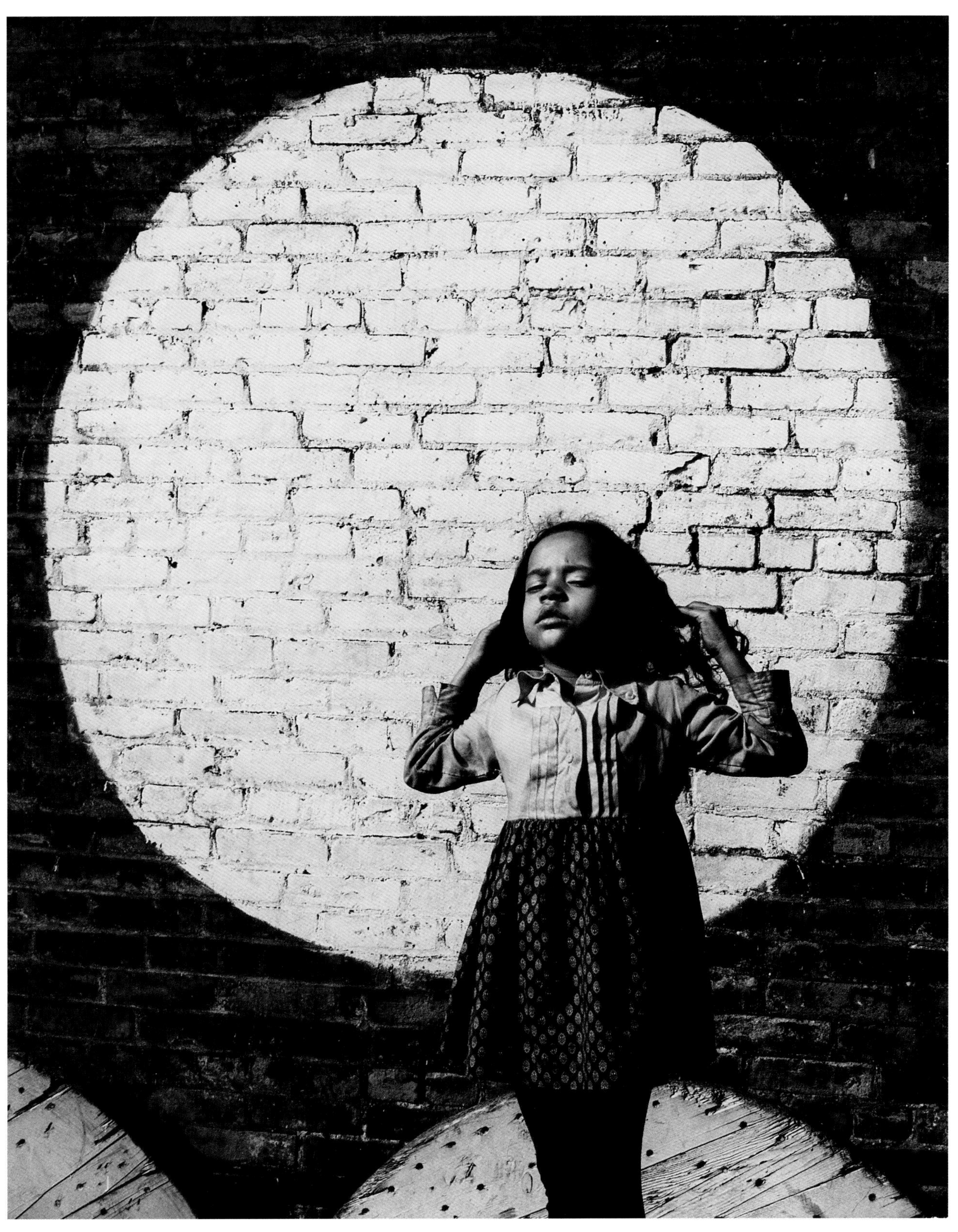

PLATE 44
Girl and Moon Dream, New York, New York, 1968

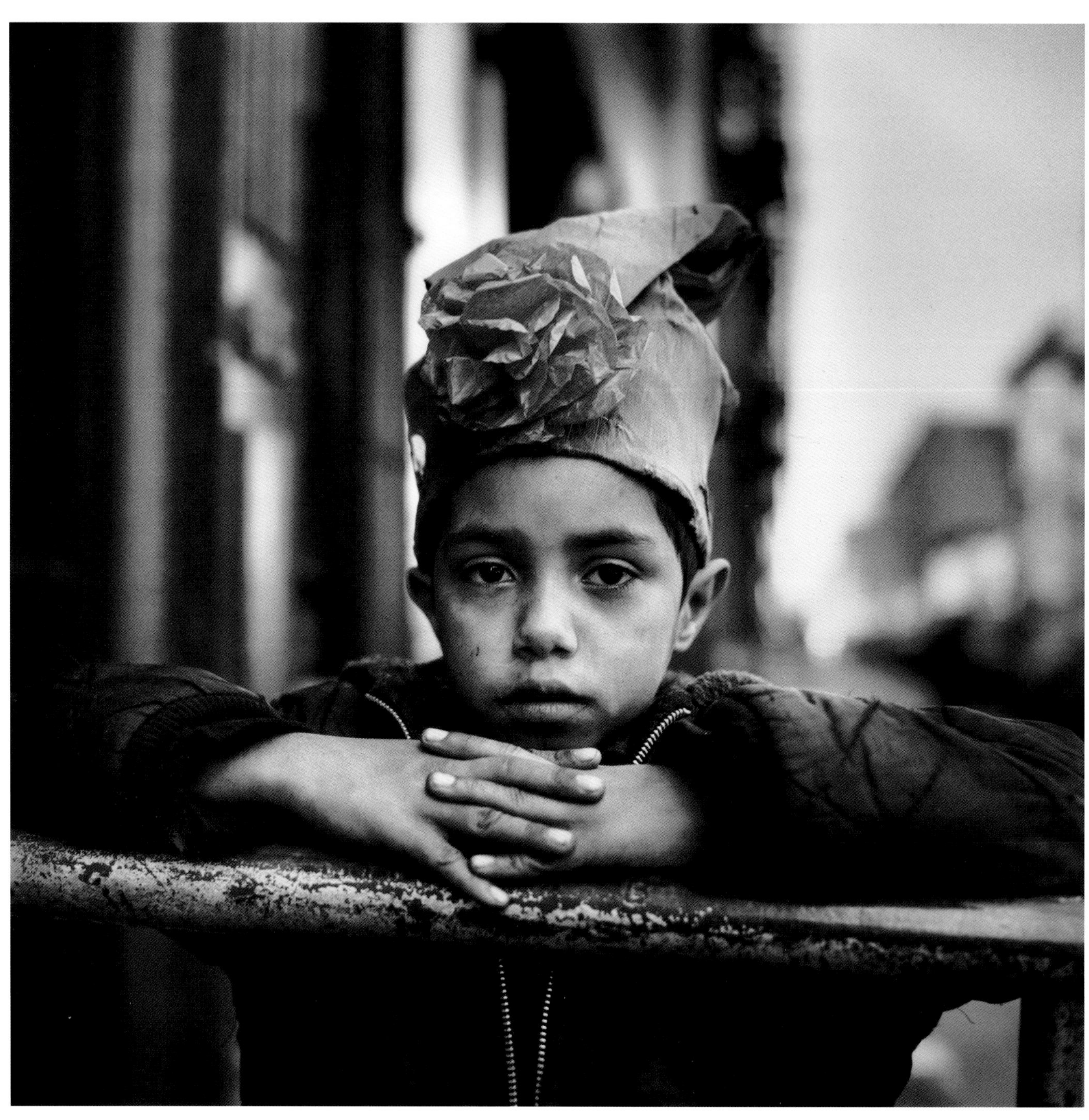

PLATE 45

Boy in Birthday Hat, Spanish Harlem, New York, negative 1970; print 2021

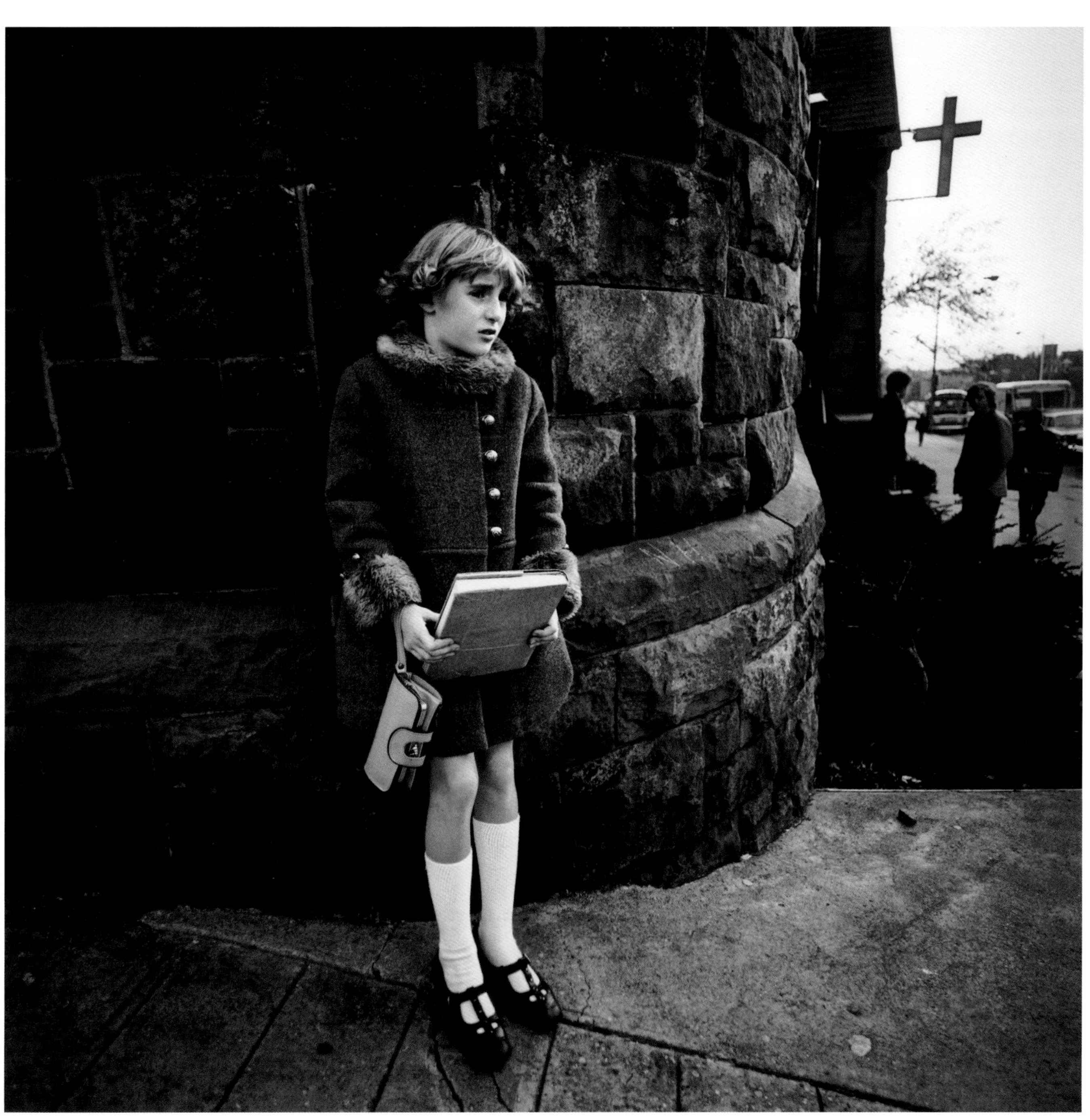

PLATE 46
Girl in Front of Parochial School, Monticello, New York, negative 1970; print 2021

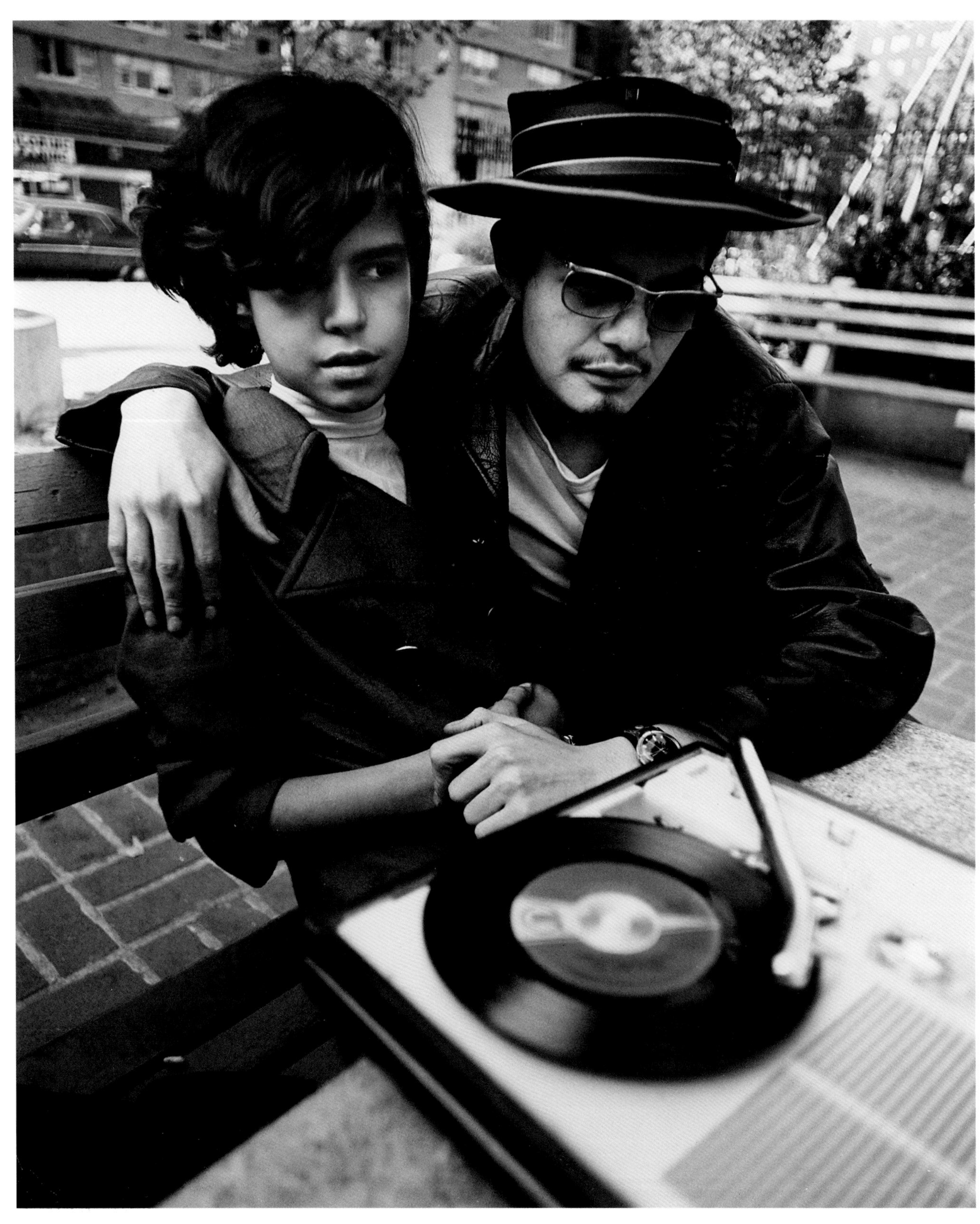

PLATE 47
Teenage Couple, New York, New York, 1970

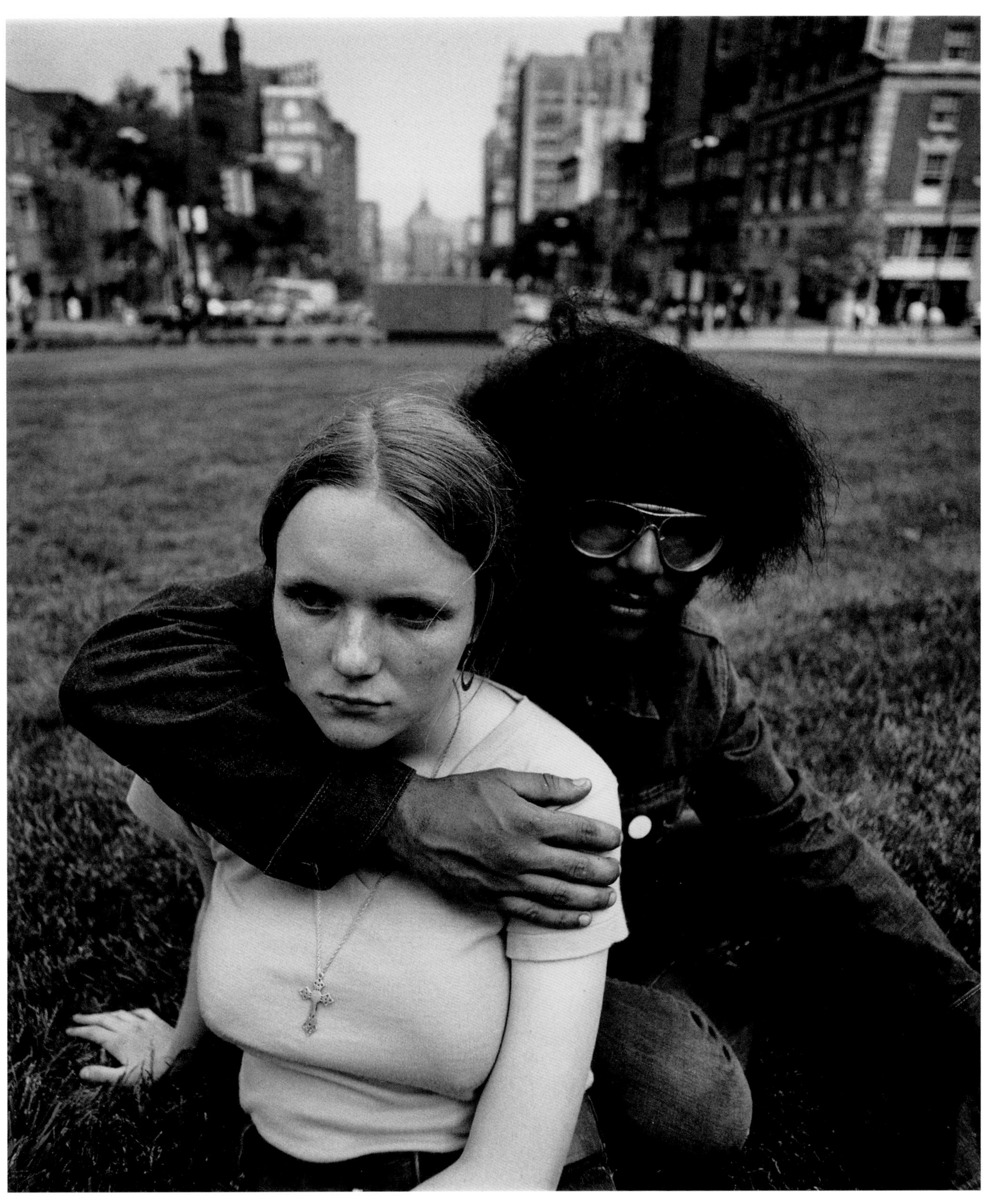

PLATE 48
Couple in Park, Albany, New York, 1970

Contact sheet, Bronx, New York, 1969
Gelatin silver print, 25.4 × 20.3 cm (10 × 8 in.)
Collection of the artist

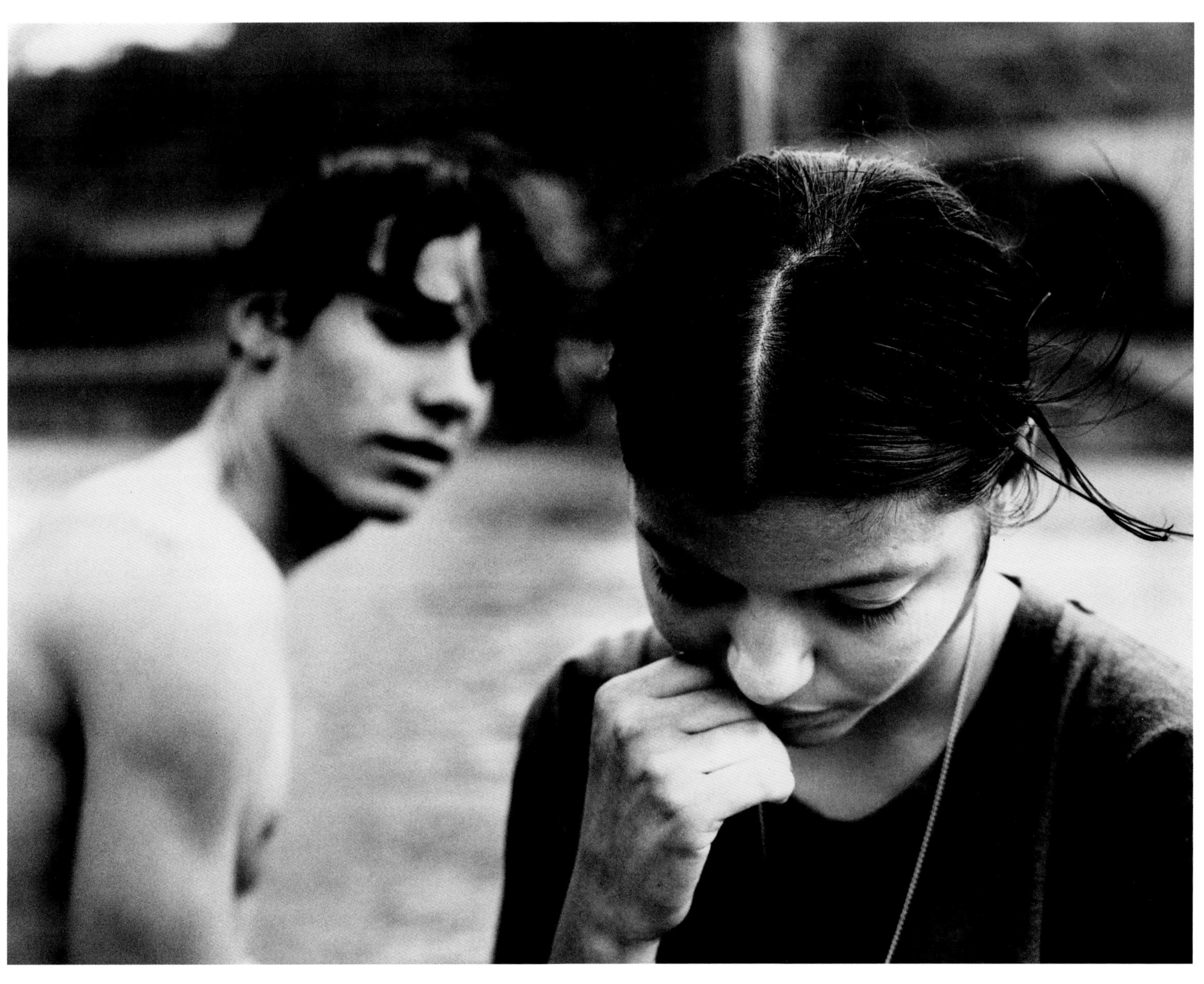

PLATE 49
Teenagers by River, Bronx, New York, 1969

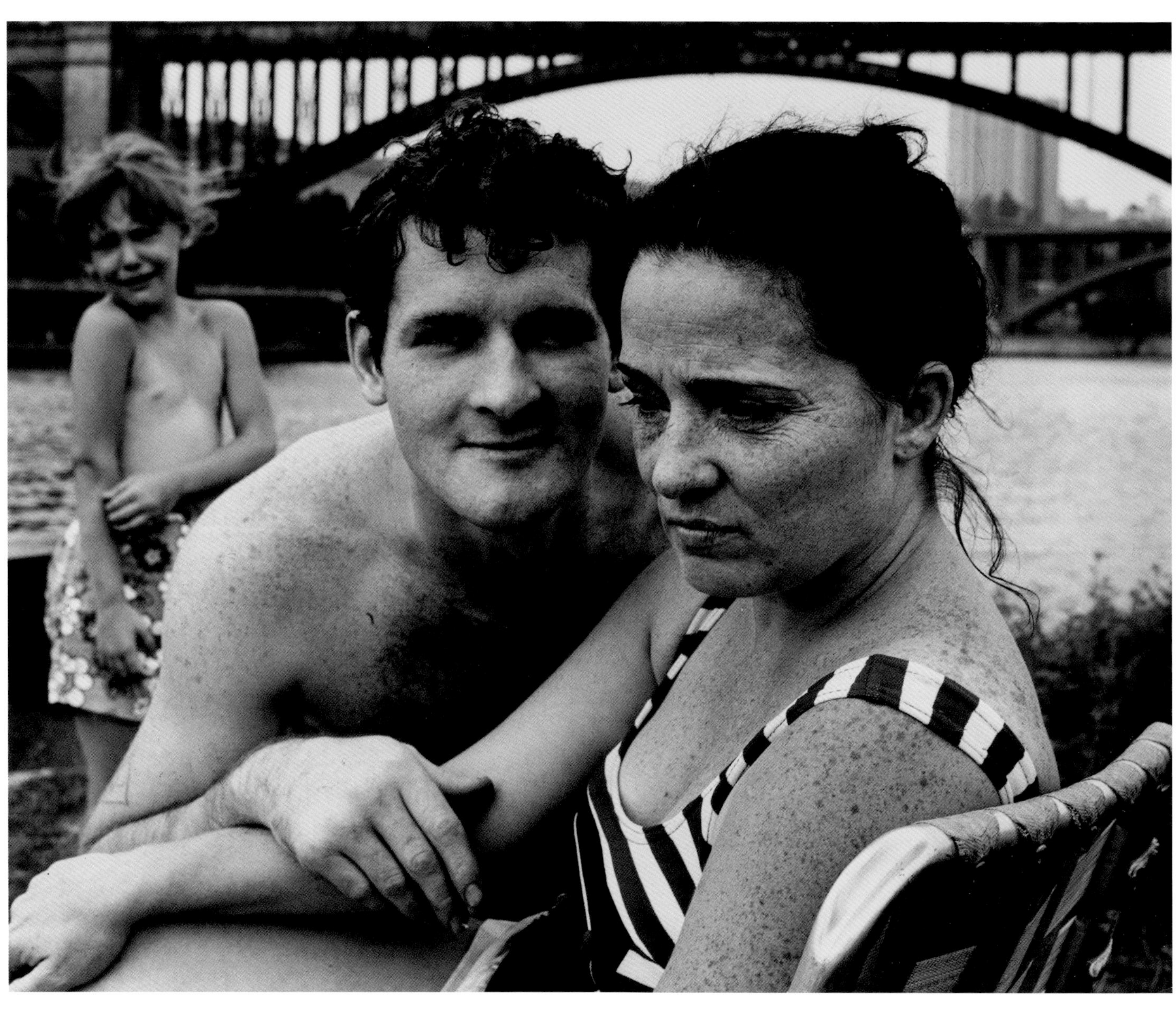

PLATE 50
Family by Harlem River, Bronx, New York, 1969

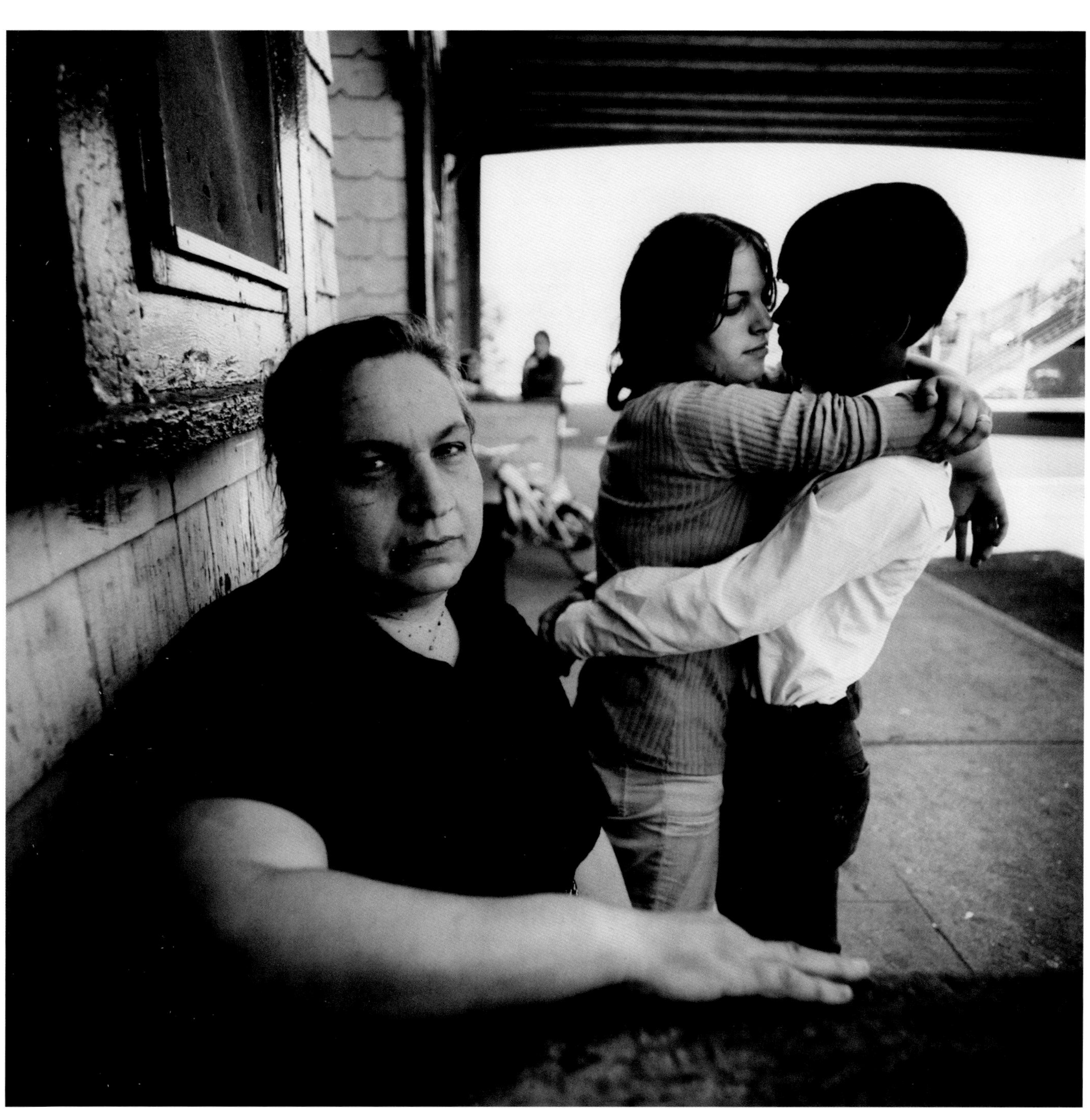

PLATE 51
Mother and Daughter and Boyfriend, Rockaway, New York, 1970

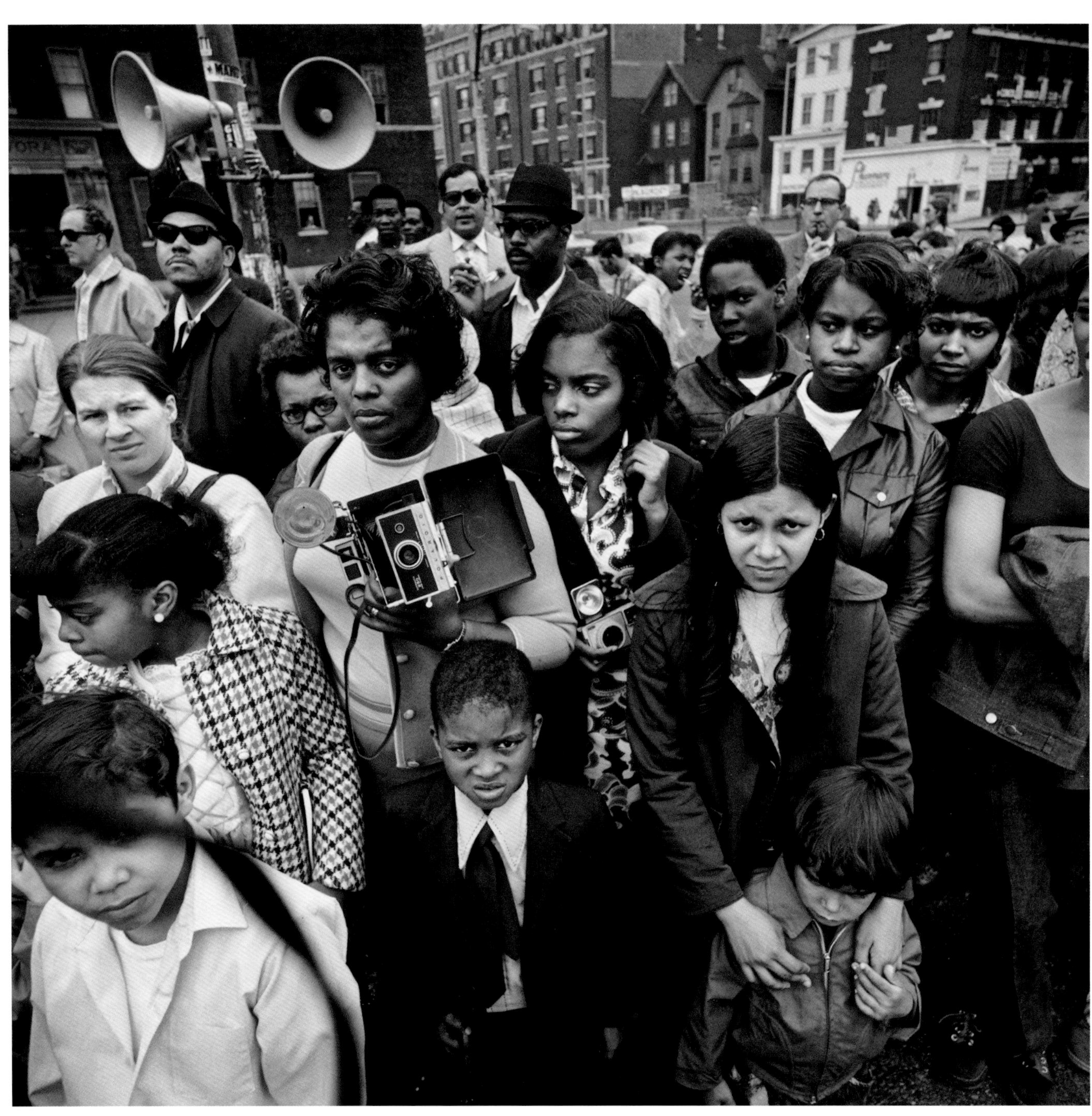

PLATE 52

Woman with Polaroid Camera at Politician's Rally, Bronx, New York, negative 1971; print 2021

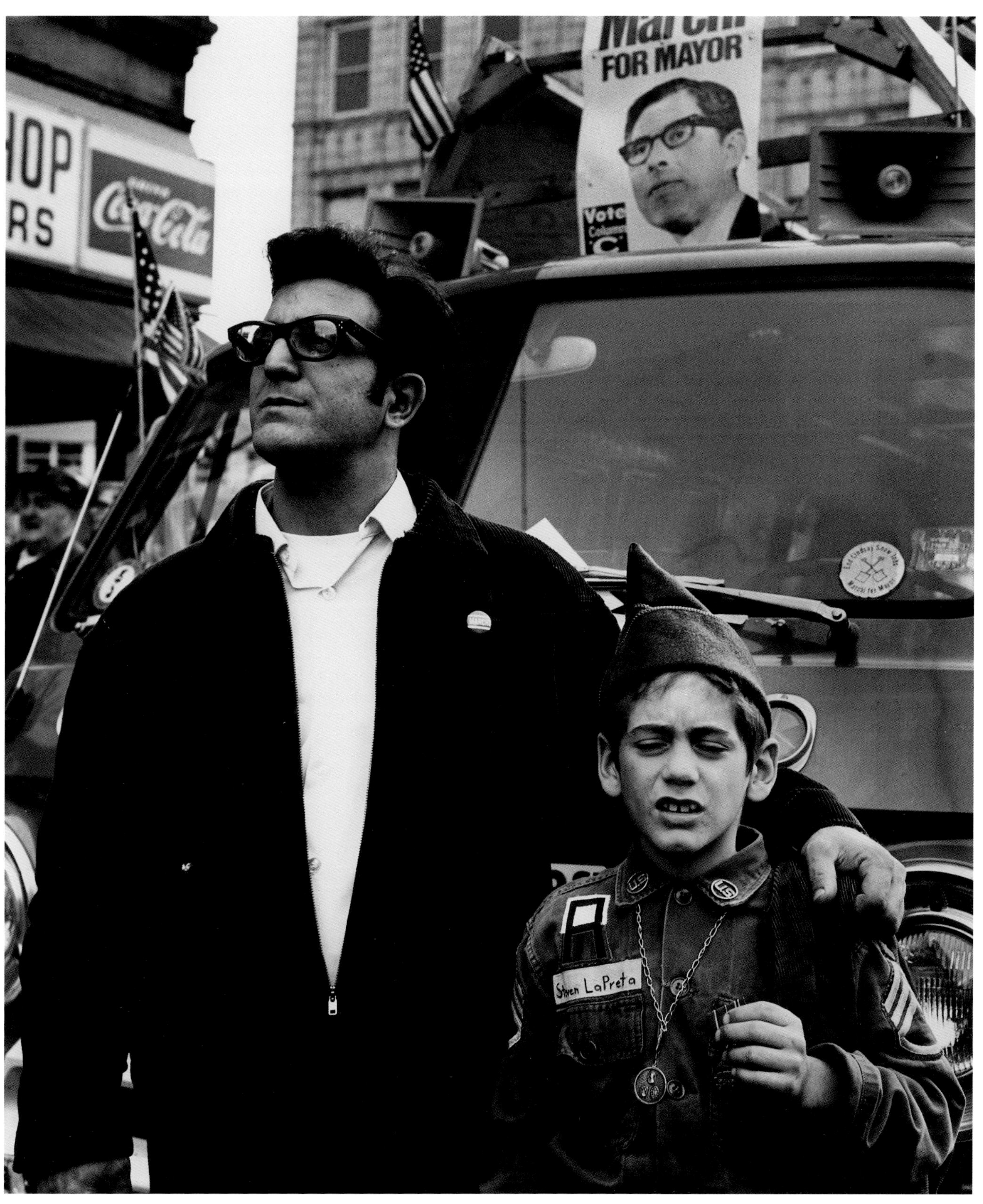

PLATE 53

Father and Son at Rally for Mayor, New York, New York, 1969

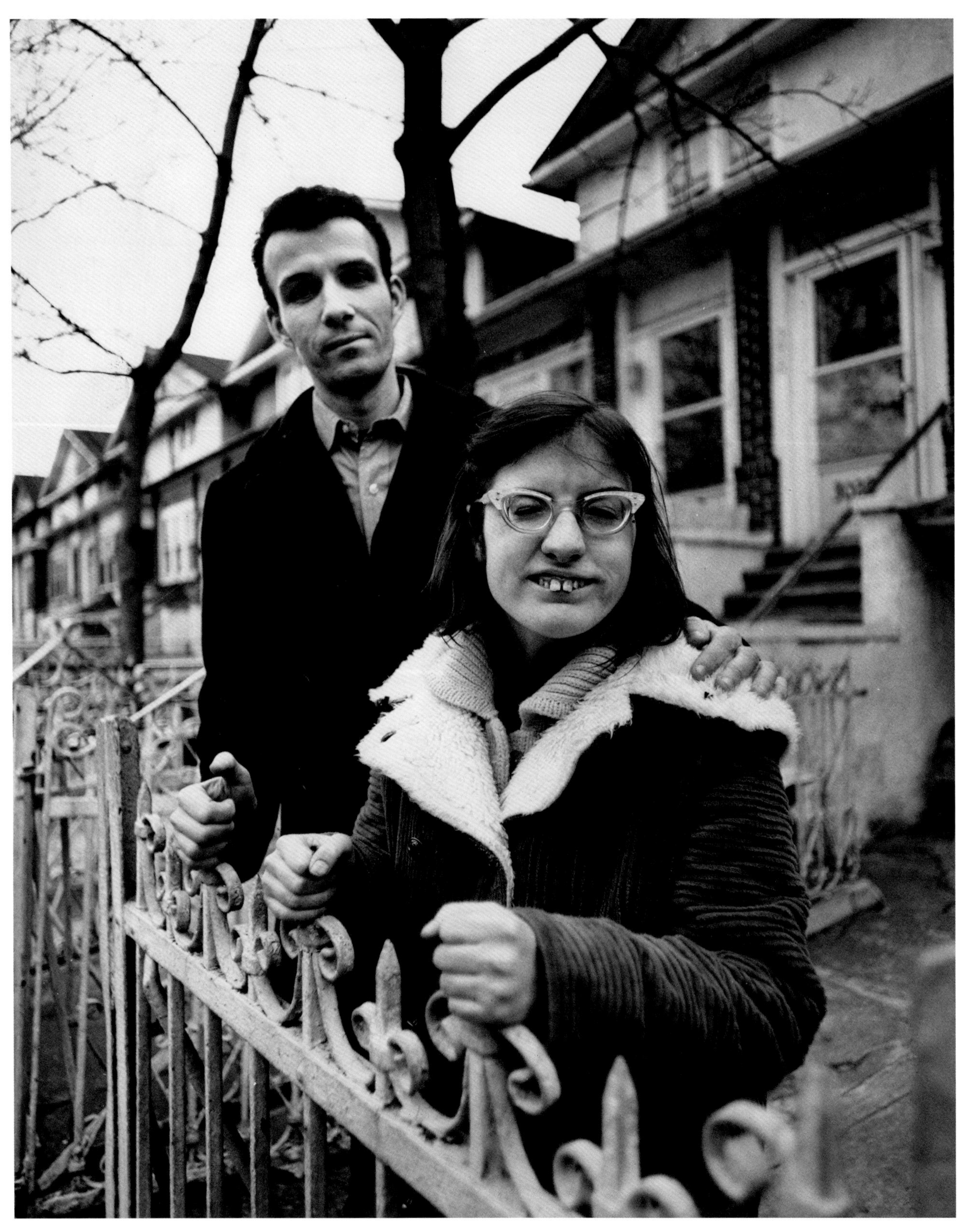

PLATE 54
Father and Daughter, Brighton Beach, New York, 1970

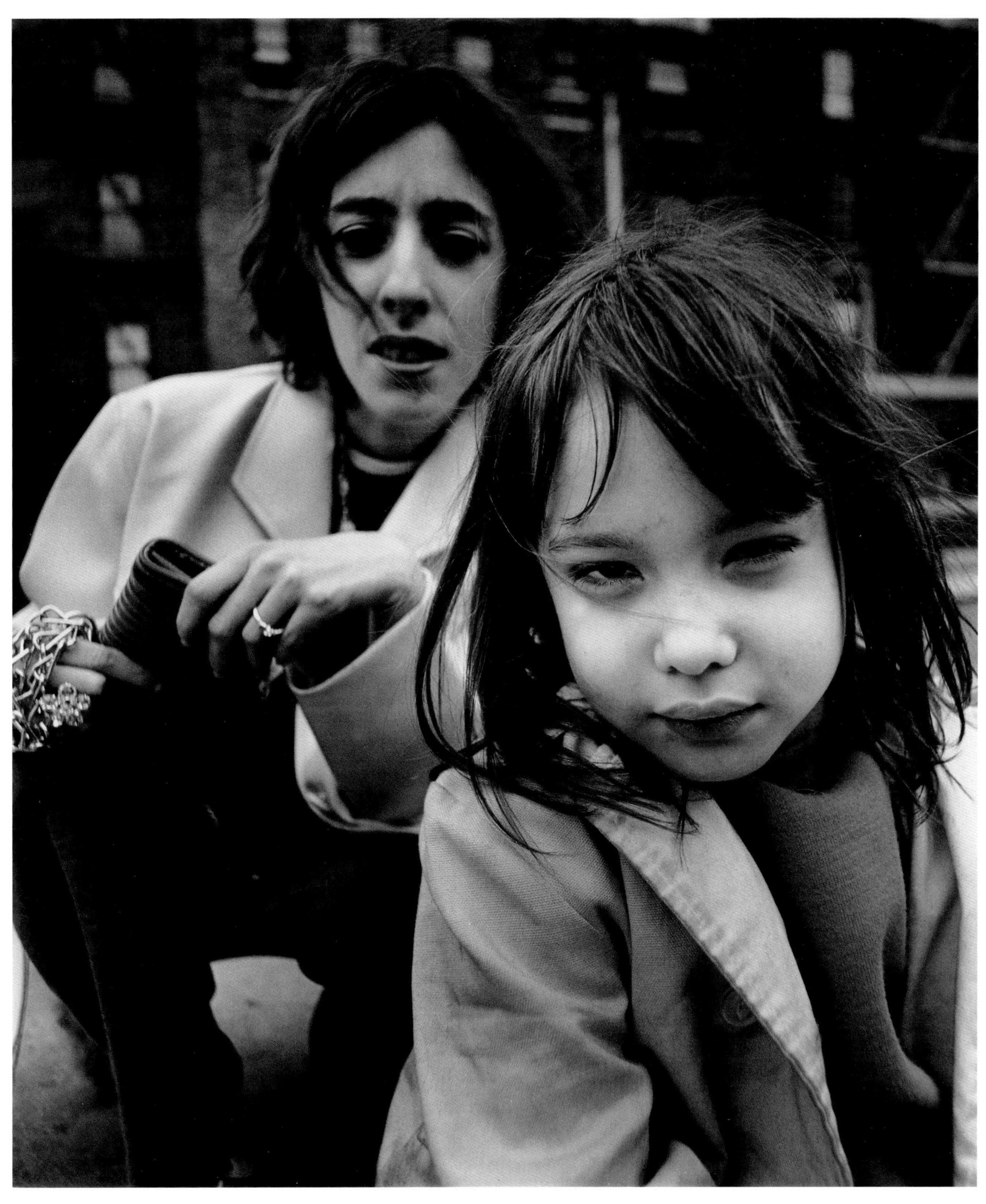

PLATE 55

Mother and Daughter, Bronx, New York, 1970

Contact sheet, Lackawanna, New York, 1970
Gelatin silver print,
25.4 × 20.3 cm
(10 × 8 in.)
Collection of the artist

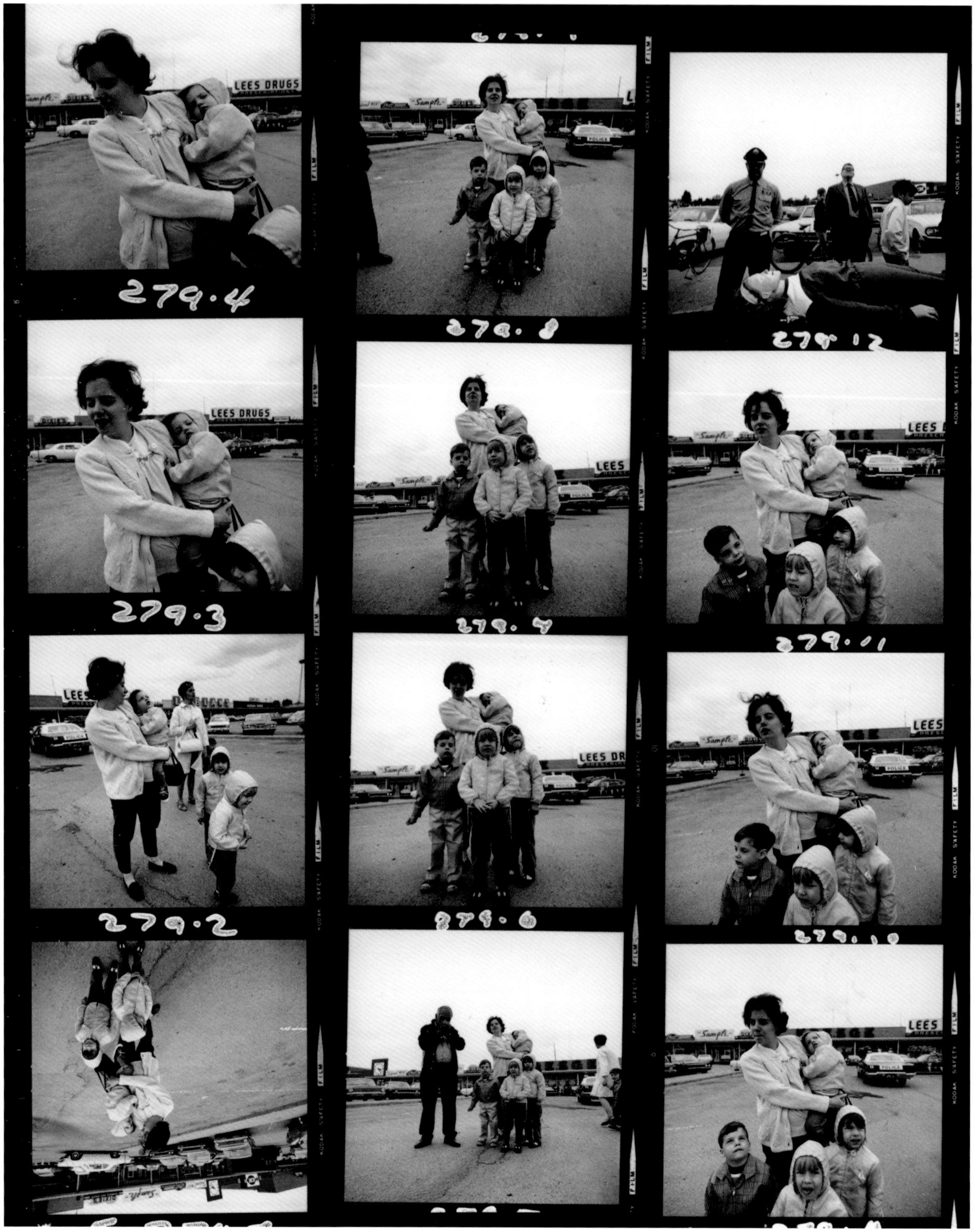

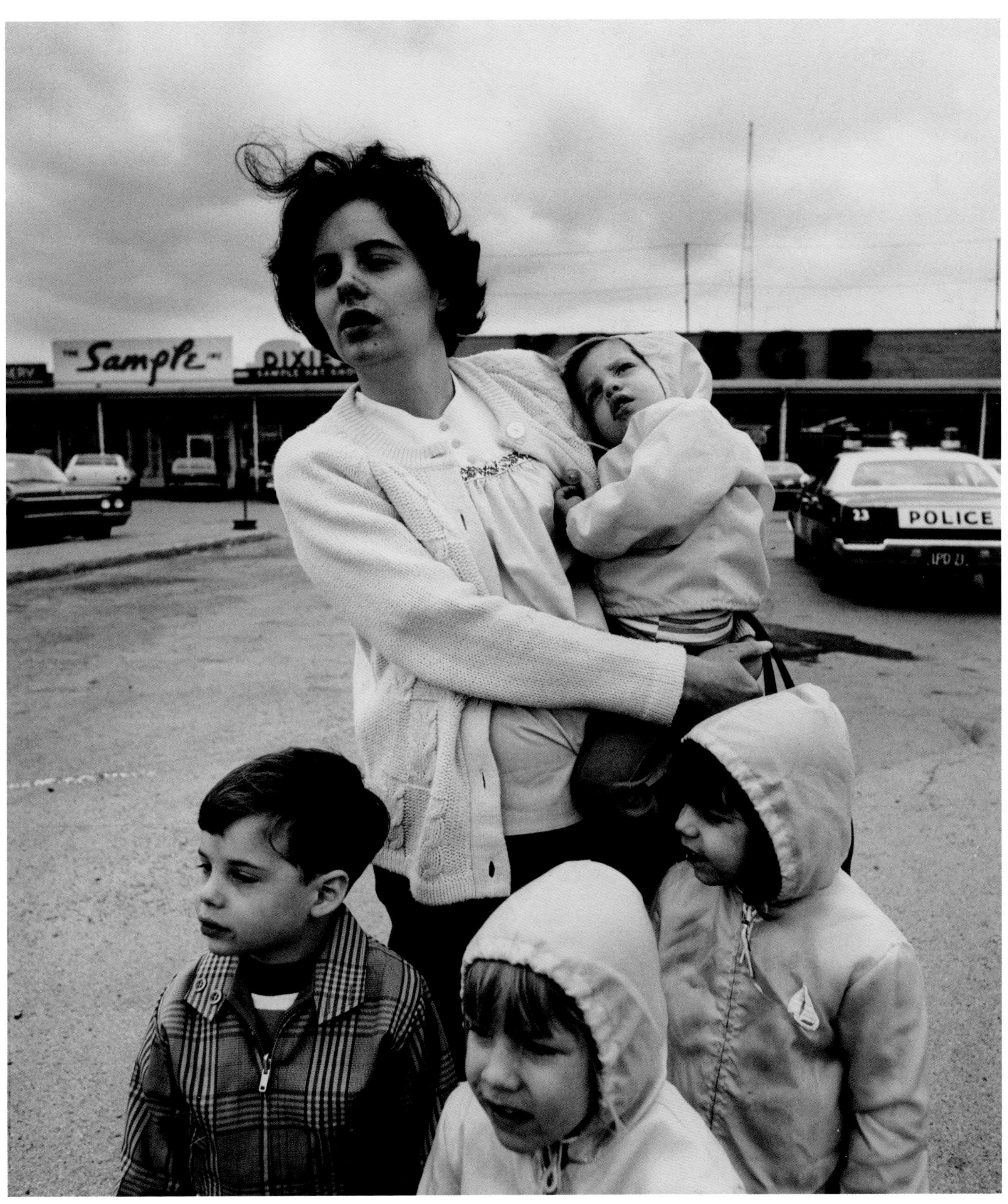

PLATE 56
Woman in Shopping Center Parking Lot, Lackawanna, New York, 1970

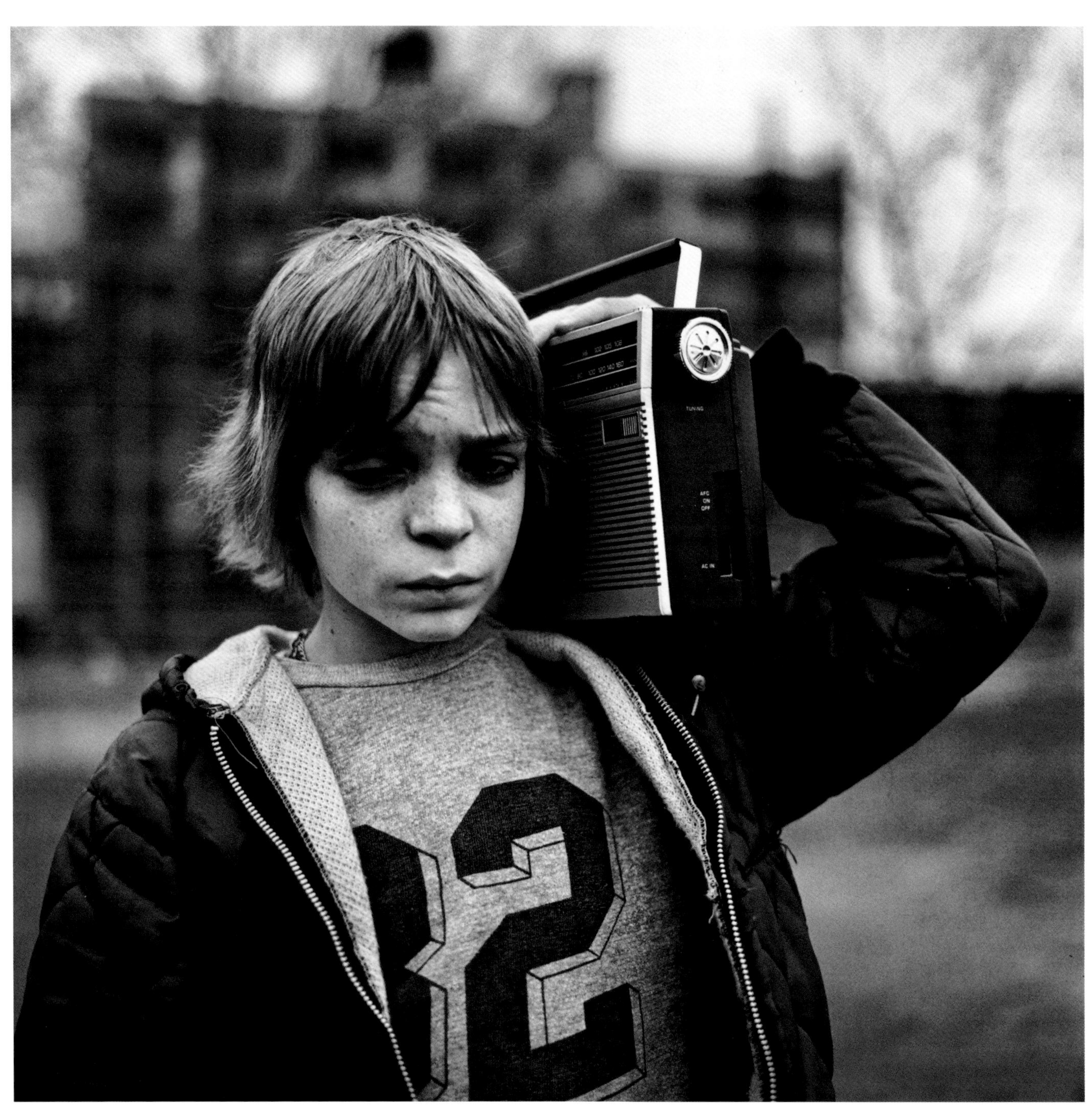

PLATE 57
Boy with Radio, Hell's Kitchen, New York, negative 1974; print 2021

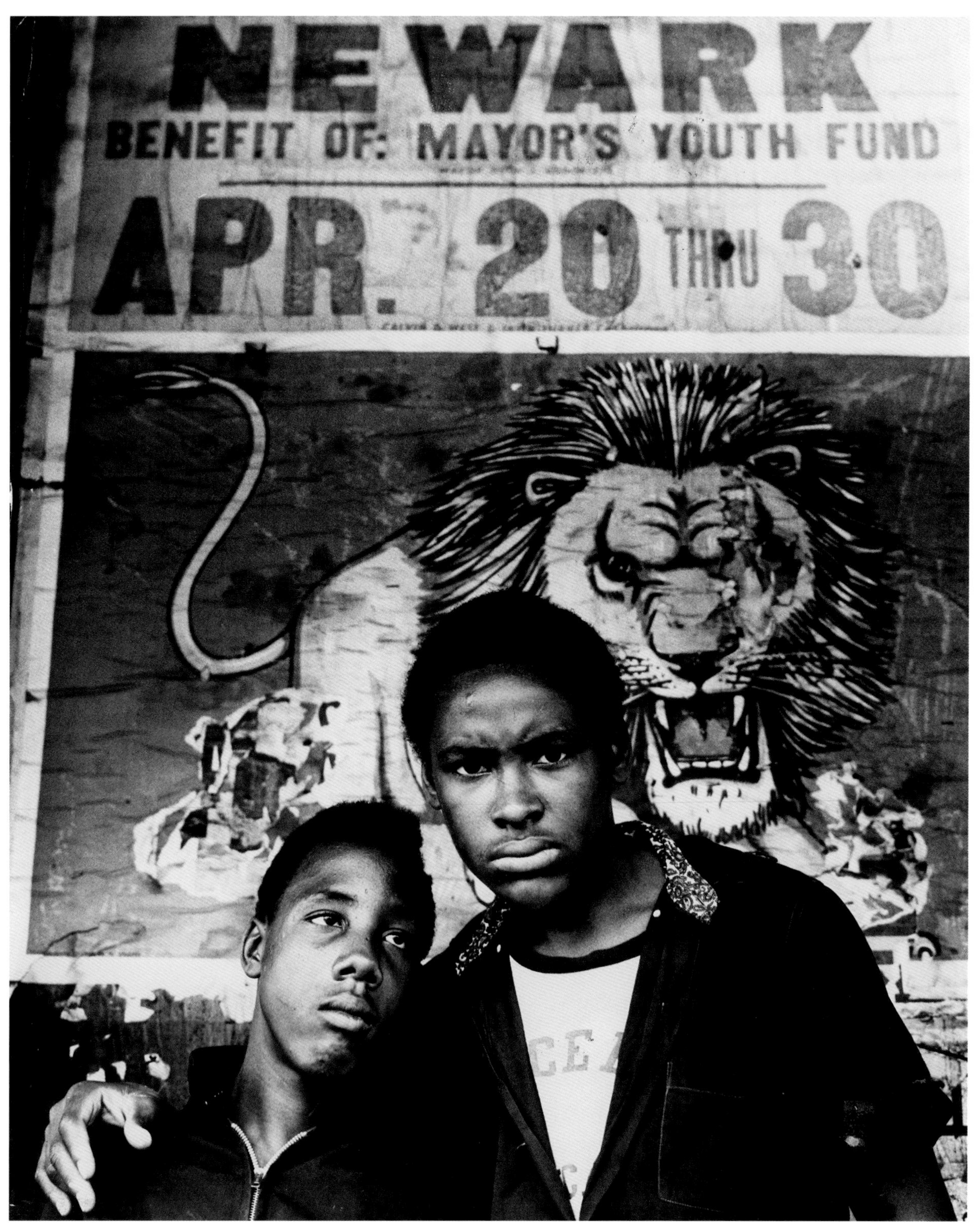

PLATE 58
Teens, Newark, New Jersey, 1970

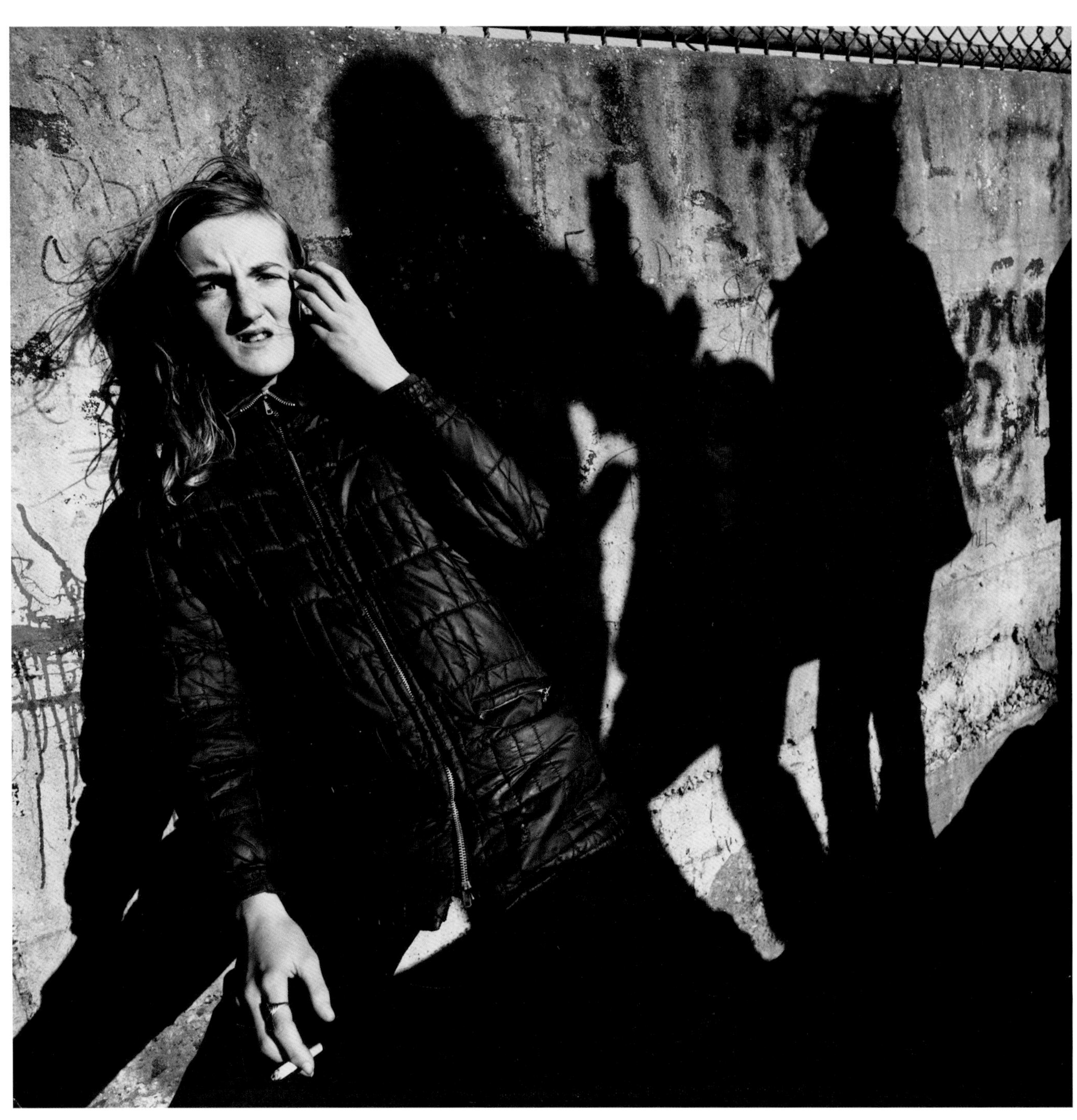

PLATE 59
Teenage Girls, Sheepshead Bay, Brooklyn, New York, 1970

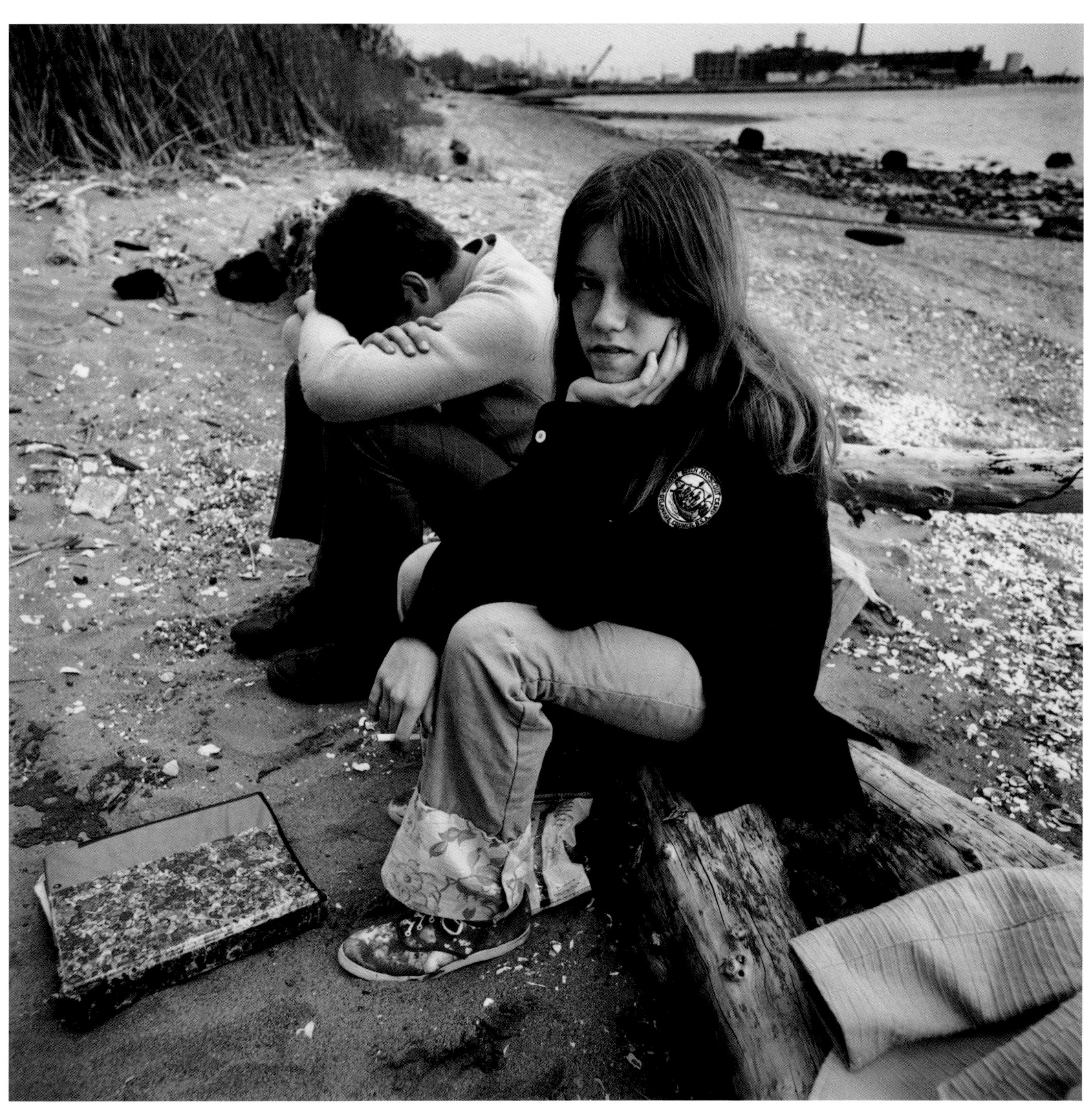

PLATE 60
Teens on Beach, Prince's Bay, Staten Island, New York, negative 1971; print 2021

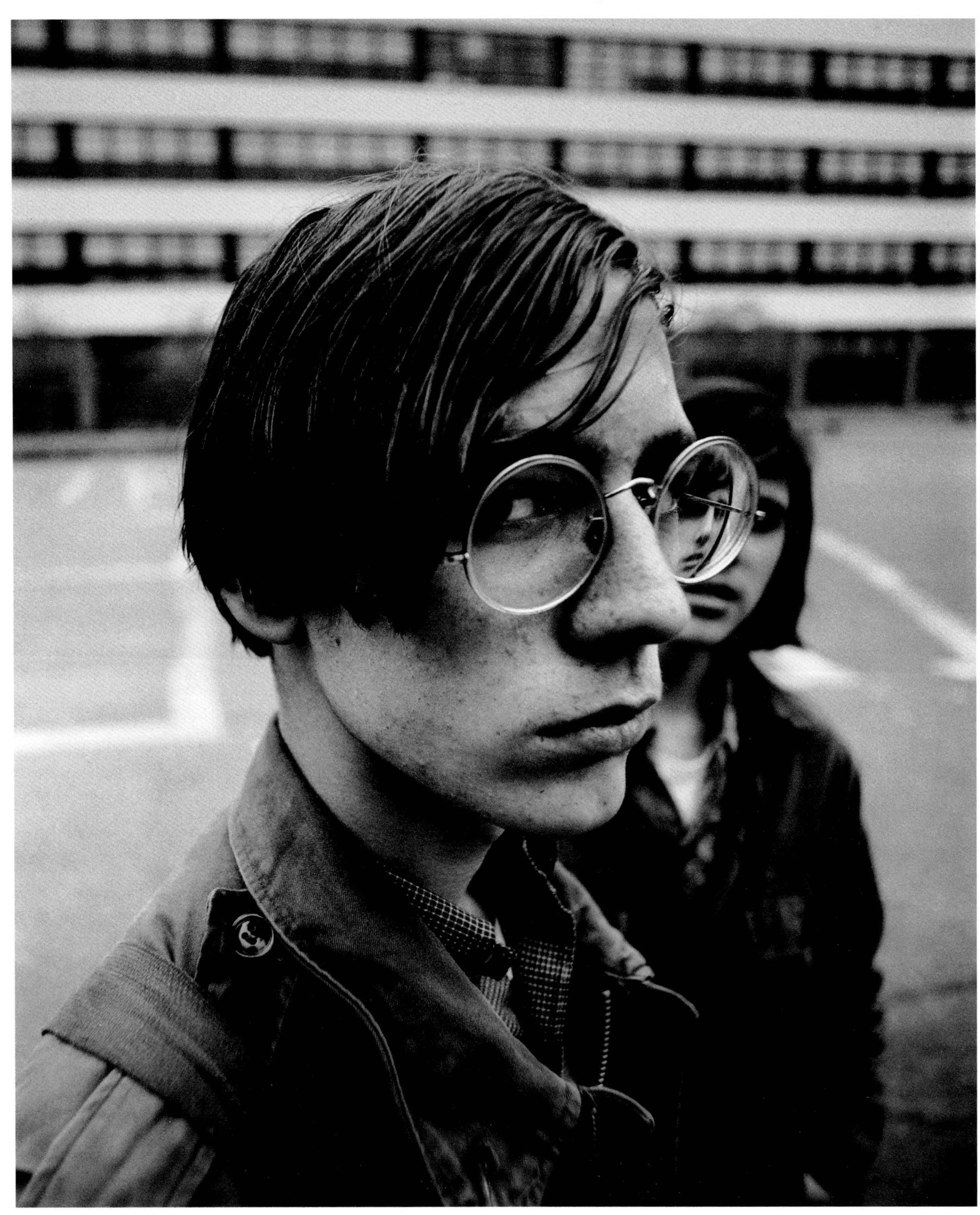

PLATE 61
Teenage Boys, Bronx High School of Science, Bronx, New York, negative 1970; print later

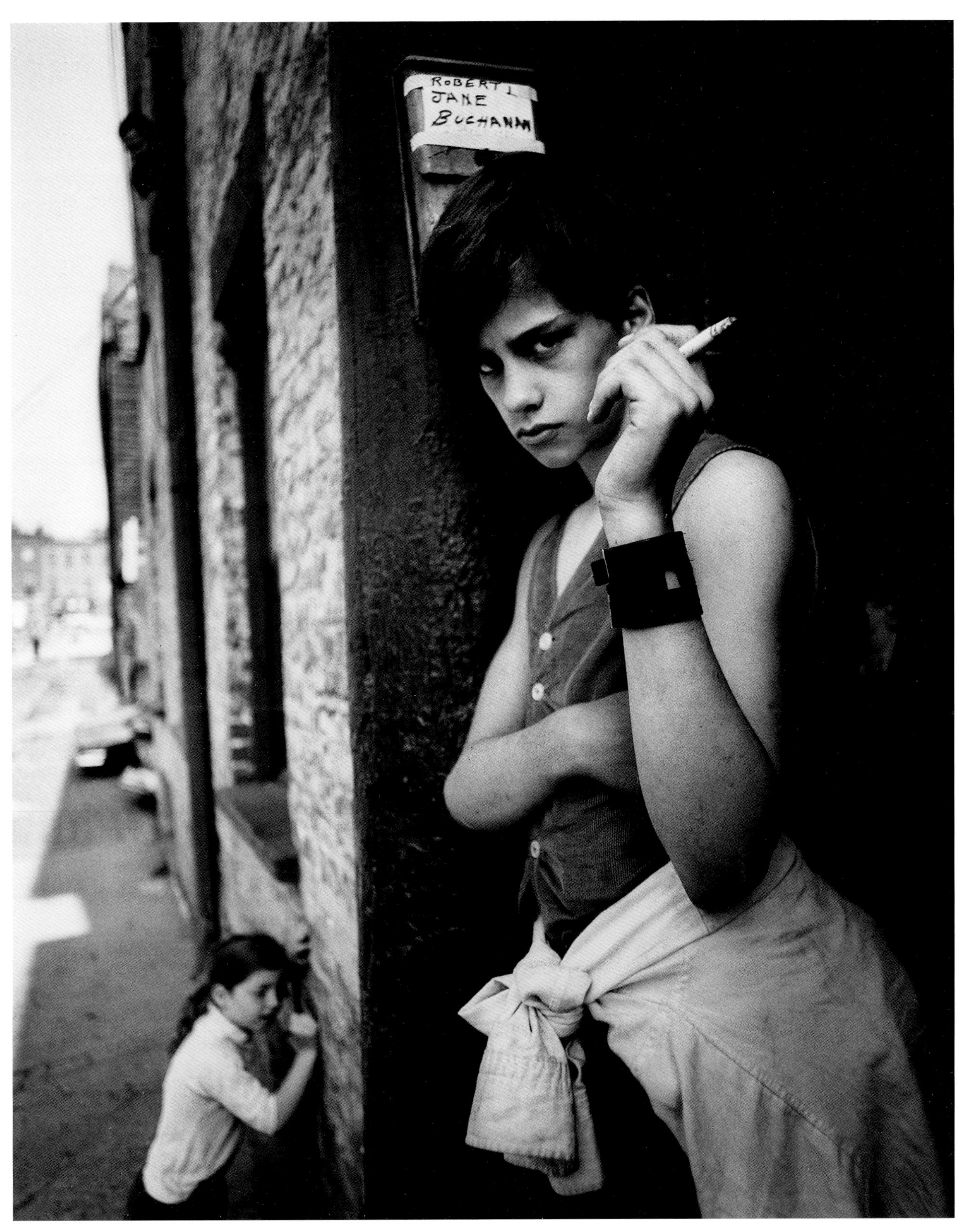

PLATE 62

Boy with Cigarette, Albany, New York, 1970

The Dream Collector

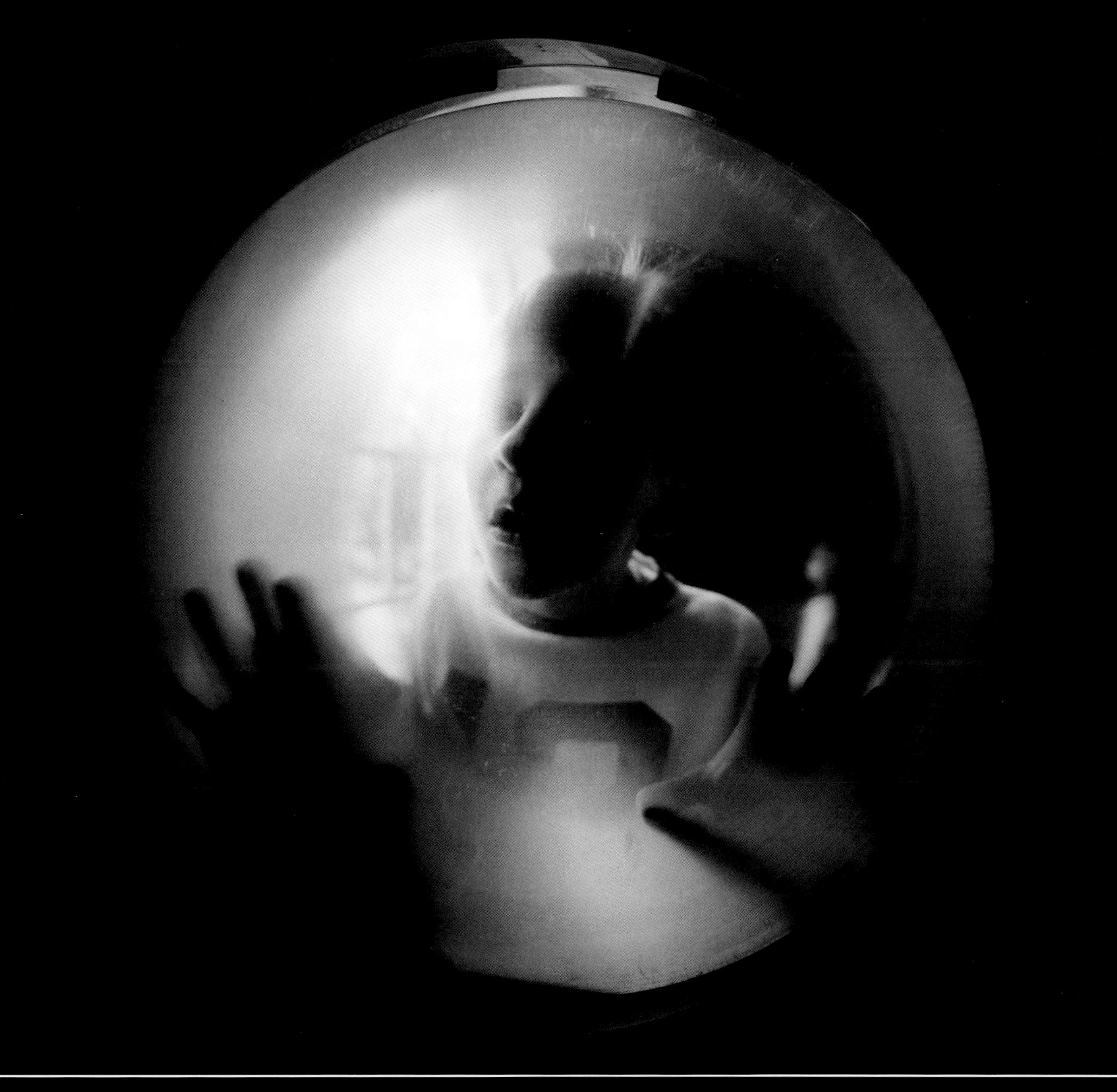

PLATE 63

Boy Looking through Window, Boston, Massachusetts, negative 1970; print 1972

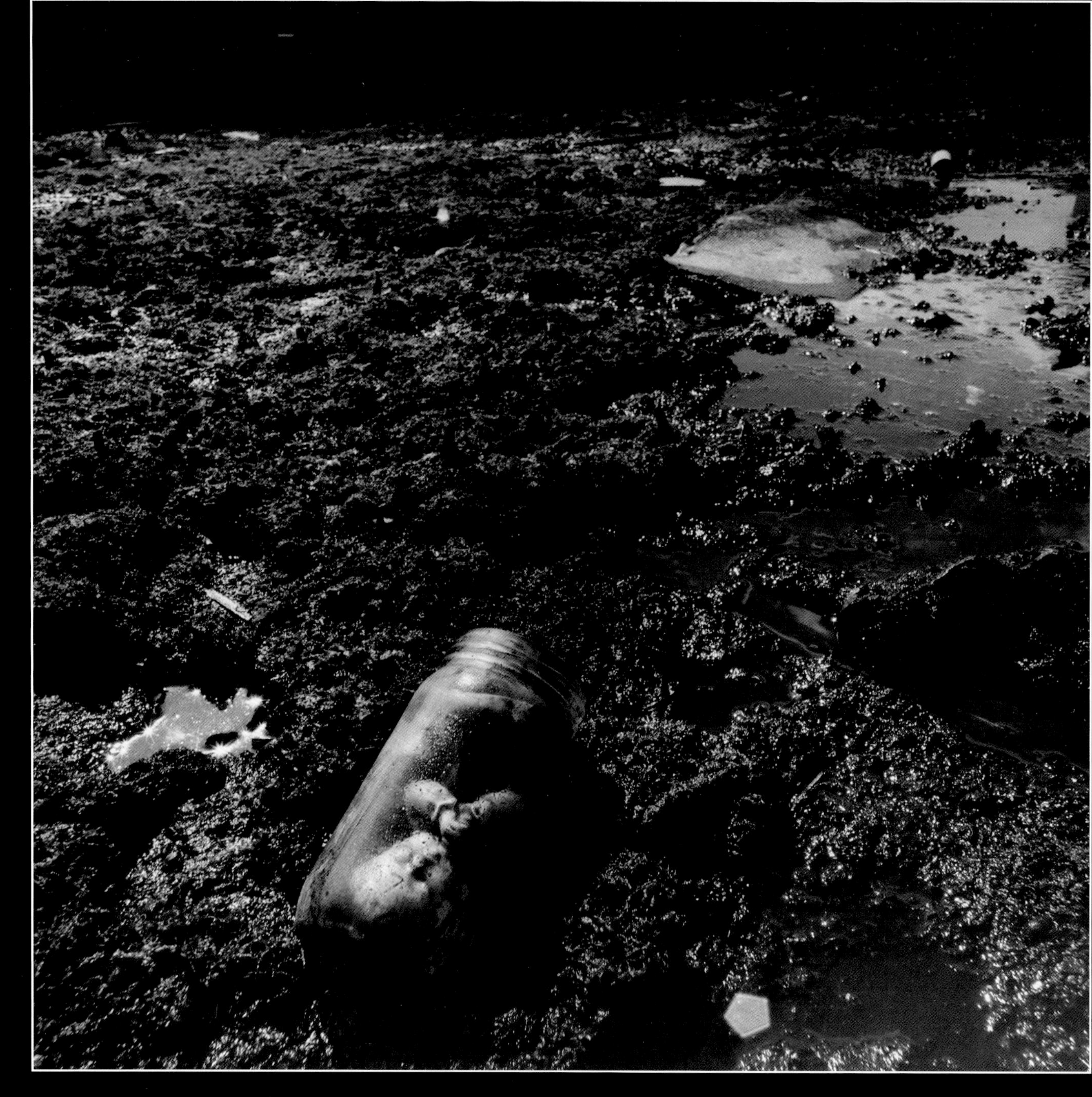

PLATE 64
Baby in Bottle, Queens, New York, 1970

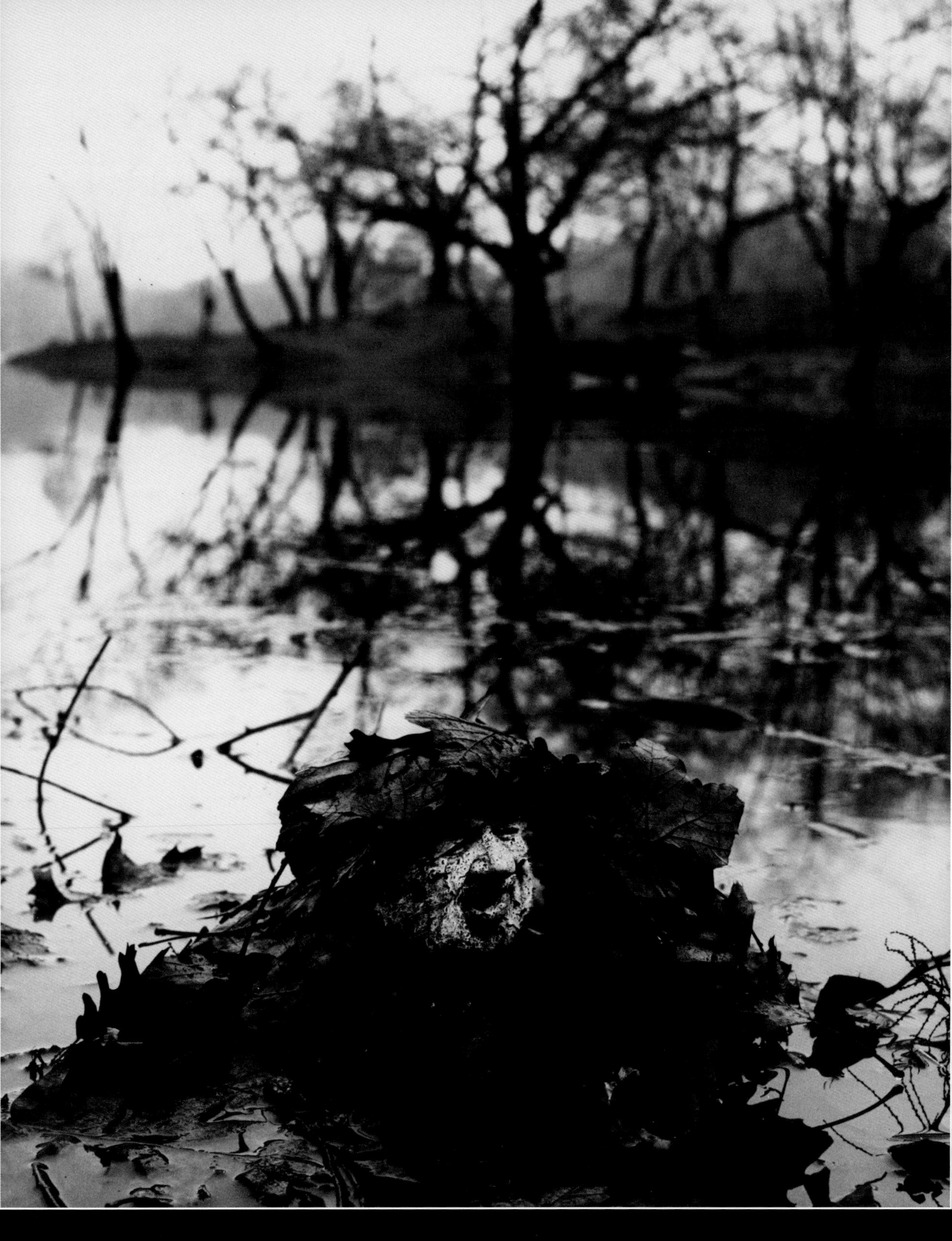

PLATE 65
Wild Man of the Forest, Central Park, New York, 1969

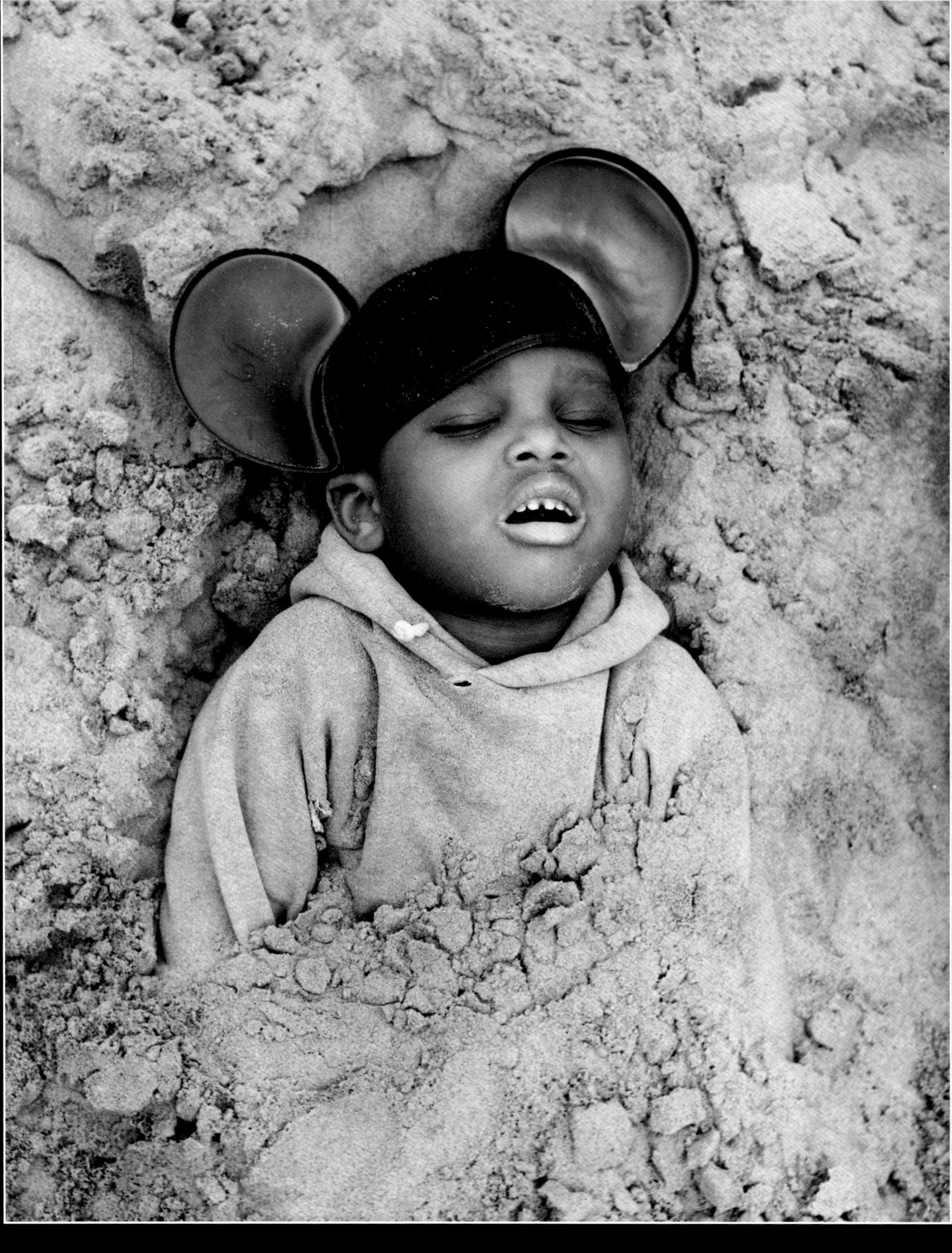

PLATE 66

Child Buried in the Sand, Coney Island, New York, 1969

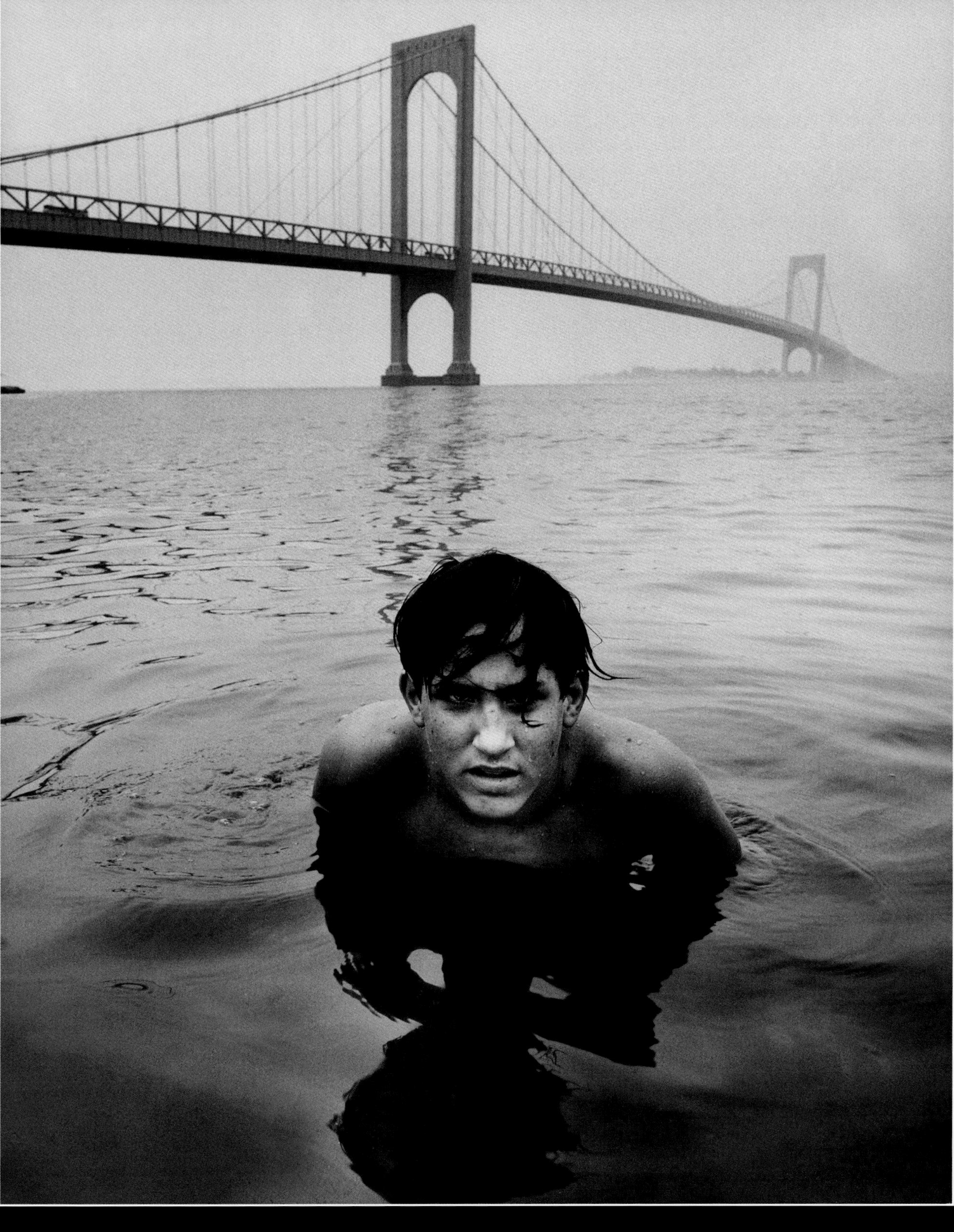

PLATE 67
Boy in Water under Bridge, Queens, New York, 1970

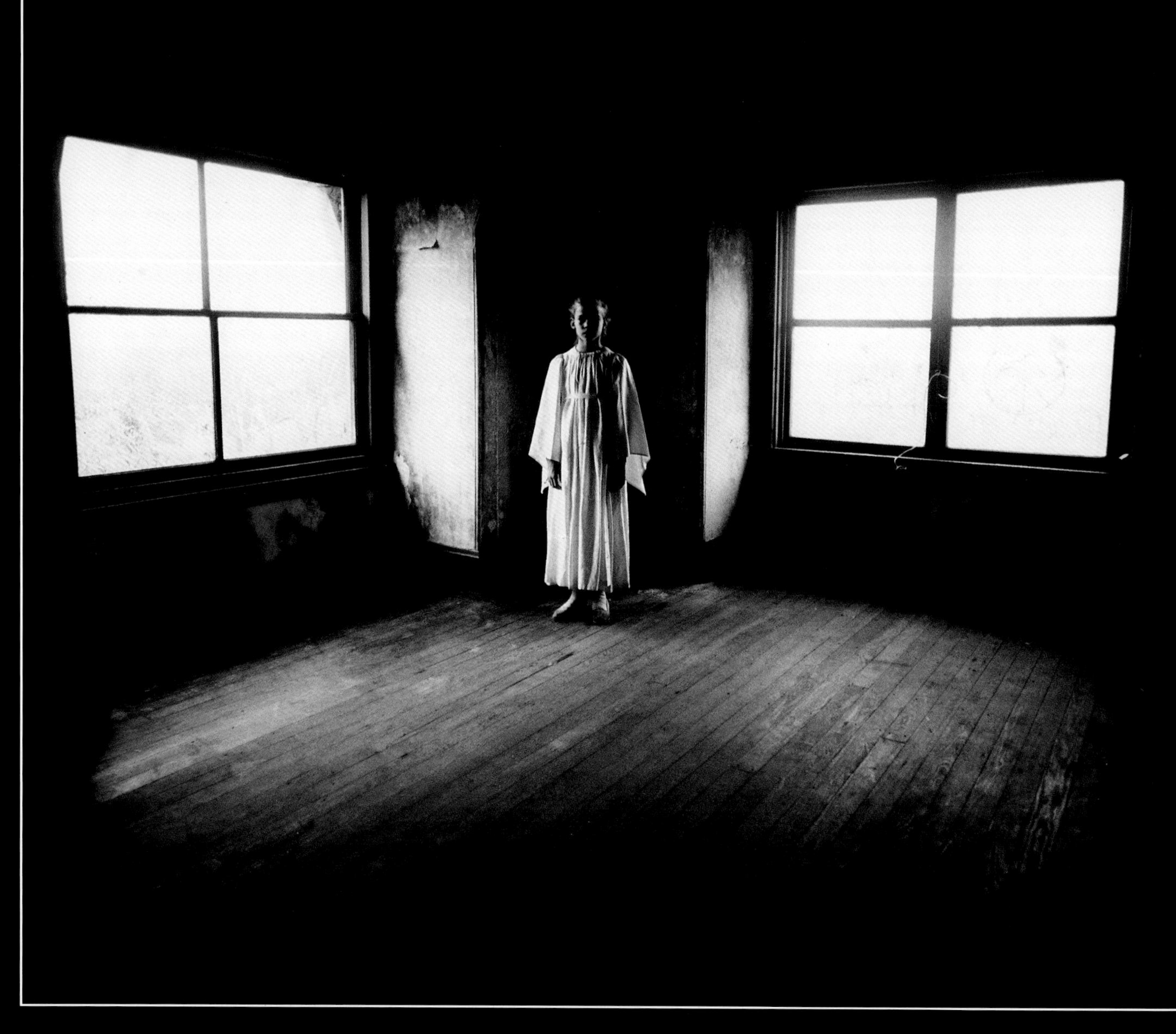

PLATE 68
Girl in White Dress (interior), Cape May, New Jersey, 1971

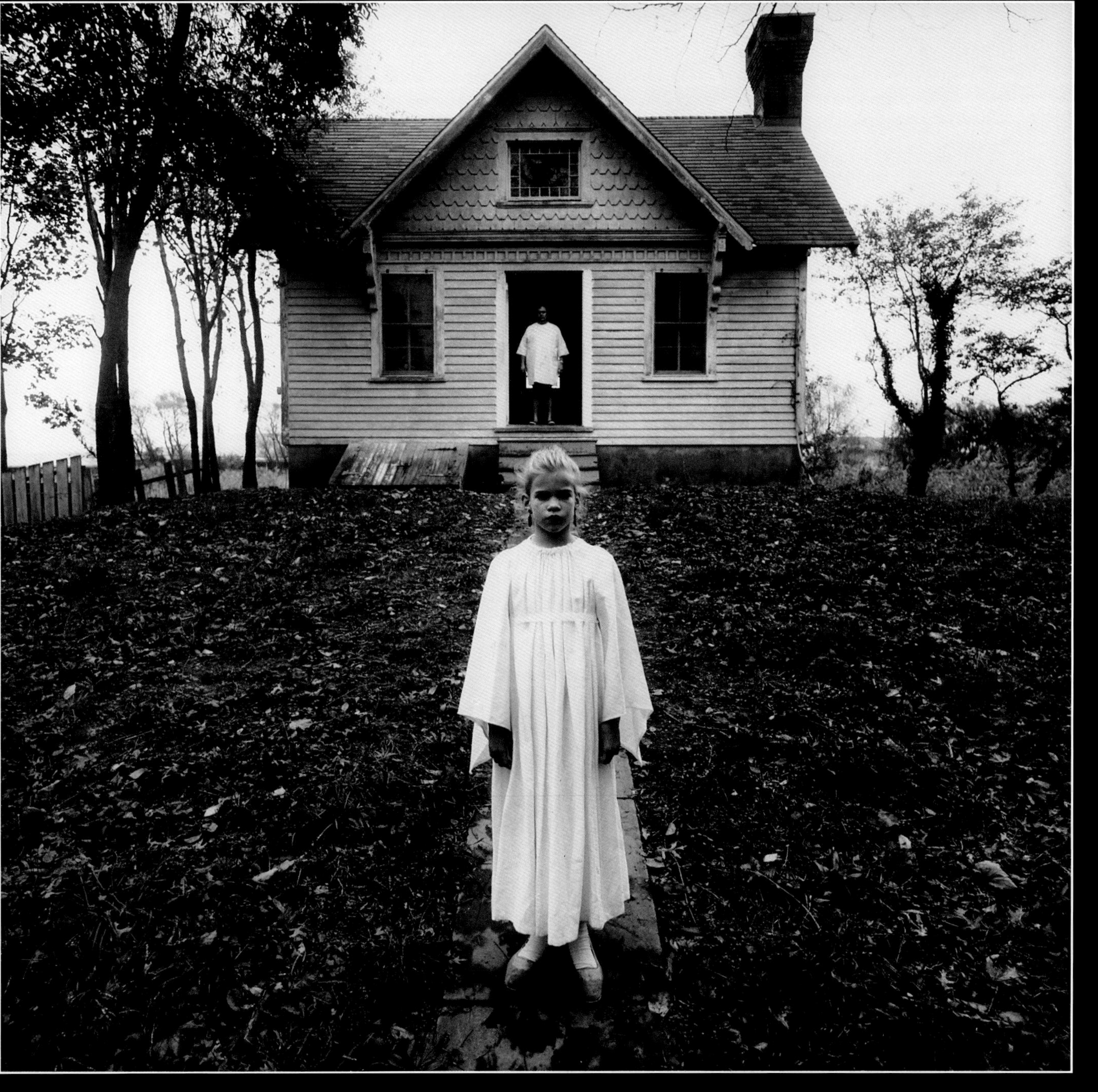

PLATE 69
Girl in White Dress (exterior), Cape May, New Jersey, 1971

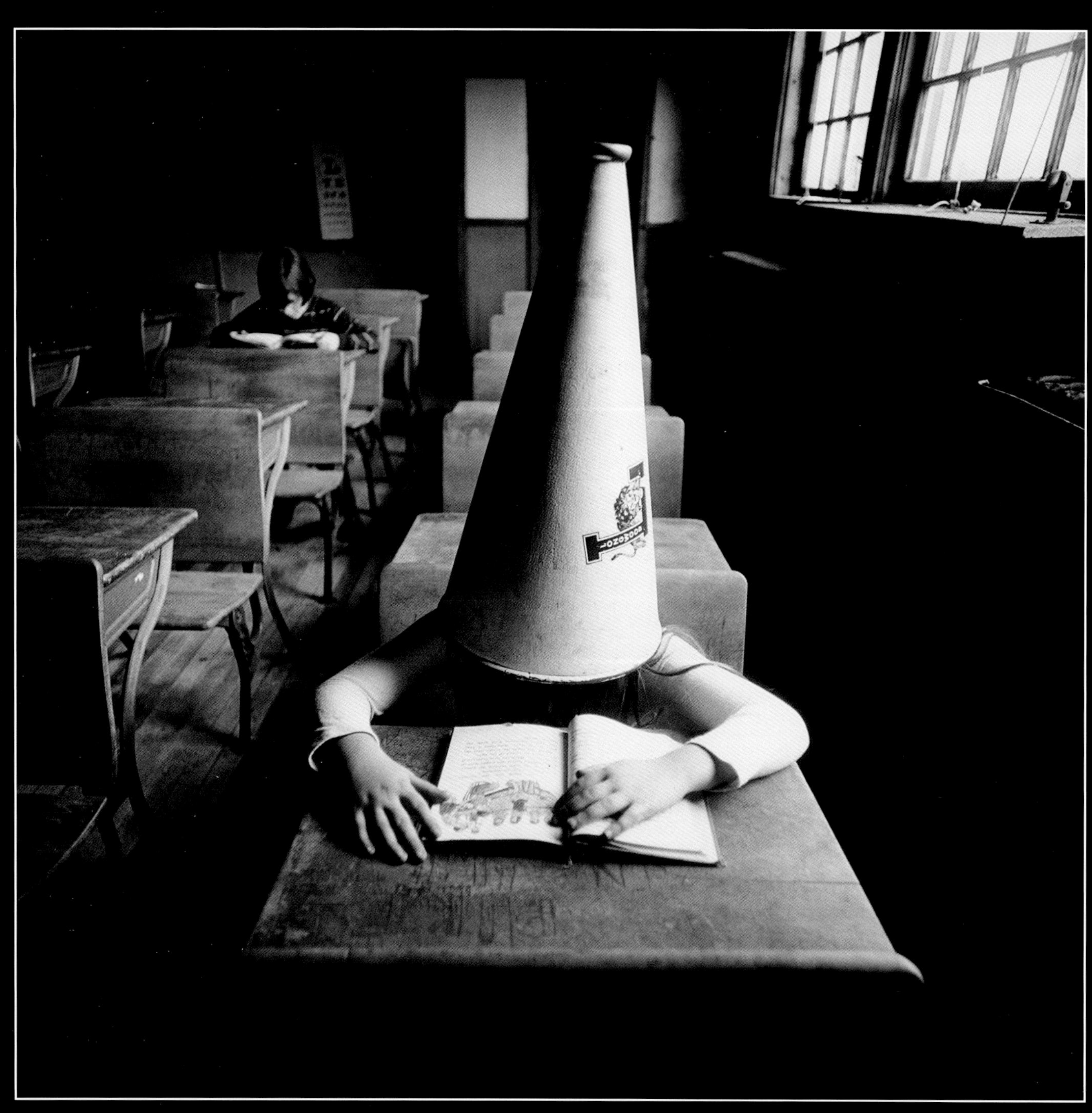

PLATE 70
Girl with Dunce Cap, P. S. 3, New York, New York, 1972

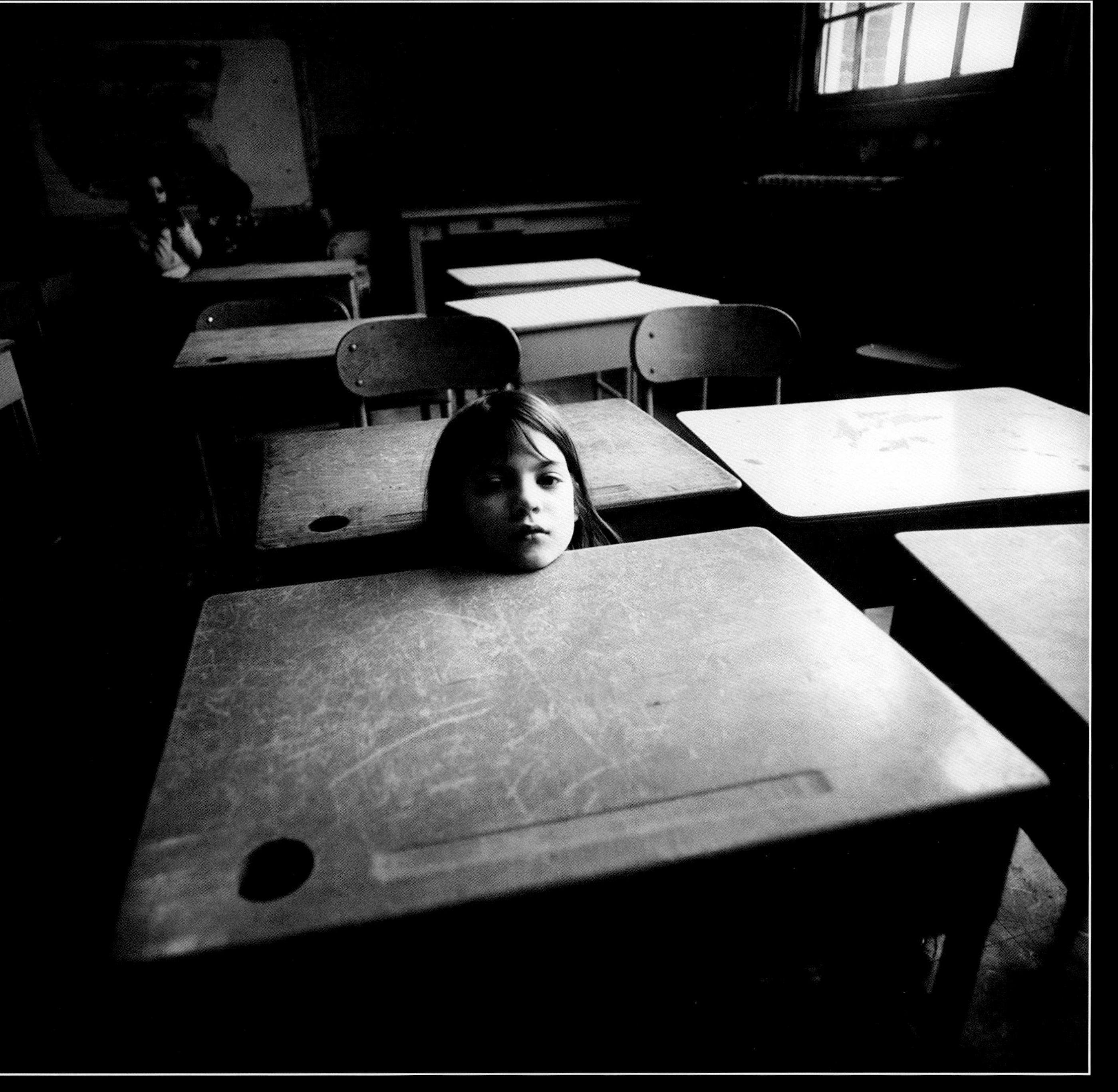

PLATE 71
School Girl's Dream, P. S. 3, New York, New York, 1972

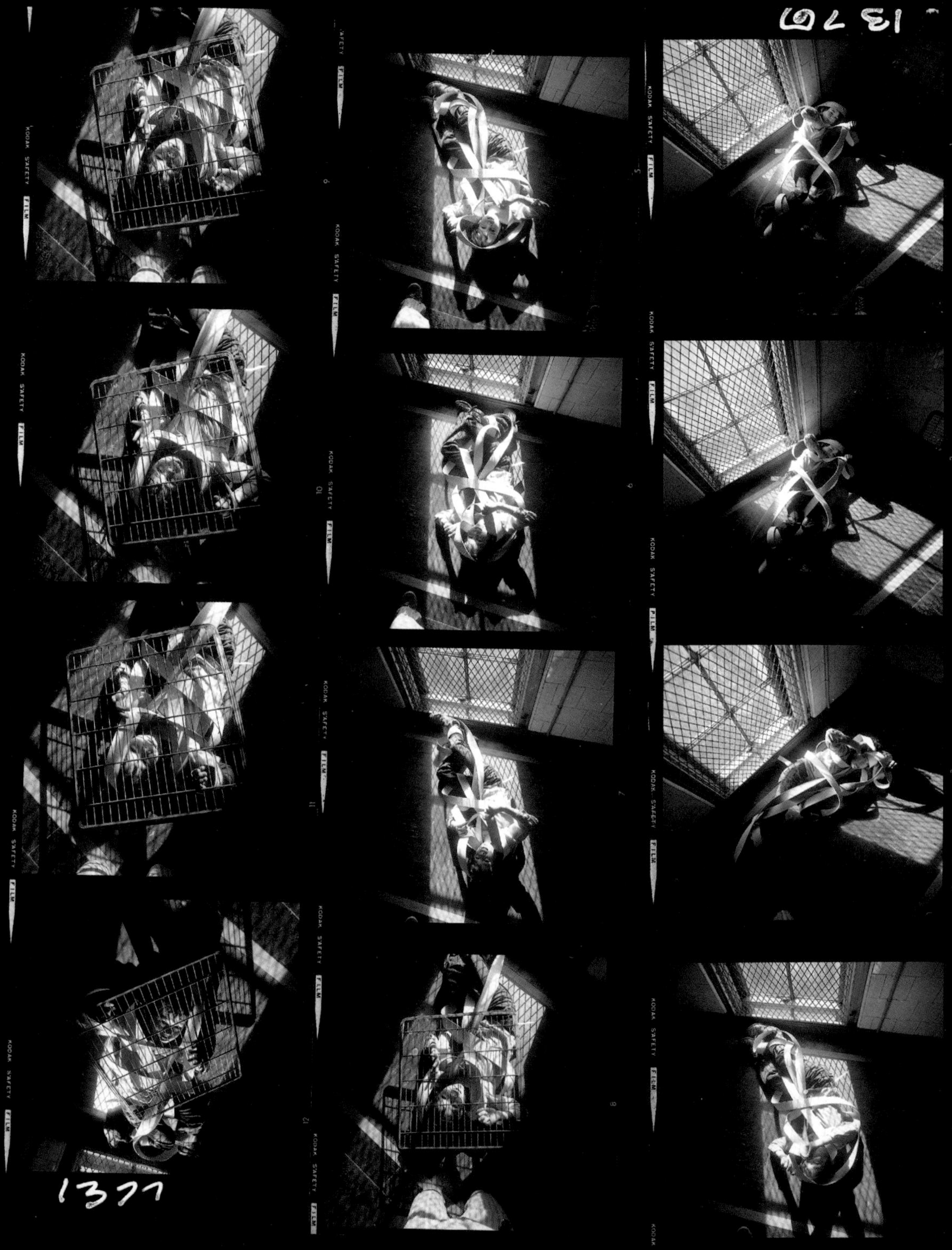

Contact sheet, P.S. 3,
New York, New York, 1972
Gelatin silver print,
25.4 × 20.3 cm
(10 × 8 in.)
Collection of the artist

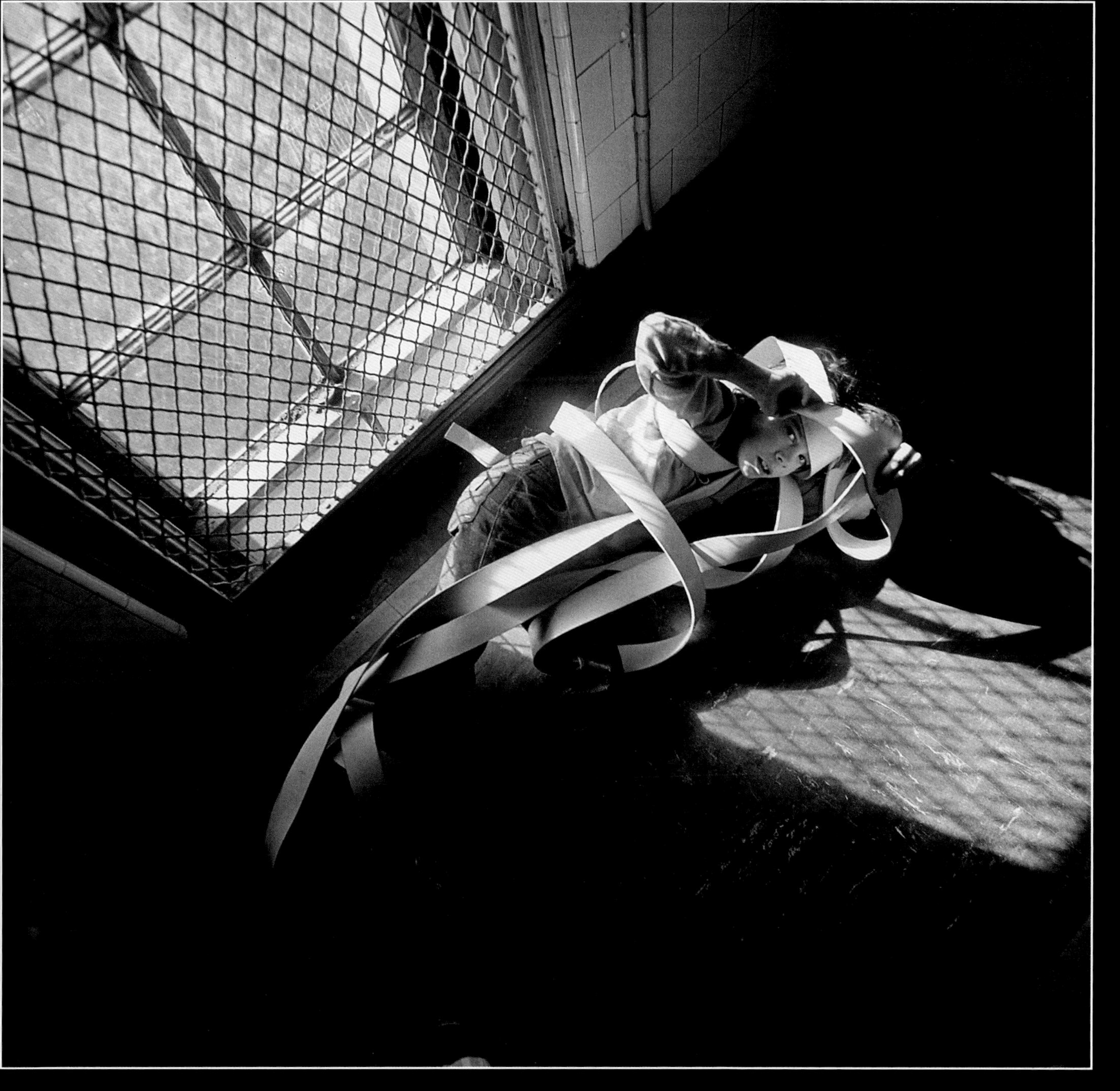

PLATE 72
Boy with Tangled Strips, P. S. 3, New York, New York, 1972

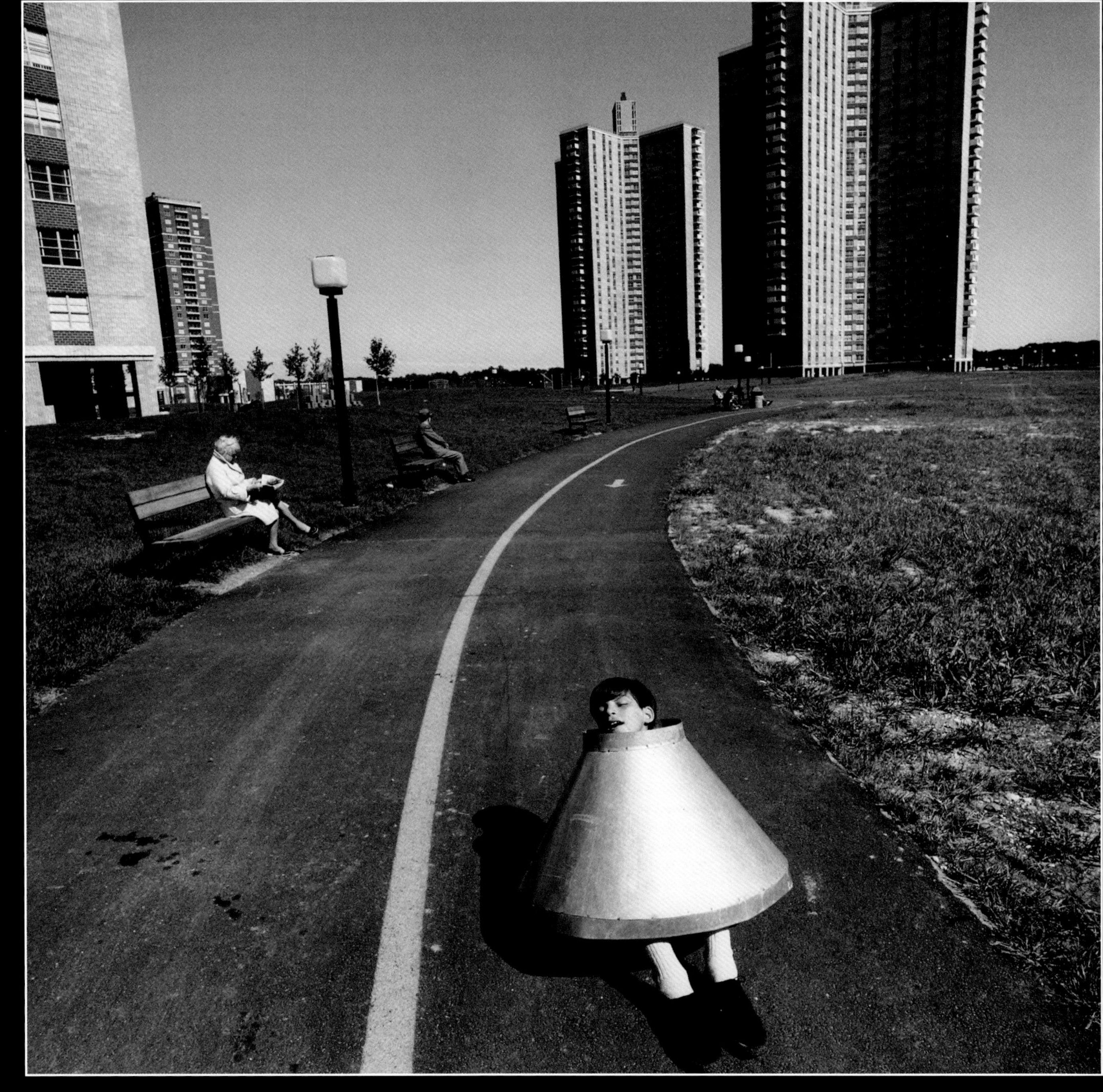

PLATE 73
Boy in Tin Cone, Bronx, New York, 1972

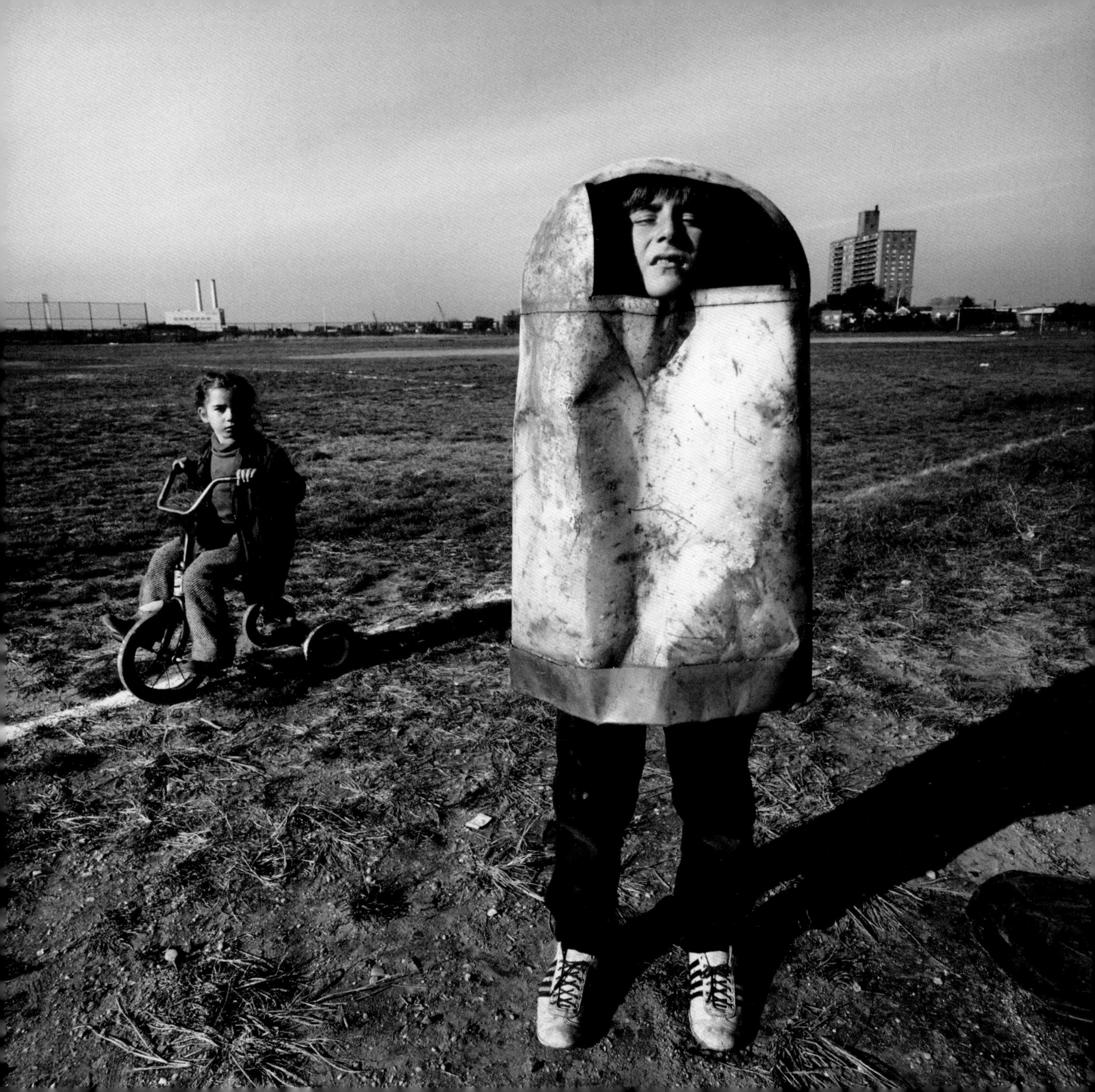

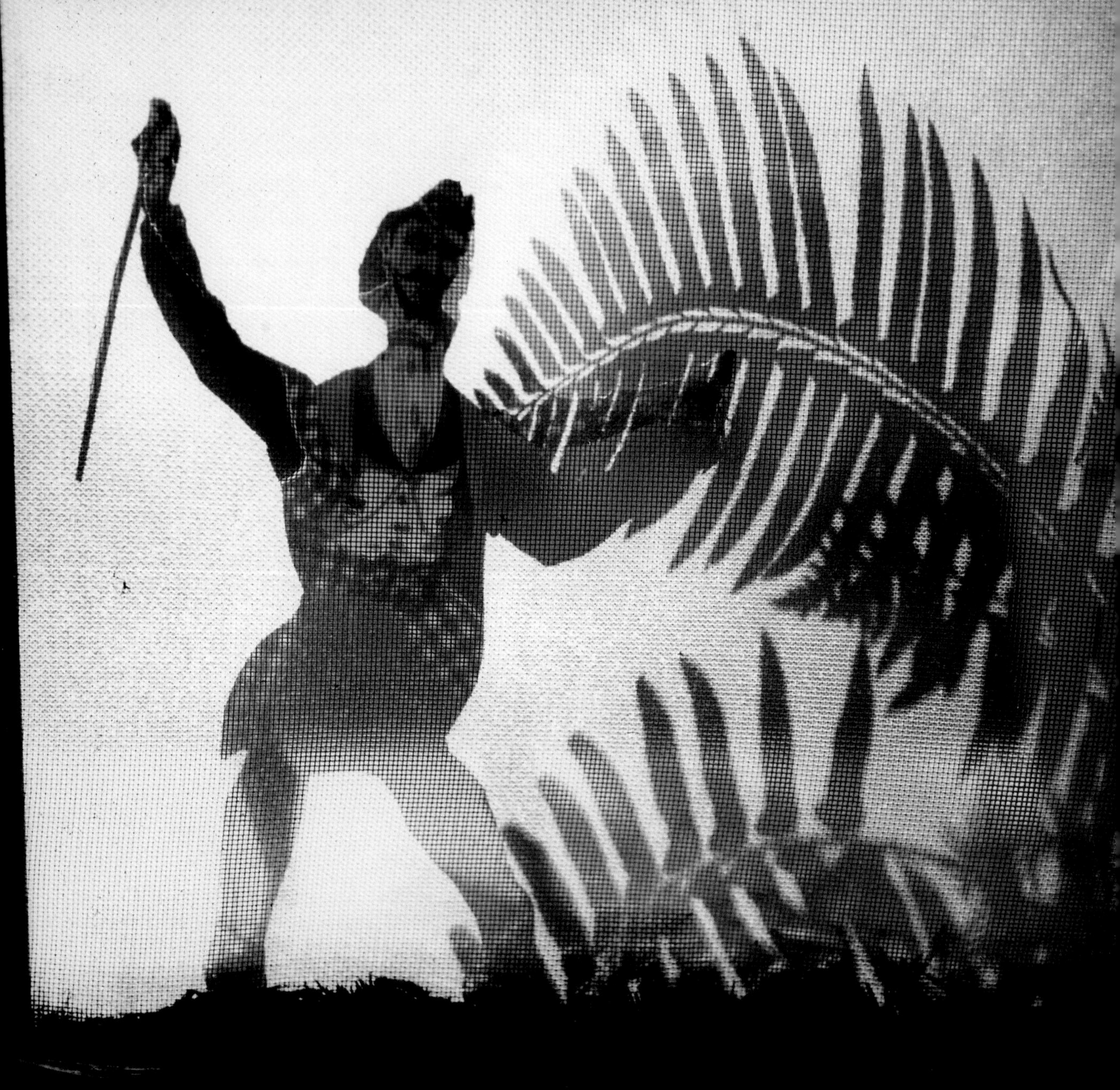

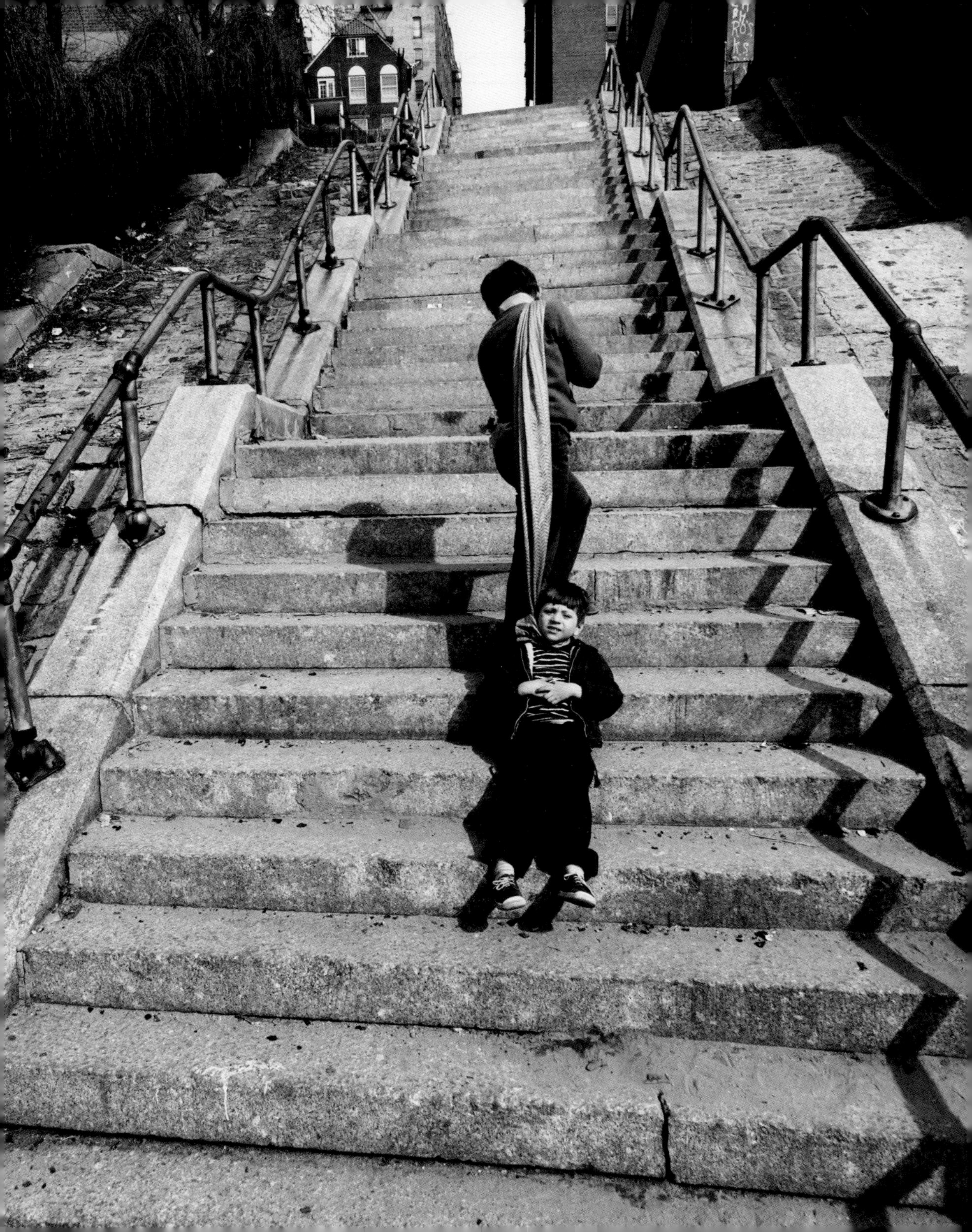

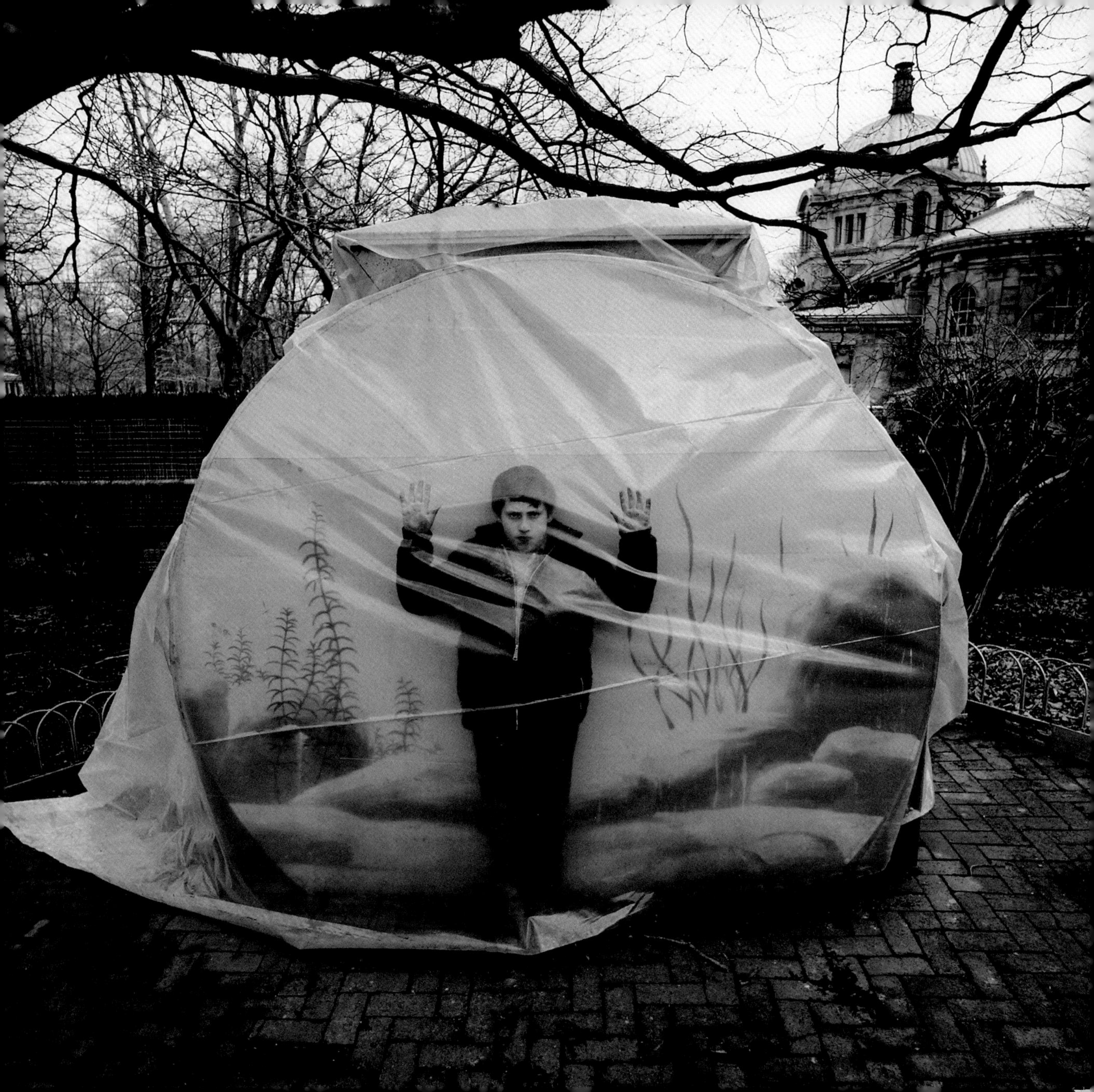

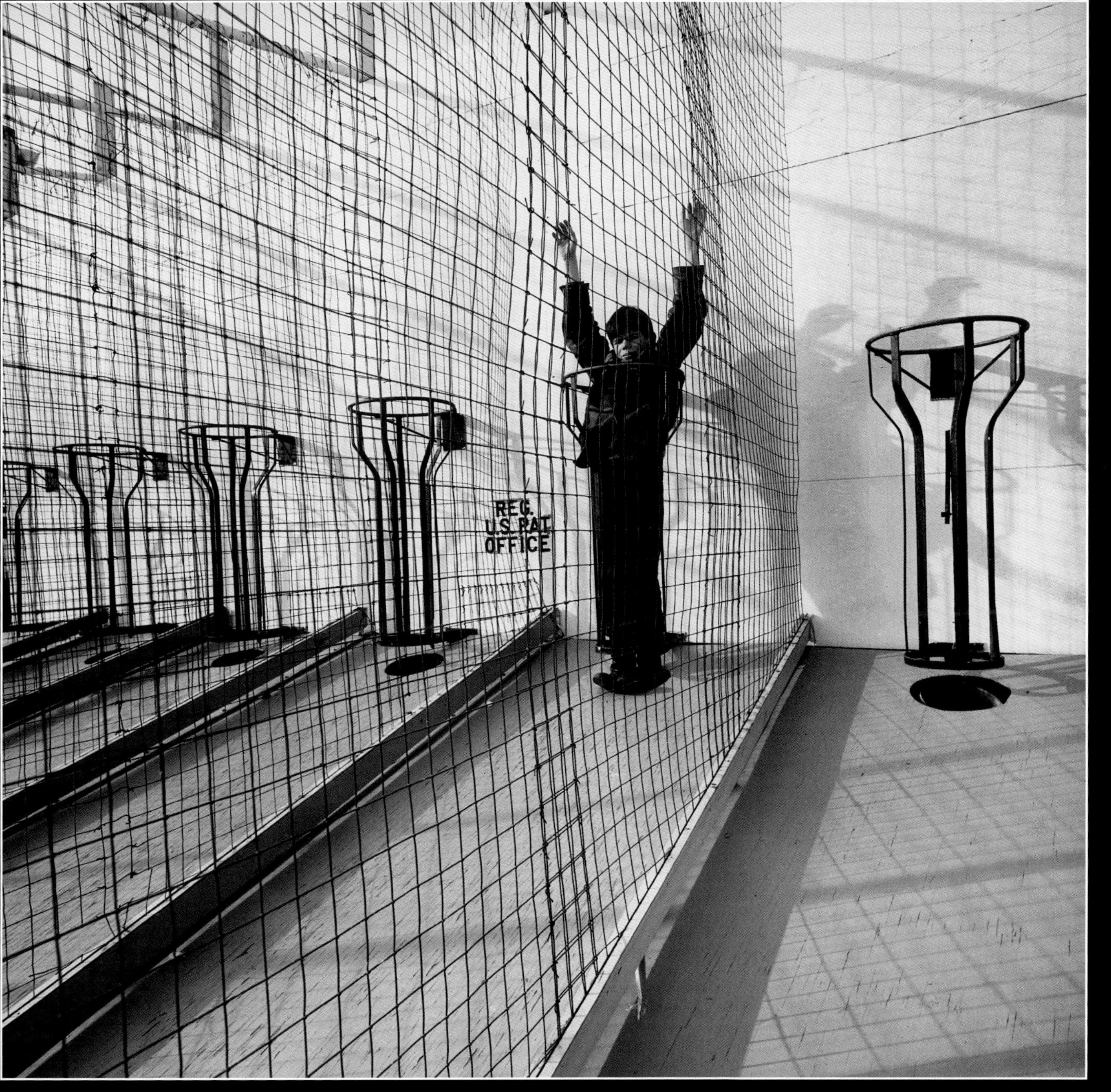

PLATE 78
Boy in Basketball Hoop, Ocean City, New Jersey, 1971

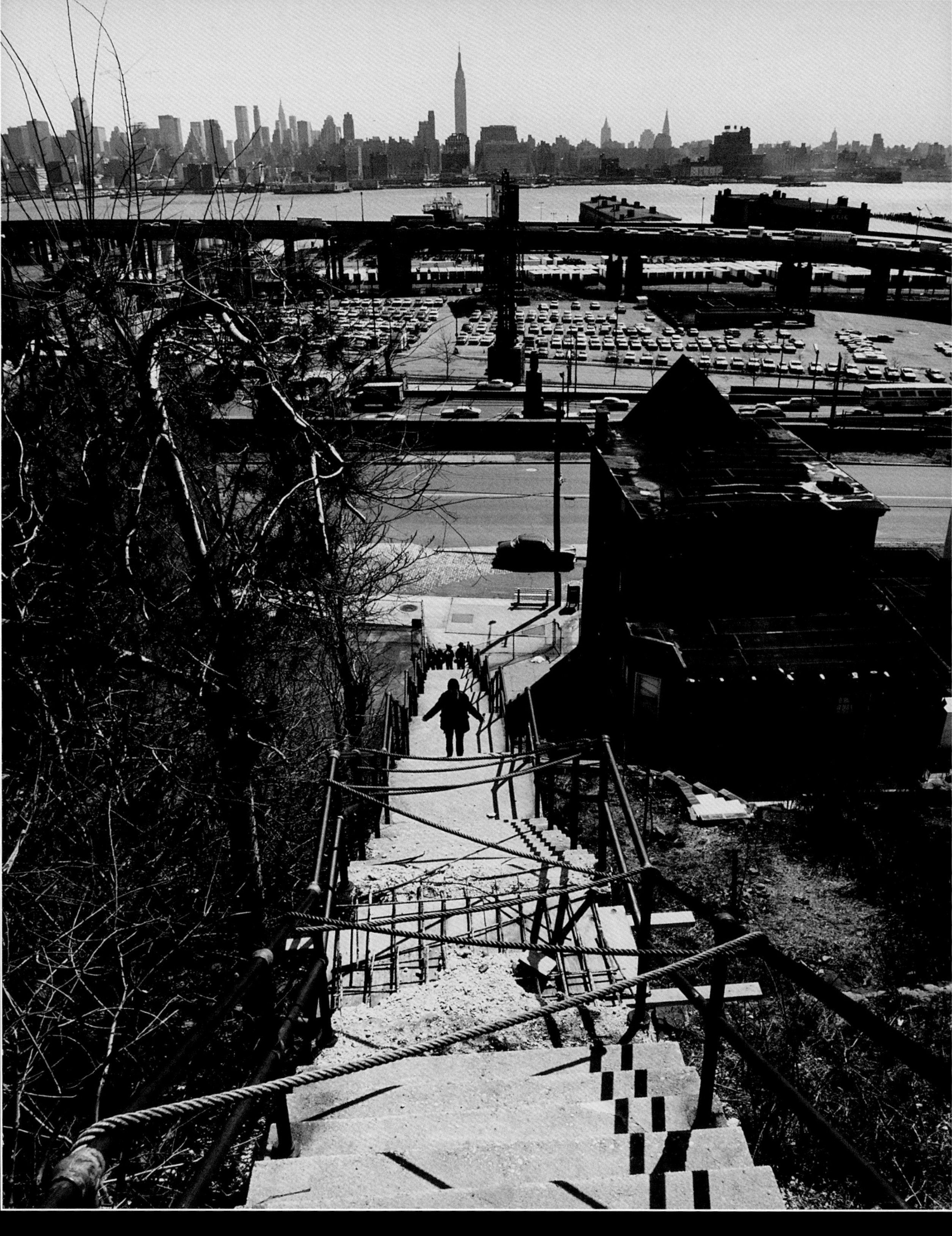

PLATE 79

Boys on Broken Staircase, Weehawken, New Jersey, 1970

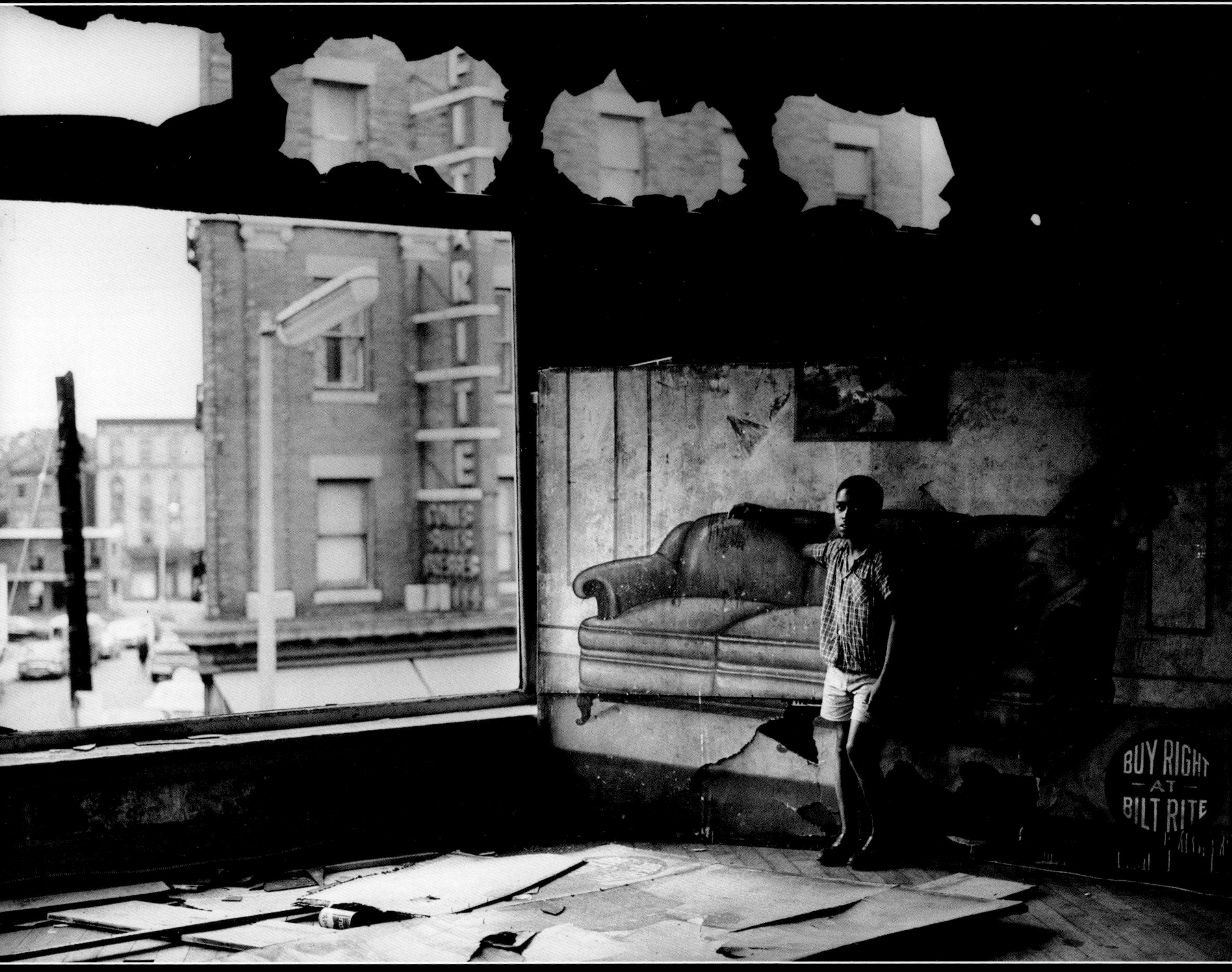

PLATE 80
Boy in Burnt-Out Furniture Store, Newark, New Jersey, 1969

Contact sheet, New York,
New York, 1971
Gelatin silver print,
25.4 × 20.3 cm
(10 × 8 in.)
Collection of the artist

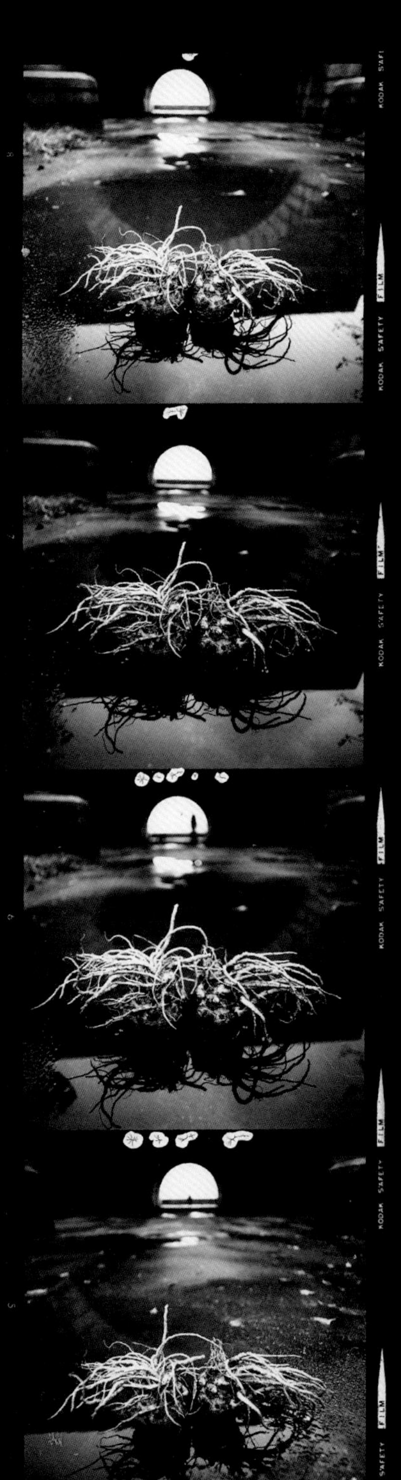

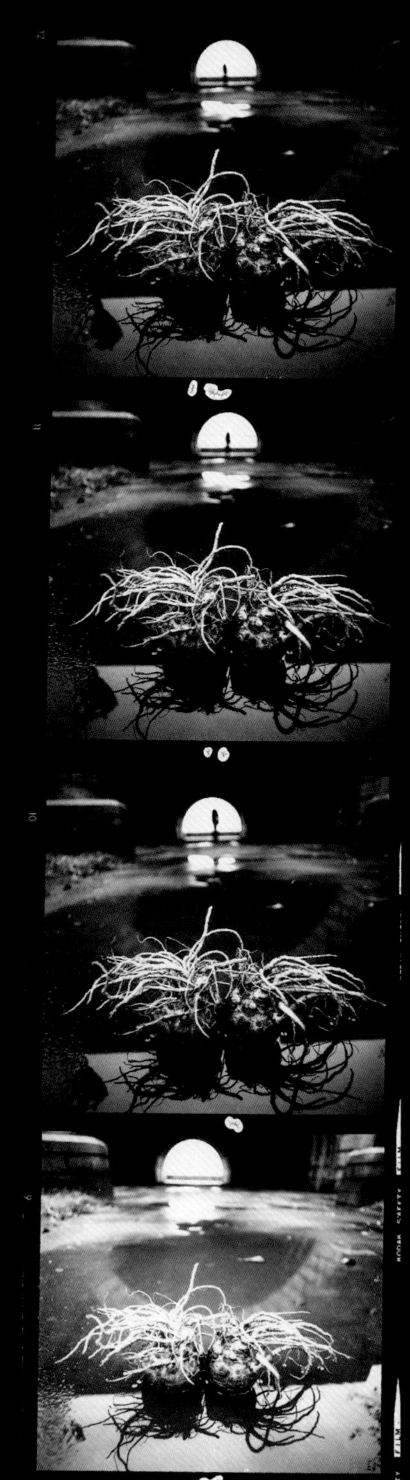

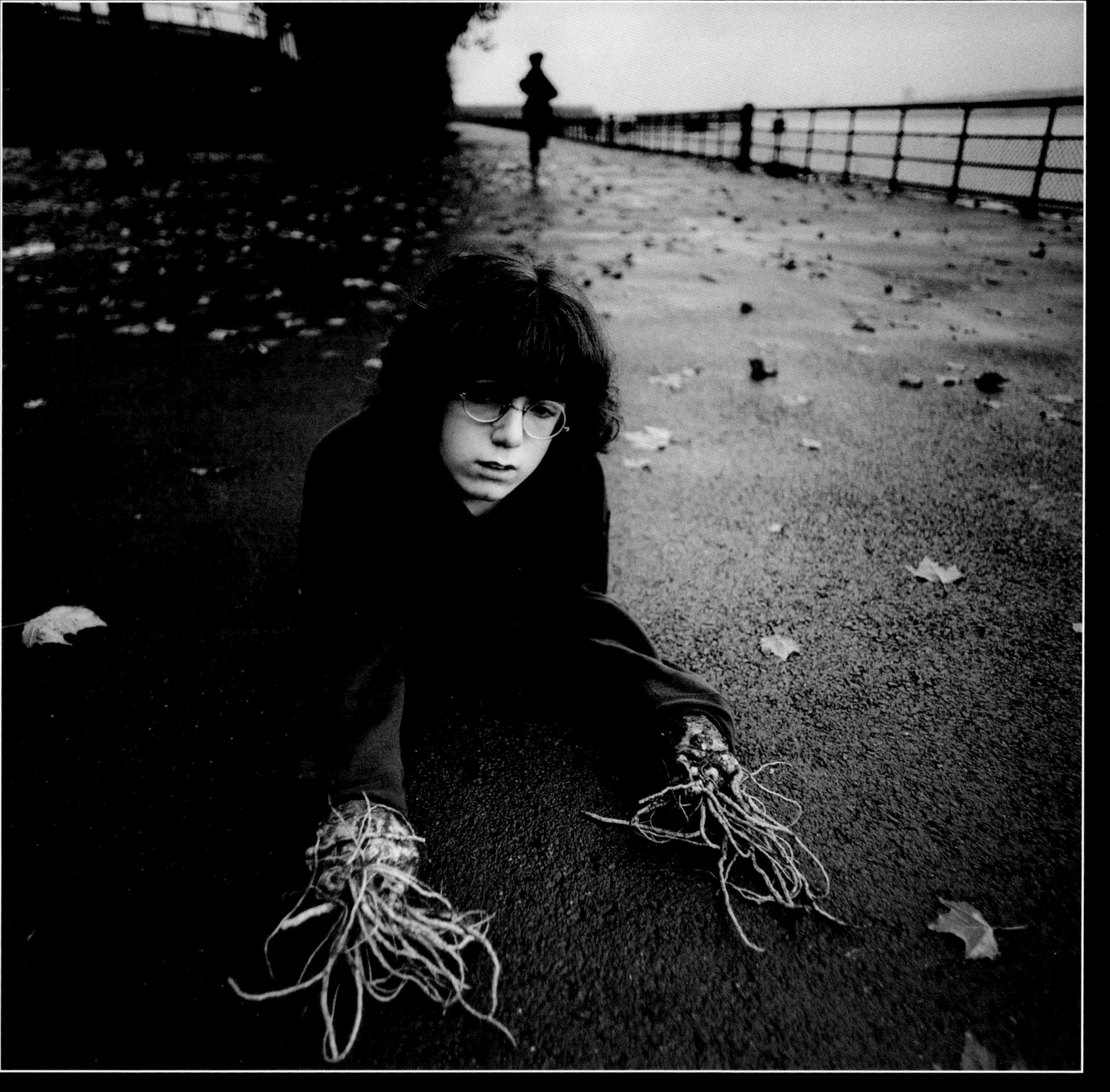

PLATE 81
Boy with Root Hands, New York, New York, 1971

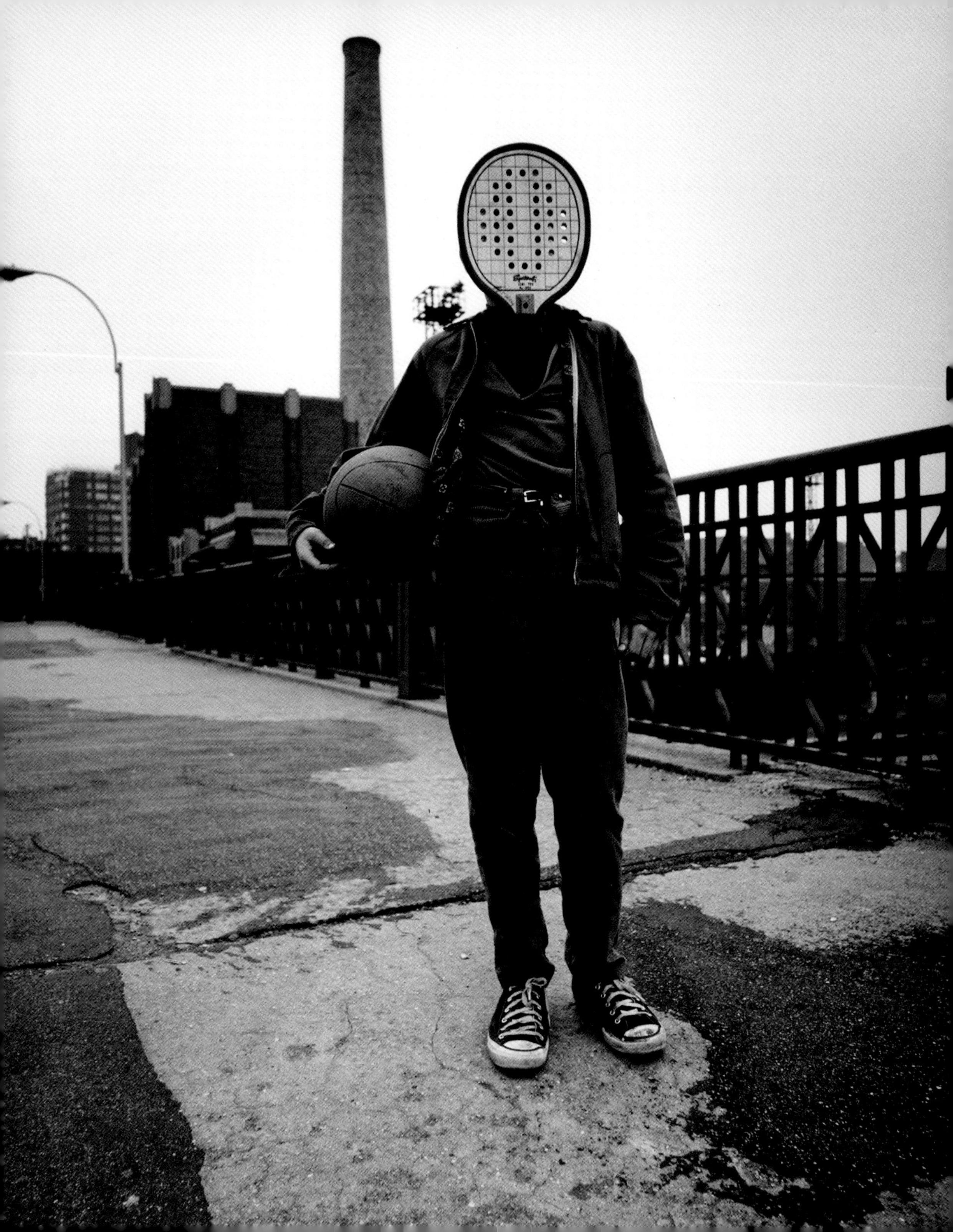

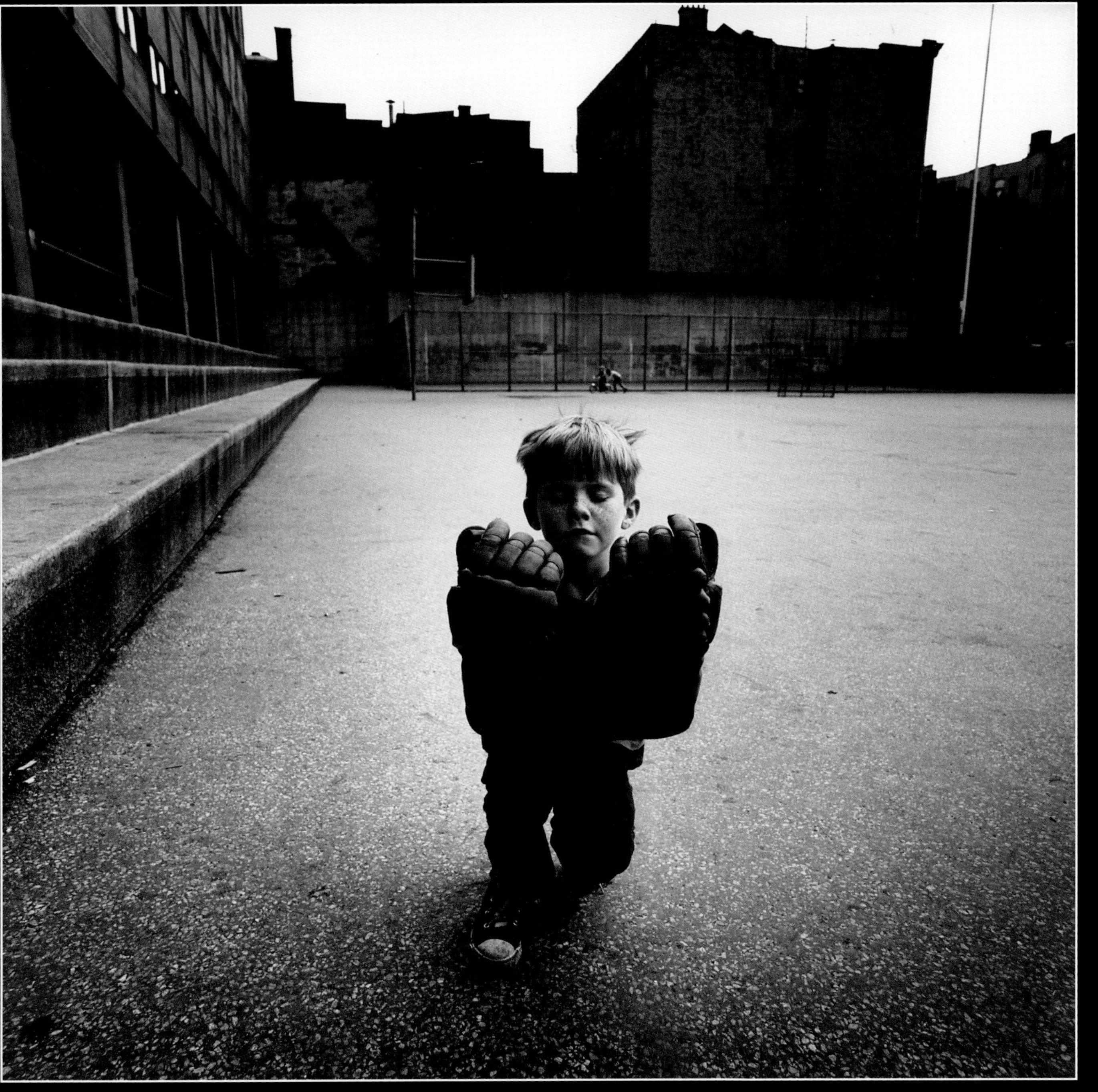

PLATE 83
Boy with Hockey Gloves, Hell's Kitchen, New York, negative 1970; print later

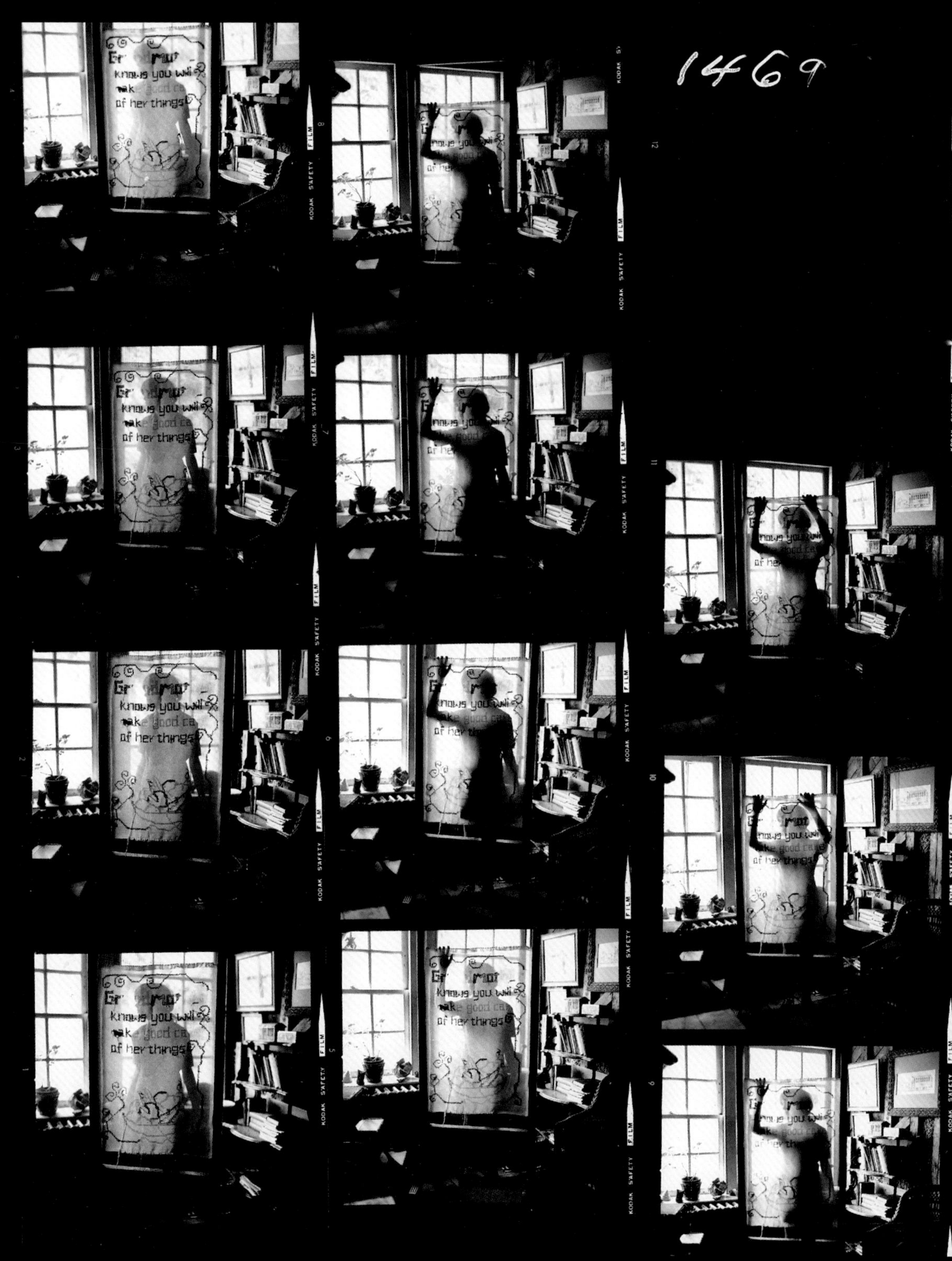

Contact sheet, Boston, Massachusetts, 1972
Gelatin silver print, 25.4 × 20.3 cm (10 × 8 in.)
Collection of the artist

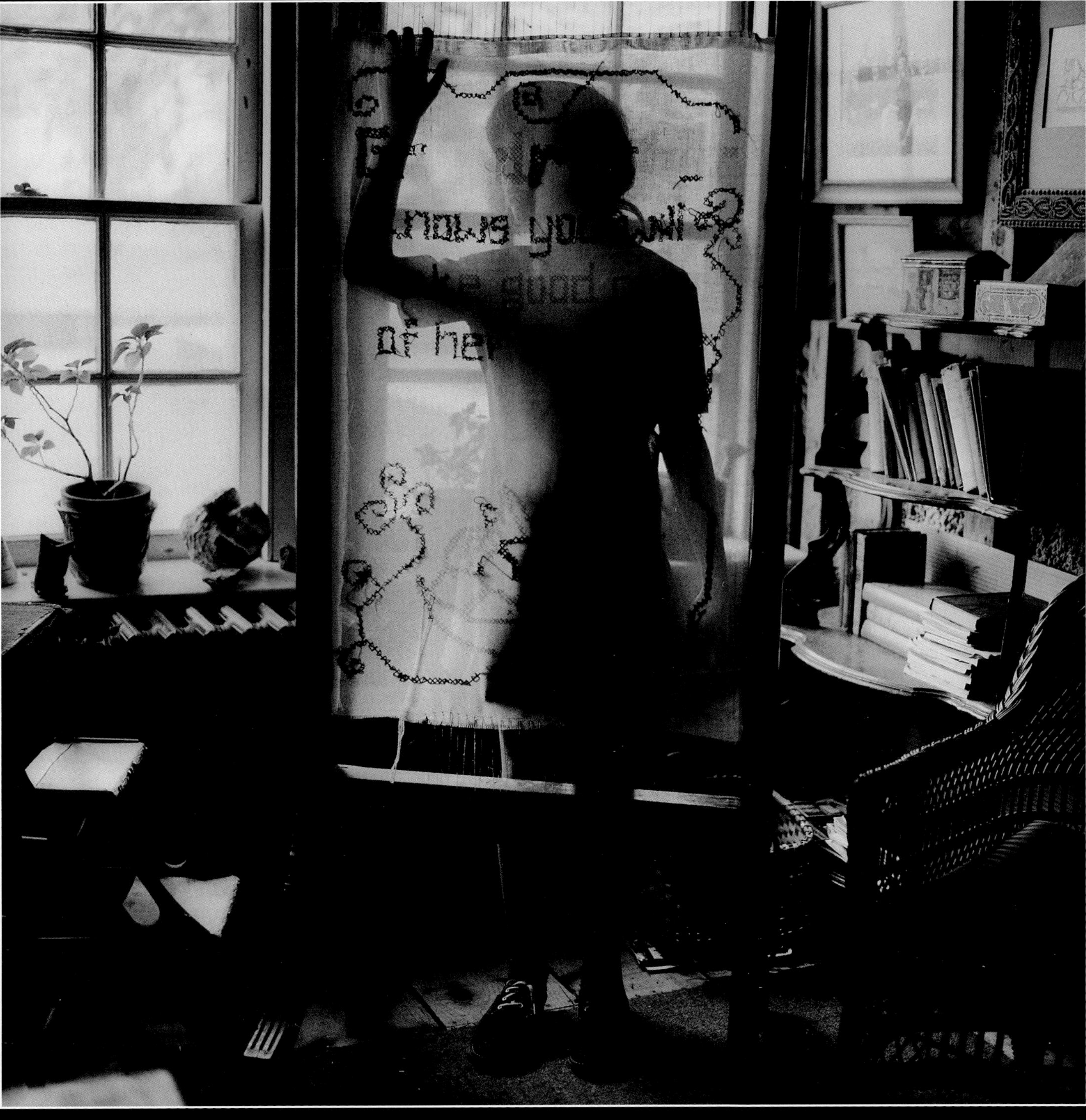

PLATE 84
Girl in Attic, Boston, Massachusetts, 1972

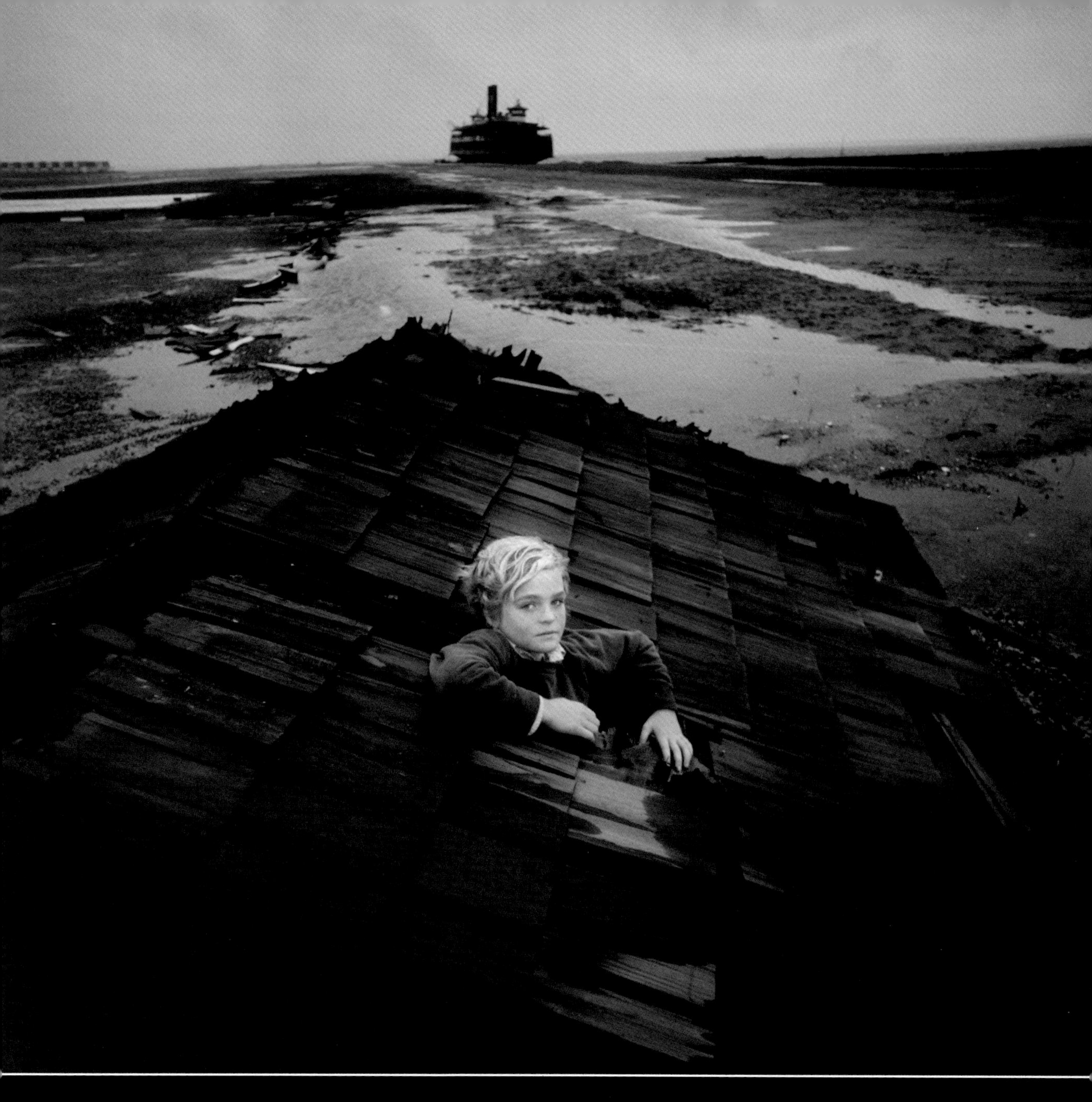

PLATE 85

Boy in Flood Dream, Ocean City, Maryland, negative 1971; print later

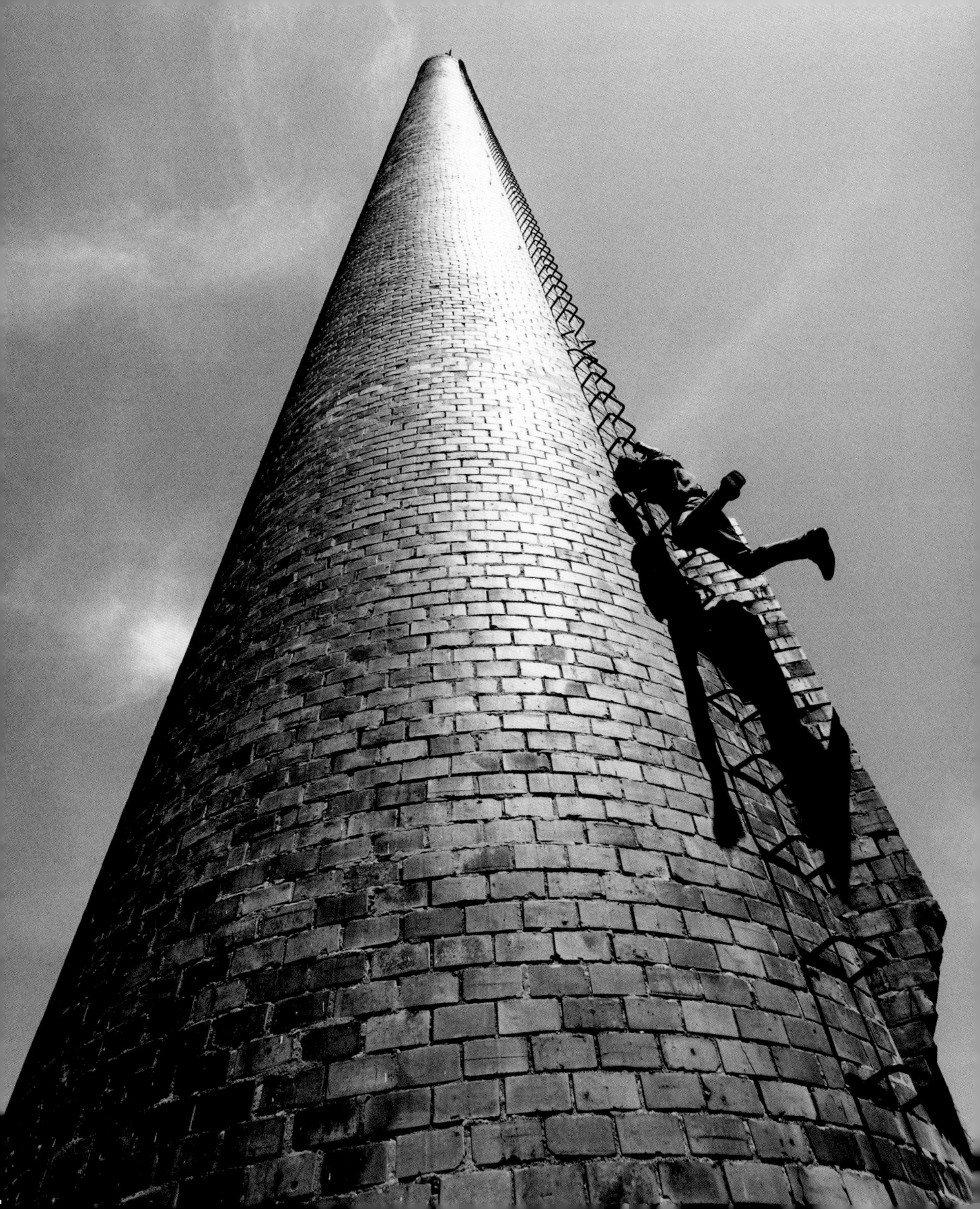

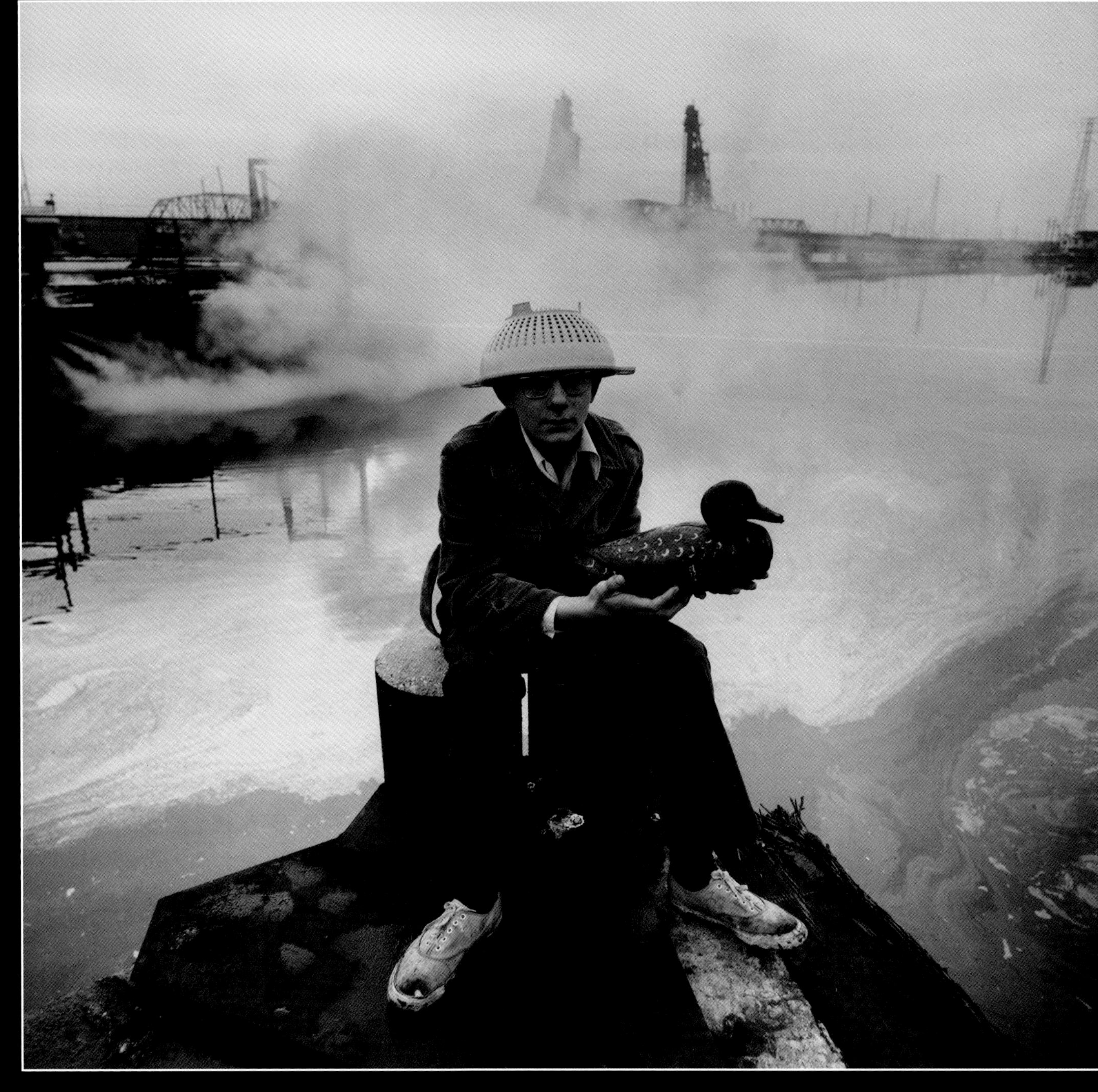

PLATE 87

Boy with Duck Decoy, Passaic, New Jersey, 1969

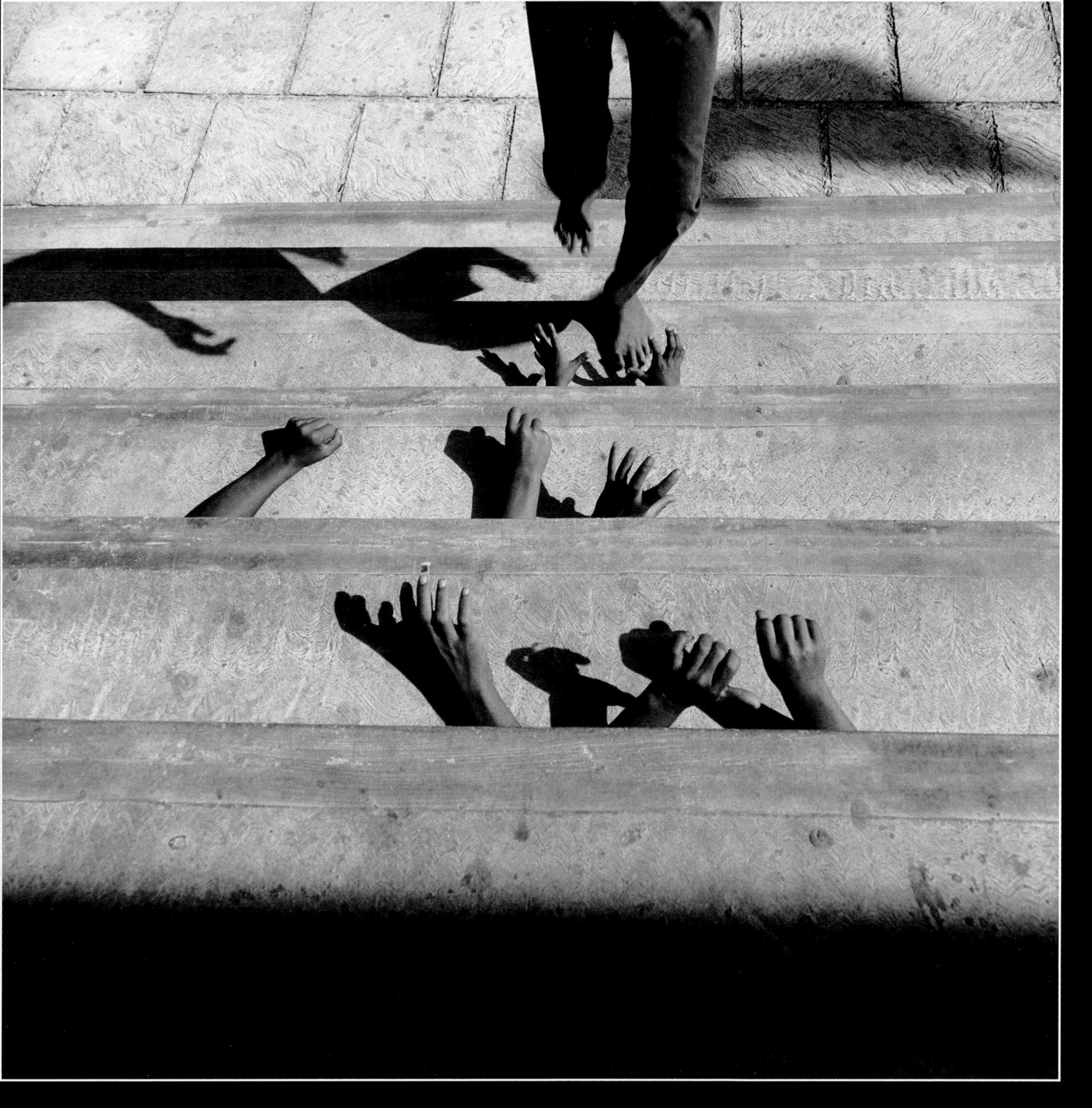

PLATE 88
Hands on the Staircase, Isla Mujeres, Mexico, 1972

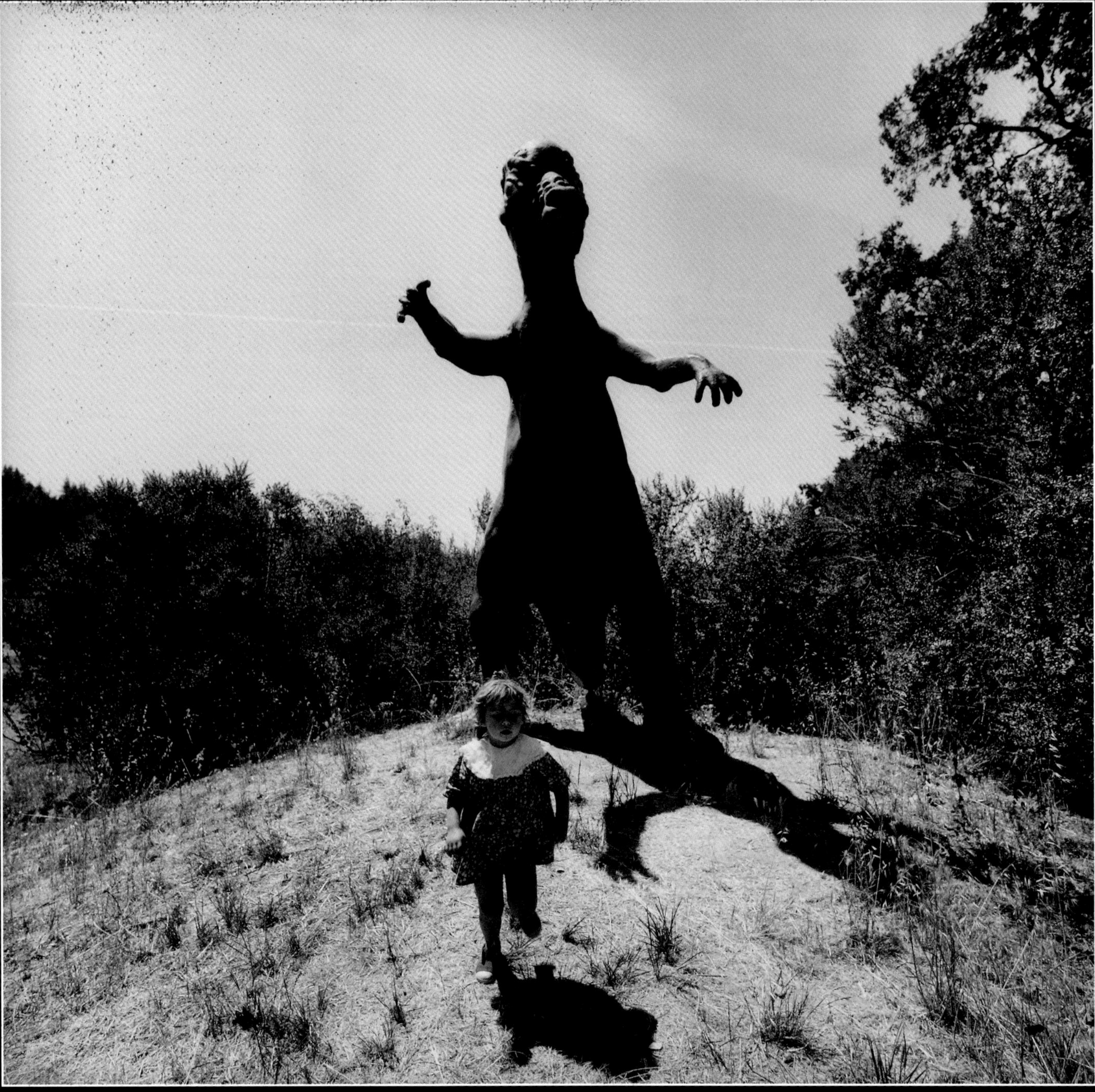

PLATE 89
Girl and Dinosaur, Santa Cruz, California, 1971

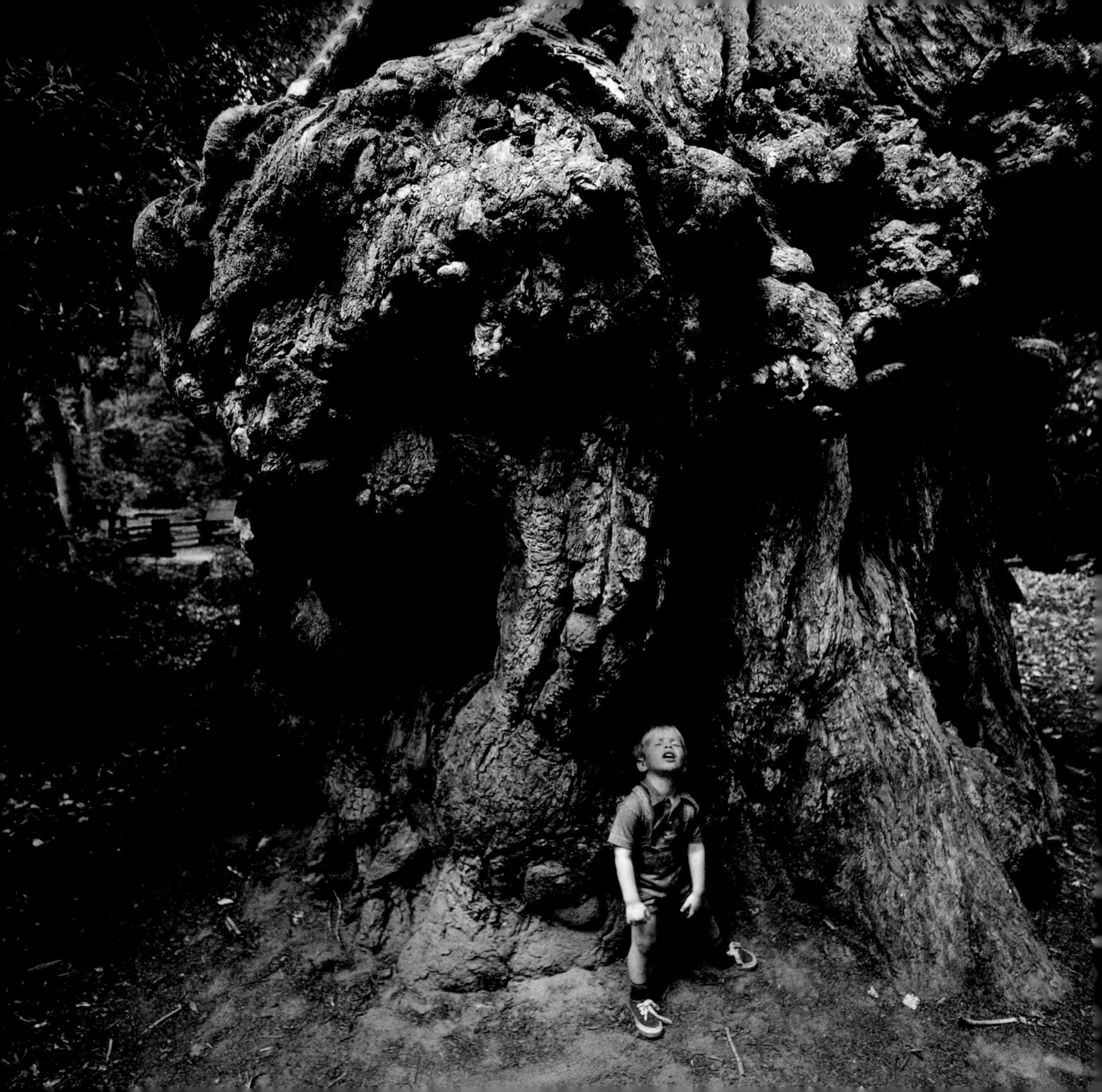

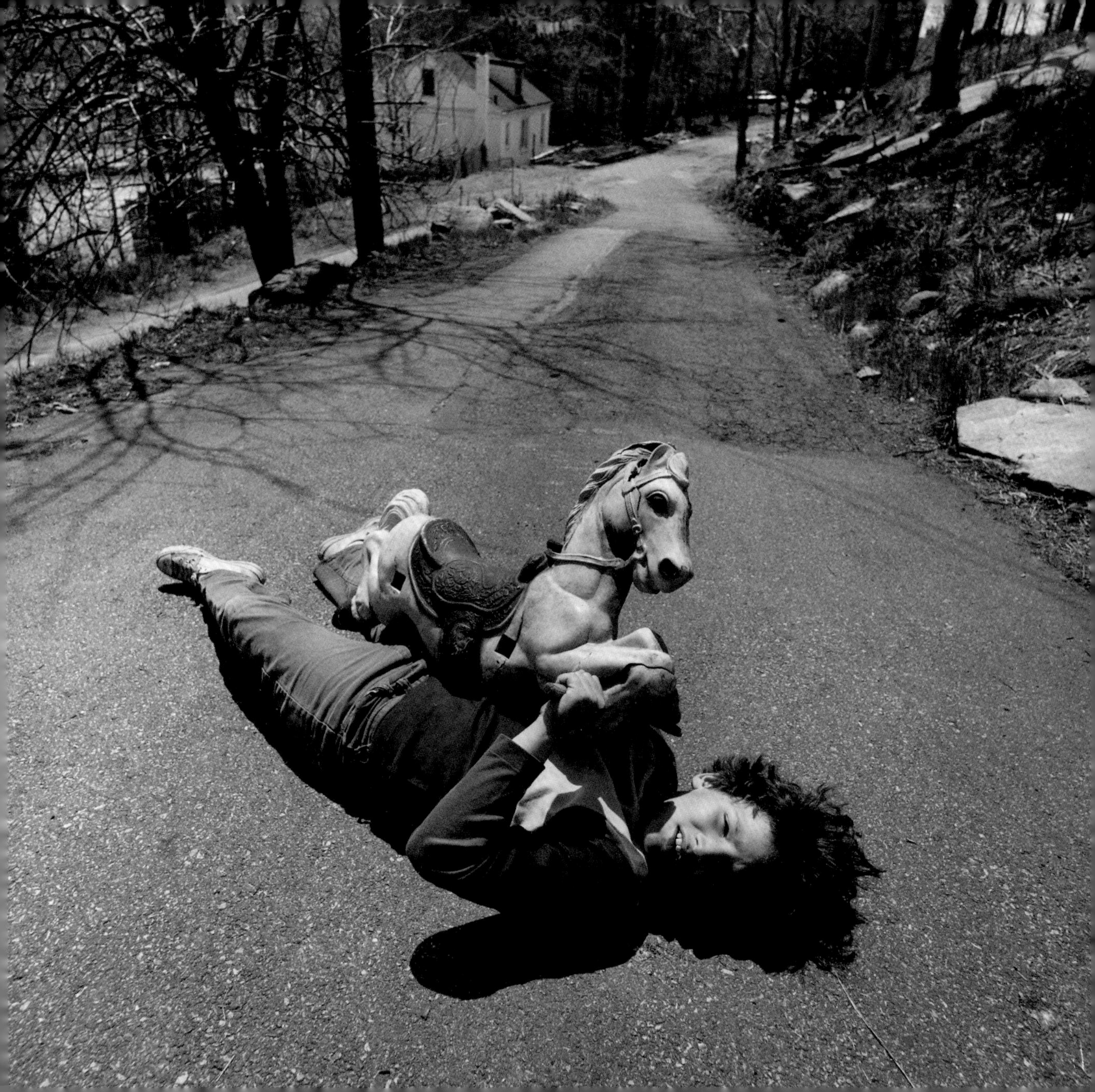

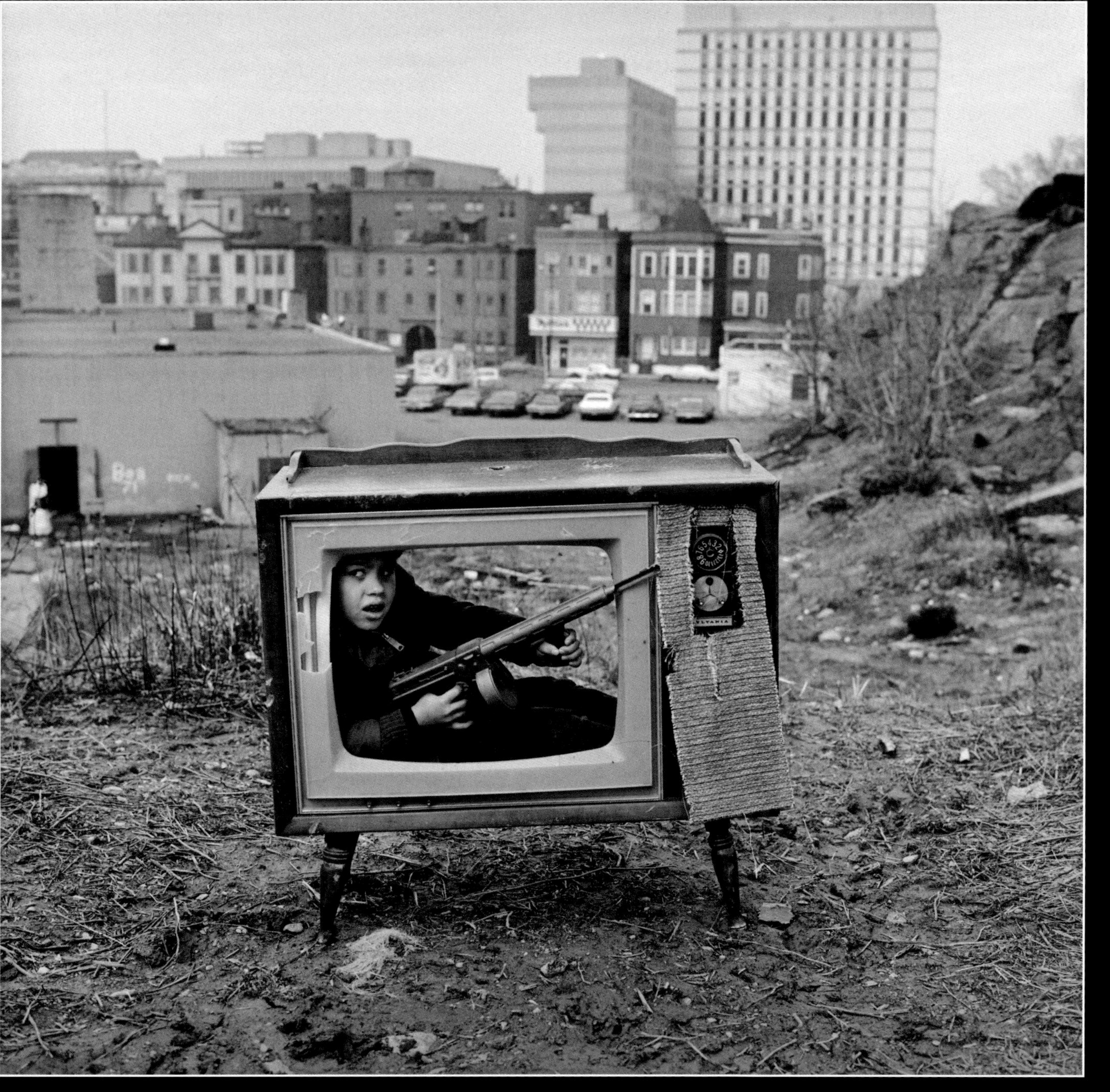

PLATE 92
Boy in TV Set, Boston, Massachusetts, 1972

Contact sheet, New York,
New York, 1971
Gelatin silver print,
25.4 × 20.3 cm
(10 × 8 in.)
Collection of the artist

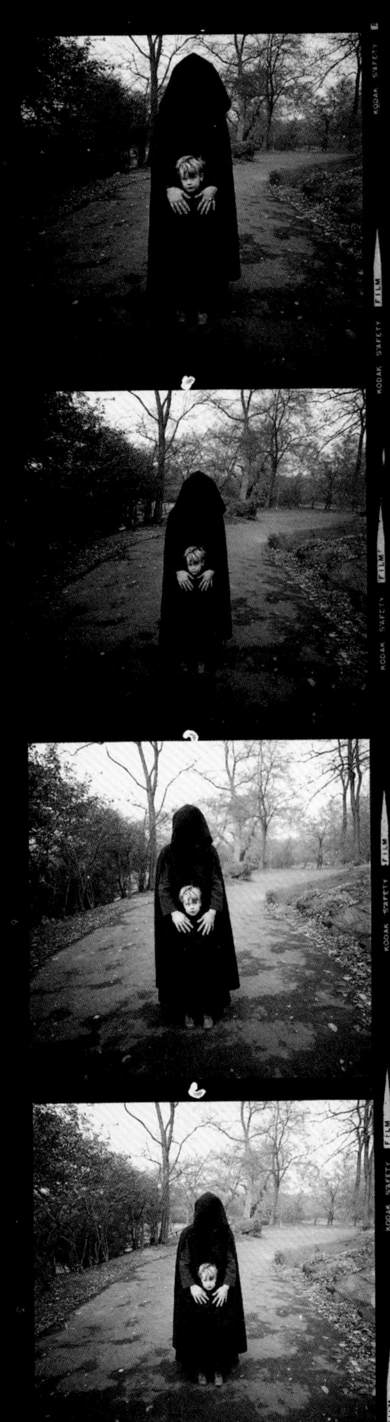

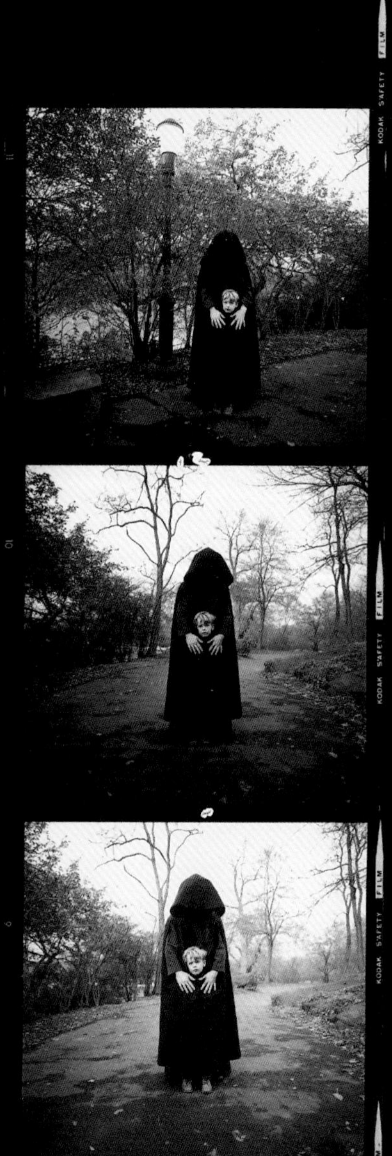

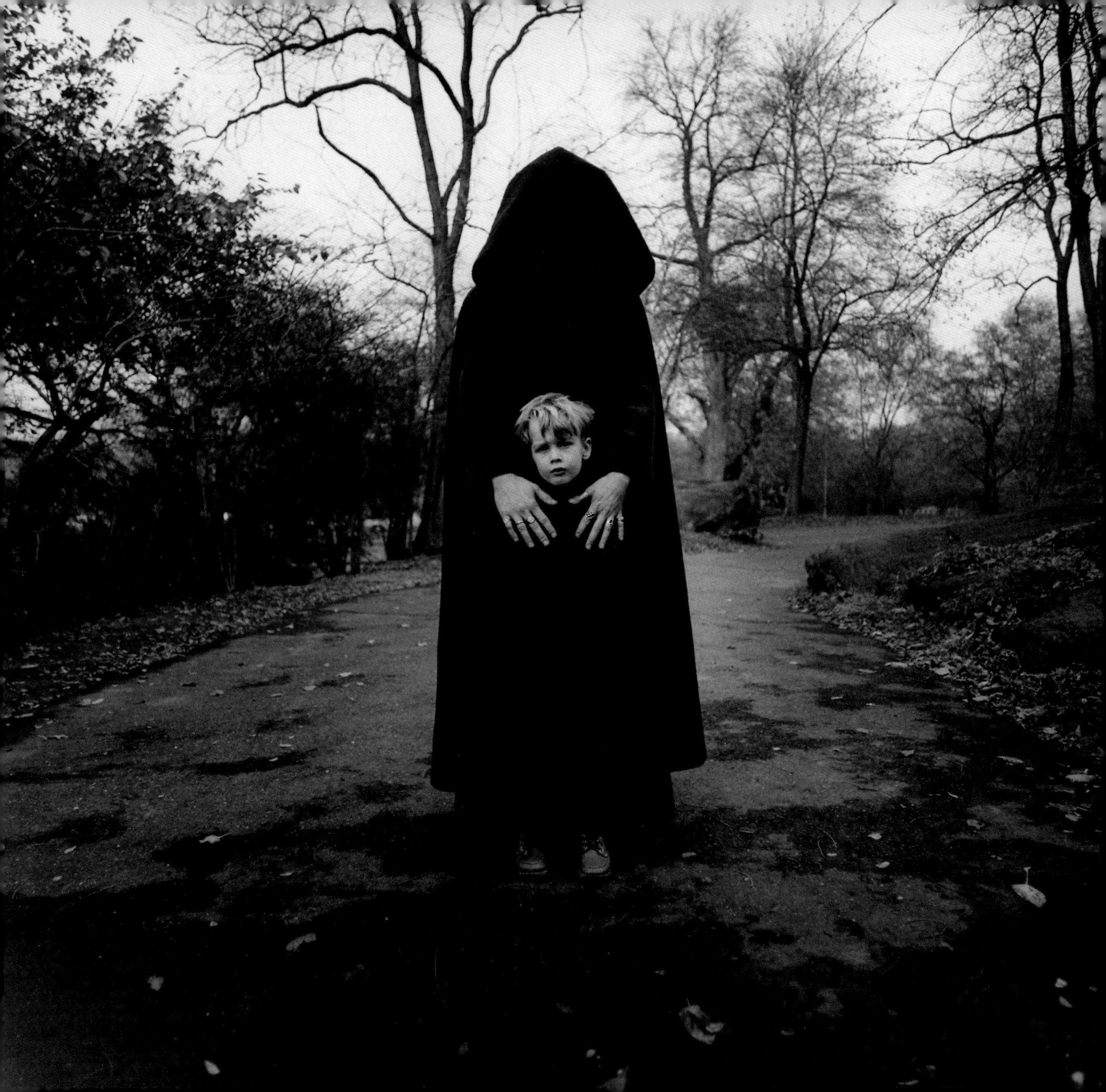

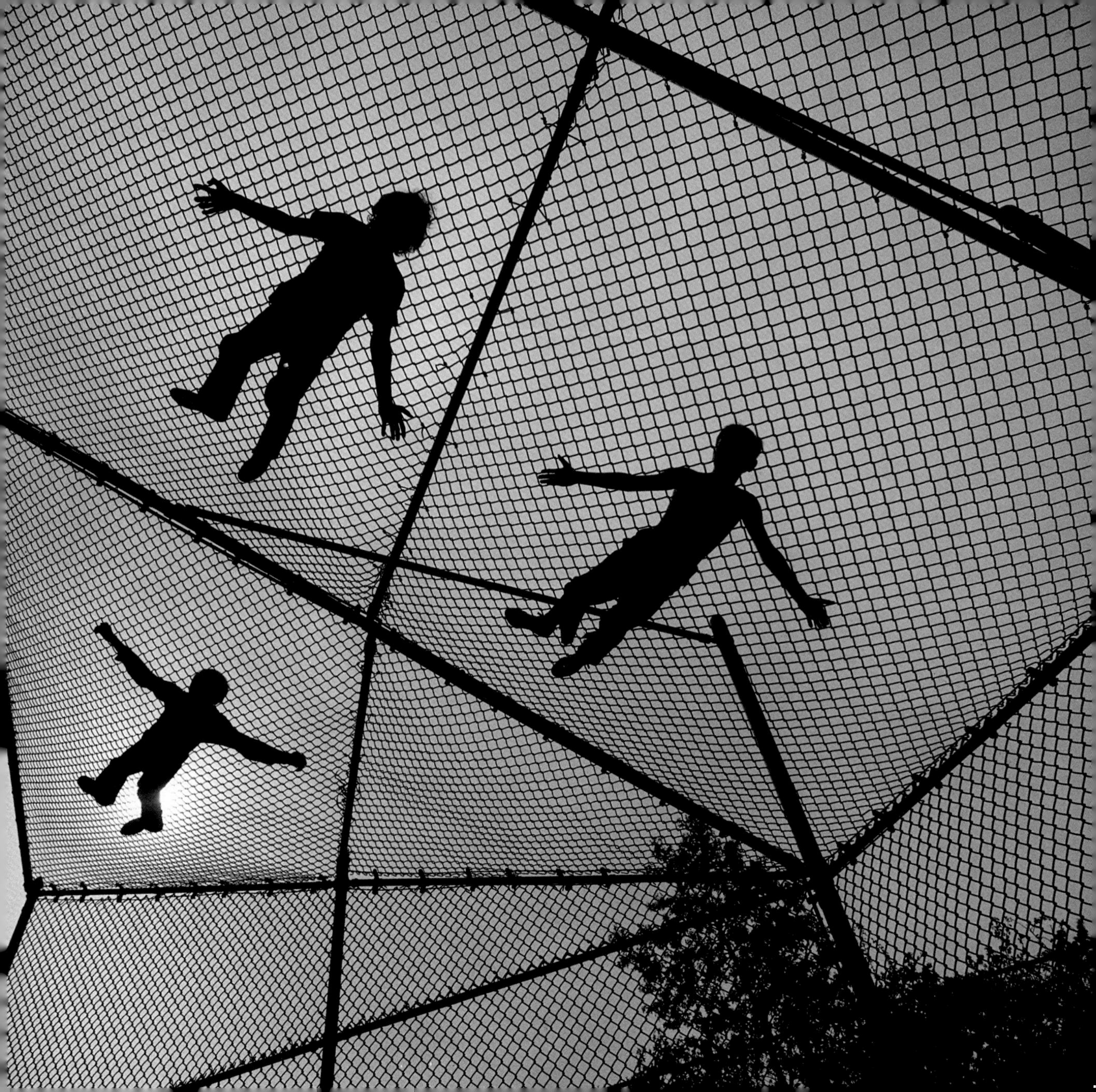

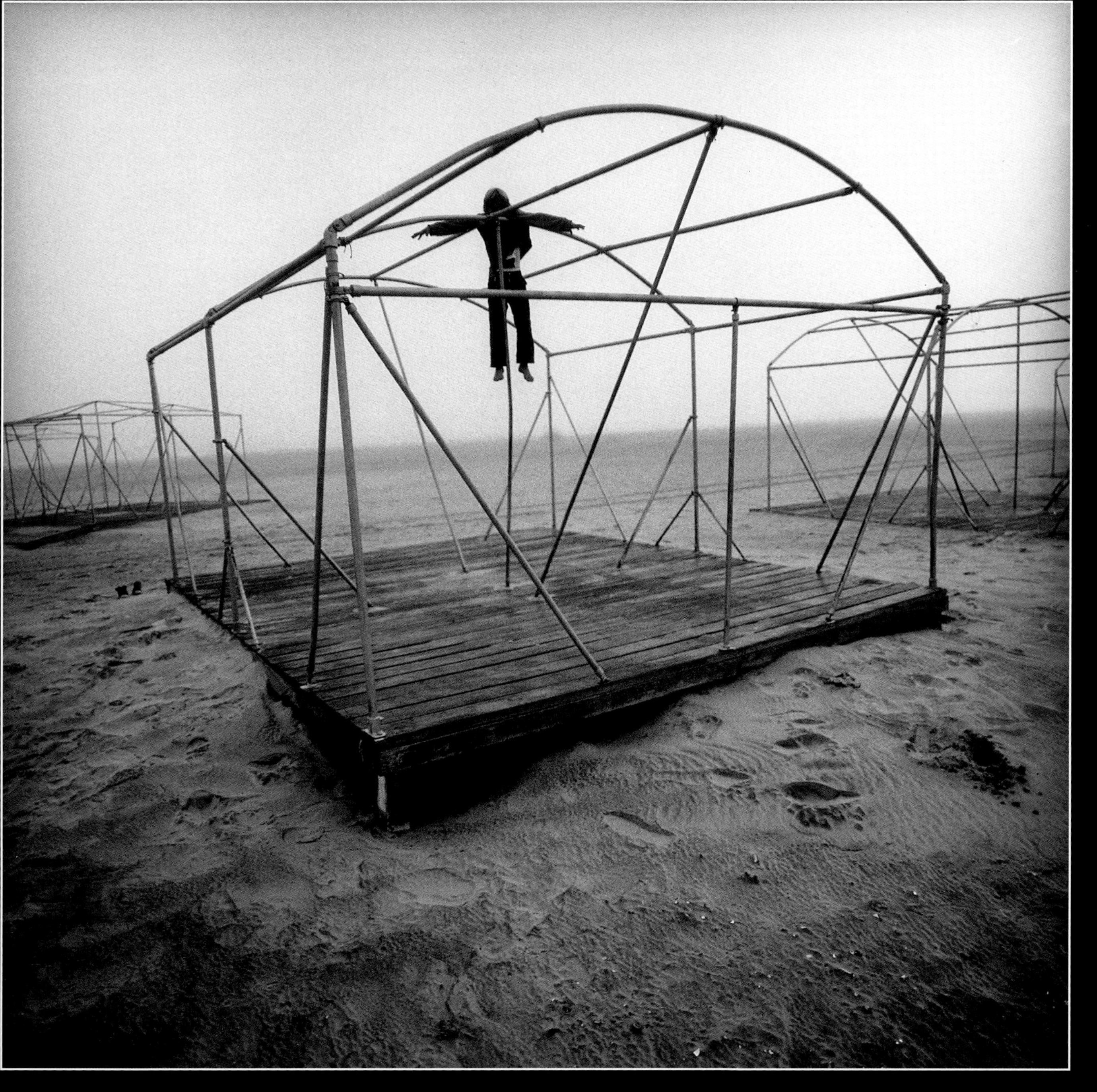

PLATE 95
Boy on Rack, Atlantic City, New Jersey, 1971

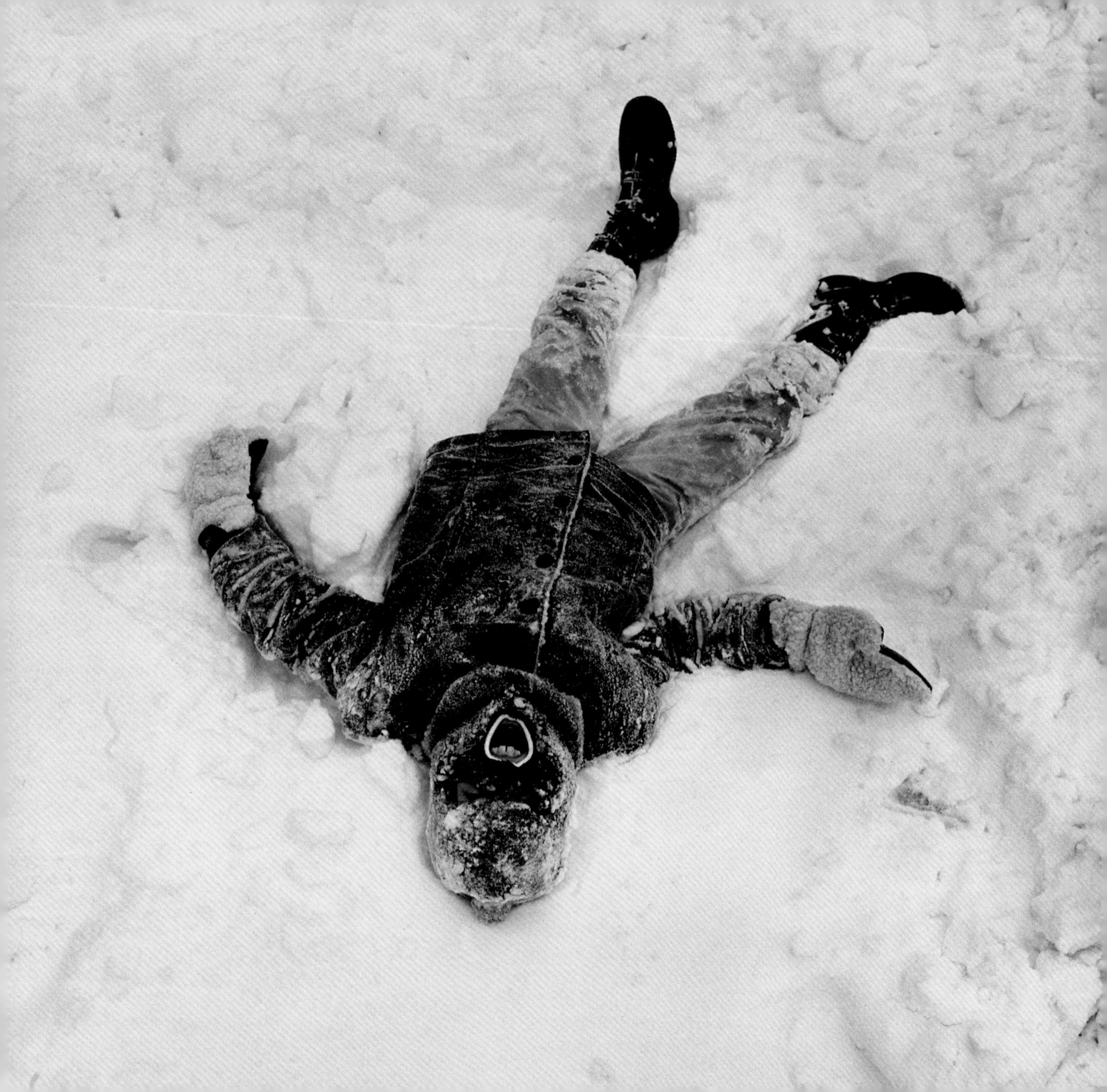

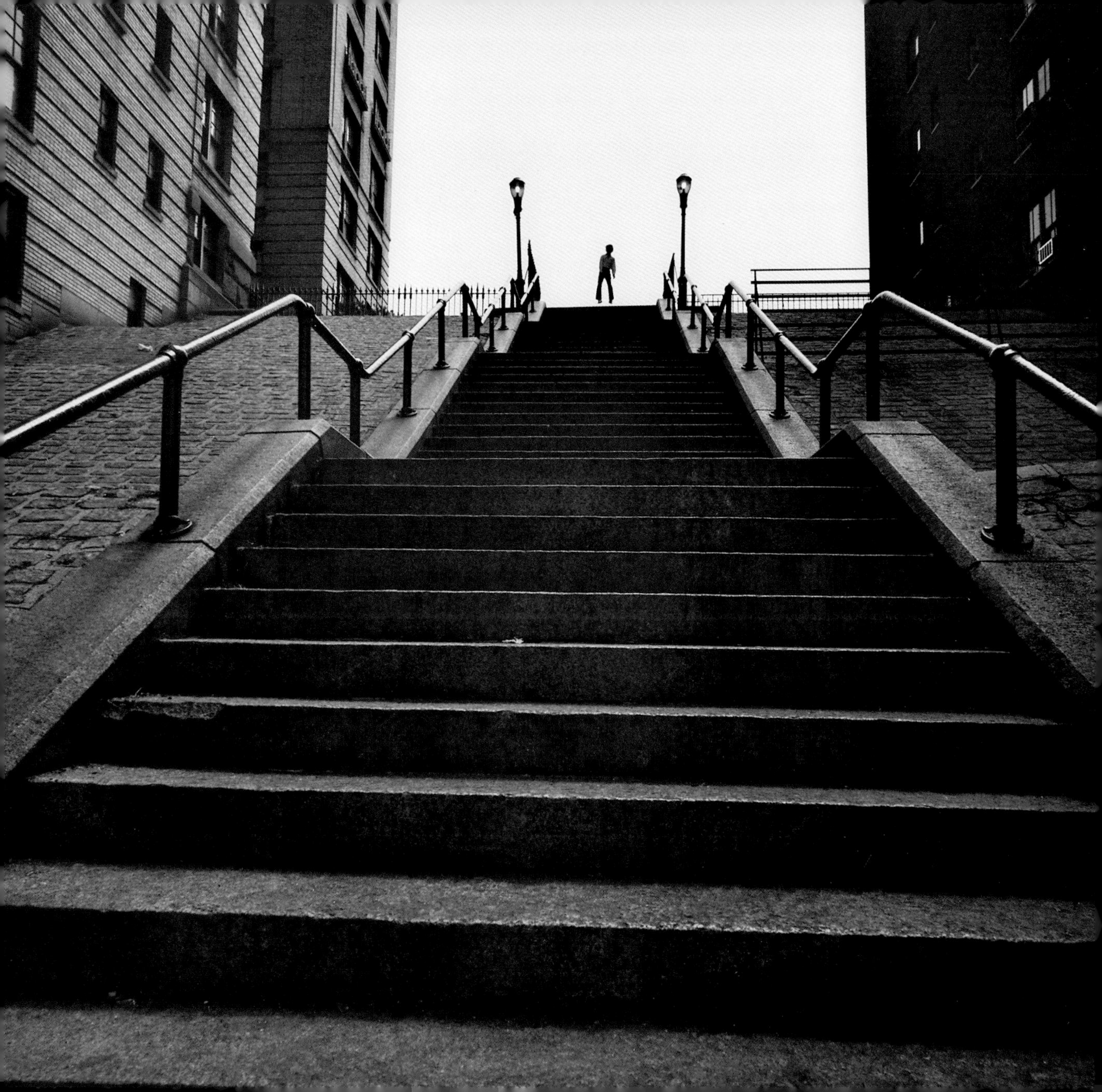

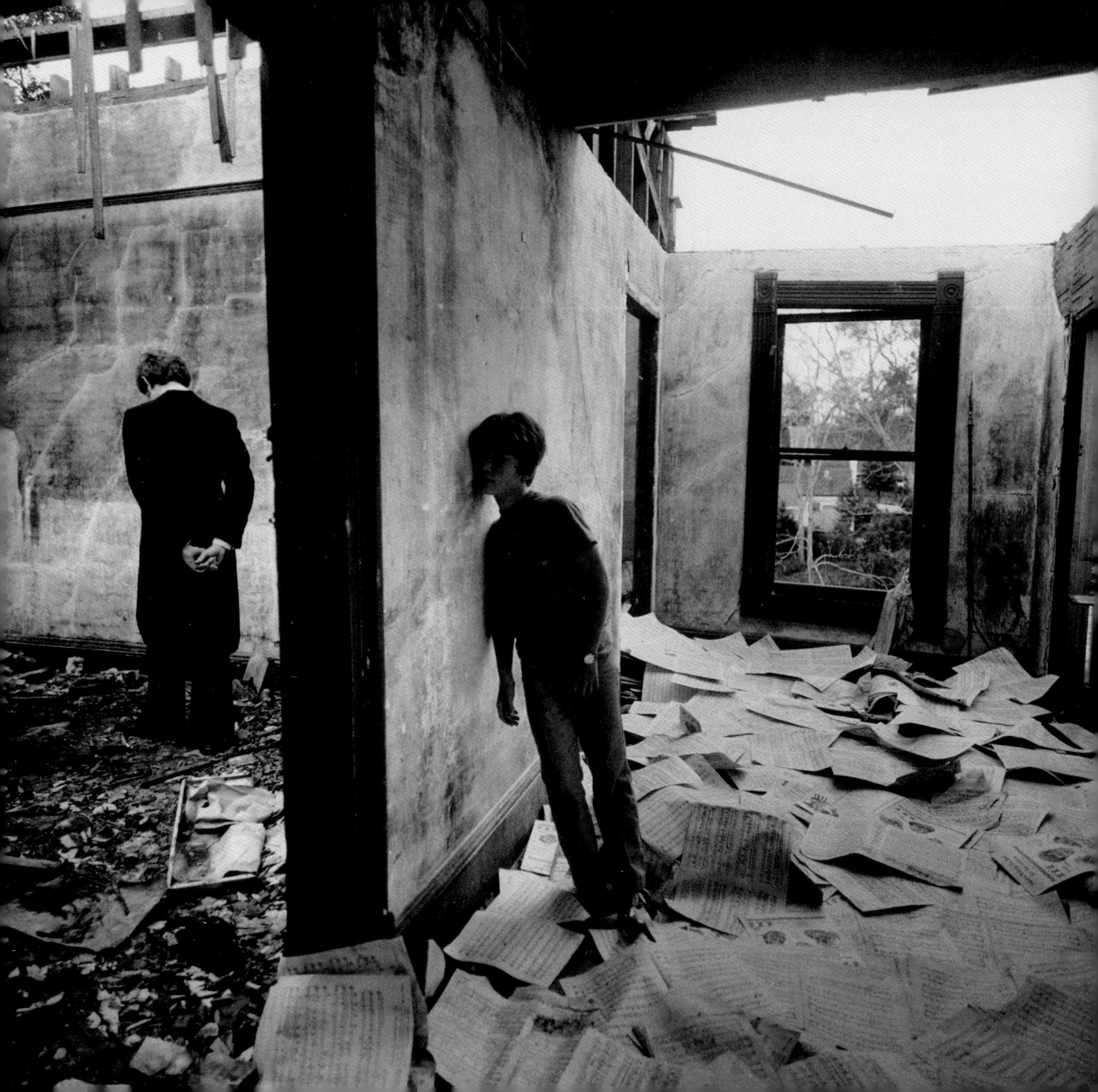

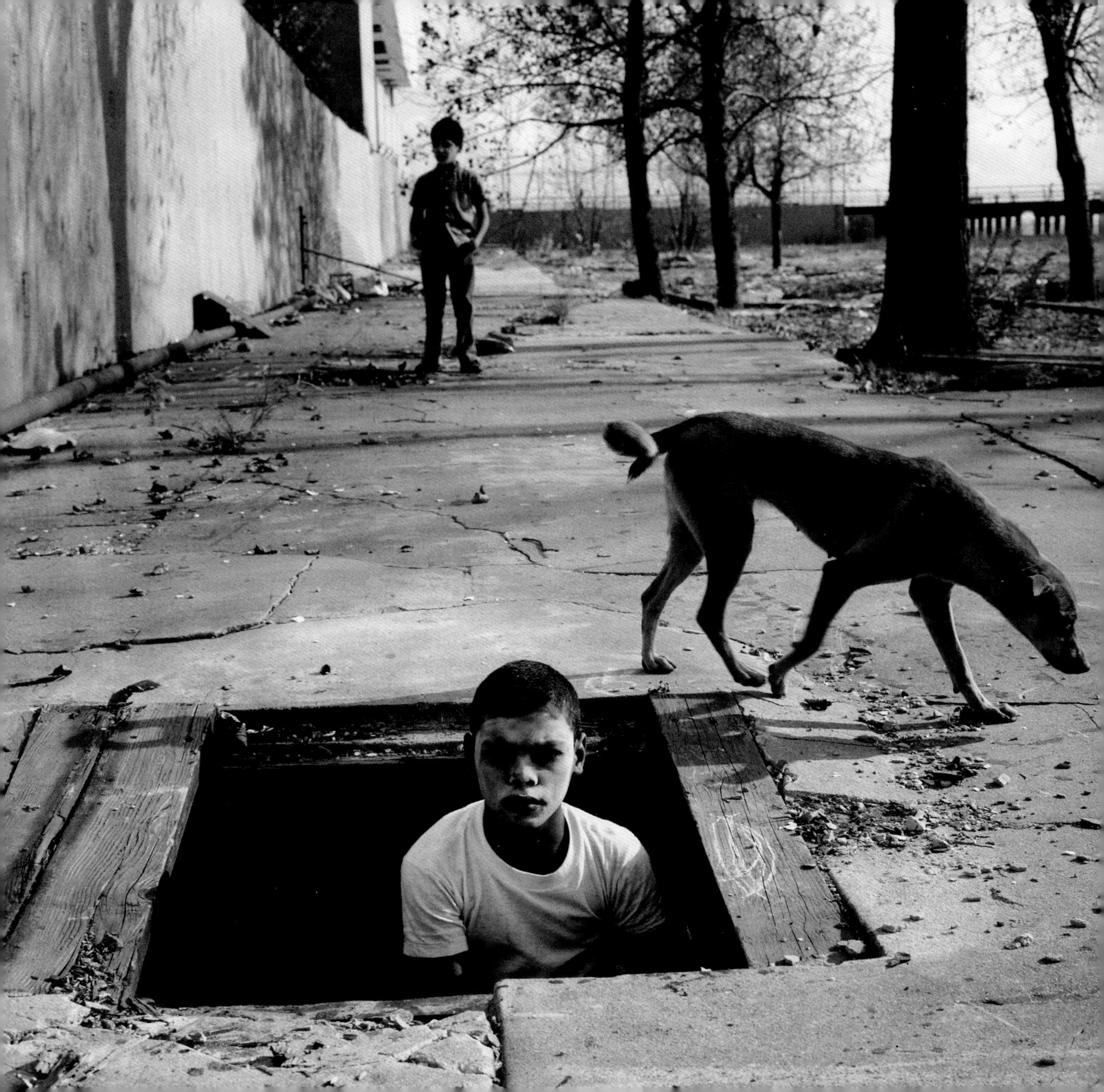

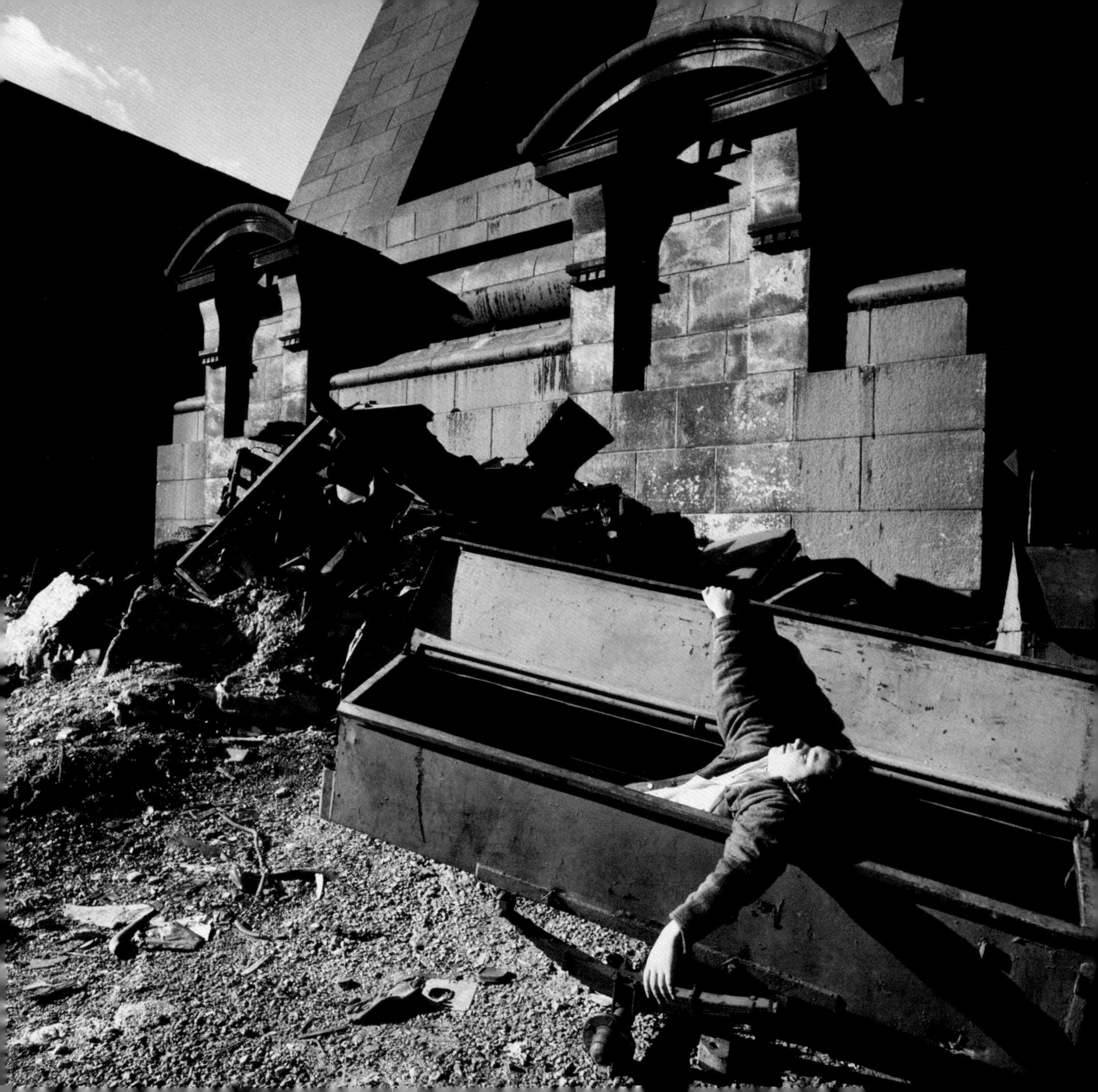

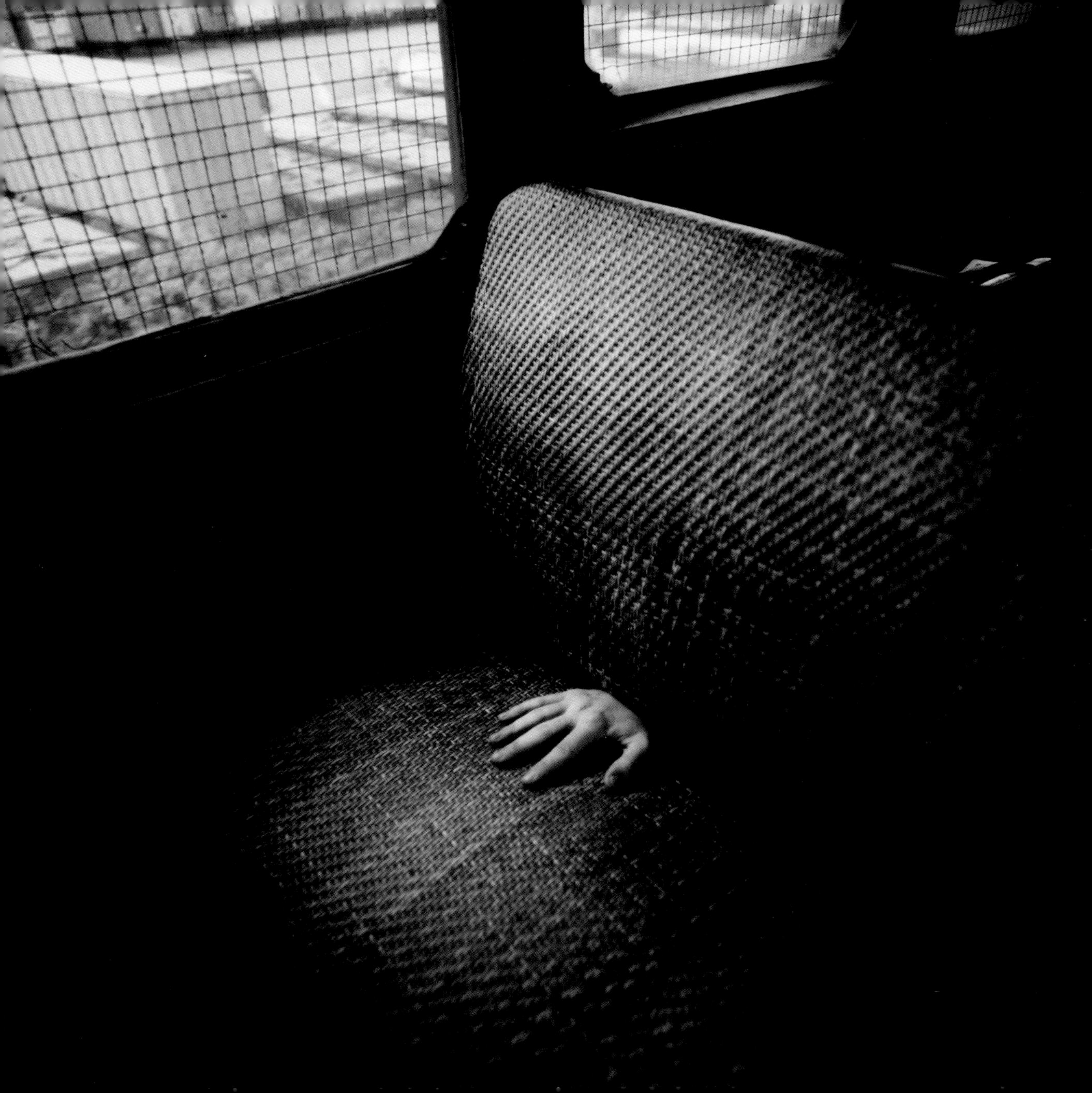

Contact sheet, East Harlem,
New York, 1969
Gelatin silver print,
25.4 × 20.3 cm (10 × 8 in.)
Collection of the artist

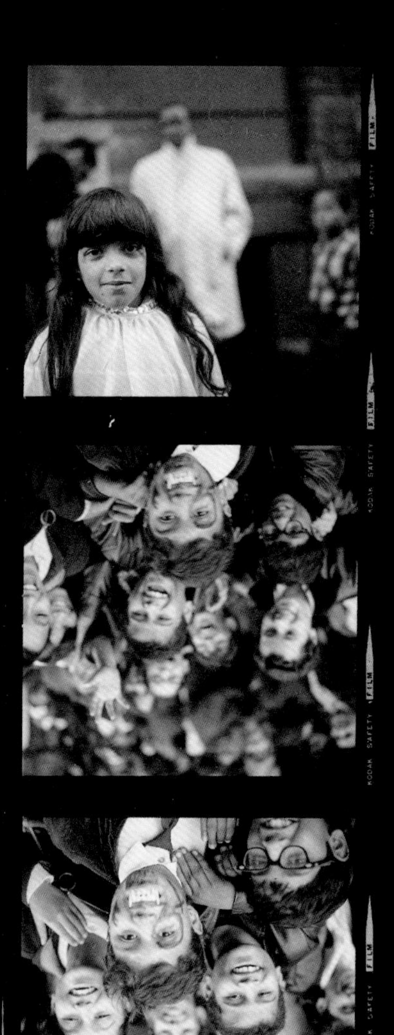

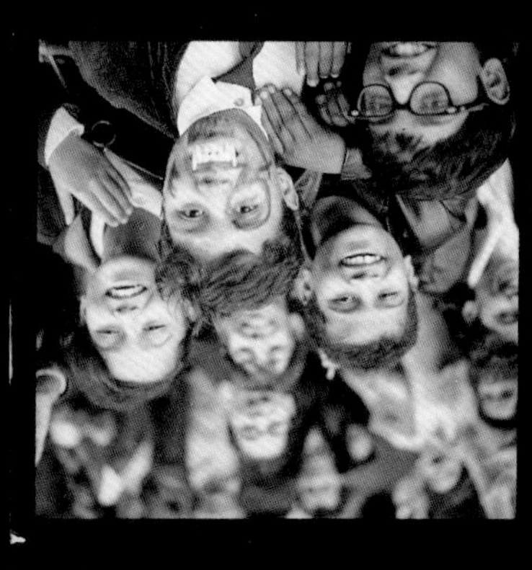

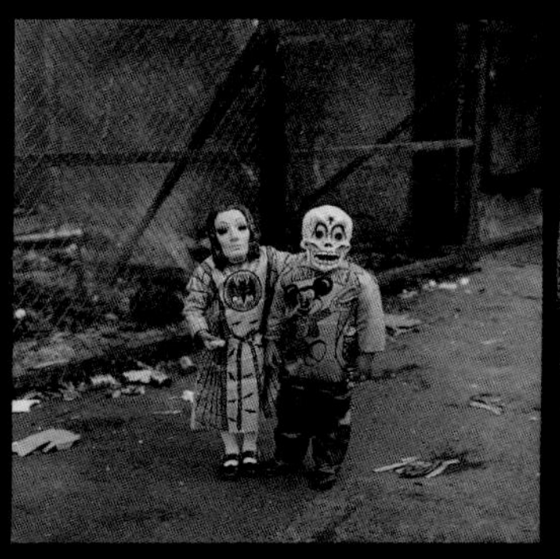

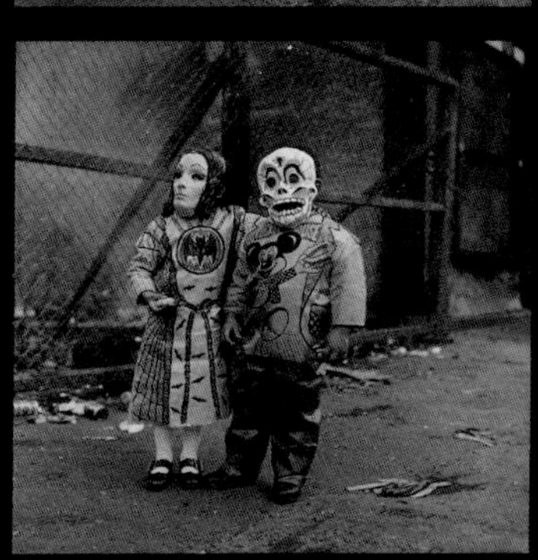

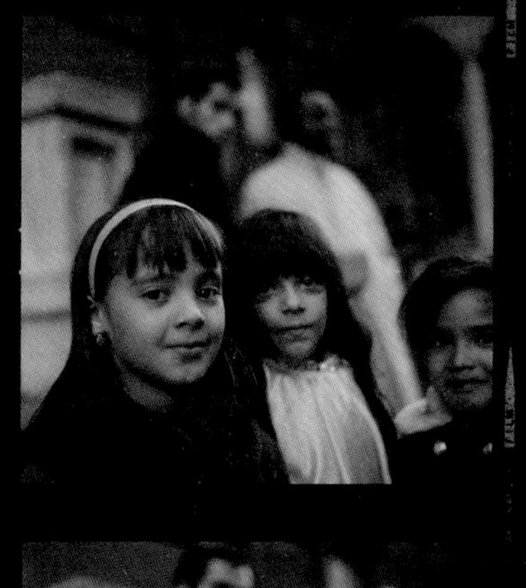

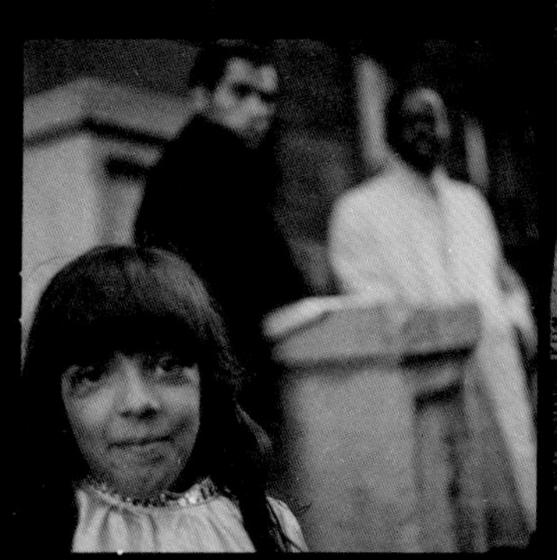

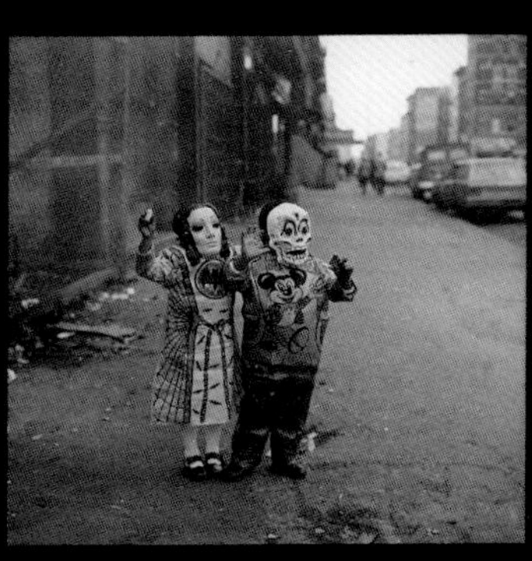

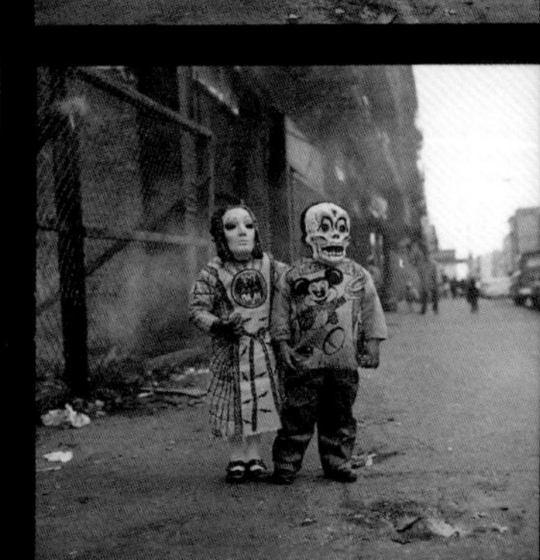

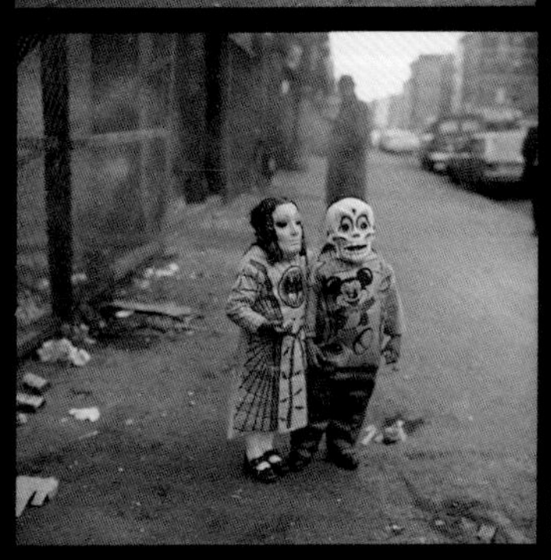

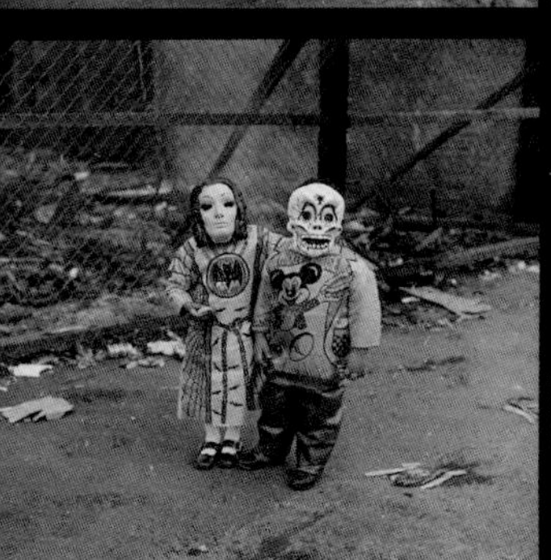

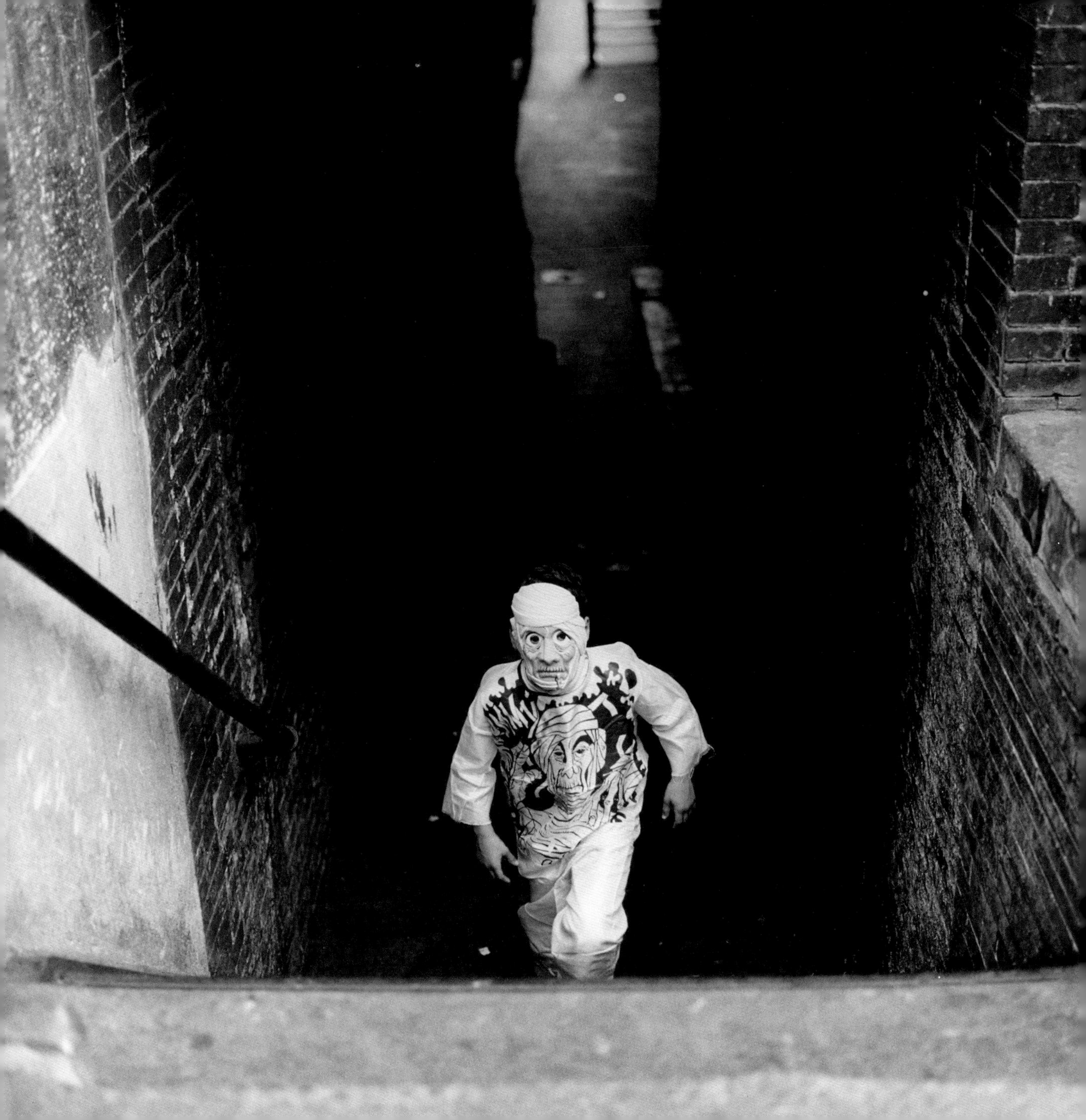

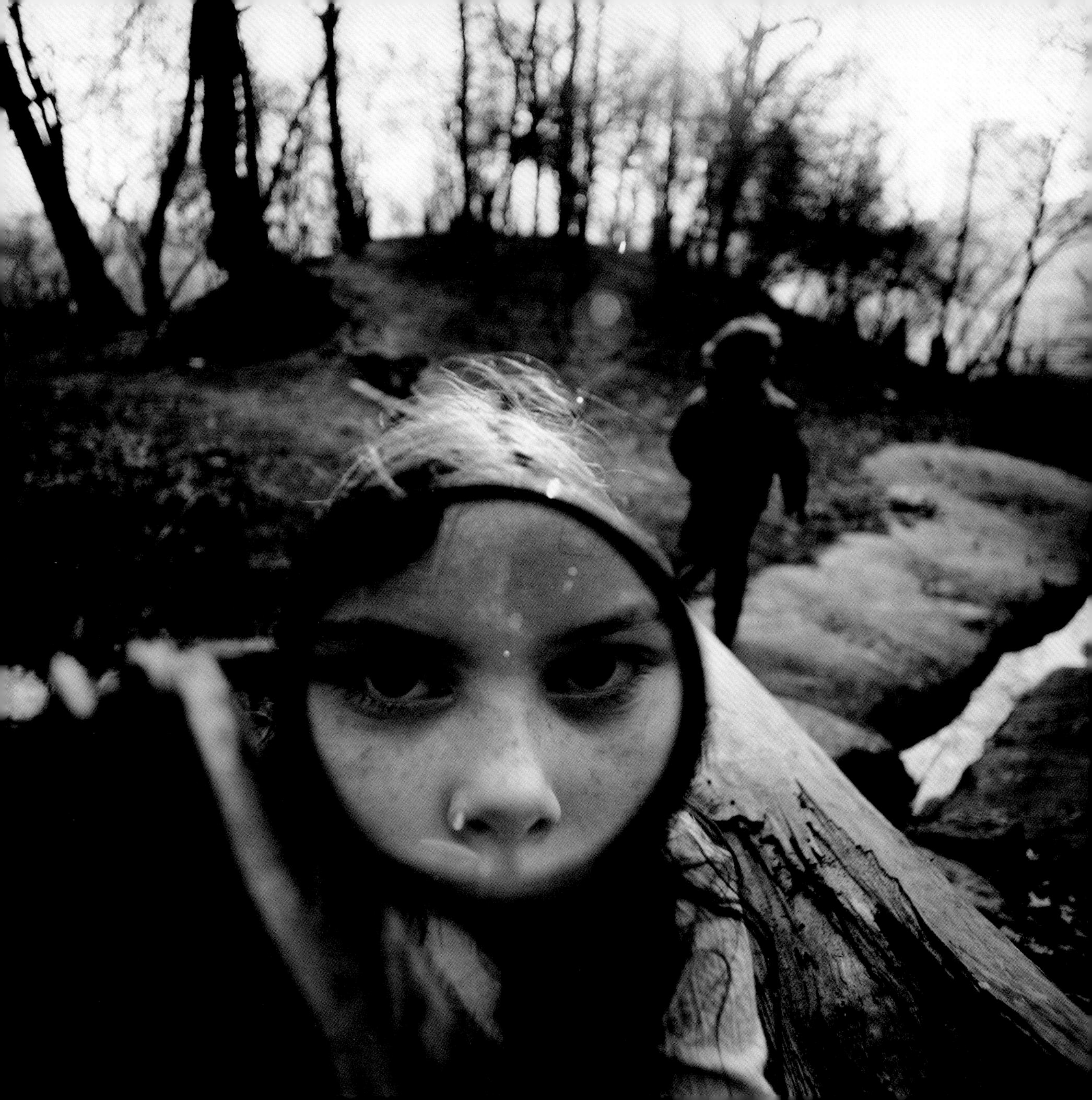

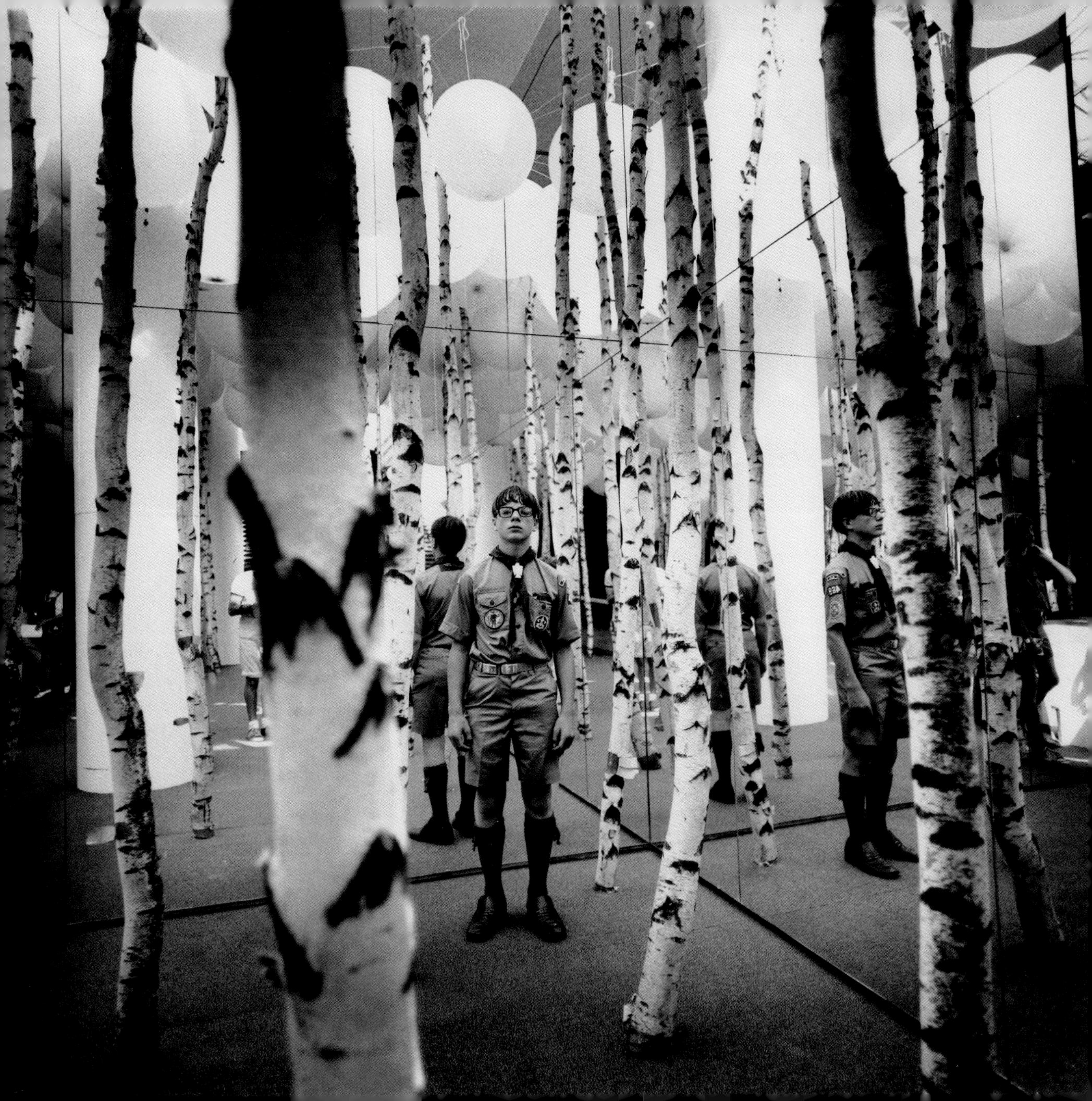

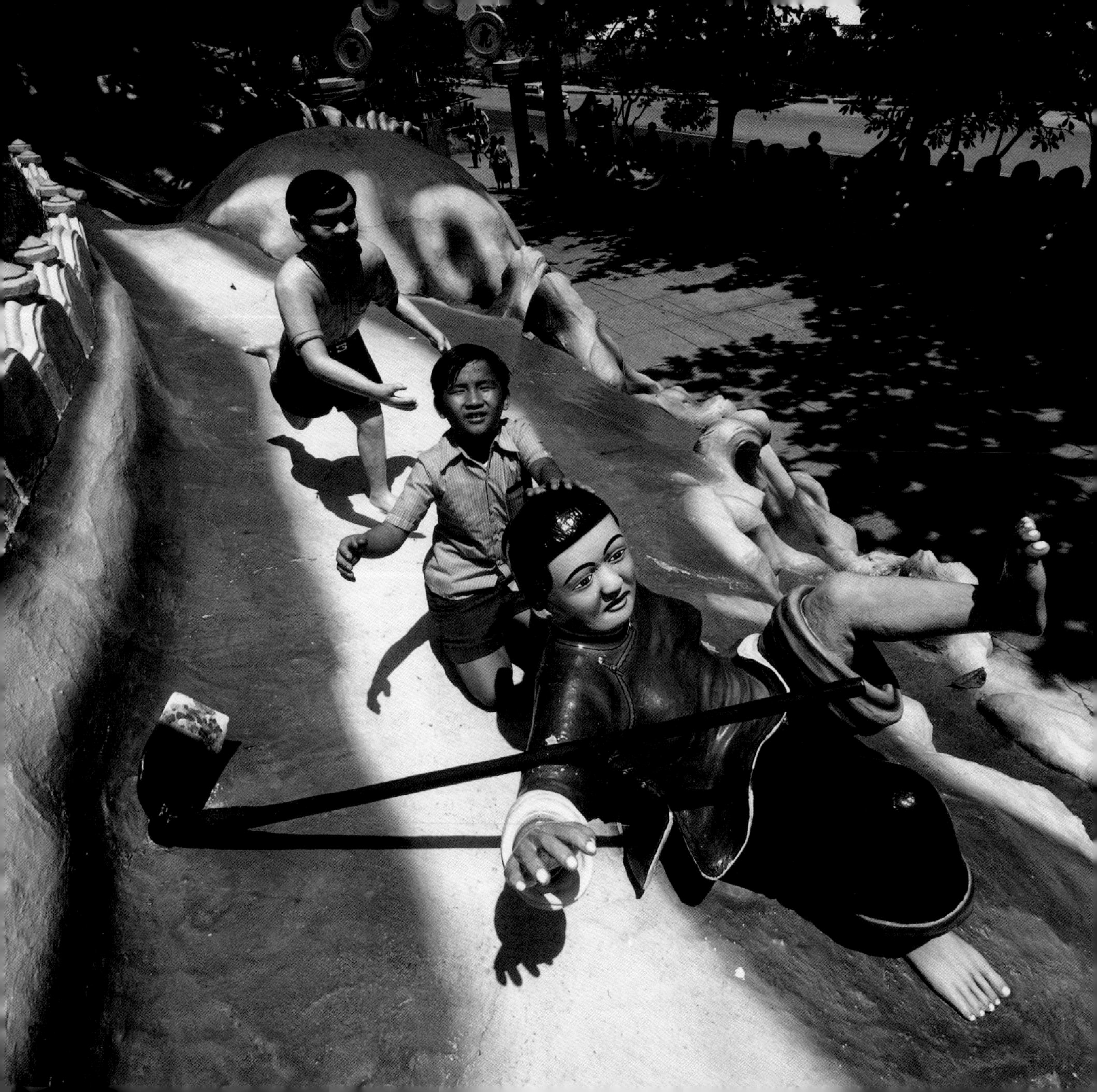

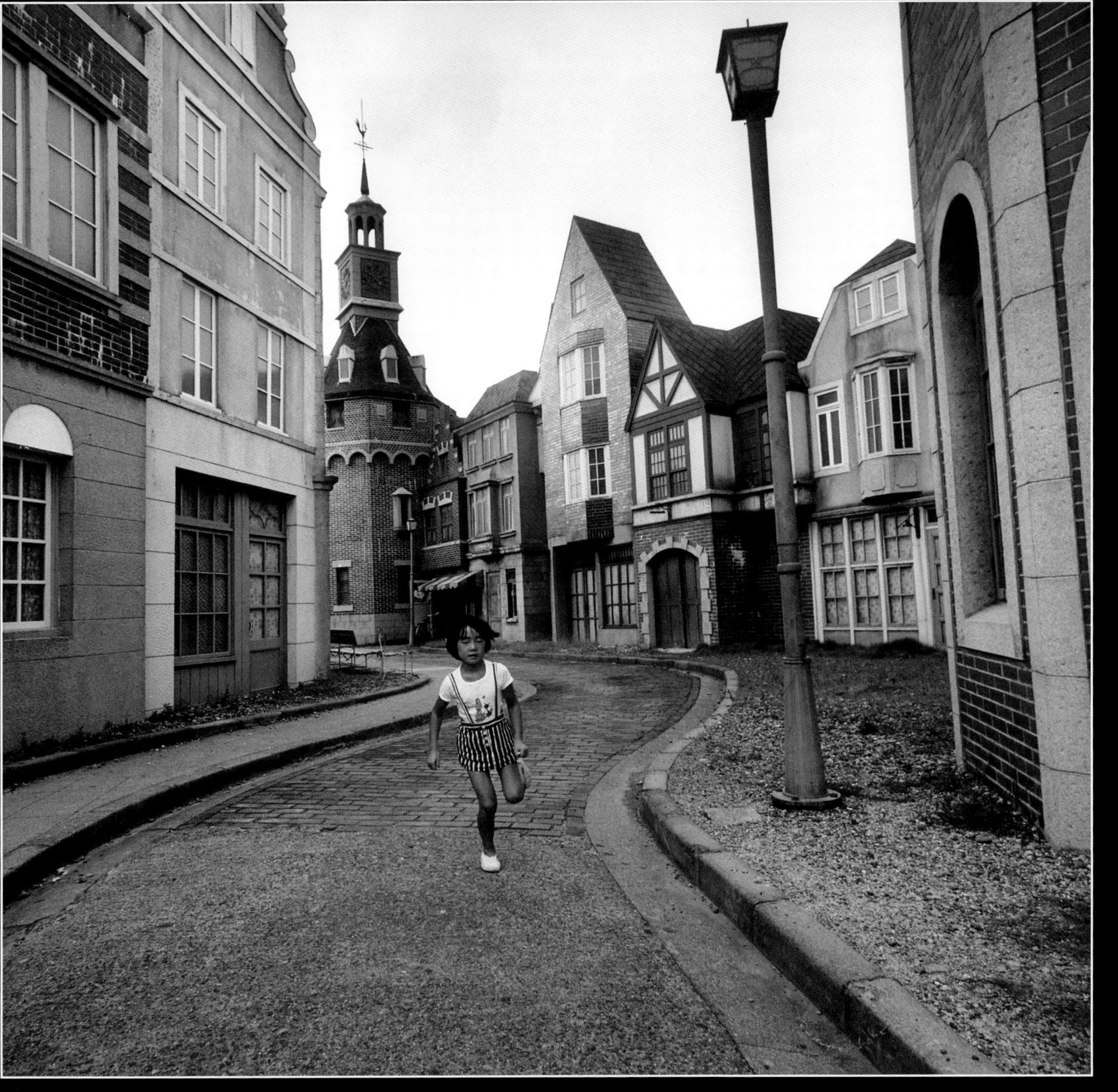

PLATE 106
Girl in Dreamland Park, Nara, Japan, negative 1974; print later

Shadow

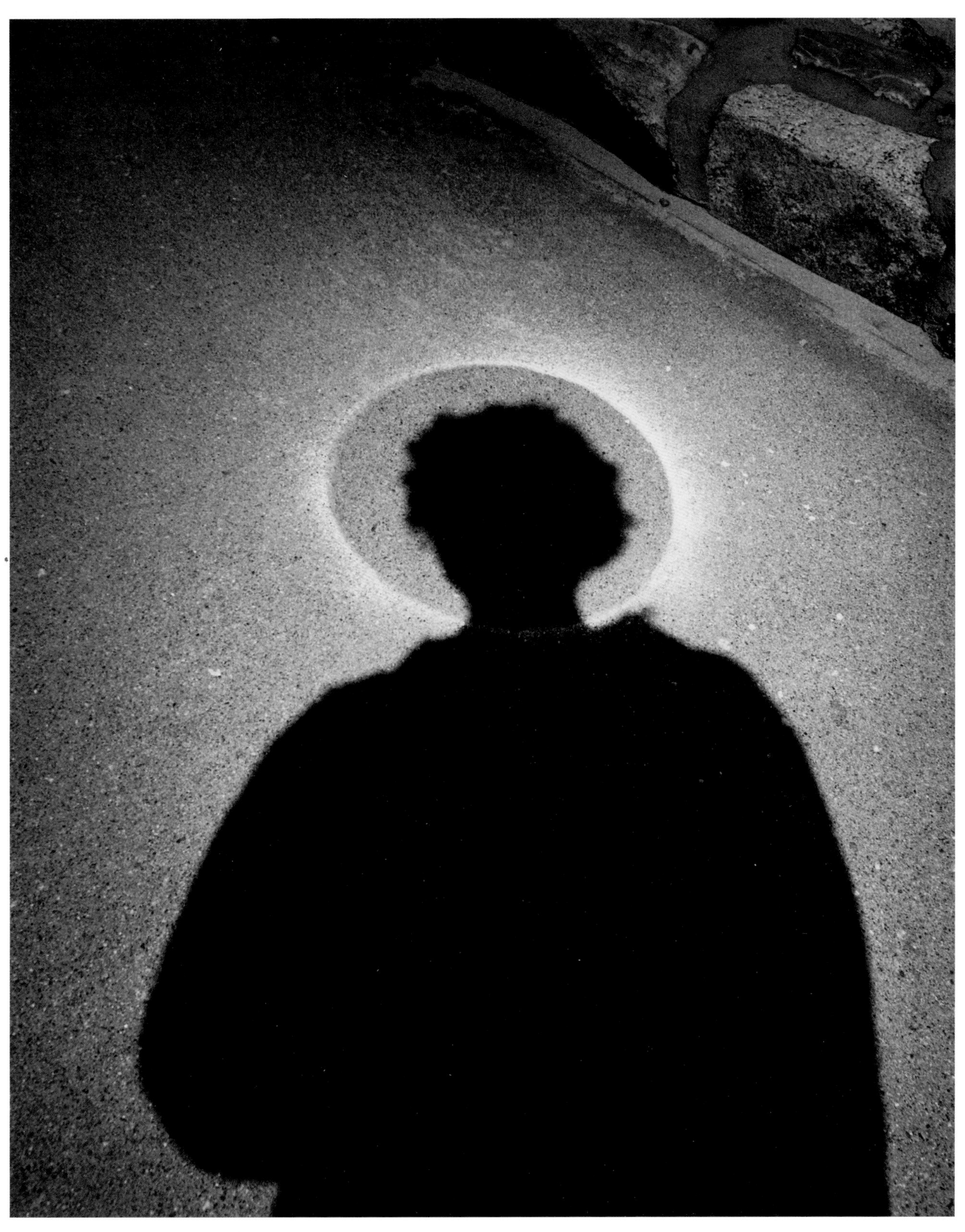

PLATE 107
Shadow Self-Portrait, New York, New York, 1970

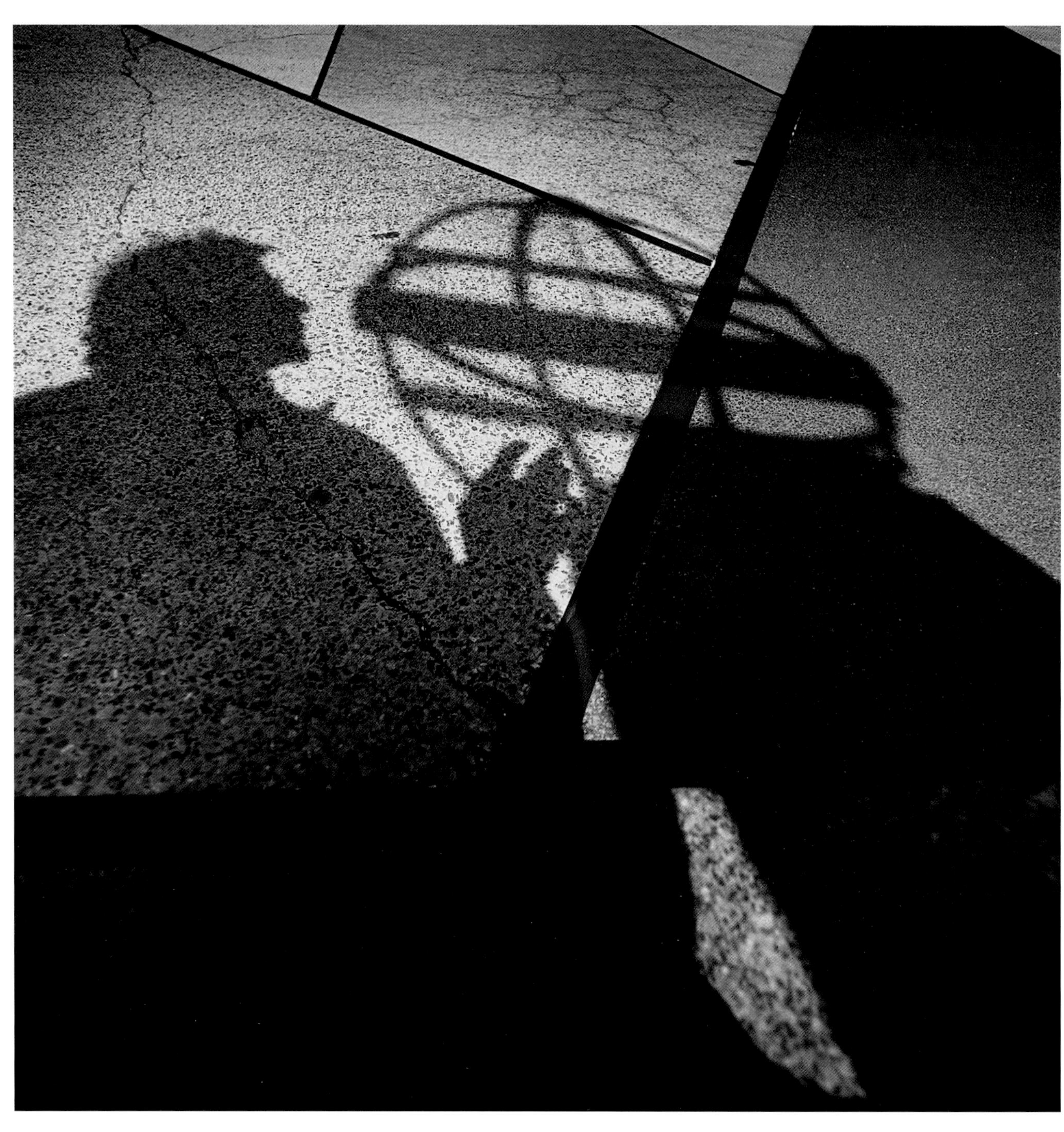

PLATE 108
Shadow, New York, New York, negative 1974; print 1975

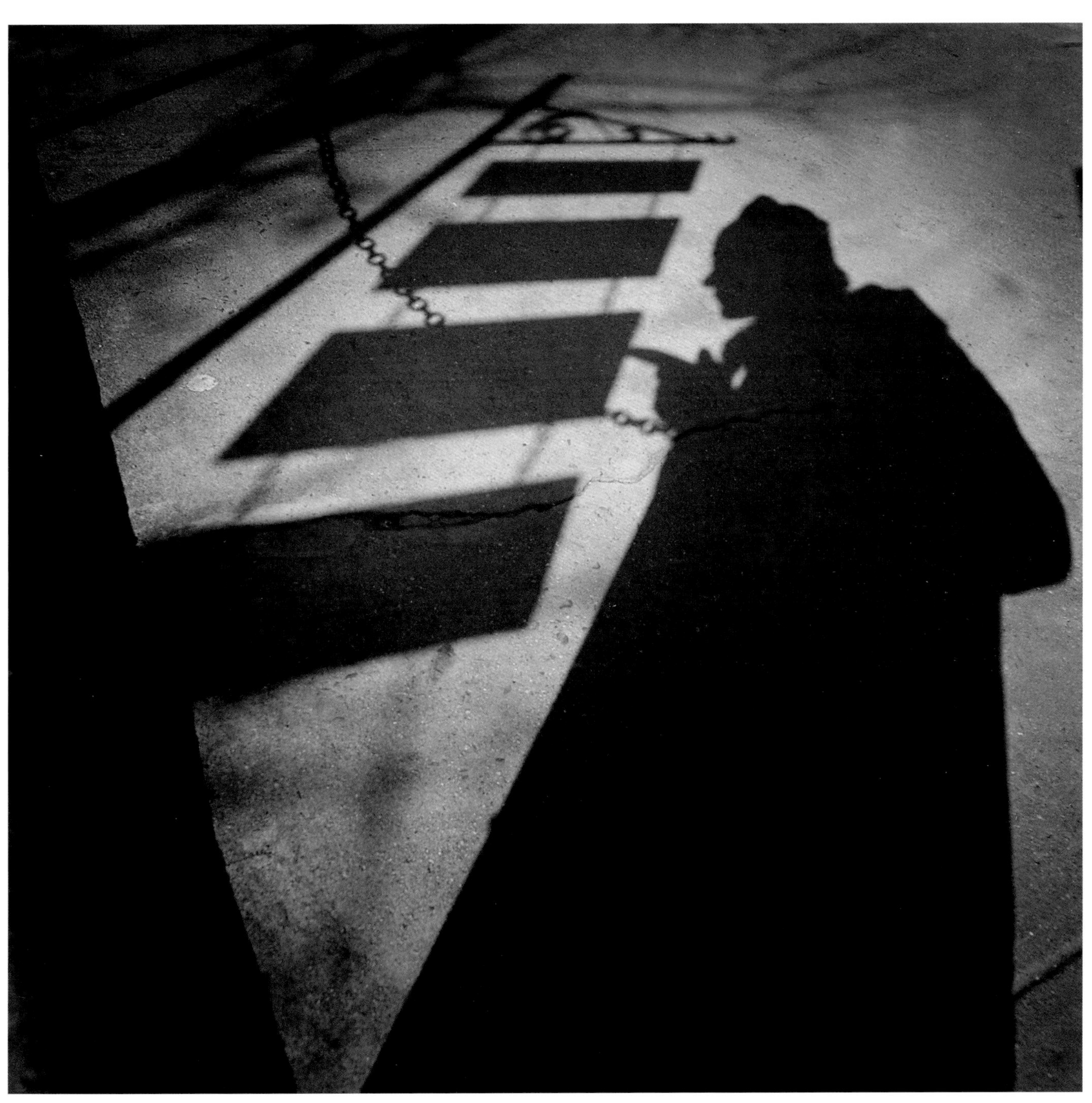

PLATE 109
Shadow, New York, New York, negative 1974; print 1975

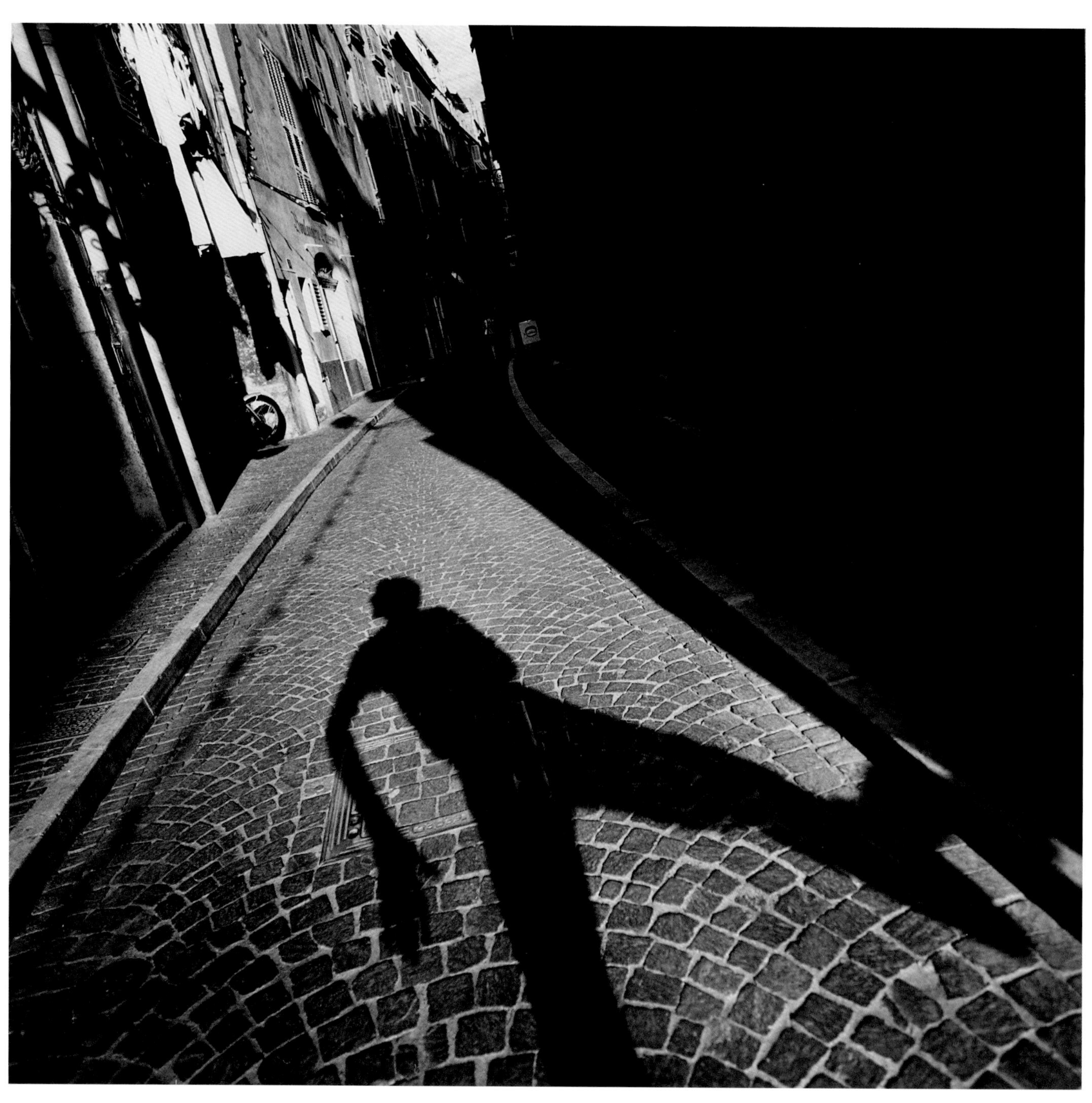

PLATE 110
Shadow, Monaco, negative 1974; print 1975

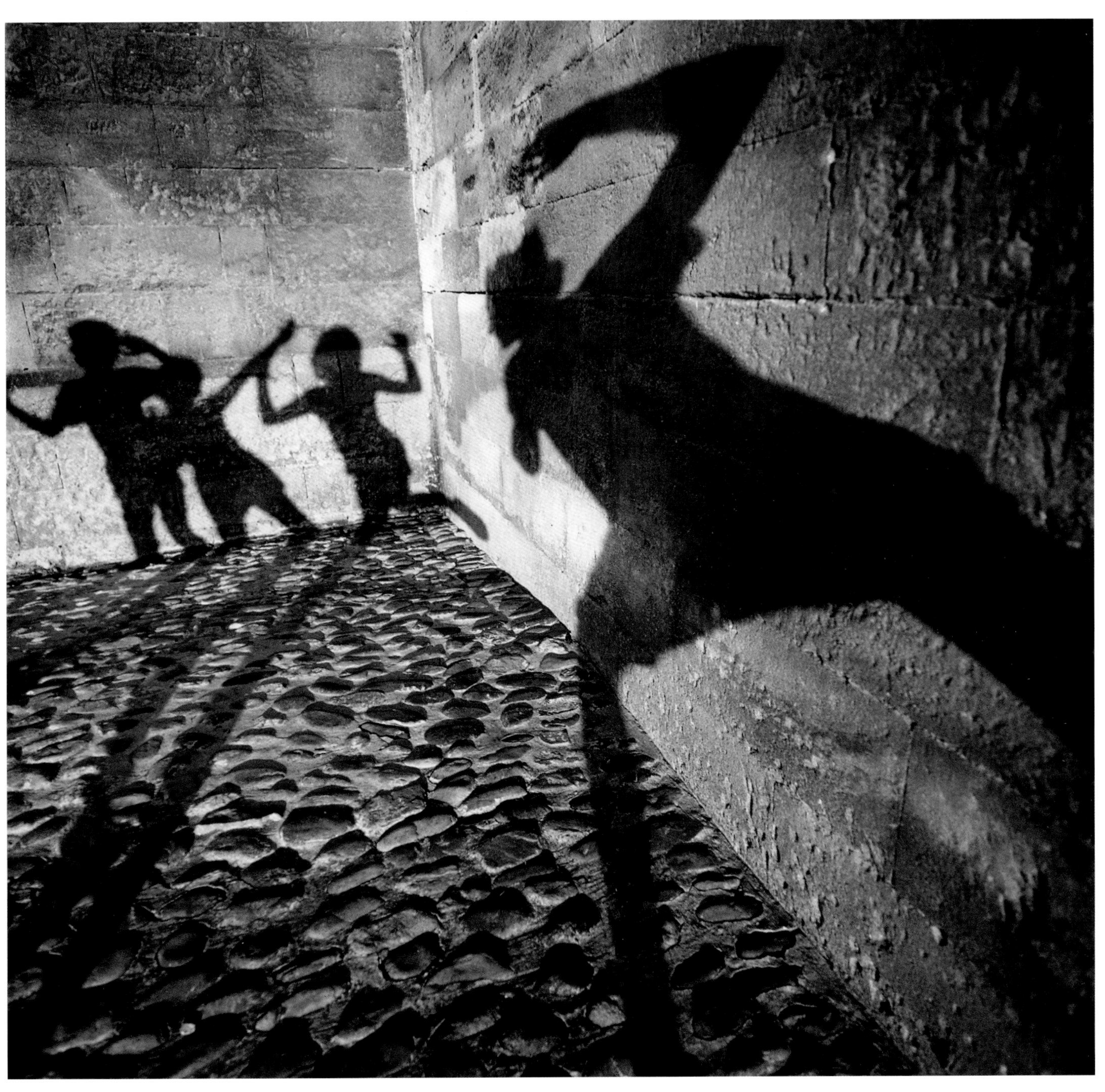

PLATE 111
Shadow, Arles, France, negative 1974; print 1975

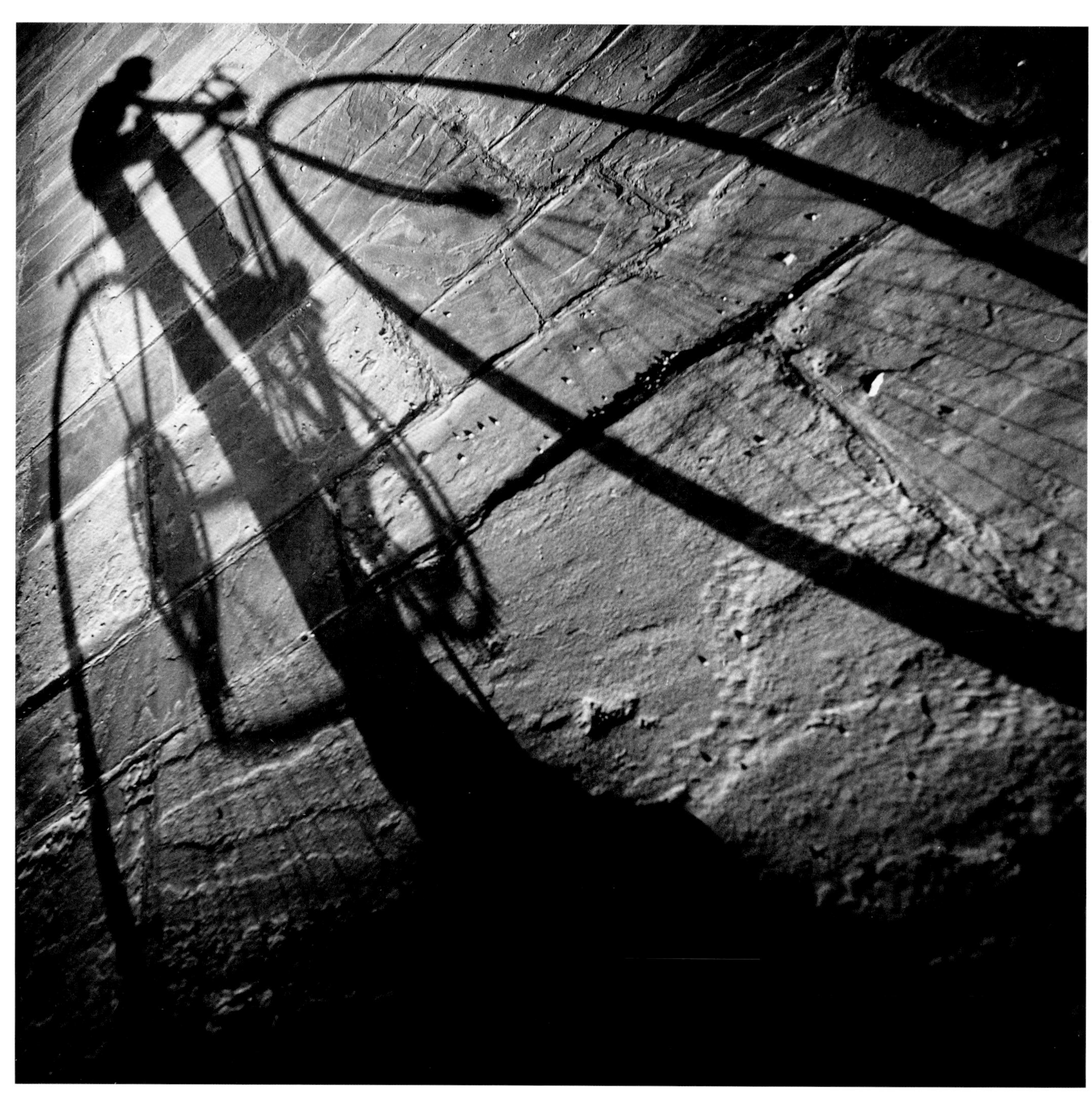

PLATE 112
Shadow, New York, New York, negative 1974; print 1975

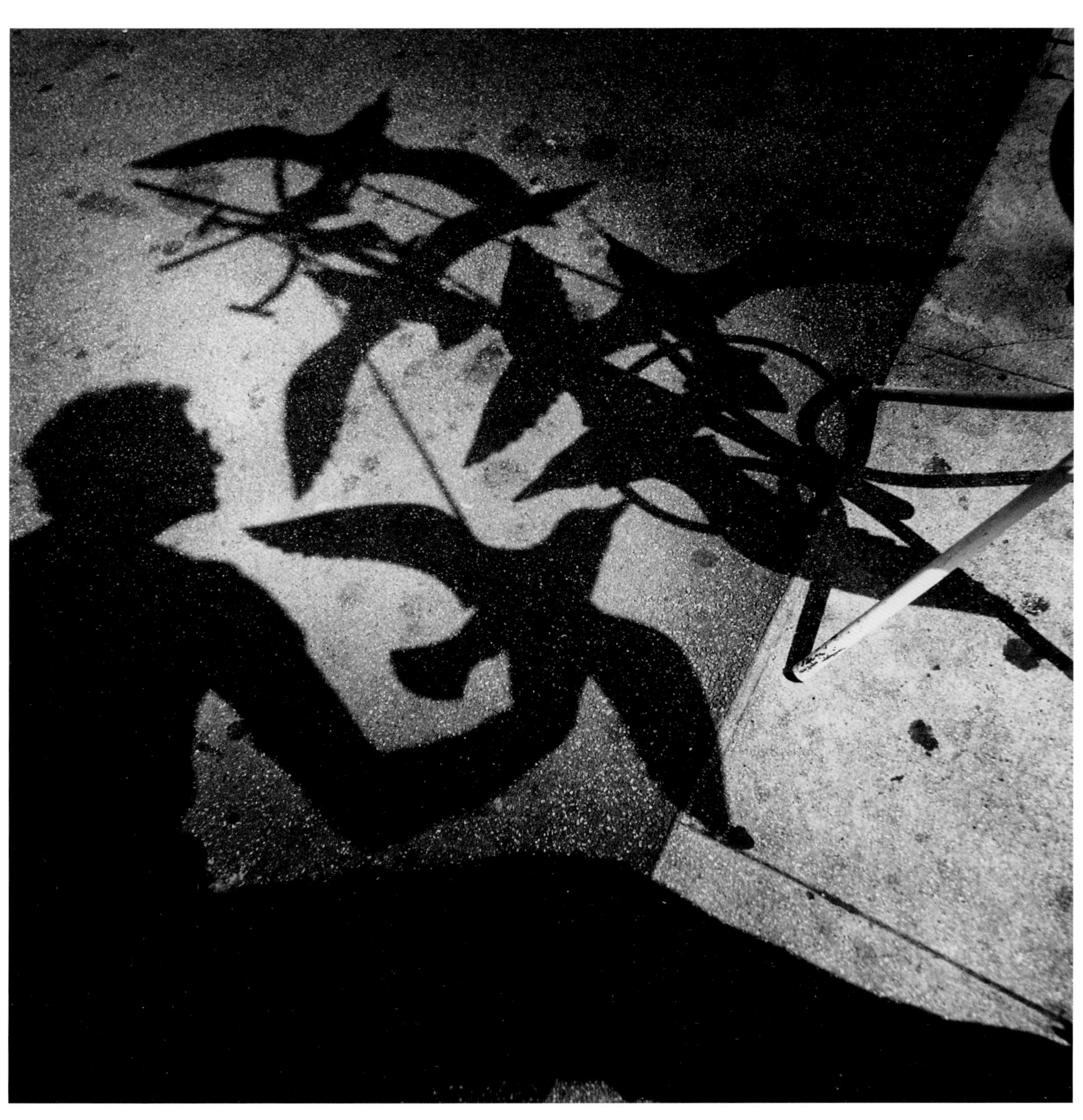

PLATE 113
Shadow, Cannes, France, negative 1974; print 1975

Contact sheet, New York,
New York, 1974
Gelatin silver print,
25.4 × 20.3 cm
(10 × 8 in.)
Collection of the artist

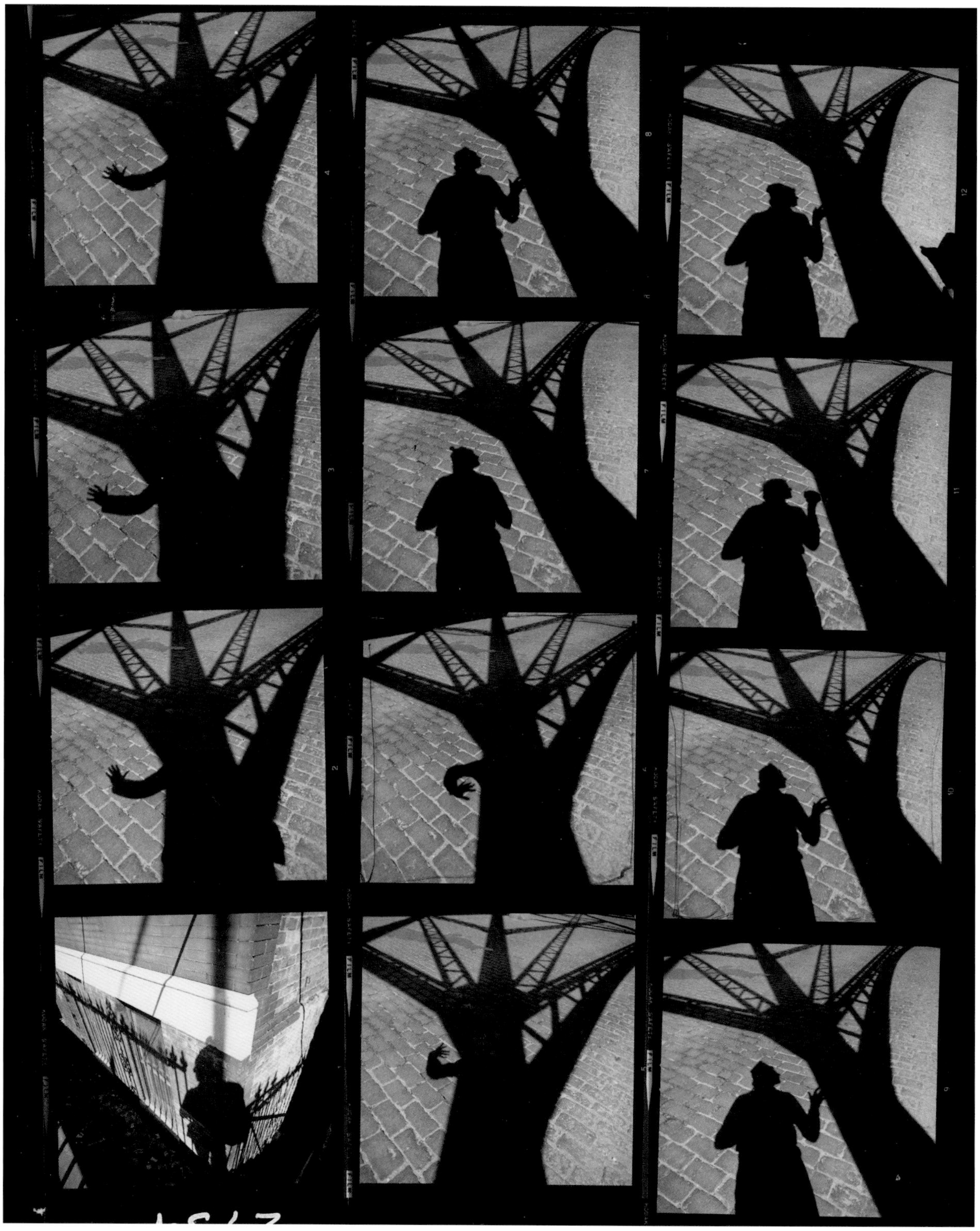

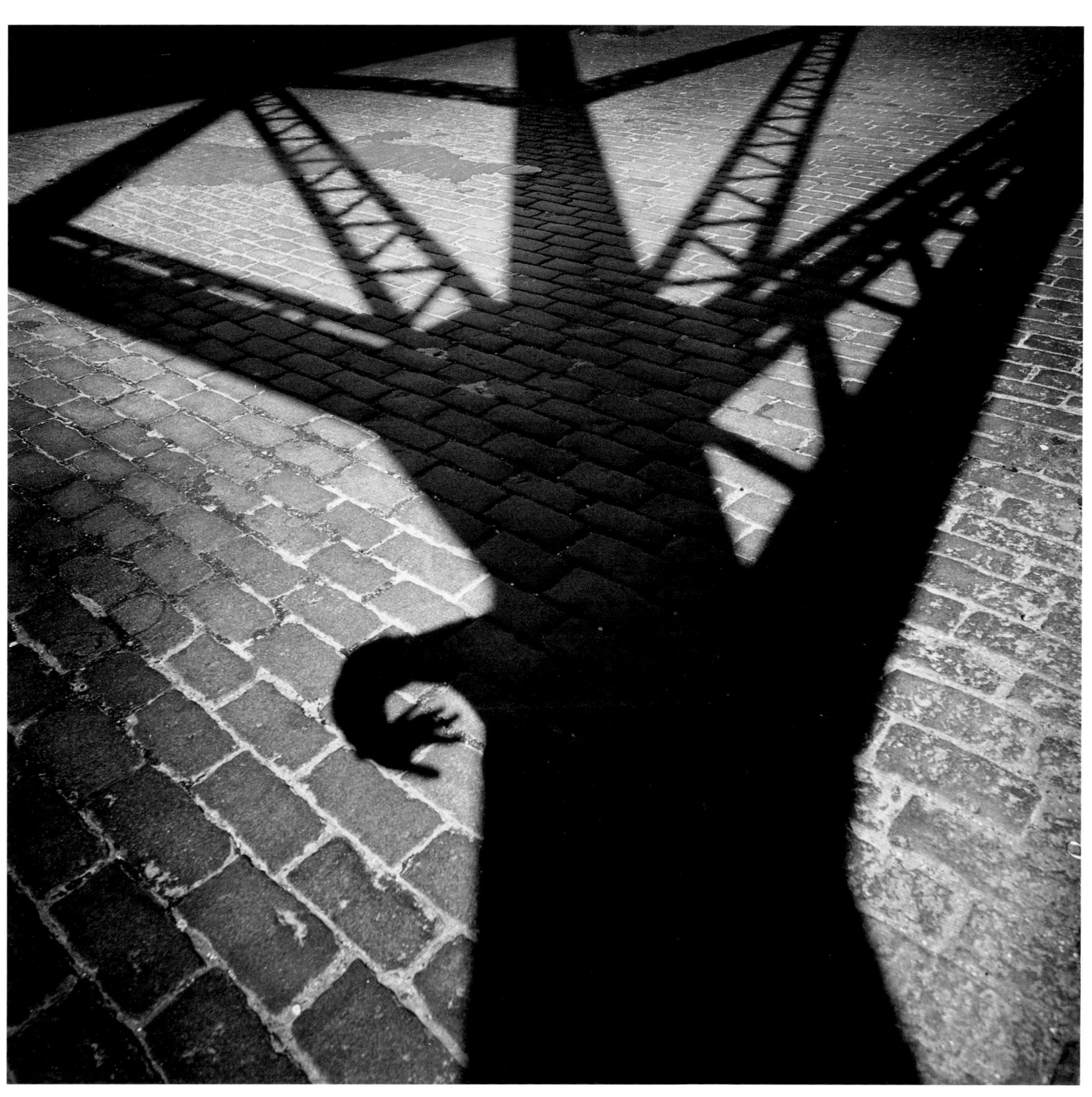

PLATE 114
Shadow, New York, New York, negative 1974; print 1975

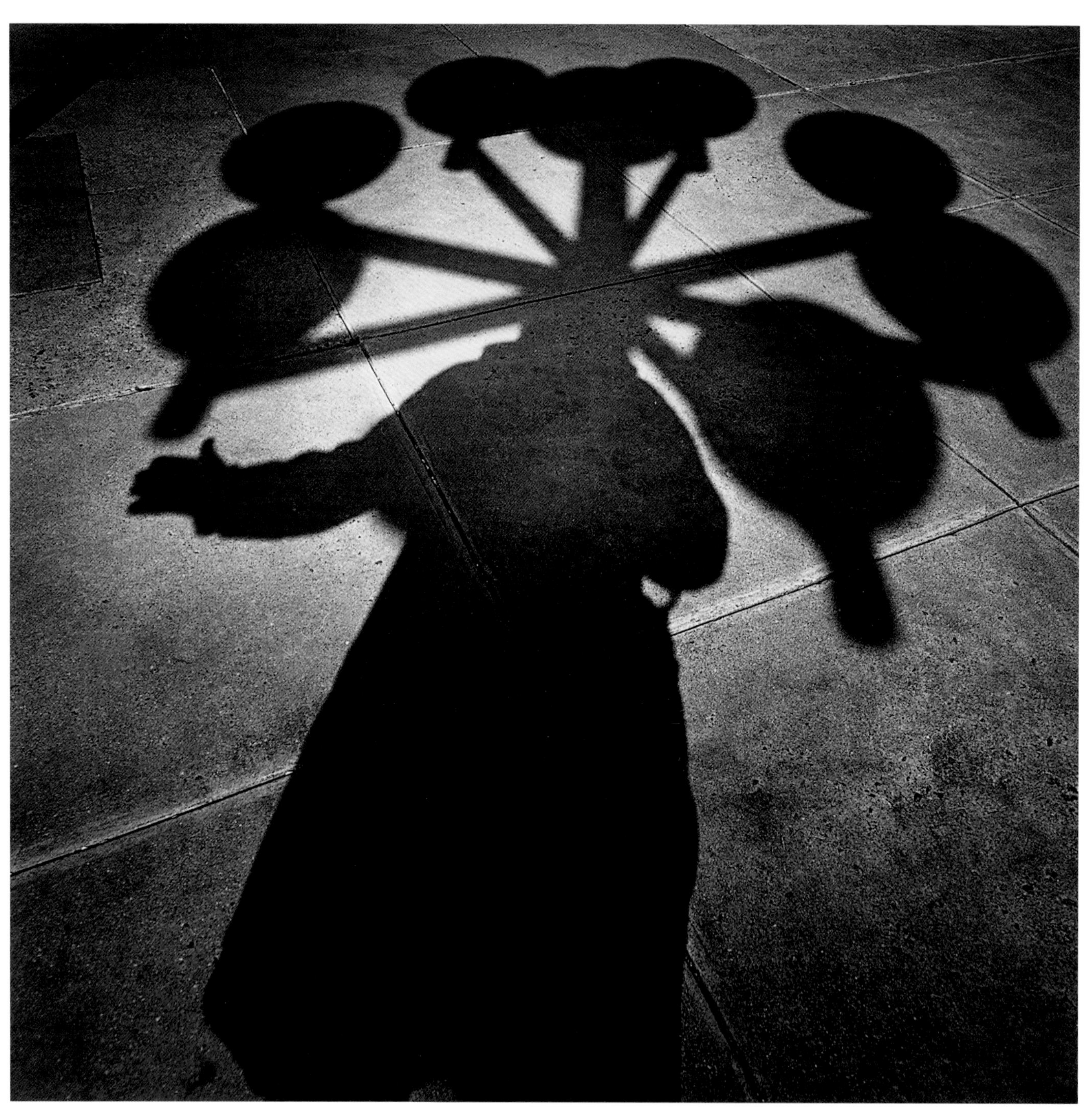

PLATE 115

Shadow, New York, New York, negative 1974; print 1975

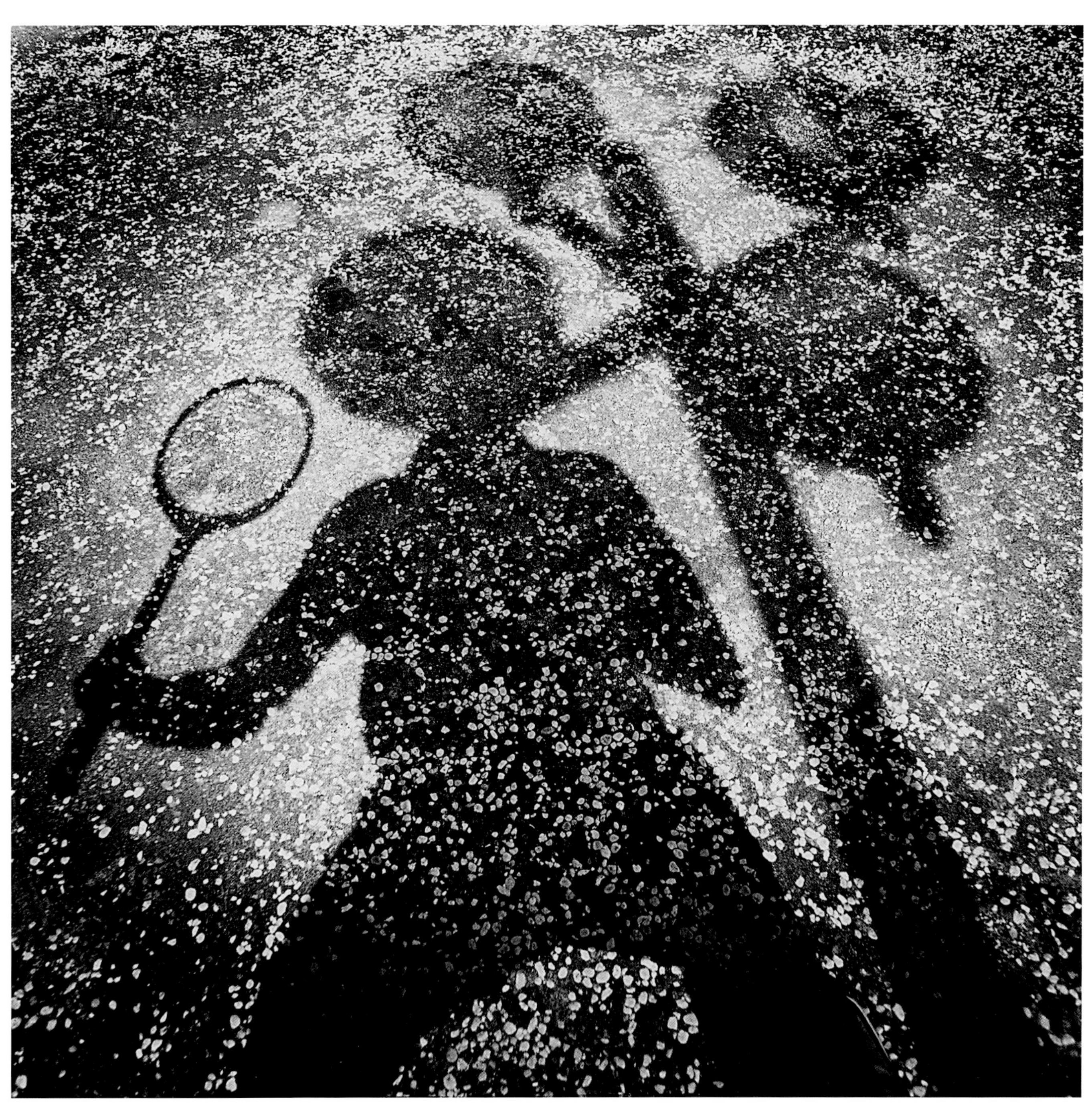

PLATE 116
Shadow, New York, New York, negative 1974; print 1975

Theater of the Mind

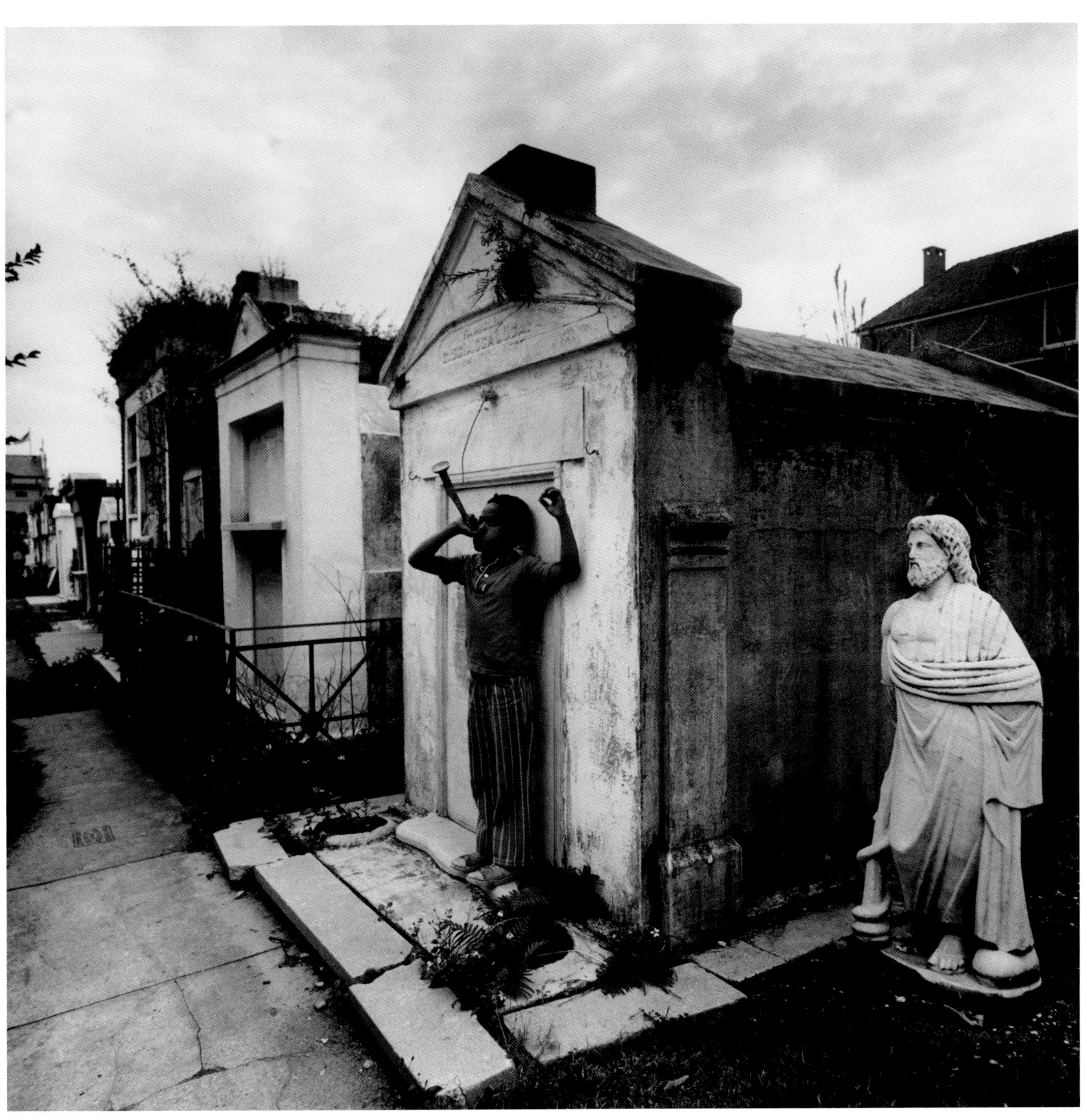

PLATE 117
Boy in Cemetery, New Orleans, Louisiana, 1974

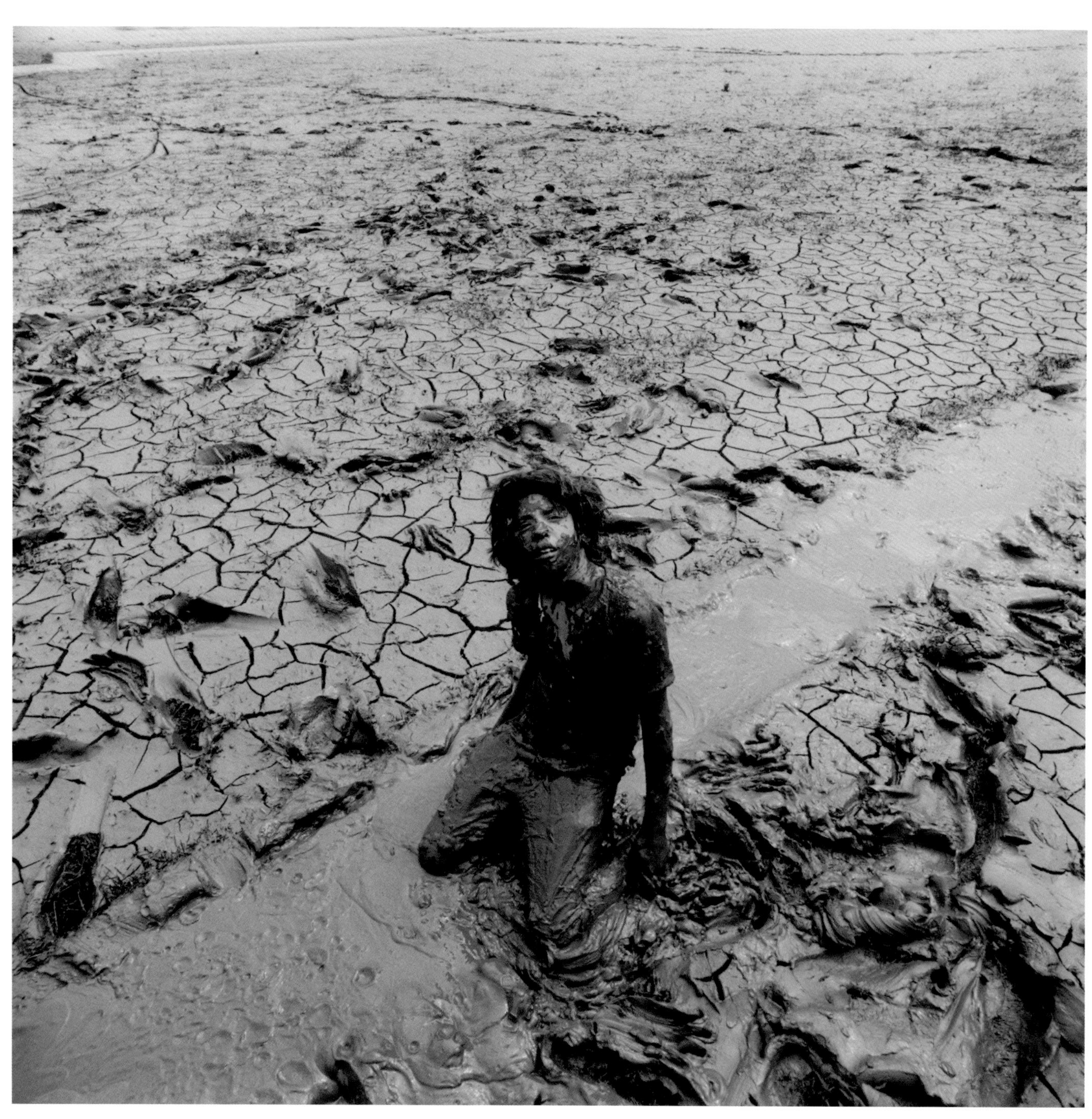

PLATE 118
Boy in Mud, Pittsburgh, Pennsylvania, negative 1972; print later

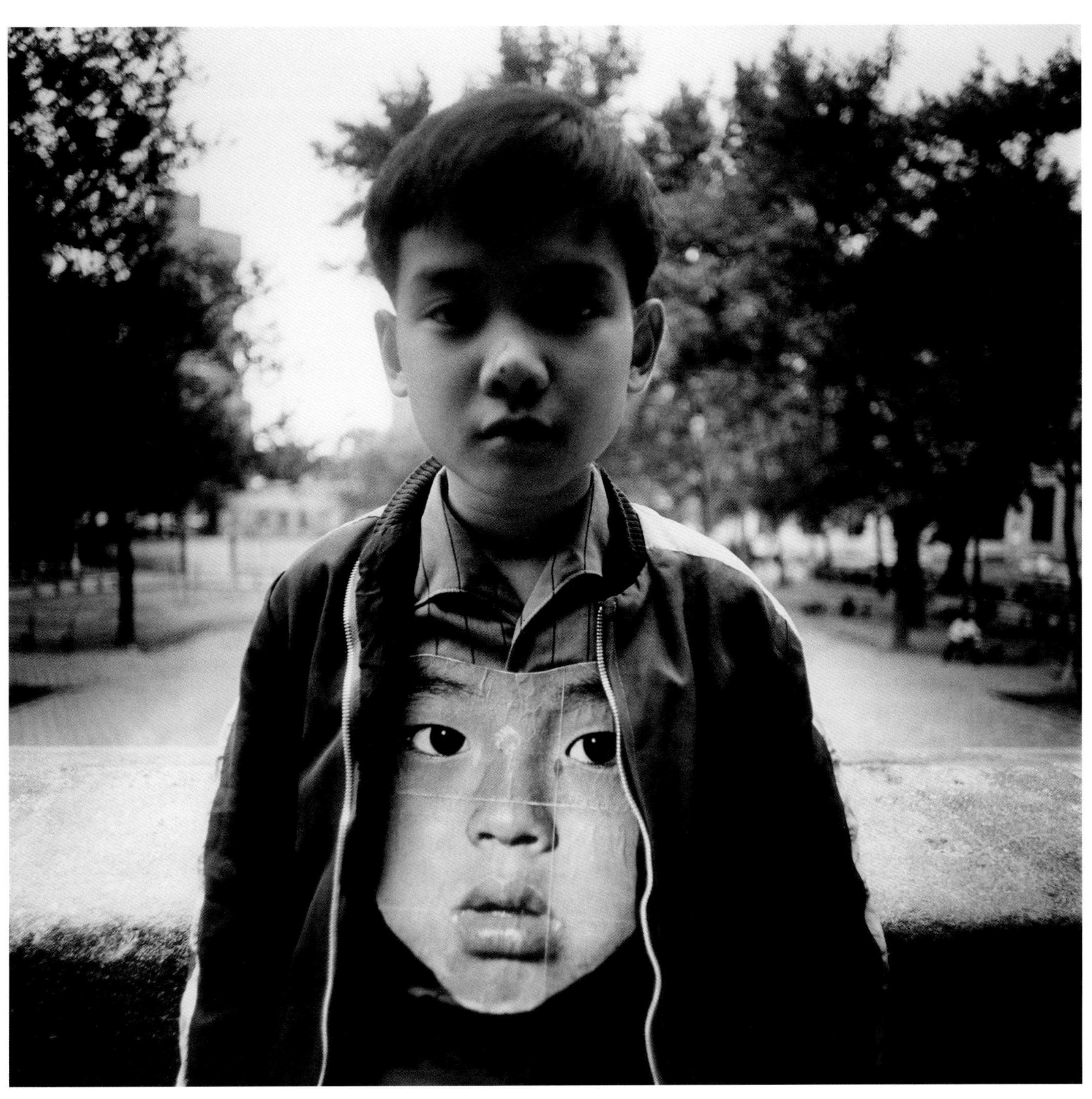

PLATE 119
Boy and Cut-Out Face, New York, New York, 1972

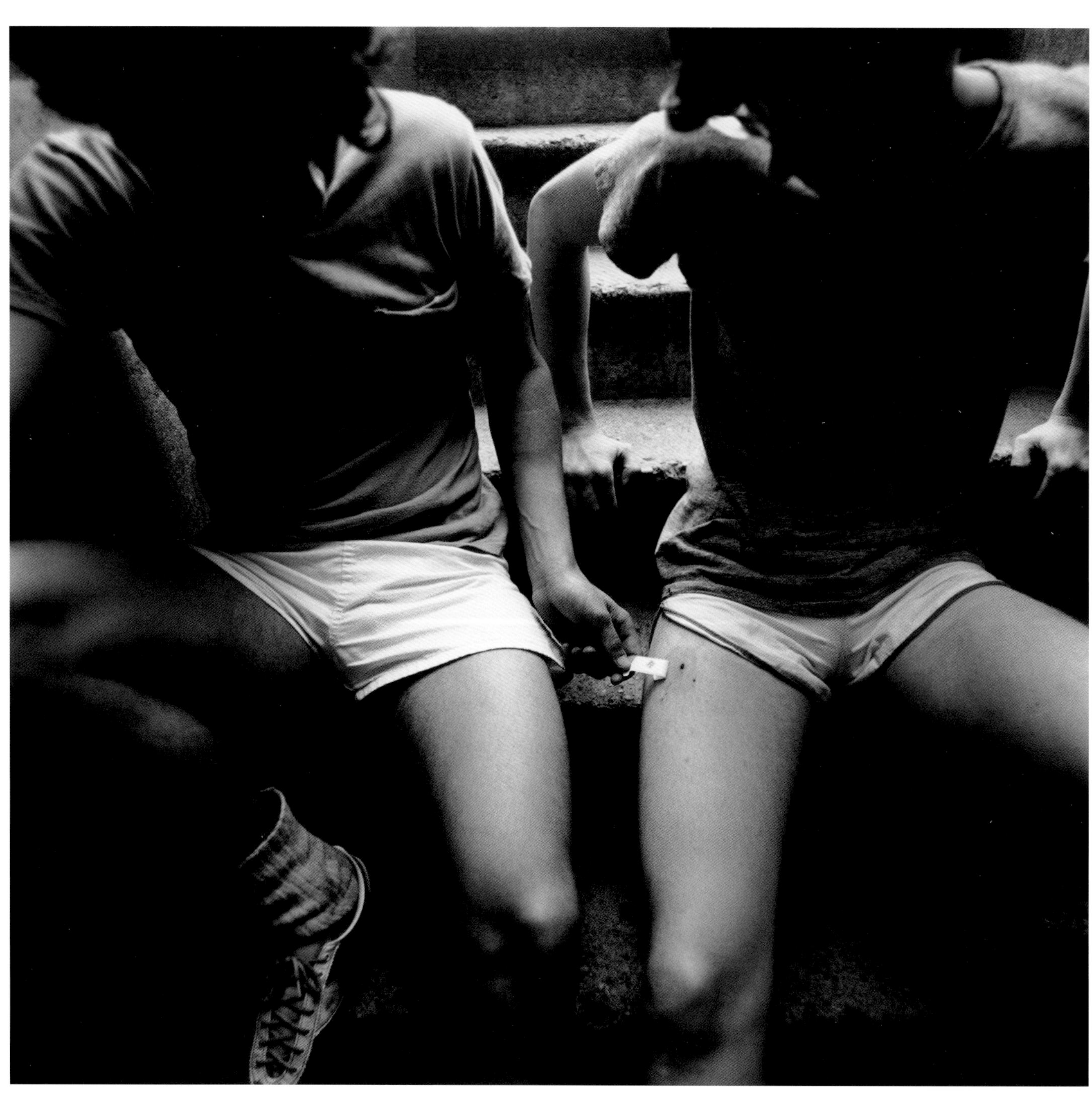

PLATE 120
Teenage Runners, New York, New York, 1976

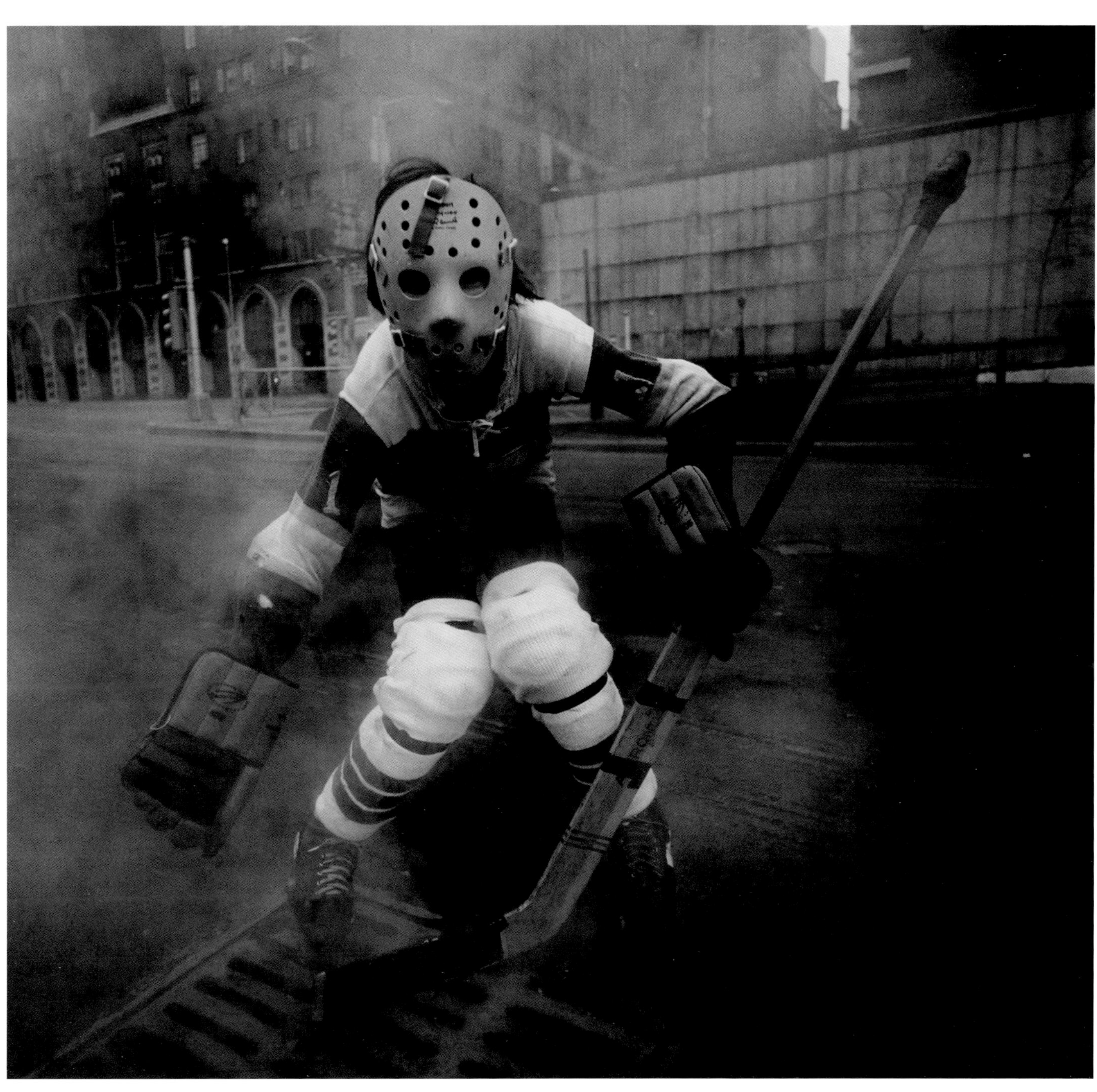

PLATE 121
Hockey Player, New York, New York, 1972

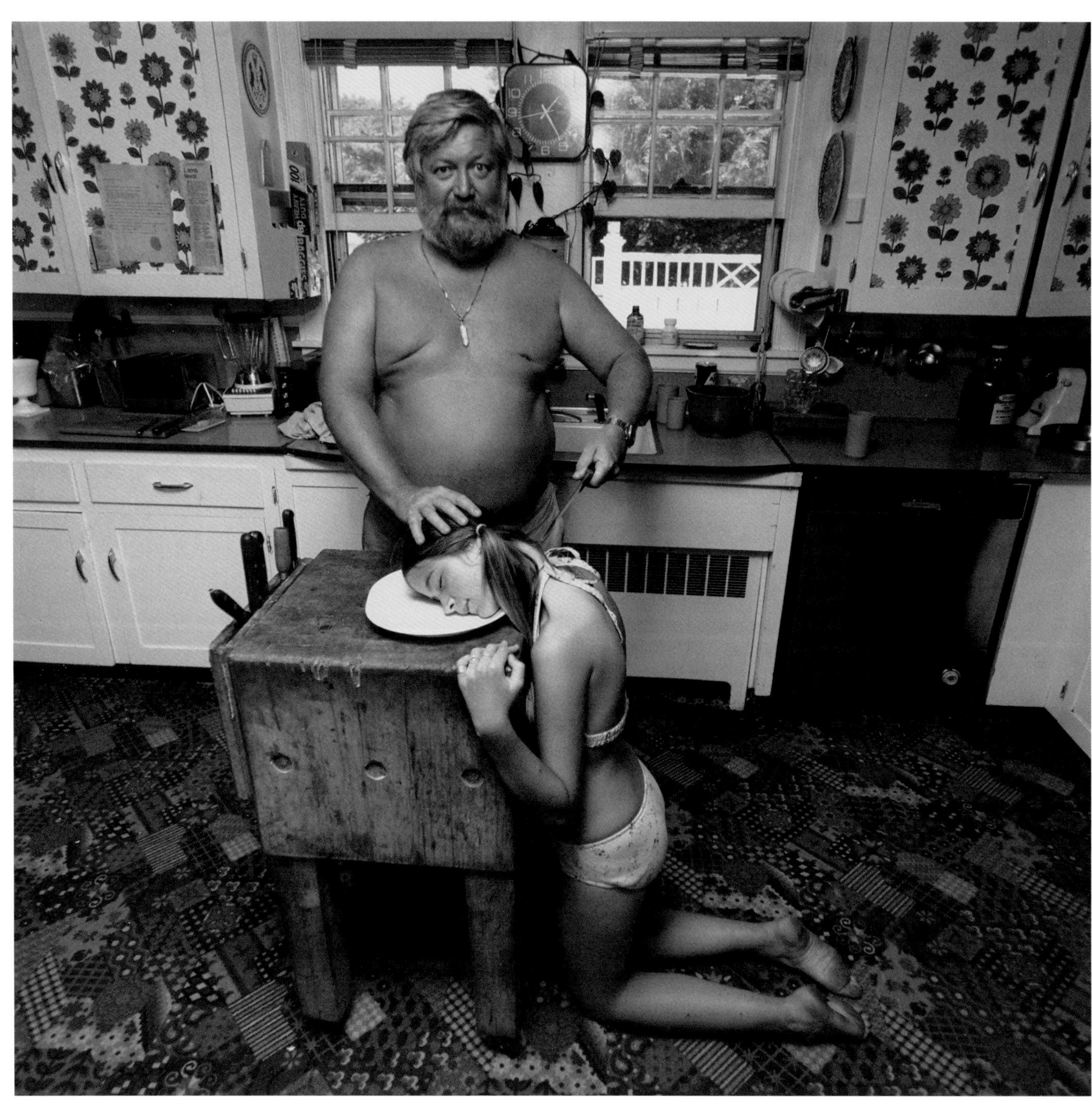

PLATE 122
Arthur Young and Daughter, Martha's Vineyard, Massachusetts, 1975

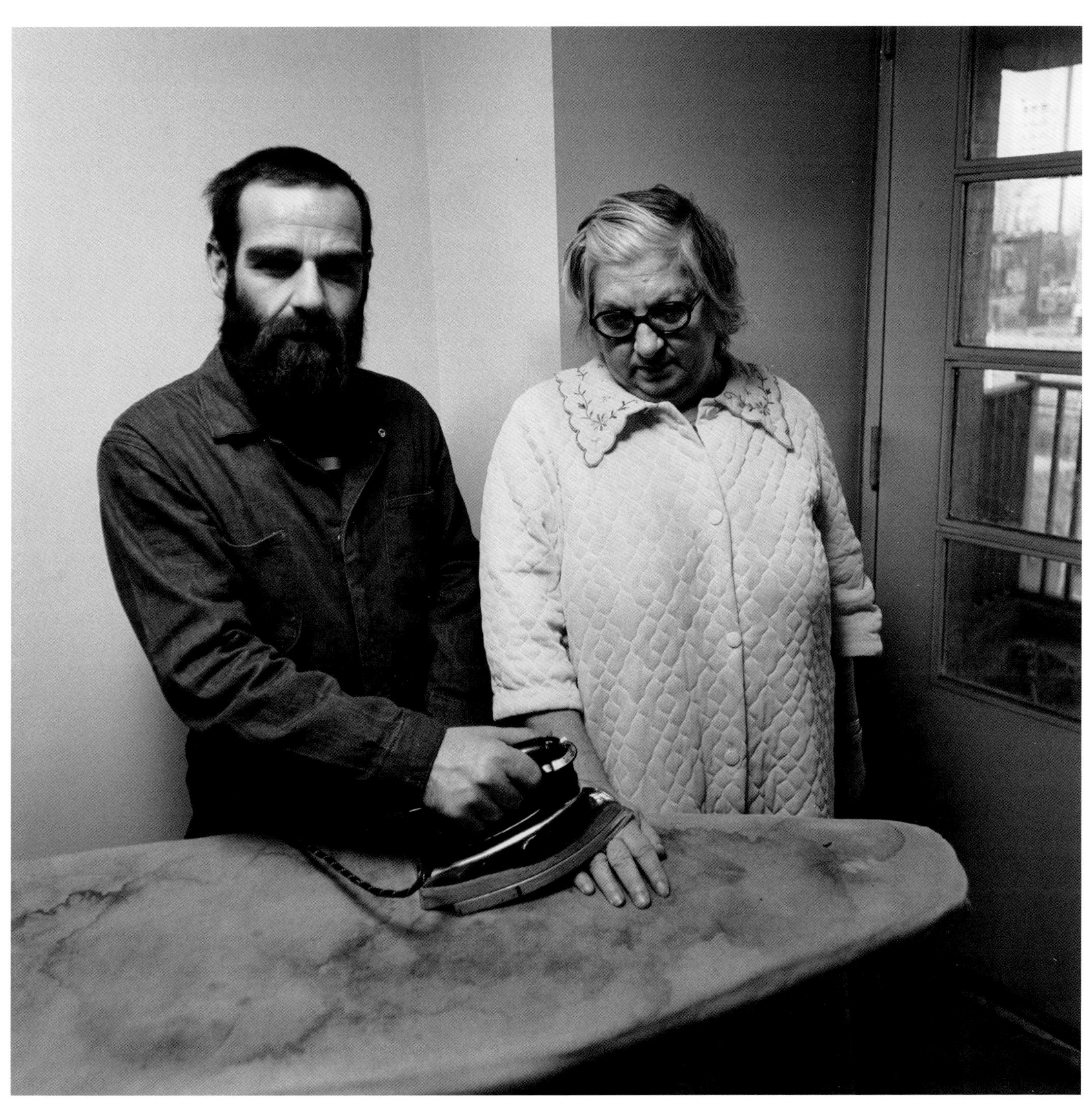

PLATE 123

Ed Berman and His Mother, Brooklyn, New York, 1975

Contact sheet, New York,
New York, 1973
Gelatin silver print,
25.4 × 20.3 cm
(10 × 8 in.)
Collection of the artist

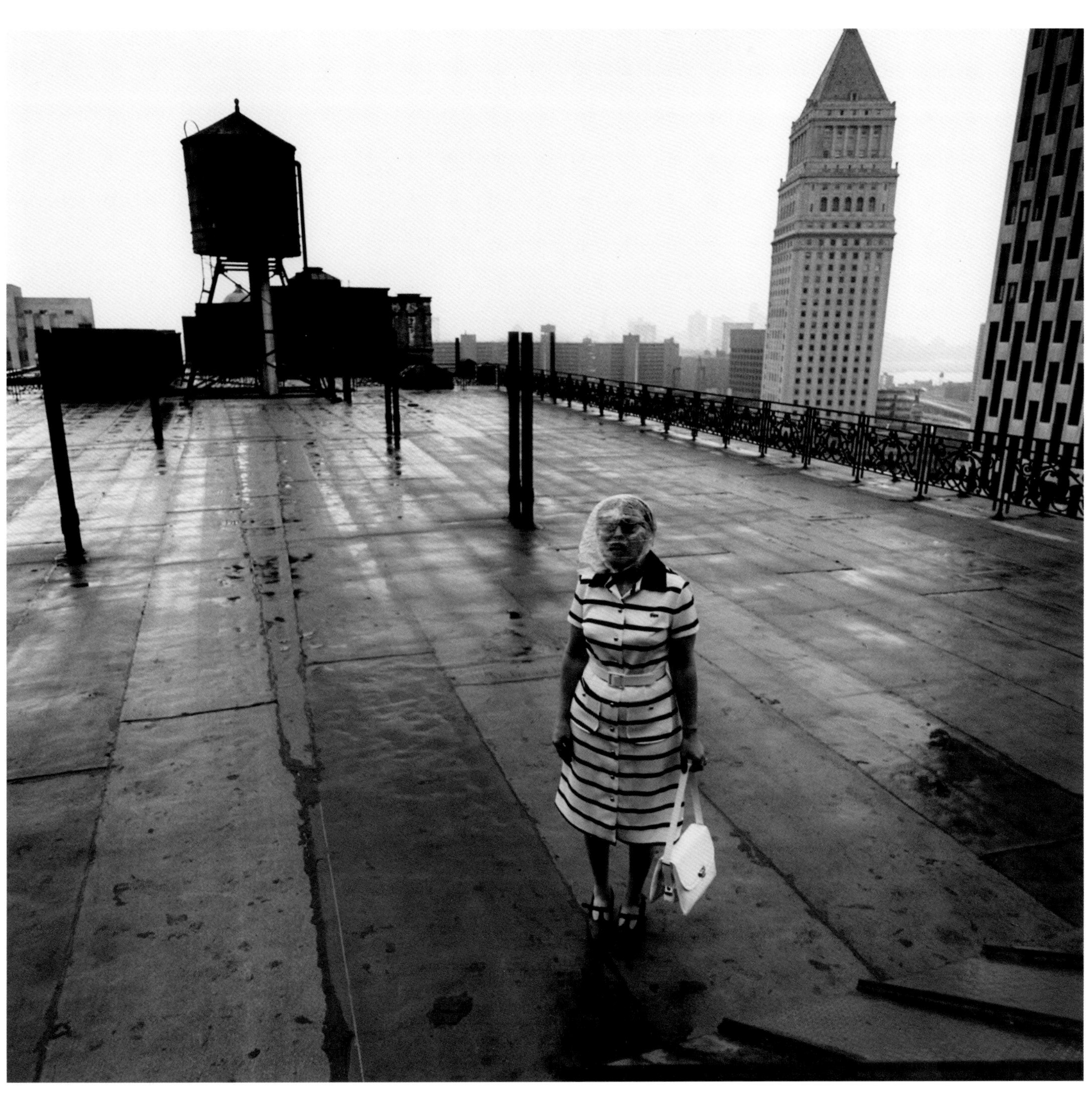

PLATE 124
Woman on Roof, Clock Tower Building, New York, New York, 1973

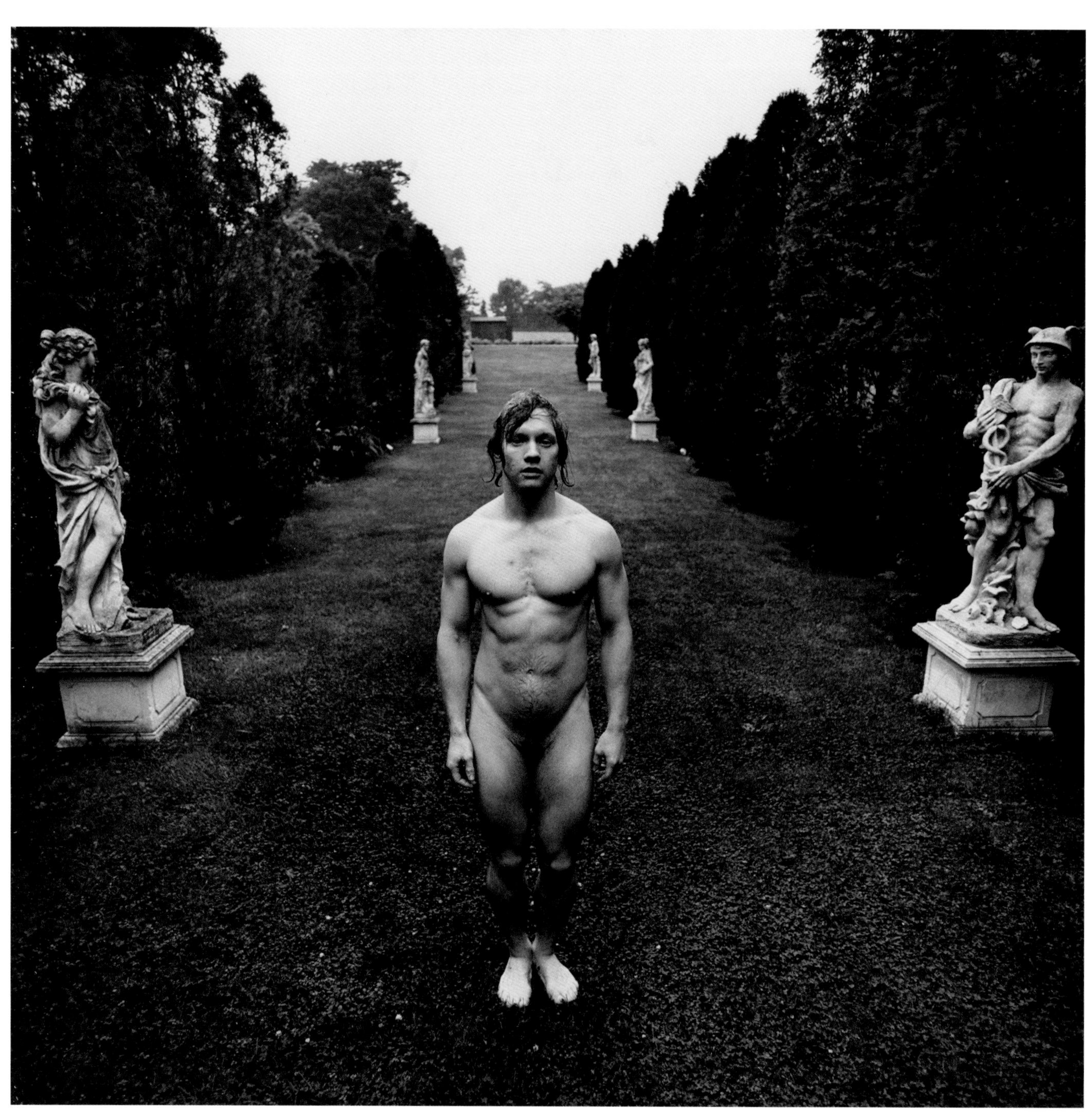

PLATE 125

Androgynous Figure between Venus and Mercury, East Hampton, New York, 1973

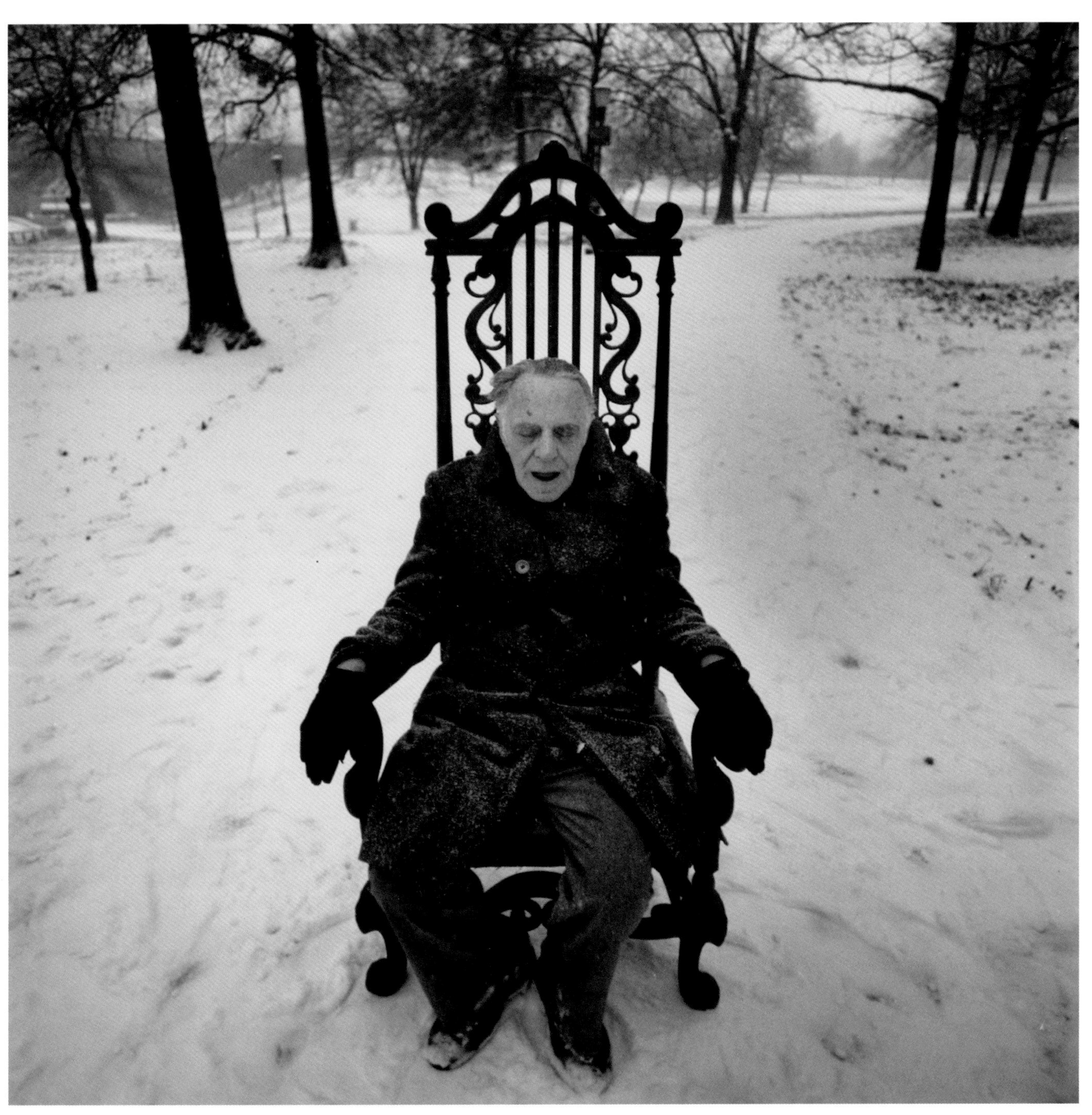

PLATE 126
Last Portrait of My Father, New York, New York, 1978

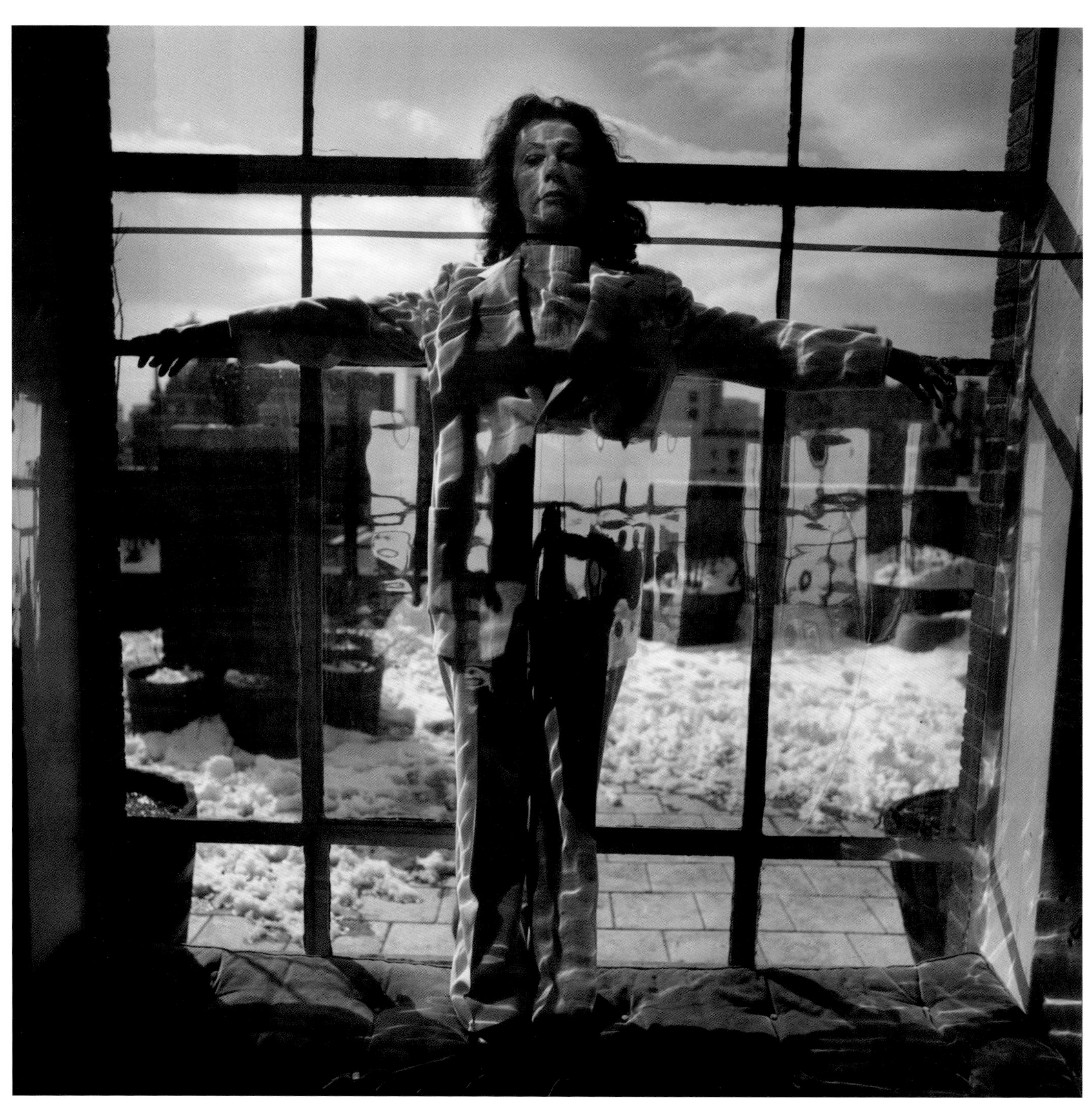

PLATE 127
Ultra Violet, New York, New York, negative 1978; print later

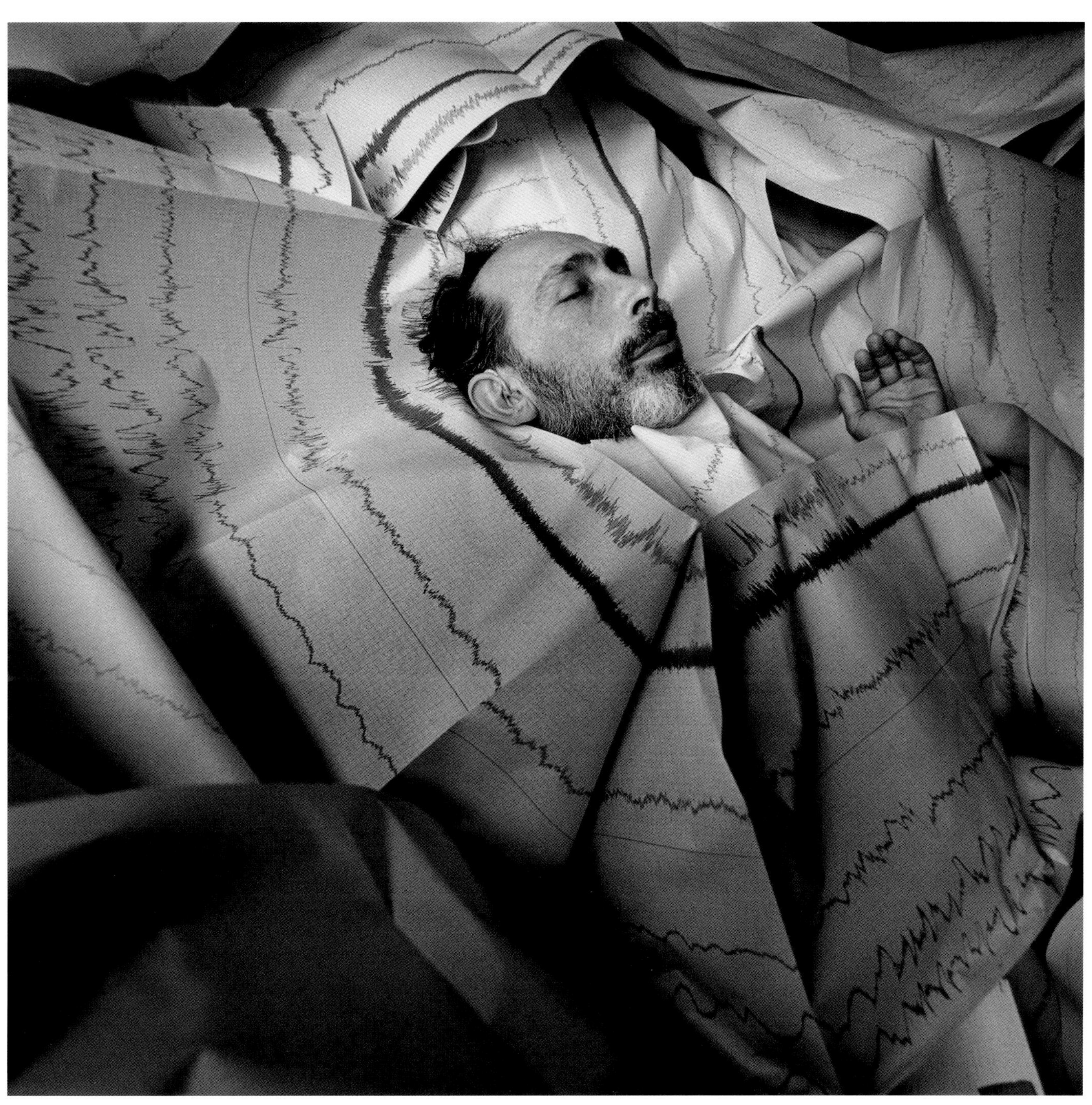

PLATE 128
Dream Therapist, Harold Ellis, New York, New York, 1975

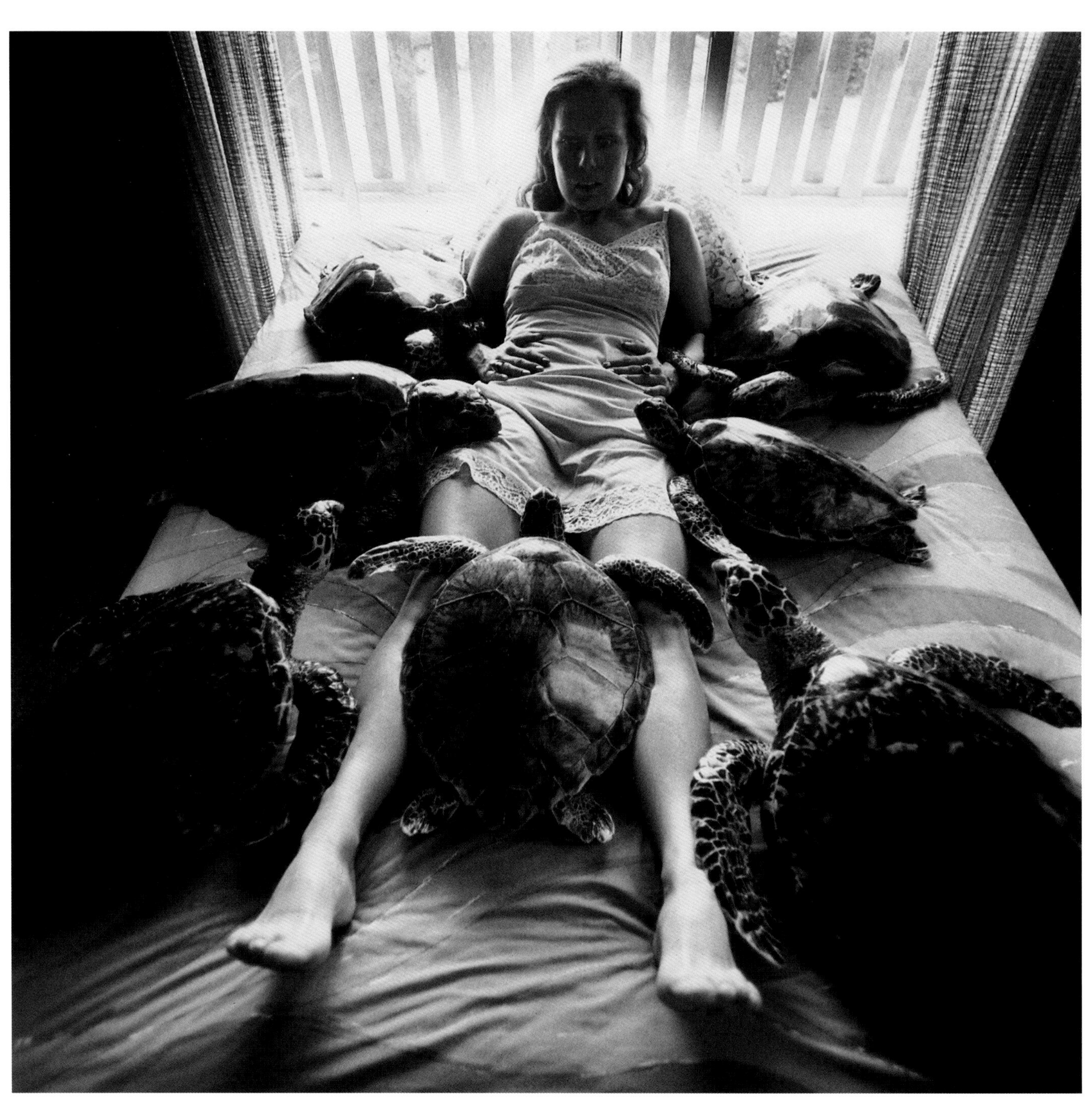

PLATE 129
Woman with Turtles, Paradise Island, Bahamas, 1975

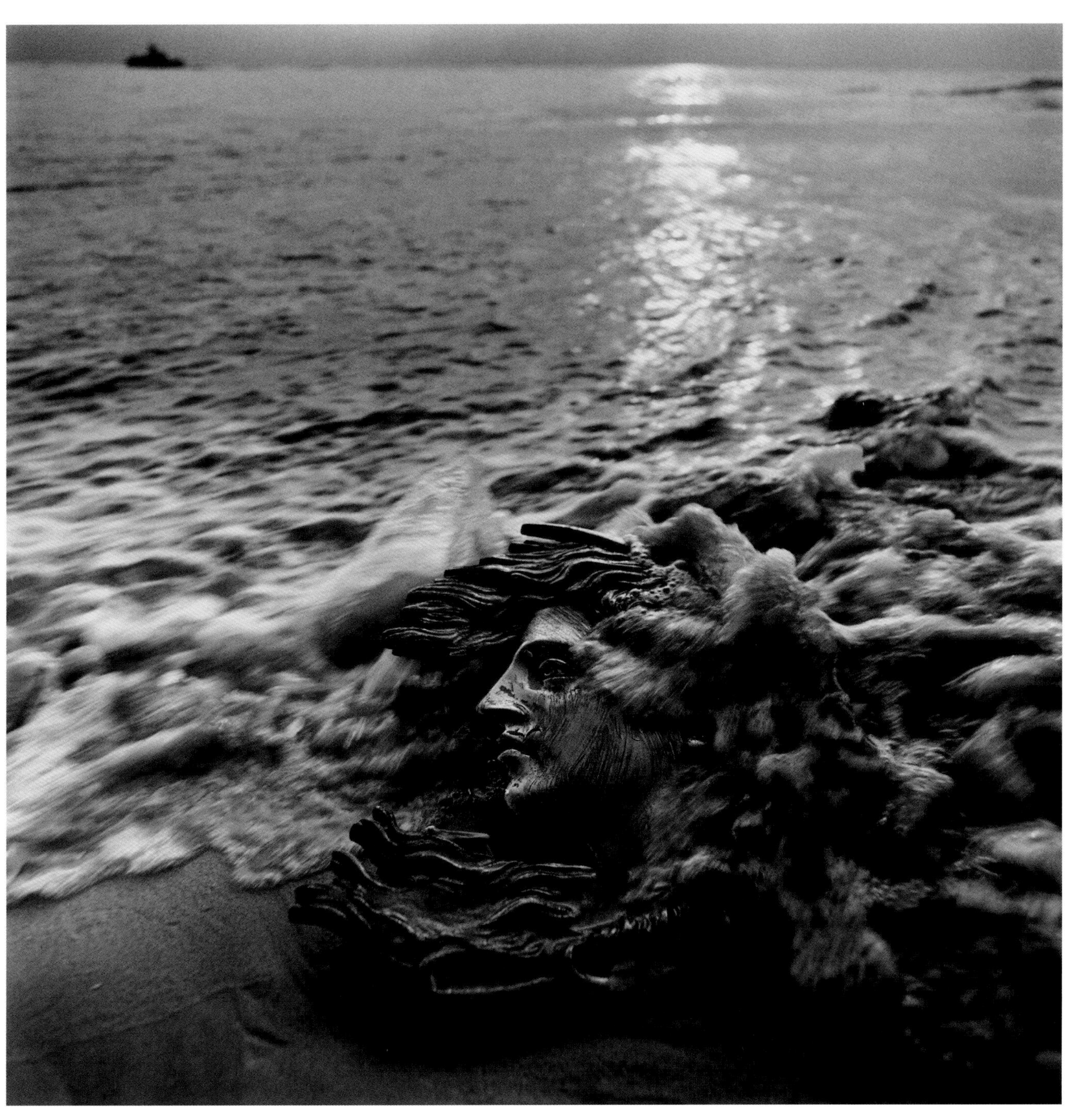

PLATE 130
Clair de Lune, Breezy Point, New York, negative 1972; print 1975

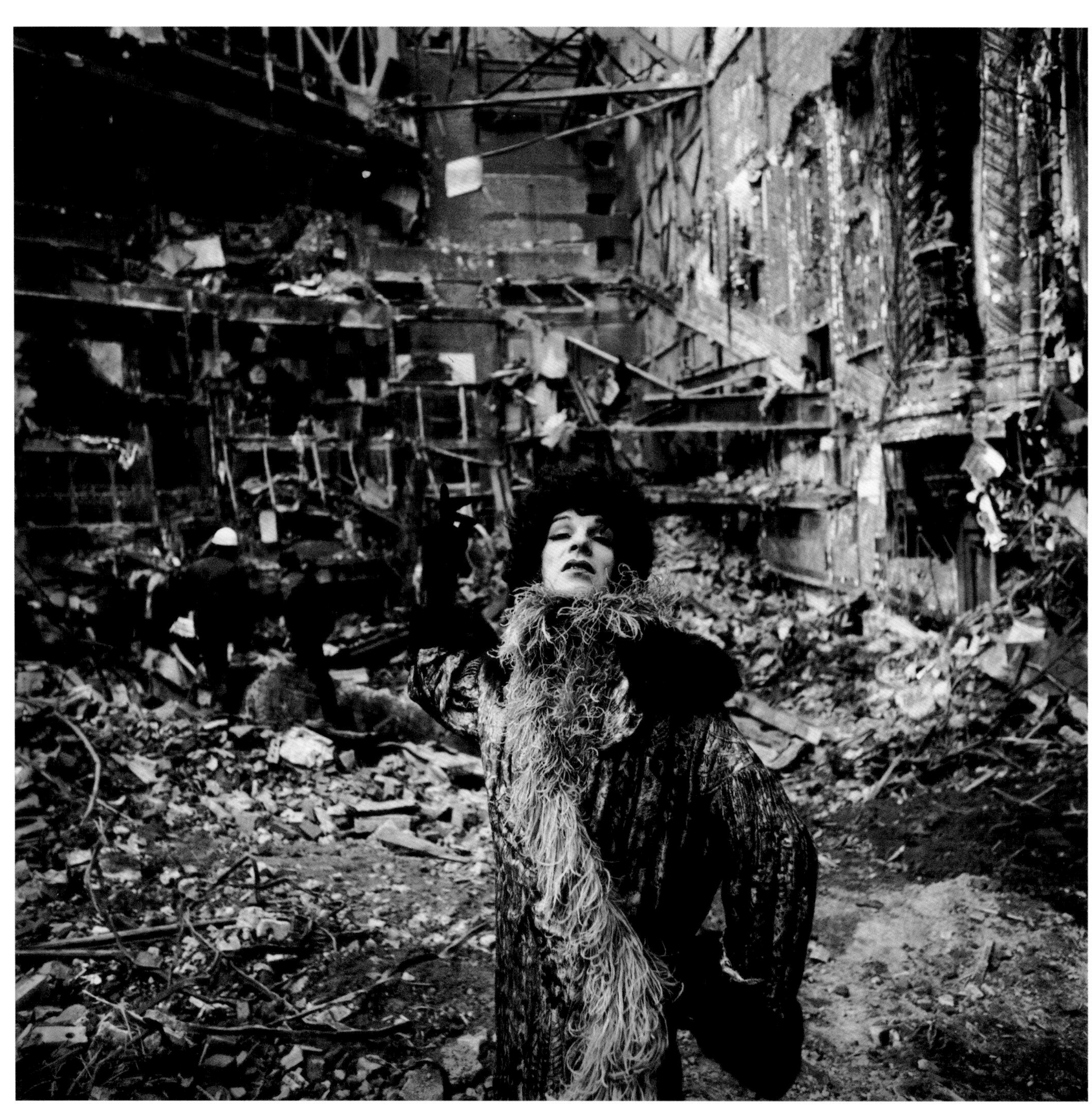

PLATE 131

Minette as Gloria Swanson in Ruins of Fox Theater, Brooklyn, New York, negative 1971; print 2021

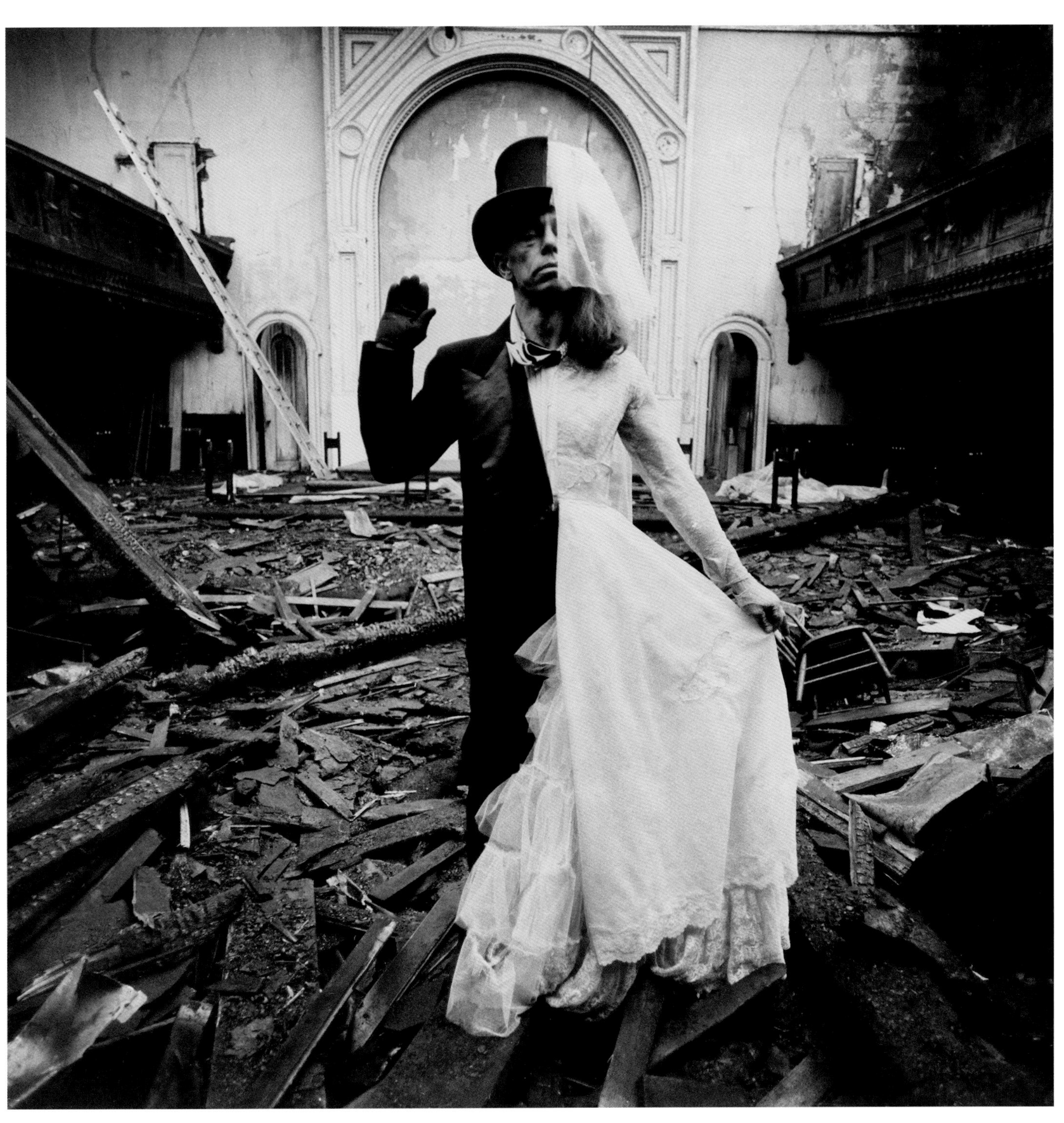

PLATE 132
Bride and Groom, New York, New York, 1970

Plate List

PLATE 1
Self-Portrait in Mirror, Coney Island, New York, 1969
Gelatin silver print
34.9 × 27.3 cm (13 3/4 × 10 3/4 in.)
Collection of David Knaus

PLATE 2
My Face in Store Window, New York, New York, 1969
Gelatin silver print
19.1 × 19.1 cm (7 1/2 × 7 1/2 in.)
Collection of David Knaus

PLATE 3
Self-Portrait in Photomat Mirror, Coney Island, New York, negative 1970; print 2021
Gelatin silver print
24.8 × 24.1 cm (9 3/4 × 9 1/2 in.)
Los Angeles, J. Paul Getty Museum, Gift of David Knaus, 2023.20.11

APPALACHIA

PLATE 4
Mrs. C. W. Boone and Her Daughter, Barnardsville, North Carolina, 1968
Gelatin silver print
21.2 × 19.4 cm (8 3/8 × 7 5/8 in.)
Los Angeles, J. Paul Getty Museum, Gift of the Ottersons, 2018.114.1

PLATE 5
Mrs. B. Riddle, Pensacola, North Carolina, 1968
Gelatin silver print
25 × 19.9 cm (9 13/16 × 7 13/16 in.)
Los Angeles, J. Paul Getty Museum, Gift of the Ottersons, 2018.114.3

PLATE 6
Jumping Jack Man and Dancing Board, Beech Creek, North Carolina, 1968
Gelatin silver print
25.1 × 20.1 cm (9 7/8 × 7 15/16 in.)
Los Angeles, J. Paul Getty Museum, Gift of the Ottersons, 2018.114.12

PLATE 7
Pearl Norwood, Maker of Raggedy Ann Dolls, Banner Elk, North Carolina, 1968
Gelatin silver print
24.5 × 19.5 cm (9 5/8 × 7 11/16 in.)
Los Angeles, J. Paul Getty Museum, Gift of the Ottersons, 2018.114.13

PLATE 8
Miner's Back, Vicco, Kentucky, 1968
Gelatin silver print
25.2 × 20.3 cm (9 15/16 × 8 in.)
Los Angeles, J. Paul Getty Museum, Gift of the Ottersons, 2018.114.16

PLATE 9
Twisted Tree Roots, Lookout, Kentucky, 1968
Gelatin silver print
25.3 × 20.4 cm (9 15/16 × 8 1/16 in.)
Los Angeles, J. Paul Getty Museum, Gift of the Ottersons, 2018.114.18

PLATE 10
Glove and Portrait, Welch, West Virginia, 1968
Gelatin silver print
18.8 × 23.7 cm (7 3/8 × 9 5/16 in.)
Los Angeles, J. Paul Getty Museum, Gift of the Ottersons, 2018.114.29

PLATE 11
Appalachian Girl Who Is Sick with Anemia, Lookout, Kentucky, 1968
Gelatin silver print
20.6 × 20.4 cm (8 1/8 × 8 1/16 in.)
Los Angeles, J. Paul Getty Museum, Gift of the Ottersons, 2018.114.31

PLATE 12
Girl with Doll's Head, Capels, West Virginia, 1968
Gelatin silver print
20.4 × 15.7 cm (8 1/16 × 6 3/16 in.)
Los Angeles, J. Paul Getty Museum, Gift of the Ottersons, 2018.114.32

THE RAMBLE

PLATE 13
Young Man on Bridge, Central Park, New York, 1969
Gelatin silver print
24.8 × 22.2 cm (9 3/4 × 8 3/4 in.)
Collection of David Knaus

PLATE 14
Watching, Central Park, New York, negative 1969; print 2007
Gelatin silver print
26.7 × 26.4 cm (10 1/2 × 10 3/8 in.)
Collection of David Knaus

PLATE 15
Young Man in Woods, Central Park, New York, 1969
Gelatin silver print
24.8 × 19.7 cm (9 3/4 × 7 3/4 in.)
Collection of David Knaus

PLATE 16
Dog Walker, Central Park, New York, negative 1969; print 2007
Gelatin silver print
26.7 × 26.4 cm (10 1/2 × 10 3/8 in.)
Collection of David Knaus

PLATE 17
In the Woods, Central Park, New York, negative 1969; print 2007
Gelatin silver print
26.7 × 26.4 cm (10 1⁄2 × 10 3⁄8 in.)
Collection of David Knaus

PLATE 18
Boy in Central Park, New York, 1969
Gelatin silver print
24.8 × 19.7 cm (9 3⁄4 × 7 3⁄4 in.)
Collection of David Knaus

PLATE 19
Two Boys in Central Park, New York, negative 1969; print 2007
Gelatin silver print
26.7 × 26.4 cm (10 1⁄2 × 10 3⁄8 in.)
Collection of David Knaus

PLATE 20
Two Men Cruising, *Central Park, New York*, 1969
Gelatin silver print
24.8 × 19.7 cm (9 3⁄4 × 7 3⁄4 in.)
Collection of David Knaus

PLATE 21
Gay Activists at First Gay Pride Parade, Christopher Street, New York, negative 1970; print 2021
Gelatin silver print
24.8 × 24.1 cm (9 3⁄4 × 9 1⁄2 in.)
Los Angeles, J. Paul Getty Museum, Gift of David Knaus, 2023.20.2

PLATE 22
Bruce at Dawn, Paper Flower Maker, East Village, New York, negative 1970; print 2021
Gelatin silver print
24.8 × 24.1 cm (9 3⁄4 × 9 1⁄2 in.)
Los Angeles, J. Paul Getty Museum, Gift of David Knaus, 2023.20.6

OPEN SPACE

PLATE 23
Cemetery, Queens, New York, 1969
Gelatin silver print
27.4 × 35.1 cm (10 13⁄16 × 13 13⁄16 in.)
Los Angeles, J. Paul Getty Museum, Gift of Trixy Castro, 2019.167.6

PLATE 24
Expressway, New York, New York, 1969
Gelatin silver print
24.8 × 19.7 cm (9 3⁄4 × 7 3⁄4 in.)
Los Angeles, J. Paul Getty Museum, Gift of David A. Cohen and Laurie K. Cohen, 2020.100.2

PLATE 25
Newton Creek, *New York*, *New York*, 1969
Gelatin silver print
24.8 × 19.7 cm (9 3⁄4 × 7 3⁄4 in.)
Los Angeles, J. Paul Getty Museum, Gift of Dr. Philip Greider, 2020.101.3

PLATE 26
Two Streets, Two Clocks, Bronx, New York, 1969
Gelatin silver print
19.9 × 19.6 cm (7 13⁄16 × 7 11⁄16 in.)
Los Angeles, J. Paul Getty Museum, Gift of Gregory V. Gooding, 2020.102.3

PLATE 27
Boy on Bike Crossing Williamsburg Bridge, New York, 1969
Gelatin silver print
40.2 × 50 cm (15 13⁄16 × 19 11⁄16 in.)
Los Angeles, J. Paul Getty Museum, Gift of Gregory V. Gooding, 2020.102.10

PLATE 28
Woman in Railroad Yard, Brooklyn, New York, 1969
Gelatin silver print
19.8 × 22.1 cm (7 13⁄16 × 8 11⁄16 in.)
Los Angeles, J. Paul Getty Museum, Gift of David A. Cohen and Laurie K. Cohen, 2020.100.4

PLATE 29
Boy on Subway Car, Williamsburg Bridge, New York, 1969
Gelatin silver print
24.2 × 19.1 cm (9 1⁄2 × 7 1⁄2 in.)
Los Angeles, J. Paul Getty Museum, Gift of Jon and Ellen Vein Family, 2019.171.4

PLATE 30
Office Workers Returning Home, New York, New York, negative 1969; print later
Gelatin silver print
18.3 × 18.4 cm (7 3⁄16 × 7 1⁄4 in.)
Los Angeles, J. Paul Getty Museum, Gift of David Knaus, 2020.99.4

PLATE 31
Woman Climbing Steps, Bronx, New York, 1969
Gelatin silver print
24.7 × 19.6 cm (9 3⁄4 × 7 11⁄16 in.)
Los Angeles, J. Paul Getty Museum, Gift of Trixy Castro, 2019.167.5

PLATE 32
Resting on Fifth Avenue, New York, New York, 1971
Gelatin silver print
19.1 × 19.2 cm (7 1⁄2 × 7 9⁄16 in.)
Los Angeles, J. Paul Getty Museum, Gift of David Knaus, 2020.99.6

PLATE 33
Jehovah's Witnesses, New York, New York, negative 1970; print 2021
Gelatin silver print
24.8 × 24.1 cm (9 3⁄4 × 9 1⁄2 in.)
Los Angeles, J. Paul Getty Museum, Gift of David Knaus, 2023.20.1

PLATE 34
Man on Way to Work Next to Wrecked Auto, New York, New York, 1976
Gelatin silver print
19.2 × 19.2 cm (7 9⁄16 × 7 9⁄16 in.)
Los Angeles, J. Paul Getty Museum, Gift of David Knaus, 2020.99.5

PLATE 35
Friends Playing Cards, Sheepshead Bay, Brooklyn, New York, 1970
Gelatin silver print
24.1 × 19.6 cm (9 1⁄2 × 7 11⁄16 in.)
Los Angeles, J. Paul Getty Museum, Gift of John V. and Laura M. Knaus, 2019.169.4

PLATE 36
Hobby Horses, Harlem River, Bronx, New York, 1970
Gelatin silver print
22.6 × 19.8 cm (8 7⁄8 × 7 13⁄16 in.)
Los Angeles, J. Paul Getty Museum, Gift of J. Patrick and Patricia A. Kennedy, 2019.168.2

PLATE 37
Abandoned Doll, Jamaica Bay, Queens, New York, 1971
Gelatin silver print
26.9 × 26.9 cm (10 9⁄16 × 10 9⁄16 in.)
Los Angeles, J. Paul Getty Museum, Gift of J. Patrick and Patricia A. Kennedy, 2019.168.5

PLATE 38
Workers' Housing, Cohoes, New York, 1970
Gelatin silver print
22.2 × 19.5 cm (8 3⁄4 × 7 11⁄16 in.)
Los Angeles, J. Paul Getty Museum, Gift of J. Patrick and Patricia A. Kennedy, 2019.168.3

PLATE 39
Boys Playing in Van Cortlandt Park, Bronx, New York, 1970
Gelatin silver print
19.5 × 24.4 cm (7 11⁄16 × 9 5⁄8 in.)
Los Angeles, J. Paul Getty Museum, Gift of David Knaus, 2020.99.7

PLATE 40
Kids with Sparklers, Lower East Side, New York, negative 1969; print 2021
Gelatin silver print
24.8 × 24.1 cm (9 3⁄4 × 9 1⁄2 in.)
Los Angeles, J. Paul Getty Museum, Gift of David Knaus, 2023.20.10

PLATE 41
Boys with Tops, Weehawken, New Jersey, 1969
Gelatin silver print
24.3 × 19.3 cm (9 9⁄16 × 7 5⁄8 in.)
Los Angeles, J. Paul Getty Museum, 2013.68.65

PLATE 42
Girl and Botanica Store, Spanish Harlem, New York, negative 1969; print 2021
Gelatin silver print
24.8 × 24.1 cm (9 3⁄4 × 9 1⁄2 in.)
Los Angeles, J. Paul Getty Museum, Gift of David Knaus, 2023.20.12

PLATE 43
Two Girls in Puerto Rican Parade, New York, New York, 1970
Gelatin silver print
18.2 × 18.4 cm (7 3⁄16 × 7 1⁄4 in.)
Los Angeles, J. Paul Getty Museum, Gift of Dr. Philip Greider, 2020.101.4

PLATE 44
Girl and Moon Dream, New York, New York, 1968
Gelatin silver print
35.3 × 27.8 cm (13 7⁄8 × 10 15⁄16 in.)
Los Angeles, J. Paul Getty Museum, Gift of David Knaus, 2020.99.14

PLATE 45
Boy in Birthday Hat, Spanish Harlem, New York, negative 1970; print 2021
Gelatin silver print
24.8 × 24.1 cm (9 3⁄4 × 9 1⁄2 in.)
Los Angeles, J. Paul Getty Museum, Gift of David Knaus, 2023.20.7

PLATE 46
Girl in Front of Parochial School, Monticello, New York, negative 1970; print 2021
Gelatin silver print
24.8 × 24.1 cm (9 3⁄4 × 9 1⁄2 in.)
Los Angeles, J. Paul Getty Museum, Gift of David Knaus, 2023.20.5

PLATE 47
Teenage Couple, New York, New York, 1970
Gelatin silver print
24.6 × 19.7 cm (9 11⁄16 × 7 3⁄4 in.)
Los Angeles, J. Paul Getty Museum, Gift of Gregory V. Gooding, 2020.102.5

PLATE 48
Couple in Park, Albany, New York, 1970
Gelatin silver print
23.9 × 19.9 cm (9 7⁄16 × 7 13⁄16 in.)
Los Angeles, J. Paul Getty Museum, Gift of J. Patrick and Patricia A. Kennedy, 2019.168.1

PLATE 49
Teenagers by River, Bronx, New York, 1969
Gelatin silver print
19.6 × 24.5 cm (7 11⁄16 × 9 5⁄8 in.)
Los Angeles, J. Paul Getty Museum, Gift of David Knaus, 2020.99.8

PLATE 50
Family by Harlem River, Bronx, New York, 1969
Gelatin silver print
19.4 × 23 cm (7 5⁄8 × 9 1⁄16 in.)
Los Angeles, J. Paul Getty Museum, Gift of David A. Cohen and Laurie K. Cohen, 2020.100.5

PLATE 51
Mother and Daughter and Boyfriend, Rockaway, New York, 1970
Gelatin silver print
27.5 × 27.3 cm (10 13⁄16 × 10 3⁄4 in.)
Los Angeles, J. Paul Getty Museum, Gift of David A. Cohen and Laurie K. Cohen, 2020.100.9

PLATE 52
Woman with Polaroid Camera at Politician's Rally, Bronx, New York, negative 1971; print 2021
Gelatin silver print
24.8 × 24.1 cm (9 3⁄4 × 9 1⁄2 in.)
Los Angeles, J. Paul Getty Museum, Gift of David Knaus, 2023.20.3

PLATE 53
Father and Son at Rally for Mayor, New York, New York, 1969
Gelatin silver print
24.2 × 19.7 cm (9 1⁄2 × 7 3⁄4 in.)
Los Angeles, J. Paul Getty Museum, Gift of Gregory V. Gooding, 2020.102.6

PLATE 54
Father and Daughter, Brighton Beach, New York, 1970
Gelatin silver print
24.2 × 19.1 cm (9 1⁄2 × 7 1⁄2 in.)
Los Angeles, J. Paul Getty Museum, Gift of Wes and Julie Nichols, 2019.170.3

PLATE 55
Mother and Daughter, Bronx, New York, 1970
Gelatin silver print
23.5 × 19.5 cm (9 1⁄4 × 7 11⁄16 in.)
Los Angeles, J. Paul Getty Museum, Gift of Wes and Julie Nichols, 2019.170.2

PLATE 56
Woman in Shopping Center Parking Lot, Lackawanna, New York, 1970
Gelatin silver print
23.3 × 19.6 cm (9 3⁄16 × 7 11⁄16 in.)
Los Angeles, J. Paul Getty Museum, Gift of J. Patrick and Patricia A. Kennedy, 2019.168.4

PLATE 57
Boy with Radio, Hell's Kitchen, New York, negative 1974; print 2021
Gelatin silver print
24.8 × 24.1 cm (9 3⁄4 × 9 1⁄2 in.)
Los Angeles, J. Paul Getty Museum, Gift of David Knaus, 2023.20.9

PLATE 58
Teens, Newark, New Jersey, 1970
Gelatin silver print
24.5 × 19.6 cm (9 5⁄8 × 7 11⁄16 in.)
Los Angeles, J. Paul Getty Museum, Gift of Gregory V. Gooding, 2020.102.4

PLATE 59
Teenage Girls, Sheepshead Bay, Brooklyn, New York, 1970
Gelatin silver print
28 × 27.2 cm (11 × 10 11⁄16 in.)
Los Angeles, J. Paul Getty Museum, Gift of Dr. Philip Greider, 2020.101.9

PLATE 60
Teens on Beach, Prince's Bay, Staten Island, New York, negative 1971; print 2021
Gelatin silver print
24.8 × 24.1 cm (9 3⁄4 × 9 1⁄2 in.)
Los Angeles, J. Paul Getty Museum, Gift of David Knaus, 2023.20.8

PLATE 61
Teenage Boys, Bronx High School of Science, Bronx, New York, negative 1970; print later
Gelatin silver print
24.9 × 19.9 cm (9 13⁄16 × 7 13⁄16 in.)
Los Angeles, J. Paul Getty Museum, Gift of Jon and Ellen Vein Family, 2019.171.2

PLATE 62
Boy with Cigarette, Albany, New York, 1970
Gelatin silver print
24.2 × 19 cm (9 1⁄2 × 7 1⁄2 in.)
Los Angeles, J. Paul Getty Museum, Gift of Gregory V. Gooding, 2020.102.2

DREAM COLLECTOR

PLATE 63
Boy Looking through Window, Boston, Massachusetts, negative 1970; print 1972
Gelatin silver print
26.3 × 26.3 cm (10 3⁄8 × 10 3⁄8 in.)
Los Angeles, J. Paul Getty Museum, 2013.68.1

PLATE 64
Baby in Bottle, Queens, New York, 1970
Gelatin silver print
26.5 × 26.1 cm (10 7⁄16 × 10 1⁄4 in.)
Los Angeles, J. Paul Getty Museum, Gift of J. Patrick and Patricia A. Kennedy, 2019.168.7

PLATE 65
Wild Man of the Forest, Central Park, New York, 1969
Gelatin silver print
34.9 × 27.3 cm (13 3⁄4 × 10 3⁄4 in.)
Los Angeles, J. Paul Getty Museum, Gift of Trixy Castro, 2019.167.11

PLATE 66
Child Buried in the Sand, Coney Island, New York, 1969
Gelatin silver print
32.9 × 25.4 cm (12 15⁄16 × 10 in.)
Los Angeles, J. Paul Getty Museum, 2013.68.2

PLATE 67
Boy in Water under Bridge, Queens, New York, 1970
Gelatin silver print
24.6 × 19.3 cm (9 11⁄16 × 7 5⁄8 in.)
Los Angeles, J. Paul Getty Museum, 2013.68.3

PLATE 68
Girl in White Dress (interior), Cape May, New Jersey, 1971
Gelatin silver print
18.6 × 18.8 cm (7 5⁄16 × 7 3⁄8 in.)
Los Angeles, J. Paul Getty Museum, 2013.68.4

PLATE 69
Girl in White Dress (exterior), Cape May, New Jersey, 1971
Gelatin silver print
26.4 × 26.4 cm (10 3⁄8 × 10 3⁄8 in.)
Los Angeles, J. Paul Getty Museum, Gift of David Knaus, 2020.99.17

PLATE 70
Girl with Dunce Cap, P.S. 3, New York, New York, 1972
Gelatin silver print
26.4 × 26.4 cm (10 3⁄8 × 10 3⁄8 in.)
Los Angeles, J. Paul Getty Museum, 2013.68.5

PLATE 71
School Girl's Dream, P.S. 3, New York, New York, 1972
Gelatin silver print
26.2 × 26.5 cm (10 5⁄16 × 10 7⁄16 in.)
Los Angeles, J. Paul Getty Museum, 2013.68.6

PLATE 72
Boy with Tangled Strips, P.S. 3, New York, New York, 1972
Gelatin silver print
26.2 × 26.5 cm (10 5⁄16 × 10 7⁄16 in.)
Los Angeles, J. Paul Getty Museum, Gift of Trixy Castro, 2019.167.12

PLATE 73
Boy in Tin Cone, Bronx, New York, 1972
Gelatin silver print
26.1 × 26 cm (10 1⁄4 × 10 1⁄4 in.)
Los Angeles, J. Paul Getty Museum, 2013.68.7

PLATE 74
Boy in Trash Can, Brooklyn, New York, 1970
Gelatin silver print
26.6 × 26.6 cm (10 1⁄2 × 10 1⁄2 in.)
Los Angeles, J. Paul Getty Museum, 2013.68.8

PLATE 75
Paper Toy Man in Window, Santa Cruz, California, 1971
Gelatin silver print
26.7 × 26.7 cm (10 1⁄2 × 10 1⁄2 in.)
Los Angeles, J. Paul Getty Museum, Gift of Trixy Castro, 2019.167.14

PLATE 76
Kidnapping Fantasy, Bronx, New York, 1970
Gelatin silver print
34.2 × 26.7 cm (13 7⁄16 × 10 1⁄2 in.)
Los Angeles, J. Paul Getty Museum, Gift of David Knaus, 2020.99.13

PLATE 77
Boy in Goldfish Bowl, Bronx, New York, 1971
Gelatin silver print
26 × 26 cm (10 1⁄4 × 10 1⁄4 in.)
Los Angeles, J. Paul Getty Museum, 2013.68.9

PLATE 78
Boy in Basketball Hoop, Ocean City, New Jersey, 1971
Gelatin silver print
26.6 × 26.7 cm (10 1⁄2 × 10 1⁄2 in.)
Los Angeles, J. Paul Getty Museum, Gift of Dr. Philip Greider, 2020.101.10

PLATE 79
Boys on Broken Staircase, Weehawken, New Jersey, 1970
Gelatin silver print
35.1 × 27.6 cm (13 13⁄16 × 10 7⁄8 in.)
Los Angeles, J. Paul Getty Museum, Gift of David A. Cohen and Laurie K. Cohen, 2020.100.10

PLATE 80
Boy in Burnt-Out Furniture Store, Newark, New Jersey, 1969
Gelatin silver print
27.2 × 35 cm (10 11⁄16 × 13 3⁄4 in.)
Los Angeles, J. Paul Getty Museum, 2013.68.10

PLATE 81
Boy with Root Hands, New York, New York, 1971
Gelatin silver print
25.5 × 25.9 cm (10 1⁄16 × 10 3⁄16 in.)
Los Angeles, J. Paul Getty Museum, 2013.68.13

PLATE 82
Boy with Basketball, Bronx, New York, 1970
Gelatin silver print
34 × 26.6 cm (13 3⁄8 × 10 1⁄2 in.)
Los Angeles, J. Paul Getty Museum, 2013.68.14

PLATE 83
Boy with Hockey Gloves, Hell's Kitchen, New York, negative 1970; print later
Gelatin silver print
27.3 × 27.5 cm (10 3⁄4 × 10 13⁄16 in.)
Los Angeles, J. Paul Getty Museum, 2013.68.15

PLATE 84
Girl in Attic, Boston, Massachusetts, 1972
Gelatin silver print
27 × 26.2 cm (10 5⁄8 × 10 5⁄16 in.)
Los Angeles, J. Paul Getty Museum, 2013.68.16

PLATE 85
Boy in Flood Dream, Ocean City, Maryland, negative 1971; print later
Gelatin silver print
47.9 × 47.9 cm (18 7⁄8 × 18 7⁄8 in.)
Collection of David Knaus

PLATE 86
Falling Dream, Coney Island, New York, 1972
Gelatin silver print
24.1 × 19.4 cm (9 1⁄2 × 7 5⁄8 in.)
Los Angeles, J. Paul Getty Museum, 2013.68.18

PLATE 87
Boy with Duck Decoy, Passaic, New Jersey, 1969
Gelatin silver print
26.3 × 26.7 cm (10 3⁄8 × 10 1⁄2 in.)
Los Angeles, J. Paul Getty Museum, 2013.68.19

PLATE 88
Hands on the Staircase, Isla Mujeres, Mexico, 1972
Gelatin silver print
26.7 × 25.7 cm (10 1⁄2 × 10 1⁄8 in.)
Los Angeles, J. Paul Getty Museum, Gift of J. Patrick and Patricia A. Kennedy, 2019.168.8

PLATE 89
Girl and Dinosaur, Santa Cruz, California, 1971
Gelatin silver print
26.4 × 26.6 cm (10 3⁄8 × 10 1⁄2 in.)
Los Angeles, J. Paul Getty Museum, 2013.68.21

PLATE 90
Child's Dream of Redwood Monster, Santa Cruz, California, 1971
Gelatin silver print
26.6 × 26.6 cm (10 1⁄2 × 10 1⁄2 in.)
Los Angeles, J. Paul Getty Museum, 2013.68.22

PLATE 91
Boy with Nightmare Horse, Bronx, New York, 1971
Gelatin silver print
26.7 × 26.5 (10 1⁄2 × 10 7⁄16 in.)
Los Angeles, J. Paul Getty Museum, Gift of Dr. Philip Greider, 2020.101.8

PLATE 92
Boy in TV Set, Boston, *Massachusetts*, 1972
Gelatin silver print
25.4 × 25.4 cm (10 × 10 in.)
Collection of David Knaus

PLATE 93
Young Boy and Hooded Figure, New York, New York, 1971
Gelatin silver print
26.6 × 26.6 cm (10 1⁄2 × 10 1⁄2 in.)
Los Angeles, J. Paul Getty Museum, 2013.68.24

PLATE 94
Flying Dream, Queens, New York, 1971
Gelatin silver print
26.5 × 26.4 cm (10 7⁄16 × 10 3⁄8 in.)
Los Angeles, J. Paul Getty Museum, Gift of Gregory V. Gooding, 2020.102.8

PLATE 95
Boy on Rack, Atlantic City, New Jersey, 1971
Gelatin silver print
26.4 × 26.4 cm (10 3⁄8 × 10 3⁄8 in.)
Los Angeles, J. Paul Getty Museum, 2013.68.25

PLATE 96
Boy in Snow, New York, New York, 1970
Gelatin silver print
26.6 × 26.6 cm (10 1⁄2 × 10 1⁄2 in.)
Los Angeles, J. Paul Getty Museum, 2013.68.26

PLATE 97
Boy Jumping Off Staircase, Bronx, New York, 1970
Gelatin silver print
26.4 × 26.4 cm (10 3⁄8 × 10 3⁄8 in.)
Los Angeles, J. Paul Getty Museum, Gift of David Knaus, 2020.99.10

PLATE 98
Boy Listening to Musician, Biloxi, Mississippi, 1971
Gelatin silver print
26.6 × 26.4 cm (10 1⁄2 × 10 3⁄8 in.)
Los Angeles, J. Paul Getty Museum, 2013.68.27

PLATE 99
Boy with Chalk Face, Coney Island, New York, 1969
Gelatin silver print
26 × 25.8 cm (10 1⁄4 × 10 3⁄16 in.)
Los Angeles, J. Paul Getty Museum, 2013.68.28

PLATE 100
Teenager in Coffin, Brooklyn, New York, 1971
Gelatin silver print
26.3 × 26.4 cm (10 3⁄8 × 10 3⁄8 in.)
Los Angeles, J. Paul Getty Museum, Gift of David A. Cohen and Laurie K. Cohen, 2020.100.8

PLATE 101
Hand on Train, Staten Island, New York, 1972
Gelatin silver print
26.6 × 26.6 cm (10 1⁄2 × 10 1⁄2 in.)
Los Angeles, J. Paul Getty Museum, 2013.68.29

PLATE 102
Halloween Child, East Harlem, New York, 1969
Gelatin silver print
28.6 × 27.6 cm (11 1⁄4 × 10 7⁄8 in.)
Los Angeles, J. Paul Getty Museum, Gift of David Knaus, 2020.99.12

PLATE 103
Girl with Magnifying Glass, New York, New York, negative 1971; print later
Gelatin silver print
26.6 × 26.6 cm (10 1⁄2 × 10 1⁄2 in.)
Los Angeles, J. Paul Getty Museum, 2013.68.45

PLATE 104
Boy in Mirrored Birch Tree Forest, Montreal, Canada, negative 1973; print later
Gelatin silver print
19.2 × 19.1 cm (7 9⁄16 × 7 1⁄2 in.)
Los Angeles, J. Paul Getty Museum, 2013.68.58

PLATE 105
Boy and Plaster Statues, Tiger Balm Gardens, Singapore, 1972
Gelatin silver print
18 × 18.1 cm (7 1⁄16 × 7 1⁄8 in.)
Los Angeles, J. Paul Getty Museum, 2013.68.57

PLATE 106
Girl in Dreamland Park, Nara, Japan, negative 1974; print later
Gelatin silver print
26.3 × 26.7 cm (10 3⁄8 × 10 1⁄2 in.)
Los Angeles, J. Paul Getty Museum, 2013.68.44

SHADOW

PLATE 107
Shadow Self-Portrait, New York, New York, 1970
Gelatin silver print
34.1 × 26.9 cm (13 7⁄16 × 10 9⁄16 in.)
Los Angeles, J. Paul Getty Museum, Gift of David Knaus, 2020.99.18

PLATE 108
Shadow, New York, New York, negative 1974; print 1975
Gelatin silver print
19.6 × 18.9 cm (7 11⁄16 × 7 7⁄16 in.)
Los Angeles, J. Paul Getty Museum, Gift of Wes and Julie Nichols, 2019.170.5

PLATE 109
Shadow, New York, New York, negative 1974; print 1975
Gelatin silver print
19.1 × 19.1 cm (7 1⁄2 × 7 1⁄2 in.)
Los Angeles, J. Paul Getty Museum, Gift of Trixy Castro, 2019.167.7

PLATE 110
Shadow, Monaco, negative 1974; print 1975
Gelatin silver print
19.2 × 19.2 cm (7 9⁄16 × 7 9⁄16 in.)
Los Angeles, J. Paul Getty Museum, Gift of Dr. Philip Greider, 2020.101.1

PLATE 111
Shadow, Arles, France, negative 1974; print 1975
Gelatin silver print
18.8 × 19 cm (7 3⁄8 × 7 1⁄2 in.)
Los Angeles, J. Paul Getty Museum, Gift of Trixy Castro, 2019.167.8

PLATE 112
Shadow, New York, New York, negative 1974; print 1975
Gelatin silver print
18.9 × 19.1 cm (7 7⁄16 × 7 1⁄2 in.)
Los Angeles, J. Paul Getty Museum, Gift of David Knaus, 2020.99.3

PLATE 113
Shadow, Cannes, France, negative 1974; print 1975
Gelatin silver print
19.4 × 19.2 cm (7 5⁄8 × 7 9⁄16 in.)
Los Angeles, J. Paul Getty Museum, Gift of John V. and Laura M. Knaus, 2019.169.6

PLATE 114
Shadow, New York, New York, negative 1974; print 1975
Gelatin silver print
18.9 × 19 cm (7 7⁄16 × 7 1⁄2 in.)
Los Angeles, J. Paul Getty Museum, Gift of David A. Cohen and Laurie K. Cohen, 2020.100.1

PLATE 115
Shadow, New York, New York, negative 1974; print 1975
Gelatin silver print
19.4 × 19 cm (7 5⁄8 × 7 1⁄2 in.)
Los Angeles, J. Paul Getty Museum, Gift of David Knaus, 2020.99.2

PLATE 116
Shadow, New York, New York, negative 1974; print 1975
Gelatin silver print
19 × 19 cm (7 ½ × 7 ½ in.)
Los Angeles, J. Paul Getty Museum, Gift of Gregory V. Gooding, 2020.102.1

THEATER OF THE MIND

PLATE 117
Boy in Cemetery, New Orleans, Louisiana, 1974
Gelatin silver print
26.7 × 26.1 cm (10 ½ × 10 ¼ in.)
Los Angeles, J. Paul Getty Museum, 2013.68.30

PLATE 118
Boy in Mud, Pittsburgh, Pennsylvania, negative 1972; print later
Gelatin silver print
22.9 × 22.9 cm (9 × 9 in.)
The Tress Archive, LLC

PLATE 119
Boy and Cut-Out Face, New York, New York, 1972
Gelatin silver print
26.3 × 26.3 cm (10 ⅜ × 10 ⅜ in.)
Los Angeles, J. Paul Getty Museum, 2013.68.33

PLATE 120
Teenage Runners, New York, New York, 1976
Gelatin silver print
25.1 × 25.4 cm (9 ⅞ × 10 in.)
Los Angeles, J. Paul Getty Museum, Gift of David Knaus, 2015.117.1

PLATE 121
Hockey Player, New York, New York, 1972
Gelatin silver print
25.4 × 25.7 cm (10 × 10 ⅛ in.)
Los Angeles, J. Paul Getty Museum, 2013.68.34

PLATE 122
Arthur Young and Daughter, Martha's Vineyard, Massachusetts, 1975
Gelatin silver print
25.7 × 25.7 cm (10 ⅛ × 10 ⅛ in.)
Los Angeles, J. Paul Getty Museum, Gift of Wes and Julie Nichols, 2019.170.6

PLATE 123
Ed Berman and His Mother, Brooklyn, New York, 1975
Gelatin silver print
26 × 26 cm (10 ¼ × 10 ¼ in.)
Los Angeles, J. Paul Getty Museum, Gift of John V. and Laura M. Knaus, 2019.169.8

PLATE 124
Woman on Roof, Clock Tower Building, New York, New York, 1973
Gelatin silver print
26 × 26.3 cm (10 ¼ × 10 ⅜ in.)
Los Angeles, J. Paul Getty Museum, Gift of David A. Cohen and Laurie K. Cohen, 2020.100.6

PLATE 125
Androgynous Figure between Venus and Mercury, East Hampton, New York, 1973
Gelatin silver print
40.1 × 39.5 cm (15 13⁄16 × 15 9⁄16 in.)
Los Angeles, J. Paul Getty Museum, Gift of David Knaus, 2020.99.15

PLATE 126
Last Portrait of My Father, New York, New York, 1978
Gelatin silver print
38.4 × 37.8 cm (15 ⅛ × 14 ⅞ in.)
Collection of David Knaus

PLATE 127
Ultra Violet, New York, New York, negative 1978; print later
Gelatin silver print
25.4 × 25.4 cm (10 × 10 in.)
The Tress Archive, LLC

PLATE 128
Dream Therapist, Harold Ellis, New York, New York, 1975
Gelatin silver print
19.1 × 19.1 cm (7 ½ × 7 ½ in.)
Los Angeles, J. Paul Getty Museum, Gift of J. Patrick and Patricia A. Kennedy, 2019.168.6

PLATE 129
Woman with Turtles, Paradise Island, Bahamas, 1975
Gelatin silver print
19.2 × 19.2 cm (7 9⁄16 × 7 9⁄16 in.)
Los Angeles, J. Paul Getty Museum, Gift of Jon and Ellen Vein Family, 2019.171.6

PLATE 130
Clair de Lune, Breezy Point, New York, negative 1972; print 1975
Gelatin silver print
38.4 × 36.8 cm (15 ⅛ × 14 ⅞ in.)
Collection of David Knaus

PLATE 131
Minette as Gloria Swanson in Ruins of Fox Theater, Brooklyn, New York, negative 1971; print 2021
Gelatin silver print
24.8 × 24.1 cm (9 ¾ × 9 ½ in.)
Los Angeles, J. Paul Getty Museum, Gift of David Knaus, 2023.20.4

PLATE 132
Bride and Groom, New York, New York, 1970
Gelatin silver print
41.7 × 40.2 cm (16 7⁄16 × 15 13⁄16 in.)
Los Angeles, J. Paul Getty Museum, Gift of Gregory V. Gooding, 2020.102.9

Selected Bibliography

The works included in this selected bibliography focus on Tress's early photography.

Photobooks by Arthur Tress

The Dream Collector. Text by John Minahan. Richmond, Va.: Westover Publishing Company, 1972; New York: Avon Books, 1973.

Shadow. New York: Avon Books, 1975.

Theater of the Mind. Texts by Duane Michals, Michel Tournier, and A. D. Coleman. Dobbs Ferry, NY: Morgan & Morgan, 1976.

Rêves. Text by Michel Tournier. Brussels: Editions Complexe, 1979.

Facing Up. Essay by Yves Navarre. New York: St. Martin's Press; Geneva: Bernard Letu, 1980.

Machinations. Introduction by Emmanuel Cooper. London: GMP Publishers, 1988.

Arthur Tress: A Retrospective. Text by Peter Weiermair. Zurich: Edition Stemmle, 1995.

Memories. Poems by Guillaume Apollinaire, translated and with an introduction by Dafydd Wood; essay by John Wood. South Dennis, MA: 21st Editions, 2003.

Transréalités. Essay by Claude Nori. Biarritz: Editions Contrejour, 2013.

Photobooks by Arthur Tress Published on Blurb.com

The Bagman Descends a Staircase (2011).

Caspar: 1964 (2011).

The Disturbed Land (2008).

Egypt: 1963 (2011).

Elmer over Time (2011).

India 1965: Toda Funeral (2011).

Open Space in the Inner City, vol. 1 (2009), vol. 2 (2010).

Passion Play: 1963 (2011).

The Ramble: 1968 (2009).

Samiland (2017).

Shooting Range: Stockholm 1966 (2011).

Spring Rain Ceremony: 1965 (2011).

To Live and Die in Dixie (2012).

Wilkes-Barre 1972: After the Flood (2017).

Women on the Edge (2013).

Selected Articles Featuring Tress Photographs

Emmer, Åke, with photographs by Arthur Tress. "Blodig Lek i Färg." *Foto och Filmteknik* 28, no. 11 (November 1966): 26–31.

Franck, Phyllis, with photographs by Arthur Tress. "On Being Hasidic in New York City." *VISTA Volunteer* 5, no. 2 (February 1969): 24–30.

Nori, Claude, with photographs by Arthur Tress. "Arthur Tress." *Progresso Fotografico* 81, no. 10 (October 1974): 42–54.

Tress, Arthur. "Amerikansk dokumentärfotografi." *Fotografisk årsbok* 25 (1970): 64–76.

———. "Arthur Tress." *Document* 1, no. 1 (January 1976): 1–20.

———. "Arthur Tress." *Hasselblad* 3 (1971): 16–29.

———. "Arthur Tress (portfolio)." *Photography Annual* (1972): 38–45.

———. "Arthur Tress." *Popular Fotografi*, no. 2 (February 1968): 40–45.

———. "Arthur Tress." *Popular Photography Annual* (1970): 32–37.

———. "Arthur Tress—bildens poesi." *Fotografisk årsbok* 23 (1968): 150–58.

———. "The Chinese Ghetto." *World Outlook* 29, no. 7 (March 1969): 20–29.

———. "Deer Dances I Have Seen." *Dance Magazine* 42, no. 9 (September 1968): 58–61, 84–85.

———. "Drömbilder." *Foto och Filmteknik* 35, no. 3 (March 1973): 20–25.

———. "Flower Power på Djurgården." *Foto och Filmteknik* 27, no. 12 (December 1967): n.p.

———. "Gallery Guide: Photographs for Show and Sale." *Creative Camera*, no. 57 (March 1969): 148–49.

———. "On Significant Texture in Photography." *Creative Camera*, no. 45 (March 1968): 94–97.

———. "Open Space in the Inner City." *Creative Camera*, no. 78 (December 1970): 362–66.

———. "Open Space in the Inner City." *World Outlook* 30, no. 1 (September 1969): 20–27.

———. "The Photograph as Magical Image." *Album*, no. 2 (March 1970): 1.

———. "Poverty and the Christian Conscience." *World Outlook* 31, no. 3 (November 1968): 18–27.

———. "Spring Rain Ceremony." *World Outlook* 30, no. 5 (January 1970): 20–27.

Urvant, Ellen, with photographs by Arthur Tress. "On Being from the Hills of Appalachia." *VISTA Volunteer* 5, no. 2 (February 1969): 4–8.

Wilansky, Eileen, with photographs by Arthur Tress. "On Being Chinese in San Francisco." *VISTA Volunteer* 5, no. 2 (February 1969): 18–22.

———. "To Live and Die in Dixie." *VISTA Volunteer* 4, no. 9 (October 1968): 3–13.

Selected Secondary Sources

Asto, Joy Celine. "Arthur Tress: Inside the Mind of the 'Dream Collector.'" *Photofocus*, April 13, 2022. https://photofocus.com/inspiration/arthur-tress-inside-the-mind-of-the-dream-collector/.

Bess, Ethel. "Arthur Tress" (interview). *Pylot*, no. 4 (Spring/Summer 2016): 54–75.

Brook, Pete. "Radical Empathy: The Photographers Challenging the Way We Think about Prison." *Huck*, no. 61 (August–September 2017): 85–90.

Davis, Julie Nelson, ed. *Arthur Tress and the Japanese Illustrated Book*. Philadelphia: University of Pennsylvania Libraries, 2022.

Ganz, James A. "Arthur Tress: Dreaming in Color." *ESOPUS*, no. 24 (2017): 197–216.

———. *Arthur Tress: San Francisco, 1964*. San Francisco: Fine Arts Museums of San Francisco and DelMonico Books, 2012.

Joslin, Russell. "Arthur Tress: The Dream Collector, Revisited" (interview). *Shots*, no. 109 (Autumn 2010): 36–45.

Livingstone, Marco, ed. *Arthur Tress: Talisman*. New York: Thames & Hudson, 1986.

Lorenz, Richard. *Fantastic Voyage: The Photographs of Arthur Tress*. Washington, DC: United States Information Agency, 1994.

———. *Arthur Tress: Fantastic Voyage, Photographs 1956–2000*. Washington, DC: Corcoran Gallery of Art, 2001.

Nieves, Evelyn. "Back in the U.S.S.R." *New York Times*, Lens blog, February 26, 2015. https://archive.nytimes.com/lens.blogs.nytimes.com/2015/02/26/back-in-the-ussr/.

Paci, Giampaolo, and Ilenia Zane. *Arthur Tress—Behind the Image*. Brescia: Paci Contemporary Gallery, 2007.

Perloff, Stephen. "Arthur Tress: The Dream Collector" (interview). *Photo Review* 15, no. 3 (Summer 1992): 12–15.

Rhem, James. "Arthur Tress: Finding Us in the Other." *Focus Magazine*, December 1, 2021. www.focusphotomag.com/photographerfocus/arthur-tress-finding-us-in-the-other/.

Soter, Tim. *Fortress: A Book about Arthur Tress*. Brooklyn, NY: The Ship Escaped, 2019.

Sprigle, David, ed. *Male of the Species: Four Decades of Photography by Arthur Tress*. Santa Monica, CA: Fotofactory Press, 1999.

Tournier, Michel. *Arthur Tress—Lux Two*. Carmel, CA: Center for Photographic Art, 1993.

Turner-Seed, Sheila. "Shadow" (interview). *Popular Photography* 79, no. 2 (August 1976): 100–103.

Wooding, Marcia. "Further Adventures in the Theater of the Mind." *35 mm Photography* (Summer 1978): 74–83, 107–15.

General Sources

Biroleau, Anne. *70': La photographie américaine*. Paris: Bibliothèque nationale de France, 2008.

Bussard, Katherine A., Alison Fisher, and Greg Foster-Rice. *The City Lost and Found: Capturing New York, Chicago, and Los Angeles, 1960–1980.* Princeton, NJ: Princeton University Art Museum, 2014.

Bustard, Bruce I. *Searching for the Seventies: The DOCUMERICA Photography Project*. London: Giles, 2013.

Cheatle, Zelda, ed. *The Photograph That Changed My Life*. London: Art Cinema, 2022.

Clarke, Kevin. *The Art of Looking: The Life and Treasures of Collector Charles Leslie*. Berlin: Bruno Gmünder, 2015.

Coleman, A. D. "The Directorial Mode: Notes toward a Definition." *Artforum* 15, no. 1 (September 1976): 55–61.

———. *The Grotesque in Photography*. New York: Summit Books, 1977.

———. "Toward Some Future History of Photography, 1965–2000: Part 1" (1999). Originally published in *21st: The Journal of Contemporary Photography*. Leo & Wolfe Publishing, Inc., 1999. www.photocriticism.com/members/archivetexts/photocriticism/coleman/colemanfuture.html.

Davis, Douglas. "The Ten 'Toughest' Photographs of 1975." *Esquire* 85, no. 2 (February 1976): 108–15.

De Gasperis, Giammaria, ed. *Contact Sheets: The Selected Photos*, vol. 1. Rome: Postcart, 2015.

Ellenzweig, Allen. *The Homoerotic Photograph: Male Images from Durieu/Delacroix to Mapplethorpe*. New York: Columbia University Press, 1992.

Garner, Gretchen. *Disappearing Witness: Change in Twentieth-Century American Photography*. Baltimore: Johns Hopkins University Press, 2003.

Goysdotter, Moa. *Impure Vision: American Staged Photography of the 1970s*. Lund: Nordic Academic Press, 2013.

Hardison, Sam, and George Stambolian. "The Art and Politics of the Male Image: A Conversation between Sam Hardison and George Stambolian." *Christopher Street* 4, no. 7 (March 1980): 14–22.

Joslin, Russell, ed. *Series of Dreams: Selections from 17 Years/68 Issues of Shots Magazine*. Oslo: Skeleton Key Press, 2018.

Kohler, Michael, ed. *Constructed Realities: The Art of Staged Photography*. Zurich: Edition Stemmle, 1995.

Lewis, Richard. *Living by Wonder: The Imaginative Life of Childhood*. New York: Touchstone Publications, 1998.

Lyons, Nathan. *Vision and Expression*. Rochester, NY: George Eastman House, 1969.

Mora, Gilles. *The Last Photographic Heroes: American Photographers of the Sixties and Seventies*. New York: Harry N. Abrams, 2007.

Ringby, Per. "Pistolteatern—Avant-Garde Performance and Political Theatre." In Benedikt Hjartarson et al., eds., *A Cultural History of the Avant-Garde in the Nordic Countries, 1950–1975*, 528–33. Leiden: Brill, 2019.

Tellgren, Anna, ed. *Reality Revisited: Photographs from the Moderna Museet Collection*. Stockholm: Moderna Museet/Steidl, 2010.

Tournier, Michel. *L'Imagerie de Michel Tournier*. Paris: Musée d'art moderne de la ville de Paris, 1987.

Travis, Bill, and Larry Davis, eds. *Photography after Stonewall*. New York: Soho Photo Gallery, 2019.

Weinberg, Jonathan, ed. *Art after Stonewall, 1969–1989*. New York: Rizzoli, 2019.

———. *Male Desire: The Homoerotic in American Art*. New York: Harry N. Abrams, 2005.

———. *Pier Groups: Art and Sex along the New York Waterfront*. University Park: Pennsylvania State University Press, 2019.

Wilson, Beth E., ed. *Taking a Different Tack: Maggie Sherwood and the Floating Foundation of Photography*. New Paltz, NY: Samuel Dorsky Museum of Art, 2009.

Wolf, Sylvia. *Visions from America: Photographs from the Whitney Museum of American Art, 1940–2001*. New York and Munich: Whitney Museum of American Art and Prestel, 2002.

Wolin, Penny. *Descendants of Light: American Photographers of Jewish Ancestry*. Cheyenne, WY: Crazy Woman Creek Press, 2015.

Acknowledgments

I wish to thank a number of individuals who contributed their expertise and encouragement to this project. I am grateful to David Knaus, Tiffany Phelan, Philip Brookman, Anna C. Lee, Robert Trujillo, James J. Shields, Richard Lewis, Neal Slavin, Julie K. Brown, Paul Roth, Per Hedström, Brian English, Margot Healey, Steve Moulton, Mark Garrett, and Eric Smith. Many Getty Museum staff members, past and present, assisted with this book and the exhibition it accompanies. Thank you to Mazie M. Harris, Paul Martineau, Claire L'Heureux, Miriam Katz, Megan Catalano, Ananya Madiraju, Sarah Freeman, Ronel Namde, Victoria Binder, Madeline Corona, David McDaniel, Jr., Stephen Heer, Ron Stroud, Marisa Weintraub, Erin Minnaugh, Kanoko Sasao, Grace Murakami, Cherie Chen, Debby Lepp, Kim Wong, Carolyn Marsden-Smith, Sharyne Nagy, Cynthia Aquino, Reena Antonishak, Virginia Heckert, Karen Hellman, Arpad Kovacs, Corey LoDuca, Olivia Chuba, Michael Smith, Tasia Johnson, Tuyet Bach, Michelle Nordon, Anne Martens, Karen Voss, Alan Konishi, Michael Mitchell, John Jacoby, Greg Sandoval, John Giurini, Valerie Tate, Janet McKillop, Emily Cregg, Judith Keller, Richard Rand, and Timothy Potts. At Getty Publications, I wish to express my deepest gratitude to Rachel Barth, Danielle Brink, Kurt Hauser, Molly McGeehan, Nola Butler, Kara Kirk, Clare Davis, Karen Levine, Katya Rice, Anne Canright, and Do Mi Stauber. Finally, I wish to extend my thanks to Arthur Tress, for his friendship, openness, and generosity.

JAMES A. GANZ

I would like to thank my family, particularly my father, Martin Tress, whose kind expressions of love and financial upkeep shielded me from the harsher realities of the world, while I had the rare luxury of finding my own true voice, and who perhaps expressed his own thwarted creative yearnings vicariously through me. Most lovingly, thank you to my older brother and sister, David and Madeleine, for their full-hearted support, both emotionally and financially—from evaporating my earliest childhood fears to enthusiastically acknowledging my slightest achievements by filling their homes and offices with my nascent artworks.

I would like to express appreciation for several teachers I've had over the years, who influenced my aesthetic sensibilities—most notably Leon Friend of Abraham Lincoln High School, with his dedicated courses in Bauhaus-style graphic design, and Heinrich Blücher, professor of philosophy at Bard College, who supported the idea of the creative person as a social critic and interpreter of the "collective consciousness." My thanks also to Duane Michals, who opened my eyes to the necessity of persistent, imaginative exploration of all photographic possibilities beyond the camera's documentary function.

I wish to applaud many of the art dealers who took on showing my work to collectors over the years—Lee Witkin, Zelda Cheatle, Richard Egan, Alex Novak, Susan Harder, Brian Clamp, Stephen Cohen, Paul Bridgewater, Laylon Whittaker, and Stephen Bulger. I am grateful to the many curators and museum professionals who went out of their way to find a home for my images and display them for wider audiences: Marco Livingstone, Richard Lorenz, Peter Weiermair, A. D. Coleman, Jonathan D. Katz, Edward de Celle, Julie Nelson Davis, Karen Sinsheimer, Jackson Davidow, Philip Brookman, and Clément Chéroux.

I am grateful to the thoughtful editors and promoters of my excursion into the world of photobook publications—most notably Peter Schults of Photo Researchers Inc. for his imaginative faith in the possibility of a volume based solely on the world of children's dreams, and the French novelist Michel Tournier, who picked up on that theme in *Rêves*. I'd like to thank Richard Lewis for his dream workshops, which opened up the world of inner wonder for me. Michael Denneny of St. Martin's Press courageously paved the way for gay authors and artists to enter the mainstream press with his publication of my 1980 book *Facing Up*. My thanks also to Goro Kuramachi of G. I. P. Tokyo, who oversaw the first Japanese edition of *The Teapot Opera*, and to Liliane De Cock, acquisitions editor at Morgan and Morgan, for believing in *Theater of the Mind*. I am grateful to Claude Nori for his enthusiasm in putting out the recent monograph *Arthur Tress: Transréalités*.

My deep thanks to David Knaus and his assistant, Tiffany Phelan, of the Arthur Tress Archive and Trust—they spent countless hours researching, collating, and transcribing much of the material that appears in the exhibition and catalogue. And, of course, thanks to the Getty publication staff, in particular designer Kurt Hauser, whose dynamic layouts made my visual concepts stand out, and to Rachel Barth, Danielle Brink, and Molly McGeehan. I am particularly grateful to Mazie Harris and Paul Martineau, whose essays amaze with their finely honed historical insights, and most of all to Jim Ganz, who over the last decade oversaw the intricate weaving together of the many disparate sections and complexities of my own biographical evolution within the larger conversation of changing photographic tastes. He also took on the challenge of correcting decades-old misconceptions by applying rigorous scholarship to iconic images to arrive at fresh insights and factual discoveries, all while remaining a close, supportive friend, encouraging me to continue working with a renewed sense of self-esteem.

I would like to thank my close San Francisco friends, who provide me with a social network as well as watch over my elderly self, keeping me from accidental harm: Eric Smith, Simon Ford, Jeffrey Braverman, Anton O'Donnell, and, in particular, Mark Garrett, who set up the connection between me and Jim Ganz that started this Getty exhibition rolling over a decade ago. Finally, thanks to my niece, Jessica Tress Masterson, for committing to further the Tress legacy as my future trustee.

ARTHUR TRESS

About the Authors

James A. Ganz is senior curator and head of the Department of Photographs at the J. Paul Getty Museum. He has lectured and published widely on topics in nineteenth- and twentieth-century art, including Impressionist Paris, the San Francisco earthquake of 1906, and the Panama-Pacific International Exposition. He curated *Arthur Tress: San Francisco 1964* at the de Young Museum in 2012.

Mazie M. Harris is assistant curator in the Department of Photographs at the J. Paul Getty Museum, where she specializes in American photography past and present, with a focus on intersections between creative and commercial concerns. Recent projects include *María Magdalena Campos-Pons: Behold* (Getty Publications, 2023), *Eye Dreaming: Photographs by Anthony Barboza* (2022), and *Paper Promises: Early American Photography* (2018).

Paul Martineau is curator in the Department of Photographs at the J. Paul Getty Museum. He has organized numerous exhibitions covering a diverse range of topics spanning the birth of photography to today. Martineau is the author of more than a dozen books and articles, including *Rodney Smith: A Leap of Faith* (2023), *Imogen Cunningham: A Retrospective* (2020), and *Icons of Style: A Century of Fashion Photography* (2018).

Illustration Credits

All artworks by Arthur Tress are © and courtesy of Arthur Tress Archive LLC.

Fig. 1: Image courtesy of Arthur Tress / Photographer unknown

Fig. 2: © Douglas Kneedler

Fig. 11: © Neil Slavin

Fig. 16: Southern Highland Craft Guild, Asheville, NC

Fig. 19: © Arthur Tress Archive LLC / Georgia Museum of Art, University of Georgia

Fig. 34: © The Touchstone Center

Fig. 38: © Ralph Gibson

Fig. 44: © 2022 Artists Rights Society (ARS), New York / VG Bild-Kunst, Bonn

Figs. 45, 46: © Arthur Tress / San Francisco Museum of Modern Art / Photo: Don Ross

Fig. 48: © Emil Schulthess / Fotostiftung Schweiz

Fig. 50: Michael Maier (1568?–1622) and Lucas Heinrich Wüthrich, *Atalanta Fugiens: Hoc Est, Emblemata Nova De Secretis Naturae Chymica* (Kassel: Bärenreiter, 1964), 161. Courtesy of HathiTrust, https://babel.hathitrust.org/cgi/pt?id=uc1.b2803751&view=1up&seq=165

Fig. 51: © Robert Mapplethorpe Foundation. Used by permission / Jointly acquired by the J. Paul Getty Trust and the Los Angeles County Museum of Art; partial gift of The Robert Mapplethorpe Foundation; partial purchase with funds provided by the J. Paul Getty Trust and the David Geffen Foundation

Fig. 53: Statens Museum for Kunst

Fig. 54: © Estate George Platt Lynes. Image Rights of Salvador Dalí reserved. Fundació Gala-Salvador Dalí, Figueres, Spain, 2023 / Image © The Metropolitan Museum of Art / Art Resource, NY

Fig. 55: © Eliot Elisofon / Harry Ransom Center, The University of Texas at Austin

Fig. 58: © The Estate of Francis Bacon. All rights reserved / DACS, London / © 2022 Artists Resource Society (ARS), New York / Photo: Rich Sanders, Des Moines, IA

Index

Page numbers in *italics* refer to images. Works without an artist or author in parentheses are by Tress.

This publication is issued on the occasion of the exhibition *Arthur Tress: Rambles, Dreams, and Shadows*, on view at the J. Paul Getty Museum at the Getty Center, Los Angeles, from October 31, 2023, to February 18, 2024.

Published by the J. Paul Getty Museum, Los Angeles
Getty Publications
1200 Getty Center Drive, Suite 500
Los Angeles, California 90049-1682
getty.edu/publications

Rachel Barth, *Project Editor*
Katya Rice, *Manuscript Editor*
Kurt Hauser, *Designer*
Molly McGeehan, *Production*
Danielle Brink, *Image and Rights Acquisition*

Distributed in the United States and Canada by the University of Chicago Press
Distributed outside the United States and Canada by Yale University Press, London

Printed in Italy by Conti Tipocolor

Library of Congress Cataloging-in-Publication Data
Names: Ganz, James A., editor. | Harris, Mazie M., contributor. | Martineau, Paul, 1967– contributor. | Tress, Arthur. | J. Paul Getty Museum, host institution, issuing body.
Title: Arthur Tress : rambles, dreams, and shadows / edited by James A. Ganz ; with essays by James A. Ganz, Mazie M. Harris, Paul Martineau.
Other titles: Arthur Tress (J. Paul Getty Museum)
Description: Los Angeles : J. Paul Getty Museum, [2024] | Issued on the occasion of the exhibition Arthur Tress: Rambles, Dreams, and Shadows, on view at the J. Paul Getty Museum at the Getty Center, Los Angeles, from October 31, 2023, to February 18, 2024. | Includes bibliographical references and index. | Summary: "This volume presents the first critical look at Arthur Tress's early photographic career, contextualizing the surreal work he became best known for by examining his other interrelated series: Appalachia: People and Places; Open Space in the Inner City; Shadow; and Theater of the Mind"—Provided by publisher.
Identifiers: LCCN 2023015393 (print) | LCCN 2023015394 (ebook) | ISBN 9781606068618 (hardback) | ISBN 9781606068625 (adobe pdf)
Subjects: LCSH: Tress, Arthur—Exhibitions. | Photography, Artistic—20th century—Exhibitions. | LCGFT: Exhibition catalogs.
Classification: LCC TR647 .T74 2023 (print) | LCC TR647 (ebook) | DDC 770.74/79494—dc23/eng/20230411
LC record available at https://lccn.loc.gov/2023015393
LC ebook record available at https://lccn.loc.gov/2023015394

Front cover: *Child's Dream of Redwood Monster, Santa Cruz, California*, 1971 (detail, plate 90)

Back cover: *Boy in Water under Bridge, Queens, New York*, 1970 (detail, plate 67)

Page 2: *Boy in Flood Dream, Ocean City, Maryland*, negative 1971; print later (detail, plate 85)

Page 3: *Shadow, New York, New York*, negative 1974; print 1975 (detail, plate 114)

Page 6: Contact sheet, Shadow, Arles, France, negative 1975; print 1975. Gelatin silver print, 25.4 × 20.3 cm (10 × 8 in.). Collection of the artist

Page 8: Contact sheet, East Harlem, New York, 1969. Gelatin silver print, 25.4 × 20.3 cm (10 × 8 in.). Collection of the artist

Page 10: Contact sheet, Queens, New York, 1971. Gelatin silver print, 25.4 × 20.3 cm (10 × 8 in.). Collection of the artist

Page 34: Contact sheet, Capels, West Virginia, 1968. Gelatin silver print, 25.4 × 20.3 cm (10 × 8 in.). Collection of the artist

Page 44: Contact sheet, Newark, New Jersey, 1969. Gelatin silver print, 25.4 × 20.3 cm (10 × 8 in.). Collection of the artist

Page 54: Contact sheet, Cape May, New Jersey, 1971. Gelatin silver print, 25.4 × 20.3 cm (10 × 8 in.). Collection of the artist

Page 70: Contact sheet, Cannes, France, 1974. Gelatin silver print, 25.4 × 20.3 cm (10 × 8 in.). Collection of the artist

Page 78: Contact sheet, New York, New York, 1970. Gelatin silver print, 25.4 × 20.3 cm (10 × 8 in.). Collection of the artist

Page 90: Contact sheet, Elementary School Mural, Daly City, California, 2020, from the series *In Recess–Covid Closed Schools of the Bay Area*. Gelatin silver print, 25.4 × 20.3 cm (10 × 8 in.). Collection of the artist

Illustration Credits
Every effort has been made to contact the owners and photographers of illustrations reproduced here whose names do not appear in the captions or in the illustration credits listed on page 259. Anyone having further information concerning copyright holders is asked to contact Getty Publications so this information can be included in future printings.

HASSELBLAD
NEGATIVE FILE
from no
New York
to no
from Jan. 19 69
Feb.
to March 19
welfare
hands on
tulips
Brooklyn
under
Bridge
TURDS in Hell
Coney Island
soldiers
Rambles
Jersey City
vacant
Lots-boys

RAMBLES
68-69
HASSELBLAD
NEGATIVE FILE
from no
NEW YORK
to no
1969
APRIL-MAY
RAMBLES
from 19
Not a public
playground 19
Brooklyn
Bridge
Gowanus
Breezy Point
Randalls
Rambles
Flasher
3 Boys
under
Aqueduct
Doll Baby
in R.S.D
Snow/salt
with skyline
warehouse
shot
Weehawken
poor kids
east side

Piano in sand
Boy dead on
Bronx Stairs
HASSELBLAD
NEGATIVE FILM
from no
800
to no
899
from March 1971
to April 1971
BRETCH BRIDE
magnifying glass
C.P.W.
Chicago stain
marked hill
marked kids
Forest Hills

Boy in Cellar
Forest Hills
3 Greek ladies
Nightmare
& Lobby Horse
HASSELBLAD
NEGATIVE FILM
from no
900-
to no
1000
from May 1971
to June 1971
Boy in leaves
Van Cortlandt
Park
Staten Island
Welfare island

sign
Staten Isle
Picnic
HASSELBLAD
NEGATIVE FILM
from no
1219
to no
1305
from Nov 1 1971
to Dec 1 1971
Cape May
Atlantic City
Wildwood
Ocean City
queens
Flushing Meadow
Boys on fence
Boys + tractor
cemetery
Long Beach
Brooklyn
Ft. Green
graves and boy
tin can
R.S.D
vacant

Gulfport
New Orleans Cem.
P.S.3 classroom
Fred Nude
New Orleans Canal
World Trade Center
Auto Show
G.M. Building
Gas Mask Flower

HASSELBLAD

NEGATIVE FILM

from no 1305

to no 1399

from Dec 1 1971

to Feb 7 1972

Jim Shields writing
Baton Rouge
East Hampton
Lonely Road -
Country clubs -
Doors with Jim
S.I. commune
R.S.D. park with hood
unemployment agency
city college
Ladies strike
Elizabeth Burge in auto junkyard

HASSELBLAD

NEGATIVE FILM

from no 1600

to no

from June 7 1972

to 19

City College
South Seaport
man with plastic in C.P.
Philadelphia flood
Wilkes Barre flood
Adam + Ruth
Prospect Park + Bronx Park

HASSELBLAD

NEGATIVE FILM

from no 1700

to no 1799

from July 1972

to August 1972
Sept 72

BALI
San Francisco
JAPAN
N.J. State Fair
Virginia State Fair
Adam + Frog
Dentist

Universal Studios
Disneyland
Staten Island
Snowman
Hockey Boy in Smoke
World Trade
2 Rakes on Chaise Lounges

HASSELBLAD

NEGATIVE FILM

from no 1800

to no 1899

from Oct 1972

to Nov. 1972

Nantucket
Provincetown
DANBURY
Virginia Beach
Norfolk
Lester Marks
DREAM CITY
CONEY ISLAND
BLANKETS
moon rock
Jessica
Harlem River
San Francisco
Barber. Violin
Starvin Marvin

STAR-TREK
Norfolk eye glasses
Santa Claus mask
Models legs C.I.
Bicycle C.I.
MIAMI BEACH
FONTAINBLEAU HOTEL POOL
Weekhawken

HASSELBLAD

NEGATIVE FILM

from no 1900

to no 1999

from Dec 1972

to Jan 1973

Statue of Liberty
Boiler Dream
Hand in Chains
Washington D.C.
MARCH.
Coney Island
Boys in Rubber
Boy in Squash
Santa Claus in Tree. P.P.
Ice. Snug Harbor. Natural History Museum
OAS MEN IN HOL
R. REYNOLDS MU
BETTY BERSH.
RED GROOMS NU
C. PARK ZOO. BRU